Identities

Race, Class, Gender, and Nationality

Edited by

Linda Martín Alcoff and Eduardo Mendieta

Blackwell Publishing

Editorial material and organization © 2003 by Linda Martín Alcoff and
Eduardo Mendieta

350 Main Street, Malden, MA 02148-5018, USA
108 Cowley Road, Oxford OX4 1JF, UK
550 Swanston Street, Carlton South, Melbourne, Victoria 3053, Australia
Kurfürstendamm 57, 10707 Berlin, Germany

First published 2003 by Blackwell Publishing Ltd

Library of Congress Cataloging-in-Publication Data has been applied for.

ISBN 0-631-21722-3 (hardback); ISBN 0-631-21723-1 (paperback)

A catalogue record for this title is available from the British Library.

Set in 9/11pt Ehrhardt
by Graphicraft Limited, Hong Kong
Printed and bound in the United Kingdom
by TJ International, Padstow, Cornwall

For further information on
Blackwell Publishing, visit our website:
http://www.blackwellpublishing.com

Contents

Notes on Authors

Georg Wilhelm Friedrich Hegel (1770–1831), German philosopher. In his youth Hegel supported the revolutionary movements in France and also Napoleon's attempt to secularize and unite Europe. The excerpt reprinted here, from *The Phenomenology of Mind* (1807), his first major work, was influential on Marx's formulation of class struggle and on subsequent accounts of the interdependence of identity, most recently, in formulations of the "politics of recognition."

Karl Marx (1818–83), German philosopher, journalist, revolutionary organizer. Marx's influence extends beyond those who identify as socialists and has altered the basic method and categories of social theory. "On the Jewish Question" (1843) is a criticism of Bruno Bauer, another member of the "Young Hegelians," who opposed supporting civil rights for Jews before there was social revolution for the working class. Marx's response has been influential on the way we understand the relationship between private identities, such as religious ones, and the state.

Sigmund Freud (1856–1939), founder of psychoanalysis. Freud based his theories on his study of medicine, psychology, neuropathology, and his clinical practice. In the excerpt reproduced here, from *The Ego and the Id* (1923), Freud, who acknowledged obsessive tendencies in his own personality, outlines his analysis of the divisions and conflicts within the self, which he developed as an explanation of irrational and neurotic human behavior. In 1939 he was forced to leave Vienna by the Nazi regime, and died in London.

George Herbert Mead (1863–1931), American pragmatist and pioneer in the field of social psychology. He was influenced by Hegel, Darwin, and Dilthey; the latter was his teacher in Berlin. Mead has been influential for his theories that the self is essentially social and that the internal life of the subject develops through a perspective that involves general, intersubjectively shared meanings. "The Self" is based on Mead's notes and on student notes from the course he taught on social psychology at the University of Chicago from 1900 to 1930.

W. E. B. Du Bois (1868–1963), historian, sociologist, novelist, editor, political activist. His writings span from 1890 to 1958. The essay reprinted here (1897) represents his early views on race, culture, and history. It is still widely influential and its interpretation is debated among leading anti-racist theorists today. Besides working for black nationalism, Du Bois also became a communist and strong supporter of African unity. In 1951, he was indicted during the height of McCarthyism on charges of treason. Although the charges were eventually dropped, he moved to Ghana in the last years of his life.

Alain Locke (1885–1954), Professor of Philosophy at Howard University with degrees from Harvard and Oxford. "The New Negro" was the lead essay he wrote for the collection, of the same name, of essays, stories, poems, and art he edited and published in 1925. Considered by many to be the "bible" of the Harlem Renaissance, it provided intellectual counterpoint to the racist denials of black humanity. Locke's stated aim was to produce a work "*of*" rather than *about* the Negro," and one that would showcase a new black sensibility emerging in the New World.

Amilcar Cabral (1924–73), political theorist and a major figure in the struggle against colonialism in Africa. In 1956 he formed with five compatriots the African Party for the Independence of Guinea and the Cape Verde Islands, which under his leadership liberated three-quarters of Guinea in ten years of revolutionary struggle. He was influential throughout the world as an outstanding theorist of anti-imperialist struggle and for his insistence on grounding ideas in the careful study of a given social reality. The speech reprinted here was delivered in 1972, a year before his assassination by Portuguese agents.

Frantz Fanon (1925–61), philosopher, psychiatrist, physician, writer, revolutionary. Originally from Martinique, he was wounded twice in World War II fighting for the French. He later moved to Algeria to work as a doctor for the poor, where he joined the struggle against French colonialism. *The Wretched of the Earth* (1961) inspired national liberation movements all over the world, including the black nationalist movement in the USA. The excerpt reprinted here is taken from *Black Skin, White Masks* (1952), which has been called the diary of a black intellectual recovering from the trauma of the white Western world.

Cheryl I. Harris, Professor of Law at the University of California, Los Angeles, began her teaching career at Chicago-Kent College of Law in 1990 after more than a decade in practice that included criminal appellate and trial work and municipal government representation as a senior attorney for the city of Chicago. Later she served as First Assistant General Attorney for the Chicago Park District. As the National Co-Chair for the National Conference of Black Lawyers for several years, she developed expertise in international human rights, particularly concerning South Africa. Her publications focus mainly on property and on critical race theory.

Stuart Hall is Emeritus Professor of Sociology at The Open University, London. His published works span almost four decades, since 1964. He was central to the formation of cultural studies as a discipline with a more inclusive approach to cultural expression and cultural politics. He has been enormously influential in conceptualizing diasporic, postcolonial, and ethnic identities, in analyzing blackness as a political identity, and in his critical and creative engagements with Marxism and postmodernism. The essay reprinted here was originally published in 1989.

Juan Flores is Professor of Puerto Rican and Black Studies at the City University of New York. Trained as a sociologist and a Germanist, he began his academic career in the German Studies Department at Stanford, was fired for his activism against the Vietnam War, and then switched institutions as well as area studies. He has become a leading theorist of Puerto Rican cultural politics, and argues that Puerto Rican communities provide a rich perspective from which to analyze global phenomena such as cultural imperialism, urbanization, identity formations, as well as the process of globalization itself.

Georg Lukács (1885–1971), political theorist and activist. Born in Budapest, he joined the Communist Party and had to spend much of his life in exile from governments of both the right and the left. He was Minister of Culture during the brief Hungarian Commune of 1919 and again during the Hungarian Revolution of 1956. His writings on culture, literature, subjectivity, and class were widely influential, and his *History and Class Consciousness*, a chapter of which is reprinted here, is considered the founding text of Western Marxism, which developed a more Hegelian, philosophical, and humanist interpretation of Marx than the scientific model emphasized by the Soviets.

Eric Hobsbawm is Professor of History at the University of London. Born in Alexandria to Jewish parents, his family was living in Vienna and Berlin during the rise of Hitler. Considered a leading Marxist historian of extraordinary breadth, he has written histories of labor, capital, nationalism, war, revolution, and jazz. His view that a partisan approach to history has the advantage of bringing new questions and challenges to existing disciplines has been influential. His career suffered during the Cold War due to his outspoken communist commitments.

E. P. Thompson (1924–93), one of England's foremost historians and social theorists. He is acclaimed as the innovator of "history from below," in which the history of everyday life is taken as key to understanding the past. He was also influential for emphasizing the importance of cultural tradition in political conflict. The excerpt reprinted here is considered a masterpiece for its original exploration of the subjective side of the emerging class consciousness.

Ranajit Guha is a historian and political economist. He is a founder of the Subaltern Studies Group, which claimed that existing Indian histories were largely elitist and that European-based concepts used in history, such as freedom, were not universal but European and limited. He puts forward the theoretical viewpoint of peasants and thus aims to unearth the political and intellectual agency of the subaltern in the colonial period. *Elementary Aspects of Peasant Insurgency in Colonial India*, published first in 1983, became the founding document of the subaltern studies school and challenged the hegemony of the concepts and categories of European Marxist social theory.

Simone de Beauvoir (1908–86), philosopher, writer, activist. She was a leader of the French left and a prolific writer whose memoirs charted the experience of the European left during her lifetime. Her most well-known book, *The Second Sex*, is a founding document of Western feminism, and all the more remarkable because it was written in the absence of a women's movement. Drawing from interviews as well as her own critiques of the existing research on women, the book was met initially with much resistance among the men in her milieu.

Monique Wittig has been a key figure of the French women's movement and of the development of radical lesbian politics. She has written several prominent essays on feminist and lesbian theory, as well as novels, short stories, and plays, and was awarded the Prix Medicis. The essay reproduced here, first delivered in 1978 and published in 1980, disputes the naturalness of women as a social category and the biological basis for the category of gender and for women's oppression. Wittig argues that lesbians are not women, according to the reigning cultural definition, and should be defined in terms of their resistance to heterosexuality rather than their erotic disposition.

Iris Marion Young is Professor of Political Science at the University of Chicago. Her first book, from which "Throwing Like a Girl" (originally presented in 1977) is taken, put forward both her socialist feminist views and also several essays that have become widely influential as phenomenological treatments of feminine bodily experience. Since then, she has become influential as a political theorist on issues of diversity and democracy; her latest book is *Inclusion and Democracy* (2000).

Kimberlé Crenshaw is Professor of Law at the University of California, Los Angeles, and Columbia University. She was a founder of the movement of Critical Race Theory, which has challenged both liberal and conservative assumptions about civil rights and racial injustice. Critical Race Theory followed *Critical Legal Studies* in its theoretical approach to the law as a discourse that rationalizes injustice, but it sought to integrate *CLS* with a liberal civil rights tradition that *CLS* had rejected for theoretical reasons. Crenshaw's work on the intersections of race and gender establishes the impossibility of separating these forms of identity.

Judith Butler is Professor of Rhetoric and Comparative Literature at Berkeley. Her theory of gender as performativity, or an imitation where there is no original, developed first in her 1990 book *Gender Trouble*, remains the most widely influential account. She sees gender identity as a regulative ideal which operates as a norm for heterosexuality; thus, rather than being the basis for feminist politics, it is the basis of women's oppression. Political organizing based on lesbian identity similarly constrains the possibilities of desire rather than liberating it.

John Boswell (1947–94), one of the most important historians of homosexuality. He avowed Christian beliefs himself, and in *Christianity, Social Tolerance and Homosexuality* (1980) argued that homosexuals were accepted by the Church before the thirteenth century. He rejected the idea that homosexual subcultures are a recent development, and he also published a study of the "Adelphopoiia" liturgy, which he argued was used for centuries as a public liturgy to celebrate erotic relationships between people of the same sex. His work has generated controversy from all sides but cannot be ignored. The essay reprinted here was first published in 1982.

David M. Halperin is Professor of Literature at the Massachusetts Institute of Technology. He is a classicist, comparatist, activist, and a leading theorist of gay studies and queer theory. He has written on Greek and Roman poetry, on Plato's erotic theory, on modern literature and film, and is a founding editor of *GLQ: A Journal of Lesbian and Gay Studies*. His influential book, *One Hundred Years of Homosexuality: The Construction of Erotic Experience in the Ancient Greek World*, contested the assumption that homosexual identity crosses cultural and historical boundaries.

Teresa de Lauretis is Professor in the History of Consciousness Department at the University of California, Santa Cruz. Originally from Italy, her work in the intersections of feminist, film, and queer theory has been widely influential. She has made creative use of psychoanalysis and semiotic theory to analyze representations of the feminine and the erasure of lesbians from popular culture. In the essay reprinted here, she explores how lesbian desire is erased even within the concept of sexual difference used by theorists such as Luce Irigaray to signify female identity.

Jason Cromwell is an anthropologist who conducts research on sex, sexuality, gender, and identity. He is a long-time member of the transcommunity and has served on the boards of directors of the Ingersoll Gender Center, International Foundation of Gender Education, and American Education Gender Information Service. The excerpt included here provides both a critique of mainstream medical and psychological discourses and also an explanation of the new vocabularies of identity being developed in transcommunities today.

Ross Poole, an Australian philosopher formerly at Macquarrie University, has written influential essays on nationalism as well as ethics, modernity, multiculturalism, and aboriginal rights. The excerpt included here provides an overview of the cutting edge debates about nationalism and national identity. He is also the author of *Morality and Modernity* (1991).

Daniel Mato is Professor of Social Sciences and Director of the Program on Globalization, Cultural Processes, and Sociopolitical Change at Universidad Central de Venezuela. He has been a visiting professor at several universities in Latin America and the USA. His work centers on representations of ethnicity and constructions of cultural identity in the context of transnational relations, and the struggle of indigenous peoples of Latin America.

Roland Robertson is Distinguished Service Professor of Sociology at the University of Pittsburgh. His work on the sociology of religion pioneered the field, and he is one of the most important thinkers in the new field of globalization theory. The essay reprinted here is his earliest and most succinct statement on globalization.

R. Radhakrishnan is Professor of English at the University of Massachusetts, Amherst. He grew up in India, studied in the USA, and has taught in both countries. His work has focused on ethical issues that arise from the formations of ethnic identities and the politics of location under postcolonial diasporic conditions.

Edward Said is Professor of English and Comparative Literature at Columbia University. Born in 1935, he grew up in Palestine, Egypt, and Lebanon, and served for 14 years in the Palestinian parliament-in-exile. He has been the foremost spokesperson for the Palestinians in the USA. *Orientalism* (1978) demonstrated in comprehensive detail that the extensive history of Western studies of Oriental societies reveal more about the self-construction of the West than about the cultures of the East. In the essay reprinted here, Said discusses Samuel Huntington's influential book, *The Clash of Civilizations*, which exhibits some of the same tendencies Said criticized in *Orientalism*.

Renato Rosaldo is a prize-winning anthropologist who has written on Southeast Asian cultures and US Latinos. He has also been influential in reformulating the model of social science based on a detached, objective observer and replacing it with a model that acknowledges subjectivity, emotion, and the inevitable narrativity of social analysis. Since 1984, he helped found the Latino Cultural Studies Working Group, the members of whom have conducted studies of Latino communities across the USA. In this context he began to develop the concept of "cultural citizenship," elaborated in the essay included here.

Mike Featherstone is Director of the Theory, Culture and Society Centre and Professor of

Sociology and Communications at Nottingham Trent University, England, and founding editor of *Theory, Culture and Society*. His work has pioneered the study of popular culture in a sociological perspective, and has also brought into dialogue the most innovative and recent work in social theory.

Ernesto Laclau is Professor of Political Theory at the University of Essex, and originally from Colombia. *Hegemony and Socialist Strategy* (1985), which he wrote with Chantal Mouffe, has become a classic text of radical democracy, offering a new theory of identity-based social movements, and uniting the philosophical lessons of postmodernism with contemporary Marxism. Laclau's subsequent work has continued his concern with developing socialist theory within late capitalist realities. The essay reprinted here explores the interdependence between universal and particular claims in relation to the politics of identity.

Donna Haraway is a Professor in the History of Consciousness Department at the University of California, Santa Cruz. She is trained in anthropology and the history of science. Her influential analysis of primate studies in *Primate Visions* (1989) documented its close connection with cultural constructions of raced and gendered identity as well as ideologies central to Western colonialism. The essay included here offers a new cyborg metaphor for human identity, one that can transcend the nature/culture divide, more accurately represent contemporary life in a high-tech age, and provide a new agenda for feminist politics.

Satya Mohanty is Professor of English at Cornell University. Born and raised in India, he studied both in India and in the USA. His work since the 1980s has pursued a comprehensive critique of postmodernist approaches to questions of identity, objectivity, and politics. He has particularly challenged the idea that if we reject essentialist accounts of identity, we must also reject the reality or the epistemic salience of identity. He has also written on topics in critical theory, twentieth-century literature, colonial and postcolonial studies, and film.

Acknowledgments

The editors and publisher gratefully acknowledge the permission granted to reproduce the copyright material in this book:

1 G. W. F. Hegel, "Independence and Dependence of Self-Consciousness," pp. 399–411 from *The Philosophy of Hegel*, ed. Carl J. Friedrich (New York: Modern Library, 1953). Copyright © 1953, 1954 by Random House, Inc. Used by permission of Modern Library, a division of Random House, Inc. This is a revised translation from the original English translation by J. B. Baillie in G. W. F. Hegel, *The Phenomenology of Mind* (New York: Harper and Row, 1931), pp. 230–40. Reprinted by permission of HarperCollins Publishers Ltd.

2 Karl Marx, "On the Jewish Question," pp. 26–46 from *The Marx-Engels Reader*, 2nd edn, ed. Robert C. Tucker (New York: W. W. Norton, 1972). Copyright © 1978, 1972 by W. W. Norton & Company, Inc. Used by permission of W. W. Norton & Company Inc.

3 Sigmund Freud, pp. 3–9 from *The Ego and the Id*, trans. Joan Riviere, revised and newly edited by James Strachey (New York: W. W. Norton, 1962). Copyright © 1960 by James Strachey. Used by permission of W. W. Norton & Company Inc.

4 George Herbert Mead, pp. 144–64 from "The Self," chapter in *Mind, Self, and Society: From the Standpoint of a Social Behaviorist* (Chicago: University of Chicago Press, 1934).

5 W. E. B. Du Bois, "The Conservation of Races," pp. 815–26 from *W. E. B. Du Bois: Writings* (New York: The Library of America, 1986).

6 Alain Locke, "The New Negro," pp. 3–16 from *The New Negro*, ed. Alain Locke (New York: Simon & Schuster, 1992). Copyright © 1925 by Albert & Charles Boni, Inc.; copyright © 1992 by Macmillan Publishing Company. Reprinted with the permission of Scribner, a division of Simon & Schuster, Inc.

7 Amilcar Cabral, "Identity and Dignity in the Context of the National Liberation Struggle," pp. 9–25 from *Return to the Source* by Amilcar Cabral (New York: Monthly Review Press, 1973). Copyright © 1973 by Monthly Review Press. Reprinted by permission of Monthly Review Foundation.

8 Frantz Fanon, "The Fact of Blackness," pp. 109–40 from *Black Skin, White Masks*, trans. Charles Lam Markmann (New York: Grove Press, 1967). Copyright © Grove Press, Inc.; used by permission of Grove/Atlantic, Inc.

9 Cheryl I. Harris, "Whiteness as Property," pp. 276–91 from *Critical Race Theory: The Key Writings that Formed the Movement*, ed. Kimberlé Crenshaw, Neil Gotanda, Gary Peller, and Kendall Thomas (New York: The New Press, 1995).

10 Stuart Hall, "New Ethnicities," pp. 441–9 from *Stuart Hall: Critical Dialogues in Cultural Studies*, ed. David Morley and Kuan-Hsing Chen (London: Routledge, 1996).

11 Juan Flores, "The Latino Imaginary," pp. 191–203 in *From Bomba to Hip-Hop: Puerto Rican Culture and Latino Identity* (New York: Columbia University Press, 2000).

12 Georg Lukács, "Class Consciousness," pp. 46–81 from *History and Class Consciousness: Studies in Marxist Dialectics*, trans. Rodney Livingstone (Cambridge: MIT Press, 1971).

13 E. J. Hobsbawm, "Class Consciousness in History," pp. 5–21 from *Aspects of History and Class Consciousness*, ed. István Mézáros (New York: Herder and Herder, 1971).

14 E. P. Thompson, "Preface," pp. 9–13 from *The Making of the English Working Class* (New York: Random House, 1966). Copyright © 1963 by E. P. Thompson. Used by permission of Pantheon Books, a division of Random House, Inc., and Victor Gollancz, a division of Orion Books, London.

15 Ranajit Guha, "Introduction," pp. 1–17 from *Elementary Aspects of Peasant Insurgency in Colonial India* (Durham: Duke University Press, 1999). Copyright © 1999, Duke University Press. All rights reserved. Reprinted with permission.

16 Simone de Beauvoir, "Introduction," pp. xv–xxxiv from *The Second Sex*, trans. and ed. H. M. Parshley (New York: Random House, 1952). Copyright © 1952 and renewed 1980 by Alfred A. Knopf Inc. Used by permission of Alfred A. Knopf, a division of Random House, Inc., and Sanford J. Greenburger, New York.

17 Monique Wittig, "One Is Not Born a Woman," pp. 9–20 from *The Straight Mind and Other Essays* (Boston: Beacon, 1992). Copyright © 1992 by Monique Wittig. Reprinted by permission of Beacon Press, Boston.

18 Iris Marion Young, "Throwing Like a Girl," pp. 141–59 from *Throwing Like a Girl and Other Essays in Feminist Philosophy and Social Theory* (Bloomington: Indiana University Press, 1990).

19 Kimberlé Crenshaw, "Mapping the Margins: Intersectionality, Identity Politics, and the Violence Against Women of Color," pp. 357–83 in *Critical Race Theory: The Key Writings that Formed the Movement*, ed. Kimberlé Crenshaw, Neil Gotanda, Gary Peller, and Kendall Thomas (New York: The New Press, 1995).

20 Judith Butler, "Gender Trouble, Feminist Theory and Psychoanalytic Discourse," pp. 324–40 from *Feminism/Postmodernism*, ed. Linda J. Nicholson (New York: Routledge, 1990).

21 John Boswell, "Revolutions, Universals, and Sexual Categories," pp. 17–36 from *Hidden From History: Reclaiming the Gay and Lesbian Past*, ed. Martin Duberman, Martha Vicinus, and George Chauncey, Jr. (New York: Penguin, 1990). Copyright © 1990 Frances Goldin Literary Agency, New York.

22 David M. Halperin, "Sex Before Sexuality: Pederasty, Politics, and Power in Classical Athens," pp. 37–53 in *Hidden From History: Reclaiming the Gay and Lesbian Past*, ed. Martin Duberman, Martha Vicinus, and George Chauncey, Jr. (New York: Penguin, 1990). Copyright © 1990 Frances Goldin Literary Agency, New York.

23 Teresa de Lauretis, "Sexual Indifference and Lesbian Representation," from *Theatre Journal* 40(2), 1988, pp. 155–77. Copyright © The Johns Hopkins University Press. Reprinted by permission of The Johns Hopkins University Press.

24 Jason Cromwell, "Transsexual Discourses and Languages of Identification," pp. 19–30 from *Transmen and FTMs: Identities, Bodies, Genders and Sexualities* (Urbana: University of Illinois Press, 1999). Copyright © 1999 by the Board of Trustees to the University of Illinois. Used with permission of the University of Illinois Press.

25 Ross Poole, "National Identity," pp. 67–74, and "Citizenship and National Identity," pp. 104–12, from *Nation and Identity* (New York: Routledge, 1999).

26 Daniel Mato, "On the Making of Transnational Identities in the Age of Globalization: The US Latina/o–'Latin' American Case," pp. 598–620 in *Cultural Studies: Theorizing Politics, Politicizing Theory* 12(4), 1998.

27 Roland Robertson, "Globalization as a Problem," pp. 8–31 from *Globalization: Social*

Theory and Global Culture (London: Sage Publications Ltd, 1994).

28 R. Radhakrishnan, "Postcoloniality and the Boundaries of Identity," from *Callaloo* 16(4), 1993, pp. 750–71. Reprinted by permission of The Johns Hopkins University Press.

29 Edward W. Said, pp. 574–8 from "The Clash of Definitions," chapter 46 in *Reflections on Exile and Other Essays* (Cambridge, Mass.: Harvard University Press, 2000). Copyright © 2000 by Edward W. Said.

30 Renato Rosaldo, "Cultural Citizenship, Inequality, and Multiculturalism," pp. 27–38 from *Latino Cultural Citizenship: Claiming Identity, Space, and Rights*, ed. William V. Flores and Rina Benmayor (Boston: Beacon Press, 1997). Copyright © 1997 by William V. Flores and Rina Benmayor. Reprinted by permission of Beacon Press, Boston.

31 Mike Featherstone, "Localism, Globalism and Cultural Identity," pp. 102–23 from *Undoing Culture* (London: Sage Publications Ltd., 1995).

32 Ernesto Laclau, "Universalism, Particularism, and the Question of Identity," pp. 20–35 from *Emancipation(s)* (London: Verso, 1996).

33 Donna J. Haraway, "A Manifesto for Cyborgs: Science, Technology, and Socialist Feminism in the 1980s," from *Socialist Review* 80, 1985, pp. 65–108.

34 Satya P. Mohanty, "The Epistemic Status of Cultural Identity," pp. 29–43 and 55–66 from *Reclaiming Identity: Realist Theory and the Predicament of Postmodernism*, ed. Paula M. L. Moya and Michael R. Hames-García (Berkeley: University of California Press, 2000). Copyright © 2000 the Regents of the University of California.

Every effort has been made to trace copyright holders and to obtain their permission for the use of copyright material. The publisher apologizes for any errors or omissions in the above list and would be grateful if notified of any corrections that should be incorporated in future reprints or editions of this book.

The editors are grateful to Chris Calvert-Minor for preparing the index. Linda would also like to thank Margaret Himley for her important editorial suggestions and Lisa Farnsworth for her secretarial help.

Introduction
Identities: Modern and Postmodern

LINDA MARTÍN ALCOFF

What goes to make up the organized self is the organization of the attitudes which are common to the group. . . . Consciousness, as frequently used, simply has reference to the field of experience, but self-consciousness refers to the ability to call out in ourselves a set of definite responses which belong to the others of the group. Consciousness and self-consciousness are not on the same level. A man alone has, fortunately or unfortunately, access to his own toothache, but that is not what we mean by self-consciousness.

George Herbert Mead (pp. 39–40 in this vol; Mind, Self and Society,
Vol. 1 162–3)

If multiculturalism is to be the goal of educational and political institutions, we need a workable notion of how a social group is unified by a common culture, as well as the ability to identify genuine cultural differences (and similarities) across groups. . . . The most basic questions about identity call for a more general reexamination of the relation between personal experience and public meanings – subjective choices and evaluations, on the one hand, and objective social location, on the other.

Satya Mohanty (p. 392 in this vol; in Moya and Hames-Garcia, 29–30)

. . . the very fact that woman *is the Other* tends to cast suspicion upon all the justifications that men have ever been able to provide for it. These have all too evidently been dictated by men's interest.

Simone de Beauvoir (p. 153 in this vol; The Second Sex xxxiii)

There is considerable interest in the question of identity today, perhaps equaled only by the considerable confusion around the question of why identities continue to exert such power, and whether they should be acknowledged and legally recognized or simply ignored in the hope that they will disappear. Everyone seems to agree that social identities such as ethnicity, sexuality, and nationality have come to the center of political mobilization since the United States' cultural revolution of the 1960s, and many construe recent global conflicts as centered around differences in fundamental aspects of cultural identity. But there is little agreement about the true causes of this emerging importance of social identities or about its most likely enduring political effects. For some, the emphasis on identity is a threat to democracy and an incitement of ceaseless conflict; for others, it is a struggle long overdue.

This volume does not pose uniform approaches to identity, but it does promise to bring the discussion to a new and more informed level. Collected here for the first time are many of the most perspicuous and influential essays on social identity and its various forms that have been written over the last 200 years, a panoply that will introduce readers to the wide expanse of serious theoretical and philosophical work on social identities, how the ones we currently live with have arisen, how they are being transformed, as well as how they *might* be transformed and how they *should* be transformed.

The differences that exist between social identities in their genesis, their manifestation, and their political effects are immense, and we agree with those who believe that each form requires extensive study and separate analysis. Yet we have opted here to collect together readings that span multiple forms of identity, not toward arguing for their essential similarity, but with two aims in mind: (1) to show that current concerns about, and deployments of, identity have not been the invention of multiculturalists but have an extensive philosophical history, and (2) to provide a "non-Balkanized" approach that will offset the usual tendency for only women's studies students to read about gender, only ethnic studies students to study race and ethnicity, and so on. All students of society and all who want to become effective citizens must become educated about the multiple identities that structure our social worlds in order to be able to understand, evaluate, and, if they choose, meaningfully participate in the struggles against identity-based forms of oppression.

Despite these aims, this collection has of course had to leave many serious issues and forms of identity out. Most significantly, we have not been able to include essays specifically on religious identities, disability-based forms of identity, or age-based forms. What we have included, however, are many of the ovarian (seminal) essays concerning the central questions of social identities in general and in many of their particulars, the most influential essays that continue to frame current debates, and a spread of topics that will reveal to readers both the important diversities and interesting similarities between analyses of race, ethnic, gender, sexual, class, and national-based identities.

In the West, the principal social struggles of the modern era can perhaps be characterized as, first, struggles of social status, then, of social class, and only then of social identity. The struggle of social status was waged against landed aristocracies and the legalized forms of caste and hierarchy that predetermined individual vocation and economic success; the struggle of social class was fought against the unbridled power of the "Mr. Moneybags" of the world to extract labor power without any protections for those suffering the extractions; and the struggles of social identity, developing most fully in the nineteenth and twentieth centuries, have been fought against the subtle social contracts by which

whole identity groups are denied basic human rights. Contra the story told by some critics of the 1960s, who lament that decade's focus on social identities such as race, gender, and sexuality, identity-based political movements did not wait until then to become politically visible and significant but began with the abolitionist, women's suffrage, and anti-apartheid struggles begun long before. Neither the struggle against discrimination based on social status, nor the one on social class or on social identity has reached completion, though there has been progress on all fronts; the movement of history has been more like a puddle of water whose concentric circles expand and increase in number than like a progress chart of upward movement.

Identity-based political movements have fought throughout the world against oppressions based on race, gender, sexuality, ethnicity, religion, culture, nationality, disability, age, and other forms of socially recognized identity. But social identities such as these operate differently from class or caste. All humanitarians might agree that the world would be a better place without class or caste categories of distinction, in which individual futures would not be constrained from birth by rigid conceptions of a person's social station and where economic production did not operate through a system in which some made world-altering decisions and reaped enormous benefits and others simply toiled for daily subsistence. In this sense liberation from class and caste forms of oppression can plausibly be articulated in terms of individual freedom. But it is not at all as clear that the future would be better off without the rich differences of life-interpretation that are developed via the social identities based on ethnicity, gender, sexuality, and other such group categories. Simply put, there are excellent reasons to eliminate class and caste as we know it, but these reasons do not apply to race, ethnicity, gender, or all other identity groups *per se*. And this means that defining liberation in terms of individual freedom may not work as well for the struggle against identity-based forms of oppression.

But surely, before we can debate the best political ends, we need to understand what identities *are*. How are they formed, and how can they be transformed? Are identities simply the congealed effect of collective historical experience, or are they imposed on individuals from external forces, always within a strategy of domination? Are identities best understood, on a psychoanalytic model, as compensatory attempts to bolster a debilitated ego?

Why are so many people the world over so attached to their ethnic identity that they are willing to go to war over it, or is this commonly heard claim quite a mistaken interpretation of the real, underlying motives behind these conflicts? Why are so many of those who have been oppressed by their identity, especially racial and gender identity, demanding respect and recognition for these identities rather than deconstruction or an escape from them? Should identities be approached as temporary political strategies with the aim of eventually dissolving all such social categories, or should the ultimate political aim be to value the diversity of identities and enhance the likelihood of collective, democratic self-formation of identity?

Despite the multiple points of view represented in this volume, there is nonetheless an important agreement about the fact that identity is not in the main an individual affair. Individuals make their own identity, but not under conditions of their own choosing. In fact, identities are often created in the crucible of colonialism, racial and sexual subordination, and national conflicts, but also in the specificity of group histories and structural position. As Stuart Hall concisely puts it, "identities are names we give to the different ways we are positioned by, and position ourselves within, the narratives of the past" (Hall 1990: 225). They are both imposed and self-made, produced through the interplay of names and social roles foisted on us by dominant narratives together with the particular choices families, communities, and individuals make over how to interpret, and resist, those impositions as well as how to grapple with their real historical experiences. But the social meanings attached to such things as skin color and body shape, the hierarchies of language and differential roles in reproduction, and the very significance accorded various identity markers, are firmly in place when a given individual is born, circumscribing their flexibility and invoking a constellation of meanings that will come into play by their appearance, or their birth certificate. To understand identities, then, we need to study psychology, culture, politics, and economics, as well as philosophy and history.

Besides their social character, another powerful aspect of social identities agreed upon by nearly all theorists is their historicity, or their evolutionary, and de-evolutionary, developments. As both Simone de Beauvoir and Judith Butler – in very different ways – argue persuasively here, biology is

insufficient to explain the vast expanse of attributes to which we have given gendered meanings and associations. In early modern France, aristocratic men spent as much time and resources on their "toilette" as any western woman today. Women have been deemed more moral and less moral, more religious and less religious, calmer and more emotional, and assorted other contradictory characterizations, often coexisting in the same culture. Biological differences confer an experiential divide between men and women over a certain range of life-events, without doubt, but there is much diversity among women in their interpretation and experience of these events, as well as among men over their reproductive experiences, that biology is simply impotent to explain. As de Beauvoir argues, "it is not upon physiology that values can be based; rather, the facts of biology take on the values that the existent bestows upon them" (Beauvoir 1989: 36). Women are made, not born, and thus they can be remade as the meanings of femininity change and mutate through historical disruptions. And if this is true of gendered identity, so much the more so for all of those identities with even less of a connection to any significant biological feature.

Thus, identities need to be analyzed not only in their cultural location but also in relation to historical epoch. The constellation of practices, beliefs about identity, the lived experiences associated with various identities, and the legal or formal recognitions of identity not only undergo constant change but can produce truly new forms of identity. Between the medieval and the modern period, "peoples" became "races," "sexes" became "genders," and "habits of perversion," at least as argued here by David Halperin, became "sexual identities." However contingent and transient these various constructions may be, it remains the case that one's placement in social categories of identity has an enormous impact on one's life, determining job prospects, career possibilities, available places to live, potential friends and lovers, reactions from police, credence from jurors, and the amount of presumptive credibility one is accorded by one's teachers, students, neighbors, and co-workers. Fanon's essay, included here, "The Fact of Blackness," is perhaps one of the most searing and rich accounts of the ways in which having a black identity can turn an individual subject into stone: "I am given no chance. I am overdetermined from without. I am the slave not of the 'idea' that others have of me but of my own appearance" (p. 64 in this vol). Fanon shows how social identities affect not only external elements of one's life in a social world but one's interior life as well, in relation to patterns of affect, belief, desire, and experience.

This Reader begins in the period known as modernity, starting from around 1800, and from here moves forward to the current transitional period we are now experiencing in our unstable present, and which has been dubbed postmodernity. In both periods social identities are the subject of intense theoretical analysis, as well as political energy, but the modern and postmodern periods are significantly different in their understanding and experience of social identities as well as in the central questions, theories, and debates posed in regard to them.

In the modern period, "Man" was first introduced as the protagonist in a play of his own making, as the lead in a story of universal progression from ignorance to enlightenment, and from tyranny to autonomy. Yet the role of "Man" was not actually played by all of humanity: some groups of people appeared only as comic relief, as a backdrop chorus singing homilies to "his" greatness, as the technical crew invisible to the audience, or as mere audience members themselves. Oddly, then, "Man" emerged at the same time as social categories of identity solidified into a carefully organized hierarchy, a "Great Chain of Being" thought to reflect the natural rank internal to the human species.

What is crucial to emphasize is that this racial imaginary did not appear at first contact or upon initial awareness of difference. Europeans traded goods with various peoples of Africa for at least 200 years before their participation in the slave trade, for example (Jordan 1968: 3–4). The English, as one of the earliest trading powers due to their maritime expertise, began trading sometime after 1550, but the concept of the Great Chain of Being was not developed and popularized until nearly the end of the eighteenth century, not coincidentally in the midst of the developing market in human flesh. The complexity of these histories of contact establish that difference in and of itself does not produce the essentialization of vilified identities, and this cuts across types of difference. For example, against the commonly heard opinion that heterosexuals develop homophobia as the natural result of seeing open homosexual relationships, empirical studies show that heterosexuals who have increased contact with out gay people actually exhibit reduced homophobia, rather than more of it. Other experi-

ments have suggested that children come to know which visible features are relevant to human classifications only after they "integrate their perceptual knowledge with ontological knowledge" (Hirschfeld 1996: 137). This is not to say that the perceptual competences are irrelevant or secondary, but that they become operable in cognition only when children adapt to what researcher Lawrence Hirschfeld calls "domain specific competences" which direct "attention to certain sorts of data" as well as positing ontological organizations of perceptible phenomena. There is more going on in the elaborations of human rank than mere ignorance or fears "naturally" elicited by encounters with difference. And differences themselves, however physically dramatic, are subject to variable valuation and recognized significance.

In this volume we reprint Hegel's mythic representation of the development of rank through a story in which two subjects meet each other initially in conditions of equality. It is because each is in the same position of insecurity *vis-à-vis* the other, because each has the same set of needs and vulnerabilities, that a struggle develops which eventually produces a division of rank and a relationship of domination. Hegel's narrative, which has been influential over countless theories of self-development and social conflict, portrayed individuals as both essentially equal and essentially interdependent.

Hegel thus was perhaps the first to open the discussion of the construction of identity in the West when he announced that a fully developed self required recognition of its status from others, and thus was not subjectively self-sufficient. Recognition from others comes not only in an abstract universalizable form but also necessarily in a substantive form, meaning that we are recognized *as* persons *with* particular qualities, features, and knowledges. In effect, Hegel's argument suggests that, rather than being extraneous to the self, socially recognized identity is a necessity of the self, in order to be able to operate as a capable moral agent, for example, or as a valid participant in civil society.

The other three essays we have included here in Part I, "Foundations," provide the further critical ingredients that have staged more current debates over identity. In his challenging essay, "The Jewish Question," which sometimes also manifests his own internalized anti-Semitism, Marx brilliantly deconstructs the political problem that group recognition is usually thought to pose – how can a state representing the general interests recognize special rights? – as colluding with the modern state's delusion that it embodies the universal interests of abstract individuals. In reality, individuals participate in the state and in civil society as tradesmen, day-laborers, landowners, Christian and Jewish, i.e. as living individuals with conflicting interests, and the universality claimed by the bourgeois political state is as yet unreal. The solution will thus not be found in setting aside the universal in order to recognize the special rights for particular groups as much as in overcoming the sources of conflict in the particularizing of community interests produced by capitalist relations of production. This essay prefigures the current debates over identity that are framed in relation to the universal versus the particular and that warn against strategies of recognizing difference that do not attend to the political contexts in which differences are produced.

In short order, Freud then offered a serious complication for this debate, uncovering the incoherence of the self, the impotence of the conscious self or ego to maintain control, and thus suggesting that illusions of "identity" are simply the symptoms of wishful thinking. Whether we are speaking of the individual or the macro-structural forces that contribute to identity formation, Freud's originality lay in his insistence that the process does not follow apparent self-interest, since the self is not transparent to itself, nor are identities the mere outward manifestations of inner selves. Neuroses, latent aggressions, paranoia, and so forth bedevil not merely the irrational or pathological individual but the most rational and even self-reflective ones among us, since the ego, or conscious self, holds only a tenuous, transitory control over the multiple and conflicting drives and fears that make up a person. Later theorists made use of Freud's theory to help explain not only individual but also collective patterns of behavior by reference to these infantile impulses or their excessive restraint, either of which can produce murderous conflict.

After Freud, questions of identity were approached much more cautiously, but the social psychologist George Herbert Mead was nonetheless capable of developing a theory of identity which avoided some of the shortcomings of pre-Freudian assumptions by suggesting that it is less correct to say that the individual self "has" a perspective than that it is "in" a perspective: that the perspective precedes the individual. "Social consciousness is organized from the outside in. The social percepts which first arise are those of other selves" (Mead 1982: 53). This is what yields Mead's idea of "objective relativism," that the shared meanings which make up our world, and our subjectivity, are broadly group-related and thus variable but also objective in that they exist in the world, not merely in our (collective) heads. Accounts such as Mead's, which situate self-formation within society, have increased in influence as individualist ontologies have slowly begun to wane. Mead's account returns us to the relational interdependence of Hegel but without a fixed teleology of outcome and with a more developed and plausible explanation of the role of the other in the self. Group identities are no longer illusions on this account, which leads us then directly back to the political questions formulated by Marx.

Essays by Hegel, Marx, Freud, and Mead thus set the stage here by encapsulating some of the preliminary stages of theoretical work on identity. Despite their differences, these thinkers opened the door to questions of identity by rejecting ontological individualism or the notion that selves have or can achieve an independence from the outside social domain. Identities are essentially social objects, gaining their intelligibility and force only within a social realm. Part I should establish the philosophical genealogy of theories of social identity.

Many theorists also agree that no less than four of the forms of identity so powerful today were invented as if from scratch in the modern period: race, arguably originating with Kant's anthropological writings and made possible by the developments in biological explanation; class, emerging as an objective social location only with the emergence of capitalism; nationality, produced along with the development of the nation-state; and sexuality, which developed as an identity rather than a practice in the context of the creation of alternative communities in which individuals could develop whole ways of life in new and different forms.

Within already existing modernist discourses, these new forms of identity were integrated into progressivist teleologies and naturalist conceptions of difference. The ordering and labeling of natural terrain, the classifying of natural types, and the typologies of "natural races" emerged simultaneously in what Foucault called the Classical episteme. Arguing via Foucault, both Cornell West and David Theo Goldberg have attempted genealogies of modern racism, meaning here not contemporary racism so much as the racism of modernism, that link the western fetishistic practices of classification, the forming of tables, and the consequent primacy of the visible with the creation of metaphysical and moral hierarchies between racialized categories of human beings (Goldberg 1993; West 1982). David Halperin has also used Foucault's work to suggest how the creation of a sexual norm in the nineteenth century produced the plethora of possible varieties of deviance, which were then studied in great detail and eventually congealed into sexual identities. And we still have endless brain studies, studies of math performance and so-called "right-brain" or "left-brain" dominance that chart differences by gender, even though the differences within each gender by all of these "yardsticks" far outweigh those between the genders. Modern discourse approaches these identities as if it is merely a matter of observing and categorizing the natural flora and fauna of human society, neglecting to consider the effects of such research on the very formation of human "types."

Modern liberalism harbored a serious paradox in this regard, and one that has not yet been resolved in either its political institutions or its political thought. Political and moral rights are based on what all persons necessarily share in common; differences are considered merely contingent and therefore either politically irrelevant or actual obstructions. Thus John Rawls, the most important theorist of liberalism in the last century, writes that neither moral judgment nor political institutions should appeal to "those contingencies [i.e. social identities] which set men at odds and allow them to be guided by their prejudices" (Rawls 1971: 19; quoted in Goldberg 1993: 6). In this climate of discourse, it has been exceedingly difficult to introduce the specific needs or rights which arise from differences of identity, such as the necessity of maternity leave, the right to speak a different language, or the need for affirmative action. These cannot even be understood as rights so long as they flow from human difference rather than commonality, unless they can be justified as transition strategies toward the aim of assimilation, a goal not everyone shares. But the paradox has been that modernism ushered in a naturalization of human differences at the same time that it was incapable of recognizing the significant political implications of these differences. Yet the political impact of these differences is no less powerful whether in the end we decide the differences are natural or humanly constructed.

To retrieve the possibility of political coherence, there seem to be only two possible strategies: either deconstruct identities as essentially inessential, or create a new political framework capable of imagining justice even where there is fundamental difference. This brings us to the postmodern present, a moment often characterized by the erosion of the great metanarratives of universal progress and also by the unsettling of identities by processes of globalization. National identities seem to be losing ground both from the transnational organization of capital as well as the increased importance of cultural, ethnic, and religious identities. The demand for a recognition of sexual identity has been challenged by those who would rather reject the very concept of essential, lifelong sexual orientations, and who argue that the demand for recognition will give the state the power to determine identity while what we should be struggling for is a freedom from state surveillance. The massive increase in immigrations and migrations, both within and between continents, has produced a new era of racial and ethnic hybridization, where a new generation experiments with ways to express and politically legitimate their complex genealogies.

Interestingly, the era of postmodernity seems to have just as much ambivalence about identity as did the modern era, but for different reasons. On the one hand, in a climate of skepticism about easy invocations of universalism, in which the hypocrisy and unequal applications of rights purported to apply to all are more and more obvious, recognizing difference has been a clarion call as an alternative to what is seen as an unworkable political discourse of universality through enforced assimilation and uniformity. Studies of difference have mushroomed throughout the academy, and groups expand their titles to reflect more possibilities: the "Gay and Lesbian Students' Association" becomes the "Gay, Lesbian, Bisexual, and Transgendered Students' Association"; "African American Studies" becomes "African American, Caribbean, and Africana Studies"; and "American Studies" begins slowly to reflect more accurately its connotation of a hemisphere rather than a single nation, as well as the divergent traditions and cultures of the peoples even within that one nation. Somewhat going against the grain, many Puerto Rican or Chicano groups are pressured into becoming (pan) "Latino" and thus more inclusive rather than differentiated, but this move is also motivated by the felt need to include more differences, so that the increasing diversification of Latinos in the US can be accommodated in one political constituency.

On the other hand, even while difference becomes the signal of a contemporary and sophisticated consciousness, postmodern thought works to deconstruct difference, to argue that it is *not* the case that "people are discriminated against *because* they are different" but, rather, "difference and the salience of different identities are produced by discrimination" (Scott 1995: 6). Because category distinctions are constructed, and perceptual practices are trained to highlight differences, the characteristics of identities themselves are argued to be made, not found, and made under conditions of oppression that should not be reenforced by the recognitions demanded by identity politics. The instability of identity categories, such that for example "blackness" signifies differently in the UK versus the US, and the essential nature of "Woman" varies across classes as well as cultures, and the plasticity of differences across historical time, are all invoked to argue that difference needs not so much an acknowledgment as a critical analysis.

The postmodern period has also inspired the development of new and speculative identities, from a cyborg imagery intended to replace natural man to various ways to embrace hybridity and diasporic identities as against constructions that assume authenticity or coherence. Even assimilation is toyed with, as long as it can be engaged in from a position of agency and power rather than forced, and moreover recognized as the two-way process it in actuality always is. This indicates the complexity of even those identities we might have considered clear-cut. The binarism of self/other begins to break down with this account, as does the assumption that either individuals or groups are clearly and neatly demarcated. Alain Locke noted in 1924:

> For generations the Negro has been the peasant matrix of that section of America which has most undervalued him, and here he has contributed not only materially in labor and in social patience, but spiritually as well. The South has unconsciously absorbed the gift of his folk-temperament. In less than half a generation it will be easier to recognize this, but the fact remains that a leaven of humor, sentiment, imagination and tropic nonchalance has gone into the making of the South from a humble, unacknowledged source. (p. 54 in this vol)

Slowly, even the mainstream begins to suspect that identities are plural, multiple, and fluid, merging into one another rather than facing each other as if from separate corners of the ring. These new images of identity then hold out the hope of resolving some of the political problems associated with the antagonisms between identities.

Yet in the midst of this celebration of hybridity, postcolonial theorists remind us that there are still operative binaries of power which alter both the lived experience and the political valence of the heterogeneity within. R. Radhakrishnan offers a sobering admonition:

> The crucial difference that one discerns between metropolitan versions of hybridity and "postcolonial" versions is that, whereas the former are characterized by an intransitive and immanent sense of *jouissance*, the latter are expressions of extreme pain and agonizing dislocations. (p. 314 in this vol)

National and class identities thus operate to mediate and alter the political texture of hybrid, cyborg, and complex identities. And as Locke's portrait suggests, hybrid appropriations of subaltern attributes by dominant groups can sometimes effect only a strengthening of the dominant without a concomitant improvement in the situation of the subaltern or even an acknowledgment of the contributions they have made to the newly diversified, culturally richer, and more resilient group in power.

Still, in the increasingly mobile and complex postmodern present, we are developing new capacities to live with ambiguity and contradictions, and in the dispersal and fragmentation of cultures is revealed new images of who we might become. This gives rise to a new practical politics of the open-ended and the impure, in which the demand for self-determination is not based on the claims of an existing, totalized "self" but on the right of historically constructed and socially situated groups to engage the processes of hybridization with some democratic supervision, to control the images and languages that dominate their cultural space, and to aim the educational directives toward goals of the group's own choosing. These new localized, group-based invocations of autonomy must replace the coercive identity enforcements which seek to discipline rogue states, uncooperative indigenous minorities, and unruly identities. Self-determination

8   *Linda Martín Alcoff*

remains the praxis of resistance, even while we relearn the true ways in which identities are formed and the realistic possibilities of autonomy in a world whose interdependence is not only economic and environmental but, just as importantly, cultural and social. The imperialist habit of presumptiveness to speak for others, to set their goals and priorities, and to dictate their values and economic practices may be unlearned through, finally, a recognition that identity makes a difference.

Note

Readers will notice inconsistencies in the forms of citation given in some of the following extracts. For the selections from Marx and Freud, we have retained the notes in their original form as given by the authors. For extracts that initially appeared in law review journals, citations follow the format typical of those journals.

References

Beauvoir, Simone de. 1989. *The Second Sex*. Translated by H. M. Parshley (New York: Vintage).

Goldberg, David Theo. 1993. *Racist Cultures: Philosophy and the Politics of Meaning* (Oxford: Basil Blackwell).

Hall, Stuart. 1990. "Cultural Identity and Diaspora." In Jonathan Rutherford, ed., *Identity: Community, Culture, Difference* (London: Lawrence and Wishart).

Hirschfeld, Lawrence A. 1996. *Race in the Making: Cognition, Culture, and the Child's Construction of Human Kinds* (Cambridge, MA.: MIT Press).

Jordan, Winthrop D. 1968. *White Over Black: American Attitudes Toward the Negro 1550–1812* (Baltimore: Penguin).

Mead, George Herbert. 1982. *The Individual and the Social Self*. Edited by David L. Miller (Chicago: University of Chicago Press).

Rawls, John. 1971. *A Theory of Justice* (Cambridge, MA: Harvard University Press).

Scott, Joan. 1995. "Multiculturalism and the Politics of Identity." In John Rajchman, ed., *The Identity in Question* (New York: Routledge).

West, Cornell. 1982. *Prophesy Deliverance!* (Philadelphia: Westminster Press).

Part I
Foundations

1

Independence and Dependence of Self-Consciousness

G. W. F. HEGEL

Master and Servant

Self-consciousness exists in itself and for itself, in that, and by the fact that it exists for another self-consciousness; that is to say, it *is* only by being acknowledged or "recognized." The conception of this its unity in its duplication, of infinitude realizing itself in self-consciousness, has many sides to it and encloses within it elements of varied significance. Thus its moments must on the one hand be strictly kept apart in detailed distinctiveness, and, on the other, in this distinction must, at the same time, also be taken as not distinguished, or must always be accepted and understood in their opposite sense. This double meaning of what is distinguished lies in the nature of self-consciousness: of its being infinite, or directly the opposite of the determinateness in which it is fixed. The detailed exposition of the notion of this spiritual unity in its duplication will bring before us the process of Recognition.

1. The Double Self-consciousness

Self-consciousness has before it another self-consciousness; it has come outside itself. This has a double significance. First, it has lost its own self, since it finds itself as an *other* being; secondly, it has thereby sublimated that other, for it does not regard the other as essentially real, but sees its own self in the other.

It must suspend this its other self. To do so is to suspend and preserve that first double meaning, and is therefore a second double meaning. First, it must set itself to suspend the other independent being, in order thereby to become certain of itself as true being; secondly, it thereupon proceeds to suspend its own self, for this other is itself.

This suspension in a double sense of its otherness in a double sense is at the same time a return in a double sense into itself. For, firstly, through suspension, it gets back itself, because it becomes one with itself again through the canceling of *its* otherness; but secondly, it likewise gives otherness back again to the other self-consciousness, for it was aware of being in the other, it cancels this its own being in the other and thus lets the other again go free.

This process of self-consciousness in relation to another self-consciousness has in this manner been represented as the action of one alone. But this action on the part of the one has itself the double significance of being at once its own action and the action of that other as well. For the other is likewise independent, shut up within itself, and there is nothing in it which is not there through itself. The first does not have the object before it in the way that object primarily exists for desire, but as an object existing independently for itself, over which therefore it has no power to do anything for its own behoof, if that object does not *per se* do what the first does to it. The process then is absolutely the double process of both self-consciousness. Each sees the other do the same as itself; each itself does what it demands on the part of the other, and for that reason does what it does, only so far as the other does the same. Action from one side only would be useless, because what is to happen can only be brought about by means of both.

The action has then a *double meaning* not only in the sense that it is an act done to itself as well as to the other, but also inasmuch as it is in its un-divided entirety the act of the one as well as of the other.

In this movement we see the process repeated which came before us as the play of forces; in the present case, however, it is found in consciousness. What in the former had effect only for us (contemplating experience), holds here for the terms themselves. The middle term is self-consciousness which breaks itself up into the extremes; and each extreme is this interchange of its own determinateness, and complete transition into the opposite. While *qua* consciousness, it no doubt comes outside itself, still, in being outside itself it is at the same time restrained within itself, it exists for itself, and its self-externalization is for consciousness. *Consciousness* finds that it immediately is and is not another consciousness, as also that this other is for itself only when it cancels itself as existing for itself, and has self-existence only in the self-existence of the other. Each is the mediating term to the other, through which each mediates and unites itself with itself; and each is to itself and to the other an immediate self-existing reality, which, at the same time, exists thus for itself only through this mediation. They recognize themselves as mutually recognizing one another.

This pure conception of recognition, of duplication of self-consciousness within its unity, we must now consider in the way its process appears for self-consciousness. It will, in the first place, present the aspect of the disparity of the two, or the break-up of the middle term into the extremes, which *qua* extremes, are opposed to one another, and of which one is merely recognized, while the other only recognizes.

2. The Conflict of the Opposed Self-consciousnesses

Self-consciousness is primarily simple being-by-itself, self-identity by exclusion of every other from itself. It takes its essential nature and absolute object to be Ego; and in this immediacy, in this bare fact of its self-existence, it is individual. That which for it is the other stands as unessential object, as object with the impress and character of negation. But the other is also a self-consciousness; an individual makes its appearance in antithesis to an individual. Appearing thus in their immediacy, they are for each other in the manner of ordinary objects. They are independent individual forms, modes of consciousness that have not risen above the bare level of life (for the existent object here has been determined as life). They are, moreover, forms of consciousness which have not yet accomplished for one another the process of absolute abstraction, of uprooting all immediate existence, and of being merely the bare, negative fact of self-identical consciousness; or, in other words, have not yet revealed themselves to each other as existing purely for themselves, i.e., as self-consciousness. Each is indeed certain of its own self, but not of the other, and hence its own certainty of itself is still without truth. For its truth would be merely that its own individual existence for itself would be shown to it to be an independent object, or, which is the same thing, that the object would be exhibited as this pure certainty of itself. By the notion of recognition, however, this is not possible, except in the form that as the other is for it, so it is for the other; each in its self through its own action and again through the action of the other achieves this pure abstraction of existence for self.

The presentation of itself, however, as pure abstraction of self-consciousness consists in showing itself as a pure negation of its objective form, or in showing that it is fettered to no determinate existence, that it is not bound at all by the particularity everywhere characteristic of existence as such, and is *not* tied up with life. The process of bringing all this out involves a twofold action – action on the part of the other, and action on the part of itself. In so far as it is the other's action, each aims at the destruction and death of the other. But in this there is implicated also the second kind of action, self-activity; for each implies that it risks its own life. The relation of both self-consciousnesses is in this way so constituted that they prove themselves and each other through a life-and-death struggle. They must enter into this struggle, for they must bring their certainty of themselves, the certainty of being for themselves, to the level of objective truth, and make this a fact both in the case of the other and in their own case as well. And it is solely by risking life, that freedom is obtained; only thus is it tried and proved that the essential nature of self-consciousness is not bare existence, is not the merely immediate form in which it at first makes its appearance, is not its mere absorption in the expanse of life. Rather it is thereby guaranteed that there is nothing present but what might be taken as a vanishing moment – that self-consciousness is merely pure self-existence, being-for-self. The individual, who has not staked his life, may, no doubt, be recognized as a person; but he has not attained the truth of this recognition as an independent self-consciousness. In the same way each must aim at the death of the other, as it risks its own life thereby; for that other is to it of no more worth than itself; the other's reality is presented to the former as an external other, as outside itself; it must cancel that externality. The other is a purely existent consciousness and entangled in manifold ways; it must regard its otherness as pure existence for itself or as absolute negation.

This trying and testing, however, by a struggle to the death cancels both the truth which was to result from it, and therewith the certainty of self altogether. For just as life is the natural "position" of consciousness, independence without absolute negativity, so death is the natural "negation" of consciousness, negation without independence, which thus remains without the requisite significance of actual recognition. Through death, doubtless, there has arisen the certainty that both did stake their life, and held it lightly both in their own case and in the case of the other; but that is not for those who underwent this struggle. They cancel their consciousness which had its place in this alien element of natural existence; in other words, they cancel themselves and are sublated, as terms or extremes seeking to have existence on their own account. But along with this there vanishes from the play of change, the essential moment, viz., that of breaking up into extremes with opposite characteristics; and the middle term collapses into a lifeless unity which is broken up into lifeless extremes, merely existent and not opposed. And the two do not mutually give and receive one another back from each other through consciousness; they let one another go quite indifferently, like things. Their act is abstract negation, not the negation characteristic of consciousness, which cancels in such a way that it preserves and maintains what is sublated, and thereby survives its being sublated.

In this experience self-consciousness becomes aware that *life* is as essential to it as pure self-consciousness. In immediate self-consciousness the simple ego is absolute object, which, however, is for us or in itself absolute mediation, and has as its essential moment substantial and solid independence. The dissolution of that simple unity is the result of the first experience; through this there is posited a pure self-consciousness, and a conscious-

ness which is not purely for itself, but for another, i.e., as an existent consciousness, consciousness in the form and shape of thinghood. Both moments are essential, since, in the first instance, they are unlike and opposed, and their reflection into unity has not yet come to light, they stand as two opposed forms or modes of consciousness. The one is independent whose essential nature is to be for itself, the other is dependent whose essence is life or existence for another. The former is the Master, or Lord, the latter the Bondsman.

3.   Master and Servant

Rule of the master

The master is the consciousness that exists *for itself*; but no longer merely the general notion of existence for the self. Rather, it is consciousness which, while existing on its own account, is mediated with itself through another consciousness, viz., bound up with an independent being or with thinghood in general. The master brings himself into relation to both these moments, to a thing as such, the object of desire, and to the consciousness whose essential character is thinghood, and since the master, *qua* notion of self-consciousness, is (a) an immediate relation of self-existence, but is now moreover at the same time (b) mediation, or a being-for-self which is for itself only through an other – he (the master) stands in relation (a) immediately to both, (b) mediately to each through the other. The master relates himself to the servant mediately through independent existence, for that is precisely what keeps the servant in bond; it is his chain, from which he could not, in the struggle, get away, and for that reason he proves himself dependent, shows that his independence consists in his being a thing. The master, however, is the power controlling this state of existence, for he has shown in the struggle that he holds existence to be merely something negative. Since he is the power dominating the negative nature of existence, while this existence again is the power controlling the other (the servant), the master holds, as a consequence, this other in subordination. In the same way the master relates himself to the thing mediately through the servant. The servant being a self-consciousness in the broad sense, also takes up a negative attitude to things and cancels them; but the thing is, at the same time, independent for him, and, in consequence, he cannot, with all his negating, get so far as to annihilate it outright and be done with it; that is to say, he merely works on it. To the master, on the other hand, by means of this mediating process, belongs the immediate relation, in the sense of the pure negation of it; in other words he gets the enjoyment. What mere desire did not attain, he now succeeds in attaining, viz., to have done with the thing, and find satisfaction in enjoyment. Desire alone did not get the length of this, because of the independence of the thing. The master, however, who has interposed the servant between it and himself, thereby relates himself merely to the dependence of the thing, and enjoys it without qualification and without reserve. The aspect of its independence he leaves to the servant, who labors upon it.

In these two moments, the master gets his recognition through another consciousness, for in them the latter affirms itself as unessential, both by working upon the thing, and, on the other hand, by the fact of being dependent on a determinate existence; in neither case can this other get the mastery over existence, and succeed in absolutely negating it. We have thus here this moment of recognition, viz., that the other consciousness cancels itself as self-existent, and *ipso facto*, itself does what the first does to it. In the same way we have the other moment, that this action on the part of the second is the action proper of the first; for what is done by the servant is properly an action on the part of the master. The latter exists only for himself, that is his essential nature; he is the negative power without qualification, a power to which the thing is nothing, and his is thus the absolutely essential action in this situation, while the servant's is not so, his is an unessential activity. But for recognition proper there is needed the moment that what the master does to the other he should also do to himself, and what the servant does to himself, he should do to the other also. On that account a form of recognition has arisen that is one-sided and unequal.

In all this, the unessential consciousness is, for the master, the object which embodies the truth of his certainty of himself. But it is evident that this object does not correspond to its notion; for, just where the master has effectively achieved rule, he really finds that something has come about quite different from an independent consciousness. It is not an independent, but rather a dependent consciousness that he has achieved. He is thus not

assured of self-existence as his truth; he finds that his truth is rather the unessential consciousness, and the fortuitous unessential action of that consciousness.

The truth of the independent consciousness is accordingly the consciousness of the servant. This doubtless appears in the first instance outside it, and not as the truth of self-consciousness. But just as the position of master showed its essential nature to be the reverse of what it wants to be, so, too, the position of servant will, when completed, pass into the opposite of what it immediately is: being a consciousness repressed within itself, it will enter into itself, and change around into real and true independence.

Anxiety

We have seen what the position of servant is only in relation to that of the master. But it is a self-consciousness, and we have now to consider what it is, in this regard, in and for itself. In the first instance, the master is taken to be the essential reality for the state of the servant; hence, for it, the truth is the independent consciousness existing for itself, although this truth is not yet taken as inherent in the servant's position itself. Still, it does in fact contain within itself this truth of pure negativity and self-existence, because it has experienced this reality within it. For this self-consciousness was not in peril and fear for this element or that, nor for this or that moment of time, it was afraid for its entire being; it felt the fear of death, it was in mortal terror of its sovereign master. It has been through that experience melted to its inmost soul, has trembled throughout its every fiber, the stable foundations of its whole being have quaked within it. This complete perturbation of its entire substance, this absolute dissolution of all its stability into fluent continuity, is, however, the simple, ultimate nature of self-consciousness, absolute negativity, pure self-referent existence, which consequently is involved in this type of consciousness. This moment of pure self-existence is moreover a fact for it; for in the master this moment is consciously his object. Further, this servant's consciousness is not only this total dissolution in a general way; in serving and toiling, the servant actually carries this out. By serving he cancels in every particular moment his dependence on and attachment to natural existence, and by his work removes this existence.

Shaping and fashioning

The feeling of absolute power, however, realized both in general and in the particular form of service, is only dissolution implicitly, and albeit the fear of his master is the beginning of wisdom, consciousness is not therein aware of being self-existent. Through work and labor, however, this consciousness of the servant comes to itself. In the moment which corresponds to desire in the case of the master's consciousness, the aspect of the non-essential relation to the thing seemed to fall to the lot of the servant, since the thing there retained its independence. Desire has reserved to itself the pure negating of the object and thereby unalloyed feeling of self. This satisfaction, however, just for that reason is itself only a state of evanescence, for it lacks objectivity or subsistence. Labor, on the other hand, is desire restrained and checked, evanescence delayed and postponed; in other words, labor shapes and fashions the thing. The negative relation to the object passes into the *form* of the object, into something that is permanent and remains; because it is just for the laborer that the object has independence. This negative mediating agency, this activity giving shape and form, is at the same time the individual existence, the pure self-existence of that consciousness, which now in the work it does is externalized and passes into the condition of permanence. The consciousness that toils and serves accordingly comes by this means to view that independent being as its self.

But again, shaping or forming the object has not only the positive significance that the servant becomes thereby aware of himself as factually and objectively self-existent; this type of consciousness has also a negative import, in contrast with its first aspect, the element of fear. For in shaping the thing it only becomes aware of its own proper negativity, its existence on its own account, as an object, through the fact that it cancels the actual form confronting it. But this objective negative element is precisely the alien, external reality, before which it trembled. Now, however, it destroys this extraneous alien negative, affirms and sets itself up as a negative in the element of permanence, and thereby becomes aware of being objectively for itself. In the master, this self-existence is felt to be an other, is only external; in fear, the self-existence is present implicitly; in fashioning the thing, self-existence comes to be felt explicitly as its own proper being, and it attains the consciousness that itself exists in

its own right and on its own account (*an und fuer sich*). By the fact that the form is objectified, it does not become something other than the consciousness molding the thing through work; for just that form is his pure self-existence, which therein becomes truly realized. Thus precisely in labor where there seemed to be merely some outsider's mind and ideas involved, the servant becomes aware, through this rediscovery of himself by himself, of having and being a "mind of his own."

For this reflection of self into self the two moments, fear and service in general, as also that of formative activity, are necessary: and at the same time both must exist in a universal manner. Without the discipline of service and obedience, fear remains formal and does not spread over the whole known reality of existence. Without the formative activity shaping the thing, fear remains inward and mute, and consciousness does not become objective for itself. Should consciousness shape and form the thing without the initial state of absolute fear, then it has merely a vain and futile "mind of its own"; for its form or negativity is not negativity *per se*, and hence its formative activity cannot furnish the consciousness of itself as essentially real. If it has endured not absolute fear, but merely some slight anxiety, the negative reality has remained external to it, its substance has not been through and through infected thereby. Since the entire content of its natural consciousness has not tottered and been shaken, it is still inherently a determinate mode of being; having a "mind of its own" (*der eigene sinn*) is simply stubbornness (*Eigensinn*), a type of freedom which does not get beyond the attitude of the servant. The less the pure form can become its essential nature, the less is that form, as overspreading and controlling particulars, a universal formative activity, an absolute conception; it is rather a piece of cleverness which has power within a certain range, but does not wield universal power and dominate the entire objective reality.

The Spirit

Reason is spirit, when its certainty of being all reality has been raised to the level of truth, and reason is consciously aware of itself as its own world, and of the world as itself. The development of spirit was indicated in the immediately preceding movement of mind, where the object of consciousness, the category pure and simple, rose to be the notion of reason. When reason "observes" this pure unity of ego and existence, the unity of subjectivity and objectivity, of for–itself–ness and in–itself–ness this unity is immanent, has the character of implicitness or of being; and consciousness of reason finds itself. But the true nature of "observation" is rather the transcendence of this instinct of finding its object lying directly at hand, and passing beyond this unconscious state of existence. The directly perceived (*angeschaut*) category, the thing simply "found," enters consciousness as the self-existence of the ego – an ego which now knows itself in the objective reality, and knows itself there as the self. But this feature of the category, viz., of being for-itself as opposed to being immanent within itself, is equally one-sided, and a moment that cancels itself. The category therefore gets for consciousness the character which it possesses in its universal truth – it is self-contained essential reality (*an und fuersich seiendes Wesen*). This character, still abstract, which constitutes the nature of absolute fact, of "fact itself," is to begin with "spiritual reality" (*das geistige Wesen*); and its mode of consciousness is here a formal knowledge of that reality, a knowledge which is occupied with the varied and manifold content thereof. This consciousness is still, in point of fact, a particular individual distinct from the general substance, and either prescribes arbitrary laws or pretends to possess within its own knowledge as such the laws as they absolutely are (*an und fuer sich*), and takes itself to be the power that passes judgment on them. Or again, looked at from the side of the substance, this is seen to be the self-contained and self-sufficient spiritual reality, which is not yet a consciousness of its own self. The self-contained and self-sufficient reality, however, which is at once aware of being actual in the form of consciousness and presents itself to itself, is Spirit.

Its essential spiritual being (*Wesen*) has been above designated as the ethical substance; spirit, however, is concrete ethical actuality (*Wirklichkeit*). Spirit is the self of the actual consciousness, to which spirit stands opposed, or rather which appears over against itself, as an objective actual world that has lost, however, all sense of strangeness for the self, just as the self has lost all sense of having a dependent or independent existence by itself, cut off and separated from that world. Being substance and universal self-identical permanent essence (*Wesen*), spirit is the immovable irreducible basis and the starting point for the action of all and every one; it is their purpose and their goal, because the ideally implicit nature (*Ansich*) of all self-consciousnesses. This substance is likewise the universal product, wrought and created by the action of each and all, and giving them unity and likeness and identity of meaning; for it is being-by-itself (*Fuersichsein*), the self-action. When considered as substance, spirit is unbending righteous self-sameness, self-identity; but when considered as being-by-itself (*Fuersichsein*), its continuity is resolved into discrete elements, it is the self-sacrificing soul of goodness, the benevolent essential nature, in which each fulfills his own special work, rends the continuum of the universal substance, and takes his own share of it. This resolution of the essence into individual forms is just the aspect of the separate action and the separate self of all the several individuals; it is the moving soul of the ethical substance, the resultant universal spiritual being. Just because this substance is a being resolved in the self, it is not a lifeless essence, but real and alive.

2

On the Jewish Question

KARL MARX

1. Bruno Bauer, *Die Judenfrage*[1]

The German Jews seek emancipation. What kind of emancipation do they want? *Civic, political* emancipation.

Bruno Bauer replies to them: In Germany no one is politically emancipated. We ourselves are not free. How then could we liberate you? You Jews are *egoists* if you demand for yourselves, as Jews, a special emancipation. You should work, as Germans, for the political emancipation of Germany, and as men, for the emancipation of mankind. You should feel the particular kind of oppression and shame which you suffer, not as an exception to the rule but rather as a confirmation of the rule.

Or do the Jews want to be placed on a footing of equality with the *Christian subjects?* If they recognize the *Christian state* as legally established they also recognize the régime of general enslavement. Why should their particular yoke be irksome when they accept the general yoke? Why should the German be interested in the liberation of the Jew, if the Jew is not interested in the liberation of the German?

The *Christian* state recognizes nothing but *privileges.* The Jew himself, in this state, has the privilege of being a Jew. As a Jew he possesses rights which the Christians do not have. Why does he want rights which he does not have but which the Christians enjoy?

In demanding his emancipation from the Christian state he asks the Christian state to abandon its *religious* prejudice. But does he, the Jew, give up *his* religious prejudice? Has he then the right to insist that someone else should forswear his religion?

The *Christian* state, *by its very nature*, is incapable of emancipating the Jew. But, adds Bauer, the Jew, by his very nature, cannot be emancipated. As long as the state remains Christian, and as long as the Jew remains a Jew, they are equally incapable, the one of conferring emancipation, the other of receiving it.

With respect to the Jews the Christian state can only adopt the attitude of a Christian state. That is, it can permit the Jew, as a matter of privilege, to isolate himself from its other subjects; but it must then allow the pressures of all the other spheres of society to bear upon the Jew, and all the more heavily since he is in *religious* opposition to the dominant religion. But the Jew likewise can only adopt a Jewish attitude, i.e. that of a foreigner, towards the state, since he opposes his illusory nationality to actual nationality, his illusory law to actual law. He considers it his right to separate himself from the rest of humanity; as a matter of principle he takes no part in the historical movement and looks to a future which has nothing in common with the future of mankind as a whole. He regards himself as a member of the Jewish people, and the Jewish people as the chosen people.

On what grounds, then, do you Jews demand emancipation? On account of your religion? But it is the mortal enemy of the state religion. As citizens? But there are no citizens in Germany. As men? But you are not men any more than are those to whom you appeal.

Bauer, after criticizing earlier approaches and solutions, formulates the question of Jewish emancipation in a new way. What, he asks, is the nature of the Jew who is to be emancipated, and the *nature* of the Christian state which is to emancipate him?

He replies by a critique of the Jewish religion, analyses the religious opposition between Judaism and
Christianity, explains the essence of the Christian
state; and does all this with dash, clarity, wit and
profundity, in a style which is as precise as it is
pithy and vigorous.

How then does Bauer resolve the Jewish question? What is the result? To formulate a question is
to resolve it. The critical study of the Jewish question is the answer to the Jewish question. Here it is
in brief: we have to emancipate ourselves before we
can emancipate others.

The most stubborn form of the opposition between Jew and Christian is the *religious* opposition.
How is an opposition resolved? By making it impossible. And how is *religious* opposition made impossible? By abolishing *religion*. As soon as Jew and
Christian come to see in their respective religions
nothing more than *stages in the development of the
human mind* – snake skins which have been cast off
by *history*, and *man* as the snake who clothed himself in them – they will no longer find themselves
in religious opposition, but in a purely critical, *scientific* and human relationship. *Science* will then
constitute their unity. But scientific oppositions are
resolved by science itself.

The *German* Jew, in particular, suffers from the
general lack of political freedom and the pronounced
Christianity of the state. But in Bauer's sense the
Jewish question has a general significance, independent of the specifically German conditions. It
is the question of the relations between religion
and the state, of the *contradiction between religious
prejudice and political emancipation*. Emancipation
from religion is posited as a condition, both for the
Jew who wants political emancipation, and for the
state which should emancipate him and itself be
emancipated.

"Very well, it may be said (and the Jew himself
says it) but the Jew should not be emancipated
because he is a Jew, because he has such an excellent and universal moral creed; the *Jew* should take
second place to the citizen, and he will be a *citizen*
although he is and desires to remain a Jew. In other
words, he is and remains a *Jew*, even though he is a
citizen and as such lives in a universal human condition; his restricted Jewish nature always finally
triumphs over his human and political obligations.
The bias persists even though it is overcome by
general principles. But if it persists, it would be
truer to say that it overcomes all the rest." "It is
only in a sophistical and superficial sense that the

Jew could remain a Jew in political life. Consequently, if he wanted to remain a Jew, this would
mean that the superficial became the essential and
thus triumphed. In other words, his life *in the state*
would be only a semblance, or a momentary exception to the essential and normal."[2]

Let us see also how Bauer establishes the role of
the state.

"France," he says, "has provided us recently,[3] in
connexion with the Jewish question (and for that
matter all other *political* questions), with the spectacle of a life which is free but which revokes its
freedom by law and so declares it to be merely an
appearance; and which, on the other hand, denies
its free laws by its acts."[4]

"In France, universal liberty is not yet established by law, nor is the *Jewish question as yet resolved*, because legal liberty, i.e. the equality of all
citizens, is restricted in actual life, which is still
dominated and fragmented by religious privileges,
and because the lack of liberty in actual life influences law in its turn and obliges it to sanction the
division of citizens who are by nature free into
oppressors and oppressed."[5]

When, therefore, would the Jewish question be
resolved in France?

"The Jew would really have ceased to be Jewish,
for example, if he did not allow his religious code
to prevent his fulfilment of his duties towards the
state and his fellow citizens; if he attended and
took part in the public business of the Chamber of
Deputies on the sabbath. It would be necessary,
further, to abolish all *religious privilege*, including
the monopoly of a privileged church. If, thereafter,
some or many or *even the overwhelming majority felt
obliged to fulfil their religious duties*, such practices
should be left *to them as an absolutely* private matter."[6] "There is no longer any religion when there
is no longer a privileged religion. Take away from
religion its power to excommunicate and it will no
longer exist."[7] "Mr. Martin du Nord has seen, in
the suggestion to omit any mention of Sunday in
the law, a proposal to declare that Christianity has
ceased to exist. With equal right (and the right is
well founded) the declaration that the law of the
sabbath is no longer binding upon the Jew would
amount to proclaiming the end of Judaism."[8]

Thus Bauer demands, on the one hand, that the
Jew should renounce Judaism, and in general that
man should renounce religion, in order to be emancipated as a citizen. On the other hand, he considers, and this follows logically, that the political

abolition of religion is the abolition of all religion. The state which presupposes religion is not yet a true or actual state. "Clearly, the religious idea gives some assurances to the state. But to what state? *To what kind of state?*"[9]

At this point we see that the Jewish question is considered only from one aspect.

It was by no means sufficient to ask: who should emancipate? who should be emancipated? The critic should ask a third question: *what kind of emancipation* is involved? What are the essential conditions of the emancipation which is demanded? The criticism of *political emancipation* itself was only the final criticism of the Jewish question and its genuine resolution into the "*general question of the age.*"

Bauer, since he does not formulate the problem at this level, falls into contradictions. He establishes conditions which are not based upon the nature of *political* emancipation. He raises questions which are irrelevant to his problem, and he resolves problems which leave his question unanswered. When Bauer says of the opponents of Jewish emancipation that "Their error was simply to assume that the Christian state was the only true one, and not to subject it to the same criticism as Judaism,"[10] we see his own error in the fact that he subjects *only* the "Christian state," and not the "state as such" to criticism, that he does not examine *the relation between political emancipation and human emancipation*, and that he, therefore, poses conditions which are only explicable by his lack of critical sense in confusing political emancipation and universal human emancipation. Bauer asks the Jews: Have you, from your standpoint, the right to demand *political emancipation*? We ask the converse question: from the standpoint of *political* emancipation can the Jew be required to abolish Judaism, or man be asked to abolish religion?

The Jewish question presents itself differently according to the state in which the Jew resides. In Germany, where there is no political state, no state as such, the Jewish question is purely *theological*. The Jew finds himself in *religious* opposition to the state, which proclaims Christianity as its foundation. This state is a theologian *ex professo*. Criticism here is criticism of theology; a double-edged criticism, of Christian and of Jewish theology. And so we move always in the domain of theology, however *critically* we may move therein.

In France, which is a *constitutional* state, the Jewish question is a question of constitutionalism, of the incompleteness *of political emancipation*. Since the *semblance* of a state religion is maintained here, if only in the insignificant and self-contradictory formula of a *religion of the majority*, the relation of the Jews to the state also retains a semblance of religious, theological opposition.

It is only in the free states of North America, or at least in some of them, that the Jewish question loses its *theological* significance and becomes a truly *secular* question. Only where the state exists in its completely developed form can the relation of the Jew, and of the religious man in general, to the political state appear in a pure form, with its own characteristics. The criticism of this relation ceases to be theological criticism when the state ceases to maintain a *theological* attitude towards religion, that is, when it adopts the attitude of a state, i.e. a *political* attitude. Criticism then becomes *criticism of the political state*. And at this point, where the question ceases to be *theological*, Bauer's criticism ceases to be critical.

"There is not, in the United States, either a state religion or a religion declared to be that of a majority, or a predominance of one religion over another. The state remains aloof from all religions."[11] There are even some states in North America in which "the constitution does not impose any religious belief or practice as a condition of political rights."[12] And yet, "no one in the United States believes that a man without religion can be an honest man."[13] And North America is preeminently the country of religiosity, as Beaumont,[14] Tocqueville[15] and the Englishman, Hamilton,[16] assure us in unison. However, the states of North America only serve as an example. The question is: what is the relation between *complete* political emancipation and religion? If we find in the country which has attained full political emancipation, that religion not only continues to *exist* but is *fresh* and *vigorous*, this is proof that the existence of religion is not at all opposed to the perfection of the state. But since the existence of religion is the existence of a defect, the source of this defect must be sought in the *nature* of the state itself. Religion no longer appears as the basis, but as the *manifestation* of secular narrowness. That is why we explain the religious constraints upon the free citizens by the secular constraints upon them. We do not claim that they must transcend their religious narrowness in order to get rid of their secular limitations. We claim that they will transcend their religious narrowness once they have overcome their secular limitations. We do not turn secular questions into theological questions; we turn theological questions into secular ones. History has for long enough been resolved into superstition; but we now resolve superstition into history. The question of the *relation between political emancipation and religion* becomes for us a question of the *relation between political emancipation and human emancipation*. We criticize the religious failings of the political state by criticizing the political state in its *secular* form, disregarding its religious failings. We express in human terms the contradiction between the state and a *particular religion*, for example *Judaism*, by showing the contradiction between the state and particular *secular elements*, between the state and *religion in general* and between the state and its general *presuppositions*.

The *political* emancipation of the Jew or the Christian – of the *religious* man in general – is the *emancipation of* the state from Judaism, Christianity, and *religion* in general. The *state* emancipates itself from religion in its own particular way, in the mode which corresponds to its nature, by emancipating itself from the *state religion*; that is to say, by giving recognition to no religion and affirming itself purely and simply as a state. To be *politically* emancipated from religion is not to be finally and completely emancipated from religion, because political emancipation is not the final and absolute form of *human* emancipation.

The limits of political emancipation appear at once in the fact that the *state* can liberate itself from a constraint without man himself being *really* liberated; that a state may be a *free state* without man himself being a *free man*. Bauer himself tacitly admits this when he makes political emancipation depend upon the following condition:

"It would be necessary, moreover, to abolish all religious privileges, including the monopoly of a privileged church. If some people, or even the *immense majority, still felt obliged to fulfil their religious duties*, this practice should be left to them as a *completely private matter*." Thus the state may have emancipated itself from religion, even though the *immense majority* of people continue to be religious. And the immense majority do not cease to be religious by virtue of being religious *in private*.

The attitude of the state, especially the *free state*, towards religion is only the attitude towards religion of the individuals who compose the state. It follows that man frees himself from a constraint in a *political* way, through the state, when he transcends his limitations, in contradiction with

himself, and in an *abstract, narrow* and partial way. Furthermore, by emancipating himself *politically*, man emancipates himself in a *devious way*, through an intermediary, however *necessary* this intermediary may be. Finally, even when he proclaims himself an atheist through the intermediary of the state, that is, when he declares the state to be an atheist, he is still engrossed in religion, because he only recognizes himself as an atheist in a roundabout way, through an intermediary. Religion is simply the recognition of man in a roundabout fashion; that is, through an intermediary. The state is the intermediary between man and human liberty. Just as Christ is the intermediary to whom man attributes all his own divinity and all his religious *bonds*, so the state is the intermediary to which man confides all his non-divinity and all his *human freedom*.

The *political* elevation of man above religion shares the weaknesses and merits of all such political measures. For example, the state as a state abolishes *private property* (i.e. man decrees by *political* means the *abolition* of private property) when it abolishes the *property qualification* for electors and representatives, as has been done in many of the North American States. Hamilton interprets this phenomenon quite correctly from the political standpoint: *The masses have gained a victory over property owners and financial wealth.*[17] Is not private property ideally abolished when the non-owner comes to legislate for the owner of property? The *property qualification* is the last *political* form in which private property is recognized.

But the political suppression of private property not only does not abolish private property; it actually presupposes its existence. The state abolishes, after its fashion, the distinctions established by *birth, social rank, education, occupation*, when it decrees that birth, social rank, education, occupation are *non-political* distinctions; when it proclaims, without regard to these distinctions, that every member of society is an *equal* partner in popular sovereignty, and treats all the elements which compose the real life of the nation from the standpoint of the state. But the state, none the less, allows private property, education, occupation, to *act* after *their* own fashion, namely as private property, education, occupation, and to manifest their *particular* nature. Far from abolishing these *effective* differences, it only exists so far as they are presupposed; it is conscious of being a *political state* and it manifests its *universality* only in opposition to these elements. Hegel, therefore, defines the relation of the political state to religion quite correctly when he says: "In order for the state to come in to existence as the *self-knowing* ethical actuality of spirit, it is essential that it should be distinct from the forms of authority and of faith. But this distinction emerges only in so far as divisions occur within the ecclesiastical sphere itself. It is only in this way that the state, above the *particular* churches, has attained to the universality of thought – its formal principle – and is bringing this universality into existence."[18] To be sure! Only in this manner, *above* the *particular* elements, can the state constitute itself as universality.

The perfected political state is, by its nature, the *species-life*[19] of man as *opposed* to his material life. All the presuppositions of this egoistic life continue to exist in *civil society outside* the political sphere, as qualities of civil society. Where the political state has attained to its full development, man leads, not only in thought, in consciousness, but in *reality*, in *life*, a double existence – celestial and terrestrial. He lives in the *political community*, where he regards himself as a *communal being*, and in *civil society* where he acts simply as a *private individual*, treats other men as means, degrades himself to the role of a mere means, and becomes the plaything of alien powers. The political state, in relation to civil society, is just as spiritual as is heaven in relation to earth. It stands in the same opposition to civil society, and overcomes it in the same manner as religion overcomes the narrowness of the profane world; i.e. it has always to acknowledge it again, re-establish it, and allow itself to be dominated by it. Man, in his *most intimate* reality, in civil society, is a profane being. Here, where he appears both to himself and to others as a real individual he is an *illusory* phenomenon. In the state, on the contrary, where he is regarded as a species-being,[20] man is the imaginary member of an imaginary sovereignty, divested of his real, individual life, and infused with an unreal universality.

The conflict in which the individual, as the professor of a *particular* religion, finds himself involved with his own quality of citizenship and with other men as members of the community, may be resolved into the *secular* schism between the *political* state and *civil society*. For man as a *bourgeois*[21] "life in the state is only an appearance or a fleeting exception to the normal and essential." It is true that the *bourgeois*, like the Jew, participates in political life only in a sophistical way, just as the *citoyen*[22] is a Jew or a *bourgeois* only in a sophistical way. But this sophistry is not personal. It is the *sophistry of the political state* itself. The difference between the religious man and the citizen is the same as that between the shopkeeper and the citizen, between the day-labourer and the citizen, between the landed proprietor and the citizen, between the *living individual* and the *citizen*. The contradiction in which the religious man finds himself with the political man, is the same contradiction in which the *bourgeois* finds himself with the citizen, and the member of civil society with his *political lion's skin*.

This secular opposition, to which the Jewish question reduces itself – the relation between the political state and its presuppositions, whether the latter are material elements such as private property, etc., or spiritual elements such as culture or religion, the conflict between the *general interest* and *private interest*, the schism between the *political* state and *civil society* – these profane contradictions, Bauer leaves intact, while he directs his polemic against their *religious* expression. "It is precisely this basis – that is, the needs which assure the existence of *civil society* and *guarantee its necessity* – which exposes its existence to continual danger, maintains an element of uncertainty in civil society, produces this continually changing compound of wealth and poverty, of prosperity and distress, and above all generates change."[23] Compare the whole section entitled "Civil society,"[24] which follows closely the distinctive features of Hegel's philosophy of right. Civil society, in its opposition to this political state, is recognized as necessary because the political state is recognized as necessary.

Political emancipation certainly represents a great progress. It is not, indeed, the final form of human emancipation, but it is the final form of human emancipation *within* the framework of the prevailing social order. It goes without saying that we are speaking here of real, practical emancipation.

Man emancipates himself *politically* from religion by expelling it from the sphere of public law to that of private law. Religion is no longer the spirit of the *state*, in which man behaves, albeit in a specific and limited way and in a particular sphere, as a species-being, in community with other men. It has become the spirit of *civil society*, of the sphere of egoism and of the *bellum omnium contra omnes*. It is no longer the essence of *community*, but the essence of *differentiation*. It has become what it was at the *beginning*, an expression of the fact that man is *separated* from the *community*, from himself and from other men. It is now only the abstract avowal of an individual folly, a private whim or caprice. The infinite fragmentation of religion in North America, for example, already gives it the *external* form of a strictly private affair. It has been relegated among the numerous private interests and exiled from the life of the community as such. But one should have no illusions about the scope of political emancipation. The division of man into the *public person* and the *private person*, the *displacement* of religion from the state to civil society – all this is not a stage in political emancipation but its consummation. Thus political emancipation does not abolish, and does not even strive to abolish, man's *real* religiosity.

The *decomposition* of man into Jew and citizen, Protestant and citizen, religious man and citizen, is not a deception practised *against* the political system nor yet an evasion of political emancipation. It is *political emancipation itself*, the *political* mode of emancipation from religion. Certainly, in periods when the political state as such comes violently to birth in civil society, and when men strive to liberate themselves through political emancipation, the state can, and must, proceed to *abolish and destroy religion*; but only in the same way as it proceeds to abolish private property, by declaring a maximum, by confiscation, or by progressive taxation, or in the same way as it proceeds to abolish life, by the *guillotine*. At those times when the state is most aware of itself, political life seeks to stifle its own prerequisites – civil society and its elements – and to establish itself as the genuine and harmonious species-life of man. But it can only achieve this end by setting itself in *violent* contradiction with its own conditions of existence, by declaring a *permanent* revolution. Thus the political drama ends necessarily with the restoration of religion, of private property, of all the elements of civil society, just as war ends with the conclusion of peace.

In fact, the perfected Christian state is not the so-called *Christian* state which acknowledges Christianity as its basis, as the state religion, and thus adopts an exclusive attitude towards other religions; it is, rather, the *atheistic* state, the democratic state, the state which relegates religion among the other elements of civil society. The state which is still theological, which still professes officially the Christian creed, and which has not yet dared to declare itself a *state*, has not yet succeeded in expressing in a human and *secular* form, in its political *reality*,

the human basis of which Christianity is the transcendental expression. The so-called Christian state is simply a *non-state*; since it is not Christianity as a religion, but only the *human core* of the Christian religion which can realize itself in truly human creations.

The so-called Christian state is the Christian negation of the state, but not at all the political realization of Christianity. The state which professes Christianity as a religion does not yet profess it in a political form, because it still has a religious attitude towards religion. In other words, such a state is not the *genuine realization* of the human basis of religion, because it still accepts the *unreal*, *imaginary* form of this human core. The so-called Christian state is an *imperfect* state, for which the Christian religion serves as the *supplement* and *sanctification* of its imperfection. Thus religion becomes necessarily one of its *means*; and so it is the *hypocritical* state. There is a great difference between saying: (i) that the *perfect* state, owing to a deficiency in the general *nature* of the state, counts religion as one of its *prerequisites*, or (ii) that the *imperfect* state, owing to a deficiency in its *particular existence* as an imperfect state, declares that religion is its *basis*. In the latter, religion becomes *imperfect politics*. In the former, the imperfection even of perfected *politics* is revealed in religion. The so-called Christian state needs the Christian religion in order to complete itself *as a state*. The democratic state, the real state, does not need religion for its political consummation. On the contrary, it can dispense with religion, because in this case the human core of religion is realized in a profane manner. The so-called Christian state, on the other hand, has a political attitude towards religion, and a religious attitude towards politics. It reduces political institutions and religion equally to mere appearances.

In order to make this contradiction clearer we shall examine Bauer's model of the Christian state, a model which is derived from his study of the German-Christian state.

"Quite recently," says Bauer, "in order to demonstrate the *impossibility* or the *non-existence* of a Christian state, those passages in the Bible have been frequently quoted with which the state *does not conform and cannot conform unless it wishes to dissolve itself entirely*."

"But the question is not so easily settled. What do these Biblical passages demand? Supernatural renunciation, submission to the authority of revelation, turning away from the state, the abolition of profane conditions. But the Christian state proclaims and accomplishes all these things. It has assimilated the *spirit of the Bible*, and if it does not reproduce it exactly in the terms which the Bible uses, that is simply because it expresses this spirit in political forms, in forms which are borrowed from the political system of this world but which, in the religious rebirth which they are obliged to undergo, are reduced to simple appearances. Man turns away from the state and by this means realizes and completes the political institutions."[25]

Bauer continues by showing that the members of a Christian state no longer constitute a nation with a will of its own. The nation has its true existence in the leader to whom it is subjected, but this leader is, by his origin and nature, alien to it since he has been imposed by God without the people having any part in the matter. The laws of such a nation are not its own work, but are direct revelations. The supreme leader, in his relations with the real nation, the masses, requires privileged intermediaries; and the nation itself disintegrates into a multitude of distinct spheres which are formed and determined by chance, are differentiated from each other by their interests and their specific passions and prejudices, and acquire as a privilege the permission to isolate themselves from each other, etc.[26]

But Bauer himself says: "Politics, if it is to be nothing more than religion, should not be politics; any more than the scouring of pans, if it is treated as a religious matter, should be regarded as ordinary housekeeping."[27] But in the German-Christian state religion is an "economic matter" just as "economic matters" are religion. In the German-Christian state the power of religion is the religion of power.

The separation of the "spirit of the Bible" from the "letter of the Bible" is an *irreligious* act. The state which expresses the Bible in the letter of politics, or in any letter other than that of the Holy Ghost, commits sacrilege, if not in the eyes of men at least in the eyes of its own religion. The state which acknowledges the Bible as its charter and Christianity as its supreme rule must be assessed according to the words of the Bible; for even the language of the Bible is sacred. Such a state, as well as the *human rubbish* upon which it is based, finds itself involved in a painful contradiction, which is insoluble from the standpoint of religious consciousness, when it is referred to those words of the Bible "with which it does not conform and *cannot con-*

form unless it wishes to dissolve itself entirely." And why does it not wish to dissolve itself entirely? The state itself cannot answer either itself or others. In its own consciousness the official Christian state is an "ought" whose realization is impossible. It cannot affirm the *reality* of its own existence without lying to itself, and so it remains always in its own eyes an object of doubt, an uncertain and problematic object. Criticism is, therefore, entirely within its rights in forcing the state, which supports itself upon the Bible, into a total disorder of thought in which it no longer knows whether it is *illusion* or *reality*; and in which the infamy of its *profane* ends (for which religion serves as a cloak) enter into an insoluble conflict with the probity of its *religious* consciousness (for which religion appears as the goal of the world). Such a state can only escape its inner torment by becoming the *myrmidon* of the Catholic Church. In the face of this Church, which asserts that secular power is entirely subordinate to its commands, the state is powerless; powerless the secular power which claims to be the rule of the religious spirit.

What prevails in the so-called Christian state is not man but alienation. The only man who counts – the *King* – is specifically differentiated from other men and is still a religious being associated directly with heaven and with God. The relations which exist here are relations still based upon *faith*. The religious spirit is still not really secularized.

But the religious spirit cannot be *really* secularized. For what is it but the *non-secular* form of a stage in the development of the human spirit? The religious spirit can only be realized if the stage of development of the human spirit which it expresses in religious form, manifests and constitutes itself in its *secular* form. This is what happens in the *democratic* state. The basis of this state is not Christianity but the *human basis* of Christianity. Religion remains the ideal, non-secular consciousness of its members, because it is the ideal form of the *stage of human development* which has been attained.

The members of the political state are religious because of the dualism between individual life and species-life, between the life of civil society and political life. They are religious in the sense that man treats political life, which is remote from his own individual existence, as if it were his true life; and in the sense that religion is here the spirit of civil society, and expresses the separation and withdrawal of man from man. Political democracy is Christian in the sense that man, not merely one man but every man, is there considered a sovereign being, a supreme being; but it is uneducated, unsocial man, man just as he is in his fortuitous existence, man as he has been corrupted, lost to himself, alienated, subjected to the rule of inhuman conditions and elements, by the whole organization of our society – in short man who is not yet a *real* species-being. Creations of fantasy, dreams, the postulates of Christianity, the sovereignty of man – but of man as an alien being distinguished from the real man – all these become, in democracy, the tangible and present reality, secular maxims.

In the perfected democracy, the religious and theological consciousness appears to itself all the more religious and theological in that it is apparently without any political significance or terrestrial aims, is an affair of the heart withdrawn from the world, an expression of the limitations of reason, a product of arbitrariness and fantasy, a veritable life in the beyond. Christianity here attains the *practical* expression of its universal religious significance, because the most varied views are brought together in the form of Christianity, and still more because Christianity does not ask that anyone should profess Christianity, but simply that he should have some kind of religion (*see* Beaumont, op. cit.). The religious consciousness runs riot in a wealth of contradictions and diversity.

We have shown, therefore, that political emancipation from religion leaves religion in existence, although this is no longer a privileged religion. The contradiction in which the adherent of a particular religion finds himself in relation to his citizenship is only *one aspect* of the universal *secular contradiction between the political state and* civil society. The consummation of the Christian state is a state which acknowledges itself simply as a state and ignores the religion of its members. The emancipation of the state from religion is not the emancipation of the real man from religion.

We do not say to the Jews, therefore, as does Bauer: you cannot be emancipated politically without emancipating yourselves completely from Judaism. We say rather: it is because you can be emancipated politically, without renouncing Judaism completely and absolutely, that *political emancipation* itself is not *human* emancipation. If you want to be politically emancipated, without emancipating yourselves humanly, the inadequacy and the contradiction is not entirely in yourselves but in the *nature* and the *category* of political emancipation. If you are preoccupied with this category you share

the general prejudice. Just as the state *evangelizes* when, although it is a state, it adopts a Christian attitude towards the Jews, the Jew *acts politically* when, though a Jew, he demands civil rights.

But if a man, though a Jew, can be emancipated politically and acquire civil rights, can he claim and acquire what are called the *rights of man*? Bauer *denies* it. "The question is whether the Jew as such, that is, the Jew who himself avows that he is constrained by his true nature to live eternally separate from men, is able to acquire and to concede to others the *universal rights of man*."

"The idea of the rights of man was only discovered in the Christian world, in the last century. It is not an innate idea; on the contrary, it is acquired in a struggle against the historical traditions in which man has been educated up to the present time. The rights of man are not, therefore, a gift of nature, nor a legacy from past history, but the reward of a struggle against the accident of birth and against the privileges which history has hitherto transmitted from generation to generation. They are the results of culture, and only he can possess them who has merited and earned them."

"But can the Jew really take possession of them? As long as he remains Jewish the limited nature which makes him a Jew must prevail over the human nature which should associate him, as a man, with other men; and it will isolate him from everyone who is not a Jew. He declares, by this separation, that the particular nature which makes him Jewish is his true and supreme nature, before which human nature has to efface itself."

"Similarly, the Christian as such cannot grant the rights of man."[28]

According to Bauer man has to sacrifice the "*privilege of faith*" in order to acquire the general rights of man. Let us consider for a moment the so-called rights of man; let us examine them in their most authentic form, that which they have among those who *discovered* them, the North Americans and the French! These rights of man are, in part, *political rights*, which can only be exercised if one is a member of a community. Their content is *participation* in the *community* life, in the *political* life of the community, the life of the state. They fall in the category of *political liberty*, of *civil rights*, which as we have seen do not at all presuppose the consistent and positive abolition of religion; nor consequently, of Judaism. It remains to consider the other part, namely the *rights of man* as distinct from the *rights of the citizen*.

Among them is to be found the freedom of conscience, the right to practise a chosen religion. The *privilege of faith* is expressly recognized, either as a *right of man* or as a consequence of a right of man, namely liberty. *Declaration of the Rights of Man and of the Citizen*, 1791, Article 10: "No one is to be disturbed on account of his opinions, even religious opinions." There is guaranteed, as one of the rights of man, "the liberty of every man to practise the *religion* to which he adheres."

The *Declaration of the Rights of Man, etc.* 1793, enumerates among the rights of man (Article 7): "The liberty of religious observance." Moreover, it is even stated, with respect to the right to express ideas and opinions, to hold meetings, to practise a religion, that: "The necessity of enunciating these *rights* presupposes either the existence or the recent memory of despotism." Compare the Constitution of 1795, Section XII, Article 354.

Constitution of Pennsylvania, Article 9, §3: "All men have received from nature the imprescriptible *right* to worship the Almighty according to the dictates of their conscience, and no one can be legally compelled to follow, establish or support against his will any religion or religious ministry. No human authority can, in any circumstances, intervene in a matter of conscience or control the forces of the soul."

Constitution of New Hampshire, Articles 5 and 6: "Among these natural rights some are by nature inalienable since nothing can replace them. The rights of conscience are among them."[29]

The incompatibility between religion and the rights of man is so little manifest in the concept of the rights of man that the *right to be religious*, in one's own fashion, and to practise one's own particular religion, is expressly included among the rights of man. The privilege of faith is a *universal right of man*.

A distinction is made between the rights of man and the rights of the citizen. Who is this *man* distinct from the *citizen*? No one but the *member of civil society*. Why is the member of civil society called "man," simply man, and why are his rights called the "rights of man"? How is this fact to be explained? By the relation between the political state and civil society, and by the nature of political emancipation.

Let us notice first of all that the so-called *rights of man*, as distinct from the *rights of the citizen*, are simply the rights of a *member of civil society*, that is, of egoistic man, of man separated from other men and from the community. The most radical constitution, that of 1793, says: *Declaration of the Rights of Man and of the Citizen*: Article 2. "These rights, etc. (the natural and imprescriptible rights) are: *equality, liberty, security, property*."

What constitutes liberty?

Article 6. "Liberty is the power which man has to do everything which does not harm the rights of others."

Liberty is, therefore, the right to do everything which does not harm others. The limits within which each individual can act without harming others are determined by law, just as the boundary between two fields is marked by a stake. It is a question of the liberty of man regarded as an isolated monad, withdrawn into himself. Why, according to Bauer, is the Jew not fitted to acquire the rights of man? "As long as he remains Jewish the limited nature which makes him a Jew must prevail over the human nature which should associate him, as a man, with other men; and it will isolate him from everyone who is not a Jew." But liberty as a right of man is not founded upon the relations between man and man, but rather upon the separation of man from man. It is the right of such separation. The right of the *circumscribed* individual, withdrawn into himself.

The practical application of the right of liberty is the right of private property. What constitutes the right of private property?

Article 16 (*Constitution* of 1793). "The right of *property* is that which belongs to every citizen of enjoying and disposing *as he will* of his goods and revenues, of the fruits of his work and industry."

The right of property is, therefore, the right to enjoy one's fortune and to dispose of it as one will; without regard for other men and independently of society. It is the right of self-interest. This individual liberty, and its application, form the basis of civil society. It leads every man to see in other men, not the *realization*, but rather the *limitation* of his own liberty. It declares above all the right "to enjoy and to dispose *as one will*, one's goods and revenues, the fruits of one's work and industry."

There remain the other rights of man, equality and security.

The term "equality" has here no political significance. It is only the equal right to liberty as defined above; namely that every man is equally regarded as a self-sufficient monad. The Constitution of 1795 defines the concept of liberty in this sense.

Article 5 (*Constitution* of 1795). "Equality consists in the fact that the law is the same for all, whether it protects or punishes."

And security?

Article 8 (*Constitution* of 1793). "Security consists in the protection afforded by society to each of its members for the preservation of his person, his rights, and his property."

Security is the supreme social concept of civil society; the concept of the police. The whole society exists only in order to guarantee for each of its members the preservation of his person, his rights and his property. It is in this sense that Hegel calls civil society "the state of need and of reason."

The concept of security is not enough to raise civil society above its egoism. Security is, rather, the *assurance* of its egoism.

None of the supposed rights of man, therefore, go beyond the egoistic man, man as he is, as a member of civil society; that is, an individual separated from the community, withdrawn into himself, wholly preoccupied with his private interest and acting in accordance with his private caprice. Man is far from being considered, in the rights of man, as a species-being; on the contrary, species-life itself – society – appears as a system which is external to the individual and as a limitation of his original independence. The only bond between men is natural necessity, need and private interest, the preservation of their property and their egoistic persons.

It is difficult enough to understand that a nation which has just begun to liberate itself, to tear down all the barriers between different sections of the people and to establish a political community, should solemnly proclaim (*Declaration* of 1791) the rights of the egoistic man, separated from his fellow men and from the community, and should renew this proclamation at a moment when only the most heroic devotion can save the nation (and is, therefore, urgently called for), and when the sacrifice of all the interests of civil society is in question and egoism should be punished as a crime. (*Declaration of the Rights of Man, etc.* 1793.) The matter becomes still more incomprehensible when we observe that the political liberators reduce citizenship, the *political community*, to a mere *means* for preserving these so-called rights of man; and consequently, that the citizen is declared to be the servant of egoistic "man," that the sphere in which man functions as a species-being is degraded to a level below the sphere where he functions as a

partial being, and finally that it is man as a bourgeois and not man as a citizen who is considered the *true* and *authentic* man.

"The end of every *political association* is the *preservation* of the natural and imprescriptible rights of man." (*Declaration of the Rights of Man, etc.* 1791, Article 2.) "Government is instituted in order to guarantee man's enjoyment of his natural and imprescriptible rights." (*Declaration, etc.* 1793, Article 1.) Thus, even in the period of its youthful enthusiasm, which is raised to fever pitch by the force of circumstances, political life declares itself to be only a *means*, whose end is the life of civil society. It is true that its revolutionary practice is in flagrant contradiction with its theory. While, for instance, security is declared to be one of the rights of man, the violation of the privacy of correspondence is openly considered. While the "unlimited freedom of the Press" (*Constitution* of 1793, Article 122), as a corollary of the right of individual liberty, is guaranteed, the freedom of the Press is completely destroyed, since "the freedom of the Press should not be permitted when it endangers public liberty."[30] This amounts to saying: the right to liberty ceases to be a right as soon as it comes into conflict with *political* life, whereas in theory political life is no more than the guarantee of the rights of man – the rights of the individual man – and should, therefore, be suspended as soon as it comes into contradiction with its *end*, these rights of man. But practice is only the exception, while theory is the rule. Even if one decided to regard revolutionary practice as the correct expression of this relation, the problem would remain as to why it is that in the minds of political liberators the relation is inverted, so that the end appears as the means and the means as the end? This optical illusion of their consciousness would always remain a problem, though a psychological and theoretical one.

But the problem is easily solved.

Political emancipation is at the same time the *dissolution* of the old society, upon which the sovereign power, the alienated political life of the people, rests. Political revolution is a revolution of civil society. What was the nature of the old society? It can be characterized in one word: *feudalism*. The old civil society had a *directly political* character; that is, the elements of civil life such as property, the family, and types of occupation had been raised, in the form of lordship, caste and guilds, to elements of political life. They determined, in this form, the relation of the individual to the *state as a whole*; that is, his *political* situation, or in other words, his separation and exclusion from the other elements of society. For this organization of national life did not constitute property and labour as social elements; it rather succeeded in *separating* them from the body of the state, and made them *distinct* societies within society. Nevertheless, at least in the feudal sense, the vital functions and conditions of civil society remained political. They excluded the individual from the body of the state, and transformed the *particular* relation which existed between his corporation and the state into a general relation between the individual and social life, just as they transformed his specific civil activity and situation into a general activity and situation. As a result of this organization, the state as a whole and its consciousness, will and activity – the general political power – also necessarily appeared as the *private* affair of a ruler and his servants, separated from the people.

The political revolution which overthrew this power of the ruler, which made state affairs the affairs of the people, and the political state a matter of *general* concern, i.e. a real state, necessarily shattered everything – estates, corporations, guilds, privileges – which expressed the separation of the people from community life. The political revolution therefore *abolished* the *political character of civil society*. It dissolved civil society into its basic elements, on the one hand *individuals*, and on the other hand the *material and cultural elements* which formed the life experience and the civil situation of these individuals. It set free the political spirit which had, so to speak, been dissolved, fragmented and lost in the various culs-de-sac of feudal society; it reassembled these scattered fragments, liberated the political spirit from its connexion with civil life and made of it the community sphere, the *general* concern of the people, in principle independent of these particular elements of civil life. A *specific* activity and situation in life no longer had any but an individual significance. They no longer constituted the general relation between the individual and the state as a whole. Public affairs as such became the general affair of each individual, and political functions became general functions.

But the consummation of the idealism of the state was at the same time the consummation of the materialism of civil society. The bonds which had restrained the egoistic spirit of civil society were removed along with the political yoke. Polit-

ical emancipation was at the same time an emancipation of civil society from politics and from even the *semblance* of a general content.

Feudal society was dissolved into its basic element, *man*; but into *egoistic* man who was its real foundation.

Man in this aspect, the member of civil society, is now the foundation and presupposition of the *political* state. He is recognized as such in the rights of man.

But the liberty of egoistic man, and the recognition of this liberty, is rather the recognition of the *frenzied* movement of the cultural and material elements which form the content of his life.

Thus man was not liberated from religion; he received religious liberty. He was not liberated from property; he received the liberty to own property. He was not liberated from the egoism of business; he received the liberty to engage in business.

The *formation of the political state*, and the dissolution of civil society into independent *individuals* whose relations are regulated by *law*, as the relations between men in the corporations and guilds were regulated by *privilege*, are accomplished by *one and the same act*. Man as a member of civil society – *non-political* man – necessarily appears as the *natural* man. The rights of man appear as natural rights because *conscious* activity is concentrated upon political *action*. Egoistic man is the *passive*, *given* result of the dissolution of society, an object of *direct apprehension* and consequently a *natural* object. The *political revolution* dissolves civil society into its elements without *revolutionizing* these elements themselves or subjecting them to criticism. This revolution regards civil society, the sphere of human needs, labour, private interests and civil law, as the *basis of its own existence*, as a self-subsistent *precondition*, and thus as its *natural basis*. Finally, man as a member of civil society is identified with *authentic man*, man as distinct from citizen, because he is man in his sensuous, individual and *immediate* existence, whereas *political* man is only abstract, artificial man, man as an *allegorical, moral* person. Thus man as he really is, is seen only in the form of *egoistic* man, and man in his *true* nature only in the form of the *abstract citizen*.

The abstract notion of political man is well formulated by Rousseau: "Whoever dares undertake to establish a people's institutions must feel himself capable of *changing*, as it were, *human nature* itself, of *transforming* each individual who, in isolation, is a complete but solitary whole, into a *part* of something greater than himself, from which in a sense, he derives his life and his being; [of changing man's nature in order to strengthen it;] of substituting a limited and moral existence for the physical and independent life [with which all of us are endowed by nature]. His task, in short, is to take from *a man his own powers*, and to give him in exchange alien powers which he can only employ with the help of other men."[31]

Every emancipation is a *restoration* of the human world and of human relationships to *man himself*.

Political emancipation is a reduction of man, on the one hand to a member of civil society, an *independent* and *egoistic* individual, and on the other hand, to a *citizen*, to a moral person.

Human emancipation will only be complete when the real, individual man has absorbed into himself the abstract citizen; when as an individual man, in his everyday life, in his work, and in his relationships, he has become a *species-being*; and when he has recognized and organized his own powers (*forces propres*) as *social* powers so that he no longer separates this social power from himself as *political* power.

Notes

1. The Jewish question. [Braunschweig, 1843. *Marx*]
2. Bauer, "Die Fähigkeit der heutigen Juden und Christen, frei zu werden," *Einundzwanzig Bogen*, p. 57. [*Marx*] Emphases added by Marx.
3. Chamber of Deputies. Debate of 26th December, 1840. [*Marx*]
4. Bauer, *Die Judenfrage*, p. 64. [*Marx*]
5. Ibid., p. 65. [*Marx*]
6. Ibid. [*Marx*]
7. Ibid., p. 71. [*Marx*]
8. Ibid., p. 66. [*Marx*]
9. Ibid., p. 97. [*Marx*]
10. Ibid., p. 3. [*Marx*]
11. Gustave de Beaumont, *Marie ou l'esclavage aux États-Unis*, Bruxelles, 1835, 2 vols., II, p. 207. [*Marx*] Marx refers to another edition, Paris, 1835.
12. Ibid., p. 216. Beaumont actually refers to *all* the States of North America.
13. Ibid., p. 217. [*Marx*]
14. G. de Beaumont, *Marie*. [*Marx*]
15. A. de Tocqueville, *De la démocratie en Amérique*. [*Marx*]
16. Thomas Hamilton, *Men and Manners in North America*, Edinburgh, 1833, 2 vols. [*Marx*] Marx quotes from the German translation, Mannheim, 1834.
17. Hamilton, *Men and Manners*, I, pp. 288, 306, 309. [*Marx*]
18. Hegel, *Grundlinien der Philosophie des Rechts*, Ier Aufgabe, 1821, p. 346. [*Marx*] See the English translation by T. M. Knox, *Hegel's Philosophy of Right*, Oxford, 1942, p. 173.
19. The terms "species-life" (*Gattungsleben*) and "species-being" (*Gattungswesen*) are derived from Feuerbach. In the first chapter of *Das Wesen des Christentums* [*The Essence of Christianity*], Leipzig, 1841, Feuerbach discusses the nature of man, and argues that man is to be distinguished from animals not by "consciousness" as such, but by a particular kind of consciousness. Man is not only conscious of himself as an individual; he is also conscious of himself as a member of the human species, and so he apprehends a "human essence" which is the same in himself and in other men. According to Feuerbach this ability to conceive of "species" is the fundamental element in the human power of reasoning: "Science is the consciousness of species." Marx, while not departing from this meaning of the terms, employs them in other contexts; and he insists more strongly than Feuerbach that since this "species-consciousness" defines the nature of man, man is only living and acting authentically (i.e. in accordance with his nature) when he lives and acts deliberately as a "species-being," that is, as a *social* being.
20. See previous note.
21. I.e. as a member of civil society.
22. I.e. the individual with political rights.
23. Bauer, *Die Judenfrage*, p. 8. [*Marx*]
24. Ibid., pp. 8–9. [*Marx*]
25. Ibid., p. 55. [*Marx*]
26. Ibid., p. 56. [*Marx*]
27. Ibid., p. 108. [*Marx*]
28. Ibid., pp. 19–20. [*Marx*]
29. Beaumont, *Marie*, II, pp. 206–7. [*Marx*]
30. Buchez et Roux, "Robespierre, jeune," *Histoire parlementaire de la Révolution française*, Tome XXVIII, p. 159. [*Marx*]
31. J. J. Rousseau, *Du contrat social*, Book II. Chapter VII, "The Legislator." Marx quoted this passage in French, and added the emphases; he omitted the portions enclosed in square brackets.

3

Consciousness and
What is Unconscious

SIGMUND FREUD

In this introductory chapter there is nothing new to be said and it will not be possible to avoid repeating what has often been said before.

The division of the psychical into what is conscious and what is unconscious is the fundamental premiss of psycho-analysis; and it alone makes it possible for psycho-analysis to understand the pathological processes in mental life, which are as common as they are important, and to find a place for them in the framework of science. To put it once more, in a different way: psycho-analysis cannot situate the essence of the psychical in consciousness, but is obliged to regard consciousness as a quality of the psychical, which may be present in addition to other qualities or may be absent.

If I could suppose that everyone interested in psychology would read this book, I should also be prepared to find that at this point some of my readers would already stop short and would go no further; for here we have the first shibboleth of psycho-analysis. To most people who have been educated in philosophy the idea of anything psychical which is not also conscious is so inconceivable that it seems to them absurd and refutable simply by logic. I believe this is only because they have never studied the relevant phenomena of hypnosis and dreams, which – quite apart from pathological manifestations – necessitate this view. Their psychology of consciousness is incapable of solving the problems of dreams and hypnosis.

"Being conscious"[1] is in the first place a purely descriptive term, resting on perception of the most immediate and certain character. Experience goes on to show that a psychical element (for instance, an idea) is not as a rule conscious for a protracted length of time. On the contrary, a state of con-

sciousness is characteristically very transitory; an idea that is conscious now is no longer so a moment later, although it can become so again under certain conditions that are easily brought about. In the interval the idea was – we do not know what. We can say that it was *latent*, and by this we mean that it was *capable of becoming conscious* at any time. Or, if we say that it was *unconscious*, we shall also be giving a correct description of it. Here "unconscious" coincides with "latent and capable of becoming conscious". The philosophers would no doubt object: "No, the term 'unconscious' is not applicable here; so long as the idea was in a state of latency it was not anything psychical at all." To contradict them at this point would lead to nothing more profitable than a verbal dispute.

But we have arrived at the term or concept of the unconscious along another path, by considering certain experiences in which mental *dynamics* play a part. We have found – that is, we have been obliged to assume – that very powerful mental processes or ideas exist (and here a quantitative or *economic* factor comes into question for the first time) which can produce all the effects in mental life that ordinary ideas do (including effects that can in their turn become conscious as ideas), though they themselves do not become conscious. It is unnecessary to repeat in detail here what has been explained so often before.[2] It is enough to say that at this point psycho-analytic theory steps in and asserts that the reason why such ideas cannot become conscious is that a certain force opposes them, that otherwise they could become conscious, and that it would then be apparent how little they differ from other elements which are admittedly psychical. The fact that in the technique of psycho-analysis a means has been found by which the opposing force can be removed and the ideas in question made conscious renders this theory irrefutable. The state in which the ideas existed before being made conscious is called by us *repression*, and we assert that the force which instituted the repression and maintains it is perceived as *resistance* during the work of analysis.

Thus we obtain our concept of the unconscious from the theory of repression. The repressed is the prototype of the unconscious for us. We see, however, that we have two kinds of unconscious – the one which is latent but capable of becoming conscious, and the one which is repressed and which is not, in itself and without more ado, capable of becoming conscious. This piece of insight into psychical dynamics cannot fail to affect terminology and description. The latent, which is unconscious only descriptively, not in the dynamic sense, we call *preconscious*; we restrict the term *unconscious* to the dynamically unconscious repressed; so that now we have three terms, conscious (*Cs.*), preconscious (*Pcs.*), and unconscious (*Ucs.*), whose sense is no longer purely descriptive. The *Pcs.* is presumably a great deal closer to the *Cs.* than is the *Ucs.*, and since we have called the *Ucs.* psychical we shall with even less hesitation call the latent *Pcs.* psychical. But why do we not rather, instead of this, remain in agreement with the philosophers and, in a consistent way, distinguish the *Pcs.* as well as the *Ucs.* from the conscious psychical? The philosophers would then propose that the *Pcs.* and the *Ucs.* should be described as two species or stages of the "psychoid", and harmony would be established. But endless difficulties in exposition would follow; and the one important fact, that these two kinds of "psychoid" coincide in almost every other respect with what is admittedly psychical, would be forced into the background in the interests of a prejudice dating from a period in which these psychoids, or the most important part of them, were still unknown.

We can now play about comfortably with our three terms, *Cs.*, *Pcs.*, and *Ucs.*, so long as we do not forget that in the descriptive sense there are two kinds of unconscious, but in the dynamic sense only one. For purposes of exposition this distinction can in some cases be ignored, but in others it is of course indispensable. At the same time, we have become more or less accustomed to this ambiguity of the unconscious and have managed pretty well with it. As far as I can see, it is impossible to avoid this ambiguity; the distinction between conscious and unconscious is in the last resort a question of perception, which must be answered "yes" or "no", and the act of perception itself tells us nothing of the reason why a thing is or is not perceived. No one has a right to complain because the actual phenomenon expresses the dynamic factor ambiguously.[3]

In the further course of psycho-analytic work, however, even these distinctions have proved to be inadequate and, for practical purposes, insufficient. This has become clear in more ways than one; but the decisive instance is as follows. We have formed the idea that in each individual there is a coherent organization of mental processes; and we call this his *ego*. It is to this ego that consciousness is attached; the ego controls the approaches to motility – that is, to the discharge of excitations into the external world; it is the mental agency which supervises all its own constituent processes, and which goes to sleep at night, though even then it exercises the censorship on dreams. From this ego proceed the repressions, too, by means of which it is sought to exclude certain trends in the mind not merely from consciousness but also from other forms of effectiveness and activity. In analysis these trends which have been shut out stand in opposition to the ego, and the analysis is faced with the task of removing the resistances which the ego displays against concerning itself with the repressed. Now we find during analysis that, when we put certain tasks before the patient, he gets into difficulties; his associations fail when they should be coming near the repressed. We then tell him that he is dominated by a resistance; but he is quite unaware of the fact, and, even if he guesses from his unpleasurable feelings that a resistance is now at work in him, he does not know what it is or how to describe it. Since, however, there can be no question but that this resistance emanates from his ego and belongs to it, we find ourselves in an unforeseen situation. We have come upon something in the ego itself which is also unconscious, which behaves exactly like the repressed – that is, which produces powerful effects without itself being conscious and which requires special work before it can be made conscious. From the point of view of analytic practice, the consequence of this discovery is that we land in endless obscurities and difficulties if we keep to our habitual forms of expression and try, for instance, to derive neuroses from a conflict between the conscious and the unconscious. We shall have to substitute for this antithesis another, taken from our insight into the structural conditions of the mind – the antithesis between the coherent ego and the repressed which is split off from it.[4]

For our conception of the unconscious, however, the consequences of our discovery are even more important. Dynamic considerations caused us to make our first correction; our insight into the structure of the mind leads to the second. We recognize that the *Ucs.* does not coincide with the repressed; it is still true that all that is repressed is *Ucs.*, but not all that is *Ucs.* is repressed. A part of the ego, too – and Heaven knows how important a part – may be *Ucs.*, undoubtedly is *Ucs.*[5] And this *Ucs.* belonging to the ego is not latent like the *Pcs.*; for if it were, it could not be activated without becoming *Cs.*, and the process of making it conscious would not encounter such great difficulties. When we find ourselves thus confronted by the necessity of postulating a third *Ucs.*, which is not repressed, we must admit that the characteristic of being unconscious begins to lose significance for us. It becomes a quality which can have many meanings, a quality which we are unable to make, as we should have hoped to do, the basis of far-reaching and inevitable conclusions. Nevertheless we must beware of ignoring this characteristic, for the property of being conscious or not is in the last resort our one beacon-light in the darkness of depth-psychology.

Notes

1. [*"Bewusst sein"* (in two words) in the original. Similarly in Chapter 2 of *Lay Analysis* (1926e), *Standard Ed.*, 20, 197. *"Bewusstsein"* is the regular German word for "consciousness", and printing it in two words emphasizes the fact that *"bewusst"* is in its form a passive participle – "being conscioused". The English "conscious" is capable of an active or a passive use; but in these discussions it is always to be taken as passive. Cf. a footnote at the end of the Editor's Note to Freud's metapsychological paper on "The Unconscious", *Standard Ed.*, 14, 165.]
2. [See, for instance, "A Note on the Unconscious" (1912g), *Standard Ed.*, 12, 262 and 264.]
3. This may be compared so far with my "Note on the Unconscious in Psycho-Analysis" (1912g). [Cf. also Sections I and II of the metapsychological paper on "The Unconscious" (1915e).] A new turn taken by criticisms of the unconscious deserves consideration at this point. Some investigators, who do not refuse to recognize the facts of psycho-analysis but who are unwilling to accept the unconscious, find a way out of the difficulty in the fact, which no one contests, that in consciousness (regarded as a phenomenon) it is possible to distinguish a great variety of gradations in intensity or clarity. Just as there are processes which are very vividly, glaringly, and tangibly conscious, so we also experience others which are only faintly, hardly even noticeably conscious; those that are most faintly conscious are, it is argued, the ones to which psycho-analysis wishes to apply the unsuitable name "unconscious". These too, however (the argument proceeds), are conscious or "in consciousness", and can be made fully and intensely conscious if sufficient attention is paid to them.

   In so far as it is possible to influence by arguments the decision of a question of this kind which depends either on convention or on emotional factors, we may make the following comments. The reference to gradations of clarity in consciousness is in no way conclusive and has no more evidential value than such analogous statements as: "There are so very many gradations in illumination – from the most glaring and dazzling light to the dimmest glimmer – therefore there is no such thing as darkness at all"; or, "There are varying degrees of vitality, therefore there is no such thing as death." Such statements may in a certain way have a meaning, but for practical purposes they are worthless. This will be seen if one tries to draw particular conclusions from them, such as, "there is therefore no need to strike a light", or, "therefore all organisms are immortal". Further, to include "what is unnoticeable" under the concept of "what is conscious" is simply to play havoc with the one and only piece of direct and certain knowledge that we have about the mind. And after all, a consciousness of which one knows nothing seems to me a good deal more absurd than something mental that is unconscious. Finally, this attempt to equate what is unnoticed with what is unconscious is obviously made without taking into account the dynamic conditions involved, which were the decisive factors in forming the psycho-analytic view. For it ignores two facts: first, that it is exceedingly difficult and requires very great effort to concentrate enough attention on something unnoticed of this kind; and secondly, that when this has been achieved the thought which was previously unnoticed is not recognized by consciousness, but often seems entirely alien and opposed to it and is promptly disavowed by it. Thus, seeking refuge from the unconscious in what is scarcely noticed or unnoticed is after all only a derivative of the preconceived belief which regards the identity of the psychical and the conscious as settled once and for all.
4. Cf. *Beyond the Pleasure Principle* (1920g) [*S.E.*, 18, 19; *I.P.L.*, 4, 13].
5. [This had already been stated not only in *Beyond the Pleasure Principle* (loc. cit.) but earlier, in "The Unconscious" (1915e), *Standard Ed.*, 14, 192–3. Indeed, it was implied in a remark at the beginning of the second paper on "The Neuro-Psychoses of Defence" (1896b).]

4

The Self

GEORGE HERBERT MEAD

The Background of the Genesis of the Self

The problem now presents itself as to how, in detail, a self arises. We have to note something of the background of its genesis. First of all there is the conversation of gestures between animals involving some sort of co-operative activity. There the beginning of the act of one is a stimulus to the other to respond in a certain way, while the beginning of this response becomes again a stimulus to the first to adjust his action to the oncoming response. Such is the preparation for the completed act, and ultimately it leads up to the conduct which is the outcome of this preparation. The conversation of gestures, however, does not carry with it the reference of the individual, the animal, the organism, to itself. It is not acting in a fashion which calls for a response from the form itself, although it is conduct with reference to the conduct of others. We have seen, however, that there are certain gestures that do affect the organism as they affect other organisms and may, therefore, arouse in the organism responses of the same character as aroused in the other. Here, then, we have a situation in which the individual may at least arouse responses in himself and reply to these responses, the condition being that the social stimuli have an effect on the individual which is like that which they have on the other. That, for example, is what is implied in language; otherwise language as significant symbol would disappear, since the individual would not get the meaning of that which he says.

The peculiar character possessed by our human social environment belongs to it by virtue of the peculiar character of human social activity; and that character, as we have seen, is to be found in the process of communication, and more particularly in the triadic relation on which the existence of meaning is based: the relation of the gesture of one organism to the adjustive response made to it by another organism, in its indicative capacity as pointing to the completion or resultant of the act it initiates (the meaning of the gesture being thus the response of the second organism to it as such, or as a gesture). What, as it were, takes the gesture out of the social act and isolates it as such – what makes it something more than just an early phase of an individual act – is the response of another organism, or of other organisms, to it. Such a response is its meaning, or gives it its meaning. The social situation and process of behavior are here presupposed by the acts of the individual organisms implicated therein. The gesture arises as a separable element in the social act, by virtue of the fact that it is selected out by the sensitivities of other organisms to it; it does not exist as a gesture merely in the experience of the single individual. The meaning of a gesture by one organism, to repeat, is found in the response of another organism to what would be the completion of the act of the first organism which that gesture initiates and indicates.

We sometimes speak as if a person could build up an entire argument in his mind, and then put it into words to convey it to someone else. Actually, our thinking always takes place by means of some sort of symbols. It is possible that one could have the meaning of "chair" in his experience without there being a symbol, but we would not be thinking about it in that case. We may sit down in a chair without thinking about what we are doing, that is, the approach to the chair is presumably already aroused in our experience, so that the meaning is there. But if one is thinking about the chair he must have some sort of a symbol for it. It may be the form of the chair, it may be the attitude that somebody else takes in sitting down, but it is more apt to be some language symbol that arouses this response. In a thought process there has to be some sort of a symbol that can refer to this meaning, that is, tend to call out this response, and also serve this purpose for other persons as well. It would not be a thought process if that were not the case.

Our symbols are all universal.[1] You cannot say anything that is absolutely particular; anything you say that has any meaning at all is universal. You are saying something that calls out a specific response in anybody else provided that the symbol exists for him in his experience as it does for you. There is the language of speech and the language of hands, and there may be the language of the expression of the countenance. One can register grief or joy and call out certain responses. There are primitive people who can carry on elaborate conversations just by expressions of the countenance. Even in these cases the person who communicates is affected by that expression just as he expects somebody else to be affected. Thinking always implies a symbol which will call out the same response in another that it calls out in the thinker. Such a symbol is a universal of discourse; it is universal in its character. We always assume that the symbol we use is one which will call out in the other person the same response, provided it is a part of his mechanism of conduct. A person who is saying something is saying to himself what he says to others; otherwise he does not know what he is talking about.

There is, of course, a great deal in one's conversation with others that does not arouse in one's self the same response it arouses in others. That is particularly true in the case of emotional attitudes. One tries to bully somebody else; he is not trying to bully himself. There is, further, a whole set of values given in speech which are not of a symbolic character. The actor is conscious of these values; that is, if he assumes a certain attitude he is, as we say, aware that this attitude represents grief. If it does he is able to respond to his own gesture in some sense as his audience does. It is not a natural situation; one is not an actor all of the time. We do at times act and consider just what the effect of our attitude is going to be, and we may deliberately use a certain tone of voice to bring about a certain result. Such a tone arouses the same response in ourselves that we want to arouse in somebody else. But a very large part of what goes on in speech has not this symbolic status.

It is the task not only of the actor but of the artist as well to find the sort of expression that will arouse in others what is going on in himself. The lyric poet has an experience of beauty with an emotional thrill to it, and as an artist using words he is seeking for those words which will answer to his emotional attitude, and which will call out in others the attitude he himself has. He can only test his results in himself by seeing whether these words do call out in him the response he wants to call out in others. He is in somewhat the same position as that of the actor. The first direct and immediate experience is not in the form of communication. We have an interesting light on this from such a poet as Wordsworth, who was very much interested in the technique of the poet's expression; and he has told us in his prefaces and also in his own poetry how his poems, as poems, arose – and uniformly the experience itself was not the immediate stimulus to the poetic expression. A period of ten years might lie between the original experience and the expression of it. This process of finding the expression in language which will call out the emotion once had is more easily accomplished when one is dealing with the memory of it than when one is in the midst of the trance-like experiences through which Wordsworth passed in his contact with nature. One has to experiment and see how the expression that is given does answer to the responses which are now had in the fainter memories of experience. Someone once said that he had very great difficulty in writing poetry; he had plenty of ideas but could not get the language he needed. He was rightly told that poetry was written in words, not in ideas.

A great deal of our speech is not of this genuinely aesthetic character; in most of it we do not deliberately feel the emotions which we arouse. We do not normally use language stimuli to call out in ourselves the emotional response which we are calling out in others. One does, of course, have sympathy in emotional situations; but what one is seeking for there is something which is, after all, that in the other which supports the individual in his own experience. In the case of the poet and actor, the stimulus calls out in the artist that which it calls out in the other, but this is not the natural function of language; we do not assume that the person who is angry is calling out the fear in himself that he is calling out in someone else. The emotional part of our act does not directly call out in us the response it calls out in the other. If a person is hostile the attitude of the other that he is interested in, an attitude which flows naturally from his angered tones, is not one that he definitely recognizes in himself. We are not frightened by a tone which we may use to frighten somebody else. On the emotional side, which is a very large part of the vocal gesture, we do not call out in ourselves in any such degree the response we call out in others as we do in the case of significant speech. Here we should call out in ourselves the type of response we are calling out in others; we must know what we are saying, and the attitude of the other which we arouse in ourselves should control what we do say. Rationality means that the type of the response which we call out in others should be so called out in ourselves, and that this response should in turn take its place in determining what further thing we are going to say and do.

What is essential to communication is that the symbol should arouse in one's self what it arouses in the other individual. It must have that sort of universality to any person who finds himself in the same situation. There is a possibility of language whenever a stimulus can affect the individual as it affects the other. With a blind person such as Helen Keller, it is a contact experience that could be given to another as it is given to herself. It is out of that sort of language that the mind of Helen Keller was built up. As she has recognized, it was not until she could get into communication with other persons through symbols which could arouse in herself the responses they arouse in other people that she could get what we term a mental content, or a self.

Another set of background factors in the genesis of the self is represented in the activities of play and the game.

Among primitive people, as I have said, the necessity of distinguishing the self and the organism was recognized in what we term the "double": the individual has a thing–like self that is affected by the individual as it affects other people and which is distinguished from the immediate organism in that it can leave the body and come back to it. This is the basis for the concept of the soul as a separate entity.

We find in children something that answers to this double, namely, the invisible, imaginary companions which a good many children produce in their own experience. They organize in this way the responses which they call out in other persons and call out also in themselves. Of course, this playing with an imaginary companion is only a peculiarly interesting phase of ordinary play. Play in this sense, especially the stage which precedes the organized games, is a play at something. A child plays at being a mother, at being a teacher, at being a policeman; that is, it is taking different rôles, as we say. We have something that suggests this in what we call the play of animals: a cat will play with her kittens, and dogs play with each other. Two dogs playing with each other will attack and defend, in a process which if carried through would amount to an actual fight. There is a combination of responses which checks the depth of the bite. But we do not have in such a situation the dogs taking a definite rôle in the sense that a child deliberately takes the rôle of another. This tendency on the part of the children is what we are working with in the kindergarten where the rôles which the children assume are made the basis for training. When a child does assume a rôle he has in himself the stimuli which call out that particular response or group of responses. He may, of course, run away when he is chased, as the dog does, or he may turn around and strike back just as the dog does in his play. But that is not the same as playing at something. Children get together to "play Indian." This means that the child has a certain set of stimuli which call out in itself the responses that they would call out in others, and which answer to an Indian. In the play period the child utilizes his own responses to these stimuli which he makes use of in building a self. The response which he has a tendency to make to these stimuli organizes them. He plays that he is, for instance, offering himself something, and he buys it; he gives a letter to himself and takes it away; he addresses himself as a parent, as a teacher; he arrests himself as a policeman. He has a set of stimuli which call out in himself the sort of responses they call out in others. He takes this group of responses and organizes them into a certain whole. Such is the simplest form of being another to one's self. It involves a temporal situation. The child says something in one character and responds in another character, and then his responding in another character is a stimulus to himself in the first character, and so the conversation goes on. A certain organized structure arises in him and in his other which replies to it, and these carry on the conversation of gestures between themselves.

If we contrast play with the situation in an organized game, we note the essential difference that the child who plays in a game must be ready to take the attitude of everyone else involved in that game, and that these different rôles must have a definite relationship to each other. Taking a very simple game such as hide-and-seek, everyone with the exception of the one who is hiding is a person who is hunting. A child does not require more than the person who is hunted and the one who is hunting. If a child is playing in the first sense he just goes on playing, but there is no basic organization gained. In that early stage he passes from one rôle to another just as a whim takes him. But in a game where a number of individuals are involved, then the child taking one rôle must be ready to take the rôle of everyone else. If he gets in a ball nine he must have the responses of each position involved in his own position. He must know what everyone else is going to do in order to carry out his own play. He has to take all of these rôles. They do not all have to be present in consciousness at the same time, but at some moments he has to have three or four individuals present in his own attitude, such as the one who is going to throw the ball, the one who is going to catch it, and so on. These responses must be, in some degree, present in his own make-up. In the game, then, there is a set of responses of such others so organized that the attitude of one calls out the appropriate attitudes of the other.

This organization is put in the form of the rules of the game. Children take a great interest in rules. They make rules on the spot in order to help themselves out of difficulties. Part of the enjoyment of the game is to get these rules. Now, the rules are the set of responses which a particular attitude calls out. You can demand a certain response in others if you take a certain attitude. These responses are all in yourself as well. There you get an organized set of such responses as that to which I have referred, which is something more elaborate than the rôles found in play. Here there is just a set of responses that follow on each other indefinitely. At such a stage we speak of a child as not yet having a fully developed self. The child responds in a fairly intelligent fashion to the immediate stimuli that come to him, but they are not organized. He does not organize his life as we would like to have him do, namely, as a whole. There is just a set of responses of the type of play. The child reacts to a certain stimulus, and the reaction is in himself that

is called out in others, but he is not a whole self. In his game he has to have an organization of these rôles; otherwise he cannot play the game. The game represents the passage in the life of the child from taking the rôle of others in play to the organized part that is essential to self-consciousness in the full sense of the term.

Play, the Game, and the Generalized Other

We were speaking of the social conditions under which the self arises as an object. In addition to language we found two illustrations, one in play and the other in the game, and I wish to summarize and expand my account on these points. I have spoken of these from the point of view of children. We can, of course, refer also to the attitudes of more primitive people out of which our civilization has arisen. A striking illustration of play as distinct from the game is found in the myths and various of the plays which primitive people carry out, especially in religious pageants. The pure play attitude which we find in the case of little children may not be found here, since the participants are adults, and undoubtedly the relationship of these play processes to that which they interpret is more or less in the minds of even the most primitive people. In the process of interpretation of such rituals, there is an organization of play which perhaps might be compared to that which is taking place in the kindergarten in dealing with the plays of little children, where these are made into a set that will have a definite structure or relationship. At least something of the same sort is found in the play of primitive people. This type of activity belongs, of course, not to the everyday life of the people in their dealing with the objects about them – there we have a more or less definitely developed self-consciousness – but in their attitudes toward the forces about them, the nature upon which they depend; in their attitude toward this nature which is vague and uncertain, there we have a much more primitive response; and that response finds its expression in taking the rôle of the other, playing at the expression of their gods and their heroes, going through certain rites which are the representation of what these individuals are supposed to be doing. The process is one which develops, to be sure, into a more or less definite technique and is controlled; and yet we can say that it has arisen out of situations similar to those in which little children play at being a parent, at being a teacher – vague personalities that are about them and which affect them and on which they depend. These are personalities which they take, rôles they play, and in so far control the development of their own personality. This outcome is just what the kindergarten works toward. It takes the characters of these various vague beings and gets them into such an organized social relationship to each other that they build up the character of the little child.[2] The very introduction of organization from outside supposes a lack of organization at this period in the child's experience. Over against such a situation of the little child and primitive people, we have the game as such.

The fundamental difference between the game and play is that in the latter the child must have the attitude of all the others involved in that game. The attitudes of the other players which the participant assumes organize into a sort of unit, and it is that organization which controls the response of the individual. The illustration used was of a person playing baseball. Each one of his own acts is determined by his assumption of the action of the others who are playing the game. What he does is controlled by his being everyone else on that team, at least in so far as those attitudes affect his own particular response. We get then an "other" which is an organization of the attitudes of those involved in the same process.

The organized community or social group which gives to the individual his unity of self may be called "the generalized other." The attitude of the generalized other is the attitude of the whole community.[3] Thus, for example, in the case of such a social group as a ball team, the team is the generalized other in so far as it enters – as an organized process or social activity – into the experience of any one of the individual members of it.

If the given human individual is to develop a self in the fullest sense, it is not sufficient for him merely to take the attitudes of other human individuals toward himself and toward one another within the human social process, and to bring that social process as a whole into his individual experience merely in these terms: he must also, in the same way that he takes the attitudes of other individuals toward himself and toward one another, take their attitudes toward the various phases or aspects of the common social activity or set of social undertakings in which, as members of an organized society or social group, they are all engaged; and he must then, by generalizing these individual attitudes of that organized society or social group itself, as a whole, act toward different social projects which at any given time it is carrying out, or toward the various larger phases of the general social process which constitutes its life and of which these projects are specific manifestations. This getting of the broad activities of any given social whole or organized society as such within the experiential field of any one of the individuals involved or included in that whole is, in other words, the essential basis and prerequisite of the fullest development of that individual's self: only in so far as he takes the attitudes of the organized social group to which he belongs toward the organized, co-operative social activity or set of such activities in which that group as such is engaged, does he develop a complete self or possess the sort of complete self he has developed. And on the other hand, the complex co-operative processes and activities and institutional functionings of organized human society are also possible only in so far as every individual involved in them or belonging to that society can take the general attitudes of all other such individuals with reference to these processes and activities and institutional functionings, and to the organized social whole of experiential relations and interactions thereby constituted – and can direct his own behavior accordingly.

It is in the form of the generalized other that the social process influences the behavior of the individuals involved in it and carrying it on, i.e., that the community exercises control over the conduct of its individual members; for it is in this form that the social process or community enters as a determining factor into the individual's thinking. In abstract thought the individual takes the attitude of the generalized other[4] toward himself, without reference to its expression in any particular other individuals; and in concrete thought he takes that attitude in so far as it is expressed in the attitudes toward his behavior of those other individuals with whom he is involved in the given social situation or act. But only by taking the attitude of the generalized other toward himself, in one or another of these ways, can he think at all; for only thus can thinking – or the internalized conversation of gestures which constitutes thinking – occur. And only through the taking by individuals of the attitude or attitudes of the generalized other toward themselves is the existence of a universe of discourse, as that system of common or social meanings which thinking presupposes at its context, rendered possible.

The self-conscious human individual, then, takes or assumes the organized social attitudes of the given social group or community (or of some one section thereof) to which he belongs, toward the social problems of various kinds which confront that group or community at any given time, and which arise in connection with the correspondingly different social projects or organized co-operative enterprises in which that group or community as such is engaged; and as an individual participant in these social projects or co-operative enterprises, he governs his own conduct accordingly. In politics, for example, the individual identifies himself with an entire political party and takes the organized attitudes of that entire party toward the rest of the given social community and toward the problems which confront the party within the given social situation; and he consequently reacts or responds in terms of the organized attitudes of the party as a whole. He thus enters into a special set of social relations with all the other individuals who belong to that political party; and in the same way he enters into various other special sets of social relations, with various other classes of individuals respectively, the individuals of each of these classes being the other members of some one of the particular organized subgroups (determined in socially functional terms) of which he himself is a member within the entire given society or social community. In the most highly developed, organized, and complicated human social communities – those evolved by civilized man – these various socially functional classes or subgroups of individuals to which any given individual belongs (and with the other individual members of which he thus enters into a special set of social relations) are of two kinds. Some of them are concrete social classes or subgroups, such as political parties, clubs, corporations, which are all actually functional social units, in terms of which their individual members are directly related to one another. The others are abstract social classes or subgroups, such as the class of debtors and the class of creditors, in terms of which their individual members are related to one another only more or less indirectly, and which only more or less indirectly function as social units, but which afford or represent unlimited possibilities for the widening and ramifying and enriching of the social relations among all the individual members of the given society as an organized and unified whole. The given individual's membership in several of these abstract social classes or subgroups makes possible his entrance into definite social relations (however indirect) with an almost infinite number of other individuals who also belong to or are included within one or another of these abstract social classes or subgroups cutting across functional lines of demarcation which divide different human social communities from one another, and including individual members from several (in some cases from all) such communities. Of these abstract social classes or subgroups of human individuals the one which is most inclusive and extensive is, of course, the one defined by the logical universe of discourse (or system of universally significant symbols) determined by the participation and communicative interaction of individuals; for of all such classes or subgroups, it is the one which claims the largest number of individual members, and which enables the largest conceivable number of human individuals to enter into some sort of social relation, however indirect or abstract it may be, with one another – a relation arising from the universal functioning of gestures as significant symbols in the general human social process of communication.

I have pointed out, then, that there are two general stages in the full development of the self. At the first of these stages, the individual's self is constituted simply by an organization of the particular attitudes of other individuals toward himself and toward one another in the specific social acts in which he participates with them. But at the second stage in the full development of the individual's self that self is constituted not only by an organization of these particular individual attitudes, but also by an organization of the social attitudes of the generalized other or the social group as a whole to which he belongs. These social or group attitudes are brought within the individual's field of direct experience, and are included as elements in the structure or constitution of his self, in the same way that the attitudes of particular other individuals are; and the individual arrives at them, or succeeds in taking them, by means of further organizing, and then generalizing, the attitudes of particular other individuals in terms of their organized social bearings and implications. So the self reaches its full development by organizing these individual attitudes of others into the organized social or group attitudes, and by thus becoming an individual reflection of the general systematic pattern of social or group behavior in which it and the others are all involved – a pattern which enters as a whole into the individual's experience in terms of these organized group attitudes which, through the mechanism of his central nervous system, he takes toward himself, just as he takes the individual attitudes of others.

The game has a logic, so that such an organization of the self is rendered possible: there is a definite end to be obtained; the actions of the different individuals are all related to each other with reference to that end so that they do not conflict; one is not in conflict with himself in the attitude of another man on the team. If one has the attitude of the person throwing the ball he can also have the response of catching the ball. The two are related so that they further the purpose of the game itself. They are interrelated in a unitary, organic fashion. There is a definite unity, then, which is introduced into the organization of other selves when we reach such a stage as that of the game, as over against the situation of play where there is a simple succession of one rôle after another, a situation which is, of course, characteristic of the child's own personality. The child is one thing at one time and another at another, and what he is at one moment does not determine what he is at another. That is both the charm of childhood as well as its inadequacy. You cannot count on the child; you cannot assume that all the things he does are going to determine what he will do at any moment. He is not organized into a whole. The child has no definite character, no definite personality.

The game is then an illustration of the situation out of which an organized personality arises. In so far as the child does take the attitude of the other and allows that attitude of the other to determine the thing he is going to do with reference to a common end, he is becoming an organic member of society. He is taking over the morale of that society and is becoming an essential member of it. He belongs to it in so far as he does allow the attitude of the other that he takes to control his own immediate expression. What is involved here is some sort of an organized process. That which is expressed in terms of the game is, of course, being continually expressed in the social life of the child, but this wider process goes beyond the immediate experience of the child himself. The importance of the game is that it lies entirely inside of the child's own experience, and the importance of our modern type of education is that it is brought as far as possible within this realm. The different attitudes that a child assumes are so organized that they

exercise a definite control over his response, as the attitudes in a game control his own immediate response. In the game we get an organized other, a generalized other, which is found in the nature of the child itself, and finds its expression in the immediate experience of the child. And it is that organized activity in the child's own nature controlling the particular response which gives unity, and which builds up his own self.

What goes on in the game goes on in the life of the child all the time. He is continually taking the attitudes of those about him, especially the rôles of those who in some sense control him and on whom he depends. He gets the function of the process in an abstract sort of a way at first. It goes over from the play into the game in a real sense. He has to play the game. The morale of the game takes hold of the child more than the larger morale of the whole community. The child passes into the game and the game expresses a social situation in which he can completely enter; its morale may have a greater hold on him than that of the family to which he belongs or the community in which he lives. There are all sorts of social organizations, some of which are fairly lasting, some temporary, into which the child is entering, and he is playing a sort of social game in them. It is a period in which he likes "to belong," and he gets into organizations which come into existence and pass out of existence. He becomes a something which can function in the organized whole, and thus tends to determine himself in his relationship with the group to which he belongs. That process is one which is a striking stage in the development of the child's morale. It constitutes him a self-conscious member of the community to which he belongs.

Such is the process by which a personality arises. I have spoken of this as a process in which a child takes the rôle of the other, and said that it takes place essentially through the use of language. Language is predominantly based on the vocal gesture by means of which co-operative activities in a community are carried out. Language in its significant sense is that vocal gesture which tends to arouse in the individual the attitude which it arouses in others, and it is this perfecting of the self by the gesture which mediates the social activities that gives rise to the process of taking the rôle of the other. The latter phrase is a little unfortunate because it suggests an actor's attitude which is actually more sophisticated than that which is involved in our own experience. To this degree it does not correctly describe that which I have in mind. We see the process most definitely in a primitive form in those situations where the child's play takes different rôles. Here the very fact that he is ready to pay out money, for instance, arouses the attitude of the person who receives money; the very process is calling out in him the corresponding activities of the other person involved. The individual stimulates himself to the response which he is calling out in the other person, and then acts in some degree in response to that situation. In play the child does definitely act out the rôle which he himself has aroused in himself. It is that which gives, as I have said, a definite content in the individual which answers to the stimulus that affects him as it affects somebody else. The content of the other that enters into one personality is the response in the individual which his gesture calls out in the other.

We may illustrate our basic concept by a reference to the notion of property. If we say "This is my property, I shall control it," that affirmation calls out a certain set of responses which must be the same in any community in which property exists. It involves an organized attitude with reference to property which is common to all the members of the community. One must have a definite attitude of control of his own property and respect for the property of others. Those attitudes (as organized sets of responses) must be there on the part of all, so that when one says such a thing he calls out in himself the response of the others. He is calling out the response of what I have called a generalized other. That which makes society possible is such common responses, such organized attitudes, with reference to what we term property, the cults of religion, the process of education, and the relations of the family. Of course, the wider the society the more definitely universal these objects must be. In any case there must be a definite set of responses, which we may speak of as abstract, and which can belong to a very large group. Property is in itself a very abstract concept. It is that which the individual himself can control and nobody else can control. The attitude is different from that of a dog toward a bone. A dog will fight any other dog trying to take the bone. The dog is not taking the attitude of the other dog. A man who says "This is my property" is taking an attitude of the other person. The man is appealing to his rights because he is able to take the attitude which everybody else in the group has with reference to property, thus arousing in himself the attitude of others.

What goes to make up the organized self is the organization of the attitudes which are common to the group. A person is a personality because he belongs to a community, because he takes over the institutions of that community into his own conduct. He takes its language as a medium by which he gets his personality, and then through a process of taking the different rôles that all the others furnish he comes to get the attitude of the members of the community. Such, in a certain sense, is the structure of a man's personality. There are certain common responses which each individual has toward certain common things, and in so far as those common responses are awakened in the individual when he is affecting other persons he arouses his own self. The structure, then, on which the self is built is this response which is common to all, for one has to be a member of a community to be a self. Such responses are abstract attitudes, but they constitute just what we term a man's character. They give him what we term his principles, the acknowledged attitudes of all members of the community toward what are the values of that community. He is putting himself in the place of the generalized other, which represents the organized responses of all the members of the group. It is that which guides conduct controlled by principles, and a person who has such an organized group of responses is a man whom we say has character, in the moral sense.

It is a structure of attitudes, then, which goes to make up a self, as distinct from a group of habits. We all of us have, for example, certain groups of habits, such as the particular intonations which a person uses in his speech. This is a set of habits of vocal expression which one has but which one does not know about. The sets of habits which we have of that sort mean nothing to us; we do not hear the intonations of our speech that others hear unless we are paying particular attention to them. The habits of emotional expression which belong to our speech are of the same sort. We may know that we have expressed ourselves in a joyous fashion but the detailed process is one which does not come back to our conscious selves. There are whole bundles of such habits which do not enter into a conscious self, but which help to make up what is termed the unconscious self.

After all, what we mean by self-consciousness is an awakening in ourselves of the group of attitudes which we are arousing in others, especially when it is an important set of responses which go to make up the members of the community. It is unfortunate to fuse or mix up consciousness, as we ordinarily use that term, and self-consciousness. Consciousness, as frequently used, simply has reference to the field of experience, but self-consciousness refers to the ability to call out in ourselves a set of definite responses which belong to the others of the group. Consciousness and self-consciousness are not on the same level. A man alone has, fortunately or unfortunately, access to his own toothache, but that is not what we mean by self-consciousness.

I have so far emphasized what I have called the structures upon which the self is constructed, the framework of the self, as it were. Of course we are not only what is common to all: each one of the selves is different from everyone else; but there has to be such a common structure as I have sketched in order that we may be members of a community at all. We cannot be ourselves unless we are also members in whom there is a community of attitudes which control the attitudes of all. We cannot have rights unless we have common attitudes. That which we have acquired as self-conscious persons makes us such members of society and gives us selves. Selves can only exist in definite relationships to other selves. No hard-and-fast line can be drawn between our own selves and the selves of others, since our own selves exist and enter as such into our experience only in so far as the selves of others exist and enter as such into our experience also. The individual possesses a self only in relation to the selves of the other members of his social group; and the structure of his self expresses or reflects the general behavior pattern of this social group to which he belongs, just as does the structure of the self of every other individual belonging to this social group.

Notes

1. Thinking proceeds in terms of or by means of universals. A universal may be interpreted behavioristically as simply the social act as a whole, involving the organization and interrelation of the attitudes of all the individuals implicated in the act, as controlling their overt responses. This organization of the different individual attitudes and interactions in a given social act, with reference to their interrelations as realized by the individuals themselves, is what we mean by a universal; and it determines what the actual overt responses of the individuals involved in the given social act will be, whether that act be concerned with a concrete project of some sort (such as the relation of physical and social means to ends desired) or with some purely abstract discussion, say the theory of relativity or the Platonic ideas.

2. ["The Relation of Play to Education," *University of Chicago Record*, I (1896–7), 140 ff.]

3. It is possible for inanimate objects, no less than for other human organisms, to form parts of the generalized and organized – the completely socialized – other for any given human individual, in so far as he responds to such objects socially or in a social fashion (by means of the mechanism of thought, the internalized conversation of gestures). Any thing – any object or set of objects, whether animate or inanimate, human or animal, or merely physical – toward which he acts, or to which he responds, socially, is an element in what for him is the generalized other; by taking the attitudes of which toward himself he becomes conscious of himself as an object or individual, and thus develops a self or personality. Thus, for example, the cult, in its primitive form, is merely the social embodiment of the relation between the given social group or community and its physical environment – an organized social means, adopted by the individual members of that group or community, of entering into social relations with that environment, or (in a sense) of carrying on conversations with it; and in this way that environment becomes part of the total generalized other for each of the individual members of the given social group or community.

4. We have said that the internal conversation of the individual with himself in terms of words or significant gestures – the conversation which constitutes the process or activity of thinking – is carried on by the individual from the standpoint of the "generalized other." And the more abstract that conversation is, the more abstract thinking happens to be, the further removed is the generalized other from any connection with particular individuals. It is especially in abstract thinking, that is to say, that the conversation involved is carried on by the individual with the generalized other, rather than with any particular individuals. Thus it is, for example, that abstract concepts are concepts stated in terms of the attitudes of the entire social group or community; they are stated on the basis of the individual's consciousness of the attitudes of the generalized other toward them, as a result of his taking these attitudes of the generalized other and then responding to them. And thus it is also that abstract propositions are stated in a form which anyone – any other intelligent individual – will accept.

Part II
Race/Ethnicity/Ethnorace

5

The Conservation of Races

W. E. B. Du Bois

The American Negro has always felt an intense personal interest in discussions as to the origins and destinies of races: primarily because back of most discussions of race with which he is familiar, have lurked certain assumptions as to his natural abilities, as to his political, intellectual and moral status, which he felt were wrong. He has, consequently, been led to deprecate and minimize race distinctions, to believe intensely that out of one blood God created all nations, and to speak of human brotherhood as though it were the possibility of an already dawning to-morrow.

Nevertheless, in our calmer moments we must acknowledge that human beings are divided into races; that in this country the two most extreme types of the world's races have met, and the resulting problem as to the future relations of these types is not only of intense and living interest to us, but forms an epoch in the history of mankind.

It is necessary, therefore, in planning our movements, in guiding our future development, that at times we rise above the pressing, but smaller questions of separate schools and cars, wage-discrimination and lynch law, to survey the whole question of race in human philosophy and to lay, on a basis of broad knowledge and careful insight, those large lines of policy and higher ideals which may form our guiding lines and boundaries in the practical difficulties of every day. For it is certain that all human striving must recognize the hard limits of natural law, and that any striving, no matter how intense and earnest, which is against the constitution of the world, is vain. The question, then, which we must seriously consider is this: What is the real meaning of Race; what has, in the past, been the law of race development, and what lessons has the past history of race development to teach the rising Negro people?

When we thus come to inquire into the essential difference of races we find it hard to come at once to any definite conclusion. Many criteria of race differences have in the past been proposed, as color, hair, cranial measurements and language. And manifestly, in each of these respects, human beings differ widely. They vary in color, for instance, from the marble-like pallor of the Scandinavian to the rich, dark brown of the Zulu, passing by the creamy Slav, the yellow Chinese, the light brown Sicilian and the brown Egyptian. Men vary, too, in the texture of hair from the obstinately straight hair of the Chinese to the obstinately tufted and frizzled hair of the Bushman. In measurement of heads, again, men vary; from the broad-headed Tartar to the medium-headed European and the narrow-headed Hottentot; or, again in language, from the highly-inflected Roman tongue to the monosyllabic Chinese. All these physical characteristics are patent enough, and if they agreed with each other it would be very easy to classify mankind. Unfortunately for scientists, however, these criteria of race are most exasperatingly intermingled. Color does not agree with texture of hair, for many of the dark races have straight hair; nor does color agree with the breadth of the head, for the yellow Tartar has a broader head than the German; nor, again, has the science of language as yet succeeded in clearing up the relative authority of these various and contradictory criteria. The final word of science, so far, is that we have at least two, perhaps three, great families of human beings – the whites and Negroes, possibly the yellow race. That other races have arisen from the intermingling of the blood of these two. This broad division of the world's races which men like Huxley and Raetzel have introduced as more nearly true than the old five-race scheme of Blumenbach, is nothing more than an acknowledgment that, so far as purely physical characteristics are concerned, the differences between men do not explain all the differences of their history. It declares, as Darwin himself said, that great as is the physical unlikeness of the various races of men their likenesses are greater, and upon this rests the whole scientific doctrine of Human Brotherhood.

Although the wonderful developments of human history teach that the grosser physical differences of color, hair and bone go but a short way toward explaining the different roles which groups of men have played in Human Progress, yet there are differences – subtle, delicate and elusive, though they may be – which have silently but definitely separated men into groups. While these subtle forces have generally followed the natural cleavage of common blood, descent and physical peculiarities, they have at other times swept across and ignored these. At all times, however, they have divided human beings into races, which, while they perhaps transcend scientific definition, nevertheless, are clearly defined to the eye of the Historian and Sociologist.

If this be true, then the history of the world is the history, not of individuals, but of groups, not of nations, but of races, and he who ignores or seeks to override the race idea in human history ignores and overrides the central thought of all history. What, then, is a race? It is a vast family of human beings, generally of common blood and language, always of common history, traditions and impulses, who are both voluntarily and involuntarily striving together for the accomplishment of certain more or less vividly conceived ideals of life.

Turning to real history, there can be no doubt, first, as to the widespread, nay, universal, prevalence of the race idea, the race spirit, the race ideal, and as to its efficiency as the vastest and most ingenious invention for human progress. We, who have been reared and trained under the individualistic philosophy of the Declaration of Independence and the laisser-faire philosophy of Adam Smith, are loath to see and loath to acknowledge this patent fact of human history. We see the Pharaohs, Caesars, Toussaints and Napoleons of history and forget the vast races of which they were but epitomized expressions. We are apt to think in our American impatience, that while it may have been true in

the past that closed race groups made history, that here in conglomerate America *nous avons changé tout cela* – we have changed all that, and have no need of this ancient instrument of progress. This assumption of which the Negro people are especially fond, can not be established by a careful consideration of history.

We find upon the world's stage today eight distinctly differentiated races, in the sense in which History tells us the word must be used. They are, the Slavs of eastern Europe, the Teutons of middle Europe, the English of Great Britain and America, the Romance nations of Southern and Western Europe, the Negroes of Africa and America, the Semitic people of Western Asia and Northern Africa, the Hindoos of Central Asia and the Mongolians of Eastern Asia. There are, of course, other minor race groups, as the American Indians, the Esquimaux and the South Sea Islanders; these larger races, too, are far from homogeneous; the Slav includes the Czech, the Magyar, the Pole and the Russian; the Teuton includes the German, the Scandinavian and the Dutch; the English include the Scotch, the Irish and the conglomerate American. Under Romance nations the widely-differing Frenchman, Italian, Sicilian and Spaniard are comprehended. The term Negro is, perhaps, the most indefinite of all, combining the Mulattoes and Zamboes of America and the Egyptians, Bantus and Bushmen of Africa. Among the Hindoos are traces of widely differing nations, while the great Chinese, Tartar, Corean and Japanese families fall under the one designation – Mongolian.

The question now is: What is the real distinction between these nations? Is it the physical differences of blood, color and cranial measurements? Certainly we must all acknowledge that physical differences play a great part, and that, with wide exceptions and qualifications, these eight great races of to-day follow the cleavage of physical race distinctions; the English and Teuton represent the white variety of mankind; the Mongolian, the yellow; the Negroes, the black. Between these are many crosses and mixtures, where Mongolian and Teuton have blended into the Slav, and other mixtures have produced the Romance nations and the Semites. But while race differences have followed mainly physical race lines, yet no mere physical distinctions would really define or explain the deeper differences – the cohesiveness and continuity of these groups. The deeper differences are spiritual, psychical, differences – undoubtedly based on the physical, but infinitely transcending them. The forces that bind together the Teuton nations are, then, first, their race identity and common blood; secondly, and more important, a common history, common laws and religion, similar habits of thought and a conscious striving together for certain ideals of life. The whole process which has brought about these race differentiations has been a growth, and the great characteristic of this growth has been the differentiation of spiritual and mental differences between great races of mankind and the integration of physical differences.

The age of nomadic tribes of closely related individuals represents the maximum of physical differences. They were practically vast families, and there were as many groups as families. As the families came together to form cities the physical differences lessened, purity of blood was replaced by the requirement of domicile, and all who lived within the city bounds became gradually to be regarded as members of the group; *i.e.*, there was a slight and slow breaking down of physical barriers. This, however, was accompanied by an increase of the spiritual and social differences between cities. This city became husbandmen, this, merchants, another warriors, and so on. The *ideals of life* for which the different cities struggled were different. When at last cities began to coalesce into nations there was another breaking down of barriers which separated groups of men. The larger and broader differences of color, hair and physical proportions were not by any means ignored, but myriads of minor differences disappeared, and the sociological and historical races of men began to approximate the present division of races as indicated by physical researches. At the same time the spiritual and physical differences of race groups which constituted the nations became deep and decisive. The English nation stood for constitutional liberty and commercial freedom; the German nation for science and philosophy; the Romance nations stood for literature and art, and the other race groups are striving, each in its own way, to develop for civilization its particular message, its particular ideal, which shall help to guide the world nearer and nearer that perfection of human life for which we all long, that "one far off Divine event."

This has been the function of race differences up to the present time. What shall be its function in the future? Manifestly some of the great races of today – particularly the Negro race – have not as yet given to civilization the full spiritual message

which they are capable of giving. I will not say that the Negro race has as yet given no message to the world, for it is still a mooted question among scientists as to just how far Egyptian civilization was Negro in its origin; if it was not wholly Negro, it was certainly very closely allied. Be that as it may, however, the fact still remains that the full, complete Negro message of the whole Negro race has not as yet been given to the world: that the messages and ideal of the yellow race have not been completed, and that the striving of the mighty Slavs has but begun. The question is, then: How shall this message be delivered; how shall these various ideals be realized? The answer is plain: By the development of these race groups, not as individuals, but as races. For the development of Japanese genius, Japanese literature and art, Japanese spirit, only Japanese, bound and welded together, Japanese inspired by one vast ideal, can work out in its fullness the wonderful message which Japan has for the nations of the earth. For the development of Negro genius, of Negro literature and art, of Negro spirit, only Negroes bound and welded together, Negroes inspired by one vast ideal, can work out in its fullness the great message we have for humanity. We cannot reverse history; we are subject to the same natural laws as other races, and if the Negro is ever to be a factor in the world's history – if among the gaily-colored banners that deck the broad ramparts of civilization is to hang one uncompromising black, then it must be placed there by black hands, fashioned by black heads and hallowed by the travail of 200,000,000 black hearts beating in one glad song of jubilee.

For this reason, the advance guard of the Negro people – the 8,000,000 people of Negro blood in the United States of America – must soon come to realize that if they are to take their just place in the van of Pan-Negroism, then their destiny is *not* absorption by the white Americans. That if in America it is to be proven for the first time in the modern world that not only Negroes are capable of evolving individual men like Toussaint, the Saviour, but are a nation stored with wonderful possibilities of culture, then their destiny is not a servile imitation of Anglo-Saxon culture, but a stalwart originality which shall unswervingly follow Negro ideals.

It may, however, be objected here that the situation of our race in America renders this attitude impossible; that our sole hope of salvation lies in our being able to lose our race identity in the commingled blood of the nation; and that any other course would merely increase the friction of races which we call race prejudice, and against which we have so long and so earnestly fought.

Here, then, is the dilemma, and it is a puzzling one, I admit. No Negro who has given earnest thought to the situation of his people in America has failed, at some time in life, to find himself at these cross-roads; has failed to ask himself at some time: What, after all, am I? Am I an American or am I a Negro? Can I be both? Or is it my duty to cease to be a Negro as soon as possible and be an American? If I strive as a Negro, am I not perpetuating the very cleft that threatens and separates Black and White America? Is not my only possible practical aim the subduction of all that is Negro in me to the American? Does my black blood place upon me any more obligation to assert my nationality than German, or Irish or Italian blood would?

It is such incessant self-questioning and the hesitation that arises from it, that is making the present period a time of vacillation and contradiction for the American Negro; combined race action is stifled, race responsibility is shirked, race enterprises languish, and the best blood, the best talent, the best energy of the Negro people cannot be marshalled to do the bidding of the race. They stand back to make room for every rascal and demagogue who chooses to cloak his selfish deviltry under the veil of race pride.

Is this right? Is it rational? Is it good policy? Have we in America a distinct mission as a race – a distinct sphere of action and an opportunity for race development, or is self-obliteration the highest end to which Negro blood dare aspire?

If we carefully consider what race prejudice really is, we find it, historically, to be nothing but the friction between different groups of people; it is the difference in aim, in feeling, in ideals of two different races; if, now, this difference exists touching territory, laws, language, or even religion, it is manifest that these people cannot live in the same territory without fatal collision; but if, on the other hand, there is substantial agreement in laws, language and religion; if there is a satisfactory adjustment of economic life, then there is no reason why, in the same country and on the same street, two or three great national ideals might not thrive and develop, that men of different races might not strive together for their race ideals as well, perhaps even better, than in isolation. Here, it seems to me, is

the reading of the riddle that puzzles so many of us. We are Americans, not only by birth and by citizenship, but by our political ideals, our language, our religion. Farther than that, our Americanism does not go. At that point, we are Negroes, members of a vast historic race that from the very dawn of creation has slept, but half awakening in the dark forests of its African fatherland. We are the first fruits of this new nation, the harbinger of that black to-morrow which is yet destined to soften the whiteness of the Teutonic to-day. We are that people whose subtle sense of song has given America its only American music, its only American fairy tales, its only touch of pathos and humor amid its mad money-getting plutocracy. As such, it is our duty to conserve our physical powers, our intellectual endowments, our spiritual ideals; as a race we must strive by race organization, by race solidarity, by race unity to the realization of that broader humanity which freely recognizes differences in men, but sternly deprecates inequality in their opportunities of development.

For the accomplishment of these ends we need race organizations: Negro colleges, Negro newspapers, Negro business organizations, a Negro school of literature and art, and an intellectual clearing house, for all these products of the Negro mind, which we may call a Negro Academy. Not only is all this necessary for positive advance, it is absolutely imperative for negative defense. Let us not deceive ourselves at our situation in this country. Weighted with a heritage of moral iniquity from our past history, hard pressed in the economic world by foreign immigrants and native prejudice, hated here, despised there and pitied everywhere; our one haven of refuge is ourselves, and but one means of advance, our own belief in our great destiny, our own implicit trust in our ability and worth. There is no power under God's high heaven that can stop the advance of eight thousand thousand honest, earnest, inspired and united people. But – and here is the rub – they *must* be honest, fearlessly criticizing their own faults, zealously correcting them; they must be *earnest*. No people that laughs at itself, and ridicules itself, and wishes to God it was anything but itself ever wrote its name in history; it *must* be inspired with the Divine faith of our black mothers, that out of the blood and dust of battle will march a victorious host, a mighty nation, a peculiar people, to speak to the nations of earth a Divine truth that shall make them free. And such a people must be united; not merely united for the organized theft of political spoils, not united to disgrace religion with whoremongers and ward-heelers; not united merely to protest and pass resolutions, but united to stop the ravages of consumption among the Negro people, united to keep black boys from loafing, gambling and crime; united to guard the purity of black women and to reduce that vast army of black prostitutes that is today marching to hell; and united in serious organizations, to determine by careful conference and thoughtful interchange of opinion the broad lines of policy and action for the American Negro.

This is the reason for being which the American Negro Academy has. It aims at once to be the epitome and expression of the intellect of the black-blooded people of America, the exponent of the race ideals of one of the world's great races. As such, the Academy must, if successful, be

(*a*) Representative in character.
(*b*) Impartial in conduct.
(*c*) Firm in leadership.

It must be representative in character; not in that it represents all interests or all factions, but in that it seeks to comprise something of the *best* thought, the most unselfish striving and the highest ideals. There are scattered in forgotten nooks and corners throughout the land, Negroes of some considerable training, of high minds, and high motives, who are unknown to their fellows, who exert far too little influence. These the Negro Academy should strive to bring into touch with each other and to give them a common mouthpiece.

The Academy should be impartial in conduct; while it aims to exalt the people it should aim to do so by truth – not by lies, by honesty – not by flattery. It should continually impress the fact upon the Negro people that they must not expect to have things done for them – they MUST DO FOR THEM-SELVES; that they have on their hands a vast work of self-reformation to do, and that a little less complaint and whining, and a little more dogged work and manly striving would do us more credit and benefit than a thousand Force or Civil Rights bills.

Finally, the American Negro Academy must point out a practical path of advance to the Negro people; there lie before every Negro today hundreds of questions of policy and right which must be settled and which each one settles now, not in accordance with any rule, but by impulse or individual preference; for instance: What should be the attitude of Negroes toward the educational qualification for voters? What should be our attitude toward separate schools? How should we meet discriminations on railways and in hotels? Such questions need not so much specific answers for each part as a general expression of policy, and nobody should be better fitted to announce such a policy than a representative honest Negro Academy.

All this, however, must come in time after careful organization and long conference. The immediate work before us should be practical and have direct bearing upon the situation of the Negro. The historical work of collecting the laws of the United States and of the various States of the Union with regard to the Negro is a work of such magnitude and importance that no body but one like this could think of undertaking it. If we could accomplish that one task we would justify our existence.

In the field of Sociology an appalling work lies before us. First, we must unflinchingly and bravely face the truth, not with apologies, but with solemn earnestness. The Negro Academy ought to sound a note of warning that would echo in every black cabin in the land: *Unless we conquer our present vices they will conquer us*; we are diseased, we are developing criminal tendencies, and an alarmingly large percentage of our men and women are sexually impure. The Negro Academy should stand and proclaim this over the housetops, crying with Garrison: *I will not equivocate, I will not retreat a single inch, and I will be heard*. The Academy should seek to gather about it the talented, unselfish men, the pure and noble-minded women, to fight an army of devils that disgraces our manhood and our womanhood. There does not stand today upon God's earth a race more capable in muscle, in intellect, in morals, than the American Negro, if he will bend his energies in the right direction; if he will

Burst his birth's invidious bar
And grasp the skirts of happy chance,
And breast the blows of circumstance,
And grapple with his evil star.

In science and morals, I have indicated two fields of work for the Academy. Finally, in practical policy, I wish to suggest the following *Academy Creed*:

1 We believe that the Negro people, as a race, have a contribution to make to civilization and humanity, which no other race can make.

2 We believe it the duty of the Americans of Negro descent, as a body, to maintain their race identity until this mission of the Negro people is accomplished, and the ideal of human brotherhood has become a practical possibility.

3 We believe that, unless modern civilization is a failure, it is entirely feasible and practicable for two races in such essential political, economic, and religious harmony as the white and colored people of America, to develop side by side in peace and mutual happiness, the peculiar contribution which each has to make to the culture of their common country.

4 As a means to this end we advocate, not such social equality between these races as would disregard human likes and dislikes, but such a social equilibrium as would, throughout all the complicated relations of life, give due and just consideration to culture, ability, and moral worth, whether they be found under white or black skins.

5 We believe that the first and greatest step toward the settlement of the present friction between the races – commonly called the Negro Problem – lies in the correction of the immorality, crime and laziness among the Negroes themselves, which still remains as a heritage from slavery. We believe that only earnest and long continued efforts on our own part can cure these social ills.

6 We believe that the second great step toward a better adjustment of the relations between the races should be a more impartial selection of ability in the economic and intellectual world, and a greater respect for personal liberty and worth, regardless of race. We believe that only earnest efforts on the part of the white people of this country will bring much needed reform in these matters.

7 On the basis of the foregoing declaration, and firmly believing in our high destiny, we, as American Negroes, are resolved to strive in every honorable way for the realization of the best and highest aims, for the development of strong manhood and pure womanhood, and for the rearing of a race ideal in America and Africa, to the glory of God and the uplifting of the Negro people.

6

The New Negro

ALAIN LOCKE

In the last decade something beyond the watch and guard of statistics has happened in the life of the American Negro and the three norns who have traditionally presided over the Negro problem have a changeling in their laps. The Sociologist, the Philanthropist, the Race-leader are not unaware of the New Negro, but they are at a loss to account for him. He simply cannot be swathed in their formulæ. For the younger generation is vibrant with a new psychology; the new spirit is awake in the masses, and under the very eyes of the professional observers is transforming what has been a perennial problem into the progressive phases of contemporary Negro life.

Could such a metamorphosis have taken place as suddenly as it has appeared to? The answer is no; not because the New Negro is not here, but because the Old Negro had long become more of a myth than a man. The Old Negro, we must remember, was a creature of moral debate and historical controversy. His has been a stock figure perpetuated as an historical fiction partly in innocent sentimentalism, partly in deliberate reactionism. The Negro himself has contributed his share to this through a sort of protective social mimicry forced upon him by the adverse circumstances of dependence. So for generations in the mind of America, the Negro has been more of a formula than a human being – a something to be argued about, condemned or defended, to be "kept down," or "in his place," or "helped up," to be worried with or worried over, harassed or patronized, a social bogey or a social burden. The thinking Negro even has been induced to share this same general attitude, to focus his attention on controversial issues, to see himself in the distorted perspective of a social problem. His shadow, so to speak, has been more real to him than his personality. Through having had to appeal from the unjust stereotypes of his oppressors and traducers to those of his liberators, friends and benefactors he has had to subscribe to the traditional positions from which his case has been viewed. Little true social or self-understanding has or could come from such a situation.

But while the minds of most of us, black and white, have thus burrowed in the trenches of the Civil War and Reconstruction, the actual march of development has simply flanked these positions, necessitating a sudden reorientation of view. We have not been watching in the right direction; set North and South on a sectional axis, we have not noticed the East till the sun has us blinking.

Recall how suddenly the Negro spirituals revealed themselves; suppressed for generations under the stereotypes of Wesleyan hymn harmony, secretive, half-ashamed, until the courage of being natural brought them out – and behold, there was folk-music. Similarly the mind of the Negro seems suddenly to have slipped from under the tyranny of social intimidation and to be shaking off the psychology of imitation and implied inferiority. By shedding the old chrysalis of the Negro problem we are achieving something like a spiritual emancipation. Until recently, lacking self-understanding, we have been almost as much of a problem to ourselves as we still are to others. But the decade that found us with a problem has left us with only a task. The multitude perhaps feels as yet only a strange relief and a new vague urge, but the thinking few know that in the reaction the vital inner grip of prejudice has been broken.

With this renewed self-respect and self-dependence, the life of the Negro community is bound to enter a new dynamic phase, the buoyancy from within compensating for whatever pressure there may be of conditions from without. The migrant masses, shifting from countryside to city, hurdle several generations of experience at a leap, but more important, the same thing happens spiritually in the life-attitudes and self-expression of the Young Negro, in his poetry, his art, his education and his new outlook, with the additional advantage, of course, of the poise and greater certainty of knowing what it is all about. From this comes the promise and warrant of a new leadership. As one of them has discerningly put it:

We have tomorrow
Bright before us
Like a flame.

Yesterday, a night-gone thing
A sun-down name.

And dawn today
Broad arch above the road we came.
We march!

This is what, even more than any "most creditable record of fifty years of freedom," requires that the Negro of to-day be seen through other than the dusty spectacles of past controversy. The day of "aunties," "uncles" and "mammies" is equally gone. Uncle Tom and Sambo have passed on, and even the "Colonel" and "George" play barnstorm rôles from which they escape with relief when the public spotlight is off. The popular melodrama has about played itself out, and it is time to scrap the fictions, garret the bogeys and settle down to a realistic facing of facts.

First we must observe some of the changes which since the traditional lines of opinion were drawn have rendered these quite obsolete. A main change has been, of course, that shifting of the Negro population which has made the Negro problem no longer exclusively or even predominantly Southern. Why should our minds remain sectionalized, when the problem itself no longer is? Then the trend of migration has not only been toward the North and the Central Midwest, but city-ward and to the great centers of industry – the problems of adjustment are new, practical, local and not peculiarly racial. Rather they are an integral part of the large industrial and social problems of our present-day demo-

cracy. And finally, with the Negro rapidly in process of class differentiation, if it ever was warrantable to regard and treat the Negro *en masse* it is becoming with every day less possible, more unjust and more ridiculous.

In the very process of being transplanted, the Negro is becoming transformed.

The tide of Negro migration, northward and city-ward, is not to be fully explained as a blind flood started by the demands of war industry coupled with the shutting off of foreign migration, or by the pressure of poor crops coupled with increased social terrorism in certain sections of the South and Southwest. Neither labor demand, the boll-weevil nor the Ku Klux Klan is a basic factor, however contributory any or all of them may have been. The wash and rush of this human tide on the beach line of the northern city centers is to be explained primarily in terms of a new vision of opportunity, of social and economic freedom, of a spirit to seize, even in the face of an extortionate and heavy toll, a chance for the improvement of conditions. With each successive wave of it, the movement of the Negro becomes more and more a mass movement toward the larger and the more democratic chance – in the Negro's case a deliberate flight not only from countryside to city, but from medieval America to modern.

Take Harlem as an instance of this. Here in Manhattan is not merely the largest Negro community in the world, but the first concentration in history of so many diverse elements of Negro life. It has attracted the African, the West Indian, the Negro American; has brought together the Negro of the North and the Negro of the South; the man from the city and the man from the town and village; the peasant, the student, the business man, the professional man, artist, poet, musician, adventurer and worker, preacher and criminal, exploiter and social outcast. Each group has come with its own separate motives and for its own special ends, but their greatest experience has been the finding of one another. Proscription and prejudice have thrown these dissimilar elements into a common area of contact and interaction. Within this area, race sympathy and unity have determined a further fusing of sentiment and experience. So what began in terms of segregation becomes more and more, as its elements mix and react, the laboratory of a great race-welding. Hitherto, it must be admitted that American Negroes have been a race more in name than in fact, or to be exact, more in

sentiment than in experience. The chief bond between them has been that of a common condition
rather than a common consciousness; a problem in
common rather than a life in common. In Harlem,
Negro life is seizing upon its first chances for group
expression and self-determination. It is – or promises at least to be – a race capital. That is why our
comparison is taken with those nascent centers of
folk-expression and self-determination which are
playing a creative part in the world to-day. Without pretense to their political significance, Harlem
has the same rôle to play for the New Negro as
Dublin has had for the New Ireland or Prague for
the New Czechoslovakia.

Harlem, I grant you, isn't typical – but it is
significant, it is prophetic. No sane observer, however sympathetic to the new trend, would contend
that the great masses are articulate as yet, but they
stir, they move, they are more than physically rest-
less. The challenge of the new intellectuals among
them is clear enough – the "race radicals" and realists who have broken with the old epoch of philanthropic guidance, sentimental appeal and protest.
But are we after all only reading into the stirrings
of a sleeping giant the dreams of an agitator? The
answer is in the migrating peasant. It is the "man
farthest down" who is most active in getting up.
One of the most characteristic symptoms of this is
the professional man, himself migrating to recapture his constituency after a vain effort to maintain
in some Southern corner what for years back seemed
an established living and clientele. The clergyman
following his errant flock, the physician or lawyer
trailing his clients, supply the true clues. In a real
sense it is the rank and file who are leading, and the
leaders who are following. A transformed and transforming psychology permeates the masses.

When the racial leaders of twenty years ago spoke
of developing race-pride and stimulating race-
consciousness, and of the desirability of race solidarity, they could not in any accurate degree have
anticipated the abrupt feeling that has surged up
and now pervades the awakened centers. Some of
the recognized Negro leaders and a powerful section
of white opinion identified with "race work" of
the older order have indeed attempted to discount
this feeling as a "passing phase," an attack of "race
nerves" so to speak, an "aftermath of the war," and
the like. It has not abated, however, if we are to
gauge by the present tone and temper of the Negro
press, or by the shift in popular support from the
officially recognized and orthodox spokesmen to

those of the independent, popular, and often radical type who are unmistakable symptoms of a new
order. It is a social disservice to blunt the fact that
the Negro of the Northern centers has reached a
stage where tutelage, even of the most interested
and well-intentioned sort, must give place to new
relationships, where positive self-direction must
be reckoned with in ever increasing measure. The
American mind must reckon with a fundamentally
changed Negro.

The Negro too, for his part, has idols of the
tribe to smash. If on the one hand the white man
has erred in making the Negro appear to be that
which would excuse or extenuate his treatment of
him, the Negro, in turn, has too often unnecessarily excused himself because of the way he has been
treated. The intelligent Negro of to-day is resolved
not to make discrimination an extenuation for his
shortcomings in performance, individual or collective; he is trying to hold himself at par, neither
inflated by sentimental allowances nor depreciated
by current social discounts. For this he must know
himself and be known for precisely what he is,
and for that reason he welcomes the new scientific
rather than the old sentimental interest. Sentimental
interest in the Negro has ebbed. We used to lament
this as the falling off of our friends; now we rejoice
and pray to be delivered both from self-pity and
condescension. The mind of each racial group has
had a bitter weaning, apathy or hatred on one side
matching disillusionment or resentment on the
other; but they face each other to-day with the
possibility at least of entirely new mutual attitudes.

It does not follow that if the Negro were better
known, he would be better liked or better treated.
But mutual understanding is basic for any subsequent cooperation and adjustment. The effort
toward this will at least have the effect of remedying
in large part what has been the most unsatisfactory
feature of our present stage of race relationships in
America, namely the fact that the more intelligent
and representative elements of the two race groups
have at so many points got quite out of vital touch
with one another.

The fiction is that the life of the races is separate, and increasingly so. The fact is that they have
touched too closely at the unfavorable and too lightly
at the favorable levels.

While inter-racial councils have sprung up in the
South, drawing on forward elements of both races,
in the Northern cities manual laborers may brush
elbows in their everyday work, but the community

and business leaders have experienced no such interplay or far too little of it. These segments must achieve contact or the race situation in America becomes desperate. Fortunately this is happening. There is a growing realization that in social effort the co-operative basis must supplant long-distance philanthropy, and that the only safeguard for mass relations in the future must be provided in the carefully maintained contacts of the enlightened minorities of both race groups. In the intellectual realm a renewed and keen curiosity is replacing the recent apathy; the Negro is being carefully studied, not just talked about and discussed. In art and letters, instead of being wholly caricatured, he is being seriously portrayed and painted.

To all of this the New Negro is keenly respons- ive as an augury of a new democracy in American culture. He is contributing his share to the new social understanding. But the desire to be under- stood would never in itself have been sufficient to have opened so completely the protectively closed portals of the thinking Negro's mind. There is still too much possibility of being snubbed or patron- ized for that. It was rather the necessity for fuller, truer self-expression, the realization of the unwis- dom of allowing social discrimination to segregate him mentally, and a counter-attitude to cramp and fetter his own living – and so the "spite-wall" that the intellectuals built over the "color-line" has happily been taken down. Much of this reopening of intellectual contacts has centered in New York and has been richly fruitful not merely in the enlarging of personal experience, but in the definite enrichment of American art and letters and in the clarifying of our common vision of the social tasks ahead.

The particular significance in the re-establish- ment of contact between the more advanced and representative classes is that it promises to offset some of the unfavorable reactions of the past, or at least to re-surface race contacts somewhat for the future. Subtly the conditions that are molding a New Negro are molding a new American attitude.

However, this new phase of things is delicate; it will call for less charity but more justice; less help, but infinitely closer understanding. This is indeed a critical stage of race relationships because of the likelihood, if the new temper is not understood, of engendering sharp group antagonism and a second crop of more calculated prejudice. In some quarters, it has already done so. Having weaned the Negro, public opinion cannot continue to paternalize. The Negro to-day is inevitably moving forward under the control largely of his own objectives. What are these objectives? Those of his outer life are happily already well and finally formulated, for they are none other than the ideals of American institutions and democracy. Those of his inner life are yet in process of formation, for the new psychology at present is more of a consensus of feeling than of opinion, of attitude rather than of program. Still some points seem to have crystallized.

Up to the present one may adequately describe the Negro's "inner objectives" as an attempt to repair a damaged group psychology and reshape a warped social perspective. Their realization has required a new mentality for the American Negro. And as it matures we begin to see its effects; at first, negative, iconoclastic, and then positive and constructive. In this new group psychology we note the lapse of sentimental appeal, then the develop- ment of a more positive self-respect and self- reliance; the repudiation of social dependence, and then the gradual recovery from hyper-sensitiveness and "touchy" nerves, the repudiation of the double standard of judgment with its special philanthropic allowances and then the sturdier desire for object- ive and scientific appraisal; and finally the rise from social disillusionment to race pride, from the sense of social debt to the responsibilities of social con- tribution, and offsetting the necessary working and commonsense acceptance of restricted conditions, the belief in ultimate esteem and recognition. There- fore the Negro to-day wishes to be known for what he is, even in his faults and shortcomings, and scorns a craven and precarious survival at the price of seeming to be what he is not. He resents being spoken of as a social ward or minor, even by his own, and to being regarded a chronic patient for the sociological clinic, the sick man of American Democracy. For the same reasons, he himself is through with those social nostrums and panaceas, the so-called "solutions" of his "problem," with which he and the country have been so liberally dosed in the past. Religion, freedom, education, money – in turn, he has ardently hoped for and peculiarly trusted these things; he still believes in them, but not in blind trust that they alone will solve his life-problem.

Each generation, however, will have its creed, and that of the present is the belief in the efficacy of collective effort, in race co-operation. This deep feeling of race is at present the mainspring of Negro life. It seems to be the outcome of the reac- tion to proscription and prejudice; an attempt, fairly successful on the whole, to convert a defensive into an offensive position, a handicap into an incentive. It is radical in tone, but not in purpose and only the most stupid forms of opposition, misunderstanding or persecution could make it otherwise. Of course, the thinking Negro has shifted a little toward the left with the world-trend, and there is an increasing group who affiliate with radical and liberal movements. But fundamentally for the present the Negro is radical on race matters, conservative on others, in other words, a "forced radical," a social protestant rather than a genuine radical. Yet under further pressure and injustice iconoclastic thought and motives will inevitably increase. Harlem's quixotic radicalisms call for their ounce of democracy to-day lest to-morrow they be beyond cure.

The Negro mind reaches out as yet to nothing but American wants, American ideas. But this forced attempt to build his Americanism on race values is a unique social experiment, and its ultimate success is impossible except through the fullest sharing of American culture and institutions. There should be no delusion about this. American nerves in sections unstrung with race hysteria are often fed the opiate that the trend of Negro advance is wholly separatist, and that the effect of its operation will be to encyst the Negro as a benign foreign body in the body politic. This cannot be – even if it were desirable. The racialism of the Negro is no limitation or reservation with respect to American life; it is only a constructive effort to build the obstructions in the stream of his progress into an efficient dam of social energy and power. Democracy itself is obstructed and stagnated to the extent that any of its channels are closed. Indeed they cannot be selectively closed. So the choice is not between one way for the Negro and another way for the rest, but between American institutions frustrated on the one hand and American ideals progressively fulfilled and realized on the other.

There is, of course, a warrantably comfortable feeling in being on the right side of the country's professed ideals. We realize that we cannot be undone without America's undoing. It is within the gamut of this attitude that the thinking Negro faces America, but with variations of mood that are if anything more significant than the attitude itself. Sometimes we have it taken with the defiant ironic challenge of McKay:

Mine is the future grinding down to-day
Like a great landslip moving to the sea,

Bearing its freight of débris far away
Where the green hungry waters restlessly
Heave mammoth pyramids, and break and roar
Their eerie challenge to the crumbling shore.

Sometimes, perhaps more frequently as yet, it is taken in the fervent and almost filial appeal and counsel of Weldon Johnson's:

O Southland, dear Southland!
Then why do you still cling
To an idle age and a musty page,
To a dead and useless thing?

But between defiance and appeal, midway almost between cynicism and hope, the prevailing mind stands in the mood of the same author's *To America*, an attitude of sober query and stoical challenge:

How would you have us, as we are?
    Or sinking 'neath the load we bear,
Our eyes fixed forward on a star,
    Or gazing empty at despair?

Rising or falling? Men or things?
    With dragging pace or footsteps fleet?
Strong, willing sinews in your wings,
    Or tightening chains about your feet?

More and more, however, an intelligent realization of the great discrepancy between the American social creed and the American social practice forces upon the Negro the taking of the moral advantage that is his. Only the steadying and sobering effect of a truly characteristic gentleness of spirit prevents the rapid rise of a definite cynicism and counter-hate and a defiant superiority feeling. Human as this reaction would be, the majority still deprecate its advent, and would gladly see it forestalled by the speedy amelioration of its causes. We wish our race pride to be a healthier, more positive achievement than a feeling based upon a realization of the shortcomings of others. But all paths toward the attainment of a sound social attitude have been difficult; only a relatively few enlightened minds have been able as the phrase puts it "to rise above" prejudice. The ordinary man has had until recently only a hard choice between the alternatives of supine and humiliating submission and stimulating but hurtful counter-prejudice. Fortunately from some inner, desperate resourcefulness has recently sprung up the simple expedient of fighting prejudice by mental passive resistance, in other words by trying to ignore it. For the few, this manna may perhaps be effective, but the masses cannot thrive upon it.

Fortunately there are constructive channels opening out into which the balked social feelings of the American Negro can flow freely.

Without them there would be much more pressure and danger than there is. These compensating interests are racial but in a new and enlarged way. One is the consciousness of acting as the advanceguard of the African peoples in their contact with Twentieth Century civilization; the other, the sense of a mission of rehabilitating the race in world esteem from that loss of prestige for which the fate and conditions of slavery have so largely been responsible. Harlem, as we shall see, is the center of both these movements; she is the home of the Negro's "Zionism." The pulse of the Negro world has begun to beat in Harlem. A Negro newspaper carrying news material in English, French and Spanish, gathered from all quarters of America, the West Indies and Africa has maintained itself in Harlem for over five years. Two important magazines, both edited from New York, maintain their news and circulation consistently on a cosmopolitan scale. Under American auspices and backing, three pan-African congresses have been held abroad for the discussion of common interests, colonial questions and the future co-operative development of Africa. In terms of the race question as a world problem, the Negro mind has leapt, so to speak, upon the parapets of prejudice and extended its cramped horizons. In so doing it has linked up with the growing group consciousness of the dark-peoples and is gradually learning their common interests. As one of our writers has recently put it: "It is imperative that we understand the white world in its relations to the non-white world." As with the Jew, persecution is making the Negro international.

As a world phenomenon this wider race consciousness is a different thing from the much asserted rising tide of color. Its inevitable causes are not of our making. The consequences are not necessarily damaging to the best interests of civilization. Whether it actually brings into being new Armadas of conflict or argosies of cultural exchange and enlightenment can only be decided by the attitude of the dominant races in an era of critical change. With the American Negro, his new internationalism is primarily an effort to recapture contact with the scattered peoples of African derivation. Garveyism may be a transient, if spectacular, phenomenon, but the possible rôle of the American Negro in the future development of Africa is one of the most constructive and universally helpful missions that any modern people can lay claim to.

Constructive participation in such causes cannot help giving the Negro valuable group incentives, as well as increased prestige at home and abroad. Our greatest rehabilitation may possibly come through such channels, but for the present, more immediate hope rests in the revaluation by white and black alike of the Negro in terms of his artistic endowments and cultural contributions, past and prospective. It must be increasingly recognized that the Negro has already made very substantial contributions, not only in his folk-art, music especially, which has always found appreciation, but in larger, though humbler and less acknowledged ways. For generations the Negro has been the peasant matrix of that section of America which has most undervalued him, and here he has contributed not only materially in labor and in social patience, but spiritually as well. The South has unconsciously absorbed the gift of his folk-temperament. In less than half a generation it will be easier to recognize this, but the fact remains that a leaven of humor, sentiment, imagination and tropic nonchalance has gone into the making of the South from a humble, unacknowledged source. A second crop of the Negro's gifts promises still more largely. He now becomes a conscious contributor and lays aside the status of a beneficiary and ward for that of a collaborator and participant in American civilization. The great social gain in this is the releasing of our talented group from the arid fields of controversy and debate to the productive fields of creative expression. The especially cultural recognition they win should in turn prove the key to that revaluation of the Negro which must precede or accompany any considerable further betterment of race relationships. But whatever the general effect, the present generation will have added the motives of self-expression and spiritual development to the old and still unfinished task of making material headway and progress. No one who understandingly faces the situation with its substantial accomplishment or views the new scene with its still more abundant promise can be entirely without hope. And certainly, if in our lifetime the Negro should not be able to celebrate his full initiation into American democracy, he can at least, on the warrant of these things, celebrate the attainment of a significant and satisfying new phase of group development, and with it a spiritual Coming of Age.

7

Identity and Dignity in the Context of the National Liberation Struggle

Amilcar Cabral

Introduction

The people's struggle for national liberation and independence from imperialist rule has become a driving force of progress for humanity and undoubtedly constitutes one of the essential characteristics of contemporary history.

An objective analysis of imperialism insofar as it is a fact or a "natural" historical phenomenon, indeed "necessary" in the context of the type of economic political evolution of an important part of humanity, reveals that imperialist rule, with all its train of wretchedness, of pillage, of crime and of destruction of human and cultural values, was not just a negative reality. The vast accumulation of capital in half-a-dozen countries of the northern hemisphere, which was the result of piracy, of the confiscation of the property of other peoples and of the ruthless exploitation of the work of these peoples, will not only lead to the monopolization of colonies, but to the division of the world and more imperialist rule.

In the rich countries, imperialist capital, constantly seeking to enlarge itself, increased the creative capacity of man and brought about a total transformation of the means of production, thanks to the rapid progress of science, of techniques, and of technology. This accentuated the pooling of labor and brought about the ascension of huge areas of population. In the colonized countries, where colonization on the whole blocked the historical process of the development of the subjected peoples or else eliminated them radically or progressively,

imperialist capital imposed new types of relationships on indigenous society, the structure of which became more complex, and it stirred up, fomented, poisoned, or resolved contradictions and social conflicts; it introduced, together with money and the development of internal and external markets, new elements in the economy; it brought about the birth of new nations from human groups or from peoples who were at different stages of historical development.

It is not to defend imperialist domination to recognize that it gave new nations to the world, the dimensions of which it reduced, and that it revealed new stages of development in human societies; and in spite of or because of the prejudices, the discrimination, and the crimes which it occasioned, it contributed to a deeper knowledge of humanity as a moving whole, as a unity in the complex diversity of the characteristics of its development.

Imperialist rule on many continents favored a multilateral and progressive (sometimes abrupt) confirmation not only between different men but also between different societies. The practice of imperialist rule – its affirmation or its negation – demanded (and still demands) a more or less accurate knowledge of the society it rules and of the historical reality (economic, social, and cultural) in the middle of which it exists. This knowledge is necessarily exposed in terms of comparison with the dominating subject and with its own historical reality. Such a knowledge is a vital necessity in the practice of imperialist rule, which results in the confrontation, mostly violent, between two identities which are totally dissimilar in their historical elements and contradictory in their different functions. The search for such a knowledge contributed to a general enrichment of human and social knowledge in spite of the fact that it was one-sided, subjective, and very often unjust.

In fact, man has never shown as much interest in knowing other men and other societies as during this century of imperialist domination. An unprecedented mass of information, of hypotheses and theories, has been built up, notably in the fields of history, ethnology, ethnography, sociology, and culture, concerning people or groups brought under imperialist domination. The concepts of race, caste, ethnicity, tribe, nation, culture, identity, dignity, and many others, have become the object of increasing attention from those who study men and the societies described as primitive or evolving.

More recently, with the rise of liberation movements, the need has arisen to analyze the character of these societies in the light of the struggle they are waging, and to decide the factors which launch or hold back this struggle. The researchers are generally agreed that, in this context, culture shows special significance. So one can argue that any attempt to clarify the true role of culture in the development of the (pre-independence) liberation movement can make a useful contribution to the broad struggle of the people against imperialist domination.

In this short lecture, we consider particularly the problems of the "return to the source," and of identity and dignity in the context of the national liberation movement.

Part I

The fact that independence movements are generally marked, even in their early stages, by an upsurge of cultural activity has led to the view that such movements are preceded by a "cultural renaissance" of the subject people. Some go as far as to suggest that culture is one means of collecting together a group, even a *weapon* in the struggle for independence.

From the experience of our own struggle and one might say that of the whole of Africa, we consider that there is a too-limited, even mistaken idea of the vital role of culture in the development of the liberation movement. In our view, this arises from a fake generalization of a phenomenon which is real but limited, which is at a particular level in the vertical structure of colonized societies – at level of the *elite* or the colonial *diasporas*. This generalization is unaware of or ignores the vital element of the problem: the indestructible character of the cultural resistance of the masses of the people when confronted with foreign domination.

Certainly imperialist domination calls for cultural oppression and attempts either directly or indirectly to do away with the most important elements of the culture of the subject people. But the people are only able to create and develop the liberation movement because they keep their culture alive despite continual and organized repression of their cultural life and because they continue to resist culturally, even when their politico-military resistance is destroyed. And it is cultural resistance which, at a given moment, can take on new forms, i.e., political, economic, armed to fight foreign domination.

With certain exceptions, *the period of colonization* was not long enough, at least in Africa, for there to be a significant degree of destruction or damage of the most important facets of the culture and traditions of the subject people. Colonial experience of imperialist domination in Africa (genocide, racial segregation, and apartheid excepted) shows that the only so-called positive solution which the colonial power put forward to repudiate the subject people's cultural resistance was *assimilation*. But the complete failure of the policy of "progressive assimilation" of native populations is the living proof both of the falsehood of this theory and of the capacity of the subject people to resist. As far as the Portuguese colonies are concerned, the maximum number of people assimilated was 0.3 percent of the total population (in Guinea), and this was after five hundred years of civilizing influence and half a century of "colonial peace."

On the other hand, even in the settlements where the overwhelming majority of the population are indigenous peoples, the area occupied by the colonial power and especially the area of *cultural influence* is usually restricted to coastal strips and to a few limited parts in the interior. Outside the boundaries of the capital and other urban centers, the influence of the colonial power's culture is almost nil. It only leaves its mark at the very top of the colonial social pyramid – which created colonialism itself – and particularly it influences what one might call the indigenous lower middle class and a very small number of workers in urban areas.

It can thus be seen that the masses in the rural areas, like a large section of the urban population, say, in all, over 99 percent of the indigenous population, are untouched or almost untouched by the culture of the colonial power. This situation is partly the result of the necessarily obscurantist character of the imperialist domination which, while it despises and suppresses indigenous culture, takes no interest in promoting culture for the masses, who are their pool for forced labor and the main object of exploitation. It is also the result of the effectiveness of cultural resistance of the people, who when they are subjected to political domination and economic exploitation find that their own culture acts as a bulwark in preserving their *identity*. Where the indigenous society has a vertical structure, this defense of their cultural heritage is further strengthened by the colonial power's interest in protecting and backing the cultural influence of the ruling classes, their allies.

The above argument implies that generally speaking there is not any marked destruction or damage to culture or tradition, neither for the masses in the subject country nor for the indigenous ruling classes (traditional chief, noble families, religious authorities). Repressed, persecuted, humiliated, betrayed by certain social groups who have compromised with the foreign power, culture took refuge in the villages, in the forests, and in the spirit of the victims of domination. Culture survives all these challenges and, through the struggle for liberation, blossoms forth again. Thus the question of a return to the source or of a cultural renaissance does not arise and could not arise for the masses of these people, for it is they who are the repository of the culture and at the same time the only social sector who can preserve and build it up and *make history*.

Thus, in Africa at least, for a true idea of the real role which culture plays in the development of the liberation movement, a distinction must be made between the situation of the masses, who preserve their culture, and that of the social groups who are assimilated or partially so, who are cut off and culturally alienated. Even though the indigenous colonial elite who emerged during the process of colonization still continues to pass on some element of indigenous culture, yet they live both materially and spiritually according to the foreign colonial culture. They seek to identify themselves increasingly with this culture, both in their social behaviors and in their appreciation of its values.

In the course of two or three generations of colonization, a social class arises made up of civil servants; people who are employed in various branches of the economy, especially commerce; professional people; and a few urban and agricultural landowners. This indigenous petite bourgeoisie, which emerged out of foreign domination and is indispensable to the system of colonial exploitation, stands midway between the masses of the working class in town and country and the small number of local representatives of the foreign ruling class. Although they may have quite strong links with the masses and with the traditional chiefs, generally speaking they aspire to a way of life which is similar if not identical with that of the foreign minority. At the same time, while they restrict their dealings with the masses, they try to become integrated into this minority, often at the cost of family or ethnic ties and always at great personal cost. Yet despite the apparent exceptions, they do not succeed in getting past the barriers thrown up by the system. They are prisoners of the cultural and social contradictions of their lives. They cannot escape from their role as a marginal class, or a "marginalized" class.

The marginal character or the "marginality" of this class both in their own country and in the diasporas established in the territory of the colonial power is responsible for the sociocultural conflicts of the colonial elite or the indigenous petite bourgeoisie, played out very much according to their material circumstances and level of acculturation but always at the individual level, never collectively.

It is within the framework of this daily drama, against the backcloth of the usually violent confrontation between the mass of the people and the ruling colonial class, that a feeling of bitterness or a *frustration complex* is bred and develops among the indigenous petite bourgeoisie. At the same time, they are becoming more and more conscious of a compelling need to question their marginal status and to rediscover an identity.

Thus they turn to the people around them, the people at the other extreme of the sociocultural conflict – the native masses. For this reason arises the problem of "return to the source," which seems to be even more pressing the greater the isolation of the petite bourgeoisie (or native elites) and their acute feelings of frustration, as in the case of African diasporas living in the colonial or racist metropolis. It comes as no surprise that the theories or "movements" such as Pan-Africanism or Negritude (two pertinent expressions arising mainly from the assumption that all black Africans have a cultural identity) were propounded outside black Africa. More recently, the black Americans' claim to an African identity is another proof, possibly rather a desperate one, of the need for a return to the source, although clearly it is influenced by a new situation: the fact that the great majority of African people are now independent.

But the return to the source is not and cannot in itself be an *act of struggle* against foreign domination (colonialist and racist), and it no longer necessarily means a return to traditions. It is the denial by the petite bourgeoisie of the pretended supremacy of the culture of the dominant power over that of the dominated people with which it must identify itself. The return to the source is therefore not a voluntary step, but the only possible reply to the demand of concrete need, historically determined and enforced by the inescapable contradiction between the colonized society and the colonial power, the mass of the people exploited and the foreign exploitive class, a contradiction in the light of which each social stratum or indigenous class must define its position.

When the return to the source goes beyond the individual and is expressed through groups or movements, the contradiction is transformed into struggle (secret or overt), and is a prelude to the pre-independence movement or of the struggle for liberation from the foreign yoke. So the return to the source is of no historical importance unless it brings not only real involvement in the struggle for independence, but also complete and absolute identification with the hopes of the mass of the people, who contest not only the foreign culture but also the foreign domination as a whole. Otherwise, the "return to the source" is nothing more than an attempt to find short-term benefits – knowingly or unknowingly, a kind of political opportunism.

One must point out that the return to the source, apparent or real, does not develop at one time and in the same way in the heart of the indigenous petite bourgeoisie. It is a slow process, broken up and uneven, whose development depends on the degree of acculturation of each individual, of the material circumstances of his life, on the forming of his ideas, and on his experience as a social being. This unevenness is the basis of the split of the indigenous petite bourgeoisie into three groups when confronted with the liberation movement: (a) a minority which, even if it wants to see an end to

foreign domination, clings to the dominant colonialist class and openly opposes the movement to protect its social position; (b) a majority of people who are hesitant and indecisive; (c) another minority of people who share in the building and leadership of the liberation movement.

But the latter group, which plays a decisive role in the development of the pre-independence movement, does not truly identify with the mass of the people (with their culture and hopes) except through struggle, the scale of this identification depending on the kind or methods of struggle, on the ideological basis of the movement, and on the level of moral and political awareness of each individual.

Part II

Identification of a section of the indigenous petite bourgeoisie with the mass of the people has an essential prerequisite: *that, in the face of destructive action by imperialist domination, the masses retain their identity*, separate and distinct from that of the colonial power. It is worthwhile therefore to decide in what circumstances this retention is possible; why, when, and at what levels of the dominated society is raised the problem of the loss or absence of identity; and in consequence it becomes necessary to assert or reassert in the framework of the pre-independence movement a separate and distinct identity from that of the colonial power.

The identity of an individual or a particular group of people is a biosociological factor outside the will of that individual or group, but which is meaningful only when it is expressed in relation to other individuals or other groups. The dialectical character of identity lies in the fact that an individual (or a group) is only similar to certain individuals (or groups) if it is also different to other individuals (or groups).

The definition of an identity, individual or collective, is at the same time the affirmation and denial of a certain number of characteristics which define the individuals or groups, through *historical* (biological and sociological) factors at a moment of their development. In fact, identity is not a constant, precisely because the biological and sociological factors which define it are in constant change. Biologically and sociologically, there are no two beings (individual or collective) completely the same or completely different, for it is always possible to find in them common or distinguishing characteristics. Therefore the identity of a being is always a relative quality, even circumstantial, for defining it demands a selection, more or less rigid and strict, of the biological and sociological characteristics of the being in question. One must point out that in the fundamental binomial in the definition of identity, the sociological factors are more determining than the biological. In fact, if it is correct that the biological element (inherited genetic patrimony) is the inescapable physical basis of the existence and continuing growth of identity, it is no less correct that the sociological element is the factor which gives it objective substance by giving content and form and allowing confrontation and comparison between individuals and between groups. To make a total definition of identity, the inclusion of the biological element is indispensable, but does not imply a sociological similarity, whereas two beings who are sociologically exactly the same must necessarily have similar biological identities.

This shows on the one hand the supremacy of the social over the individual condition, for society (human, for example) is a higher form of life. It shows, on the other hand, the need not to confuse the *original identity*, of which the biological element is the main determinant, and the *actual identity*, of which the main determinant is the sociological element. Clearly, the identity of which one must take account at a given moment of the growth of a being (individual or collective) is the actual identity, and awareness of that being reached only on the basis of his original identity is incomplete, partial and false, for it leaves out or does not comprehend the decisive influence of social conditions on the content and form of identity.

In the formation and development of individual or collective identity, the social condition is an objective agent, arising from economic, political, social, and cultural aspects which are characteristic of the growth and history of the society in question. If one argues that the economic aspect is fundamental, one can assert that identity is in a certain sense the expression of an economic reality. This reality, whatever the geographical context and the path of development of the society, is defined by the level of productive forces (the relationship between man and nature) and by the means of production (the relations between men and between classes within this society). But if one accepts that culture is a dynamic synthesis of the material and spiritual conditions of the society and expresses relationships both between man and nature and

between the different classes within a society, one can assert that identity is, at the individual and collective level and beyond the economic condition, the expression of culture. This is why to attribute, recognize, or declare the identity of an individual or group is above all to place that individual or group in the framework of a culture. Now as we all know, the main prop of culture in any society is the social structure. One can therefore draw the conclusion that the possibility of a movement group keeping (or losing) its identity in the face of foreign domination depends on the extent of the destruction of its social structure under the stresses of that domination.

As for the effects of imperialist domination on the social structure of the dominated people, one must look here at the case of classic colonialism, against which the pre-independence movement is contending. In that case, whatever the stage of historical development of the dominated society, the social structure can be subjected to the following experiences: (a) *total destruction*, mixed with immediate or gradual liquidation of the indigenous people and replacement by a foreign people; (b) *partial destruction*, with the settling of a more or less numerous foreign population; (c) *ostensible preservation*, brought about by the restriction of the indigenous people in geographical areas or special reserves usually without means of living, and the massive influx of a foreign population.

The fundamentally horizontal character of the social structure of African people, due to the profusion of ethnic groups, means that the cultural resistance and degree of retention of identity are not uniform. So even where ethnic groups have broadly succeeded in keeping their identity, we observe that the most *resistant* groups are those which have had the most violent battles with the colonial power during the period of effective occupation or those who because of their geographical location have had least contact with the foreign presence.

One must point out that the attitude of the colonial power towards the ethnic groups creates an insoluble contradiction: on the one hand it must divide or keep divisions in order to rule, and for that reason favors separation if not conflict between ethnic groups; on the other hand, to try to keep the permanency of its domination, it needs to destroy the social structure, culture, and by implication identity, of these groups. Moreover, it must protect the ruling class of those groups (like, for example, the Fula tribe or nation in our country) which have given decisive support during the colonial conquest – a policy which favors the preservation of the identity of these groups.

As has already been said, there are not usually important changes in respect of culture in the upright shape of the indigenous social pyramids (groups or societies with a state). Each level or class keeps its identity, linked with that of the group but separate from that of other social classes. Conversely, in the urban centers as in some of the interior regions of the country where the cultural influence of the colonial power is felt, the problem of identity is more complicated. While the bottom and the top of the social pyramid (that is, the mass of the working class drawn from different ethnic groups and the foreign dominant class) keep their identities, the middle level of this pyramid (the indigenous petite bourgeoisie), culturally uprooted, alienated, or more or less assimilated, engages in a sociological battle in search of its identity. One must also point out that though united by a new identity – granted by the colonial power – the foreign dominant class can not free itself from the contradictions of its own society, which it brings to the colonized country.

When at the initiative of a minority of the indigenous petite bourgeoisie allied with the indigenous masses the pre-independence movement is launched, the masses have no need to assert or reassert their identity, which they have never confused nor would have known how to confuse with that of the colonial power. This need is felt only by the indigenous petite bourgeoisie, which finds itself obliged to take up a position in the struggle which opposes the masses to the colonial power. However, the reassertion of identity distinct from that of the colonial power is not always achieved by all the petite bourgeoisie. It is only a minority who do this, while another minority asserts, often in a noisy manner, the identity of the foreign dominant class, while the silent majority is trapped in indecision.

Moreover, even when there is a reassertion of an identity distinct from that of the colonial power, therefore the same as that of the masses, it does not show itself in the same way everywhere. One part of the middle-class minority engaged in the pre-independence movement uses the foreign cultural norms, calling on literature and art, to express the discovery of its identity rather than to express the hopes and sufferings of the masses. And precisely because he uses the language and speech of the minority colonial power, he only occasionally manages to influence the masses, generally illiterate and familiar with other forms of artistic expression. This does not, however, remove the value of the contribution of the development of the struggle made by this petite bourgeoise minority, for it can at the same time influence a sector of the uprooted or those who are late-comers to its own class and an important sector of public opinion in the colonial metropolis, notably the class of intellectuals.

The other part of the lower middle class which from the start joins in the pre-independence movement finds, in its prompt share in the liberation struggle and in integration with the masses, the best means of expression of identity distinct from that of the colonial power.

That is why identification with the masses and reassertion of identity can be temporary or definitive, apparent or real, in the light of the daily efforts and sacrifices demanded by the struggle itself. A struggle which, while being the organized political expression of a culture, is also and necessarily a proof not only of identity but also of dignity.

In the course of the process of colonialist domination, the masses, whatever the characteristic of the social structure of the group to which they belong, do not stop resisting the colonial power. In a first phase – that of conquest, cynically called pacification – they resist, gun in hand, foreign occupation. In a second phase – that of the golden age of triumphant colonialism – they offer the foreign domination passive resistance, almost silent, but blazoned with many revolts, usually individual and once in a while collective. The revolt is particularly in the field of work and taxes, even in social contacts with the representatives, foreign or indigenous, of the colonial power. In a third phase – that of the liberation struggle – it is the masses who provide the main strength which employs political or armed resistance to challenge and to destroy foreign domination. Such a prolonged and varied resistance is possible only because, while keeping their culture and identity, the masses keep intact the sense of their individual and collective dignity, despite the worries, humiliations, and brutalities to which they are often subjected.

The assertion or reassertion by the indigenous petite bourgeoisie of identity distinct from that of the colonial power does not and could not bring about restoration of a sense of dignity to that class alone. In this context, we see that the sense of dignity of the petite bourgeoisie class depends on the objective moral and social feeling of each individual, on his subjective attitude towards the two poles of the colonial conflict, between which he is forced to live out the daily drama of colonization. This drama is the more shattering to the extent to which the petite bourgeoisie, in fulfilling its role, is made to live alongside both the foreign dominating class and the masses. On one side, the petite bourgeoisie is the victim of frequent if not daily humiliation by the foreigner, and on the other side it is aware of the injustice to which the masses are subjected and of their resistance and spirit of rebel-lion. Hence arises the apparent paradox of colonial domination: it is from within the indigenous petite bourgeoisie, a social class which grows from colonialism itself, that arise the first important steps towards mobilizing and organizing the masses for the struggle against the colonial power.

The struggle, in the face of all kinds of obstacles and in a variety of forms, reflects the awareness or grasp of a complete identity, generalizes and consolidates the sense of dignity strengthened by the development of political awareness, and derives from the culture or cultures of the masses in revolt one of its principal strengths.

8

The Fact of Blackness

Frantz Fanon

"Dirty nigger!" Or simply, "Look, a Negro!"

I came into the world imbued with the will to find a meaning in things, my spirit filled with the desire to attain to the source of the world, and then I found that I was an object in the midst of other objects.

Sealed into that crushing objecthood, I turned beseechingly to others. Their attention was a liberation, running over my body suddenly abraded into nonbeing, endowing me once more with an agility that I had thought lost, and by taking me out of the world, restoring me to it. But just as I reached the other side, I stumbled, and the movements, the attitudes, the glances of the other fixed me there, in the sense in which a chemical solution is fixed by a dye. I was indignant; I demanded an explanation. Nothing happened. I burst apart. Now the fragments have been put together again by another self.

As long as the black man is among his own, he will have no occasion, except in minor internal conflicts, to experience his being through others. There is of course the moment of "being for others," of which Hegel speaks, but every ontology is made unattainable in a colonized and civilized society. It would seem that this fact has not been given sufficient attention by those who have discussed the question. In the *Weltanschauung* of a colonized people there is an impurity, a flaw that outlaws any ontological explanation. Someone may object that this is the case with every individual, but such an objection merely conceals a basic problem. Ontology – once it is finally admitted as leaving existence by the wayside – does not permit us to understand the being of the black man. For not only must the black man be black; he must be black in relation to

the white man. Some critics will take it on themselves to remind us that this proposition has a converse. I say that this is false. The black man has no ontological resistance in the eyes of the white man. Overnight the Negro has been given two frames of reference within which he has had to place himself. His metaphysics, or, less pretentiously, his customs and the sources on which they were based, were wiped out because they were in conflict with a civilization that he did not know and that imposed itself on him.

The black man among his own in the twentieth century does not know at what moment his inferiority comes into being through the other. Of course I have talked about the black problem with friends, or, more rarely, with American Negroes. Together we protested, we asserted the equality of all men in the world. In the Antilles there was also that little gulf that exists among the almost-white, the mulatto, and the nigger. But I was satisfied with an intellectual understanding of these differences. It was not really dramatic. And then. . . .

And then the occasion arose when I had to meet the white man's eyes. An unfamiliar weight burdened me. The real world challenged my claims. In the white world the man of color encounters difficulties in the development of his bodily schema. Consciousness of the body is solely a negating activity. It is a third-person consciousness. The body is surrounded by an atmosphere of certain uncertainty. I know that if I want to smoke, I shall have to reach out my right arm and take the pack of cigarettes lying at the other end of the table. The matches, however, are in the drawer on the left, and I shall have to lean back slightly. And all these movements are made not out of habit but out of implicit knowledge. A slow composition of my *self* as a body in the middle of a spatial and temporal world – such seems to be the schema. It does not impose itself on me; it is, rather, a definitive structuring of the self and of the world – definitive because it creates a real dialectic between my body and the world.

For several years certain laboratories have been trying to produce a serum for "denegrification"; with all the earnestness in the world, laboratories have sterilized their test tubes, checked their scales, and embarked on researches that might make it possible for the miserable Negro to whiten himself and thus to throw off the burden of that corporeal malediction. Below the corporeal schema I had sketched a historico-racial schema. The elements that I used had been provided for me not by "residual sensations and perceptions primarily of a tactile, vestibular, kinesthetic, and visual character,"[1] but by the other, the white man, who had woven me out of a thousand details, anecdotes, stories. I thought that what I had in hand was to construct a physiological self, to balance space, to localize sensations, and here I was called on for more.

"Look, a Negro!" It was an external stimulus that flicked over me as I passed by. I made a tight smile.

"Look, a Negro!" It was true. It amused me.

"Look, a Negro!" The circle was drawing a bit tighter. I made no secret of my amusement.

"Mama, see the Negro! I'm frightened!" Frightened! Frightened! Now they were beginning to be afraid of me. I made up my mind to laugh myself to tears, but laughter had become impossible.

I could no longer laugh, because I already knew that there were legends, stories, history, and above all *historicity*, which I had learned about from Jaspers. Then, assailed at various points, the corporeal schema crumbled, its place taken by a racial epidermal schema. In the train it was no longer a question of being aware of my body in the third person but in a triple person. In the train I was given not one but two, three places. I had already stopped being amused. It was not that I was finding febrile coordinates in the world. I existed triply: I occupied space. I moved toward the other . . . and the evanescent other, hostile but not opaque, transparent, not there, disappeared. Nausea. . . .

I was responsible at the same time for my body, for my race, for my ancestors. I subjected myself to an objective examination, I discovered my blackness, my ethnic characteristics; and I was battered down by tom-toms, cannibalism, intellectual deficiency, fetishism, racial defects, slave-ships, and above all else, above all: "Sho' good eatin'."

On that day, completely dislocated, unable to be abroad with the other, the white man, who unmercifully imprisoned me, I took myself far off from my own presence, far indeed, and made myself an object. What else could it be for me but an amputation, an excision, a hemorrhage that spattered my whole body with black blood? But I did not want this revision, this thematization. All I wanted was to be a man among other men. I wanted to come lithe and young into a world that was ours and to help to build it together.

But I rejected all immunization of the emotions. I wanted to be a man, nothing but a man. Some identified me with ancestors of mine who had been enslaved or lynched: I decided to accept this. It was on the universal level of the intellect that I understood this inner kinship – I was the grandson of slaves in exactly the same way in which President Lebrun was the grandson of tax-paying, hardworking peasants. In the main, the panic soon vanished.

In America, Negroes are segregated. In South America, Negroes are whipped in the streets, and Negro strikers are cut down by machine-guns. In West Africa, the Negro is an animal. And there beside me, my neighbor in the university, who was born in Algeria, told me: "As long as the Arab is treated like a man, no solution is possible."

"Understand, my dear boy, color prejudice is something I find utterly foreign. . . . But of course, come in, sir, there is no color prejudice among us. . . . Quite, the Negro is a man like ourselves. . . . It is not because he is black that he is less intelligent than we are. . . . I had a Senegalese buddy in the army who was really clever. . . ."

Where am I to be classified? Or, if you prefer, tucked away?

"A Martinican, a native of 'our' old colonies."

Where shall I hide?

"Look at the nigger! . . . Mama, a Negro! . . . Hell, he's getting mad. . . . Take no notice, sir, he does not know that you are as civilized as we. . . ."

My body was given back to me sprawled out, distorted, recolored, clad in mourning in that white winter day. The Negro is an animal, the Negro is bad, the Negro is mean, the Negro is ugly; look, a nigger, it's cold, the nigger is shivering, the nigger is shivering because he is cold, the little boy is trembling because he is afraid of the nigger, the nigger is shivering with cold, that cold that goes through your bones, the handsome little boy is trembling because he thinks that the nigger is quivering with rage, the little white boy throws himself into his mother's arms: Mama, the nigger's going to eat me up.

All round me the white man, above the sky tears at its navel, the earth rasps under my feet, and there is a white song, a white song. All this whiteness that burns me. . . .

I sit down at the fire and I become aware of my uniform. I had not seen it. It is indeed ugly. I stop there, for who can tell me what beauty is?

Where shall I find shelter from now on? I felt an easily identifiable flood mounting out of the countless facets of my being. I was about to be angry. The fire was long since out, and once more the nigger was trembling.

"Look how handsome that Negro is! . . ."

"Kiss the handsome Negro's ass, madame!"

Shame flooded her face. At last I was set free from my rumination. At the same time I accomplished two things: I identified my enemies and I made a scene. A grand slam. Now one would be able to laugh.

The field of battle having been marked out, I entered the lists.

What? While I was forgetting, forgiving, and wanting only to love, my message was flung back in my face like a slap. The white world, the only honorable one, barred me from all participation. A man was expected to behave like a man. I was expected to behave like a black man – or at least like a nigger. I shouted a greeting to the world and the world slashed away my joy. I was told to stay within bounds, to go back where I belonged.

They would see, then! I had warned them, anyway. Slavery? It was no longer even mentioned, that unpleasant memory. My supposed inferiority? A hoax that it was better to laugh at. I forgot it all, but only on condition that the world not protect itself against me any longer. I had incisors to test. I was sure they were strong. And besides. . . .

What! When it was I who had every reason to hate, to despise, I was rejected? When I should have been begged, implored, I was denied the slightest recognition? I resolved, since it was impossible for me to get away from an *inborn complex*, to assert myself as a BLACK MAN. Since the other hesitated to recognize me, there remained only one solution: to make myself known.

In *Anti-Semite and Jew* (p. 95), Sartre says: "They [the Jews] have allowed themselves to be poisoned by the stereotype that others have of them, and they live in fear that their acts will correspond to this stereotype. . . . We may say that their conduct is perpetually overdetermined from the inside."

All the same, the Jew can be unknown in his Jewishness. He is not wholly what he is. One hopes, one waits. His actions, his behavior are the final determinant. He is a white man, and, apart from some rather debatable characteristics, he can sometimes go unnoticed. He belongs to the race of those who since the beginning of time have never known cannibalism. What an idea, to eat one's father! Simple enough, one has only not to be a nigger. Granted, the Jews are harassed – what am I thinking of? They are hunted down, exterminated, cremated. But these are little family quarrels. The Jew is disliked from the moment he is tracked down. But in my case everything takes on a *new* guise. I am given no chance. I am overdetermined from without. I am the slave not of the "idea" that others have of me but of my own appearance.

I move slowly in the world, accustomed now to seek no longer for upheaval. I progress by crawling. And already I am being dissected under white eyes, the only real eyes. I am *fixed*. Having adjusted their microtomes, they objectively cut away slices of my reality. I am laid bare. I feel, I see in those white faces that it is not a new man who has come in, but a new kind of man, a new genus. Why, it's a Negro!

I slip into corners, and my long antennae pick up the catch-phrases strewn over the surface of things – nigger underwear smells of nigger – nigger teeth are white – nigger feet are big – the nigger's barrel chest – I slip into corners, I remain silent, I strive for anonymity, for invisibility. Look, I will accept the lot, as long as no one notices me!

"Oh, I want you to meet my black friend. . . . Aimé Césaire, a black man and a university graduate. . . . Marian Anderson, the finest of Negro singers. . . . Dr. Cobb, who invented white blood, is a Negro. . . . Here, say hello to my friend from Martinique (be careful, he's extremely sensitive). . . ."

Shame. Shame and self-contempt. Nausea. When people like me, they tell me it is in spite of my color. When they dislike me, they point out that it is not because of my color. Either way, I am locked into the infernal circle.

I turn away from these inspectors of the Ark before the Flood and I attach myself to my brothers, Negroes like myself. To my horror, they too reject me. They are almost white. And besides they are about to marry white women. They will have children faintly tinged with brown. Who knows, perhaps little by little. . . .

I had been dreaming.

"I want you to understand, sir, I am one of the best friends the Negro has in Lyon."

The evidence was there, unalterable. My blackness was there, dark and unarguable. And it tormented me, pursued me, disturbed me, angered me.

Negroes are savages, brutes, illiterates. But in my own case I knew that these statements were false. There was a myth of the Negro that had to be destroyed at all costs. The time had long since passed when a Negro priest was an occasion for wonder. We had physicians, professors, statesmen. Yes, but something out of the ordinary still clung to such cases. "We have a Senegalese history teacher. He is quite bright. . . . Our doctor is colored. He is very gentle."

It was always the Negro teacher, the Negro doctor; brittle as I was becoming, I shivered at the slightest pretext. I knew, for instance, that if the physician made a mistake it would be the end of him and of all those who came after him. What could one expect, after all, from a Negro physician? As long as everything went well, he was praised to the skies, but look out, no nonsense, under any conditions! The black physician can never be sure how close he is to disgrace. I tell you, I was walled in: No exception was made for my refined manners, or my knowledge of literature, or my understanding of the quantum theory.

I requested, I demanded explanations. Gently, in the tone that one uses with a child, they introduced me to the existence of a certain view that was held by certain people, but, I was always told, "We must hope that it will very soon disappear." What was it? Color prejudice.

It [colour prejudice] is nothing more than the unreasoning hatred of one race for another, the contempt of the stronger and richer peoples for those whom they consider inferior to themselves, and the bitter resentment of those who are kept in subjection and are so frequently insulted. As colour is the most obvious outward manifestation of race it has been made the criterion by which men are judged, irrespective of their social or educational attainments. The light-skinned races have come to despise all those of a darker colour, and the dark-skinned peoples will no longer accept without protest the inferior position to which they have been relegated.[2]

I had read it rightly. It was hate; I was hated, despised, detested, not by the neighbor across the street or my cousin on my mother's side, but by an entire race. I was up against something unreasoned. The psychoanalysts say that nothing is more traumatizing for the young child than his encounters with what is rational. I would personally say that for a man whose only weapon is reason there is nothing more neurotic than contact with unreason.

I felt knife blades open within me. I resolved to defend myself. As a good tactician, I intended to rationalize the world and to show the white man that he was mistaken.

In the Jew, Jean-Paul Sartre says, there is

a sort of impassioned imperialism of reason: for he wishes not only to convince others that he is right; his goal is to persuade them that there is an absolute and unconditioned value to rationalism. He feels himself to be a missionary of the universal; against the universality of the Catholic religion, from which he is excluded, he asserts the "catholicity" of the rational, an instrument by which to attain to the truth and establish a spiritual bond among men.[3]

And, the author adds, though there may be Jews who have made intuition the basic category of their philosophy, their intuition

has no resemblance to the Pascalian subtlety of spirit, and it is this latter – based on a thousand imperceptible perceptions – which to the Jew seems his worst enemy. As for Bergson, his philosophy offers the curious appearance of an anti-intellectualist doctrine constructed entirely by the most rational and most critical of intelligences. It is through argument that he establishes the existence of pure duration, of philosophic intuition; and that very intuition which discovers duration or life, is itself universal, since anyone may practice it, and it leads toward the universal, since its objects can be named and conceived.[4]

With enthusiasm I set to cataloguing and probing my surroundings. As times changed, one had seen the Catholic religion at first justify and then condemn slavery and prejudices. But by referring everything to the idea of the dignity of man, one had ripped prejudice to shreds. After much reluctance, the scientists had conceded that the Negro was a human being; *in vivo* and *in vitro* the Negro had been proved analogous to the white man: the same morphology, the same histology. Reason was confident of victory on every level. I put all the parts back together. But I had to change my tune.

That victory played cat and mouse; it made a fool of me. As the other put it, when I was present, it was not; when it was there, I was no longer. In the abstract there was agreement: The Negro is a human being. That is to say, amended the less firmly convinced, that like us he has his heart on the left side. But on certain points the white man remained intractable. Under no conditions did he wish any intimacy between the races, for it is a truism that "crossings between widely different races can lower the physical and mental level. . . . Until we have a more definite knowledge of the effect of race-crossings we shall certainly do best to avoid crossings between widely different races."[5]

For my own part, I would certainly know how to react. And in one sense, if I were asked for a definition of myself, I would say that I am one who waits; I investigate my surroundings, I interpret everything in terms of what I discover, I become sensitive.

In the first chapter of the history that the others have compiled for me, the foundation of cannibalism has been made eminently plain in order that I may not lose sight of it. My chromosomes were supposed to have a few thicker or thinner genes representing cannibalism. In addition to the *sex-linked*, the scholars had now discovered the *racial-linked*.[6] What a shameful science!

But I understand this "psychological mechanism." For it is a matter of common knowledge that the mechanism is only psychological. Two centuries ago I was lost to humanity, I was a slave forever. And then came men who said that it all had gone on far too long. My tenaciousness did the rest; I was saved from the civilizing deluge. I have gone forward.

Too late. Everything is anticipated, thought out, demonstrated, made the most of. My trembling hands take hold of nothing; the vein has been mined out. Too late! But once again I want to understand.

Since the time when someone first mourned the fact that he had arrived too late and everything had been said, a nostalgia for the past has seemed to persist. Is this that lost original paradise of which Otto Rank speaks? How many such men, apparently rooted to the womb of the world, have devoted their lives to studying the Delphic oracles or exhausted themselves in attempts to plot the wanderings of Ulysses! The pan-spiritualists seek to prove the existence of a soul in animals by using this argument: A dog lies down on the grave of his master and starves to death there. We had to wait for Janet to demonstrate that the aforesaid dog, in contrast to man, simply lacked the capacity to liquidate the past. We speak of the glory of Greece, Artaud says; but, he adds, if modern man can no longer understand the *Choephoroi* of Aeschylus, it is Aeschylus who is to blame. It is tradition to which the anti-Semites turn in order to ground the validity of their "point of view." It is tradition, it is that long historical past, it is that blood relation between Pascal and Descartes, that is invoked when the Jew is told, "There is no possibility of your finding a place in society." Not long ago, one of those good Frenchmen said in a train where I was sitting: "Just let the real French virtues keep going and the race is safe. Now more than ever, national union must be made a reality. Let's have an end of internal strife! Let's face up to the foreigners (here he turned toward my corner) no matter who they are."

It must be said in his defense that he stank of cheap wine; if he had been capable of it, he would have told me that my emancipated-slave blood could not possibly be stirred by the name of Villon or Taine.

An outrage!

The Jew and I: Since I was not satisfied to be racialized, by a lucky turn of fate I was humanized. I joined the Jew, my brother in misery.

An outrage!

At first thought it may seem strange that the anti-Semite's outlook should be related to that of the Negrophobe. It was my philosophy professor, a native of the Antilles, who recalled the fact to me one day: "Whenever you hear anyone abuse the Jews, pay attention, because he is talking about you." And I found that he was universally right – by which I meant that I was answerable in my body and in my heart for what was done to my brother. Later I realized that he meant, quite simply, an anti-Semite is inevitably anti-Negro.

You come too late, much too late. There will always be a world – a white world – between you and us. . . . The other's total inability to liquidate the past once and for all. In the face of this affective ankylosis of the white man, it is understandable that I could have made up my mind to utter my Negro cry. Little by little, putting out pseudopodia here and there, I secreted a race. And that race staggered under the burden of a basic element. What was it? *Rhythm!* Listen to our singer, Léopold Senghor:

It is the thing that is most perceptible and least material. It is the archetype of the vital element. It is the first condition and the hallmark of Art, as breath is of life: breath, which accelerates or slows, which becomes even or agitated according to the tension in the individual, the degree and the nature of his emotion. This is rhythm in its primordial purity, this is rhythm in the masterpieces of Negro art, especially sculpture. It is composed of a theme – sculptural form – which is set in opposition to a sister theme, as inhalation is to exhalation, and that is repeated. It is not the kind of symmetry that gives rise to monotony; rhythm is alive, it is free. . . . This is how rhythm affects what is least intellectual in us, tyrannically, to make us penetrate to the spirituality of the object; and that character of abandon which is ours is itself rhythmic.[7]

Had I read that right? I read it again with redoubled attention. From the opposite end of the white world a magical Negro culture was hailing me. Negro sculpture! I began to flush with pride. Was this our salvation?

I had rationalized the world and the world had rejected me on the basis of color prejudice. Since no agreement was possible on the level of reason, I threw myself back toward unreason. It was up to the white man to be more irrational than I. Out of the necessities of my struggle I had chosen the method of regression, but the fact remained that it was an unfamiliar weapon; here I am at home; I am made of the irrational; I wade in the irrational. Up to the neck in the irrational. And now how my voice vibrates!

Those who invented neither gunpowder nor the
   compass
Those who never learned to conquer steam or
   electricity

Those who never explored the seas or the skies
But they know the farthest corners of the land
   of anguish
Those who never knew any journey save that of
   abduction
Those who learned to kneel in docility
Those who were domesticated and Christianized
Those who were injected with bastardy. . . .

Yes, all those are my brothers – a "bitter brotherhood" imprisons all of us alike. Having stated the minor thesis, I went overboard after something else.

. . . But those without whom the earth would
   not be the earth
Tumescence all the more fruitful
than
the empty land
still more the land
Storehouse to guard and ripen all
on earth that is most earth
My blackness is no stone, its deafness
hurled against the clamor of the day
My blackness is no drop of lifeless water
on the dead eye of the world
My blackness is neither a tower nor a cathedral
It thrusts into the red flesh of the sun
It thrusts into the burning flesh of the sky
It hollows through the dense dismay of its own
   pillar of patience.[8]

Eyah! the tom-tom chatters out the cosmic message. Only the Negro has the capacity to convey it, to decipher its meaning, its import. Astride the world, my strong heels spurring into the flanks of the world, I stare into the shoulders of the world as the celebrant stares at the midpoint between the eyes of the sacrificial victim.

But they abandon themselves, possessed, to the essence of all things, knowing nothing of externals but possessed by the movement of all things

uncaring to subdue but playing the play of
   the world
truly the eldest sons of the world
open to all the breaths of the world
meeting-place of all the winds of the world
undrained bed of all the waters of the world
spark of the sacred fire of the World
flesh of the flesh of the world, throbbing
   with the very movement of the world![9]

Blood! Blood! . . . Birth! Ecstasy of becoming! Three-quarters engulfed in the confusions of the day, I feel myself redden with blood. The arteries of all the world, convulsed, torn away, uprooted, have turned toward me and fed me.

"Blood! Blood! All our blood stirred by the male heart of the sun."[10]

Sacrifice was a middle point between the creation and myself – now I went back no longer to sources but to The Source. Nevertheless, one had to distrust rhythm, earth-mother love, this mystic, carnal marriage of the group and the cosmos.

In *La vie sexuelle en Afrique noire*, a work rich in perceptions, De Pédrals implies that always in Africa, no matter what field is studied, it will have a certain magicosocial structure. He adds:

> All these are the elements that one finds again on a still greater scale in the domain of secret societies. To the extent, moreover, to which persons of either sex, subjected to circumcision during adolescence, are bound under penalty of death not to reveal to the uninitiated what they have experienced, and to the extent to which initiation into a secret society always excites to acts of *sacred love*, there is good ground to conclude by viewing both male and female circumcision and the rites that they embellish as constitutive of minor secret societies.[11]

I walk on white nails. Sheets of water threaten my soul on fire. Face to face with these rites, I am doubly alert. Black magic! Orgies, witches' sabbaths, heathen ceremonies, amulets. Coitus is an occasion to call on the gods of the clan. It is a sacred act, pure, absolute, bringing invisible forces into action. What is one to think of all these manifestations, all these initiations, all these acts? From every direction I am assaulted by the obscenity of dances and of words. Almost at my ear there is a song:

> First our hearts burned hot
> Now they are cold
> All we think of now is Love
> When we return to the village
> When we see the great phallus
> Ah how then we will make Love
> For our parts will be dry and clean.[12]

The soil, which only a moment ago was still a tamed steed, begins to revel. Are these virgins, these nymphomaniacs? Black Magic, primitive mentality, animism, animal eroticism, it all floods over me. All of it is typical of peoples that have not kept pace with the evolution of the human race. Or, if one prefers, this is humanity at its lowest. Having reached this point, I was long reluctant to commit myself. Aggression was in the stars. I had to choose. What do I mean? I had no choice. . . .

Yes, we are – we Negroes – backward, simple, free in our behavior. That is because for us the body is not something opposed to what you call the mind. We are in the world. And long live the couple, Man and Earth! Besides, our men of letters helped me to convince you; your white civilization overlooks subtle riches and sensitivity. Listen:

> Emotive sensitivity. *Emotion is completely Negro as reason is Greek*.[13] Water rippled by every breeze? Unsheltered soul blown by every wind, whose fruit often drops before it is ripe? Yes, in one way, the Negro today is richer *in gifts than in works*.[14] But the tree thrusts its roots into the earth. The river runs deep, carrying precious seeds. And, the Afro-American poet, Langston Hughes, says:

> > I have known rivers
> > ancient dark rivers
> > my soul has grown deep
> > like the deep rivers.

The very nature of the Negro's emotion, of his sensitivity, furthermore, explains his attitude toward the object perceived with such basic intensity. It is an abandon that becomes need, an active state of communion, indeed of identification, however negligible the action – I almost said the personality – of the object. A rhythmic attitude: The adjective should be kept in mind.[15]

So here we have the Negro rehabilitated, "standing before the bar," ruling the world with his intuition, the Negro recognized, set on his feet again, sought after, taken up, and he is a Negro – no, he is not a Negro but the Negro, exciting the fecund antennae of the world, placed in the foreground of the world, raining his poetic power on the world, "open to all the breaths of the world." I embrace the world! I am the world! The white man has never understood this magic substitution. The white man wants the world; he wants it for himself alone. He finds himself predestined master of this world. He enslaves it. An acquisitive relation is established between the world and him. But there exist other values that fit only my forms. Like a magician, I robbed the white man of "a certain world," forever after lost to him and his. When that happened, the white man must have been rocked backward by a force that he could not identify, so little used as he is to such reactions. Somewhere beyond the objective world of farms and banana trees and rubber trees, I had subtly brought the real world into being. The essence of the world was my fortune. Between the world and me a relation of coexistence was established. I had discovered the primeval One. My "speaking hands" tore at the hysterical throat of the world. The white man had the anguished feeling that I was escaping from him and that I was taking something with me. He went through my pockets. He thrust probes into the least circumvolution of my brain. Everywhere he found only the obvious. So it was obvious that I had a secret. I was interrogated; turning away with an air of mystery, I murmured:

Tokowaly, uncle, do you remember the nights gone by
When my head weighed heavy on the back of your patience or
Holding my hand your hand led me by shadows and signs
The fields are flowers of glowworms, stars hang on the bushes, on the trees
Silence is everywhere
Only the scents of the jungle hum, swarms of reddish bees that overwhelm the crickets' shrill sounds,
And covered tom-tom, breathing in the distance of the night.
You, Tokowaly, you listen to what cannot be heard, and you explain to me what the ancestors are saying in the liquid calm of the constellations,
The bull, the scorpion, the leopard, the elephant, and the fish we know,
And the white pomp of the Spirits in the heavenly shell that has no end,
But now comes the radiance of the goddess Moon and the veils of the shadows fall.
Night of Africa, my black night, mystical and bright, black and shining.[16]

I made myself the poet of the world. The white man had found a poetry in which there was nothing poetic. The soul of the white man was corrupted, and, as I was told by a friend who was a teacher in the United States, "The presence of the Negroes beside the whites is in a way an insurance policy on humanness. When the whites feel that they have become too mechanized, they turn to the men of color and ask them for a little human sustenance." At last I had been recognized, I was no longer a zero.

I had soon to change my tune. Only momentarily at a loss, the white man explained to me that, genetically, I represented a stage of development: "Your properties have been exhausted by us. We have had earth mystics such as you will never approach. Study our history and you will see how far this fusion has gone." Then I had the feeling that I was repeating a cycle. My originality had been torn out of me. I wept a long time, and then I began to live again. But I was haunted by a galaxy of erosive stereotypes: the Negro's *sui generis* odor . . . the Negro's *sui generis* good nature . . . the Negro's *sui generis* gullibility. . . .

I had tried to flee myself through my kind, but the whites had thrown themselves on me and hamstrung me. I tested the limits of my essence; beyond all doubt there was not much of it left. It was here that I made my most remarkable discovery. Properly speaking, this discovery was a rediscovery.

I rummaged frenetically through all the antiquity of the black man. What I found there took away my breath. In his book *L'abolition de l'esclavage* Schoelcher presented us with compelling arguments. Since then, Frobenius, Westermann, Delafosse – all of them white – had joined the chorus: Ségou, Djenné, cities of more than a hundred thousand people; accounts of learned blacks (doctors of theology who went to Mecca to interpret the Koran). All of that, exhumed from the past, spread with its insides out, made it possible for me to find a valid historic place. The white man was wrong, I was not a primitive, not even a half-man, I belonged to a race that had already been working in gold and silver two thousand years ago. And too there was something else, something else that the white man could not understand. Listen:

What sort of men were these, then, who had been torn away from their families, their countries, their religions, with a savagery unparalleled in history?

Gentle men, polite, considerate, unquestionably superior to those who tortured them – that collection of adventurers who slashed and violated and spat on Africa to make the stripping of her the easier.

The men they took away knew how to build houses, govern empires, erect cities, cultivate fields, mine for metals, weave cotton, forge steel.

Their religion had its own beauty, based on mystical connections with the founder of the city. Their customs were pleasing, built on unity, kindness, respect for age.

No coercion, only mutual assistance, the joy of living, a free acceptance of discipline.

Order – Earnestness – Poetry and Freedom.

From the untroubled private citizen to the almost fabulous leader there was an unbroken chain of understanding and trust. No science? Indeed yes; but also, to protect them from fear, they possessed great myths in which the most subtle observation and the most daring imagination were balanced and blended. No art? They had their magnificent sculpture, in which human feeling erupted so unrestrained yet always followed the obsessive laws of rhythm in its organization of the major elements of a material called upon to capture, in order to redistribute, the most secret forces of the universe. . . .[17]

Monuments in the very heart of Africa? Schools? Hospitals? Not a single good burgher of the twentieth century, no Durand, no Smith, no Brown even suspects that such things existed in Africa before the Europeans came. . . .

But Schoelcher reminds us of their presence, discovered by Caillé, Mollien, the Cander brothers. And, though he nowhere reminds us that when the Portuguese landed on the banks of the Congo in 1498, they found a rich and flourishing state there and that the courtiers of Ambas were dressed in robes of silk and brocade, at least he knows that Africa had brought itself up to a juridical concept of the state, and he is aware, living in the very flood of imperialism, that European civilization, after all, is only one more civilization among many – and not the most merciful.[18]

I put the white man back into his place; growing bolder, I jostled him and told him point-blank, "Get used to me, I am not getting used to anyone." I shouted my laughter to the stars. The white man, I could see, was resentful. His reaction time lagged interminably. . . . I had won. I was jubilant.

"Lay aside your history, your investigations of the past, and try to feel yourself into our rhythm. In a society such as ours, industrialized to the high-

est degree, dominated by scientism, there is no longer room for your sensitivity. One must be tough if one is to be allowed to live. What matters now is no longer playing the game of the world but subjugating it with integers and atoms. Oh, certainly, I will be told, now and then when we are worn out by our lives in big buildings, we will turn to you as we do to our children – to the innocent, the ingenuous, the spontaneous. We will turn to you as to the childhood of the world. You are so real in your life – so funny, that is. Let us run away for a little while from our ritualized, polite civilization and let us relax, bend to those heads, those adorably expressive faces. In a way, you reconcile us with ourselves."

Thus my unreason was countered with reason, my reason with "real reason." Every hand was a losing hand for me. I analyzed my heredity. I made a complete audit of my ailment. I wanted to be typically Negro – it was no longer possible. I wanted to be white – that was a joke. And, when I tried, on the level of ideas and intellectual activity, to reclaim my negritude, it was snatched away from me. Proof was presented that my effort was only a term in the dialectic:

> But there is something more important: The Negro, as we have said, creates an anti-racist racism for himself. In no sense does he wish to rule the world: He seeks the abolition of all ethnic privileges, wherever they come from; he asserts his solidarity with the oppressed of all colors. At once the subjective, existential, ethnic idea of *negritude* "passes," as Hegel puts it, into the objective, positive, exact idea of *proletariat*. "For Césaire," Senghor says, "the white man is the symbol of capital as the Negro is that of labor. . . . Beyond the black-skinned men of his race it is the battle of the world proletariat that is his song."

That is easy to say, but less easy to think out. And undoubtedly it is no coincidence that the most ardent poets of negritude are at the same time militant Marxists.

But that does not prevent the idea of race from mingling with that of class: The first is concrete and particular, the second is universal and abstract; the one stems from what Jaspers calls understanding and the other from intellection; the first is the result of a psychobiological syncretism and the second is a methodical construction based on experience. In fact, negritude appears as the minor term of a dialectical progression: The theoretical and practical assertion of the supremacy of the white man is its thesis; the position of negritude as an antithetical value is the moment of negativity. But this negative moment is insufficient by itself, and the Negroes who employ it know this very well; they know that it is intended to prepare the synthesis or realization of the human in a society without races. Thus negritude is the root of its own destruction, it is a transition and not a conclusion, a means and not an ultimate end.[19]

When I read that page, I felt that I had been robbed of my last chance. I said to my friends, "The generation of the younger black poets has just suffered a blow that can never be forgiven." Help had been sought from a friend of the colored peoples, and that friend had found no better response than to point out the relativity of what they were doing. For once, that born Hegelian had forgotten that consciousness has to lose itself in the night of the absolute, the only condition to attain to consciousness of self. In opposition to rationalism, he summoned up the negative side, but he forgot that this negativity draws its worth from an almost substantive absoluteness. A consciousness committed to experience is ignorant, has to be ignorant, of the essences and the determinations of its being.

Orphée Noir is a date in the intellectualization of the *experience* of being black. And Sartre's mistake was not only to seek the source of the source but in a certain sense to block that source:

Will the source of Poetry be dried up? Or will the great black flood, in spite of everything, color the sea into which it pours itself? It does not matter: Every age has its own poetry; in every age the circumstances of history choose a nation, a race, a class to take up the torch by creating situations that can be expressed or transcended only through Poetry; sometimes the poetic impulse coincides with the revolutionary impulse, and sometimes they take different courses. Today let us hail the turn of history that will make it possible for the black men to utter "the great Negro cry with a force that will shake the pillars of the world" (Césaire).[20]

And so it is not I who make a meaning for myself, but it is the meaning that was already there,

pre-existing, waiting for me. It is not out of my bad nigger's misery, my bad nigger's teeth, my bad nigger's hunger that I will shape a torch with which to burn down the world, but it is the torch that was already there, waiting for that turn of history.

In terms of consciousness, the black consciousness is held out as an absolute density, as filled with itself, a stage preceding any invasion, any abolition of the ego by desire. Jean-Paul Sartre, in this work, has destroyed black zeal. In opposition to historical becoming, there had always been the unforeseeable. I needed to lose myself completely in negritude. One day, perhaps, in the depths of that unhappy romanticism. . . .

In any case I *needed* not to know. This struggle, this new decline had to take on an aspect of completeness. Nothing is more unwelcome than the commonplace: "You'll change, my boy; I was like that too when I was young . . . you'll see, it will all pass."

The dialectic that brings necessity into the foundation of my freedom drives me out of myself. It shatters my unreflected position. Still in terms of consciousness, black consciousness is immanent in its own eyes. I am not a potentiality of something, I am wholly what I am. I do not have to look for the universal. No probability has any place inside me. My Negro consciousness does not hold itself out as a lack. It *is*. It is its own follower.

But, I will be told, your statements show a misreading of the processes of history. Listen then:

Africa I have kept your memory Africa
you are inside me
Like the splinter in the wound
like a guardian fetish in the center of the village
make me the stone in your sling
make my mouth the lips of your wound
make my knees the broken pillars of your
    abasement
AND YET
I want to be of your race alone
workers peasants of all lands . . .
. . . white worker in Detroit black peon in
    Alabama
uncountable nation in capitalist slavery
destiny ranges us shoulder to shoulder
repudiating the ancient maledictions of blood
    taboos
we roll away the ruins of our solitudes
If the flood is a frontier
we will strip the gully of its endless

covering flow
If the Sierra is a frontier
we will smash the jaws of the volcanoes
upholding the Cordilleras
and the plain will be the parade ground of the
    dawn
where we regroup our forces sundered
by the deceits of our masters
As the contradiction among the features
creates the harmony of the face
we proclaim the oneness of the suffering
and the revolt
of all the peoples on all the face of the earth and
    we mix the mortar of the age of brotherhood
    out of the dust of idols.[21]

Exactly, we will reply, Negro experience is not a
whole, for there is not merely *one* Negro, there are
Negroes. What a difference, for instance, in this
other poem:

The white man killed my father
Because my father was proud
The white man raped my mother
Because my mother was beautiful
The white man wore out my brother in the hot
    sun of the roads
Because my brother was strong
Then the white man came to me
His hands red with blood
Spat his contempt into my black face
Out of his tyrant's voice:
"Hey boy, a basin, a towel, water."[22]

Or this other one:

My brother with teeth that glisten at the com-
    pliments of hypocrites
My brother with gold-rimmed spectacles
Over eyes that turn blue at the sound of the
    Master's voice
My poor brother in dinner jacket with its silk
    lapels
Clucking and whispering and strutting through
    the drawing rooms of Condescension
How pathetic you are
The sun of your native country is nothing more
    now than a shadow
On your composed civilized face
And your grandmother's hut
Brings blushes into cheeks made white by years
    of abasement and *Mea culpa*

But when regurgitating the flood of lofty empty
    words
Like the load that presses on your shoulders
You walk again on the rough red earth of Africa
These words of anguish will state the rhythm
    of your uneasy gait
I feel so alone, so alone here![23]

From time to time one would like to stop. To
state reality is a wearing task. But, when one has
taken it into one's head to try to express existence,
one runs the risk of finding only the nonexistent.
What is certain is that, at the very moment when I
was trying to grasp my own being, Sartre, who
remained The Other, gave me a name and thus
shattered my last illusion. While I was saying to
him:

"My negritude is neither a tower nor a cathedral,
    it thrusts into the red flesh of the sun,
    it thrusts into the burning flesh of the sky,
    it hollows through the dense dismay of its own
        pillar of patience . . ."

while I was shouting that, in the paroxysm of my
being and my fury, he was reminding me that my
blackness was only a minor term. In all truth, in all
truth I tell you, my shoulders slipped out of the
framework of the world, my feet could no longer
feel the touch of the ground. Without a Negro
past, without a Negro future, it was impossible for
me to live my Negrohood. Not yet white, no longer
wholly black, I was damned. Jean-Paul Sartre had
forgotten that the Negro suffers in his body quite
differently from the white man.[24] Between the white
man and me the connection was irrevocably one of
transcendence.[25]

But the constancy of my love had been forgotten. I defined myself as an absolute intensity of
beginning. So I took up my negritude, and with
tears in my eyes I put its machinery together again.
What had been broken to pieces was rebuilt, recon-
structed by the intuitive lianas of my hands.

My cry grew more violent: I am a Negro, I am a
Negro, I am a Negro. . . .

And there was my poor brother – living out
his neurosis to the extreme and finding himself
paralyzed:

THE NEGRO: I can't, ma'am.
LIZZIE: Why not?
THE NEGRO: I can't shoot white folks.

LIZZIE: Really! That would bother them, wouldn't it?

THE NEGRO: They're white folks, ma'am.

LIZZIE: So what? Maybe they got a right to bleed you like a pig just because they're white?

THE NEGRO: But they're white folks.

A feeling of inferiority? No, a feeling of non-existence. Sin is Negro as virtue is white. All those white men in a group, guns in their hands, cannot be wrong. I am guilty. I do not know of what, but I know that I am no good.

THE NEGRO: That's how it goes, ma'am. That's how it always goes with white folks.

LIZZIE: You too? You feel guilty?

THE NEGRO: Yes, ma'am.[26]

It is Bigger Thomas – he is afraid, he is terribly afraid. He is afraid, but of what is he afraid? Of himself. No one knows yet who he is, but he knows that fear will fill the world when the world finds out. And when the world knows, the world always expects something of the Negro. He is afraid lest the world know, he is afraid of the fear that the world would feel if the world knew. Like that old woman on her knees who begged me to tie her to her bed:

"I just know, Doctor: Any minute that thing will take hold of me."

"What thing?"

"The wanting to kill myself. Tie me down, I'm afraid."

In the end, Bigger Thomas acts. To put an end to his tension, he acts, he responds to the world's anticipation.[27]

So it is with the character in *If He Hollers Let Him Go*[28] – who does precisely what he did not want to do. That big blonde who was always in his way, weak, sensual, offered, open, fearing (desiring) rape, became his mistress in the end.

The Negro is a toy in the white man's hands; so, in order to shatter the hellish cycle, he explodes. I cannot go to a film without seeing myself. I wait for me. In the interval, just before the film starts, I wait for me. The people in the theater are watching me, examining me, waiting for me. A Negro groom is going to appear. My heart makes my head swim.

The crippled veteran of the Pacific war says to my brother, "Resign yourself to your color the way I got used to my stump; we're both victims."[29]

Nevertheless with all my strength I refuse to accept that amputation. I feel in myself a soul as immense as the world, truly a soul as deep as the deepest of rivers, my chest has the power to expand without limit. I am a master and I am advised to adopt the humility of the cripple. Yesterday, awakening to the world, I saw the sky turn upon itself utterly and wholly. I wanted to rise, but the disemboweled silence fell back upon me, its wings paralyzed. Without responsibility, straddling Nothingness and Infinity, I began to weep.

Notes

1. Jean Lhermitte, *L'Image de notre corps* (Paris, Nouvelle Revue critique, 1939), p. 17.
2. Sir Alan Burns, *Colour Prejudice* (London, Allen and Unwin, 1948), p. 16.
3. *Anti-Semite and Jew* (New York, Grove Press, 1960), pp. 112–13.
4. Ibid., p. 115.
5. Jon Alfred Mjoen, "Harmonic and Disharmonic Race-crossings," The Second International Congress of Eugenics (1921), *Eugenics in Race and State*, vol. II, p. 60, quoted in Sir Alan Burns, *Colour Prejudice*, p. 120.
6. In English in the original. (Translator's note.)
7. "Ce que l'homme noir apporte," in Claude Nordey, *L'Homme de couleur* (Paris, Plon, 1939), pp. 309–10.
8. Aimé Césaire, *Cahier d'un retour au pays natal* (Paris, Présence Africaine, 1956), pp. 77–8.
9. Ibid., p. 78.
10. Ibid., p. 79.
11. De Pédrals, *La Vie sexuelle en Afrique noire* (Paris, Payot), p. 83.
12. A. M. Vergiat, *Les Rites secrets des primitifs de l'Oubangui* (Paris, Payot, 1951), p. 113.
13. My italics – F.F.
14. My italics – F.F.
15. Léopold Senghor, "Ce que l'homme noir apporte," p. 205.
16. Léopold Senghor, *Chants d'ombre* (Paris, Editions du Seuil, 1945).
17. Aimé Césaire, Introduction to Victor Schoelcher, *Esclavage et colonisation* (Paris, Presses Universitaires de France, 1948), p. 7.
18. Ibid., p. 8.
19. Jean-Paul Sartre, *Orphée Noir*, preface to *Anthologie de la nouvelle poésie nègre et malgache* (Paris, Presses Universitaires de France, 1948), pp. xl ff.
20. Ibid., p. xliv.
21. Jacques Roumain, "Bois-d'Ebène," Prelude, in *Anthologie de la nouvelle poésie nègre et malgache*, p. 113.

22. David Diop, "Le temps du martyre," in ibid., p. 174.

23. David Diop, "Le Renégat."

24. Though Sartre's speculations on the existence of The Other may be correct (to the extent, we must remember, to which *Being and Nothingness* describes an alienated consciousness), their application to a black consciousness proves fallacious. That is because the white man is not only The Other but also the master, whether real or imaginary.

25. In the sense in which the word is used by Jean Wahl in *Existence humaine et transcendance* (Neuchâtel, La Baconnière, 1944).

26. Jean-Paul Sartre, *The Respectful Prostitute*, in *Three Plays* (New York, Knopf, 1949), pp. 189, 191. Originally, *La Putain respectueuse* (Paris, Gallimard, 1947). See also *Home of the Brave*, a film by Mark Robson.

27. Richard Wright, *Native Son* (New York, Harper, 1940).

28. By Chester Himes (Garden City, Doubleday, 1945).

29. *Home of the Brave.*

9

Whiteness as Property

CHERYL I. HARRIS

she walked into forbidden worlds
impaled on the weapon of her own pale skin
she was a sentinel
at impromptu planning sessions
of her own destruction. . . .

Cheryl I. Harris, "Poem for Alma"

[P]etitioner was a citizen of the United States and a resident of the state of Louisiana of mixed descent, in the proportion of seven eighths Caucasian and one eighth African blood; that the mixture of colored blood was not discernible in him, and that he was entitled to every recognition, right, privilege and immunity secured to the citizens of the United States of the white race by its Constitution and laws . . . and thereupon entered a passenger train and took possession of a vacant seat in a coach where passengers of the white race were accommodated.

Plessy v. Ferguson[1]

I. Introduction

In the thirties, some years after my mother's family became part of the great river of black migration that flowed north, my Mississippi-born grandmother was confronted with the harsh matter of economic survival for herself and her two daughters. Having separated from my grandfather, who himself was trapped on the fringes of economic marginality, she took one long hard look at her choices and presented herself for employment at a major retail store in Chicago's central business district. This decision would have been unremarkable for a white woman in similar circumstances, but for my grandmother it was an act of both great daring and self-denial – for in so doing she was presenting herself as a white woman. In the parlance of racist America, she was "passing."

Her fair skin, straight hair, and aquiline features had not spared her from the life of sharecropping into which she had been born in anywhere/nowhere, Mississippi – the outskirts of Yazoo City. In the burgeoning landscape of urban America, though, anonymity was possible for a black person with "white" features. She was transgressing

boundaries, crossing borders, spinning on margins, traveling between dualities of Manichean space, rigidly bifurcated into light/dark, good/bad, white/black. No longer immediately identifiable as "Lula's daughter," she could thus enter the white world, albeit on a false passport, not merely passing but trespassing.

Every day my grandmother rose from her bed in her house in a black enclave on the south side of Chicago, sent her children off to a black school, boarded a bus full of black passengers, and rode to work. No one at her job ever asked if she was black; the question was unthinkable. By virtue of the employment practices of the "fine establishment" in which she worked, she could not have been. Catering to the upper middle class, understated tastes required that blacks not be allowed.

She quietly went about her clerical tasks, not once revealing her true identity. She listened to the women with whom she worked discuss their worries – their children's illnesses, their husband's disappointments, their boyfriends' infidelities – all of the mundane yet critical things that made up their lives. She came to know them but they did not know her, for my grandmother occupied a completely different place. That place – where white supremacy and economic domination meet – was unknown turf to her white co-workers. They remained oblivious to the worlds within worlds that existed just beyond the edge of their awareness and yet were present in their very midst.

Each evening, my grandmother, tired and worn, retraced her steps home, laid aside her mask, and reentered herself. Day in and day out, she made herself invisible, then visible again, for a price too inconsequential to do more than barely sustain her family and at a cost too precious to conceive. She left the job some years later, finding the strain too much to bear.

From time to time, as I later sat with her, she would recollect that period, and the cloud of some painful memory would pass across her face. Her voice would remain subdued, as if to contain the still-remembered tension. On rare occasions, she would wince, recalling some particularly racist comment made in her presence because of her presumed shared group affiliation. Whatever retort might have been called for had been suppressed long before it reached her lips, for the price of her family's well-being was her silence. Accepting the risk of self-annihilation was the only way to survive.

Although she never would have stated it this way, the clear and ringing denunciations of racism she delivered from her chair when advanced arthritis had rendered her unable to work were informed by those experiences. The fact that self-denial had been a logical choice and had made her complicit in her own oppression at times fed the fire in her eyes when she confronted some daily outrage inflicted on black people. Later, these painful memories forged her total identification with the civil rights movement. Learning about the world at her knee as I did, these experiences also came to inform my outlook and my understanding of the world.

My grandmother's story is far from unique. Indeed, there are many who crossed the color line never to return. Passing is well known among black people in the United States; it is a feature of race subordination in all societies structured on white supremacy. Notwithstanding the purported benefits of black heritage in an era of affirmative action, passing is not an obsolete phenomenon that has slipped into history.

The persistence of passing is related to the historical and continuing pattern of white racial domination and economic exploitation, which has invested passing with a certain economic logic. It was a given for my grandmother that being white automatically ensured higher economic returns in the short term and greater economic, political, and social security in the long run. Becoming white meant gaining access to a whole set of public and private privileges that materially and permanently guaranteed basic subsistence needs and, therefore, survival. Becoming white increased the possibility of controlling critical aspects of one's life rather than being the object of others' domination.

My grandmother's story illustrates the valorization of whiteness as treasured property in a society structured on racial caste. In ways so embedded that it is rarely apparent, the set of assumptions, privileges, and benefits that accompany the status of being white have become a valuable asset – one that whites sought to protect and those who passed sought to attain, by fraud if necessary. Whites have come to expect and rely on these benefits, and over time these expectations have been affirmed, legitimated, and protected by the law. Even though the law is neither uniform nor explicit in all instances, in protecting settled expectations based on white privilege, American law has recognized a property interest in whiteness that, although unacknowledged, now forms the background against which legal disputes are framed, argued, and adjudicated.

This article investigates the relationships between concepts of race and property, and it reflects on how rights in property are contingent on, intertwined with, and conflated with race. Through this entangled relationship between race and property, historical forms of domination have evolved to reproduce subordination in the present. [. . .]

II. The Construction of Race and the Emergence of Whiteness as Property

The racialization of identity and the racial subordination of blacks and Native Americans provided the ideological basis for slavery and conquest. Although the systems of oppression of blacks and Native Americans differed in form – the former involving the seizure and appropriation of labor, the latter entailing the seizure and appropriation of land – undergirding both was a racialized conception of property implemented by force and ratified by law.

The origins of property rights in the United States are rooted in racial domination. Even in the early years of the country, it was not the concept of race alone that operated to oppress blacks and Indians; rather, it was the interaction between conceptions of race and property which played a critical role in establishing and maintaining racial and economic subordination.

The hyperexploitation of black labor was accomplished by treating black people themselves as objects of property. Race and property were thus conflated by establishing a form of property contingent on race: only blacks were subjugated as slaves and treated as property. Similarly, the conquest, removal, and extermination of Native American life and culture were ratified by conferring and acknowledging the property rights of whites in Native American land. Only white possession and occupation of land was validated and therefore privileged as a basis for property rights. These distinct forms of exploitation each contributed in varying ways to the construction of whiteness as property.

A. FORMS OF RACIALIZED PROPERTY: RELATIONSHIPS BETWEEN SLAVERY, RACE, AND PROPERTY

1. The convergence of racial and legal status

Although the early colonists were cognizant of race, racial lines were neither consistently nor sharply delineated among or within all social groups. Captured Africans sold in the Americas were distinguished from the population of indentured or bond servants – "unfree" white labor – but it was not an irrebuttable presumption that all Africans were "slaves," or that slavery was the only appropriate status for them. The distinction between African and white indentured labor grew, however, as decreasing terms of service were introduced for white bond servants. Simultaneously, the demand for labor intensified, resulting in a greater reliance on African labor and a rapid increase in the number of Africans imported to the colonies.

The construction of white identity and the ideology of racial hierarchy were intimately tied to the evolution and expansion of the system of chattel slavery. The further entrenchment of plantation slavery was in part an answer to a social crisis produced by the eroding capacity of the landed class to control the white labor population. The dominant paradigm of social relations, however, was that while not all Africans were slaves, virtually all slaves were not white. It was their racial Otherness that

came to justify the subordinated status of blacks. The result was a classification system that "key[ed] official rules of descent to national origin" so that "[m]embership in the new social category of 'Negro' became itself sufficient justification for enslaveability."[2] Although the cause of the increasing gap between the status of African and white labor is contested by historians, it is clear that "[t]he economic and political interests defending Black slavery were far more powerful than those defending indentured servitude."[3]

By the 1660s, the especially degraded status of blacks as chattel slaves was recognized by law. Between 1680 and 1682, the first slave codes appeared, enshrining the extreme deprivations of liberty already existing in social practice. Many laws parceled out differential treatment based on racial categories: blacks were not permitted to travel without permits, to own property, to assemble publicly, or to own weapons – nor were they to be educated. Racial identity was further merged with stratified social and legal status: "black" racial identity marked who was subject to enslavement, whereas "white" racial identity marked who was "free" or, at minimum, not a slave. The ideological and rhetorical move from "slave" and "free" to "black" and "white" as polar constructs marked an important step in the social construction of race.

2. Implications for property

The social relations that produced racial identity as a justification for slavery also had implications for the conceptualization of property. This result was predictable, as the institution of slavery, lying at the very core of economic relations, was bound up with the idea of property. Through slavery, race and economic domination were fused.[4]

Slavery produced a peculiar, mixed category of property and humanity – a hybrid with inherent instabilities that were reflected in its treatment and ratification by the law. The dual and contradictory character of slaves as property and persons was exemplified in the Representation Clause of the Constitution. Representation in the House of Representatives was apportioned on the basis of population computed by counting all persons and "three-fifths of all other persons" – slaves. Gouveneur Morris's remarks before the Constitutional Convention posed the essential question: "Upon what principle is it that slaves shall be computed in the representation? Are they men? Then make them Citizens & let them vote? Are they property? Why then is no other property included?"[5]

The cruel tension between property and humanity was also reflected in the law's legitimation of the use of blackwomen's bodies as a means of increasing property.[6] In 1662, the Virginia colonial assembly provided that "[c]hildren got by an Englishman upon a Negro woman shall be bond or free according to the condition of the mother. . . ."[7] In reversing the usual common law presumption that the status of the child was determined by the father, the rule facilitated the reproduction of one's own labor force. Because the children of blackwomen assumed the status of their mother, slaves were bred through blackwomen's bodies. The economic significance of this form of exploitation of female slaves should not be underestimated. Despite Thomas Jefferson's belief that slavery should be abolished, like other slaveholders, he viewed slaves as economic assets, noting that their value could be realized more efficiently from breeding than from labor. A letter he wrote in 1805 stated, "I consider the labor of a breeding woman as no object, and that a child raised every 2 years is of more profit than the crop of the best laboring man."[8]

Even though there was some unease in slave law, reflective of the mixed status of slaves as humans and property, the critical nature of social relations under slavery was the commodification of human beings. Productive relations in early American society included varying forms of sale of labor capacity, many of which were highly oppressive; but slavery was distinguished from other forms of labor servitude by its permanency and the total commodification attendant to the status of the slave. Slavery as a legal institution treated slaves as property that could be transferred, assigned, inherited, or posted as collateral.[9] For example, in *Johnson* v. *Butler*,[10] the plaintiff sued the defendant for failing to pay a debt of $496 on a specified date; because the covenant had called for payment of the debt in "money or negroes," the plaintiff contended that the defendant's tender of one negro only, although valued by the parties at an amount equivalent to the debt, could not discharge the debt. The court agreed with the plaintiff. This use of Africans as a stand-in for actual currency highlights the degree to which slavery "propertized" human life.

Because the "presumption of freedom [arose] from color [white]" and the "black color of the race [raised] the presumption of slavery," whiteness became a shield from slavery, a highly volatile and unstable form of property. In the form adopted in the United States, slavery made human beings market-alienable and in so doing, subjected human life and personhood – that which is most valuable – to the ultimate devaluation. Because whites could not be enslaved or held as slaves, the racial line between white and black was extremely critical; it became a line of protection and demarcation from the potential threat of commodification, and it determined the allocation of the benefits and burdens of this form of property. White identity and whiteness were sources of privilege and protection; their absence meant being the object of property.

Slavery as a system of property facilitated the merger of white identity and property. Because the system of slavery was contingent on and conflated with racial identity, it became crucial to be "white," to be identified as white, to have the property of being white. Whiteness was the characteristic, the attribute, the property of free human beings. [. . .]

B. CRITICAL CHARACTERISTICS OF PROPERTY AND WHITENESS

1. *Whiteness as a traditional form of property*

Whiteness fits the broad historical concept of property described by classical theorists. In James Madison's view, for example, property "embraces every thing to which a man may attach a value and have a right," referring to all of a person's legal rights. Property as conceived in the founding era included not only external objects and people's relationships to them, but also all of those human rights, liberties, powers, and immunities that are important for human well-being, including freedom of expression, freedom of conscience, freedom from bodily harm, and free and equal opportunities to use personal faculties.

Whiteness defined the legal status of a person as slave or free. White identity conferred tangible and economically valuable benefits, and it was jealously guarded as a valued possession, allowed only to those who met a strict standard of proof. Whiteness – the right to white identity as embraced by the law – is property if by "property" one means all of a person's legal rights.

Other traditional theories of property emphasize that the "natural" character of property is derivative of custom, contrary to the notion that property is the product of a delegation of sovereign power. This "bottom-up" theory holds that the law of property merely codifies existing customs and social relations. Under that view, government-created rights such as social welfare payments cannot constitute legitimate property interests because they are positivistic in nature. Other theorists have challenged this conception, and argued that even the most basic of "customary" property rights – the rule of first possession, for example – is dependent on its acceptance or rejection in particular instances by the government. Citing custom as a source of property law begs the central question: Whose custom?

Rather than remaining within the bipolar confines of custom or command, it is crucial to recognize the dynamic and multifaceted relationship among custom, command, and law, as well as the extent to which positionality determines how each may be experienced and understood. Indian custom was obliterated by force and replaced with the regimes of common law which embodied the customs of the conquerors. The assumption of American law as it related to Native Americans was that conquest did give rise to sovereignty. Indians experienced the property laws of the colonizers and the emergent American nation as acts of violence perpetuated by the exercise of power and ratified through the rule of law. At the same time, these laws were perceived as custom and "common sense" by the colonizers. The founders, for instance, so thoroughly embraced Lockean labor theory as the basis for a right of acquisition because it affirmed the right of the New World settlers to settle on and acquire the frontier. It confirmed and ratified their experience.

The law's interpretation of those encounters between whites and Native Americans not only inflicted vastly different results on them but also established a pattern – a custom – of valorizing whiteness. As the forms of racialized property were perfected, the value and protection extended to whiteness increased. Regardless of which theory of property one adopts, the concept of whiteness – established by centuries of custom (illegitimate custom, but custom nonetheless) and codified by law – may be understood as a property interest.

2. Property and expectations

"Property is nothing but the basis of expectation," according to Jeremy Bentham, "consist[ing] in an established expectation, in the persuasion of being able to draw such and such advantage from the thing possessed."[11] The relationship between expectations and property remains highly significant, as the law "has recognized and protected even the expectation of rights as actual legal property."[12] This theory does not suggest that all values or all expectations give rise to property, but those expectations in tangible or intangible things which are valued and protected by the law are property.

In fact, the difficulty lies not in identifying expectations as a part of property but, rather, in distinguishing which expectations are reasonable and therefore merit the protection of the law as property. Although the existence of certain property rights may seem self-evident, and the protection of certain expectations may seem essential for social stability, property is a legal construct by which selected private interests are protected and upheld. In creating property "rights," the law draws boundaries and enforces or reorders existing regimes of power. The inequalities that are produced and reproduced are not givens or inevitabilities; rather, they are conscious selections regarding the structuring of social relations. In this sense, it is contended that property rights and interests are not "natural" but "creation[s] of law." In a society structured on racial subordination, white privilege became an expectation and, to apply Margaret Radin's concept, whiteness became the quintessential property for personhood. The law constructed "whiteness" as an objective fact, although in reality it is an ideological proposition imposed through subordination. This move is the central feature of "reification": "Its basis is that a relation between people takes on the character of a thing and thus acquires a 'phantom objectivity,' an autonomy that seems so strictly rational and all-embracing as to conceal every trace of its fundamental nature: the relation between people."[13] Whiteness was an "object" over which continued control was – and is – expected. . . .

Because the law recognized and protected expectations grounded in white privilege (albeit not explicitly in all instances), these expectations became tantamount to property that could not permissibly be intruded upon without consent. As the law explicitly ratified those expectations in continued privilege or extended ongoing protection to those illegitimate expectations by failing to expose or to disturb them radically, the dominant and subordinate positions within the racial hierarchy were reified in law. When the law recognizes, either implicitly or explicitly, the settled expectations of

whites built on the privileges and benefits produced by white supremacy, it acknowledges and
reinforces a property interest in whiteness that
reproduces black subordination.

3. *The property functions of whiteness*

In addition to the theoretical descriptions of property, whiteness also meets the functional criteria of
property. Specifically, the law has accorded "holders" of whiteness the same privileges and benefits
accorded holders of other types of property. The
liberal view of property is that it includes the exclusive rights of possession, use, and disposition.
Its attributes are the right to transfer or alienability, the right to use and enjoyment, and the right
to exclude others. Even when examined against
this limited view, whiteness conforms to the general contours of property. It may be a "bad" form
of property, but it is property nonetheless.

a. *Rights of disposition*

Property rights are traditionally described as fully
alienable. Because fundamental personal rights are
commonly understood to be inalienable, it is problematic to view them as property interests. However, as Margaret Radin notes, "inalienability" is
not a transparent term; it has multiple meanings
that refer to interests that are nonsalable, nontrans-
ferable, or non-market-alienable. The common core
of inalienability is the negation of the possibility of
separation of an entitlement, right, or attribute from
its holder.

 Classical theories of property identified alienability as a requisite aspect of property; thus, that
which is inalienable cannot be property. As the
major exponent of this view, John Stuart Mill
argued that public offices, monopoly privileges, and
human beings – all of which were or should have
been inalienable – should not be considered property at all. Under this account, if inalienability
inheres in the concept of property, then whiteness,
incapable of being transferred or alienated either
inside or outside the market, would fail to meet a
criterion of property.

 As Radin notes, however, even under the classical
view, alienability of certain property was limited.
Mill also advocated certain restraints on alienation
in connection with property rights in land and,
probably, other natural resources. In fact, the law
has recognized various kinds of inalienable property. For example, entitlements of the regulatory

and welfare states, such as transfer payments and
government licenses, are inalienable; yet they have
been conceptualized and treated as property by law.
Although this "new property" has been criticized
as being improper – that is, not appropriately cast
as property – the principal objection has been based
on its alleged lack of productive capacity, not on its
inalienability.

 The law has also acknowledged forms of inalienable property derived from nongovernmental sources.
In the context of divorce, courts have held that professional degrees or licenses held by one party and
financed by the labor of the other is marital property
whose value is subject to allocation by the court.
A medical or law degree is not alienable either in
the market or by voluntary transfer. Nevertheless,
it is included as property when dissolving a legal
relationship.

 Indeed, Radin argues that as a deterrent to
the dehumanization of universal commodification,
market-inalienability may be justified to protect
property important to the person and to safeguard
human flourishing. She suggests that noncommodi-
fication or market-inalienability of personal property
or those things essential to human flourishing is
necessary to guard against the objectification of
human beings. To avoid that danger, "we must cease
thinking that market alienability is inherent in the
concept of property." Following this logic, then,
the inalienability of whiteness should not preclude
the consideration of whiteness as property. Paradoxically, its inalienability may be more indicative
of its perceived enhanced value rather than of its
disqualification as property.

b. *Right to use and enjoyment*

Possession of property includes the rights of use
and enjoyment. If these rights are essential aspects
of property, it is because "the problem of property
in political philosophy dissolves into . . . questions
of the will and the way in which we use the things
of this world."[14] As whiteness is simultaneously an
aspect of identity and a property interest, it is something that can both be experienced and deployed
as a resource. Whiteness can move from being a
passive characteristic as an aspect of identity to an
active entity that – like other types of property – is
used to fulfill the will and to exercise power. The
state's official recognition both of a racial identity
that subordinated blacks and of privileged rights in
property based on race, elevated whiteness from a
passive attribute to an object of law and a resource

deployable at the social, political, and institutional level to maintain control. Thus, a white person "used and enjoyed" whiteness whenever she took advantage of the privileges accorded white people simply by virtue of their whiteness – when she exercised any number of rights reserved for the holders of whiteness. Whiteness as the embodiment of white privilege transcended mere belief or preference; it became usable property, the subject of the law's regard and protection. In this respect, whiteness, as an active property, has been used and enjoyed.

c. ...

The conception of reputation as property found its origins in early concepts of property which encompassed things (such as land and personalty), income (such as revenues from leases, mortgages, and patent monopolies), and one's life, liberty, and labor. . . . The idea of self-ownership, then, was particularly fertile ground for the idea that reputation, as an aspect of identity earned through effort, was similarly property. Moreover, the loss of reputation was capable of being valued in the market.

The direct manifestation of the law's legitimation of whiteness as reputation is revealed in the well-established doctrine that to call a white person "black" is to defame her.[15] Although many of the cases were decided in an era when the social and legal stratification of whites and blacks was more absolute, as late as 1957 the principle was reaffirmed, notwithstanding significant changes in the legal and political status of blacks. As one court noted, "there is still to be considered the social distinction existing between the races," and the allegation was likely to cause injury.[16] A black person, however, could not sue for defamation if she was called "white." Because the law expressed and reinforced the social hierarchy as it existed, it was presumed that no harm could flow from such a reversal.

Private identity based on racial hierarchy was legitimated as public identity in law, even after the end of slavery and the formal end of legal race segregation. Whiteness as interpersonal hierarchy was recognized externally as race reputation. Thus, whiteness as public reputation and personal property was affirmed.

d.   The absolute right to exclude
Many theorists have traditionally conceptualized property as including the exclusive rights of use,

disposition, and possession, with possession embracing the absolute right to exclude. The right to exclude was the central principle, too, of whiteness as identity, for whiteness in large part has been characterized not by an inherent unifying characteristic but by the exclusion of others deemed to be "not white." The possessors of whiteness were granted the legal right to exclude others from the privileges inhering in whiteness; whiteness became an exclusive club whose membership was closely and grudgingly guarded. The courts played an active role in enforcing this right to exclude – determining who was or was not white enough to enjoy the privileges accompanying whiteness. In that sense, the courts protected whiteness as they did any other form of property.

Moreover, as it emerged, the concept of whiteness was premised on white supremacy rather than on mere difference. "White" was defined and constructed in ways that increased its value by reinforcing its exclusivity. Indeed, just as whiteness as property embraced the right to exclude, whiteness as a theoretical construct evolved for the very purpose of racial exclusion. Thus, the concept of whiteness is built on exclusion and racial subjugation. This fact was particularly evident during the period of the most rigid racial exclusion, for whiteness signified racial privilege and took the form of status property.

At the individual level, recognizing oneself as "white" necessarily assumes premises based on white supremacy: it assumes that black ancestry in any degree, extending to generations far removed, automatically disqualifies claims to white identity, thereby privileging "white" as unadulterated, exclusive, and rare. Inherent in the concept of "being white" was the right to own or hold whiteness to the exclusion and subordination of blacks. Because "[i]dentity is . . . continuously being constituted through social interactions,"[17] the assigned political, economic, and social inferiority of blacks necessarily shaped white identity. In the commonly held popular view, the presence of black "blood" – including the infamous "one-drop" – consigned a person to being "black" and evoked the "metaphor . . . of purity and contamination" in which black blood is a contaminant and white racial identity is pure. Recognizing or identifying oneself as white is thus a claim of racial purity, an assertion that one is free of any taint of black blood. The law has played a critical role in legitimating this claim.

C. White Legal Identity: The Law's Acceptance and Legitimation of Whiteness as Property

The law assumed the crucial task of racial classification, and accepted and embraced the then-current theories of race as biological fact. This core precept of race as a physically defined reality allowed the law to fulfill an essential function – to "parcel out social standing according to race" and to facilitate systematic discrimination by articulating "seemingly precise definitions of racial group membership." This allocation of race and rights continued a century after the abolition of slavery.

The law relied on bounded, objective, and scientific definitions of race – what Neil Gotanda has called "historical-race"[18] – to construct whiteness as not merely race, but race plus privilege. By making race determinant and the product of rationality and science, dominant and subordinate positions within the racial hierarchy were disguised as the product of natural law and biology rather than as naked preferences. Whiteness as racialized privilege was then legitimated by science and was embraced in legal doctrine as "objective fact."

Case law that attempted to define race frequently struggled over the precise fractional amount of black "blood" – traceable black ancestry – that would defeat a claim to whiteness. Although the courts applied varying fractional formulas in different jurisdictions to define "black" or, in the terms of the day, "negro" or "colored," the law uniformly accepted the rule of hypodescent[19] – racial identity was governed by blood, and white was preferred.

This legal assumption of race as blood-borne was predicated on the pseudo-sciences of eugenics and craniology, which saw their major development during the eighteenth and nineteenth centuries. The legal definition of race was the "objective" test propounded by racist theorists of the day, who described race to be immutable, scientific, biologically determined – an unsullied fact of the blood rather than a volatile and violently imposed regime of racial hierarchy.

In adjudicating who was "white," courts sometimes noted that, by physical characteristics, the individual whose racial identity was at issue appeared to be white and, in fact, had been regarded as white in the community. Yet if an individual's blood was tainted, she could not claim to be "white" as the law understood, regardless of the fact that phenotypically she may have been completely in-distinguishable from a white person, may have lived as a white person, and may have descended from a family that lived as whites. Although socially accepted as white, she could not legally be white. Blood as "objective fact" predominated over appearance and social acceptance, which were socially fluid and subjective measures.

In fact, though, "blood" was no more objective than that which the law dismissed as subjective and unreliable. The acceptance of the fiction that the racial ancestry could be determined with the degree of precision called for by the relevant standards or definitions rested on false assumptions that racial categories of prior ancestors had been accurately reported, that those reporting in the past shared the definitions currently in use, and that racial purity actually existed in the United States.[20] Ignoring these considerations, the law established rules that extended equal treatment to those of the "same blood," albeit of different complexions, because it was acknowledged that, "[t]here are white men as dark as mulattoes, and there are pure-blooded albino Africans as white as the whitest Saxons."[21]

The standards were designed to accomplish what mere observation could not: "That even Blacks who did not look Black were kept in their place."[22] Although the line of demarcation between black and white varied from rules that classified as black a person containing "any drop of Black blood" to more liberal rules that defined persons with a preponderance of white blood to be white,[23] the courts universally accepted the notion that white status was something of value that could be accorded only to those persons whose proofs established their whiteness as defined by the law.[24] Because legal recognition of a person as white carried material benefits, "false" or inadequately supported claims were denied like any other unsubstantiated claim to a property interest. Only those who could lay "legitimate" claims to whiteness could be legally recognized as white, because allowing physical attributes, social acceptance, or self-identification to determine whiteness would diminish its value and destroy the underlying presumption of exclusivity. In effect, the courts erected legal "no trespassing" signs.

In the realm of social relations, racial recognition in the United States is thus an act of race subordination. In the realm of legal relations, judicial definition of racial identity based on white supremacy reproduced that race subordination at the institutional level. In transforming white to whiteness, the law masked the ideological content of racial definition and the exercise of power required to maintain it: "It convert[ed an] abstract concept into [an] entity."[25]

1. Whiteness as racialized privilege

The material benefits of racial exclusion and subjugation functioned, in the labor context, to stifle class tensions among whites. White workers perceived that they had more in common with the bourgeoisie than with fellow workers who were black. Thus, W. E. B. Du Bois's classic historical study of race and class, *Black Reconstruction*,[26] noted that, for the evolving white working class, race identification became crucial to the ways that it thought of itself and conceived its interests. There were, he suggested, obvious material benefits, at least in the short term, to the decision of white workers to define themselves by their whiteness: their wages far exceeded those of blacks and were high even in comparison with world standards. Moreover, even when the white working class did not collect increased pay as part of white privilege, there were real advantages not paid in direct income: whiteness still yielded what Du Bois termed a "public and psychological wage" vital to white workers.[27] Thus, Du Bois noted that whites

> were given public deference . . . because they were white. They were admitted freely with all classes of white people, to public functions, to public parks. . . . The police were drawn from their ranks, and the courts, dependent on their votes, treated them with . . . leniency. . . . Their vote selected public officials, and while this had small effect upon the economic situation, it had great effect on their personal treatment. . . . White schoolhouses were the best in the community, and conspicuously placed, and they cost anywhere from twice to ten times as much per capita as the colored schools.[28]

The central feature of the convergence of "white" and "worker" lay in the fact that racial status and privilege could ameliorate and assist in "evad[ing] rather than confront[ing class] exploitation."[29] Although not accorded the privileges of the ruling class, in both the North and South, white workers could accept their lower class position in the hierarchy "by fashioning identities as 'not slaves' and as 'not Blacks.' "[30] Whiteness produced – and was

reproduced by – the social advantage that accompanied it.

Whiteness was also central to national identity and to the republican project. The amalgamation of various European strains into an American identity was facilitated by an oppositional definition of black as Other. As Andrew Hacker suggests, fundamentally, the question was not so much "who is white" but, rather, "who may be considered white," for the historical pattern was that various immigrant groups of different ethnic origins were accepted into a white identity shaped around Anglo-American norms. Current members then "ponder[ed] whether they want[ed] or need[ed] new members as well as the proper pace of new admissions into this exclusive club."[31] Through minstrel shows in which white actors masquerading in blackface played out racist stereotypes, the popular culture put the black at " 'solo spot centerstage, providing a relational model in contrast to which masses of Americans could establish a positive and superior sense of identity,' . . . [one] . . . established by an infinitely manipulable negation comparing whites with a construct of a socially defenseless group."[32]

It is important to note the effect of this hypervaluation of whiteness. Owning white identity as property affirmed the self-identity and liberty of whites and, conversely, denied the self-identity and liberty of blacks. The attempts to lay claim to whiteness through "passing" painfully illustrate the effects of the law's recognition of whiteness. The embrace of a lie, undertaken by my grandmother and the thousands like her, could occur only when oppression makes self-denial and the obliteration of identity rational and, in significant measure, beneficial. The economic coercion of white supremacy on self-definition nullifies any suggestion that passing is a logical exercise of liberty or self-identity. The decision to pass as white was not a choice, if by that word one means voluntariness or lack of compulsion. The fact of race subordination was coercive, and it circumscribed the liberty to define oneself. Self-determination of identity was not a right for all people but a privilege accorded on the basis of race. The effect of protecting whiteness at law was to devalue those who were not white by coercing them to deny their identity in order to survive.

2. Whiteness, rights, and national identity

The concept of whiteness was carefully protected because so much was contingent upon it. Whiteness conferred on its owners aspects of citizenship which were all the more valued because they were denied to others. Indeed, the very fact of citizenship itself was linked to white racial identity. The Naturalization Act of 1790 restricted citizenship to persons who resided in the United States for two years, who could establish their good character in court, and who were "white." Moreover, the trajectory of expanding democratic rights for whites was accompanied by the contraction of the rights of blacks in an ever-deepening cycle of oppression. The franchise, for example, was broadened to extend voting rights to unpropertied white men at the same time that black voters were specifically disenfranchised, arguably shifting the property required for voting from land to whiteness. This racialized version of republicanism – this *Herrenvolk* republicanism – constrained any vision of democracy from addressing the class hierarchies adverse to many who considered themselves white.

The inherent contradiction between the bondage of blacks and republican rhetoric that championed the freedom of "all" men was resolved by positing that blacks were different. The laws did not mandate that blacks be accorded equality under the law because nature – not man, not power, not violence – had determined their degraded status. Rights were for those who had the capacity to exercise them, a capacity denoted by racial identity. This conception of rights was contingent on race, on whether one could claim whiteness – a form of property. This articulation of rights that were contingent on property ownership was a familiar paradigm, as similar requirements had been imposed on the franchise in the early part of the Republic. For the first two hundred years of the country's existence, the system of racialized privilege in the public and private spheres carried through this linkage of rights and inequality, of rights and property. Whiteness as property was the critical core of a system that affirmed the hierarchical relations between white and black. [. . .]

III.   The Persistence of Whiteness as Property

A.   THE PERSISTENCE OF WHITENESS AS VALUED SOCIAL IDENTITY

Even as the capacity of whiteness to deliver is arguably diminished by the elimination of rigid racial stratifications, whiteness continues to be perceived as materially significant. Because real power and wealth never have been accessible to more than a narrowly defined ruling elite, for many whites the benefits of whiteness as property, in the absence of legislated privilege, may have been reduced to a claim of relative privilege only in comparison to people of color. Nevertheless, whiteness retains its value as a "consolation prize": it does not mean that all whites will win, but simply that they will not lose, if losing is defined as being on the bottom of the social and economic hierarchy – the position to which blacks have been consigned.

Andrew Hacker, in his 1992 book *Two Nations*,[33] recounts the results of a recent exercise that probed the value of whiteness according to the perceptions of whites. The study asked a group of white students how much money they would seek if they were changed from white to black. "Most seemed to feel that it would not be out of place to ask for $50 million, or $1 million for each coming black year." Whether this figure represents an accurate amortization of the societal cost of being black in the United States, it is clear that whiteness is still perceived to be valuable. The wages of whiteness are available to all whites, regardless of class position – even to those whites who are without power, money, or influence. Whiteness, the characteristic that distinguishes them from blacks, serves as compensation even to those who lack material wealth. It is the relative political advantages extended to whites, rather than actual economic gains, that are crucial to white workers. Thus, as Kimberlé Crenshaw points out, whites have an actual stake in racism.[34] Because blacks are held to be inferior, although no longer on the basis of science as antecedent determinant but, rather, by virtue of their position at the bottom, it allows whites – all whites – to "include themselves in the dominant circle. [Although most whites] hold no real power, [all can claim] their privileged racial identity."[35]

White workers often identify themselves primarily as white rather than as workers because it is through their whiteness that they are afforded access to a host of public, private, and psychological benefits. It is through the concept of whiteness that class-consciousness among white workers is subordinated and attention is diverted from class oppression.

Although dominant societal norms have embraced the ideas of fairness and nondiscrimination, removal of privilege and antisubordination principles are actively rejected or at best ambiguously received, because expectations of white privilege are bound up with what is considered essential for self-realization. Among whites, the idea persists that their whiteness is meaningful. Whiteness is an aspect of racial identity surely, but it is much more; it remains a concept based on relations of power, a social construct predicated on white dominance and black subordination.

B. Subordination through Denial of Group Identity

Whiteness as property is also constituted through the reification of expectations in the continued right of white-dominated institutions to control the legal meaning of group identity. This reification manifests itself in the law's dialectical misuse of the concept of group identity as it pertains to racially subordinated peoples. The law has recognized and codified racial group identity as an instrument of exclusion and exploitation; however, it has refused to recognize group identity when asserted by racially oppressed groups as a basis for affirming or claiming rights. The law's approach to group identity reproduces subordination, in the past through "race-ing" a group – that is, by assigning a racial identity that equated with inferior status and, in the present, by erasing racial group identity.

In part, the law's denial of the existence of racial groups is not only predicated on the rejection of the ongoing presence of the past, but it is also grounded on a basic tenet of liberalism – that constitutional protections inhere in individuals, not in groups. As informed by the Lockean notion of the social contract, the autonomous, free will of the individual is central; indeed, it is the individual who, in concert with other individuals, elects to enter into political society and to form a state of limited powers. This philosophical view of society is closely aligned with the antidiscrimination principle – the idea being that equality mandates only the equal treatment of individuals under the law. Within this framework, the idea of the social group has no place.

Although the law's determination of any "fact," including that of group identity, is not infinitely flexible, its studied ignorance of the issue of racial group identity ensures wrong results by assuming a pseudo-objective posture that does not permit it to hear the complex dialogue concerning identity questions, particularly as they pertain to historically dominated groups.

Instead, the law holds to the basic premise that definition from above can be fair to those below, that beneficiaries of racially conferred privilege have the right to establish norms for those who have historically been oppressed pursuant to those norms, and that race is not historically contingent. Although the substance of race definitions has changed, what persists is the expectation of white-controlled institutions in the continued right to determine meaning – the reified privilege of power – that reconstitutes the property interest in whiteness in contemporary form.

[. . .]

IV. Delegitimating the Property Interest in Whiteness Through Affirmative Action

Within the worlds of de jure and de facto segregation, whiteness has value, whiteness is valued, and whiteness is expected to be valued in law. The legal affirmation of whiteness and white privilege allowed expectations that originated in injustice to be naturalized and legitimated. The relative economic, political, and social advantages dispensed to whites under systematic white supremacy in the United States were reinforced through patterns of oppression of blacks and Native Americans. Materially, these advantages became institutionalized privileges; ideologically, they became part of the settled expectations of whites – a product of the unalterable original bargain. The law masks as natural what is chosen; it obscures the consequences of social selection as inevitable. The result is that the distortions in social relations are immunized from truly effective intervention, because the existing inequities are obscured and rendered nearly invisible. The existing state of affairs is considered neutral and fair, however unequal and unjust it is in substance. Although the existing state of inequitable distribution is the product of institutionalized white supremacy and economic exploitation, it is seen by whites as part of the natural order of things, something that cannot legitimately be disturbed. Through legal doctrine, expectation of continued privilege based on white domination was reified; whiteness as property was reaffirmed.

The property interest in whiteness has proven to be resilient and adaptive to new conditions. Over time it has changed in form but it has retained its essential exclusionary character and continued to distort outcomes of legal disputes by favoring and protecting settled expectations of white privilege. The law expresses the dominant conception of constructs such as "rights," "equality," "property," "neutrality," and "power": rights mean shields from interference; equality means formal equality; property means the settled expectations that are to be protected; neutrality means the existing distribution, which is natural; and power is the mechanism for guarding all of this. . . .

Affirmative action begins the essential work of rethinking rights, power, equality, race, and property from the perspective of those whose access to each of these has been limited by their oppression. [. . .] From this perspective, affirmative action is required on moral and legal grounds to delegitimate the property interest in whiteness – to dismantle the actual and expected privilege that has attended "white" skin since the founding of the country. Like "passing," affirmative action undermines the property interest in whiteness. Unlike passing, which seeks the shelter of an assumed whiteness as a means of extending protection at the margins of racial boundaries, affirmative action denies the privileges of whiteness and seeks to remove the legal protections of the existing hierarchy spawned by race oppression. What passing attempts to circumvent, affirmative action moves to challenge.

Rereading affirmative action to delegitimate the property interest in whiteness suggests that if, historically, the law has legitimated and protected the settled whites' expectations in white privilege, delegitimation should be accomplished not merely by implementing equal treatment but also by equalizing treatment among the groups that have been illegitimately privileged or unfairly subordinated by racial stratification. Obviously, the meaning of equalizing treatment would vary, because the extent of privilege and subordination is not constant with reference to all societal goods. In some instances, the advantage of race privilege to poorer whites may be materially insignificant when compared to their class disadvantage against more privileged whites. But exposing the critical core of whiteness as property – the unconstrained right to exclude – directs attention toward questions of redistribution and property that are crucial under both race and class analysis. The conceptions of rights, race, property, and affirmative action as currently understood are unsatisfactory and insufficient to facilitate the self-realization of oppressed people. [. . .]

A.   AFFIRMATIVE ACTION: A NEW FORM OF STATUS PROPERTY?

If whiteness as property is the reification, in law, of expectations of white privilege, then according privilege to blacks through systems of affirmative action might be challenged as performing the same ideological function, but on the other side of the racial line. As evidence of a property interest in blackness, some might point out that, recently, some whites have sought to characterize themselves as belonging to a racial minority. Equating affirmative action with whiteness as property, however, is false and can only be maintained if history is ignored or inverted while the premises inherent in the existing racial hierarchy are retained. Whiteness as property is derived from the deep historical roots of systematic white supremacy which have given rise to definitions of group identity predicated on the racial subordination of the Other, and have reified expectations of continued white privilege. This reification differs in crucial ways from the premises, intent, and objectives of affirmative action.

Fundamentally, affirmative action does not reestablish a property interest in blackness, because black identity is not the functional opposite of whiteness. Even today, whiteness is still intertwined with the degradation of blacks and is still valued because "the artifact of 'whiteness' . . . sets a floor on how far [whites] can fall." Acknowledging black identity does not involve the systematic subordination of whites, nor does it even set up a danger of doing so. Affirmative action is based on principles of anti-subordination, not principles of black superiority.

The removal of white privilege pursuant to a program of affirmative action would not be implemented under an ideology of subordination, nor would it be situated in the context of the historical or present exploitation of whites. It is thus not a matter of implementing systematic disadvantage to whites or installing mechanisms of group exploitation. Whites are not an oppressed people and are not at risk of becoming so. Those whites who are disadvantaged in society suffer not because of their race but in spite of it. Refusing to implement affirmative action as a remedy for racial subordination will not alleviate the class oppression of poor whites; indeed, failing to do so will reinforce the existing regime of race and class domination which leaves lower-class whites more vulnerable to class exploitation. Affirmative action does not institute a regime of racialized hierarchy in which all whites, because they are white, are deprived of economic, social, and political benefits. It does not reverse the hierarchy; rather, it levels the racial privilege.

Even if one rejects the notion that properly constructed affirmative action policies cause whites no injustice, affirmative action does not implement a set of permanent, never-ending privileges for blacks. Affirmative action does not distort black expectations because it does not naturalize these expectations. Affirmative action can only be implemented through conscious intervention, and it requires constant monitoring and reevaluation – so it does not function behind a mask of neutrality in the realm beyond scrutiny. Affirmative action for blacks does not reify existing patterns of privilege, nor does it produce subordination of whites as a group. If anything, it might fairly be said that affirmative action creates a property interest in true equal opportunity – opportunity and means that are equalized.

B.   WHAT AFFIRMATIVE ACTION HAS BEEN; WHAT AFFIRMATIVE ACTION MIGHT BECOME

The truncated application of affirmative action as a policy has obscured affirmative action as a concept. The ferocious and unending debate on affirmative action cannot be understood unless the concept of affirmative action is considered and conceptually disengaged from its application in the United States.

As policy, affirmative action does not have a clearly identifiable pedigree; rather, it was one of the limited concessions offered in official response to demands for justice pressed by black constituencies. Despite uneven implementation in the areas of public employment, higher education, and government contracts, it translated into the attainment by blacks of jobs, admissions to universities, and contractual opportunities. Affirmative action programs did not, however, stem the tide of growing structural unemployment and underemployment among black workers, nor did it prevent the decline in material conditions for blacks as a whole. Such programs did not change the subordinated status of blacks, in part because of structural changes in the economy, and in part because the programs were not designed to do so.

However, affirmative action is more than a program: it is a principle, internationally recognized, based on a theory of rights and equality. Formal equality overlooks structural disadvantage and requires mere nondiscrimination or "equal treatment"; by contrast, affirmative action calls for equalizing treatment by redistributing power and resources in order to rectify inequities and to achieve real equality. The current polarized debate on affirmative action and the intense political and judicial opposition to the concept is thus grounded in the fact that, in its requirement of equalizing treatment, affirmative action implicitly challenges the sanctity of the original and derivative present distribution of property, resources, and entitlements, and it directly confronts the notion that there is a protectable property interest in "whiteness." If affirmative action doctrine were freed from the constraint of protecting the property interest in whiteness – if, indeed, it were conceptualized from the perspective of those on the bottom – it might assist in moving away from a vision of affirmative action as an uncompensated taking and inspire a new perspective on identity as well. The fundamental precept of whiteness, the core of its value, is its exclusivity; but exclusivity is predicated not on any intrinsic characteristic, but on the existence of the symbolic Other, which functions to "create an illusion of unity" among whites. Affirmative action might challenge the notion of property and identity as the unrestricted right to exclude. In challenging the property interest in whiteness, affirmative action could facilitate the destruction of the false premises of legitimacy and exclusivity inherent in whiteness and break the distorting link between white identity and property.

Affirmative action in the South African context offers a point of comparison. It has emerged as one of the democratic movement's central demands, appearing in both the constitutional guidelines and draft Bill of Rights issued by the African National Congress. These documents simultaneously denounce all forms of discrimination and embrace affirmative action as a mechanism for rectifying the gross inequities in South African society.

The South African conception of affirmative action expands the application of affirmative action to a much broader domain than has typically been envisioned in the United States. That is, South Africans consider affirmative action a strategic measure to address directly the distribution of property and power, with particular regard to the maldistribution of land and the need for housing. This policy has not yet been clearly defined, but what is implied by this conception of affirmative action is that existing distributions of property will be modified by rectifying unjust loss and inequality. Property rights will then be respected, but they will not be absolute; rather, they will be considered against a societal requirement of affirmative action. In essence, this conception of affirmative action is moving toward the reallocation of power and the right to have a say. This conception is in fact consistent with the fundamental principle of affirmative action and effectively removes the constraint imposed in the American model, which strangles affirmative action principles by protecting the property interest in whiteness.

V. Conclusion

Whiteness as property has carried and produced a heavy legacy. It is a ghost that has haunted the political and legal domains in which claims for justice have been inadequately addressed for far too long. Only rarely declaring its presence, it has warped efforts to remediate racial exploitation. It has blinded society to the systems of domination that work against so many by retaining an unvarying focus on vestiges of systemic racialized privilege which subordinates those perceived as a particularized few – the Others. It has thwarted not only conceptions of racial justice but also conceptions of property which embrace more equitable possibilities. In protecting the property interest in whiteness, property is assumed to be no more than the right to prohibit infringement on settled expectations, ignoring countervailing equitable claims predicated on a right to inclusion. It is long past time to put the property interest in whiteness to rest. Affirmative action can assist in that task. If properly conceived and implemented, it is not only consistent with norms of equality but also essential to shedding the legacy of oppression.

Notes

1. 163 U.S. 537, 538 (1896).
2. N. Gotanda, "A Critique of 'Our Constitution is ColorBlind,' " 44 *Stan L. Rev.*, 1, 34 (1991).
3. D. Roediger, *The Wages of Whiteness*, at 32 (1991).
4. The system of racial oppression grounded in slavery was driven in large measure (although by no means exclusively) by economic concerns.
5. M. Farrand, ed., 2 *The Records of the Federal Convention of 1787*, at 222 (1911).
6. My use of the term "blackwomen" is an effort to use language that more clearly reflects the unity of identity as "black" and "woman," with neither aspect primary or subordinate to the other. It is an attempt to realize in practice what has been identified in theory – that, as Kimberlé Crenshaw notes, blackwomen exist "at the crossroads of gender and race hierarchies"; K. Crenshaw, "Whose Story Is It, Anyway? Feminist and Antiracist Appropriations of Anita Hill," in Toni Morrison, ed., *Race-ing Justice, En-gendering Power: Essays on Anita Hill, Clarence Thomas, and the Construction of Social Reality*, 402, 403 (1992).
7. A. L. Higginbotham, Jr., *In the Matter of Color: Race and the American Legal Process*, at 43 (1978).
8. Letter from Thomas Jefferson to John Jordan (Dec. 21, 1805), cited in R. Takaki, *Iron Cages: Race and Culture in Nineteenth-Century America*, at 44 (1990).
9. By 1705, Virginia had classified slaves as real property; see Higginbotham, *In the Matter of Color*, at 52. In Massachusetts and South Carolina, slaves were identified as chattels; ibid., at 78, 211.
10. 4 Ky. (1 Bibb) 97 (1815).
11. Jeremy Bentham, "Security and Equality in Property," in C. B. Macpherson, ed., *Property: Mainstream and Critical Positions*, at 51–2 (1978).
12. Ibid., at 366.
13. G. Lukacs, *History and Class Consciousness*, 83, trans. R. Livingstone (1971).
14. K. R. Minogue, "The Concept of Property and Its Contemporary Significance," in J. R. Pennock and J. W. Chapman, eds., *Nomos XXII: Property*, at 15 (1980).
15. See J. H. Crabb, "Annotation, Libel and Slander: Statements Respecting Race, Color, or Nationality as Actionable," 46 *A. L. R.*, 2d 1287, 1289 (1956) ("The bulk of the cases have arisen from situations in which it was stated erroneously that a white person was a Negro. According to the majority rule, this is libelous per se").
16. *Bowen v. Independent Publishing Co.*, 96 S.E.2d 564, 565 (S.C. 1957).
17. R. C. Post, "The Social Foundations of Defamation Law: Reputation and the Constitution," 74 *Cal. L. Rev.*, 691, 709 (1986).
18. Gotanda defines "historical-race" as socially constructed formal categories predicated on race subordination that included presumed substantive characteristics relating to "ability, disadvantage, or moral culpability."
19. "Hypodescent" is the term used by anthropologist Marvin Harris to describe the American system of racial classification in which the subordinate classification is assigned to the offspring if there is one "superordinate" and one "subordinate" parent. Under this system, the child of a black parent and a white parent is black; M. Harris, *Patterns of Race in the Americas*, 37, 56 (1964).

20. It is not at all clear that even the slaves imported from abroad represented "pure negro races." As Gunner Myrdal noted, many of the tribes imported from Africa had intermingled with peoples of the Mediterranean, among them Portuguese slave traders. Other slaves brought to the United States came via the West Indies, where some Africans had been brought directly, but still others had been brought via Spain and Portugal, countries in which extensive interracial sexual relations had occurred. By the mid-nineteenth century it was, therefore, a virtual fiction to speak of "pure blood" as it relates to racial identification in the United States; see G. Myrdal, *An American Dilemma*, at 123 (1944).

21. *People v. Dean*, 14 Mich. 406, 422 (1866).

22. R. T. Diamond and R. J. Cottrol, "Codifying Caste: Louisiana's Racial Classification Scheme and the Fourteenth Amendment," 29 *Loy. L. Rev.*, 255, 281 (1983).

23. See, for example, *Gray v. Ohio*, 4 Ohio 353, 355 (1831).

24. The courts adopted this standard even as they critiqued the legitimacy of such rules and definitions. For example, in *People v. Dean*, 14 Mich. 406 (1886), the court, in interpreting the meaning of the word "white" for the purpose of determining whether the defendant had voted illegally, criticized as "absurd" the notion that "a preponderance of mixed blood, on one side or the other of any given standard, has the remotest bearing upon personal fitness or unfitness to possess political privileges"; ibid., at 417. Yet it held that the electorate that had voted for racial exclusion had the right to determine voting privileges; see ibid., at 416.

25. S. J. Gould, *The Mismeasure of Man*, 24 (1981).

26. W. E. B. Du Bois, *Black Reconstruction* (1976) [1935].

27. Ibid., at 700.

28. Ibid., at 700–1.

29. Roediger, *The Wages of Whiteness*, at 13.

30. Ibid.

31. Ibid., at 9.

32. Ibid., at 118 (quoting Alan W. C. Green, " 'Jim Crow,' 'Zip Coon': The Northern Origin of Negro Minstrelsy," 11 *Mass. Rev.*, 385, 395 (1970)).

33. A. Hacker, *Two Nations*, 155 (1992).

34. See K. W. Crenshaw, "Race, Reform, and Retrenchment: Transformation and Legitimation in Anti-discrimination Law," 101 *Harv. L. Rev.*, 1331, 1381 (1988).

35. Roediger, *The Wages of Whiteness*, at 5.

10

New Ethnicities

Stuart Hall

I have centred my remarks on an attempt to identify and characterize a significant shift that has been
going on (and is still going on) in black cultural
politics. This shift is not definitive, in the sense
that there are two clearly discernible phases – one
in the past which is now over and the new one
which is beginning – which we can neatly counter-
pose to one another. Rather, they are two phases of
the same movement, which constantly overlap and
interweave. Both are framed by the same historical
conjuncture and both are rooted in the politics of
anti-racism and the post-war black experience
in Britain. Nevertheless I think we can identify
two different "moments" and that the difference
between them is significant.

It is difficult to characterize these precisely, but
I would say that the first moment was grounded in
a particular political and cultural analysis. Politically, this is the moment when the term "black"
was coined as a way of referencing the common
experience of racism and marginalization in Britain
and came to provide the organizing category of
a new politics of resistance, among groups and
communities with, in fact, very different histories,
traditions and ethnic identities. In this moment,
politically speaking. "The black experience", as
a singular and unifying framework based on the
building up of identity across ethnic and cultural
difference between the different communities,
became "hegemonic" over other ethnic/racial
identities – though the latter did not, of course,
disappear. Culturally, this analysis formulated
itself in terms of a critique of the way blacks were
positioned as the unspoken and invisible "other"
of predominantly white aesthetic and cultural
discourses.

This analysis was predicated on the marginalization of the black experience in British culture;
not fortuitously occurring at the margins, but placed,
positioned at the margins, as the consequence of a
set of quite specific political and cultural practices
which regulated, governed and "normalized" the
representational and discursive spaces of English
society. These formed the conditions of existence
of a cultural politics designed to challenge, resist
and, where possible, to transform the dominant
regimes of representation – first in music and style,
later in literary, visual and cinematic forms. In these
spaces blacks have typically been the objects, but
rarely the subjects, of the practices of representation. The struggle to come into representation was
predicated on a critique of the degree of fetishization, objectification and negative figuration which
are so much a feature of the representation of the
black subject. There was a concern not simply with
the absence or marginality of the black experience
but with its simplification and its stereotypical
character.

The cultural politics and strategies which developed around this critique had many facets, but
its two principal objects were: first the question of
access to the rights to representation by black artists
and black cultural workers themselves. Second, the
contestation of the marginality, the stereotypical
quality and the fetishized nature of images of blacks,
by the counter-position of a "positive" black imagery. These strategies were principally addressed
to changing what I would call the "relations of
representation".

I have a distinct sense that in the recent period
we are entering a new phase. But we need to be
absolutely clear what we mean by a "new" phase

because, as soon as you talk of a new phase, people instantly imagine that what is entailed is the *substitution* of one kind of politics for another. I am quite distinctly not talking about a shift in those terms. Politics does not necessarily proceed by way of a set of oppositions and reversals of this kind, though some groups and individuals are anxious to "stage" the question in this way. The original critique of the predominant relations of race and representation and the politics which developed around it have not and cannot possibly disappear while the conditions which gave rise to it – cultural racism in its Dewsbury form – not only persists but positively flourishes under Thatcherism.[1] There is no sense in which a new phase in black cultural politics could replace the earlier one. Nevertheless it is true that as the struggle moves forward and assumes new forms, it does to some degree *displace*, reorganize and reposition the different cultural strategies in relation to one another. If this can be conceived in terms of the "burden of representation", I would put the point in this form: that black artists and cultural workers now have to struggle, not on one, but on *two* fronts. The problem is, how to characterize this shift – if indeed, we agree that such a shift has taken or is taking place – and if the language of binary oppositions and substitutions will no longer suffice. The characterization that I would offer is tentative, proposed in the context of this essay mainly to try and clarify some of the issues involved, rather than to pre-empt them.

The shift is best thought of in terms of a change from a struggle over the relations of representation to a politics of representation itself. It would be useful to separate out such a "politics of representation" into its different elements. We all now use the word representation, but, as we know, it is an extremely slippery customer. It can be used, on the one hand, simply as another way of talking about how one images a reality that exists "outside" the means by which things are represented: a conception grounded in a mimetic theory of representation. On the other hand the term can also stand for a very radical displacement of that unproblematic notion of the concept of representation. My own view is that events, relations, structures do have conditions of existence and real effects, outside the sphere of the discursive; but that it is only within the discursive, and subject to its specific conditions, limits and modalities, do they have or can they be constructed within meaning. Thus, while not wanting to expand the territorial claims

of the discursive infinitely, how things are represented and the "machineries" and regimes of representation in a culture do play a *constitutive*, and not merely a reflexive, after-the-event, role. This gives questions of culture and ideology, and the scenarios of representation – subjectivity, identity, politics – a formative, not merely an expressive, place in the constitution of social and political life. I think it is the move towards this second sense of representation which is taking place and which is transforming the politics of representation in black culture.

This is a complex issue. First, it is the effect of a theoretical encounter between black cultural politics and the discourses of a Eurocentric, largely white, critical cultural theory which, in recent years, has focused so much analysis of the politics of representation. This is always an extremely difficult, if not dangerous, encounter. (I think particularly of black people encountering the discourses of poststructuralism, postmodernism, psychoanalysis and feminism.) Second, it marks what I can only call "the end of innocence", or the end of the innocent notion of the essential black subject. Here again, the end of the essential black subject is something which people are increasingly debating, but they may not have fully reckoned with its political consequences. What is at issue here is the recognition of the extraordinary diversity of subjective positions, social experiences and cultural identities which compose the category "black"; that is, the recognition that "black" is essentially a politically and culturally *constructed* category, which cannot be grounded in a set of fixed trans-cultural or transcendental racial categories and which therefore has no guarantees in nature. What this brings into play is the recognition of the immense diversity and differentiation of the historical and cultural experience of black subjects. This inevitably entails a weakening or fading of the notion that "race" or some composite notion of race around the term black will either guarantee the effectivity of any cultural practice or determine in any final sense its aesthetic value.

We should put this as plainly as possible. Films are not necessarily good because black people make them. They are not necessarily "right-on" by virtue of the fact that they deal with the black experience. Once you enter the politics of the end of the essential black subject you are plunged headlong into the maelstrom of a continuously contingent, unguaranteed, political argument and debate: a critical politics, a politics of criticism. You can no longer conduct black politics through the strategy of a simple set of reversals, putting in the place of the bad old essential white subject, the new essentially good black subject. Now, that formulation may seem to threaten the collapse of an entire political world. Alternatively, it may be greeted with extraordinary relief at the passing away of what at one time seemed to be a necessary fiction. Namely, either that all black people are good or indeed that all black people are *the same*. After all, it is one of the predicates of racism that "you can't tell the difference because they all look the same". This does not make it any easier to conceive of how a politics can be constructed which works with and through difference, which is able to build those forms of solidarity and identification which make common struggle and resistance possible but without suppressing the real heterogeneity of interests and identities, and which can effectively draw the political boundary lines without which political contestation is impossible, without fixing those boundaries for eternity. It entails the movement in black politics, from what Gramsci called the "war of manoeuvre" to the "war of position" – the struggle around positionalities. But the difficulty of conceptualizing such a politics (and the temptation to slip into a sort of endlessly sliding discursive liberal-pluralism) does not absolve us of the task of developing such a politics.

The end of the essential black subject also entails a recognition that the central issues of race always appear historically in articulation, in a formation, with other categories and divisions and are constantly crossed and recrossed by the categories of class, of gender and ethnicity. (I make a distinction here between race and ethnicity to which I shall return.) To me, films like *Territories, Passion of Remembrance, My Beautiful Laundrette* and *Sammy and Rosie Get Laid*, for example, make it perfectly clear that this shift has been engaged; and that the question of the black subject cannot be represented without reference to the dimensions of class, gender, sexuality and ethnicity.

Difference and Contestation

A further consequence of this politics of representation is the slow recognition of the deep ambivalence of identification and desire. We think about identification usually as a simple process, structured around fixed "selves" which we either are or are not. The play of identity and difference which

constructs racism is powered not only by the positioning of blacks as the inferior species but also, and at the same time, by an inexpressible envy and desire; and this is something the recognition of which fundamentally *displaces* many of our hitherto stable political categories, since it implies a process of identification and otherness which is more complex than we had hitherto imagined.

Racism, of course, operates by constructing impassable symbolic boundaries between racially constituted categories, and its typically binary system of representation constantly marks and attempts to fix and naturalize the difference between belongingness and otherness. Along this frontier there arises what Gayatri Spivak calls the "epistemic violence" of the discourses of the Other – of imperialism, the colonized, Orientalism, the exotic, the primitive, the anthropological and the folk-lore.[2] Consequently the discourse of anti-racism had often been founded on a strategy of reversal and inversion, turning the "Manichean aesthetic" of colonial discourse upside-down. However, as Fanon constantly reminded us, the epistemic violence is both outside and inside, and operates by a process of splitting on both sides of the division – in here as well as out here. That is why it is a question, not only of "black-skin" but of *"Black-Skin, White Masks"* – the internalization of the self-as-other. Just as masculinity always constructs femininity as double – simultaneously Madonna and Whore – so racism constructs the black subject: noble savage and violent avenger. And in the doubling, fear and desire double for one another and play across the structures of otherness, complicating its politics.

Recently I have read several articles about the photographic text of Robert Mapplethorpe – especially his inscription of the nude, black male – all written by black critics or cultural practitioners.[3] These essays properly begin by identifying in Mapplethorpe's work the tropes of fetishization, the fragmentation of the black image and its objectification, as the forms of their appropriation within the white, gay gaze. But, as I read, I know that something else is going on as well in both the production and the reading of those texts. The continuous circling around Mapplethorpe's work is not exhausted by being able to place him as the white fetishistic, gay photographer; and this is because it is also marked by the surreptitious return of desire – that deep ambivalence of identification which makes the categories in which we have previously thought and argued about black cultural politics and the black cultural text extremely problematic. This brings to the surface the unwelcome fact that a great deal of black politics, constructed, addressed and developed directly in relation to questions of race and ethnicity, has been predicated on the assumption that the categories of gender and sexuality would stay the same and remain fixed and secured. What the new politics of representation does is to put that into question, crossing the questions of racism irrevocably with questions of sexuality. That is what is so disturbing, finally, to many of our settled political habits about *Passion of Remembrance*. This double fracturing entails a different kind of politics because, as we know, black radical politics has frequently been stabilized around particular conceptions of black masculinity, which are only now being put into question by black women and black gay men. At certain points, black politics has also been underpinned by a deep absence or more typically an evasive silence with reference to class.

Another element inscribed in the new politics of representation has to do with the question of ethnicity. I am familiar with all the dangers of "ethnicity" as a concept and have written myself about the fact that ethnicity, in the form of a culturally constructed sense of Englishness and a particularly closed, exclusive and regressive form of English national identity, is one of the core characteristics of British racism today.[4] I am also well aware that the politics of anti-racism has often constructed itself in terms of a contestation of "multi-ethnicity" or "multi-culturalism". On the other hand, as the politics of representation around the black subject shifts, I think we will begin to see a renewed contestation over the meaning of the term "ethnicity" itself.

If the black subject and black experience are not stabilized by Nature or by some other essential guarantee, then it must be the case that they are constructed historically, culturally, politically – and the concept which refers to this is "ethnicity". The term ethnicity acknowledges the place of history, language and culture in the construction of subjectivity and identity, as well as the fact that all discourse is placed, positioned, situated, and all knowledge is contextual. Representation is possible only because enunciation is always produced within codes which have a history, a position within the discursive formations of a particular space and time. The displacement of the "centred" discourses of the West entails putting in question its universalist character and its transcendental claims to speak

for everyone, while being itself everywhere and nowhere. The fact that this grounding of ethnicity in difference was deployed, in the discourse of racism, as a means of disavowing the realities of racism and repression does not mean that we can permit the term to be permanently colonized. That appropriation will have to be contested, the term dis-articulated from its position in the discourse of "multi-culturalism" and transcoded, just as we previously had to recuperate the term "black" from its place in a system of negative equivalences. The new politics of representation therefore also sets in motion an ideological contestation around the term "ethnicity". But in order to pursue that movement further, we will have to re-theorize the concept of *difference*.

It seems to me that, in the various practices and discourses of black cultural production, we are beginning to see constructions of just such a new conception of ethnicity: a new cultural politics which engages rather than suppresses *difference* and which depends, in part, on the cultural construction of new ethnic identities. Difference, like representation, is also a slippery and, therefore, contested concept. There is the "difference" which makes a radical and unbridgable separation: and there is a "difference" which is positional, conditional and conjunctural, closer to Derrida's notion of *différance*, though if we are concerned to maintain a politics it cannot be defined exclusively in terms of an infinite sliding of the signifier. We still have a great deal of work to do to *decouple* ethnicity, as it functions in the dominant discourse, from its equivalence with nationalism, imperialism, racism and the state, which are the points of attachment around which a distinctive British or, more accurately, English ethnicity have been constructed. Nevertheless, I think such a project is not only possible but necessary. Indeed, this decoupling of ethnicity from the violence of the state is implicit in some of the new forms of cultural practice that are going on in films like *Passion* and *Handsworth Songs*. We are beginning to think about how to represent a non-coercive and a more diverse conception of ethnicity, to set against the embattled, hegemonic conception of "Englishness" which, under Thatcherism, stabilizes so much of the dominant political and cultural discourses, and which, because it is hegemonic, does not represent itself as an ethnicity at all.

This marks a real shift in the point of contestation, since it is no longer only between anti-racism

and multi-culturalism but *inside* the notion of ethnicity itself. What is involved is the splitting of the
notion of ethnicity between, on the one hand, the
dominant notion which connects it to nation and
"race" and, on the other hand, what I think is the
beginning of a positive conception of the ethnicity
of the margins, of the periphery. That is to say, a
recognition that we all speak from a particular place,
out of a particular history, out of a particular experience, a particular culture, without being contained
by that position as "ethnic artists" or film-makers.
We are all, in that sense, *ethnically* located and our
ethnic identities are crucial to our subjective sense
of who we are. But this is also a recognition that
this is not an ethnicity which is doomed to survive,
as Englishness was, only by marginalizing, dispos-
sessing, displacing and forgetting other ethnicities.
This precisely is the politics of ethnicity predicated
on difference and diversity.

The final point which I think is entailed in this
new politics of representation has to do with an
awareness of the black experience as a *diaspora*
experience, and the consequences which this carries for the process of unsettling, recombination,
hybridization and "cut-and-mix" – in short, the process of cultural *diaspora-ization* (to coin an ugly
term) which it implies. In the case of the young
black British films and film-makers under discussion,
the diaspora experience is certainly profoundly fed
and nourished by, for example, the emergence of
Third World cinema; by the African experience;
the connection with Afro-Caribbean experience; and
the deep inheritance of complex systems of representation and aesthetic traditions from Asian and
African culture. But, in spite of these rich cultural "roots", the new cultural politics is operating
on new and quite distinct ground – specifically,
contestation over what it means to be "British".
The relation of this cultural politics to the past;
to its different "roots" is profound, but complex.
It cannot be simple or unmediated. It is (as a
film like *Dreaming Rivers* reminds us) complexly
mediated and transformed by memory, fantasy and
desire. Or, as even an explicitly political film like
Handsworth Songs clearly suggests, the relation
is inter-textual – mediated, through a variety of
other "texts". There can, therefore, be no simple
"return" or "recovery" of the ancestral past which
is not re-experienced through the categories of the
present: no base for creative enunciation in a simple reproduction of traditional forms which are not
transformed by the technologies and the identities

of the present. This is something that was signalled
as early as a film like *Blacks Britannica* and as recently as Paul Gilroy's important book, *There Ain't
No Black in the Union Jack*.[5] Fifteen years ago we
didn't care, or at least I didn't care, whether there
was any black in the Union Jack. Now not only do
we care, we *must*.

This last point suggests that we are also
approaching what I would call the end of a certain
critical innocence in black cultural politics. And
here, it might be appropriate to refer, glancingly,
to the debate between Salman Rushdie and myself
in the *Guardian* some months ago. The debate
was not about whether *Handsworth Songs* or *The
Passion of Remembrance* were great films or not,
because, in the light of what I have said, once you
enter this particular problematic, the question of
what good films are, which parts of them are good
and why, is open to the politics of criticism. Once
you abandon essential categories, there is no place
to go apart from the politics of criticism and to
enter the politics of criticism in black culture is to
grow up, to leave the age of critical innocence.

It was not Salman Rushdie's particular judgement that I was contesting, so much as the mode in
which he addressed them. He seemed to me to be
addressing the films as if from the stable, well-
established critical criteria of a *Guardian* reviewer.
I was trying, perhaps unsuccessfully, to say that I
thought this an inadequate basis for a political criticism and one which overlooked precisely the signs
of innovation, and the constraints, under which
these film-makers were operating. It is difficult to
define what an alternative mode of address would
be. I certainly didn't want Salman Rushdie to say
he thought the films were good because they were
black. But I also didn't want him to say that he
thought they weren't good because "we creative
artists all know what good films are", since I no
longer believe we can resolve the questions of
aesthetic value by the use of these transcendental,
canonical cultural categories. I think there is
another position, one which locates itself *inside* a
continuous struggle and politics around black representation, but which then is able to open up a
continuous critical discourse about themes, about
the forms of representation, the subjects of representation, above all, the regimes of representation.
I thought it was important, at that point, to intervene to try and get that mode of critical address
right, in relation to the new black film-making. It is
extremely tricky, as I know, because as it happens,

in intervening, I got the mode of address wrong too! I failed to communicate the fact that, in relation to his *Guardian* article, I thought Salman was hopelessly wrong about *Handsworth Songs*, which does not in any way diminish my judgement about the stature of *Midnight's Children*. I regret that I couldn't get it right, exactly, because the politics of criticism has to be able to get both things right.

Such a politics of criticism has to be able to say (just to give one example) why *My Beautiful Laundrette* is one of the most riveting and important films produced by a black writer in recent years and precisely for the reason that made it so controversial: its refusal to represent the black experience in Britain as monolithic, self-contained, sexually stabilized and always "right-on" – in a word, always and only "positive", or what Hanif Kureishi has called "cheering fictions":

> the writer as public relations officer, as hired liar. If there is to be a serious attempt to understand Britain today, with its mix of races and colours, its hysteria and despair, then, writing about it has to be complex. It can't apologize or idealize. It can't sentimentalize and it can't represent only one group as having a monopoly on virtue.[6]

Laundrette is important particularly in terms of its control, of knowing what it is doing, as the text crosses those frontiers between gender, race, ethnicity, sexuality and class. *Sammy and Rosie* is also a bold and adventurous film, though in some ways less coherent, not so sure of where it is going, overdriven by an almost uncontrollable, cool anger. One needs to be able to offer that as a critical judgement and to argue it through, to have one's mind changed, without undermining one's essential commitment to the project of the politics of black representation.

Notes

1. The Yorkshire town of Dewsbury became the focus of national attention when white parents withdrew their children from a local school with predominantly Asian pupils, on the grounds that "English" culture was no longer taught on the curriculum. The contestation of multicultural education from the right also underpinned the controversies around Bradford headmaster Ray Honeyford. See Paul Gordon, "The New Right, race and education", *Race and Class* XXIX (3), Winter 1987.
2. Gayatri C. Spivak, in *Other Worlds: Essays in Cultural Politics*, Methuen, 1987.
3. Kobena Mercer, "Imaging the black man's sex", in Patricia Holland et al. (eds), *Photography/ Politics: Two*, Comedia/Methuen, 1987, and various articles in *Ten.8* 22, 1986, an issue on "Black experiences" edited by David A. Bailey.
4. Stuart Hall, "Racism and reaction", in *Five Views on Multi-Racial Britain*, Commission for Racial Equality, 1978.
5. Paul Gilroy, *There Ain't No Black in the Union Jack: The Cultural Politics of Race and Nation*, Hutchinson, 1988.
6. Hanif Kureishi, "Dirty washing", *Time Out*, 14–20 November 1985.

11

The Latino Imaginary: Meanings of Community and Identity

Juan Flores

Is that Hispanic or Latino? What's in a name? A bewildered public puzzles over alternative signifiers, and even over who is being so designated, and how. "What do we call them? What do they want to be called? What do they call themselves?" Or, as the title of a thoughtful article on just this problem of megalabels has it, "What's the Problem with 'Hispanic'? Just Ask a 'Latino.' "[1]

The broadest identifying term, of course, long used as shorthand even by many Latinos themselves, has been "Spanish," as in Spanish restaurant or Spanish television, where the idea of a unifying language culture conspires with the suggestion of Iberian origins and characteristics. The ideological undertones of that label, which are of course retained in slight variation in both "Hispanic" and "Latino," go unquestioned, as does the reality that many of those so designated do not even speak Spanish as a first language, or at all. The need for elastic and flexible usages stretches the field of reference so far that Spaniards, and even Italians and French, sometimes find their place under that hopelessly porous umbrella. The signifying net is cast so wide that what would seem the defining experiences, migration and resettlement, become of secondary importance, and all of Latin America is swept conveniently into the "Hispanic" bin. Or, to complicate the picture beyond recognition, there is even the suggestion that "Latinos" be used "to refer to those citizens from the Spanish-speaking world living *in* the United States" and "Hispanics" to "those living elsewhere."[2]

With all the slippages and evident arbitrariness, though, what would seem a terminological free-for-all actually does mark off limits and contexts, and pressing issues of power. "Where I come from,

in New Mexico, nobody uses Latino, most people never even heard the term. We're Mexicanos, Chicanos, Mexican-Americans, Raza, Hispanic, but never Latino. Anyone who comes around talking about Latino this or Latino that is obviously an outsider." Or, from a contrary perspective, it is "Hispanic" that raises the red flag: "Hispanic? For me, a Hispanic is basically a sellout, *un vendido*. Anyone who calls himself Hispanic, or refers to our community as Hispanic, just wants to be an American and forget about our roots."

Bits of conversation like these point up the range of contention over the choice of words to name a people, a culture, a community.[3] Behind the war of words, of course, there lurks the real battle, which has to do with attitudes, interpretations, and positions. In the dismissive indifference of many Americans there is often that undertone of annoyance which, when probed a little further, only turns out to be a cover for other, submerged emotions like ignorance, fear, and of course disdain. The gaps among Latinos or Hispanics themselves can be as polarized as they appear here, with one usage thoroughly discrediting the other. But usually the options are more flexible, operational, and mediated by a whole span of qualifying terms, tones, and situations. And over against those who use the words at all, there are many Mexican Americans, Puerto Ricans, Colombians, Cubans, or Dominicans who have no use for any such catchall phrases and would rather stick to distinct national designations.[4]

Yet this disparity over nomenclature, sharp as it is in the case of Latinos, should not be mistaken for a total lack of consensus or collective identity, nor as proof that any identification of the group or "community" is no more than a label imposed from outside, and above. Regardless of what anyone chooses to name it, the Latino or Hispanic community exists because for much of the history of the hemisphere, and multiplying exponentially the closer we approach the present, people have moved from Latin America to the United States, while portions of Latin America have been incorporated into what has become the United States. Along with their increase in numbers there has also been a deepening of their impact, real and potential, on the doings, and the destiny, of this country.

It is becoming clear that any discussion of an "American community" must be inclusive of Latinos and cognizant of the existence of a "Latino community" intrinsic to historical discourses about U.S. culture. The real challenge, though, is that the Latino presence makes it necessary to recognize that the very meaning of the word, the concept of *community* itself, is relative according to the perspective or position of the group in question: there is both a "Latino community" and a "community" in the Latino sense of the word.

Comunidad: the Spanish word, even more clearly than the English, calls to mind two of the key terms – *común* and *unidad* – in the conceptualization of this notoriously elusive idea. What do we have in "common," and what "unites" us, what are our commonalities and what makes for our unity? It is important to note that though the two terms point in the same semantic direction they are not synonymous, and their apparent coupling in the same word, *comunidad*, is not a redundancy. For while *común* refers to sharing – that is, those aspects in the cultures of the various constitutive groups that overlap – the sense of *unidad* is that which bonds the groups above and beyond the diverse particular commonalities. The point of this admittedly rather willful deconstruction is, once again, that the Latino "experience," the group's demonstrable reality and existence, includes but is not coterminous with its self-consciousness: *común* stands for the community *in* itself, while *unidad* refers to the community *for* itself, the way that it thinks, conceives of, imagines itself.

The "Latino community" is an "imagined community" – to summon Benedict Anderson's well-worn though useful phrase – a compelling present-day example of a social group being etched and composed out of a larger, impinging geopolitical landscape.[5] The role of the social imagination and the imaginary in the self-conception of nationally, ethnically, and "racially" kindred groups is of course central, but must always be assessed with a view toward *how* they are being imagined (i.e., from "within" or "without") and to what ends and outcomes. Distinguishing between interior and exterior perspectives is thus a necessary step, and given that in the case of Latinos the outside representation is the dominant one, any instance of cultural expression by Latinos themselves may serve as a healthy corrective to the ceaseless barrage of stereotypes that go to define what is "Latino" in the public mind.

But the marking off of "us" and "them," though the foundational exercise in "imagining" communities, has its own limits, as it becomes evident that there is from both angles as much blurring involved as clear and meaningful bounding. Vexing questions like who's Latino and who isn't, and what kind of Latina(o)(s) we are talking about, quickly press in on any too facile dichotomy. Beyond the issue of names and labels, and even who is using them, there are differing levels or modes of meaning simultaneously at work in the very act of apprehending and conceptualizing the "community" and "identity" in question. "Latino" or "Hispanic" not only mean different things to different people; they also "mean" in different ways and refer to different dimensions of collective social experience.

I would suggest that by distinguishing between a *demographic*, an *analytic*, and an *imaginary* approach to Latino unity and diversity it is possible effectively to complicate and deepen our understanding of cultural expression, identity, and politics without becoming paralyzed by the sheer complexity and contradictoriness of it all. Whether Latinos or Hispanics are thought of as an enumerated aggregate of people, an analytically differentiated set of constituent groups, or a historically imagined cultural "community" or "ethnoscape," is at the core of ongoing debates and confusions.[6] Not that these diverse conceptualizations are mutually exclusive, nor are they to be considered in any mechanically sequential or hierarchical way. On the contrary, as I seek to describe them it will be obvious that all three are necessary, and that they are complementary. That is, they are really different methodological and epistemological emphases rather than discrete forms of explanation. But scrutinizing them in hypothetical discreteness not only helps understand their interrelation but may also enhance our analysis and appreciation of the voices and images of Latino art.[7]

The demographic conception of Latinos, or of a "Latino community," refers to an aggregate of people whose existence is established on the basis of numerical presence: count them, therefore they are. Here Latinos – or more commonly at this level, Hispanics – comprise not so much a community as a "population," a quantified slice of the social whole. As limited as such a means of identification may seem, it is nevertheless the dominant one, serving as it does both government bureaucracies and corporate researchers in setting public taste and policy. This definition of the Hispanic community by official measurement is thus inherently instrumental, since the immediate goal is really to identify, not so much social groups or lines of cultural unity and diversity, but voting blocs and consumer markets. From this angle, Latinos appear as a homogeneous, passive mass, a "target" public, with any concern for internal differentiation or possible social agency itself geared toward those same pragmatic goals of electoral or commercial utility.[8]

But it is not only campaign managers and admen for whom Latinos are, first of all, numbers. The labels and tallies they arrive at for their convenience – be it Hispanic or Latino, at whatever percentile – are made visible, credible, "real," by means of a whole sensorium of images, sounds, and flavors. The demographic label thus aims not only to buy the Hispanic package but to sell it; it targets not only potential customers but merchandise, or even movers of merchandise. Whatever the particular purpose, though, the means and result are usually the same – stereotyped images offering up distorted, usually offensive, and in any case, superficial portrayals of Latino people.[9] And these are the only images of Latinos that many people in the United States, and around the world, are ever exposed to, which makes it difficult for the public to gauge their accuracy. It is important to recognize these images as products not just of opportunist politicians or greedy marketeers but also of the demographic mentality itself. Numbers call forth labels, which in turn engender generic, homogenized representations – stereotypes. According to the same logic, holding economic and political power relies on the work of both the census-taker and the cameraman.

The most loudly proclaimed finding of this aggregative endeavor, by now a demographic truism of our times, is that Hispanics are the nation's "fastest-growing minority," on course to become the "largest" minority at some (variously defined)

point early in the coming century. Whether greeted by alarmist jitters or triumphalist joy, this momentous news item rests on an abiding confidence in the validity of the count, and an unquestioned consensus that like social units are being summed and demarcated from unlike, incompatible ones. The often unspoken allusion, of course, is to African Americans, who are thus cast as the main rival in the numbers race and the main instance, among "minorities," of the non-Hispanic other. Asian Americans, too, are in the running, with all lines of historical interaction and congruency again erased from the calculation. In both cases, it is clear how tools of advertent inclusion and conjunction may at the same time serve as wedges between and among groups whose social placement and experience in the United States could just as well, given a different political agenda, point to commonalities as to differences. The tactics of divide and conquer are still prominent in the arsenal of power, and nowhere more so in the contemporary equation than in the talk of Hispanics as undifferentiated numeraries.

The process of adding up is accompanied by the need to break down, to identify not the sum total but the constituent parts. The analytical approach – the business, above all, of positivist social science – is bent on deaggregation; it presumes to move closer to Latino "reality" by recognizing and tabulating the evident diversity of Latino groups and experiences. Such varying factors as country of origin, time in the United States (generation), region or place of settlement, occupation and socioeconomic status, educational background, and the like, move into focus as the only meaningful units or vantages of analysis, with any cohesion among Latinos referred to only in the plural: typically, there are only Latino "populations," groups, or at best "communities."

This analytical account of Latino multiplicity is indeed often helpful in counteracting stereotypes and monolithic categories, and the elaborate discussion of "modes of incorporation" certainly allows for a sense of the dynamic relation among a too hastily posited aggregate of structurally differentiated social experiences.[10] But resting as it overwhelmingly does on socially constructed statistical evidence and an objectification of collective historical actors, it is still close kin to the demographic approach. Even the census evidences an increasing official need to break the composite down, with "Hispanics" now grouped into Mexican, Puerto

Rican, Cuban origin, Central and South American origin, and "Other Hispanic," subcategories which then serve as the basis for much quantitative research. Commercially geared demographics are also far along in their analytical enterprise, having persuasively charted both a "pan-Hispanic" as well as regionally differentiated Los Angeles, Miami, and New York centered markets, along with countless other target-specific variables.

To this extent, and in many social scientific studies, the pluralizing "analysis" of Latino reality is still dealing with a community "in itself," constructed in terms of relatively inert categories with their appropriate labels and generic representations. The focus on "labor market experience" as the "key factor in the structuring of [Hispanic] ethnicity," for example, while an invaluable starting point for differentiating social positions among the groups and subgroups in question, leaves unaddressed what would seem the crucial issue of "the complexities of the interaction between social and ethnic identities," that is, the "interdependency between socioeconomic placement and cultural (self-) identification."[11]

Ultimately, the limitation of analytical methodologies of this kind is not the act of differentiation itself, but a failure to differentiate among differences, and among kinds and levels of difference. For example, the vast research on Latinos as part of immigration studies, perhaps the most prevalent paradigm for treating Latino social experience, tends to stumble in the face of the glaring fact that the majority of Latinos, comprising the largest national groups within the composite, are not even "immigrants" in any quantifiable or recognized sense: because of their citizenship status, Puerto Ricans are not counted among the nation's immigrant populations, and a large share of the Mexican Americans are here not because they crossed the border, but because "the border crossed them." Characteristically, this most severe and telling divide among the Latino pan-ethnicity, the difference between immigrant and "resident minority" Latinos having much to do with issues of colonial status and class, tends to elude even the most thorough and cautious scrutiny of Latino realities, which as a result arrive at misleading conclusions. Even historically informed and critically "balanced" accounts of Latino immigration and communities, such as those of Roberto Suro and Rubén G. Rumbaut among others, lose interpretive cogency because of this overly "objectivist" method and inattention to such

structurally larger but less readily quantifiable dimensions of contrastive analysis, and lead to continual equivocation and inconsistency – like that of Rumbaut – as to the validity of any unifying concept at all, or, in the case of Suro's *Strangers Among Us* (1998), to an inadequately critical relation to "culture of poverty" and "underclass" theory in speaking of "Puerto Rican-like poverty," a central message of his book being that "the entire nation will suffer if the Puerto Rican fate is repeated" by "today's Latino newcomers."[12]

Yet Latinos are also social agents and not just passive objects in this analyzing process, nor do they tend to sidestep the task of "telling Hispanics apart." Consciously and intuitively, personally and collectively, Puerto Ricans, Mexicans, Cubans, Dominicans, and each of the other groups most often project their own respective national backgrounds as a first and primary axis of identity and on that basis, fully mindful of differences and distances, negotiate their relation to some more embracing "Latino" or "Hispanic" composite. Here the force of analysis, rather than an extension of demographic aggregation and labeling, stands in direct opposition to it, an instinctive reaction against instrumental measuring and its pernicious consequences. Of course, there are interests involved here too, but in this case they are the interests of the "object" of analysis itself, the Latino peoples and communities.

From a Latino perspective understood in this way, analysis is guided above all by lived experience and historical memory, factors that tend to be relegated by prevailing sociological approaches as either inaccessible or inconsequential. Rather than as slices or cross-sections, the various groups and their association may be seen in dynamic, relational terms, with traditions and continuities weighing off subtly against changes and reconfigurations. At this level of conceptualization, differences are drawn among and within the groups not so as to divide or categorize for the sake of more efficient manipulation, but to assure that social identities, actions, and alliances are adequately grounded in the specific historical experiences and cultural practices that people recognize as their own, with appropriate attention to the sometimes sharp class and racial cleavages that always cross-cut any too hasty presumption of equivalence. The logic is that solidarity can only be posited when the lines of social differentiation are fully in view, but the goal, nevertheless, is solidarity.

It is this critical, historically based approach to diverse and changing Latino realities that underlies and sustains what I refer to as the "Latino imaginary," another sense or conceptual space of pan-group aggregation that is too often and too easily confused with the official, demographic version. Not that calculation is itself foreign to an "imagined" Latino community; in fact it is at this epistemological level that the very act and authority of counting and measuring become issues of vital social contestation. The "imaginary" in this sense does not signify the "not real," some make-believe realm oblivious to the facts, but a projection beyond the "real" as the immediately present and rationally discernible. It is the "community" represented "for itself," a unity fashioned creatively on the basis of shared memory and desire, congruent histories of misery and struggle, and intertwining utopias.

The Latino historical imaginary refers, first of all, to home countries in Latin America, the landscapes, life-ways, and social struggles familiar, if not personally, at least to one's family and people, and in any case indispensable to Latinos in situating themselves in U.S. society. Mexico, Puerto Rico, and Cuba are very different points of imaginative reference, to be sure, and again, it is always through their particular national optics that Latinos tend to envision some generic Latin American or Latino "We." But the features of José Martí's "nuestra América" do stand out in the Latino historical unconscious in that long narrative of Spanish and North American colonial conquest, the enslavement and subjugation of indigenous and African peoples, the troubled consolidation of nations under the thumb of international power, and the constant migratory movement of peoples, cultures, and things which has been attendant to all aspects of the Latino saga. For Latinos in the United States, the passage to, and from, "el Norte" assumes such prominence in the social imaginary that migration is often confounded with life itself, and any fixity of the referential homeland gives way to an image of departure and arrival, the abandoned and the reencountered.

This nomadic, migratory dimension of the Latino imaginary is anchored in the historical reasons for coming here, and in the placement assigned most Latinos in U.S. society. Unlike earlier waves of European immigrants, Latinos typically move to this country as a direct result of the economic and political relationship of their homelands, and home region, to the United States. However much Cuba, Mexico, and Puerto Rico may vary in status and

social arrangement – and if we add the Dominican Republic and Colombia the range could hardly be wider in present-day geopolitics – huge portions of their respective populations have come to live in the United States because of the gravitational pull of metropolitan power and dependency at work in each and all of their histories. Since World War II, its economy on a course of shrinkage and transition rather than unbridled expansion, the United States has been tapping its colonial reserves to fill in its lower ranks, and its Latin American and Caribbean neighbors have proven to be the closest and most abundant sources at hand.

Colonial relations of hemispheric inequality underlie not only the historical logic of Latino migration but also the position and conditions of Latinos here in this society. Differential treatment is of course rampant, as has been dramatically evident in recent years in the contrasting fates of Cubans and Haitians arriving on the same rafts from their beleaguered home islands. Yet today even many Cuban Americans, recent arrivals and long-standing citizens alike, are finding the red carpets and gold-paved streets illusory at best, and are coming to resent being cited as the exception to the rule of Latino disadvantage. For the Latino imaginary, even when the relatively "privileged" Cuban Americans are reckoned in, rests on the recognition of ongoing oppression and discrimination, racism and exploitation, closed doors and patrolled borders. Whether sanguine or enraged, this recognition structures the negotiated relations among Latinos, between Latinos and the dominant culture, and with other groups such as African Americans and Native Americans.

Memory fuels desire: the past as imagined from a Latino perspective awakens an anticipatory sense of what is, or might be, in store. The alarmist hysteria over the prospect of "America's fastest-growing minority" overrunning the society is directed not only at Latino people themselves but at the ground shift in power relations implied in that new calculus. For the desire that these demographic trends awaken in Latinos is directed first of all toward recognition and justice in this society, but wider, hemispheric changes always figure somewhere on the agenda. The Latino imaginary infuses the clamor for civil rights with a claim to sovereignty on an international scale; retribution involves reversing the history of conquest and subordination, including its inherent migratory imperative. A full century after its initial pronouncement,

Martí's profile of "nuestra América" still looms like a grid over the map of the entire continent, with the northern co-optation of the name America demanding special scrutiny and revision.

But Latino memory and desire, though standing as a challenge to prevailing structures of power, are not just reactive. The imaginary articulates more than a reflexive response to negative conditions and unfavorably weighted relations which, though oppositional, is as a response still ultimately mimetic and confined to extrinsically set terms. It is important to recognize that the Latino imaginary, like that of other oppressed groups, harbors the elements of an alternative ethos, an ensemble of cultural values and practices created in its own right and to its own ends. Latinos listen to their own kinds of music, eat their own kinds of food, dream their dreams and snap their photos not just to express their difference from, or opposition to, the way the "gringos" do it. These choices and preferences, though arrived at under circumstances of dependency and imposition, also attest to a deep sense of autonomy and self-referentiality. Latino identity is imagined not as the negation of the non-Latino, but as the affirmation of cultural and social realities, myths and possibilities, as they are inscribed in their own human trajectory.

The conditions for the emergence of a Latino cultural ethos were set around midcentury, as it began to become clear that these "new immigrants" filing in from the southern backyard make for a different kind of social presence than that constituted by European arrivals of earlier years. Of course, the histories of each of the major U.S. Latino groups extend much further back than that: Cubans and Puerto Ricans to the mid- to later nineteenth century, when colonies of artisans and political exiles formed in New York and Florida, while today's "Chicanos" were "here" all along, for centuries before the fateful year 1848 when the northern third of their nation was rudely moved in on and annexed by the bearers of Manifest Destiny. In fact, in the long historical view, the literary and cultural presence of Spanish-speaking people in the territory now called the United States actually precedes that of the English. And if we add to that the Indian American and Afro-American dimensions of "nuestra América," a full-scale revision, or inversion, of the national history results, with the supposed "core," Anglo-Saxon culture appearing as the real intruder, the original illegal alien.

It is a serious fallacy, therefore, to think of Latinos in the United States as "recent arrivals," as is often the tendency in their treatment in scholarly research on immigration.[13] But despite their longstanding, constitutive role in North American history, sheer demographic growth and diversification point to a markedly new structural positioning and cultural dynamic for Latinos in the second half of the twentieth century. Now more than ever, in the present, "postcolonial" era, many Latinos are here as colonial migrants, whose very locations and movements are defined by the status of their "home" countries within the system of transnational economic power. Rather than an ethnic, minority, or immigrant group, those trusty old concepts of cultural pluralism, Latinos may now be more accurately described as a diasporic community or, more suggestively in view of the intensified transnational linkages, as an "ethnoscape" or "world tribe." But a still more satisfactory neologism to characterize the social and cultural space occupied by Latinos is that of the "delocalized transnation," of whom it is also said that they "become doubly loyal to their nations of origin and thus ambivalent about their loyalties to America."[14] Precisely because of the persisting hierarchies of transnational power, if convergences among today's Latinos involve the formation of a "Hispanic nation," it promises to be decidedly less an "American" nation, less a "step toward joining America," than commentators like Geoffrey Fox might propose.[15]

The social consciousness and cultural expression of this new geopolitical reality burst forth in the late 1960s and early 1970s, surely the watershed years in the construction of a new language of Latino identity. Inspired by the Civil Rights movement, the opposition to the war against Vietnam, and the Cuban Revolution, countless movements, causes, and organizations rallied thousands of Chicanos and Puerto Ricans to the cries of "¡Viva la Raza!" and "¡Despierta Boricua!" The political horizon of the Latino imaginary was set in those spirited movements and found vibrant artistic expression in such diverse forms as wall murals, bilingual poetry and street theater, and hybrid music and dance styles like boogaloo, Chicano rock, Latin soul, and salsa. *Talleres* (workshops) and *conjuntos* (musical groups), readings and *actos* (dramatic sketches) proliferated, lending voice and vision to the fervent political struggles of Latino and Latin American peoples and often attesting to close cultural affinities and political solidarities with other, non-Latino groups, notably African Americans and American Indians.

By our time, in the 1990s, that heyday is long past, hardly even a living memory for many young Latinos; all too frequently in the burgeoning scholarly and journalistic literature on Latinos of recent years, the importance of that foundational period in the story of Latino identity-formation is minimized or erased. But the Brown Berets and the Young Lords Party, the Chicano Moratorium and the Lincoln Hospital takeover, the causes of the farmworkers and Puerto Rican independence, along with many other manifestations of cultural and political activism, are still an inspiration and a model of militancy and righteous defiance for the present generation of Latinos of all nationalities as they sharpen their social awareness. For although the immediacy, intensity, and cultural effervescence has no doubt waned in the intervening decades, Latinos in the United States have just as assuredly continued to grow as a social movement to be reckoned with, nationally and internationally, in the years ahead. This is true demographically in the striking (for some startling) multiplication in their numbers, and analytically in the equally sharp diversification of their places of origin and settlement. As contrasted with earlier stages, the Latino concept is today a far more differentiated site of intersecting social identities, especially along sexual, racial, and class lines.

But the persistence and expansion of the Latino social movements are most prominent as a cultural imaginary, a still emergent space or "community" of memory and desire. In the present generation, Latino youth from many backgrounds have played a formative role in the creation of hip-hop and its inflection toward Latino expression and experience; though not always explicitly political in intention, the Latino contribution to contemporary popular music, dance, performance, and visual imaging has accompanied important signs of social organization and self-identification among young Latinos in many parts of the country. The emergence of "Latino literature," though in important ways a marketing and canonizing category having the effect of concealing distinctions necessary for purposes of literary history and criticism, has also involved expanded horizons and greater intercultural exchange than had been true in the previous, Nuyorican and Chicano generation. In the case of the "casitas" in the New York barrios – another richly suggestive and often-cited example from recent Latino experi-

ence – entire neighborhoods across generational and many other lines are drawn together by way of sharing in the enactment of collective cultural memory.[16] Present-day considerations and representations of Latino life which would do justice to that complex reality find it necessary to incorporate such instances of cultural innovation and "invented traditions" by way of complementing their reliance on social scientific insights.[17]

Hispanic? Latino? Settling on a name never comes easy, and when it comes to an all-embracing term for Mexicans, Puerto Ricans, Cubans, Dominicans, Colombians, Salvadorans, Panamanians, and an array of other Latin American and Caribbean peoples in the United States, consensus does not seem to be near at hand. But the search for a name, more than an act of classification, is actually a process of historical imagination and a struggle over social meaning at diverse levels of interpretation. Rigorous demographic and social science analysis is no doubt essential to the task of circumscribing that process, and especially for identifying structural variations in the placement of the different national groups relative to hierarchies of power and attendant histories of racialization. But only a fully interdisciplinary approach, guided by an attention to cultural expression and identity claims and transcending the bounds set by positivist analysis, allows for an integral understanding of Latino experience. In that sense the search for Latino identity and community, the ongoing articulation of a panethnic and transnational imaginary, is also a search for a new map, a new ethos, a new *América*.

Notes

1. David González, "What's the Problem with 'Hispanic'? Just Ask a 'Latino,' " *New York Times*, November 15, 1992, sec. 4, p. 6.
2. llan Stavans, *The Hispanic Condition: Reflections on Culture and Identity in America* (New York: HarperCollins, 1995), 27. Another such unusual, and in my view confusing, usage of the terms may be found in William Luis, *Dance Between Two Cultures: Latino Caribbean Literature Written in the United States* (Nashville: Vanderbilt University Press, 1997), x–xi; here "Latino" refers to those of Latin American background born and raised in the United States, while "Hispanic" is taken to refer to those "born and raised in their parents' home country." Though the terminological distinction is questionable

and remote from common parlance, Luis is accurate in calling for distinctions in group denomination when he states that "it would be incongruous to group Hispanics from privileged families who have superior educational backgrounds, traveling to the United States to pursue a post-secondary education, with Latinos living in the ghettos of East Harlem or East Los Angeles, attending inferior schools and lacking the economic support necessary to overcome the limitations of their existence" (xi). For an example of the overemphasis on language and an excessively expansive sense of "Latino" and "Hispanic," see Geoffrey Fox, *Hispanic Nation: Culture, Politics, and the Constructing of Identity* (Secaucus, NJ: Carol, 1996).

3. The opening citations are renderings of statements I have encountered during the course of conversations and interviews, or in newspaper accounts. Examples of the abundant published discussion of the terms *Hispanic* and *Latino* may be found in Suzanne Oboler, *Ethnic Labels, Latino Lives: Identity and the Politics of (Re)Presentation in the United States* (Minneapolis: University of Minnesota, 1995); Earl Shorris, *Latinos: A Biography of the People* (New York: Norton, 1992); and *Latin American Perspectives* 19.4 (Fall 1992). See also my essay, "Pan-Latino/Trans-Latino: Puerto Ricans in the 'New Nueva York'," in *From Bomba to Hip-Hop: Puerto Rican Culture and Latino Identity* (New York: Columbia University Press, 2000).

4. Documentation of this widespread preference for national designations may be found in Rodolfo O. de la Garza et al., "Latino National Political Survey," as published in de la Garza, ed., *Latino Voices: Mexican, Puerto Rican, and Cuban Perspectives on American Politics* (Boulder, Colo.: Westview, 1992). For a response, see Luis Fraga et al., *Still Looking for America: Beyond the Latino National Political Survey* (Stanford, Calif.: Stanford Center for Chicano Research, 1994).

5. Benedict Anderson, *Imagined Communities: Reflections on the Origin and Spread of Nationalism* (London: Verso, 1983). As useful as Anderson's coinage may be for characterizing the cultural convergences among Latinos, to posit the idea of a "Hispanic nation," as in Geoffrey Fox's book of that title, would seem premature at best, and misleading in taking Anderson's analysis too literally (see Fox, *Hispanic Nation*, esp. 1–18).

6. The range of theoretical approaches from strictly quantitative to comparative to ideological is evident in the growing published literature on "Hispanics" or "Latinos," as cited in note 2 above. See in addition, for example, Marta Tienda and Vilma Ortíz, " 'Hispanicity' and the 1980 Census," *Social Science Quarterly* 67 (1986): 3–20; Félix Padilla, *Latino Ethnic Consciousness: The Case of Mexican Americans*

and Puerto Ricans in Chicago (Notre Dame: Notre Dame University Press, 1985); Rebecca Morales and Frank Bonilla, eds., *Latinos in a Changing U.S. Economy* (Newbury Park, Calif.: Sage, 1993). The concept of "ethnoscape" is set forth by Arjun Appadurai, *Modernity at Large: Cultural Dimensions of Globalization* (Minneapolis: University of Minnesota Press, 1996), esp. 27–65.

7. The present essay was originally intended as a general theoretical introduction to the projected catalogue of "Latino Voices," the first international festival of Latino photography, which opened in Houston in November 1994. The idea of conceptualizing and circumscribing a "Latino imaginary" arose while pre-viewing slides of images by Chicano, Puerto Rican, and Cuban photographers included in that historic exhibition, and deciding how best to present their theoretical and cultural significance to a broad United States audience of the 1990s. Although the catalogue did not materialize, I have presented the paper in a variety of settings across the country, incorporating insights as I went along. I especially thank Wendy Watriss, Frances Aparicio, and Marvette Pérez for their critical responses, though they are in no way to be held responsible for the arguments of the essay as it stands.

8. The most extended discussion of these instrumental uses of the "Hispanic" label may be found in Oboler's *Ethnic Labels, Latino Lives*, though I also find of some interest the exchange between Fernando Treviño and David Hayes-Bautista in the *American Journal of Public Health* 77.1 (January 1987): 61–71.

9. For examples of "Hispanics" in advertisements and other commercial uses, see Flores and George Yúdice, "Living Borders/Buscando América: Languages of Latino Self-Formation," *Social Text* 24 (1990): 57–84. That essay also appeared in my book *Divided Borders: Essays on Puerto Rican Identity* (Houston: Arte Público, 1993), 199–224. See also Arlene Dávila, *Latinos Inc: The Marketing and Making of a People* (Berkeley: University of California Press, 2001).

10. On the vast research on "modes of incorporation," see especially Alejandro Portes and Robert L. Bach, *Latin Journey: Cuban and Mexican Immigrants in the United States* (Berkeley: University of California Press, 1985), and Alejandro Portes and Rubén G. Rumbaut, *Immigrant America: A Portrait* (Berkeley: University of California Press, 2nd edn., 1996).

11. See Candace Nelson and Marta Tienda, "The Structuring of Hispanic Ethnicity: Historical and Contemporary Perspectives," in Mary Romero, Pierrette Hondagneu-Sotelo, and Vilma Ortiz, eds., *Challenging Fronteras* (New York: Routledge, 1997), 7–29 (quotations from 26).

12. Roberto Suro, *Strangers Among Us: How Latino Immigration Is Transforming America* (New York:

Knopf, 1998), 146–7. For Rumbaut, see the valuable essay, "The Americans: Latin American and Caribbean Peoples in the United States," in Alfred Stepan, ed., *Americas: New Interpretive Essays* (New York: Oxford University Press, 1992), 275–307; it is worth noting that while the author seems to have little difficulty speaking of "Latinos" as a group when contrasting them with African Americans, he otherwise voices skepticism as to the value of pan-ethnic, or what he terms "supranational," identities.

13. See, for example, Silvia Pedraza, "The Contribution of Latino Studies to Social Science Research on Immigration," JSRI Occasional Paper no. 36 (East Lansing: Julian Samora Research Institute, Michigan State University, 1998). Even broad historical overviews of Latino immigration may tend to abbreviate the duration of Latino presence in the United States; see, for example, Rubén G. Rumbaut, "The Americans," where preponderant attention goes to the post-1960s period.

14. See Arjun Appadurai, "Patriotism and Its Futures," *Modernity at Large*, 158–77.

15. See Fox, *Hispanic Nation*, esp. 237ff.

16. On Latino rap, see my "Puerto Rocks: Rap, Roots, and Amnesia," in *From Bomba to Hip-Hop*. For an interpretation of the casita phenomenon, see my "Salvación Casita: Space, Performance, and Community," in ibid.

17. See, for example, Peter Winn, "North of the Border," in *Americas: The Changing Face of Latin America and the Caribbean* (New York: Pantheon, 1992), 550–600. This chapter, like the book as a whole, is intended as the accompaniment to the ten-part public television series on contemporary Latin America. "North of the Border," the final chapter and segment, is about U.S. Latinos and is based on the research of Alejandro Portes and Rubén G. Rumbaut; their social science findings are significantly amplified by extensive references to rap music, casitas, and other cultural phenomena. See also Fox, *Hispanic Nation*, esp. 223ff.

Part III
Class and Identity

12

Class Consciousness

Georg Lukács

The question is not what goal is *envisaged* for the time being by this or that member of the proletariat, or even by the proletariat as a whole. The question is *what is the proletariat* and what course of action will it be forced historically to take in conformity with its own *nature*.

Marx: *The Holy Family*

Marx's chief work breaks off just as he is about to embark on the definition of class. This omission was to have serious consequences both for the theory and the practice of the proletariat. For on this vital point the later movement was forced to base itself on interpretations, on the collation of occasional utterances by Marx and Engels and on the independent extrapolation and application of their method. In Marxism the division of society into classes is determined by position within the process of production. But what, then, is the meaning of class consciousness? The question at once branches out into a series of closely interrelated problems. First of all, how are we to understand class consciousness (in theory)? Second, what is the (practical) function of class consciousness, so understood, in the context of the class struggle? This leads to the further question: is the problem of class consciousness a "general" sociological problem or does it mean one one thing for the proletariat and another for every other class to have emerged hitherto? And lastly, is class consciousness homogeneous in nature and function or can we discern different gradations and levels in it? And if so, what are their practical implications for the class struggle of the proletariat?

1

In his celebrated account of historical materialism[1] Engels proceeds from the assumption that although the essence of history consists in the fact that "nothing happens without a conscious purpose or an intended aim", to understand history it is necessary to go further than this. For on the one hand, "the many individual wills active in history for the most part produce results quite other than those intended – often quite the opposite; *their motives, therefore, in relation to the total result are likewise of only secondary importance*. On the other hand, the further question arises: *what driving forces in turn stand behind these motives?* What are the historical causes which transform themselves into these motives in the brain of the actors?" He goes on to argue that these driving forces ought themselves to be determined, in particular those which "set in motion great masses, whole peoples and again whole classes of the people; and which create *a lasting action resulting in a great transformation.*" The essence of scientific Marxism consists, then, in the realisation that the real motor forces of history are independent of man's (psychological) consciousness of them.

At a more primitive stage of knowledge this independence takes the form of the belief that these forces belong, as it were, to nature and that in them and in their causal interactions it is possible to discern the "eternal" laws of nature. As Marx says of bourgeois thought: "Man's reflections on the forms of social life and consequently also his scientific analysis of those forms, take a course directly opposite to that of their actual historical development. He begins post festum, with the results of the process of development ready to hand before him. The characters . . . have already acquired the stability of natural self-understood forms of social life, before man seeks to decipher not their historical character (for in his eyes they are immutable) but their meaning."[2]

This is a dogma whose most important spokesmen can be found in the political theory of classical German philosophy and in the economic theory of Adam Smith and Ricardo. Marx opposes to them a critical philosophy, a theory of theory and a consciousness of consciousness. This critical philosophy implies above all historical criticism. It dissolves the rigid, unhistorical, natural appearance of social institutions; it reveals their historical origins and shows therefore that they are subject to history in every respect including historical decline. Consequently history does not merely unfold *within* the terrain mapped out by these institutions. It does not resolve itself into the evolution of *contents*, of men and situations, etc., while the *principles* of society remain eternally valid. Nor are these institutions the *goal* to which all history aspires, such that when they are realised history will have fulfilled her mission and will then be at an end. On the contrary, history is precisely *the history of these institutions*, of the changes they undergo *as* institutions which bring men together in societies. Such institutions start by controlling economic relations between men and go on to permeate all human relations (and hence also man's relations with himself and with nature, etc.).

At this point bourgeois thought must come up against an insuperable obstacle, for its starting-point and its goal are always, if not always consciously, an apologia for the existing order of things or at least the proof of their immutability.[3] "Thus there has been history, but there is no longer any,"[4] Marx observes with reference to bourgeois economics, a dictum which applies with equal force to all attempts by bourgeois thinkers to understand the process of history. (It has often been pointed out that this is also one of the defects of Hegel's philosophy of history.) As a result, while bourgeois thought is indeed able to conceive of history as a problem, it remains an *intractable* problem. Either it is forced to abolish the process of history and regard the institutions of the present as eternal laws of nature which for "mysterious" reasons and in a manner wholly at odds with the principles of a rational science were held to have failed to establish themselves firmly, or indeed at all, in the past. (This is characteristic of bourgeois sociology.) Or else, everything meaningful or purposive is banished from history. It then becomes impossible to advance beyond the mere "individuality" of the

various epochs and their social and human representatives. History must then insist with Ranke that every age is "equally close to God", i.e. has attained an equal degree of perfection and that – for quite different reasons – there is no such thing as historical development.

In the first case it ceases to be possible to understand the *origin* of social institutions.[5] The objects of history appear as the objects of immutable, eternal laws of nature. History becomes fossilised in a *formalism* incapable of comprehending that the real nature of socio-historical institutions is that they consist of *relations between men*. On the contrary, men become estranged from this, the true source of historical understanding and cut off from it by an unbridgeable gulf. As Marx points out,[6] people fail to realise "that these definite social relations are just as much the products of men as linen, flax, etc.".

In the second case, history is transformed into the irrational rule of blind forces which is embodied at best in the "spirit of the people" or in "great men". It can therefore only be described pragmatically but it cannot be rationally understood. Its only possible organisation would be aesthetic, as if it were a work of art. Or else, as in the philosophy of history of the Kantians, it must be seen as the instrument, senseless in itself, by means of which timeless, suprahistorical, ethical principles are realised.

Marx resolves this dilemma by exposing it as an illusion. The dilemma means only that the contradictions of the capitalist system of production are reflected in these mutually incompatible accounts of the same object. For in this historiography with its search for "sociological" laws or its formalistic rationale, we find the reflection of man's plight in bourgeois society and of his helpless enslavement by the forces of production. "To them, *their own social action*", Marx remarks,[7] "takes the form of the action of objects which rule the producers instead of being ruled by them". This law was expressed most clearly and coherently in the purely natural and rational laws of classical economics. Marx retorted with the demand for a historical critique of economics which resolves the totality of the reified objectivities of social and economic life into *relations between men*. Capital and with it every form in which the national economy objectifies itself is, according to Marx, "not a thing but a social relation between persons mediated through things".[8]

However, by reducing the objectivity of the social institutions so hostile to man to relations between men, Marx also does away with the false implications of the irrationalist and individualist principle, i.e. the other side of the dilemma. For to eliminate the objectivity attributed both to social institutions inimical to man and to their historical evolution means the restoration of this objectivity to their underlying basis, to the relations between men; it does not involve the elimination of laws and objectivity independent of the will of man and in particular the wills and thoughts of individual men. It simply means that this objectivity is the self-objectification of human society at a particular stage in its development; its laws hold good only within the framework of the historical context which produced them and which is in turn determined by them.

It might look as though by dissolving the dilemma in this manner we were denying consciousness any decisive role in the process of history. It is true that the conscious reflexes of the different stages of economic growth remain historical facts of great importance; it is true that while dialectical materialism is itself the product of this process, it does not deny that men perform their historical deeds themselves and that they do so consciously. But as Engels emphasises in a letter to Mehring,[9] this consciousness is false. However, the dialectical method does not permit us simply to proclaim the "falseness" of this consciousness and to persist in an inflexible confrontation of true and false. On the contrary, it requires us to investigate this "false consciousness" concretely as an aspect of the historical totality and as a stage in the historical process.

Of course bourgeois historians also attempt such concrete analyses; indeed they reproach historical materialists with violating the concrete uniqueness of historical events. Where they go wrong is in their belief that the concrete can be located in the empirical individual of history ("individual" here can refer to an individual man, class or people) and in his empirically given (and hence psychological or mass-psychological) consciousness. And just when they imagine that they have discovered the most concrete thing of all: *society as a concrete totality*, the system of production at a given point in history and the resulting division of society into classes – they are in fact at the furthest remove from it. In missing the mark they mistake something wholly abstract for the concrete. "These relations", Marx states, "are not those between one individual and another, but between worker and capitalist, tenant and landlord, etc. Eliminate these relations and you abolish the whole of society; your Prometheus will then be nothing more than a spectre without arms or legs. . . ."[10]

Concrete analysis means then: the relation to society *as a whole*. For only when this relation is established does the consciousness of their existence that men have at any given time emerge in all its essential characteristics. It appears, on the one hand, as something which is *subjectively* justified in the social and historical situation, as something which can and should be understood, i.e. as "right". At the same time, *objectively*, it by-passes the essence of the evolution of society and fails to pinpoint it and express it adequately. That is to say, objectively, it appears as a "false consciousness". On the other hand, we may see the same consciousness as something which fails *subjectively* to reach its self-appointed goals, while furthering and realising the *objective* aims of society of which it is ignorant and which it did not choose.

This twofold dialectical determination of "false consciousness" constitutes an analysis far removed from the naïve description of what men *in fact* thought, felt and wanted at any moment in history and from any given point in the class structure. I do not wish to deny the great importance of this, but it remains after all merely the *material* of genuine historical analysis. The relation with concrete totality and the dialectical determinants arising from it transcend pure description and yield the category of objective possibility. By relating consciousness to the whole of society it becomes possible to infer the thoughts and feelings which men would have in a particular situation if they were *able* to assess both it and the interests arising from it in their impact on immediate action and on the whole structure of society. That is to say, it would be possible to infer the thoughts and feelings appropriate to their objective situation. The number of such situations is not unlimited in any society. However much detailed researches are able to refine social typologies there will always be a number of clearly distinguished basic types whose characteristics are determined by the types of position available in the process of production. Now class consciousness consists in fact of the appropriate and rational reactions "imputed" [zugerechnet] to a particular typical position in the process of production.[11] This consciousness is, therefore, neither the sum nor the average of what is thought or felt by the single individuals who make up the class. And yet the historically significant actions of the class as a whole are determined in the last resort by this consciousness and not by the thought of the individual – and these actions can be understood only by reference to this consciousness.

This analysis establishes right from the start the distance that separates class consciousness from the empirically given, and from the psychologically describable and explicable ideas which men form about their situation in life. But it is not enough just to state that this distance exists or even to define its implications in a formal and general way. We must discover, firstly, whether it is a phenomenon that differs according to the manner in which the various classes are related to society as a whole and whether the differences are so great as to produce *qualitative distinctions*. And we must discover, secondly, the *practical* significance of these different possible relations between the objective economic totality, the imputed class consciousness and the real, psychological thoughts of men about their lives. We must discover, in short, the *practical, historical function* of class consciousness.

Only after such preparatory formulations can we begin to exploit the category of objective possibility systematically. The first question we must ask is how far is it *in fact* possible to discern the whole economy of a society from inside it? It is essential to transcend the limitations of particular individuals caught up in their own narrow prejudices. But it is no less vital not to overstep the frontier fixed for them by the economic structure of society and establishing their position in it.[12] Regarded abstractly and formally, then, class consciousness implies a class-conditioned *unconsciousness* of ones own socio-historical and economic condition.[13] This condition is given as a definite structural relation, a definite formal nexus which appears to govern the whole of life. The "falseness", the illusion implicit in this situation is in no sense arbitrary; it is simply the intellectual reflex of the objective economic structure. Thus, for example, "the value or price of labour-power takes on the appearance of the price or value of labour itself . . ." and "the illusion is created that the totality is paid labour. . . . In contrast to that, under slavery even that portion of labour which is paid for appears unpaid for."[14] Now it requires the most painstaking historical analysis to use the category of objective possibility so as to isolate the conditions in which this illusion can be exposed and a real connection with the totality

established. For if from the vantage point of a particular class the totality of existing society is not visible; if a class thinks the thoughts imputable to it and which bear upon its interests right through to their logical conclusion and yet fails to strike at the heart of that totality, then such a class is doomed to play only a subordinate role. It can never influence the course of history in either a conservative or progressive direction. Such classes are normally condemned to passivity, to an unstable oscillation between the ruling and the revolutionary classes, and if perchance they do erupt then such explosions are purely elemental and aimless. They may win a few battles but they are doomed to ultimate defeat.

For a class to be ripe for hegemony means that its interests and consciousness enable it to organise the whole of society in accordance with those interests. The crucial question in every class struggle is this: which class possesses this capacity and this consciousness at the decisive moment? This does not preclude the use of force. It does not mean that the class-interests destined to prevail and thus to uphold the interests of society as a whole can be guaranteed an automatic victory. On the contrary, such a transfer of power can often only be brought about by the most ruthless use of force (as e.g. the primitive accumulation of capital). But it often turns out that questions of class consciousness prove to be decisive in just those situations where force is unavoidable and where classes are locked in a life-and-death-struggle. Thus the noted Hungarian Marxist Erwin Szabó is mistaken in criticising Engels for maintaining that the Great Peasant War (of 1525) was essentially a reactionary movement. Szabó argues that the peasants' revolt was suppressed *only* by the ruthless use of force and that its defeat was not grounded in socio-economic factors and in the class consciousness of the peasants. He overlooks the fact that the deepest reason for the weakness of the peasantry and the superior strength of the princes is to be sought in class consciousness. Even the most cursory student of the military aspects of the Peasants' War can easily convince himself of this.

It must not be thought, however, that all classes ripe for hegemony have a class consciousness with the same inner structure. Everything hinges on the extent to which they can become conscious of the actions they need to perform in order to obtain and organise power. The question then becomes: how far does the class concerned perform the actions history has imposed on it "consciously" or "unconsciously"? And is that consciousness "true" or "false"? These distinctions are by no means academic. Quite apart from problems of culture where such fissures and dissonances are crucial, in all practical matters too the fate of a class depends on its ability to elucidate and solve the problems with which history confronts it. And here it becomes transparently obvious that class consciousness is concerned neither with the thoughts of individuals, however advanced, nor with the state of scientific knowledge. For example, it is quite clear that ancient society was broken economically by the limitations of a system built on slavery. But it is equally clear that neither the ruling classes nor the classes that rebelled against them in the name of revolution or reform could perceive this. In consequence the practical emergence of these problems meant that the society was necessarily and irremediably doomed.

The situation is even clearer in the case of the modern bourgeoisie, which, armed with its knowledge of the workings of economics, clashed with feudal and absolutist society. For the bourgeoisie was quite unable to perfect its fundamental science, its own science of classes: the reef on which it foundered was its failure to discover even a theoretical solution to the problem of crises. The fact that a scientifically acceptable solution does exist is of no avail. For to accept that solution, even in theory, would be tantamount to observing society *from a class standpoint other than that of the bourgeoisie*. And no class can do that – unless it is willing to abdicate its power freely. Thus the barrier which converts the class consciousness of the bourgeoisie into "false" consciousness is objective; it is the class situation itself. It is the objective result of the economic set-up, and is neither arbitrary, subjective nor psychological. The class consciousness of the bourgeoisie may well be able to reflect all the problems of organisation entailed by its hegemony and by the capitalist transformation and penetration of total production. But it becomes obscured as soon as it is called upon to face problems that remain within its jurisdiction but which point beyond the limits of capitalism. The discovery of the "natural laws" of economics is pure light in comparison with mediaeval feudalism or even the mercantilism of the transitional period, but by an internal dialectical twist they became "natural laws based on the unconsciousness of those who are involved in them".[15]

It would be beyond the scope of these pages to advance further and attempt to construct a historical and systematic typology of the possible degrees of class consciousness. That would require – in the first instance – an exact study of the point in the total process of production at which the interests of the various classes are most immediately and vitally involved. Secondly, we would have to show how far it would be in the interest of any given class to go beyond this immediacy, to annul and transcend its immediate interest by seeing it as a factor within a totality. And lastly, what is the nature of the totality that is then achieved? How far does it really embrace the true totality of production? It is quite evident that the quality and structure of class consciousness must be very different if, e.g. it remains stationary at the separation of consumption from production (as with the Roman *Lumpen-proletariat*) or if it represents the formation of the interests of circulation (as with merchant capital). Although we cannot embark on a systematic typology of the various points of view it can be seen from the foregoing that these specimens of "false" consciousness differ from each other both qualitatively, structurally and in a manner that is crucial for the activity of the classes in society.

2

It follows from the above that for pre-capitalist epochs and for the behaviour of many strata within capitalism whose economic roots lie in pre-capitalism, class consciousness is unable to achieve complete clarity and to influence the course of history consciously.

This is true above all because class interests in pre-capitalist society never achieve full (economic) articulation. Hence the structuring of society into castes and estates means that economic elements are *inextricably* joined to political and religious factors. In contrast to this, the rule of the bourgeoisie means the abolition of the estates-system and this leads to the organisation of society along class lines. (In many countries vestiges of the feudal system still survive, but this does not detract from the validity of this observation.)

This situation has its roots in the profound difference between capitalist and pre-capitalist economics. The most striking distinction, and the one that directly concerns us, is that pre-capitalist societies are much less *cohesive* than capitalism. The various parts are much more self-sufficient and less closely interrelated than in capitalism. Commerce plays a smaller role in society, the various sectors were more autonomous (as in the case of village communes) or else plays no part at all in the economic life of the community and in the process of production (as was true of large numbers of citizens in Greece and Rome). In such circumstances the state, i.e. the organised unity, remains insecurely anchored in the real life of society. One sector of society simply lives out its "natural" existence in what amounts to a total independence of the fate of the state. "The simplicity of the organisation for production in these self-sufficient communities that constantly reproduce themselves in the same form, and when accidentally destroyed, spring up again on the spot and with the same name – this simplicity supplies the key to the secret of the immutability of Asiatic societies, an immutability in such striking contrast with the constant dissolution and refounding of Asiatic states, and the never-ceasing changes of dynasty. The structure of the economic elements of society remains untouched by the storm-clouds of the political sky."[16]

Yet another sector of society is – economically – completely parasitic. For this sector the state with its power apparatus is not, as it is for the ruling classes under capitalism, a means whereby to put into practice the principles of its economic power – if need be with the aid of force. Nor is it the instrument it uses to create the conditions for its economic dominance (as with modern colonialism). That is to say, the state is not a *mediation* of the economic control of society: it is that *unmediated dominance itself*. This is true not merely in cases of the straightforward theft of land or slaves, but also in so-called peaceful economic relations. Thus in connection with labour-rent Marx says: "Under such circumstances the surplus labour can be extorted from them for the benefit of the nominal landowner only by other than economic pressure." In Asia "rent and taxes coincide, or rather there is no tax other than this form of ground-rent".[17]

Even commerce is not able, in the forms it assumes in pre-capitalist societies, to make decisive inroads on the basic structure of society. Its impact remains superficial and the process of production, above all in relation to labour, remains beyond its control. "A merchant could buy every commodity, but labour as a commodity he could not buy. He existed only on sufferance, as a dealer in the products of the handicrafts."[18]

Despite all this, every such society constitutes an economic unity. The only question that arises is whether this unity enables the individual sectors of society to relate to society as a whole in such a way that their imputed consciousness can assume an economic form. Marx emphasises[19] that in Greece and Rome the class struggle "chiefly took the form of a conflict between debtors and creditors". But he also makes the further, very valid point: "Nevertheless, the money-relationship – and the relationship of creditor to debtor is one of money – reflects only the deeper-lying antagonism between the economic conditions of existence." Historical materialism showed that this reflection was no more than a reflection, but we must go on to ask: was it at all possible – objectively – for the classes in such a society to become conscious of the economic basis of these conflicts and of the economic problems with which the society was afflicted? Was it not inevitable that these conflicts and problems should assume either natural, religious forms,[20] or else political and legal ones, depending on circumstances?

The division of society into estates or castes means in effect that conceptually and organisationally these "natural" forms are established without their economic basis ever becoming conscious. It means that there is no mediation between the pure traditionalism of natural growth and the legal institutions it assumes.[21] In accordance with the looser economic structure of society, the political and legal institutions (here the division into estates, privileges, etc.) have different functions objectively and subjectively from those exercised under capitalism. In capitalism these institutions merely imply the stabilisation of purely economic forces so that – as Karner has ably demonstrated[22] – they frequently adapt themselves to changed economic structures without changing themselves in form or content. By contrast, in pre-capitalist societies legal institutions intervene *substantively* in the interplay of economic forces. In fact there are no purely economic categories to appear or to be given legal form (and according to Marx, economic categories are "forms of existence, determinations of life").[23] Economic and legal categories are objectively and *substantively so interwoven as to be inseparable*. (Consider here the instances cited earlier of labour-rent, and taxes, of slavery, etc.) In Hegel's parlance the economy has not even objectively reached the stage of being-for-itself. There is therefore no possible position within such a society from which the economic basis of all social relations could be made conscious.

This is not of course to deny the objective economic foundations of social institutions. On the contrary, the history of [feudal] estates shows very clearly that what in origin had been a "natural" economic existence cast into stable forms begins gradually to disintegrate as a result of subterranean, "unconscious" economic development. That is to say, it ceases to be a real unity. Their economic content destroys the unity of their juridical form. (Ample proof of this is furnished both by Engels in his analysis of the class struggles of the Reformation period and by Cunow in his discussion of the French Revolution.) However, despite this conflict between juridical form and economic content, the juridical (privilege-creating) forms retain a great and often absolutely crucial importance for the consciousness of estates in the process of disintegration. For the form of the estates conceals the connection between the – real but "unconscious" – economic existence of the estate and the economic totality of society. It fixates consciousness directly on its privileges (as in the case of the knights during the Reformation) or else – no less directly – on the particular element of society from which the privileges emanated (as in the case of the guilds).

Even when an estate has disintegrated, even when its members *have been absorbed economically into a number of different classes*, it still retains this (objectively unreal) ideological coherence. For the relation to the whole created by the consciousness of one's status is not directed to the real, living economic unity but to a past state of society as constituted by the privileges accorded to the estates. Status-consciousness – a real historical factor – masks class consciousness; in fact it prevents it from emerging at all. A like phenomenon can be observed under capitalism in the case of all "privileged" groups whose class situation lacks any immediate economic base. The ability of such a class to adapt itself to the real economic development can be measured by the extent to which it succeeds in "capitalising" itself, i.e. transforming its privileges into economic and capitalist forms of control (as was the case with the great landowners).

Thus class consciousness has quite a different relation to history in pre-capitalist and capitalist periods. In the former case the classes could only be deduced from the immediately given historical reality *by the methods of historical materialism*. In capitalism they themselves constitute this immediately given historical *reality*. It is therefore no accident that (as Engels too has pointed out) this

knowledge of history only became possible with the advent of capitalism. Not only – as Engels believed – because of the greater simplicity of capitalism in contrast to the "complex and concealed relations" of earlier ages. But primarily because only with capitalism does economic class interest emerge in all its starkness as the motor of history. In pre-capitalist periods man could never become conscious (not even by virtue of an "imputed" consciousness) of the "true driving forces which stand behind the motives of human actions in history". They remained hidden behind motives and were in truth the blind forces of history. Ideological factors do not merely "mask" economic interests, they are not merely the banners and slogans: they are the parts, the components of which the real struggle is made. Of course, if historical materialism is deployed to discover the *sociological meaning* of these struggles, economic interests will doubtless be revealed as the decisive *factors in any explanation*.

But there is still an unbridgeable gulf between this and capitalism where economic factors are not concealed "behind" consciousness but are present *in* consciousness itself (albeit unconsciously or repressed). With capitalism, with the abolition of the feudal estates and with the creation of a society with a *purely economic* articulation, class consciousness arrived at the point where *it could become conscious*. From then on social conflict was reflected in an ideological struggle for consciousness and for the veiling or the exposure of the class character of society. But the fact that this conflict became possible points forward to the dialectical contradictions and the internal dissolution of pure class society. In Hegel's words, "When philosophy paints its gloomy picture a form of life has grown old. It cannot be rejuvenated by the gloomy picture, but only understood. Only when dusk starts to fall does the owl of Minerva spread its wings and fly."

3

Bourgeoisie and proletariat are the only pure classes in bourgeois society. They are the only classes whose existence and development are entirely dependent on the course taken by the modern evolution of production and only from the vantage point of these classes can a plan for the total organisation of society *even be imagined*. The outlook of the other classes (petty bourgeois or peasants) is ambiguous or sterile because their existence is not based exclusively on their role in the capitalist system of production but is indissolubly linked with the vestiges of feudal society. Their aim, therefore, is not to advance capitalism or to transcend it, but to reverse its action or at least to prevent it from developing fully. Their class interest concentrates on *symptoms of development* and not on development itself, and on elements of society rather than on the construction of society as a whole.

The question of consciousness may make its appearance in terms of the objectives chosen or in terms of action, as for instance in the case of the petty bourgeoisie. This class lives at least in part in the capitalist big city and every aspect of its existence is directly exposed to the influence of capitalism. Hence it cannot possibly remain wholly unaffected by the *fact* of class conflict between bourgeoisie and proletariat. But as a "transitional class in which the interests of two other classes become simultaneously blunted . . ." it will imagine itself "to be above all class antagonisms".[24] Accordingly it will search for ways whereby it will "not indeed eliminate the two extremes of capital and wage labour, but will weaken their antagonism and transform it into harmony".[25] In all decisions crucial for society its actions will be irrelevant and it will be forced to fight for both sides in turn but always without consciousness. In so doing its own objectives – which exist exclusively in its own consciousness – must become progressively weakened and increasingly divorced from social action. Ultimately they will assume purely "ideological" forms. The petty bourgeoisie will only be able to play an active role in history as long as these objectives happen to coincide with the real economic interests of capitalism. This was the case with the abolition of the feudal estates during the French Revolution. With the fulfilment of this mission its utterances, which for the most part remain unchanged in form, become more and more remote from real events and turn finally into mere caricatures (this was true, e.g. of the Jacobinism of the Montagne 1848–51).

This isolation from society as a whole has its repercussions on the internal structure of the class and its organisational potential. This can be seen most clearly in the development of the peasantry. Marx says on this point:[26] "The small-holding peasants form a vast mass whose members live in similar conditions but without entering into manifold relations with each other. Their mode of production isolates them from one another instead of bringing them into mutual intercourse. . . . Every single

peasant family . . . thus acquires its means of life more through exchange with nature than in intercourse with society. . . . In so far as millions of families live under economic conditions of existence that separate their mode of life, their interests and their culture from those of other classes and place them in opposition to them, they constitute a class. In so far as there is only a local connection between the small-holding peasants, and the identity of their interests begets no community, no national unity and no political organisation, they do not constitute a class." Hence *external* upheavals, such as war, revolution in the towns, etc. are needed before these masses can coalesce in a unified movement, and even then they are incapable of organising it and supplying it with slogans and a positive direction corresponding to their own interests.

Whether these movements will be progressive (as in the French Revolution of 1789 or the Russian Revolution of 1917), or reactionary (as with Napoleon's coup d'état) will depend on the position of the other classes involved in the conflict, and on the level of consciousness of the parties that lead them. For this reason, too, the *ideological* form taken by the class consciousness of the peasants changes its content more frequently than that of other classes: this is because it is always borrowed from elsewhere. Hence parties that base themselves wholly or in part on this class consciousness always lack really firm and secure support in critical situations (as was true of the Socialist Revolutionaries in 1917 and 1918). This explains why it is possible for peasant conflicts to be fought out under opposing flags. Thus it is highly characteristic of both Anarchism and the "class consciousness" of the peasantry that a number of counter-revolutionary rebellions and uprisings of the middle and upper strata of the peasantry in Russia should have found the anarchist view of society to be a satisfying ideology. We cannot really speak of class consciousness in the case of these classes (if, indeed, we can even speak of them as classes in the strict Marxist sense of the term): for a full consciousness of their situation would reveal to them the hopelessness of their particularist strivings in the face of the inevitable course of events. Consciousness and self-interest then are *mutually incompatible* in this instance. And as class consciousness was defined in terms of the problems of imputing class interests the failure of their class consciousness to develop in the immediately given historical reality becomes comprehensible philosophically.

With the bourgeoisie, also, class consciousness stands in opposition to class interest. But here the antagonism is *not contradictory but dialectical.*

The distinction between the two modes of contradiction may be briefly described in this way: in the case of the other classes, a class consciousness is prevented from emerging by their position within the process of production and the interests this generates. In the case of the bourgeoisie, however, these factors combine to produce a class consciousness but one which is cursed by its very nature with the tragic fate of developing an insoluble contradiction at the very zenith of its powers. As a result of this contradiction it must annihilate itself.

The tragedy of the bourgeoisie is reflected historically in the fact that even before it had defeated its predecessor, feudalism, its new enemy, the proletariat, had appeared on the scene. Politically, it became evident when at the moment of victory, the "freedom", in whose name the bourgeoisie had joined battle with feudalism, was transformed into a new repressiveness. Sociologically, the bourgeoisie did everything in its power to eradicate the fact of class conflict from the consciousness of society, even though class conflict had only emerged in its purity and became established as an historical fact with the advent of capitalism. Ideologically, we see the same contradiction in the fact that the bourgeoisie endowed the individual with an unprecedented importance, but at the same time that same individuality was annihilated by the economic conditions to which it was subjected, by the reification created by commodity production.

All these contradictions, and the list might be extended indefinitely, are only the reflection of the deepest contradictions in capitalism itself as they appear in the consciousness of the bourgeoisie in accordance with their position in the total system of production. For this reason they appear as dialectical contradictions in the class consciousness of the bourgeoisie. They do not merely reflect the inability of the bourgeoisie to grasp the contradictions inherent in its own social order. For, on the one hand, capitalism is the first system of production able to achieve a total economic penetration of society,[27] and this implies that in theory the bourgeoisie should be able to progress from this central point to the possession of an (imputed) class consciousness of the whole system of production. On the other hand, the position held by the capitalist class and the interests which determine its actions ensure that it will be unable to control its own system of production even in theory.

There are many reasons for this. In the first place, it only seems to be true that for capitalism production occupies the centre of class consciousness and hence provides the theoretical starting-point for analysis. With reference to Ricardo "who had been reproached with an exclusive concern with production", Marx emphasised[28] that he "defined distribution as the sole subject of economics". And the detailed analysis of the process by which capital is concretely realised shows in every single instance that the interest of the capitalist (who produces not goods but commodities) is necessarily confined to matters that must be peripheral in terms of production. Moreover, the capitalist, enmeshed in what is for him the decisive process of the expansion of capital, must have a standpoint from which the most important problems become quite invisible.[29]

The discrepancies that result are further exacerbated by the fact that there is an insoluble contradiction running through the internal structure of capitalism between the social and the individual principle, i.e. between the function of capital as private property and its objective economic function. As the *Communist Manifesto* states: "Capital is a social force and not a personal one." But it is a social force whose movements are determined by the individual interests of the owners of capital – who cannot see and who are necessarily indifferent to all the social implications of their activities. Hence the social principle and the social function implicit in capital can only prevail unbeknown to them and, as it were, against their will and behind their backs. Because of this conflict between the individual and the social, Marx rightly characterised the stock companies as the "negation of the capitalist mode of production itself".[30] Of course, it is true that stock companies differ only in inessentials from individual capitalists and even the so-called abolition of the anarchy in production through cartels and trusts only shifts the contradiction elsewhere, without, however, eliminating it. This situation forms one of the decisive factors governing the class consciousness of the bourgeoisie. It is true that the bourgeoisie acts as a class in the objective evolution of society. But it understands the process (which it is itself instigating) as something external which is subject to objective laws which it can only experience passively.

Bourgeois thought observes economic life consistently and necessarily from the standpoint of the

individual capitalist and this naturally produces a
sharp confrontation between the individual and the
overpowering supra-personal "law of nature" which
propels all social phenomena.[31] This leads both to
the antagonism between individual and class interests in the event of conflict (which, it is true, rarely
becomes as acute among the ruling classes as in the
bourgeoisie), and also to the logical impossibility of
discovering theoretical and practical solutions to
the problems created by the capitalist system of
production.

"This sudden reversion from a system of credit
to a system of hard cash heaps theoretical fright on
top of practical panic; and the dealers by whose
agency circulation is effected shudder before the
impenetrable mystery in which their own economic
relations are shrouded."[32] This terror is not unfounded, that is to say, it is much more than the
bafflement felt by the individual capitalist when
confronted by his own individual fate. The facts
and the situations which induce this panic force
something into the consciousness of the bourgeoisie which is too much of a brute fact for its existence to be wholly denied or repressed. But equally
it is something that the bourgeoisie can never fully
understand. For the recognisable background to
this situation is the fact that "the *real barrier* of
capitalist production is *capital itself*".[33] And if this
insight were to become conscious it would indeed
entail the self-negation of the capitalist class.

In this way the objective limits of capitalist production become the limits of the class consciousness of the bourgeoisie. The older "natural" and
"conservative" forms of domination had left un-
molested[34] the forms of production of whole sections of the people they ruled and therefore exerted
by and large a traditional and unrevolutionary influence. Capitalism, by contrast, is a revolutionary
form par excellence. *The fact that it must necessarily
remain in ignorance of the objective economic limitations of its own system expresses itself as an internal,
dialectical contradiction in its class consciousness.*

This means that *formally* the class consciousness
of the bourgeoisie is geared to economic consciousness. And indeed the highest degree of unconsciousness, the crassest form of "false consciousness"
always manifests itself when the conscious mastery
of economic phenomena appears to be at its greatest. From the point of view of the relation of consciousness to society this contradiction is expressed
as the *irreconcilable antagonism between ideology and
economic base*. Its dialectics are grounded in the

irreconcilable antagonism between the (capitalist)
individual, i.e. the stereotyped individual of capitalism, and the "natural" and inevitable process of
development, i.e. the process not subject to consciousness. In consequence theory and practice are
brought into irreconcilable opposition to each other.
But the resulting dualism is anything but stable; in
fact it constantly strives to harmonise principles
that have been wrenched apart and thenceforth
oscillate between a new "false" synthesis and its
subsequent cataclysmic disruption.

This internal dialectical contradiction in the class
consciousness of the bourgeoisie is further aggrav-
ated by the fact that the objective limits of capitalism do not remain purely negative. That is to
say that capitalism does not merely set "natural"
laws in motion that provoke crises which it cannot
comprehend. On the contrary, those limits acquire
a historical embodiment with its own consciousness and its own actions: the proletariat.

Most "normal" shifts of perspective produced
by the capitalist point of view in the image of the
economic structure of society tend to "obscure and
mystify the true origin of surplus value".[35] In the
"normal", purely theoretical view this mystification only attaches to the organic composition of
capital, viz. to the place of the employer in the
productive system and the economic function of
interest, etc., i.e. it does no more than highlight
the failure of observers to perceive the true driving forces that lie beneath the surface. But when
it comes to practice this mystification touches
upon the central fact of capitalist society: the class
struggle.

In the class struggle we witness the emergence
of all the hidden forces that usually lie concealed
behind the façade of economic life, at which the
capitalists and their apologists gaze as though trans-
fixed. These forces appear in such a way that they
cannot possibly be ignored. So much so that even
when capitalism was in the ascendant and the proletariat could only give vent to its protests in the
form of vehement spontaneous explosions, even
the ideological exponents of the rising bourgeoisie
acknowledged the class struggle as a basic fact of
history. (For example, Marat and later historians
such as Mignet.) But in proportion as the theory
and practice of the proletariat made society conscious of this unconscious, revolutionary principle
inherent in capitalism, the bourgeoisie was thrown
back increasingly on to a conscious defensive. The
dialectical contradiction in the "false" consciousness

of the bourgeoisie became more and more acute: the "false" consciousness was converted into a mendacious consciousness. What had been at first an objective contradiction now became subjective also: the theoretical problem turned into a moral posture which decisively influenced every practical class attitude in every situation and on every issue.

Thus the situation in which the bourgeoisie finds itself determines the function of its class consciousness in its struggle to achieve control of society. The hegemony of the bourgeoisie really does embrace the whole of society; it really does attempt to organise the whole of society in its own interests (and in this it has had some success). To achieve this it was forced both to develop a coherent theory of economics, politics and society (which in itself presupposes and amounts to a "Weltanschauung"), and also to make conscious and sustain its faith in its own *mission* to control and organise society. The tragic dialectics of the bourgeoisie can be seen in the fact that it is not only desirable but essential for it to clarify its own class interests on *every particular issue*, while at the same time such a clear awareness becomes fatal when it is extended to *the question of the totality*. The chief reason for this is that the rule of the bourgeoisie can only be the rule of a minority. Its hegemony is exercised not merely *by* a minority but *in the interest* of that minority, so the need to deceive the other classes and to ensure that their class consciousness remains amorphous is inescapable for a bourgeois regime. (Consider here the theory of the state that stands "above" class antagonisms, or the notion of an "impartial" system of justice.)

But the veil drawn over the nature of bourgeois society is indispensable to the bourgeoisie itself. For the insoluble internal contradictions of the system become revealed with increasing starkness and so confront its supporters with a choice. Either they must consciously ignore insights which become increasingly urgent or else they must suppress their own moral instincts in order to be able to support with a good conscience an economic system that serves only their own interests.

Without overestimating the efficacy of such ideological factors it must be agreed that the fighting power of a class grows with its ability to carry out its own mission with a good conscience and to adapt all phenomena to its own interests with unbroken confidence in itself. If we consider Sismondi's criticism of classical economics, German criticisms of natural law and the youthful critiques of Carlyle, it becomes evident that from a very early stage the ideological history of the bourgeoisie was *nothing but a desperate resistance to every insight into the true nature of the society it had created and thus to a real understanding of its class situation.* When the *Communist Manifesto* makes the point that the bourgeoisie produces its own gravediggers this is valid ideologically as well as economically. The whole of bourgeois thought in the nineteenth century made the most strenuous efforts to mask the real foundations of bourgeois society; everything was tried: from the greatest falsifications of fact to the "sublime" theories about the "essence" of history and the state. But in vain: with the end of the century the issue was resolved by the advances of science and their corresponding effects on the consciousness of the capitalist elite.

This can be seen very clearly in the bourgeoisie's greater readiness to accept the idea of conscious organisation. A greater measure of concentration was achieved first in the stock companies and in the cartels and trusts. This process revealed the social character of capital more and more clearly without affecting the general anarchy in production. What it did was to confer near-monopoly status on a number of giant individual capitalists. Objectively, then, the social character of capital was brought into play with great energy but in such a manner as to keep its nature concealed from the capitalist class. Indeed this illusory elimination of economic anarchy successfully diverted their attention from the true situation. With the crises of the War and the post-war period this tendency has advanced still further: the idea of a "planned" economy has gained ground at least among the more progressive elements of the bourgeoisie. Admittedly this applies only within quite narrow strata of the bourgeoisie and even there it is thought of more as a theoretical experiment than as a practical way out of the impasse brought about by the crises.

When capitalism was still expanding it rejected every sort of social organisation on the grounds that it was "an inroad upon such sacred things as the rights of property, freedom and unrestricted play for the initiative of the individual capitalist".[36] If we compare that with current attempts to harmonise a "planned" economy with the class interests of the bourgeoisie, we are forced to admit that what we are witnessing is *the capitulation of the class consciousness of the bourgeoisie before that of the proletariat.* Of course, the section of the bourgeoisie that accepts the notion of a "planned" economy does not mean by it the same as does the proletariat: it regards it as a last attempt to save capitalism by driving its internal contradictions to breaking-point. Nevertheless this means jettisoning the last theoretical line of defence. (As a strange counterpart to this we may note that *at just this point in time* certain sectors of the proletariat *capitulate before the bourgeoisie* and adopt this, the most problematic form of bourgeois organisation.)

With this the whole existence of the bourgeoisie and its culture is plunged into the most terrible crisis. On the one hand, we find the utter sterility of an ideology divorced from life, of a more or less conscious attempt at forgery. On the other hand, a cynicism no less terribly jejune lives on in the world-historical irrelevances and nullities of its own existence and concerns itself only with the defence of that existence and with its own naked self-interest. This ideological crisis is an unfailing sign of decay. The bourgeoisie has already been thrown on the defensive; however aggressive its *weapons* may be, it is fighting for self-preservation. *Its power to dominate has vanished beyond recall.*

4

In this struggle for consciousness historical materialism plays a crucial role. Ideologically no less than economically, the bourgeoisie and the proletariat are mutually interdependent. The same process that the bourgeoisie experiences as a permanent crisis and gradual dissolution appears to the proletariat, likewise in crisis-form, as the gathering of strength and the springboard to victory. Ideologically this means that the same growth of insight into the nature of society, which reflects the protracted death struggle of the bourgeoisie, entails a steady growth in the strength of the proletariat. For the proletariat the truth is a weapon that brings victory; and the more ruthless, the greater the victory. This makes more comprehensible the desperate fury with which bourgeois science assails historical materialism: for as soon as the bourgeoisie is forced to take up its stand on this terrain, it is lost. And, at the same time, this explains why the proletariat and *only* the proletariat can discern in the correct understanding of *the nature of society* a power-factor of the first, and perhaps decisive importance.

The unique function of consciousness in the class struggle of the proletariat has consistently been overlooked by the vulgar Marxists who have substituted a petty "Realpolitik" for the great battle of principle which reaches back to the ultimate problems of the objective economic process. Naturally we do not wish to deny that the proletariat must proceed from the facts of a given situation. But it is to be distinguished from other classes by the fact that it goes beyond the contingencies of history; far from being driven forward by them, it is itself their driving force and impinges centrally upon the process of social change. When the vulgar Marxists detach themselves from this central point of view, i.e. from the point where a proletarian class consciousness arises, *they thereby place themselves on the level of consciousness of the bourgeoisie.* And that the bourgeoisie fighting on its own ground will prove superior to the proletariat both economically and ideologically can come as a surprise only to a vulgar Marxist. Moreover only a vulgar Marxist would infer from this fact, which after all derives exclusively from his own attitude, that the bourgeoisie *generally* occupies the stronger position. For quite apart from the very real force at its disposal, it is self-evident that the bourgeoisie *fighting on its own ground* will be both more experienced and more expert. Nor will it come as a surprise if the bourgeoisie automatically obtains the upper hand when its opponents abandon their own position for that of the bourgeoisie.

As the bourgeoisie has the intellectual, organisational and every other advantage, the superiority of the proletariat must lie exclusively in its ability to see society from the centre, as a coherent whole. This means that it is able to act in such a way as to change reality; in the class consciousness of the proletariat theory and practice coincide and so it can consciously throw the weight of its actions onto the scales of history – and this is the deciding factor. When the vulgar Marxists destroy this unity they cut the nerve that binds proletarian theory to proletarian action. They reduce theory to the "scientific" treatment of the symptoms of social change and as for practice they are themselves reduced to being buffeted about aimlessly and uncontrollably by the various elements of the process they had hoped to master.

The class consciousness that springs from this position must exhibit the same internal structure as that of the bourgeoisie. But when the logic of events drives the same dialectical contradictions to the surface of consciousness the consequences for the proletariat are even more disastrous than for the bourgeoisie. For despite all the dialectical contradictions, despite all its objective falseness, the self-deceiving "false" consciousness that we find in the bourgeoisie is at least in accord with its class situation. It cannot save the bourgeoisie from the constant exacerbation of these contradictions and so from destruction, but it can enable it to continue the struggle and even engineer victories, albeit of short duration.

But in the case of the proletariat such a consciousness not only has to overcome these internal (bourgeois) contradictions, but it also conflicts with the course of action to which the economic situation necessarily commits the proletariat (regardless of its own thoughts on the subject). The proletariat must act in a proletarian manner, but its own vulgar Marxist theory blocks its vision of the right course to adopt. The dialectical contradiction between necessary proletarian action and vulgar Marxist (bourgeois) theory becomes more and more acute. As the decisive battle in the class struggle approaches, the power of a true or false theory to accelerate or retard progress grows in proportion. The "realm of freedom", the end of the "prehistory of mankind" means precisely that the power of the objectified, reified relations between men begins to revert to *man*. The closer this process comes to its goal the more urgent it becomes for the proletariat to understand its own historical mission and the more vigorously and directly proletarian class consciousness will determine each of its actions. For the blind power of the forces at work will only advance "automatically" to their goal of self-annihilation as long as that goal is not within reach. When the moment of transition to the "realm of freedom" arrives this will become apparent just because the blind forces really will hurtle blindly towards the abyss, and only the conscious will of the proletariat will be able to save mankind from the impending catastrophe. In other words, when the final economic crisis of capitalism develops, *the fate of the revolution (and with it the fate of mankind) will depend on the ideological maturity of the proletariat, i.e. on its class consciousness.*

We have now determined the unique function of the class consciousness of the proletariat in contrast to that of other classes. The proletariat cannot liberate itself as a class without simultaneously abolishing class society as such. For that reason its consciousness, the last class consciousness in the history of mankind, must both lay bare the nature of society and achieve an increasingly inward fusion of theory and practice. "Ideology" for the proletariat

is no banner to follow into battle, nor is it a cover for its true objectives: it is the objective and the weapon itself. Every non-principled or unprincipled use of tactics on the part of the proletariat debases historical materialism to the level of mere "ideology" and forces the proletariat to use bourgeois (or petty bourgeois) tactics. It thereby robs it of its greatest strength by forcing class consciousness into the secondary or inhibiting role of a bourgeois consciousness, instead of the active role of a proletarian consciousness.

5

The relationship between class consciousness and class situation is really very simple in the case of the proletariat, but the obstacles which prevent its consciousness being realised in practice are correspondingly greater. In the first place this consciousness is divided within itself. It is true that society as such is highly unified and that it evolves in a unified manner. But in a world where the reified relations of capitalism have the appearance of a natural environment it looks as if there is not a unity but a diversity of mutually independent objects and forces.

The most striking division in proletarian class consciousness and the one most fraught with consequences is the separation of the economic struggle from the political one. Marx repeatedly exposed[37] the fallacy of this split and demonstrated that it is in the nature of every economic struggle to develop into a political one (and vice versa). Nevertheless it has not proved possible to eradicate this heresy from the theory of the proletariat. The cause of this aberration is to be found in the dialectical separation of immediate objectives and ultimate goal and, hence, in the dialectical division within the proletarian revolution itself.

Classes that successfully carried out revolutions in earlier societies had their task made easier *subjectively* by this very fact of the discrepancy between their own class consciousness and the objective economic set-up, i.e. by their very unawareness of their own function in the process of change. They had only to use the power at their disposal to enforce their *immediate* interests while the social import of their actions was hidden from them and left to the "ruse of reason" of the course of events.

But as the proletariat has been entrusted by history with the task of *transforming society consciously*, its class consciousness must develop a dialectical contradiction between its immediate interests and its long-term objectives, and between the discrete factors and the whole. For the discrete factor, the concrete situation with its concrete demands is by its very nature an integral part of the existing capitalist society; it is governed by the laws of that society and is subject to its economic structure. Only when the immediate interests are integrated into a total view and related to the final goal of the process do they become revolutionary, pointing concretely and consciously beyond the confines of capitalist society.

This means that subjectively, i.e. for the class consciousness of the proletariat, the dialectical relationship between immediate interests and objective impact on the whole of society is located *in the consciousness of the proletariat itself.* It does not work itself out as a purely objective process quite apart from all (imputed) consciousness – as was the case with all classes hitherto. Thus the revolutionary victory of the proletariat does not imply, as with former classes, *the immediate realisation of the socially given existence of the class*, but, as the young Marx clearly saw and defined, *its self-annihilation.* The *Communist Manifesto* formulates this distinction in this way: "All the preceding classes that got the upper hand, sought to fortify their already acquired status by subjecting society at large to their conditions of appropriation. The proletarians cannot become masters of the productive forces of society, except *by abolishing their own previous mode of appropriation*, and thereby every other previous mode of appropriation." (My italics.)

This inner dialectic makes it hard for the proletariat to develop its class consciousness in opposition to that of the bourgeoisie which by cultivating the crudest and most abstract kind of empiricism was able to make do with a superficial view of the world. Whereas even when the development of the proletariat was still at a very primitive stage it discovered that one of the elementary rules of class warfare was to advance beyond what was immediately given. (Marx emphasises this as early as his observations on the Weavers' Uprising in Silesia.)[38] For because of its situation this contradiction is introduced directly into the consciousness of the proletariat, whereas the bourgeoisie, from its situation, saw the contradictions confronting it as the outer limits of its consciousness.

Conversely, this contradiction means that "false" consciousness is something very different for the proletariat than for every preceding class. Even correct statements about particular situations or aspects of the development of bourgeois class consciousness reveal, when related to the whole of society, the limits of that consciousness and unmask its "falseness". Whereas the proletariat *always aspires towards the truth* even in its "false" consciousness and in its substantive errors. It is sufficient here to recall the social criticism of the Utopians or the proletarian and revolutionary extension of Ricardo's theory. Concerning the latter, Engels places great emphasis on the fact that it is "formally incorrect economically", but he adds at once: "What is false from a formal economic point of view can be true in the perspective of world history. . . . Behind the formal economic error may lie concealed a very true economic content."[39]

Only with the aid of this distinction can there be any resolution of the contradiction in the class consciousness of the proletariat; only with its aid can that contradiction become a conscious factor in history. For the objective aspiration towards truth which is immanent even in the "false" consciousness of the proletariat does not at all imply that this aspiration can come to light without the active intervention of the proletariat. On the contrary, the mere aspiration towards truth can only strip off the veils of falseness and mature into historically significant and socially revolutionary knowledge by the potentiating of consciousness, by conscious action and conscious self-criticism. Such knowledge would of course be unattainable were it not for the objective aspiration, and here we find confirmation of Marx's dictum that "mankind only ever sets itself tasks which it can accomplish".[40] But the aspiration only *yields the possibility.* The accomplishment can only be the fruit of the *conscious* deeds of the proletariat.

The dialectical cleavage in the consciousness of the proletariat is a product of the same structure that makes the historical mission of the proletariat possible by pointing forward and beyond the existing social order. In the case of the other classes we found an antagonism between the class's self-interest and that of society, between individual deed and social consequences. This antagonism set an external limit to consciousness. Here, in the centre of proletarian class consciousness we discover an antagonism between momentary interest and ultimate goal. The outward victory of the proletariat can only be achieved if this antagonism is inwardly overcome.

As we stressed in the motto to this essay the existence of this conflict enables us to perceive that class consciousness is identical with neither the psychological consciousness of individual members of the proletariat, nor with the (mass-psychological) consciousness of the proletariat as a whole; but it is, on the contrary, *the sense, become conscious, of the historical role of the class.* This sense will objectify in particular interests of the moment which may only be omitted at the price of allowing the proletarian class struggle to slip back into the most primitive Utopianism. Every momentary interest may have either of two functions: either it will be a step towards the ultimate goal or else it will conceal it. Which of the two it will be depends *entirely upon the class consciousness of the proletariat and not on victory or defeat in isolated skirmishes.* Marx drew attention very early on[41] to this danger, which is particularly acute on the economic "trade-union" front: "At the same time the working class ought not to exaggerate to themselves the ultimate consequences of these struggles. They ought not to forget that they are fighting with effects, but not with the causes of those effects . . . , that they are applying palliatives, not curing the malady. They ought, therefore, not to be exclusively absorbed in these unavoidable guerilla fights . . . instead of simultaneously trying to cure it, instead of using their organised forces as a lever for the final emancipation of the working class, that is to say, the ultimate abolition of the wages system."

We see here the source of every kind of opportunism which begins always with effects and not causes, parts and not the whole, symptoms and not the thing itself. It does not regard the particular interest and the struggle to achieve it as a means of education for the final battle whose outcome depends on closing the gap between the psychological consciousness and the imputed one. Instead it regards the particular as a valuable achievement in itself or at least as a step along the path towards the ultimate goal. In a word, opportunism *mistakes the actual, psychological state of consciousness of proletarians for the class consciousness of the proletariat.*

The practical damage resulting from this confusion can be seen in the great loss of unity and cohesiveness in proletarian praxis when compared to the unity of the objective economic tendencies. The superior strength of true, practical class consciousness lies in the ability to look beyond the divisive symptoms of the economic process to the unity of the total social system underlying it. In the age of capitalism it is not possible for the total system to become directly visible in external phenomena. For instance, the economic basis of a world crisis is undoubtedly unified and its coherence can be understood. But its actual appearance in time and space will take the form of a disparate succession of events in different countries at different times and even in different branches of industry in a number of countries.

When bourgeois thought "transforms the different limbs of society into so many separate societies"[42] it certainly commits a grave theoretical error. But the immediate practical consequences are nevertheless in harmony with the interests of capitalism. The bourgeoisie is unable in theory to understand more than the details and the symptoms of economic processes (a failure which will *ultimately* prove its undoing). In the short term, however, it is concerned above all to impose its mode of life upon the day-to-day actions of the proletariat. In this respect (and in this respect alone) its superiority in organisation is clearly visible, while the wholly different organisation of the proletariat, *its capacity for being organised as a class,* cannot become effective.

The further the economic crisis of capitalism advances, the more clearly this unity in the economic process becomes *comprehensible in practice.* It was there, of course, in so-called periods of normality, too, and was therefore visible from the class standpoint of the proletariat, but the gap between appearance and ultimate reality was too great for that unity to have any practical consequences for proletarian action.

In periods of crisis the position is quite different. The unity of the economic process now moves within reach. So much so that even capitalist theory cannot remain wholly untouched by it, though it can never fully adjust to it. In this situation the fate of the proletariat, and hence of the whole future of humanity, hangs on whether or not it will take *the step that has now become objectively possible.* For even if the particular symptoms of crisis appear separately (according to country, branch of industry, in the form of "economic" or "political" crisis, etc.), and even if in consequence the reflex of the crisis is fragmented in the immediate psychological consciousness of the workers, it is still possible and necessary to advance beyond this consciousness. And this is *instinctively* felt to be a necessity by larger and larger sections of the proletariat.

Opportunism had – as it seemed – merely served to inhibit the objective tendency until the crisis became acute. Now, however, it adopts a *course directly opposed to it.* Its aim now is to scotch the development of proletarian class consciousness in its progress from that which is merely given to that which conforms to the objective total process; even more, it hopes *to reduce the class consciousness of the proletariat to the level of* the psychologically given and thus to divert into the opposite direction what had hitherto been the purely instinctive tendency. As long as the unification of proletarian class consciousness was not a practical possibility this theory could – with some charity – be regarded as a mere error. But in this situation it takes on the character of a conscious deception (regardless of whether its advocates are psychologically conscious of this or not). In contrast with the right instincts of the proletariat it plays the same role as that played hitherto by capitalist theory: it denounces the correct view of the overall economic situation and the correct class consciousness of the proletariat together with its organised form, the Communist Party, as something unreal and inimical to the "true" interests of the workers (i.e. their immediate, national or professional interests) and as something alien to their "genuine" class consciousness (i.e. that which is psychologically given).

To say that class consciousness has no psychological reality does not imply that it is a mere fiction. Its reality is vouched for by its ability to explain the infinitely painful path of the proletarian revolution, with its many reverses, its constant return to its starting-point and the incessant self-criticism of which Marx speaks in the celebrated passage in *The Eighteenth Brumaire.*

Only the consciousness of the proletariat can point to the way that leads out of the impasse of capitalism. As long as this consciousness is lacking, the crisis remains permanent, it goes back to its starting-point, repeats the cycle until after infinite sufferings and terrible detours the school of history completes the education of the proletariat and confers upon it the leadership of mankind. But the proletariat is not given any choice. As Marx says, it must become a class not only "as against capital" but also "for itself";[43] that is to say, the class struggle must be raised from the level of economic necessity to the level of conscious aim and effective class consciousness. The pacifists and humanitarians of the class struggle whose efforts tend whether they will or no to retard this lengthy, painful and crisis-ridden process would be horrified if they could but see what sufferings they inflict on the proletariat by extending this course of education. But the pro-

letariat cannot abdicate its mission. The only question at issue is how much it has to suffer before it achieves ideological maturity, before it acquires a true understanding of its class situation and a true class consciousness.

Of course this uncertainty and lack of clarity are themselves the symptoms of the crisis in bourgeois society. As the product of capitalism the proletariat must necessarily be subject to the modes of existence of its creator. This mode of existence is inhumanity and reification. No doubt the very existence of the proletariat implies criticism and the negation of this form of life. But until the objective crisis of capitalism has matured and until the proletariat has achieved true class consciousness, and the ability to understand the crisis fully, it cannot go beyond the criticism of reification and so it is only negatively superior to its antagonist. Indeed, if it can do no more than negate some aspects of capitalism, if it cannot at least aspire to a critique of the whole, then it will not even achieve a negative superiority. This applies to the petty-bourgeois attitudes of most trade unionists. Such criticism from the standpoint of capitalism can be seen most strikingly in the separation of the various theatres of war. The bare fact of separation itself indicates that the consciousness of the proletariat is still fettered by reification. And if the proletariat finds the economic inhumanity to which it is subjected easier to understand than the political, and the political easier than the cultural, then all these separations point to the extent of the still unconquered power of capitalist forms of life in the proletariat itself.

The reified consciousness must also remain hopelessly trapped in the two extremes of crude empiricism and abstract utopianism. In the one case, consciousness becomes either a completely passive observer moving in obedience to laws which it can never control. In the other it regards itself as a power which is able of its own – subjective – volition to master the essentially meaningless motion of objects. We have already identified the crude empiricism of the opportunists in its relation to proletarian class consciousness. We must now go on to see utopianism as characteristic of the internal divisions within class consciousness. (The separation of empiricism from utopianism undertaken here for purely methodological reasons should not be taken as an admission that the two cannot occur together in particular trends and even individuals. On the contrary, they are frequently found together and are joined by an internal bond.)

The philosophical efforts of the young Marx were largely directed towards the refutation of the various false theories of consciousness (including both the "idealism" of the Hegelian School and the "materialism" of Feuerbach) and towards the discovery of a correct view of the role of consciousness in history. As early as the Correspondence of 1843 [with Ruge] he conceives of consciousness as immanent in history. Consciousness does not lie outside the real process of history. It does not have to be introduced into the world by philosophers; therefore to gaze down arrogantly upon the petty struggles of the world and to despise them is indefensible. "We only show it [the world] what its struggles are about and consciousness is a thing that it must needs acquire whether it will or not." What is needed then is only "to explain its own actions to it".[44] The great polemic against Hegel in *The Holy Family* concentrates mainly on this point.[45] Hegel's inadequacy is that he only seems to allow the absolute spirit to make history. The resulting otherworldliness of consciousness *vis-à-vis* the real events of history becomes, in the hands of Hegel's disciples, an arrogant – and reactionary – confrontation of "spirit" and "mass". Marx mercilessly exposes the flaws and absurdities and the reversions to a pre-Hegelian stage implicit in this approach.

Complementing this is his – aphoristic – critique of Feuerbach. The materialists had elaborated a view of consciousness as of something appertaining to this world. Marx sees it as merely one stage in the process, the stage of "bourgeois society". He opposes to it the notion of consciousness as "practical critical activity" with the task of "changing the world".

This provides us with the philosophical foundation we need to settle accounts with the utopians. For their thought contains this very duality of social process and the consciousness of it. Consciousness approaches society from another world and leads it from the false path it has followed back to the right one. The utopians are prevented by the undeveloped nature of the proletarian movement from seeing the true bearer of historical movement in history itself, in the way the proletariat organises itself as a class and, hence, in the class consciousness of the proletariat. They are not yet able to "take note of what is happening before their very eyes and to become its mouthpiece".[46]

It would be foolish to believe that this criticism and the recognition that a post–utopian attitude to history has become *objectively possible* means that utopianism can be dismissed as a factor in the proletariat's struggle for freedom. This is true only for those stages of class consciousness that have really achieved the unity of theory and practice described by Marx, the real and practical intervention of class consciousness in the course of history and hence the practical understanding of reification. And this did not all happen at a single stroke and in a coherent manner. For there are not merely national and "social" stages involved but there are also gradations within the class consciousness of workers in the same strata. The separation of economics from politics is the most revealing and also the most important instance of this. It appears that some sections of the proletariat have quite the right instincts as far as the economic struggle goes and can even raise them to the level of class consciousness. At the same time, however, when it comes to political questions they manage to persist in a completely utopian point of view. It does not need to be emphasised that there is no question here of a mechanical duality. The utopian view of the function of politics must impinge dialectically on their views about economics and, in particular, on their notions about the economy as a totality (as, for example, in the Syndicalist theory of revolution). In the absence of a real understanding of the interaction between politics and economics a war against the whole economic system, to say nothing of its reorganisation, is quite out of the question.

The influence enjoyed even today by such completely utopian theories as those of Ballod or of guild-socialism shows the extent to which utopian thought is still prevalent, even at a level where the direct life-interests of the proletariat are most nearly concerned and where the present crisis makes it possible to read off from history the correct course of action to be followed.

This syndrome must make its appearance even more blatantly where it is not yet possible to see society as a whole. This can be seen at its clearest in purely ideological questions, in questions of culture. These questions occupy an almost wholly isolated position in the consciousness of the proletariat; the organic bonds connecting these issues with the immediate life-interests of the proletariat as well as with society as a whole have not even begun to penetrate its consciousness. The achievement in this area hardly ever goes beyond the self-criticism of capitalism – carried out here by the proletariat. What is positive here in theory and practice is almost entirely utopian.

These gradations are, then, on the one hand, objective historical necessities, nuances in the objective possibilities of consciousness (such as the relative cohesiveness of politics and economics in comparison to cultural questions). On the other hand, where consciousness already exists as an objective possibility, they indicate degrees of distance between the psychological class consciousness and the adequate understanding of the total situation. *These* gradations, however, can no longer be referred back to socio-economic causes. *The objective theory of class consciousness is the theory of its objective possibility.* The stratification of the problems and economic interests *within* the proletariat is, unfortunately, almost wholly unexplored, but research would undoubtedly lead to discoveries of the very first importance. But however useful it would be to produce a typology of the various strata, we would still be confronted at every turn with the problem of whether it is actually possible to make the objective possibility of class consciousness into a reality. Hitherto this question could only occur to extraordinary individuals (consider Marx's completely non-utopian prescience with regard to the problems of dictatorship). Today it has become a real and relevant question for a whole class: the question of the inner transformation of the proletariat, of its development to the stage of its own objective historical mission. It is an ideological crisis which must be solved before a practical solution to the world's economic crisis can be found.

In view of the great distance that the proletariat has to travel ideologically it would be disastrous to foster any illusions. But it would be no less disastrous to overlook the forces at work within the proletariat which are tending towards the ideological defeat of capitalism. Every proletarian revolution has created workers' councils in an increasingly radical and conscious manner. When this weapon increases in power to the point where it becomes the organ of state, this is a sign that the class consciousness of the proletariat is on the verge of overcoming the bourgeois outlook of its leaders.

The revolutionary workers' council (not to be confused with its opportunist caricatures) is one of the forms which the consciousness of the proletariat has striven to create ever since its inception. The fact that it exists and is constantly developing shows that the proletariat already stands on the threshold of its own consciousness and hence on the threshold of victory. The workers' council spells the political and economic defeat of reification. In the period following the dictatorship it will eliminate the bourgeois separation of the legislature, administration and judiciary. During the struggle for control its mission is twofold. On the one hand, it must overcome the fragmentation of the proletariat in time and space, and on the other, it has to bring economics and politics together into the true synthesis of proletarian praxis. In this way it will help to reconcile the dialectical conflict between immediate interests and ultimate goal.

Thus we must never overlook the distance that separates the consciousness of even the most revolutionary worker from the authentic class consciousness of the proletariat. But even this situation can be explained on the basis of the Marxist theory of class struggle and class consciousness. *The proletariat only perfects itself by annihilating and transcending itself, by creating the classless society through the successful conclusion of its own class struggle.* The struggle for this society, in which the dictatorship of the proletariat is merely a phase, is not just a battle waged against an external enemy, the bourgeoisie. It is equally the struggle of the proletariat *against itself*: against the devastating and degrading effects of the capitalist system upon its class consciousness. The proletariat will only have won the real victory when it has overcome these effects within itself. The separation of the areas that should be united, the diverse stages of consciousness which the proletariat has reached in the various spheres of activity are a precise index of what has been achieved and what remains to be done. The proletariat must not shy away from self-criticism, for victory can only be gained by the truth and self-criticism must, therefore, be its natural element.

Notes

1. *Feuerbach and the End of Classical German Philosophy*, S.W. II, pp. 354 ff.
2. *Capital* I, p. 75.
3. And also of the "pessimism" which *perpetuates* the present state of affairs and represents it as the uttermost limit of human development just as much as does "optimism". In this respect (and in this respect alone) Hegel and Schopenhauer are on a par with each other.
4. *The Poverty of Philosophy*, p. 135.
5. Ibid., p. 117.
6. Ibid., p. 122.
7. *Capital* I, p. 75 (my italics). Cf. also Engels, *The Origin of the Family, Private Property and the State*, S.W. II, pp. 292–3.
8. *Capital* I, p. 766. Cf. also *Wage Labour and Capital*, S.W. II, p. 83; on machines see *The Poverty of Philosophy*, p. 149; on money, ibid., p. 89, etc.

9. *Dokumente des Sozialismus* II, p. 76.
10. *The Poverty of Philosophy*, p. 112.
11. In this context it is unfortunately not possible to discuss in greater detail some of the ramifications of these ideas in Marxism, e.g. the very important category of the "economic persona". Even less can we pause to glance at the relation of historical materialism to comparable trends in bourgeois thought (such as Max Weber's ideal types).
12. This is the point from which to gain an historical understanding of the great utopians such as Plato or Sir Thomas More. Cf. also Marx on Aristotle, *Capital* I, pp. 59–60.
13. "But although ignorant of this, yet he says it," Marx says of Franklin, *Capital* I, p. 51. And similarly: "They know not what they do, but they do it." Ibid., p. 74.
14. *Wages, Price and Profit*, S.W. I, pp. 388–9.
15. Engels, *Umriss zu einer Kritik der Nationalökonomie*, Nachlass I, p. 449.
16. *Capital* I, p. 358.
17. *Capital* III, p. 770 (my italics).
18. *Capital* I, pp. 358–9. This probably explains the politically reactionary role played by merchants' capital as opposed to industrial capital in the beginnings of capitalism. Cf. *Capital* III, p. 322.
19. *Capital* I, pp. 135–6.
20. Marx and Engels repeatedly emphasise the naturalness of these social formations, *Capital* I, pp. 339, 351, etc. The whole structure of evolution in Engels' *Origin of the Family* is based on this idea. I cannot enter here into the controversies on this issue – controversies involving Marxists too; I should just like to stress that here also I consider the views of Marx and Engels to be more profound and historically more correct than those of their "improvers".
21. Cf. *Capital* I, p. 339.
22. *Die soziale Funktion der Rechtsinstitute*, Marx-Studien, Vol. I.
23. *A Contribution to the Critique of Political Economy*, p. 302.
24. *The Eighteenth Brumaire of Louis Bonaparte*, S.W. I, p. 252.
25. Ibid., p. 249.
26. Ibid., pp. 302–3.
27. But no more than the tendency. It is Rosa Luxemburg's great achievement to have shown that this is not just a passing phase but that capitalism can only survive – economically – while it moves society in the direction of capitalism but has not yet fully penetrated it. This economic self-contradiction of any purely capitalist society is undoubtedly one of the reasons for the contradictions in the class consciousness of the bourgeoisie.
28. *A Contribution to the Critique of Political Economy*, p. 285.

29. *Capital* III, pp. 136, 307–8, 318, etc. It is self-evident that the different groups of capitalists, such as industrialists and merchants, etc., are differently placed; but the distinctions are not relevant in this context.
30. Ibid., p. 428.
31. On this point cf. the essay "The Marxism of Rosa Luxemburg".
32. *A Contribution to the Critique of Political Economy*, p. 198.
33. *Capital* III, pp. 245 and also 252.
34. This applies also to e.g. primitive forms of hoarding (see *Capital* I, p. 131) and even to certain expressions of (what is relatively) "pre-capitalist" merchants' capital. Cf. *Capital* III, p. 329.
35. *Capital* III, pp. 165 and also 151, 373–6, 383, etc.
36. *Capital* I, p. 356.
37. *The Poverty of Philosophy*, p. 197. Letters and extracts from letters to F. A. Sorge and others, p. 42, etc.
38. Nachlass II, p. 54. [Kritische Randglossen zu dem Artikel: Der König von Preussen und die Sozialreform.]
39. Preface to *The Poverty of Philosophy*, p. 197.
40. *A Contribution to the Critique of Political Economy*, p. 12.
41. *Wages, Price and Profit*, S.W. I, pp. 404–5.
42. *The Poverty of Philosophy*, pp. 123–4.
43. Ibid., p. 195.
44. Nachlass I, p. 382. [Correspondence with Ruge 1843.]
45. Cf. the essay "What is Orthodox Marxism?"
46. *The Poverty of Philosophy*, p. 140. Cf. also the *Communist Manifesto*, S.W. I, pp. 58–9.

References

Nachlass = *Aus dem literarischen Nachlass von Karl Marx, Friedrich Engels und Ferdinand Lasalle*. Stuttgart: Herausgegeben von Franz Mehring (4 vols.), 1902.

S.W. = Marx/Engels, *Selected Works* (2 vols.). London: Lawrence and Wishart, 1950.

Lukacs, Georg. 1957. "What is Orthodox Marxism?" trans. Michael Harrington. *New International*, Summer.

Lukacs, Georg. 1971. "The Marxism of Rosa Luxemburg." In Georg Lukacs, *History and Class Consciousness: Studies in Marxist Dialectics*, trans. Rodney Livingstone. Cambridge, Mass.: MIT Press.

Marx, Karl. 1961/1962. *Capital* (3 vols.). Moscow: Foreign Language Publishing House.

Marx, Karl. n.d. *The Poverty of Philosophy*. Moscow: Foreign Languages Publishing House.

Marx, Karl and Engels, Friedrich. 1904. *A Contribution to a Critique of Political Economy*, trans. N. I. Stone. New York and London.

13

Class Consciousness in History

E. J. Hobsbawm

The title of this series of lectures is taken from the well-known but largely unread book by George Lukács, *History and Class Consciousness*, a collection of studies published in 1923, strongly criticized within the Communist movement, and virtually unobtainable for some thirty or forty years thereafter. In fact, since no English version of it was in print until recently, it is still little more than a title to most people in this country. My task in this introductory lecture is, however, rather wider than that of providing a simple commentary or crib to Lukács's book. I want to reflect, as a historian, on the nature and role of class consciousness in history, on the assumption that we are all agreed about one basic proposition: that social classes, class conflict and class consciousness exist and play a role in history. We may well disagree on what role they play, or on its importance, but for the sake of the present argument further general agreement is not necessary. Nevertheless, in fairness both to the subject and to the thinker whose name is so obviously associated with it, I ought perhaps to begin by explaining where my own reflections connect with Lukács's own extremely interesting argument (which is, of course, derived from Marx) and where they do not.

As most people with a moderate acquaintance with Marxism know, there is a certain ambiguity in Marx's treatment of social classes, which is perhaps due to the fact that he never wrote systematically about this subject. The manuscript of *Capital* breaks off at the very point where this systematic exposition was due to begin, so that Chapter 52 of Volume III of *Capital* on Classes cannot even be considered an outline or torso. Elsewhere Marx used the term "class" in two rather different senses,

according to context. First, it could stand for those broad aggregates of people which can be classified together by an objective criterion – because they stand in a similar relationship to the means of production – and more especially the groupings of exploiters and exploited which, for purely economic reasons, are found in all human societies beyond the primitive communal and, as Marx would argue, until the triumph of proletarian revolution. "Class" is used in this sense in the celebrated opening passage of the *Communist Manifesto* ("The history of all hitherto existing society is the history of class struggles") and for the general purposes of what we might call Marx's macro-theory. I do not claim that this simple formulation exhausts the meaning of "class" in the first sense of Marx's usage, but it will at least serve to distinguish it from the second sense, which introduces a subjective element into the concept of class – namely, *class consciousness*. For the purposes of the historian, i.e. the student of micro-history, or of history "as it happened" (and of the present "as it happens") as distinct from the general and rather abstract models of the historical transformation of societies, class and the problem of class consciousness are inseparable. "Class" in the full sense only comes into existence at the historical moment when classes begin to acquire consciousness of themselves as such. It is no accident that the *locus classicus* of Marx's discussion of class consciousness is a piece of contemporary history, dealing in years, months, or even weeks and days – namely, that work of genius, *The Eighteenth Brumaire of Louis Bonaparte*. The two senses of "class" are not, of course, in conflict. Each has its place in Marx's thought.

Lukács's treatment, if I understand him correctly, starts with this duality. He distinguishes between the objective fact of class and the theoretical deductions from this which could be and/or which are drawn by men. But he makes a further distinction: between the *actual* ideas which men form about class, and which are the subject matter of historical study[1] and what he calls "ascribed" (*zugerechnetes*) class consciousness. This consists of "the ideas, sentiments, etc., which men in a given situation of life *would* have, *if they were able to grasp in its entirety* this situation, and the interests deriving from it, both as regards immediate action and as regards the structure of society which (would) correspond to those interests".[2] In other words, it is what, let us say, an ideally rational bourgeois or proletarian would think. It is a theoretical construct, based on a theoretical model of society, and not an empirical generalization about what people actually think. Lukács further argues that in different classes the "distance" between actual and ascribed class consciousness is larger or smaller, and may be so large as to constitute not only a difference of degree, but one of kind.

Lukács derives some very interesting ideas from this distinction, but these are not my concern here. I do not say that the historian *qua* historian must only be concerned with the actual facts. If he is a Marxist or indeed if he tries to answer any of the really significant questions about the historical transformations of society in any way, he must also have at the back of his mind a theoretical model of societies and transformations, and the contrast between actual and rational behaviour cannot but concern him, if only because he must be concerned with the historical effectiveness of the actions and ideas he studies, which – at least up to and including the era of bourgeois society – do not normally correspond to the intentions of the individuals and organizations which undertake them or hold them. For instance, it is important to note – as Lukács and Marx did, incidentally – that the class consciousness of peasants is normally quite ineffective, except when organized and led by non-peasants with non-peasant ideas; and why this is so. Or it is important to note the divergence between the actual, i.e. observable class consciousness of proletarians, which is programmatically rather modest, and the kind of wider class consciousness not merely "ascribable" (in the Lukácsian sense) to them, but actually embodied in the working class through the socialist labour movements which this class devel-

oped. However, though historians cannot overlook such matters, they are naturally more concerned professionally with what actually happened (including what might under specified circumstances have happened), than they are with what ought really to happen. I shall therefore leave aside much of Lukács's discussion as irrelevant to my purpose, which is the rather modest one of the historian.

The first point I wish to make is one which was also made by both Marx and Lukács. While classes in the objective sense can be said to have existed ever since the break-up of a society based essentially on kinship, class consciousness is a phenomenon of the modern industrial era. This is familiar to historians, who have often traced the transition from the pre-industrial concept of "rank" or "estate" to the modern one of "class", from such terms as "the populace" or "the labouring poor" to "the proletariat" or "the working class" (via the intermediate "the working classes"), and the, historically slightly earlier, formation of such terms as "middle class" or "bourgeoisie" out of the old "middle rank(s) of society". In Western Europe this change occurred roughly in the first half of the nineteenth century, probably before 1830–40. Why is class consciousness so late to emerge?

In my view Lukács's argument is persuasive. He points out that economically speaking all precapitalist societies have incomparably less cohesion as a single entity than the capitalist economy. Their various parts are far more independent of one another, their mutual economic dependence far less. The smaller the role of commodity exchange in an economy, the more parts of society are either economically self-sufficient (like the parts of the rural economy) or have no particular economic function except perhaps parasitic consumption (as in classical antiquity), the more distant, indirect, "unreal" are the links between what people actually experience as economy, polity or society, and what actually constitutes the wider economic, political, etc. framework within which they operate.[3]

Contrariwise, one might add, the relatively few and numerically small strata whose actual experience coincides with this larger framework may develop something like a class consciousness much sooner than the rest. This is true, for instance, of nobility and gentry, who are few in number, interrelated, and who function in part through their direct relationship to institutions which express or symbolize society as a whole – such as king, the court, parliament, etc. I note in passing that some historians have used this phenomenon as an argument against Marxist interpretations of class and class struggles in history. As will be evident, it is in fact specifically provided for in Marxist analysis.

In other words, under capitalism class is an immediate and in some sense a directly *experienced* historical reality, whereas in pre-capitalist epochs it may merely be an analytical construct which makes sense of a complex of facts otherwise inexplicable. This distinction must not, of course, be confused with the more familiar Marxist proposition that in the course of capitalist development class structure is simplified and polarized until, in extreme cases such as Britain at some periods, one can operate in practice with a simple two-class system of "middle class" and "working class". This may also be true, but that is part of another line of thought. Incidentally, it does not imply, and Marx never suggested that it implied, a perfect homogeneity of each class. For certain purposes we need not trouble about their internal heterogeneities, as, for instance, when defining certain crucial relations between classes, such as that between employers and workers. For other purposes we cannot leave them out of account. Neither Marx nor Engels neglected the social complexities, stratifications, etc., within classes in their directly historical writings or their analyses of contemporary politics. However, this is by the way.

If we try to look at the consciousness of social strata in the pre-capitalist epochs, we therefore find a situation of some complexity. At the top we have groups such as the high aristocracy which come close to class consciousness on the modern scale, i.e. on what, using an anachronism, we might call the "national" scale (the scale of the large state), or even in some respects the international scale. However, it is highly likely that even in such cases of "class consciousness" the criterion of self-definition will be primarily non-economic, whereas in modern classes it is primarily economic. It may be impossible to be a noble without holding land and dominating peasants, and abstaining from manual labour, but these characteristics would not be enough to define a noble to the satisfaction of a medieval society. This would require also kinship ("blood"), special legal status and privileges, a special relationship to the king, or various others.

At the bottom of the social hierarchy, on the other hand, the criteria of social definition are either too narrow or too global for class consciousness. In one sense they may be entirely localized, since the village community, the district, or some other limited area is in fact the only *real* society and economy that matters, the rest of the world making only remote and occasional incursions into it. So far as men living in such circumstances are concerned, the man from the next valley may not merely be a foreigner, but an enemy, however similar his social situation. Political programmes and perspectives are by definition localized. I was once told by a political organizer in Latin America who worked among Indians: "It is no use telling them the tiller has a right to the soil. What they understand is only this: 'You have a right to this piece of land which belonged to your community in your grandfather's day and which has since been stolen from you by the landlords. Now you can claim it back.'" Yet in another sense these criteria may be so general and universal as to exclude any properly social self-classification. Peasants may be so convinced that all the world, except for a marginal few, consists of them, that they may merely define themselves as "people" or (as in Russian language) "Christians". (This leads to unconscious historical ironies, such as that of the revolutionary atheist libertarian leader in Andalusia who told his defeated comrades, "Every Christian had better hide in the hills" or the Red Army sergeant who was overheard during the last war addressing his platoon as "True Believers".) Or else they may simply define themselves as "countrymen" against the cities (*campesinos, contadinos, paysans*). One might argue that the well-known affinity of peasants for millennial or messianic movements reflects this social reality. The unit of their organized action is either the parish pump or the universe. There is nothing in between.

Once again confusion must be avoided. What I have been talking about is the absence of a specific class consciousness. This is *not* the same as that low degree of class consciousness which Marx and other observers have noted, e.g. among the peasantry in the capitalist era. Marx ascribed this, at any rate in the case of nineteenth-century France, to the fact that being a peasant implied being exactly like a great many other peasants, but lacking mutual economic relationships with them.[4] Each peasant household is, economically speaking, largely isolated from the others. This may well be true under capitalist conditions, and it may help to distinguish peasants as a class from workers as a class, for concentration in groups of mutual co-operation is the basic social reality of proletarian existence. Marx's argument suggests, in my view correctly and fruitfully, that there are degrees of class cohesion. As Theodore Shanin once put it,[5] the peasantry is "a class of low classness", and conversely one might say that the industrial proletariat is a class of extremely high "classness". (It is, after all, the only class which has developed genuine political mass movements held together specifically and primarily by class consciousness, e.g. as "parties of the working class" – Labour parties, *Partis Ouvriers*, etc.)

However, the point I have noted about precapitalist societies is not this, but a different one. In such societies, it may be suggested, the social consciousness of the "lower ranks" or subaltern classes will be fragmented into local or other segments even when their social reality is one of economic and social co-operation and mutual aid, as is the case in several kinds of village community. There will frequently be not high or low "classness", but, in the sense of consciousness, no "classness" at all, beyond the miniature scale. Alternatively, it may be suggested, the unity felt by the subaltern groups will be so global as to go beyond class and state. There will not be peasants, but "people" or "countrymen"; there will be not workers, but an indiscriminate "common people" or "labouring poor", distinguished from the rich merely by poverty, from the idle (whether rich or poor) by the compulsion to live by the sweat of their brow, and from the powerful by the unspoken or explicit corollary of weakness and helplessness.

Between the top and the bottom of the preindustrial social hierarchies, we find a conglomerate of local, sectional and other groups, each with its multiple horizons, and far too complex for cursory analysis, or for that matter for more than the rarest common action on the "national" scale. Within a locality, such as a city state, these may in fact be profitably analysed in terms of class and class struggles, as indeed contemporaries and historians have habitually done from the days of the ancient Greek cities. However, even here the realities of socio-economic stratification are likely to be overlaid, in the minds of men, by the non-economic – e.g. the legal – classifications which tend to prevail in such societies. This is obvious where the new reality of a society divided frankly by economics comes into conflict with the old models of a hierarchically stratified society, the reality of socio-economic transformation with the ideal of socio-economic fixity. Then we can see the conflicting criteria of social consciousness locked in battle, e.g. the declining corporate or guild consciousness of journeymen craftsmen and the rising class consciousness of proletarians, skilled or otherwise. How far such consciousness of status (which is, of course, itself economic, in so far as legal or quasi-legal privilege implies economic advantage) persists or can revive under modern capitalism is an interesting subject for enquiry, which I cannot pursue. Lukács has a few suggestive observations on this point, to which I draw your attention.[6]

Can we therefore say that class consciousness is absent from pre-capitalist societies? Not entirely, for even if we leave aside the history of small and locally enclosed communities such as city states, and the special case of ruling classes, we encounter two types of social movement which plainly operate on a more than local and less than ecumenical scale. These are, first, those of the "common people" or "labouring poor" against the "top people" ("When Adam delved and Eve span, who was then the gentleman?") and, second, the phenomenon of peasant wars, sometimes actually recognized and named as such by contemporaries. The absence of class consciousness in the modern sense does not imply the absence of classes and class conflict. But it is evident that in the modern economy this changes quite fundamentally.

How? Let me begin with a general but very significant observation. The scale of modern class consciousness is wider than in the past, but it is essentially "national" and not global: that is to say it operates within the frameworks of the territorial states which, in spite of the marked development of a single interdependent world economy, have remained to this day the main units of economic development. In this sense our situation is still analogous to that of pre-capitalist societies though on a higher level. The decisive aspects of economic reality may be global, but the *palpable*, the experienced economic reality, the things which directly and obviously affect the lives and livelihoods of people, are those of Britain, the USA, France, etc. It is not impossible that we may today be entering the era of a directly global economy. Some numerically small strata of the population do indeed already function internationally, subject to linguistic limitations, as, for instance, scientists and some other types of academics, a fact both expressed and symbolized by their rapid movement between jobs in different parts of the world. However, for most people this is not yet the case, and indeed in important ways the increasing management of the economy and of social affairs by governments has intensified the national character of social consciousness. To this extent global classes are still the same sort of theoretical constructs as they were in pre-capitalist days, except at rare moments of global revolutionary ferment. The real and effective classes are national. The links of "international solidarity" between French and British workers, or even between their socialist movements, are far more tenuous than the links which bind British workers to one another.

Within these limits, what of the consciousness of the different classes? I do not want to go through the list of the classes and strata which historians and sociologists might or might not agree to recognize as the major ones. Instead, I wish to draw your attention to two aspects of the problem.

The first is the question of the relation between class consciousness and socio-economic reality. There are "class" slogans and programmes which have very little chance of realization, because they run dead against the current of history, and others which are more practicable, because they run with it. Peasant movements and those of the classical petty bourgeoisie of small artisans, shopkeepers, petty entrepreneurs, etc., belong to the first kind. Politically these strata may be extremely formidable, because of their numerical strength or for other reasons, but historically they are inevitable victims, even when they ensure the victory of whatever cause they attach themselves to. At most they may become powerful sectional vested interests of negation, and even these have rather limited strength in countries where the dominant economic or political forces are extremely dynamic. The immense political strength of the North American farmers and small towns has not significantly slowed down the decline of either the farmers as a class, or the economic concentration against which the Populists fought so strenuously. The Nazis, who were borne to power on the mass mobilization of such strata, and some of whom actually tried to some extent to realize their programme, turned out to be a régime of monopolist and state capitalism, not because they set out to be, but because the programme of the "little man" was simply a non-starter. If the socialist perspectives of the working-class movement are

excluded, then the only alternative in western industrial states is a régime of big business-cum-big government.

The relation between peasant movements and the régimes they have brought to power in the twentieth century is analogous. These revolutions, as Eric Wolf has pointed out, have been victorious primarily because they have mobilized the peasantry, and above all the most traditionally-minded strata of the peasantry.[7] Yet the actual social outcome of these transformations has been very different from the aspirations of the peasants who made them possible, even when they received the land. History has more than confirmed the Marxists against the Narodniks: post-revolutionary systems have not been constructed on the foundations of the pre-capitalist village communities, but on its ruins. (However, it is only fair to add that they confirmed the Narodniks against some of the Marxists on another point: the most effective rural revolutionaries have been neither the proto-capitalist *kulaks* nor the proletarianized village labourers, but the middle peasantry.)

More interesting than such cases of what might be called blind-alley class consciousness is the situation of classes whose relation to social reality changes. The case of the bourgeoisie is both instructive and familiar. Around, say, 1860, bourgeois class consciousness, even in an unsophisticated form, did in fact reflect and – at a very superficial level – explain the reality of bourgeois society. In 1960 this was plainly not so any longer, even though our society can still be described as capitalist. We can still read the sort of opinions which every good Liberal *pater-familias* took for granted at the time Lincoln was assassinated, mostly in the leader columns of the *Daily Telegraph* and the speeches of a few back-bench Conservative MPs. They are indeed still taken for granted in good suburban homes. It is patent that today these views have about as much relation to reality as the speeches of William Jennings Bryan about the Bible. Conversely, it is today evident that the pure programme of nineteenth-century economic liberalism, as put forward, say, in the Presidential campaign of Barry Goldwater in 1964, is as unrealizable as the peasant or petty-bourgeois utopias. The difference between them is that the Goldwater ideology did once serve to transform the world economy, but no longer does so, whereas the other ideologies of the "little men" never did. In brief, the development of capitalism has left its former carrier, the bourgeoisie, behind. The contradiction between the social nature of production and the private nature of appropriation in this system has always existed, but was (economically speaking) secondary up to a certain point. Unrestricted competitive private enterprise by owner-managed family firms and state abstention was not merely an ideal, or even a social reality, but at a certain stage the most effective model for the rapid economic growth of industrial economies. Today the contradiction is dramatic and obvious. The capitalism of vast corporations intertwined with vast states remains a system of private appropriation, and its basic problems arise from this fact. However, even in its ordinary business operations it finds the economic liberalism of the nineteenth century quite irrelevant, and the class which carried it, the classical bourgeoisie, unnecessary.

The point I wish to make is this. Some forms of class consciousness, and the ideologies based on them, are, as it were, in tune with historical development, and others not. Some, having once been in tune, cease to be. Who today are the rising classes whose consciousness and ideology point to the future? The question is important not only in political terms, but (if we follow Marx) for our understanding of epistemology, at least in the social sciences. I cannot, however, pursue it further here.

The second aspect I want to discuss concerns the relation between class consciousness and organization. Let me begin with some obvious historic differences between bourgeois or "middle-class" and working-class consciousness. Bourgeois movements were based on a very powerful class consciousness. In fact, we can probably still say that the class struggle is normally fought or felt with much greater or more consistent bitterness on the bourgeois side of the front (where the menace of revolution is the dominant sentiment) than on the proletarian side (where hope, a civilized emotion, is at least as important as hatred). However, they were rarely *explicit* class movements. The few parties which have called themselves specifically "middle-class" parties, or by some similar title, are normally pressure groups for particular and generally modest purposes, such as keeping down rates and taxes. The bourgeois movements waved liberal, conservative, or other ideological banners, but claimed to be socially classless or all-embracing even when they were visibly not. Proletarian movements, on the other hand, are based on explicit class consciousness and class cohesion. At the same time bourgeois movements were organized much

more loosely and informally, often apparently for limited purposes, and involved much less loyalty and discipline than working-class ones, though in actual fact their political perspectives might be very ambitious. In this respect the contrast between the Anti-Corn Law League, the prototype as it were of bourgeois-class movements, and the Chartists, the prototype of mass-proletarian ones, is instructive.

As we have noted, the difference is not necessarily in the scope of the political objectives pursued. Both may be equally ambitious in so far as they aimed at the overthrow of one kind of society and its replacement by another. The difference may lie in the nature of the social experience of the classes or strata, their composition, and their social function. This point could be formulated in various ways. The bourgeoisie or "upper middle class" was or is an élite group of cadres, not because its members are specially selected for ability or enterprise (as they always felt sure they were), but because it consists essentially of people who are, at least potentially, in positions of command or influence, however local; of people who can make things happen as individuals, or in small numbers. (This statement does not apply to the petty bourgeoisie or lower middle class as a group.) The characteristic "campaign" of the modern British professional strata – against the location of an airport, the routing of a motorway, or some other piece of administrative steam-rollering – is effective out of all proportion to the number of persons involved in it for this reason. On the other hand, the working class, like the peasantry, consists almost by definition of people who cannot make things happen except collectively, though, unlike peasants, their experience of labour demonstrates every day that they must act collectively or not at all. But even their collective action requires structure and leadership to be effective. Without a formal organization for action, except under certain circumstances at the place of work, they are unlikely to be effective; without one which is capable of exercising hegemony (to use Gramsci's phrase), they will remain as subaltern as the common people of the pre-industrial past. The fact that history may, as Marxists argue, have cast them as the grave-diggers of an old and the foundation of a new society (although this requires some rethinking or at least reformulation) does not change this characteristic of their social existence here and now. In other words, bourgeois or middle-class movements can operate as "stage armies of the good"; proletarian ones can only operate as real armies with real generals and staffs.

The matter may be put another way. Each class has two levels of aspiration, at least until it becomes politically victorious: the immediate, day-by-day specific demands, and the more general demand for the kind of society which suits it. (Once it is victorious this second demand turns into conservatism.) There may, of course, be conflicts between these two levels of aspiration, as when sections of the nineteenth-century bourgeoisie, whose general demand was for government abstention from economic interference, found themselves appealing to government for specific aid and protection. In the case of a class like the bourgeoisie both these levels of aspirations can be pursued with only relatively loose or *ad hoc* kinds of organization, though not without a general ideology to hold them together, such as economic liberalism. Even the nineteenth-century class parties of liberalism were not mass parties or movements (except in so far as they appealed to the lower orders), but coalitions of notables, of influential individuals or small groups.[8]

On the other hand, working-class consciousness at both levels implies formal organization; and organization which is itself the carrier of class ideology, which without it would be little more than a complex of informal habits and practices. The organization (the "union," "party" or "movement") thus becomes an extension of the individual worker's personality, which it supplements and completes. When working-class militants or party supporters, faced with some novel political situation, refuse to express their own opinion and send visiting journalists to "the union" (or whatever else the title of the organization may be), it expresses not the abdication of their private judgment before some superior authority's, but the assumption that the "union's" words are their words; they are what they would say if they had the private capacity to say it.[9]

Nevertheless, the types of consciousness and organization which correspond to each of the two levels are normally distinct, though sometimes linked or combined. The lower level is represented by what Lenin called (with his usual sharp and realistic eye for social realities) "trade union consciousness", the higher by "socialist consciousness" (or possibly, but much more rarely, some other consciousness which envisages the total transformation of society). The former is (as Lenin also

observed) the more spontaneously generated, but also the more limited. Without the latter the class consciousness of the working class is incomplete, historically speaking, and its very presence as a class may, as in the USA, be – quite mistakenly – questioned. Without either, the workers may, for political purposes, be completely negligible, indeed "invisible", like the very substantial mass of "Tory working men" who have always existed in Britain, without affecting, in more than the most fleeting and marginal way, the structure, policy and programme of the Conservative Party, which could not win a single election without them.

Once again the distinction between proletariat and peasants must be made. The latter, also a historically subaltern class, require even the most elementary class consciousness and organization on the national (i.e. the politically effective) scale to be brought to them from outside, whereas the more elementary forms of class consciousness, class action, and organization tend to develop spontaneously within the working class. The development of significant trade union movements is almost universal in societies of industrial capitalism (unless prevented by physical coercion). The development of "labour" or "socialist" parties has been so common in such societies that the infrequent cases where they have not developed (as in the USA) are commonly treated as in some sense exceptional, and requiring special explanation. This is not so with autonomous peasant movements and even less with so-called "peasant parties", whose structure is in any case rather different from that of "labour parties". Proletarian movements have a built-in potential for hegemony, which peasant movements lack.

"Socialist consciousness" *through* organization is thus an essential complement of working-class consciousness. But it is neither automatic nor inevitable, and what is more, it is not class consciousness in the obvious sense in which spontaneous "trade-unionist" consciousness is, whether in its moderate reformist or in its politically less stable and effective radical, even revolutionary "syndicalist" form. And at this point the problem of class consciousness in history turns into an acute problem of twentieth-century politics. For the necessary mediation of organization implies a difference, and, with greater or smaller probability, a divergence, between "class" and "organization", i.e. on the political level, "party". The further we move from the elementary social units and situations in which class and organization mutually control one another –

e.g. in the classic case, the socialist or communist union lodge in the mining village – and into the vast and complex area where the major decisions about society are taken, the greater the potential divergence. In the extreme case of what left-wing discussion has baptized "substitutionism", the movement replaces the class, the party the movement, the apparatus of functionaries the party, the (formally elected) leadership the apparatus, and, in well-known historical examples, the inspired general secretary or other leader the central committee. The problems which arise out of this, to some extent, inevitable divergence affect the entire concept of the nature of socialism, though it may also be argued that, with the increasing irrelevance to contemporary capitalism of the old type of nineteenth-century entrepreneurial bourgeoisie, controlling significant quantities of the means of production *as individuals or families*, they may also be arising within the present system. They are problems, partly of the apparatus of administration, planning, executive and political decision, etc., which any complex modern society must possess, and especially one of economic and social planning and management under present circumstances (i.e. problems of "bureaucracy"), and partly of the nature of societies and régimes arising out of the labour and socialist movements. These are not the same, though the loose and emotional usage of such terms as "bureaucracy" in left-wing discussion tends to confuse them: they are congruent only where a formal bureaucracy is *ex officio* a ruling "class" in the technical sense, as perhaps among the imperial Chinese scholar-gentry, or today among the senior managers of corporate capitalism, whose interest is one of ownership as well as salaried management.[10]

The crucial problem for socialists is that revolutionary socialist régimes, unlike bourgeois ones, arise not out of a class, but out of the characteristic combination of class and organization. It is not the working class itself which takes power and exercises hegemony, but the working-class *movement* or *party*, and (short of taking an anarchist view) it is difficult to see how it could be otherwise. In this respect the historical development of the USSR has been quite logical, though not necessarily inevitable. The "party" became the effective and formal ruling group, on the assumption that it "stood for" the working class. The systematic subordination of state to party has reflected this. In due course, equally logically, the party absorbed and assimilated the effective individual cadres of the new society as

they emerged – its officers, administrators, executives, scientists, etc. – so that at a certain point of Soviet history success in almost any socially significant career implied the invitation to join it. (This did not imply that these "functional" recruits acquired an equal possibility to form policy with the old members for whom politics was a career, but then there was an analogous difference in the bourgeoisie between those recognized as belonging to the ruling class and those within this body who belonged to the *governing* group.) The fact that the original social basis of the party, the small industrial proletariat of Tsarist Russia, was dispersed or destroyed during the Revolution and Civil War obviously facilitated this evolution of the Communist Party. The fact that, after a generation of the new régime, the individual cadres of the new society were largely recruited from men and women of worker or peasant origins, who had made their career entirely in and through it, and only in a rapidly diminishing proportion from the members or children of former bourgeois and aristocratic families, whom the régime naturally tried to exclude, speeded the process up further. Nevertheless, it may be suggested that a process of this kind was implicit in the "proletarian revolution", unless systematic counter-measures were taken.[11]

The moment when "proletarian revolution" is successful is therefore the critical one. It is at this moment, when the formerly reasonable assumption of a virtual identity between class and organization opens the way to the subordination of the former to the latter, that "substitutionism" becomes dangerous. So long as the organization continues to maintain its *automatic* general identity with the class, and denies the possibility of more than the most temporary and superficial divergences, the way to extreme abuses, up to and including Stalinism, lies wide open. Indeed, some degree of abuse is hardly to be avoided, for the organization is likely to assume that its views and actions represent the *real* views (or in Lukácsian terms, the "ascribed" consciousness) of the class, and where the actual views of the class diverge from it these divergences are due to ignorance, lack of understanding, hostile infiltration, etc., and must be ignored if not suppressed. The stronger the concentration of party-cum-state power, the greater the temptation to ignore or suppress; and conversely, the weaker this concentration, the greater the temptation to strengthen it.

Hence problems of political democracy, of pluralist structures, freedom of expression, etc., become *more* important than before, a statement which does not imply that the solution of such problems must or should be those of bourgeois liberalism. To take an obvious example. If under socialist systems trade unions lose their old functions and strikes are outlawed, then, whatever the general justification and the possible overall gains for the workers, these have lost an essential means for influencing the condition of their lives, and unless they acquire some other means for the purpose theirs is a net loss. The classical bourgeoisie could defend the equivalent of its "trade–union–conscious" interests in various more or less informal ways, where they conflicted with the wider interests of the class as interpreted by governments. The working class, even in socialist systems, can do so only through organization, i.e. only through a political system of multiple organizations *or* through a single movement which makes itself sensitive to the views of its rank and file, i.e. through effective internal democracy.

But is this exclusively a problem of proletarian revolutions and socialist systems? As we have already noted in passing, similar problems are arising out of the changing structure of the modern capitalist economy itself. Increasingly the constitutional, legal, political and other devices by means of which people were traditionally supposed to ensure some influence over the shaping of their lives and their society – if only negative influence – are becoming ineffective. This is not so merely in the sense in which they have always been ineffective for the "labouring poor" in any but a trivial manner, but in the sense that they are increasingly irrelevant to the actual machinery of technocratic and bureaucratized decision. "Politics" are reduced to public relations and manipulations. Decisions as vital as war and peace not merely by-pass the official organs for them, but may be taken – by a handful of central bankers, by a president or prime minister with one or two backroom advisers, by an even less identifiable interlocking of technicians and executives – in ways which are not even formally open to political control. The classical machinery of nineteenth-century "real" politics increasingly revolves in a void: the leading articles of the "heavy" newspapers are read by back-bench MPs whose opinions are negligible or by ministers who are dispensable; and their respective speeches are only a little less insignificant than their private *démarches*

with those who actually take decisions, assuming they can be identified. Even the members of "the Establishment" (or ruling class) may as individuals be little more influential than the shareholders in whose interests capitalist firms are still (in legal theory) conducted. Increasingly the real members of the ruling class today are not so much real persons as organizations; not the Krupps or Rockefellers, but General Motors and IBM, not to mention the organization of government and the public sector, with whom they readily interchange executives.[12]

The political dimensions of class consciousness and especially the relation between members of the class and organizations are therefore rapidly changing. The problems of the relations of the proletariat with working-class states, or even the large-scale organizations of their movement under capitalism, are only a special case within a more general situation, which the imperatives of technology and large-scale public or corporate management have transformed. This observation should not be used merely to score debating points. Nothing is more futile and infuriating than pots calling kettles black and assuming that in so doing they have solved the problem of blackness. Classes continue and have consciousness. It is the practical expression of this consciousness which is today in question, given the changes in its historic context. But at this point the historian may fall silent, not without relief. His professional concern is not the present or future, though he ought to throw some light on it, but the past. What is likely to happen, and what we can or ought to do about it, cannot be discussed here.

Notes

1. *Geschichte und Klassenbewusstsein*, Berlin, 1923, p. 62. All my references are to this original edition.
2. Ibid., p. 62.
3. Ibid., p. 67.
4. The relevant passage from *Eighteenth Brumaire*, VII, is famous, but will not be harmed by yet another quotation: "The small peasants form a vast mass, the members of which live in similar conditions, but without entering into manifold relations with one another. Their mode of production isolates them from one another, instead of bringing them into mutual intercourse. . . . Their field of production, the small holding, admits of no division of labour in its cultivation, no application of science and,

therefore, no multiplicity of development, no diversity of talents, no wealth of social relationships. Each individual peasant family is almost self-sufficient; it itself directly produces the major part of its consumption and thus acquires its means of life more through exchange with nature than in intercourse with society. The small holding, the peasant and his family; alongside them another small holding, another peasant and another family. A few score of these make up a village, and a few score villages make up a Department. In this way the great mass of the French nation is formed by simple addition of homologous magnitudes, much as potatoes in a sack form a sackful of potatoes. Insofar as millions of families live under economic conditions of existence that divide their mode of life, their interests and their culture from those of other classes, and put them in hostile contrast to the latter, they form a class. Insofar as there is merely a local interconnection among these small peasants, and the identity of their interests begets no unity, no national union and no political organisation, they do not form a class."

5. "The Peasantry as a political factor" (*Sociol. Rev.*, XIV, 1, 1966), pp. 5–27.
6. E.g. *Geschichte und Klassenbewusstsein*, p. 70.
7. "On Peasant Rebellions" (*New Society*, 4.9.1969).
8. Once again, this does not apply to parties of the lower middle class, which tended and tend to be mass movements, though, reflecting the socio-economic isolation of the members of these strata, mass movements of a particular kind. Marx's prophetic insight into the relation of the French peasants with Napoleon III is relevant here: "They cannot represent themselves, they must be represented. Their representative must at the same time appear as their master, as an authority over them."
9. The most striking instances of such identification are normally found in the comparatively early stages of labour organization, before labour movements have become part of the official political system of operations, and at times or in places where the movement consists of a single organization which represents, i.e. literally "stands for", the class.

10. A ruling group may or may not be bureaucratized, though in European history it has rarely been so; it may operate with or through a bureaucratized administrative system, as in twentieth-century Britain, or an unbureaucratized one, as in eighteenth-century Britain. The same, allowing for the different social status – ruling parties are not classes – may be true in socialist societies. The CPSU is bureaucratic, and operates through a very bureaucratized state and economic administration. The Maoist "cultural revolution" has, if I understand it correctly, attempted to destroy the bureaucratization of the Chinese CP, but it is a fairly safe bet that the country continues to be administered by means of a bureaucratic system. It is not even impossible to discover examples of a bureaucratized ruling group with a non-bureaucratic, i.e. without an effective, administrative system, as perhaps in some ecclesiastical states of the past.
11. I am not discussing the possible developments which might lead large numbers of the individual cadres, in particular historical circumstances, to prefer *not* to join the formal organization of "top people", i.e. the party.
12. At a lower level, it also seems that the differences between formally liberal-democratic and other political systems may be diminishing sharply. Neither President de Gaulle, whose constitution guaranteed him against excessive electoral or parliamentary interference, nor President Johnson, who was not so safeguarded, were significantly affected by the pressures recognized in liberal systems. Both were vulnerable only to quite different pressures, operating outside such systems.

14

Preface from *The Making of the English Working Class*

E. P. Thompson

This book has a clumsy title, but it is one which meets its purpose. *Making*, because it is a study in an active process, which owes as much to agency as to conditioning. The working class did not rise like the sun at an appointed time. It was present at its own making.

Class, rather than classes, for reasons which it is one purpose of this book to examine. There is, of course, a difference. "Working classes" is a descriptive term, which evades as much as it defines. It ties loosely together a bundle of discrete phenomena. There were tailors here and weavers there, and together they make up the working classes.

By class I understand an historical phenomenon, unifying a number of disparate and seemingly unconnected events, both in the raw material of experience and in consciousness. I emphasise that it is an *historical* phenomenon. I do not see class as a "structure", nor even as a "category", but as something which in fact happens (and can be shown to have happened) in human relationships.

More than this, the notion of class entails the notion of historical relationship. Like any other relationship, it is a fluency which evades analysis if we attempt to stop it dead at any given moment and anatomise its structure. The finest-meshed sociological net cannot give us a pure specimen of class, any more than it can give us one of deference or of love. The relationship must always be embodied in real people and in a real context. Moreover, we cannot have two distinct classes, each with an independent being, and then bring them *into* relationship with each other. We cannot have love without lovers, nor deference without squires and labourers. And class happens when some men, as a result of common experiences (inherited or shared),

feel and articulate the identity of their interests as between themselves, and as against other men whose interests are different from (and usually opposed to) theirs. The class experience is largely determined by the productive relations into which men are born – or enter involuntarily. Class-consciousness is the way in which these experiences are handled in cultural terms: embodied in traditions, value-systems, ideas, and institutional forms. If the experience appears as determined, class-consciousness does not. We can see a *logic* in the responses of similar occupational groups undergoing similar experiences, but we cannot predicate any *law*. Consciousness of class arises in the same way in different times and places, but never in *just* the same way.

There is today an ever-present temptation to suppose that class is a thing. This was not Marx's meaning, in his own historical writing, yet the error vitiates much latter-day "Marxist" writing. "It", the working class, is assumed to have a real existence, which can be defined almost mathematically – so many men who stand in a certain relation to the means of production. Once this is assumed it becomes possible to deduce the class-consciousness which "it" ought to have (but seldom does have) if "it" was properly aware of its own position and real interests. There is a cultural superstructure, through which this recognition dawns in inefficient ways. These cultural "lags" and distortions are a nuisance, so that it is easy to pass from this to some theory of substitution: the party, sect, or theorist, who disclose class-consciousness, not as it is, but as it ought to be.

But a similar error is committed daily on the other side of the ideological divide. In one form, this is a plain negative. Since the crude notion of class attributed to Marx can be faulted without difficulty, it is assumed that any notion of class is a pejorative theoretical construct, imposed upon the evidence. It is denied that class has happened at all. In another form, and by a curious inversion, it is possible to pass from a dynamic to a static view of class. "It" – the working class – exists, and can be defined with some accuracy as a component of the social structure. Class-consciousness, however, is a bad thing, invented by displaced intellectuals, since everything which disturbs the harmonious co-existence of groups performing different "social rôles" (and which thereby retards economic growth) is to be deplored as an "unjustified disturbance-symptom".[1] The problem is to determine how best "it" can be conditioned to accept its social rôle, and how its grievances may best be "handled and channelled".

If we remember that class is a relationship, and not a thing, we can not think in this way. "It" does not exist, either to have an ideal interest or consciousness, or to lie as a patient on the Adjustor's table. Nor can we turn matters upon their heads, as has been done by one authority who (in a study of class obsessively concerned with methodology, to the exclusion of the examination of a single real class situation in a real historical context) has informed us:

> Classes are based on the differences in legitimate power associated with certain positions, i.e. on the structure of social rôles with respect to their authority expectations. . . . An individual becomes a member of a class by playing a social rôle relevant from the point of view of authority. . . . He belongs to a class because he occupies a position in a social organisation; i.e. class membership is derived from the incumbency of a social rôle.[2]

The question, of course, is how the individual got to be in this "social rôle", and how the particular social organisation (with its property-rights and structure of authority) got to be there. And these are historical questions. If we stop history at a given point, then there are no classes but simply a multitude of individuals with a multitude of experiences. But if we watch these men over an adequate period of social change, we observe patterns in their relationships, their ideas, and their institutions. Class is defined by men as they live their own history, and, in the end, this is its only definition.

If I have shown insufficient understanding of the methodological preoccupations of certain sociologists, nevertheless I hope this book will be seen as a contribution to the understanding of class. For I am convinced that we cannot understand class unless we see it as a social and cultural formation, arising from processes which can only be studied as they work themselves out over a considerable historical period. This book can be seen as a biography of the English working class from its adolescence until its early manhood. In the years between 1780 and 1832 most English working people came to feel an identity of interests as between themselves, and as against their rulers and employers. This ruling class was itself much divided, and in fact only gained in cohesion over the same years because certain antagonisms were resolved (or faded into relative insignificance) in the face of an insurgent working class. Thus the working-class presence was, in 1832, the most significant factor in British political life.

The book is written in this way. In Part One I consider the continuing popular traditions in the 18th century which influenced the crucial Jacobin agitation of the 1790s. In Part Two I move from subjective to objective influences – the experiences of groups of workers during the Industrial Revolution which seem to me to be of especial significance. I also attempt an estimate of the character of the new industrial work-discipline, and the bearing upon this of the Methodist Church. In Part Three I pick up the story of plebeian Radicalism, and carry it through Luddism to the heroic age at the close of the Napoleonic Wars. Finally, I discuss some aspects of political theory and of the consciousness of class in the 1820s and 1830s.

This is a group of studies, on related themes, rather than a consecutive narrative. In selecting these themes I have been conscious, at times, of writing against the weight of prevailing orthodoxies. There is the Fabian orthodoxy, in which the great majority of working people are seen as passive victims of *laissez faire*, with the exception of a handful of far-sighted organisers (notably, Francis Place). There is the orthodoxy of the empirical economic historians, in which working people are seen as a labour force, as migrants, or as the data for statistical series. There is the "Pilgrim's Progress" orthodoxy, in which the period is ransacked for forerunners – pioneers of the Welfare State, progenitors of a Socialist Commonwealth, or (more recently) early exemplars of rational industrial relations. Each of these orthodoxies has a certain validity. All have added to our knowledge. My quarrel with the first and second is that they tend to obscure the agency of working people, the degree to which they contributed, by conscious efforts, to the making of history. My quarrel with the third is that it reads history in the light of subsequent preoccupations, and not as in fact it occurred. Only the successful (in the sense of those whose aspirations anticipated subsequent evolution) are remembered. The blind alleys, the lost causes, and the losers themselves are forgotten.

I am seeking to rescue the poor stockinger, the Luddite cropper, the "obsolete" hand-loom weaver, the "utopian" artisan, and even the deluded follower of Joanna Southcott, from the enormous condescension of posterity. Their crafts and traditions may have been dying. Their hostility to the new industrialism may have been backward-looking. Their communitarian ideals may have been fantasies. Their insurrectionary conspiracies may have been foolhardy. But they lived through these times of acute social disturbance, and we did not. Their aspirations were valid in terms of their own experience; and, if they were casualties of history, they remain, condemned in their own lives, as casualties.

Our only criterion of judgement should not be whether or not a man's actions are justified in the light of subsequent evolution. After all, we are not at the end of social evolution ourselves. In some of the lost causes of the people of the Industrial Revolution we may discover insights into social evils which we have yet to cure. Moreover, this period now compels attention for two particular reasons. First, it was a time in which the plebeian movement placed an exceptionally high valuation upon egalitarian and democratic values. Although

we often boast our democratic way of life, the events of these critical years are far too often forgotten or slurred over. Second, the greater part of the world today is still undergoing problems of industrialisation, and of the formation of democratic institutions, analogous in many ways to our own experience during the Industrial Revolution. Causes which were lost in England might, in Asia or Africa, yet be won.

Finally, a note of apology to Scottish and Welsh readers. I have neglected these histories, not out of chauvinism, but out of respect. It is because class is a cultural as much as an economic formation that I have been cautious as to generalising beyond English experience. (I have considered the Irish, not in Ireland, but as immigrants to England.) The Scottish record, in particular, is quite as dramatic, and as tormented, as our own. The Scottish Jacobin agitation was more intense and more heroic. But the Scottish story is significantly different. Calvinism was not the same thing as Methodism, although it is difficult to say which, in the early 19th century, was worse. We had no peasantry in England comparable to the Highland migrants. And the popular culture was very different. It is possible, at least until the 1820s, to regard the English and Scottish experiences as distinct, since trade union and political links were impermanent and immature.

Notes

1. An example of this approach, covering the period of this book, is to be found in the work of a colleague of Professor Talcott Parsons: N. J. Smelser, *Social Change in the Industrial Revolution* (1959).
2. R. Dahrendorf, *Class and Class Conflict in Industrial Society* (1959), pp. 148–9.

15

Introduction from *Elementary Aspects of Peasant Insurgency in Colonial India*

Ranajit Guha

The historiography of peasant insurgency in colonial India is as old as colonialism itself. It originated at the intersection of the East India Company's political concerns and a characteristically eighteenth-century view of history – a view of history as politics and of the past as a guide to the future – which they brought with them. They were concerned to stop their newly acquired dominions from disintegrating like the moribund empire of the Mughals under the impact of peasant insurrections. For agrarian disturbances in many forms and on scales ranging from local riots to war-like campaigns spread over many districts were endemic throughout the first three quarters of British rule until the very end of the nineteenth century. At a simple count[1] there are no fewer than 110 known instances of these even for the somewhat shorter period of 117 years – from the Rangpur *dhing* to the Birsaite *ulgulan* – spanned by the present work. The formative layers of the developing state were ruptured again and again by these seismic upheavals until it was to learn to adjust to its unfamiliar site by trial and error and consolidate itself by the increasing sophistication of legislative, administrative and cultural controls.

Insurgency was thus the necessary antithesis of colonialism during the entire phase between its incipience and coming of age. The tension of this relationship required a record for the regime to refer to so that it could understand the nature and motivation of any considerable outbreak of violence in the light of previous experience and by understanding suppress it. Historiography stepped in here to provide that vital discourse for the state.

This is how the very first accounts of peasant uprisings in the period of British rule came to be written up as administrative documents of one kind or another – despatches on counter-insurgency operations, departmental minutes on measures to deal with a still active insurrection and reports of investigation into some of the more important cases of unrest. In all this literature, known to the profession as "primary sources", one can see the official mind struggling to comprehend these apparently unanticipated phenomena by means of analogy, that is, to say it after Saussure, by an "awareness and understanding of a relation between forms".[2] Just as one learns the use of a new language by feeling one's way from the known elements to the unknown, comparing and contrasting unfamiliar sounds and meanings with familiar ones, so did the early administrators try to make sense of a peasant revolt in terms of what made it similar to or different from other incidents of the same kind. Thus the Chota Nagpur uprisings of 1801 and 1817 and the Barasat *bidroha* of 1831 served as points of reference in some of the most authoritative policy statements on the Kol insurrection of 1831–2, the latter in its turn figured in official thinking at the highest level on the occasion of the Santal *hool* of 1855, and that last event was cited by the Deccan Riots Commission as a historic parallel to the subject of its investigation – the Kunbi uprising of 1875 in Poona and Ahmadnagar districts.[3]

The discourse on peasant insurgency thus made its debut quite clearly as a discourse of power. Rational in its representation of the past as linear and secular rather than cyclical and mythic, it had nothing but reasons of state as its *raison d'être*. Drafted into the service of the regime as a direct instrument of its will it did not even bother to conceal its partisan character. Indeed, it often merged, both in its narrative and analytic forms, into what was explicitly official writing. For administrative practice turned it almost into a convention that a magistrate or a judge should construct his report on a local uprising as a historical narrative, as witness the classic series, "Narrative of Events", produced by the heads of the districts caught up in the disturbances of the Mutiny years. And again, causal explanation, used in the West to arrive at what its practitioners believed to be the historical truth, served in colonialist historiography merely as an apology for law and order – the truth of the force by which the British had annexed the subcontinent. As the judicial authorities in Calcutta put it in a statement soon after the insurrection led by Titu Mir, it was "an object of paramount importance" for the government "that the cause which gave rise to [those disturbances] should be fully investigated in order that the motives which activated the insurgents [might] be rightly understood and such measures adopted as [were] deemed expedient to prevent a recurrence of similar disorders".[4] Causality was harnessed thus to counter-insurgency and the sense of history converted into an element of administrative concern.

The importance of such representation can hardly be over-estimated. By making the security of the state into the central problematic of peasant insurgency, it assimilated the latter as merely an element in the career of colonialism. In other words, the peasant was denied recognition as a subject of history in his own right even for a project that was all his own. This denial came eventually to be codified into the dominant, indeed, the only mode of historiography on this subject. Even when a writer was apparently under no obligation to think like a bureaucrat affected by the trauma of a recent jacquerie, he was conditioned to write the history of a peasant revolt as if it were some other history – that of the Raj, or of Indian nationalism, or of socialism, depending on his particular ideological bent. The result, for which the responsibility must be shared equally by all schools and tendencies, has been to exclude the insurgent as the subject of his own history.[5]

To acknowledge the peasant as the maker of his own rebellion is to attribute, as we have done in this work, a consciousness to him. Hence, the word "insurgency" has been used in the title and the text as the name of that consciousness which informs the activity of the rural masses known as jacquerie, revolt, uprising, etc. or to use their Indian designations – dhing, bidroha, ulgulan, hool, *fituri* and so on. This amounts, of course, to a rejection of the idea of such activity as purely spontaneous – an idea that is elitist as well as erroneous. It is elitist because it makes the mobilization of the peasantry altogether contingent on the intervention of charismatic leaders, advanced political organizations or upper classes. Consequently, bourgeois-nationalist historiography has to wait until the rise of Mahatma Gandhi and the Congress Party to explain the peasant movements of the colonial period so that all major events of this genre up to the end of the First World War may then be treated as the pre-history of the "Freedom Movement". An equally elitist view inclined to the left discerns in the same events a pre-history of the socialist and communist movements in the subcontinent. What both of these assimilative interpretations share is a "scholastic and academic historico-political outlook which sees as real and worthwhile only such movements of revolt as are one hundred per cent conscious, i.e. movements that are governed by plans worked out in advance to the last detail or in line with abstract theory (which comes to the same thing)".[6]

But as Antonio Gramsci whose words are quoted above has said, there is no room for pure spontaneity in history. This is precisely where they err who fail to recognize the trace of consciousness in the apparently unstructured movements of the masses. The error derives more often than not from two nearly interchangeable notions of organization and politics. What is conscious is presumed in this view to be identical with what is organized in the sense that it has, first, a "conscious leadership", secondly, some well-defined aim, and thirdly, a programme specifying the components of the latter as particular objectives and the means of achieving them. (The second and the third conditions are often collapsed in some versions.) The same equation is often written with politics as a substitute for organization. To those who prefer this device it offers the special advantage of identifying consciousness with their own political ideals and norms so that the activity of the masses found wanting in these terms may then be characterized as unconscious, hence pre-political.

The image of the pre-political peasant rebel in societies still to be fully industrialized owes a great deal to E. J. Hobsbawm's pioneering work published over two decades ago.[7] He has written there of "pre-political people" and "pre-political populations". He uses this term again and again to describe a state of supposedly absolute or near absence of political consciousness or organization which he believes to have been characteristic of such people. Thus, "the social brigand appears", according to him, "only before the poor have reached *political consciousness* or acquired *more effective methods of social agitation*", and what he means by such expressions (emphasized by us) is made clear in the next sentence when he says: "The bandit is a *pre-political phenomenon* and his strength is in *inverse* proportion to that of *organized revolutionism* and *Socialism* or *Communism*." He finds the "traditional forms of peasant discontent" to have been "virtually devoid of any explicit ideology, *organization* or *programme*". In general, "*pre-political* people" are defined as those "who have not yet found, or only begun to find, a specific language in which to express their aspirations about the world".

Hobsbawm's material is of course derived almost entirely from the European experience and his generalizations are perhaps in accord with it, although one detects a certain contradiction when he says at the same time that "social banditry has next to *no organization or ideology*", and that "in one sense banditry is a rather primitive form of *organized social protest*". Again his characterization, in *Captain Swing*, of the English agricultural labourers' movement of 1830 as "spontaneous and unorganized" does not match fully the observation of his co-author George Rudé to the effect that many of its militant "undertakings" such as wage-riots, machine-breaking and the "mobbing" of overseers and parsons "even if erupting spontaneously, quickly developed the nucleus of a local organisation".

Whatever its validity for other countries the notion of pre-political peasant insurgency helps little in understanding the experience of colonial India. For there was nothing in the militant movements of its rural masses that was not political. This could hardly have been otherwise under the conditions in which they worked, lived and conceptualized the world. Taking the subcontinent as a whole capitalist development in agriculture remained merely incipient and weak throughout the period of a century and a half until 1900. Rents constituted the most substantial part of income

yielded by property in land. Its incumbents related to the vast majority of agricultural producers as landlords to tenant-cultivators, sharecroppers, agricultural labourers and many intermediate types with features derived from each of these categories. The element that was constant in this relationship with all its variety was the extraction of the peasant's surplus by means determined rather less by the free play of the forces of a market economy than by the extra-economic force of the landlord's standing in local society and in the colonial polity. In other words, it was a relationship of dominance and subordination – a political relationship of the feudal type, or as it has been appropriately described, a semi-feudal relationship which derived its material sustenance from pre-capitalist conditions of production and its legitimacy from a traditional culture still paramount in the superstructure.

The authority of the colonial state, far from being neutral to this relationship, was indeed one of its constitutive elements. For under the Raj the state assisted directly in the reproduction of landlordism. Just as Murshid Quli Khan had reorganized the fiscal system of Bengal in such a way as to substitute a solvent and relatively vigorous set of landlords for a bankrupt and effete landed aristocracy,[8] so did the British infuse new blood for old in the proprietary body by the Permanent Settlement in the east, ryotwari in the south and some permutations of the two in most other parts of the country. The outcome of all this was to revitalize a quasi-feudal structure by transferring resources from the older and less effective members of the landlord class to younger and, for the regime politically and financially, more dependable ones. For the peasant this meant not less but in many cases more intensive and systematic exploitation: the crude medieval type of oppression in the countryside emanating from the arbitrary will of local despots under the previous system was replaced now by the more regulated will of a foreign power which for a long time to come was to leave the landlords free to collect *abwab* and *mathot* from their tenants and rack-rent and evict them. Obliged under pressure eventually to legislate against such abuses, it was unable to eliminate them altogether because its law-enforcing agencies at the local level served as instruments of landlord authority, and the law, so right on paper, allowed itself to be manipulated by court officials and lawyers in favour of landlordism. The Raj even left the power of punishment, that ultimate power of the state, to be shared to some extent by the rural elite in the name of respect for indigenous tradition, which meant in effect turning a blind eye to the gentry dispensing criminal justice either as members of the dominant class operating from *kachari* and *gadi* or as those of dominant castes entrenched in village panchayats. The collusion between *sarkar* and zamindar was indeed a part of the common experience of the poor and the subaltern at the local level nearly everywhere.

One important consequence of this revitalization of landlordism under British rule was a phenomenal growth of peasant indebtedness. For with a land market flourishing under the triple impact of agrarian legislation, demographic increase and a progressively larger money supply, many *mahajans* and *banias* bought up estates by the dozen at auctions from impoverished landlords and evicted tenants. Set up as rural proprietors they brought to bear all their usurious skill on their function as rentiers. They were encouraged to do so by a whole set of factors specific to colonial rule – the near or total absence of rent laws to protect tenant-cultivators until towards the last quarter of the nineteenth century, the lack of any effective and enforceable ceilings on local interest rates, the want of coordination between a harvest calendar geared to traditional agricultural practices and a fiscal calendar geared to the routine of imperial management, and the development of a market economy luring the peasant with little or no capital to turn his field into a frontier of commercial agriculture and consequently himself into a perpetual debtor. A cumulative result of all this was to make landlords into moneylenders – as much as 46 per cent of all peasant debt in the then United Provinces was owed to landlords in 1934[9] – and give rise to yet another of those historic paradoxes characteristic of the Raj – that is, to assign to the most advanced capitalist power in the world the task of fusing landlordism and usury in India so well as to impede the development of capitalism both in agriculture and in industry.

It was thus that the hitherto discrete powers of the landlord, the moneylender and the official came to form, under colonial rule, a composite apparatus of dominance over the peasant. His subjection to this triumvirate – *sarkari, sahukari* and zamindari – was primarily political in character, economic exploitation being only one, albeit the most obvious, of its several instances. For the appropriation of his surplus was brought about by the authority wielded over local societies and markets by the landlord-moneylenders and a secondary capitalism working closely with them and by the encapsulation of that authority in the power of the colonial state. Indeed, the element of coercion was so explicit and so ubiquitous in all their dealings with the peasant that he could hardly look upon his relationship with them as anything but political. By the same token too in undertaking to destroy this relationship he engaged himself in what was essentially a political task, a task in which the existing power nexus had to be turned on its head as a necessary condition for the redress of any particular grievance.

There was no way for the peasant to launch into such a project in a fit of absent-mindedness. For this relationship was so fortified by the power of those who had the most to benefit from it and their determination, backed by the resources of a ruling culture, to punish the least infringement, that he risked all by trying to subvert or destroy it by rebellion. This risk involved not merely the loss of his land and chattels but also that of his moral standing derived from an unquestioning subordination to his superiors, which tradition had made into his dharma. No wonder, therefore, that the preparation of an uprising was almost invariably marked by much temporization and weighing of pros and cons on the part of its protagonists. In many instances they tried at first to obtain justice from the authorities by deputation (e.g. Titu's bidroha, 1831), petition (e.g. Khandesh riots, 1852), and peaceful demonstration (e.g. Indigo rebellion, 1860) and took up arms only as a last resort when all other means had failed. Again, an *émeute* was preceded in most cases by consultation among the peasants in various forms, depending on the organization of the local society where it originated. There were meetings of clan elders and caste panchayats, neighbourhood conventions, larger mass gatherings, and so on. These consultative processes were often fairly protracted and could take weeks or even months to build up the necessary consensus at various levels until most of an entire community was mobilized for action by the systematic use of primordial networks and many different means of verbal and non-verbal communication.

There was nothing spontaneous about all this in the sense of being unthinking and wanting in deliberation. The peasant obviously knew what he was doing when he rose in revolt. The fact that this was designed primarily to destroy the authority of the superordinate elite, and carried no elaborate blueprint for its replacement, does not put it outside the realm of politics. On the contrary, insurgency affirmed its political character precisely by its negative and inversive procedure. By trying to force a mutual substitution of the dominant and the dominated in the power structure it left nothing to doubt about its own identity as a project of power. As such it was perhaps less primitive than it is often presumed to be. More often than not it lacked neither in leadership nor in aim nor even in some rudiments of a programme, although none of these attributes could compare in maturity or sophistication with those of the historically more advanced movements of the twentieth century. The evidence is ample and unambiguous on this point. Of the many cases discussed in this work there is none that could be said to have been altogether leaderless. Almost each had indeed some sort of a central leadership to give it a name and some cohesion, although in no instance was it fully in control of the many local initiatives originating with grassroot leaders whose authority was as fragmented as their standing short in duration. Quite clearly one is dealing here with a phenomenon that was nothing like a modern party leadership but could perhaps be best described, in Gramsci's words, as "multiple elements of 'conscious leadership' but no one of them . . . predominant". Which is of course a very different thing from stigmatizing these loosely oriented struggles as "sub-political" outbreaks of mass impetuosity without any direction and form.

Again, if aim and programme are a measure of politics, the militant mobilizations of our period must be regarded as more or less political. Not one of them was quite aimless, although the aim was more elaborately and precisely defined in some events than in others. The Barasat peasantry led by Titu Mir, the Santals under the *Subah* brothers and the Mundas under Birsa all stated their objectives to be power in one form or another. Peasant kings were a characteristic product of rural revolt throughout the subcontinent, and an anticipation of power was indexed on some occasions by the rebels designating themselves as a formally constituted army (*fauj*), their commanders as law-enforcing personnel (e.g. *daroga*, *subahdar*, *nazir*, etc.), and other leaders as ranked civilian officials (e.g. *dewan*, *naib*, etc.) – all by way of simulating the functions of a state apparatus. That the raj they wanted to substitute for the one they were out to destroy did not quite conform to the model of a secular and national state, and their concept of power failed

to rise above localism, sectarianism and ethnicity, does not take away from the essentially political character of their activity but defines the quality of that politics by specifying its limitations.

It would be wrong of course to overestimate the maturity of this politics and read into it the qualities of a subsequent phase of more intensified class conflict, widespread anti-imperialist struggle and generally a higher level of militancy among the masses. Compared to these, the peasant movements of the first three-quarters of British rule represented a somewhat inchoate and naive state of consciousness. Yet we propose to focus on this consciousness as our central theme, because it is not possible to make sense of the experience of insurgency merely as a history of events without a subject. It is in order to rehabilitate that subject that we must take the peasant-rebel's awareness of his own world and his will to change it as our point of departure.

For however feeble and tragically ineffective this awareness and will might have been, they were still nothing less than the elements of a consciousness which was learning to compile and classify the individual and disparate moments of experience and organize these into some sort of generalizations. These were, in other words, the very beginnings of a theoretical consciousness. Insurgency was indeed the site where the two mutually contradictory tendencies within this still imperfect, almost embryonic, theoretical consciousness – that is, a conservative tendency made up of the inherited and uncritically absorbed material of the ruling culture and a radical one oriented towards a practical transformation of the rebel's conditions of existence[10] – met for a decisive trial of strength.

The object of this work is to try and depict this struggle not as a series of specific encounters but in its general form. The elements of this form derive from the very long history of the peasant's subalternity and his striving to end it. Of these the former is of course more fully documented and represented in elite discourse because of the interest it has always had for its beneficiaries. However, subordination can hardly be justified as an ideal and a norm without acknowledging the fact and possibility of insubordination, so that the affirmation of dominance in the ruling culture speaks eloquently too of its Other, that is, resistance. They run on parallel tracks over the same stretches of history as mutually implied but opposed aspects of a pair of antagonistic consciousnesses.

It is thus that the oppression of the peasantry and the latter's revolt against it figure again and again in our past not only as intermingled matters of fact but also as hostile but concomitant traditions. Just as the time-honoured practice of holding the rural masses in thraldom has helped to develop codes of deference and loyalty, so has the recursive practice of insurgency helped to develop fairly well-established structures of defiance over the centuries. These are operative in a weak and fragmentary manner even in everyday life and in individual and small-group resistance, but come into their own in the most emphatic and comprehensive fashion when those masses set about turning things upside down and the moderating rituals, cults and ideologies help no longer to maintain the contradiction between subaltern and superordinate at a non-antagonistic level. In their detail of course these larger structures of resistance vary according to differences between regional cultures as well as between styles of dominance and the relative weights of the dominant groups in any given situation. But since insurgency with all its local variations relates antagonistically to this dominance everywhere throughout the historical period under study, there is much to it that combines into patterns cutting across its particular expressions. For, as it has been said:

> The history of all past society has consisted in the development of class antagonisms, antagonisms that assumed different forms at different epochs. But whatever form they may have taken, one fact is common to all past ages, viz. the exploitation of one part of society by the other. No wonder, then, that the social consciousness of past ages, despite all the multiplicity and variety it displays, moves within certain common forms, or general ideas, which cannot completely vanish except with the total disappearance of class antagonisms.[11]

It will be our aim in this work to try and identify some of these "common forms or general ideas" in rebel consciousness during the colonial period. However, within that category we have chosen to concentrate on "the first elements" which make it possible for the general ideas to combine in complex formations and constitute what Gramsci has described as "the pillars of politics and of any collective action whatsoever".[12] These *elementary aspects*, as we propose to call them, are subject to a high degree of redundancy: precisely because they recur again and again and almost everywhere in

our agrarian movements, they are the ones which are the most overlooked. The result has been not merely to exclude politics from the historiography of Indian peasant insurgency but to reduce the latter to a mere embellishment, a sort of decorative and folklorist detail serving primarily to enliven the *curricula vitae* of the indigenous and foreign elites. By contrast, it is rebel consciousness which will be allowed to dominate the present exercise. We want to emphasize its sovereignty, its consistency and its logic in order to compensate for its absence from the literature on the subject and to act, if possible, as a corrective to the eclecticism common to much writing on this theme.

[. . .]

Most, though not all, of this evidence is elitist in origin. This has come down to us in the form of official records of one kind or another – police reports, army despatches, administrative accounts, minutes and resolutions of governmental departments, and so on. Non-official sources of our information on the subject, such as newspapers or the private correspondence between persons in authority, too, speak in the same elitist voice, even if it is that of the indigenous elite or of non-Indians outside officialdom. Staple of most historical writing on colonial themes, evidence of this type has a way of stamping the interests and outlook of the rebels' enemies on every account of our peasant rebellions.

One obvious way of combating such bias could perhaps be to summon folklore, oral as well as written, to the historian's aid. Unfortunately however there is not enough to serve for this purpose either in quantity or quality in spite of populist beliefs to the contrary. For one thing, the actual volume of evidence yielded by songs, rhymes, ballads, anecdotes, etc. is indeed very meagre, to the point of being insignificant, compared to the size of documentation available from elitist sources on almost any agrarian movement of our period. This is a measure not only of the monopoly which the peasant's enemies had of literacy under the Raj, but of their concern to watch and record every hostile gesture among the rural masses. They simply had too much to lose, and fear, which haunts all authority based on force, made careful archivists of them. Take, for instance, the Santal hool of 1855 which is richer than many others in this respect. Yet what we know about it from the *Judicial Proceedings* series of the West Bengal State Archives alone, that is, not counting the district records, far outweighs the information to be had from Jugia Harom's and Chotrae Desmanjhi's reminiscences taken together with the folklore collected by Sen, Baskay, and Archer and Culshaw.[13] For most other events the proportion is perhaps even higher in favour of the elitist sources. Indeed, for one of the most important of these, namely, the Barasat revolt of 1832, it would be hard to find anything at all that does not derive from a quarter identified with opinions hostile to Titu and his followers.

An equally disappointing aspect of the folklore relating to peasant militancy is that it can be elitist too. Not all singers and balladeers took a sympathetic view of it. Some of them belonged to upper-caste families fallen on hard times or to other impoverished groups within the middle strata of rural society. Cut off from the tillers of the soil by status if not by wealth, they hung on to the rural gentry for patronage and expressed the latter's anxieties and prejudices in their compositions on the theme of agrarian disturbances. Thus, the insurgent voice which comes through the Mundari poetry and homiletics published by Singh, or the anti-survey song in Sandip dialect published by Grierson, is more than balanced out in folk literature by the representation of an obviously landlord point of view in some of the verses cited in Saha's account of the Pabna bidroha, Ray's of the Pagalpanthi insurrection, and so on.[14]

How then are we to get in touch with the consciousness of insurgency when our access to it is barred thus by the discourse of counter-insurgency? The difficulty is perhaps less insurmountable than it seems to be at first sight. For counter-insurgency, which derives directly from insurgency and is determined by the latter in all that is essential to its form and articulation, can hardly afford a discourse that is not fully and compulsively involved with the rebel and his activities. It is of course true that the reports, despatches, minutes, judgments, laws, letters, etc. in which policemen, soldiers, bureaucrats, landlords, usurers and others hostile to insurgency register their sentiments amount to a representation of their will. But these documents do not get their content from that will alone, for the latter is predicated on another will – that of the insurgent. It should be possible therefore to read the presence of a rebel consciousness as a necessary and pervasive element within that body of evidence.

There are two ways in which this presence makes itself felt. In the first place, it comes as a direct reporting of such rebel utterances as are intercepted by the authorities from time to time and used for pacification campaigns, legal enactments, judicial proceedings and other interventions of the regime against its adversaries. Witness to a sort of official eavesdropping, this discourse enters into the records of counter-insurgency variously as messages and rumours circulating within a rural community, snatches of conversation overheard by spies, statements made by captives under police interrogation or before courts, and so on. Meant to assist the Raj in suppressing rebellion and incriminating rebels, its usefulness in that particular respect was a measure of its authenticity as a documentation of the insurgent's will. In other words, intercepted discourse of this type testifies no less to the consciousness of the rebel peasantry than to the intentions of their enemies, and may quite legitimately serve as evidence for a historiography not compromised by the latter's point of view.

The presence of this consciousness is also affirmed by a set of indices within elite discourse. These have the function of expressing the hostility of the British authorities and their native protégés towards the unruly troublemakers in the countryside. The words, phrases and, indeed, whole chunks of prose addressed to this purpose are designed primarily to indicate the immorality, illegality, undesirability, barbarity, etc. of insurgent practice and to announce by contrast the superiority of the elite on each count. A measure of the difference between two mutually contradictory perceptions, they have much to tell us not only about elite mentality but also about that to which it is opposed – namely, subaltern mentality. The antagonism is indeed so complete and so firmly structured that from the terms stated for one it should be possible, by reversing their values, to derive the implicit terms of the other. When, therefore, an official document speaks of badmashes as participants in rural disturbances, this does not mean (going by the normal sense of that Urdu word) any ordinary collection of rascals but peasants involved in a militant agrarian struggle. In the same context, a reference to any "dacoit village" (as one comes across so often in the Mutiny narratives) would indicate the entire population of a village united in resistance to the armed forces of the state; "contagion" – the enthusiasm and solidarity generated by an uprising among various rural groups within a region; "fanatics" – rebels inspired by some kinds of revivalist or puritanical doctrines; "lawlessness" – the defiance by the people of what they had come to regard as bad laws, and so on. Indeed, the pressures exercised by insurgency on elite discourse force it to reduce the semantic range of many words and expressions, and assign to them specialized meanings in order to identify peasants as rebels and their attempt to turn the world upside down as crime. Thanks to such a process of narrowing down it is possible for the historian to use this impoverished and almost technical language as a clue to the antonymies which speak for a rival consciousness – that of the rebel. Some of that consciousness which is so firmly inscribed in elite discourse will, we hope, be made visible in our reading of it in this work.

Notes

References to manuscripts and printed works have been indicated by abbreviations or by authors (see References), and *not* by titles.

A Roman numeral after a colon specifies the volume(s) and an Arabic numeral the page(s) of a publication.

An Arabic numeral before an oblique indicates chapter or section and that after it verse or paragraph in a Sanskrit text or its translation.

A date enclosed in brackets after an author's name distinguishes that publication from his other writings.

1. The estimate is based on events catalogued in three standard works, viz. Chaudhuri (1955) and Ray (1966, 1970). A complete list, yet to be put together by historians as a serious project for research, will of course show a much higher total, for it should be obvious to scholars working on particular regions that these compilations, based on published sources and secondary works, do not include numerous local instances still to be retrieved from the archives and oral literature.
2. Saussure: 165.
3. BC 1363 (54227): Vice-President's Minute (30 Mar. 1832); Blunt's Minutes (24 Mar. and 4 Apr. 1832). BC 1363 (54228): Neave to Government (29 Mar. 1832). JP, 19 July 1855: Elliott to Grey (15 July 1855). JP, 8 Nov. 1855: Lieutenant-Governor's Minute (19 Oct. 1855).
4. JC, 22 Nov. 1831 (no. 91).
5. For a more elaborate presentation of the argument stated so far, see Guha (1983).
6. This and other observations attributed to Gramsci on the question of spontaneity are taken from "Spontaneity and Conscious Leadership" in Gramsci: 196–200.
7. For the citations and attributions in this and the next paragraph, see Hobsbawm: 2, 5, 13, 23, 96, 118 and Hobsbawm and Rudé: 19, 205.
8. Sarkar: 409–10.
9. Bengal: I 98.
10. Gramsci: 333.
11. Marx and Engels: VI 504.
12. Gramsci: 144.
13. For these, see Mare Hapram K. Reak Katha: *passim*, but especially pp. *clxxvi–viii*; Culshaw and Archer: 218–39; Sen (1926): 265–71; Baskay: *passim*.
14. Singh: Appendices H, I, K; Grierson: 257; Saha: III 97–100; Ray (1966): 235.

References

Archival material

BC, JC and JP = Board's Collections in the India Office Library, London.

Works cited

Baskay, Dhirendranath. 1976. *Saontal Ganasamgramer Itihas*. Calcutta.

Bengal, Government of. 1940. *Report of the Land Revenue Commission*, vol. 1. Alipore.

Chaudhuri, S. B. 1955. *Civil Disturbances during the British Rule in India*. Calcutta.

Culshaw, W. J. and Archer, W. G. 1945. "The Santal Rebellion," in *Man in India*, vol. 25 (4), pp. 208–17, December.

Gramsci, A. 1971. *Selections from the Prison Notebooks*. London.

Grierson, G. A. 1968. *Linguistic Survey of India*, vol. 5, pt. 1. Reprint. Delhi.

Guha, Ranajit. 1983. "The Prose of Counter-Insurgency," in R. Guha (ed.), *Subaltern Studies*, vol. 2. Delhi.

Hobsbawm, E. J. 1959. *Primitive Rebels*. Manchester.

Hobsbawm, E. J. and Rudé, G. 1969. *Captain Swing*. London.

Mare Hapram Ko Reak Katha (The Traditions and Institutions of the Saontals). 1953. Translated by Baidyanath Hansdah. In *Census 1951, West Bengal District Handbooks: Bankura* Appendix V, pp. lxxxvii–clxxi.

Marx, K. and Engels, F. 1975–8. *Collected Works*, vols. 3, 6, 10, 11. London.

Ray, Suprakash. 1966. *Bharater Krishak-bidroha O Ganatantrik Samgram*, vol. 1. Calcutta.

Ray, Suprakash. 1970. *Bharater Baiplabik Samgramer Itihas*, Calcutta.

Saha, Radharaman. 1923–6. *Pabna Jelar Itihas*, 3 vols. Bengali Years: 1330–3. Pabna.

Sarkar, Jadunath (ed.). 1948. *The History of Bengal*, vol. 2. Dacca.

Saussure, Ferdinand de. 1974. *Course in General Linguistics*. Glasgow.

Sen, Dinesh Chandra (ed.). 1926. *Eastern Bengal Ballads*, vol. 2, pt. 1. Calcutta.

Singh, Suresh. 1966. *Dust Storm and Hanging Mist*. Calcutta.

Part IV
Gender/Sexuality

16

Introduction from *The Second Sex*

SIMONE DE BEAUVOIR

For a long time I have hesitated to write a book on woman. The subject is irritating, especially to women; and it is not new. Enough ink has been spilled in the quarreling over feminism, now practically over, and perhaps we should say no more about it. It is still talked about, however, for the voluminous nonsense uttered during the last century seems to have done little to illuminate the problem. After all, is there a problem? And if so, what is it? Are there women, really? Most assuredly the theory of the eternal feminine still has its adherents who will whisper in your ear: "Even in Russia women still are *women*"; and other erudite persons – sometimes the very same – say with a sigh: "Woman is losing her way, woman is lost." One wonders if women still exist, if they will always exist, whether or not it is desirable that they should, what place they occupy in this world, what their place should be. "What has become of women?" was asked recently in an ephemeral magazine.[1]

But first we must ask: what is a woman? "*Tota mulier in utero*," says one, "woman is a womb." But in speaking of certain women, connoisseurs declare that they are not women, although they are equipped with a uterus like the rest. All agree in recognizing the fact that females exist in the human species; today as always they make up about one half of humanity. And yet we are told that femininity is in danger; we are exhorted to be women, remain women, become women. It would appear, then, that every female human being is not necessarily a woman; to be so considered she must share in that mysterious and threatened reality known as femininity. Is this attribute something secreted by the ovaries? Or is it a Platonic essence, a product of the philosophic imagination? Is a rustling petticoat enough to bring it down to earth? Although some women try zealously to incarnate this essence, it is hardly patentable. It is frequently described in vague and dazzling terms that seem to have been borrowed from the vocabulary of the seers, and indeed in the times of St. Thomas it was considered an essence as certainly defined as the somniferous virtue of the poppy.

But conceptualism has lost ground. The biological and social sciences no longer admit the existence of unchangeably fixed entities that determine given characteristics, such as those ascribed to woman, the Jew, or the Negro. Science regards any characteristic as a reaction dependent in part upon a *situation*. If today femininity no longer exists, then it never existed. But does the word *woman*, then, have no specific content? This is stoutly affirmed by those who hold to the philosophy of the enlightenment, of rationalism, of nominalism; women, to them, are merely the human beings arbitrarily designated by the word *woman*. Many American women particularly are prepared to think that there is no longer any place for woman as such; if a backward individual still takes herself for a woman, her friends advise her to be psychoanalyzed and thus get rid of this obsession. In regard to a work, *Modern Woman: The Lost Sex*, which in other respects has its irritating features, Dorothy Parker has written: "I cannot be just to books which treat of woman as woman. . . . My idea is that all of us, men as well as women, should be regarded as human beings." But nominalism is a rather inadequate doctrine, and the antifeminists have had no trouble in showing that women simply *are not* men. Surely woman is, like man, a human being;

but such a declaration is abstract. The fact is that every concrete human being is always a singular, separate individual. To decline to accept such notions as the eternal feminine, the black soul, the Jewish character, is not to deny that Jews, Negroes, women exist today – this denial does not represent a liberation for those concerned, but rather a flight from reality. Some years ago a well-known woman writer refused to permit her portrait to appear in a series of photographs especially devoted to women writers; she wished to be counted among the men. But in order to gain this privilege she made use of her husband's influence! Women who assert that they are men lay claim none the less to masculine consideration and respect. I recall also a young Trotskyite standing on a platform at a boisterous meeting and getting ready to use her fists, in spite of her evident fragility. She was denying her feminine weakness; but it was for love of a militant male whose equal she wished to be. The attitude of defiance of many American women proves that they are haunted by a sense of their femininity. In truth, to go for a walk with one's eyes open is enough to demonstrate that humanity is divided into two classes of individuals whose clothes, faces, bodies, smiles, gaits, interests, and occupations are manifestly different. Perhaps these differences are superficial, perhaps they are destined to disappear. What is certain is that right now they do most obviously exist.

If her functioning as a female is not enough to define woman, if we decline also to explain her through "the eternal feminine," and if nevertheless we admit, provisionally, that women do exist, then we must face the question: what is a woman?

To state the question is, to me, to suggest, at once, a preliminary answer. The fact that I ask it is in itself significant. A man would never get the notion of writing a book on the peculiar situation of the human male.[2] But if I wish to define myself, I must first of all say: "I am a woman"; on this truth must be based all further discussion. A man never begins by presenting himself as an individual of a certain sex; it goes without saying that he is a man. The terms *masculine* and *feminine* are used symmetrically only as a matter of form, as on legal papers. In actuality the relation of the two sexes is not quite like that of two electrical poles, for man represents both the positive and the neutral, as is indicated by the common use of *man* to designate human beings in general; whereas woman represents only the negative, defined by limiting criteria,

without reciprocity. In the midst of an abstract discussion it is vexing to hear a man say: "You think thus and so because you are a woman"; but I know that my only defense is to reply: "I think thus and so because it is true," thereby removing my subjective self from the argument. It would be out of the question to reply: "And you think the contrary because you are a man," for it is understood that the fact of being a man is no peculiarity. A man is in the right in being a man; it is the woman who is in the wrong. It amounts to this: just as for the ancients there was an absolute vertical with reference to which the oblique was defined, so there is an absolute human type, the masculine. Woman has ovaries, a uterus; these peculiarities imprison her in her subjectivity, circumscribe her within the limits of her own nature. It is often said that she thinks with her glands. Man superbly ignores the fact that his anatomy also includes glands, such as the testicles, and that they secrete hormones. He thinks of his body as a direct and normal connection with the world, which he believes he apprehends objectively, whereas he regards the body of woman as a hindrance, a prison, weighed down by everything peculiar to it. "The female is a female by virtue of a certain *lack* of qualities," said Aristotle; "we should regard the female nature as afflicted with a natural defectiveness." And St. Thomas for his part pronounced woman to be an "imperfect man," an "incidental" being. This is symbolized in Genesis where Eve is depicted as made from what Bossuet called "a supernumerary bone" of Adam.

Thus humanity is male and man defines woman not in herself but as relative to him; she is not regarded as an autonomous being. Michelet writes: "Woman, the relative being. . . ." And Benda is most positive in his *Rapport d'Uriel*: "The body of man makes sense in itself quite apart from that of woman, whereas the latter seems wanting in significance by itself. . . . Man can think of himself without woman. She cannot think of herself without man." And she is simply what man decrees; thus she is called "the sex," by which is meant that she appears essentially to the male as a sexual being. For him she is sex – absolute sex, no less. She is defined and differentiated with reference to man and not he with reference to her; she is the incidental, the inessential as opposed to the essential. He is the Subject, he is the Absolute – she is the Other.[3]

The category of the *Other* is as primordial as consciousness itself. In the most primitive societies, in the most ancient mythologies, one finds the expression of a duality – that of the Self and the Other. This duality was not originally attached to the division of the sexes; it was not dependent upon any empirical facts. It is revealed in such works as that of Granet on Chinese thought and those of Dumézil on the East Indies and Rome. The feminine element was at first no more involved in such pairs as Varuna-Mitra, Uranus-Zeus, Sun-Moon, and Day-Night than it was in the contrasts between Good and Evil, lucky and unlucky auspices, right and left, God and Lucifer. Otherness is a fundamental category of human thought.

Thus it is that no group ever sets itself up as the One without at once setting up the Other over against itself. If three travelers chance to occupy the same compartment, that is enough to make vaguely hostile "others" out of all the rest of the passengers on the train. In small-town eyes all persons not belonging to the village are "strangers" and suspect; to the native of a country all who inhabit other countries are "foreigners"; Jews are "different" for the anti-Semite, Negroes are "inferior" for American racists, aborigines are "natives" for colonists, proletarians are the "lower class" for the privileged.

Lévi-Strauss, at the end of a profound work on the various forms of primitive societies, reaches the following conclusion: "Passage from the state of Nature to the state of Culture is marked by man's ability to view biological relations as a series of contrasts; duality, alternation, opposition, and symmetry, whether under definite or vague forms, constitute not so much phenomena to be explained as fundamental and immediately given data of social reality."[4] These phenomena would be incomprehensible if in fact human society were simply a *Mitsein* or fellowship based on solidarity and friendliness. Things become clear, on the contrary, if, following Hegel, we find in consciousness itself a fundamental hostility toward every other consciousness; the subject can be posed only in being opposed – he sets himself up as the essential, as opposed to the other, the inessential, the object.

But the other consciousness, the other ego, sets up a reciprocal claim. The native traveling abroad is shocked to find himself in turn regarded as a "stranger" by the natives of neighboring countries. As a matter of fact, wars, festivals, trading, treaties, and contests among tribes, nations, and classes tend to deprive the concept *Other* of its absolute sense and to make manifest its relativity; willy-nilly, individuals and groups are forced to realize the reciprocity of their relations. How is it, then, that this reciprocity has not been recognized between the sexes, that one of the contrasting terms is set up as the sole essential, denying any relativity in regard to its correlative and defining the latter as pure otherness? Why is it that women do not dispute male sovereignty? No subject will readily volunteer to become the object, the inessential; it is not the Other who, in defining himself as the Other, establishes the One. The Other is posed as such by the One in defining himself as the One. But if the Other is not to regain the status of being the One, he must be submissive enough to accept this alien point of view. Whence comes this submission in the case of woman?

There are, to be sure, other cases in which a certain category has been able to dominate another completely for a time. Very often this privilege depends upon inequality of numbers – the majority imposes its rule upon the minority or persecutes it. But women are not a minority, like the American Negroes or the Jews; there are as many women as men on earth. Again, the two groups concerned have often been originally independent; they may have been formerly unaware of each other's existence, or perhaps they recognized each other's autonomy. But a historical event has resulted in the subjugation of the weaker by the stronger. The scattering of the Jews, the introduction of slavery into America, the conquests of imperialism are examples in point. In these cases the oppressed retained at least the memory of former days; they possessed in common a past, a tradition, sometimes a religion or a culture.

The parallel drawn by Bebel between women and the proletariat is valid in that neither ever formed a minority or a separate collective unit of mankind. And instead of a single historical event it is in both cases a historical development that explains their status as a class and accounts for the membership of *particular individuals* in that class. But proletarians have not always existed, whereas there have always been women. They are women in virtue of their anatomy and physiology. Throughout history they have always been subordinated to men, and hence their dependency is not the result of a historical event or a social change – it was not something that *occurred*. The reason why otherness in this case seems to be an absolute is in part that it lacks the contingent or incidental nature of historical facts. A condition brought about at a certain time can be abolished at some other time, as the Negroes of Haiti and others have proved; but it might seem that a natural condition is beyond the possibility of change. In truth, however, the nature of things is no more immutably given, once for all, than is historical reality. If woman seems to be the inessential which never becomes the essential, it is because she herself fails to bring about this change. Proletarians say "We"; Negroes also. Regarding themselves as subjects, they transform the bourgeois, the whites, into "others." But women do not say "We," except at some congress of feminists or similar formal demonstration; men say "women," and women use the same word in referring to themselves. They do not authentically assume a subjective attitude. The proletarians have accomplished the revolution in Russia, the Negroes in Haiti, the Indo-Chinese are battling for it in Indo-China; but the women's effort has never been anything more than a symbolic agitation. They have gained only what men have been willing to grant; they have taken nothing, they have only received.[5]

The reason for this is that women lack concrete means for organizing themselves into a unit which can stand face to face with the correlative unit. They have no past, no history, no religion of their own; and they have no such solidarity of work and interest as that of the proletariat. They are not even promiscuously herded together in the way that creates community feeling among the American Negroes, the ghetto Jews, the workers of Saint-Denis, or the factory hands of Renault. They live dispersed among the males, attached through residence, housework, economic condition, and social standing to certain men – fathers or husbands – more firmly than they are to other women. If they belong to the bourgeoisie, they feel solidarity with men of that class, not with proletarian women; if they are white, their allegiance is to white men, not to Negro women. The proletariat can propose to massacre the ruling class, and a sufficiently fanatical Jew or Negro might dream of getting sole possession of the atomic bomb and making humanity wholly Jewish or black; but woman cannot even dream of exterminating the males. The bond that unites her to her oppressors is not comparable to any other. The division of the sexes is a biological fact, not an event in human history. Male and female stand opposed within a primordial *Mitsein*, and woman has not broken it. The couple is a fundamental unity with its two halves riveted together, and the cleavage of society along the line

of sex is impossible. Here is to be found the basic trait of woman: she is the Other in a totality of which the two components are necessary to one another.

One could suppose that this reciprocity might have facilitated the liberation of woman. When Hercules sat at the feet of Omphale and helped with her spinning, his desire for her held him captive; but why did she fail to gain a lasting power? To revenge herself on Jason, Medea killed their children; and this grim legend would seem to suggest that she might have obtained a formidable influence over him through his love for his offspring. In *Lysistrata* Aristophanes gaily depicts a band of women who joined forces to gain social ends through the sexual needs of their men; but this is only a play. In the legend of the Sabine women, the latter soon abandoned their plan of remaining sterile to punish their ravishers. In truth woman has not been socially emancipated through man's need – sexual desire and the desire for offspring – which makes the male dependent for satisfaction upon the female.

Master and slave, also, are united by a reciprocal need, in this case economic, which does not liberate the slave. In the relation of master to slave the master does not make a point of the need that he has for the other; he has in his grasp the power of satisfying this need through his own action; whereas the slave, in his dependent condition, his hope and fear, is quite conscious of the need he has for his master. Even if the need is at bottom equally urgent for both, it always works in favor of the oppressor and against the oppressed. That is why the liberation of the working class, for example, has been slow.

Now, woman has always been man's dependent, if not his slave; the two sexes have never shared the world in equality. And even today woman is heavily handicapped, though her situation is beginning to change. Almost nowhere is her legal status the same as man's, and frequently it is much to her disadvantage. Even when her rights are legally recognized in the abstract, long-standing custom prevents their full expression in the mores. In the economic sphere men and women can almost be said to make up two castes; other things being equal, the former hold the better jobs, get higher wages, and have more opportunity for success than their new competitors. In industry and politics men have a great many more positions and they monopolize the most important posts. In addition to all this, they enjoy a traditional prestige that the education of children tends in every way to support, for the present enshrines the past – and in the past all history has been made by men. At the present time, when women are beginning to take part in the affairs of the world, it is still a world that belongs to men – they have no doubt of it at all and women have scarcely any. To decline to be the Other, to refuse to be a party to the deal – this would be for women to renounce all the advantages conferred upon them by their alliance with the superior caste. Man-the-sovereign will provide woman-the-liege with material protection and will undertake the moral justification of her existence; thus she can evade at once both economic risk and the metaphysical risk of a liberty in which ends and aims must be contrived without assistance. Indeed, along with the ethical urge of each individual to affirm his subjective existence, there is also the temptation to forgo liberty and become a thing. This is an inauspicious road, for he who takes it – passive, lost, ruined – becomes henceforth the creature of another's will, frustrated in his transcendence and deprived of every value. But it is an easy road; on it one avoids the strain involved in undertaking an authentic existence. When man makes of woman the *Other*, he may, then, expect her to manifest deep-seated tendencies toward complicity. Thus, woman may fail to lay claim to the status of subject because she lacks definite resources, because she feels the necessary bond that ties her to man regardless of reciprocity, and because she is often very well pleased with her role as the *Other*.

But it will be asked at once: how did all this begin? It is easy to see that the duality of the sexes, like any duality, gives rise to conflict. And doubtless the winner will assume the status of absolute. But why should man have won from the start? It seems possible that women could have won the victory; or that the outcome of the conflict might never have been decided. How is it that this world has always belonged to the men and that things have begun to change only recently? Is this change a good thing? Will it bring about an equal sharing of the world between men and women?

These questions are not new, and they have often been answered. But the very fact that woman *is the Other* tends to cast suspicion upon all the justifications that men have ever been able to provide for it. These have all too evidently been dictated by men's interest. A little-known feminist of the seventeenth century, Poulain de la Barre,

put it this way: "All that has been written about women by men should be suspect, for the men are at once judge and party to the lawsuit." Everywhere, at all times, the males have displayed their satisfaction in feeling that they are the lords of creation. "Blessed be God . . . that He did not make me a woman," say the Jews in their morning prayers, while their wives pray on a note of resignation: "Blessed be the Lord, who created me according to His will." The first among the blessings for which Plato thanked the gods was that he had been created free, not enslaved; the second, a man, not a woman. But the males could not enjoy this privilege fully unless they believed it to be founded on the absolute and the eternal; they sought to make the fact of their supremacy into a right. "Being men, those who have made and compiled the laws have favored their own sex, and jurists have elevated these laws into principles," to quote Poulain de la Barre once more.

Legislators, priests, philosophers, writers, and scientists have striven to show that the subordinate position of woman is willed in heaven and advantageous on earth. The religions invented by men reflect this wish for domination. In the legends of Eve and Pandora men have taken up arms against women. They have made use of philosophy and theology, as the quotations from Aristotle and St. Thomas have shown. Since ancient times satirists and moralists have delighted in showing up the weaknesses of women. We are familiar with the savage indictments hurled against women throughout French literature. Montherlant, for example, follows the tradition of Jean de Meung, though with less gusto. This hostility may at times be well founded, often it is gratuitous; but in truth it more or less successfully conceals a desire for self-justification. As Montaigne says, "It is easier to accuse one sex than to excuse the other." Sometimes what is going on is clear enough. For instance, the Roman law limiting the rights of woman cited "the imbecility, the instability of the sex" just when the weakening of family ties seemed to threaten the interests of male heirs. And in the effort to keep the married woman under guardianship, appeal was made in the sixteenth century to the authority of St. Augustine, who declared that "woman is a creature neither decisive nor constant," at a time when the single woman was thought capable of managing her property. Montaigne understood clearly how arbitrary and unjust was woman's appointed lot: "Women are not in the wrong when they decline to accept the rules laid down for them, since the men make these rules without consulting them. No wonder intrigue and strife abound." But he did not go so far as to champion their cause.

It was only later, in the eighteenth century, that genuinely democratic men began to view the matter objectively. Diderot, among others, strove to show that woman is, like man, a human being. Later John Stuart Mill came fervently to her defense. But these philosophers displayed unusual impartiality. In the nineteenth century the feminist quarrel became again a quarrel of partisans. One of the consequences of the industrial revolution was the entrance of women into productive labor, and it was just here that the claims of the feminists emerged from the realm of theory and acquired an economic basis, while their opponents became the more aggressive. Although landed property lost power to some extent, the bourgeoisie clung to the old morality that found the guarantee of private property in the solidity of the family. Woman was ordered back into the home the more harshly as her emancipation became a real menace. Even within the working class the men endeavored to restrain woman's liberation, because they began to see the women as dangerous competitors – the more so because they were accustomed to work for lower wages.

In proving woman's inferiority, the antifeminists then began to draw not only upon religion, philosophy, and theology, as before, but also upon science – biology, experimental psychology, etc. At most they were willing to grant "equality in difference" to the *other* sex. That profitable formula is most significant; it is precisely like the "equal but separate" formula of the Jim Crow laws aimed at the North American Negroes. As is well known, this so-called equalitarian segregation has resulted only in the most extreme discrimination. The similarity just noted is in no way due to chance, for whether it is a race, a caste, a class, or a sex that is reduced to a position of inferiority, the methods of justification are the same. "The eternal feminine" corresponds to "the black soul" and to "the Jewish character." True, the Jewish problem is on the whole very different from the other two – to the anti-Semite the Jew is not so much an inferior as he is an enemy for whom there is to be granted no place on earth, for whom annihilation is the fate desired. But there are deep similarities between the situation of woman and that of the Negro. Both are being emancipated today from a like paternalism,

and the former master class wishes to "keep them in their place" – that is, the place chosen for them. In both cases the former masters lavish more or less sincere eulogies, either on the virtues of "the good Negro" with his dormant, childish, merry soul – the submissive Negro – or on the merits of the woman who is "truly feminine" – that is, frivolous, infantile, irresponsible – the submissive woman. In both cases the dominant class bases its argument on a state of affairs that it has itself created. As George Bernard Shaw puts it, in substance, "The American white relegates the black to the rank of shoeshine boy; and he concludes from this that the black is good for nothing but shining shoes." This vicious circle is met with in all analogous circumstances; when an individual (or a group of individuals) is kept in a situation of inferiority, the fact is that he *is* inferior. But the significance of the verb *to be* must be rightly understood here; it is in bad faith to give it a static value when it really has the dynamic Hegelian sense of "to have become." Yes, women on the whole *are* today inferior to men; that is, their situation affords them fewer possibilities. The question is: should that state of affairs continue?

Many men hope that it will continue; not all have given up the battle. The conservative bourgeoisie still see in the emancipation of women a menace to their morality and their interests. Some men dread feminine competition. Recently a male student wrote in the *Hebdo-Latin*: "Every woman student who goes into medicine or law robs us of a job." He never questioned his rights in this world. And economic interests are not the only ones concerned. One of the benefits that oppression confers upon the oppressors is that the most humble among them is made to *feel* superior; thus, a "poor white" in the South can console himself with the thought that he is not a "dirty nigger" – and the more prosperous whites cleverly exploit this pride.

Similarly, the most mediocre of males feels himself a demigod as compared with women. It was much easier for M. de Montherlant to think himself a hero when he faced women (and women chosen for his purpose) than when he was obliged to act the man among men – something many women have done better than he, for that matter. And in September 1948, in one of his articles in the *Figaro littéraire*, Claude Mauriac – whose great originality is admired by all – could[6] write regarding woman: "*We* listen on a tone [*sic!*] of polite indifference . . . to the most brilliant among them, well knowing that her wit reflects more or less luminously ideas that come from *us*." Evidently the speaker referred to is not reflecting the ideas of Mauriac himself, for no one knows of his having any. It may be that she reflects ideas originating with men, but then, even among men there are those who have been known to appropriate ideas not their own; and one can well ask whether Claude Mauriac might not find more interesting a conversation reflecting Descartes, Marx, or Gide rather than himself. What is really remarkable is that by using the questionable *we* he identifies himself with St. Paul, Hegel, Lenin, and Nietzsche, and from the lofty eminence of their grandeur looks down disdainfully upon the bevy of women who make bold to converse with him on a footing of equality. In truth, I know of more than one woman who would refuse to suffer with patience Mauriac's "tone of polite indifference."

I have lingered on this example because the masculine attitude is here displayed with disarming ingenuousness. But men profit in many more subtle ways from the otherness, the alterity of woman. Here is miraculous balm for those afflicted with an inferiority complex, and indeed no one is more arrogant toward women, more aggressive or scornful, than the man who is anxious about his virility. Those who are not fear-ridden in the presence of their fellow men are much more disposed to recognize a fellow creature in woman; but even to these the myth of woman, the Other, is precious for many reasons.[7] They cannot be blamed for not cheerfully relinquishing all the benefits they derive from the myth, for they realize what they would lose in relinquishing woman as they fancy her to be, while they fail to realize what they have to gain from the woman of tomorrow. Refusal to pose oneself as the Subject, unique and absolute, requires great self-denial. Furthermore, the vast majority of men make no such claim explicitly. They do not *postulate* woman as inferior, for today they are too thoroughly imbued with the ideal of democracy not to recognize all human beings as equals.

In the bosom of the family, woman seems in the eyes of childhood and youth to be clothed in the same social dignity as the adult males. Later on, the young man, desiring and loving, experiences the resistance, the independence of the woman desired and loved; in marriage, he respects woman as wife and mother, and in the concrete events of conjugal life she stands there before him as a free being. He can therefore feel that social subordina-

tion as between the sexes no longer exists and that on the whole, in spite of differences, woman is an equal. As, however, he observes some points of inferiority – the most important being unfitness for the professions – he attributes these to natural causes. When he is in a co-operative and benevolent relation with woman, his theme is the principle of abstract equality, and he does not base his attitude upon such inequality as may exist. But when he is in conflict with her, the situation is reversed: his theme will be the existing inequality, and he will even take it as justification for denying abstract equality.[8]

So it is that many men will affirm as if in good faith that women *are* the equals of man and that they have nothing to clamor for, while *at the same time* they will say that women can never be the equals of man and that their demands are in vain. It is, in point of fact, a difficult matter for man to realize the extreme importance of social discriminations which seem outwardly insignificant but which produce in woman moral and intellectual effects so profound that they appear to spring from her original nature. The most sympathetic of men never fully comprehend woman's concrete situation. And there is no reason to put much trust in the men when they rush to the defense of privileges whose full extent they can hardly measure. We shall not, then, permit ourselves to be intimidated by the number and violence of the attacks launched against women, nor to be entrapped by the self-seeking eulogies bestowed on the "true woman," nor to profit by the enthusiasm for woman's destiny manifested by men who would not for the world have any part of it.

We should consider the arguments of the feminists with no less suspicion, however, for very often their controversial aim deprives them of all real value. If the "woman question" seems trivial, it is because masculine arrogance has made of it a "quarrel"; and when quarreling, one no longer reasons well. People have tirelessly sought to prove that woman is superior, inferior, or equal to man. Some say that, having been created after Adam, she is evidently a secondary being; others say on the contrary that Adam was only a rough draft and that God succeeded in producing the human being in perfection when He created Eve. Woman's brain is smaller; yes, but it is relatively larger. Christ was made a man; yes, but perhaps for his greater humility. Each argument at once suggests its opposite, and both are often fallacious. If we are to gain understanding, we must get out of these ruts; we must discard the vague notions of superiority, inferiority, equality which have hitherto corrupted every discussion of the subject and start afresh.

Very well, but just how shall we pose the question? And, to begin with, who are we to propound it at all? Man is at once judge and party to the case; but so is woman. What we need is an angel – neither man nor woman – but where shall we find one? Still, the angel would be poorly qualified to speak, for an angel is ignorant of all the basic facts involved in the problem. With a hermaphrodite we should be no better off, for here the situation is most peculiar; the hermaphrodite is not really the combination of a whole man and a whole woman, but consists of parts of each and thus is neither. It looks to me as if there are, after all, certain women who are best qualified to elucidate the situation of woman. Let us not be misled by the sophism that because Epimenides was a Cretan he was necessarily a liar; it is not a mysterious essence that compels men and women to act in good or in bad faith, it is their situation that inclines them more or less toward the search for truth. Many of today's women, fortunate in the restoration of all the privileges pertaining to the estate of the human being, can afford the luxury of impartiality – we even recognize its necessity. We are no longer like our partisan elders; by and large we have won the game. In recent debates on the status of women the United Nations has persistently maintained that the equality of the sexes is now becoming a reality, and already some of us have never had to sense in our femininity an inconvenience or an obstacle. Many problems appear to us to be more pressing than those which concern us in particular, and this detachment even allows us to hope that our attitude will be objective. Still, we know the feminine world more intimately than do the men because we have our roots in it, we grasp more immediately than do men what it means to a human being to be feminine; and we are more concerned with such knowledge. I have said that there are more pressing problems, but this does not prevent us from seeing some importance in asking how the fact of being women will affect our lives. What opportunities precisely have been given us and what withheld? What fate awaits our younger sisters, and what directions should they take? It is significant that books by women on women are in general animated in our day less by a wish to demand our rights than by an effort toward clarity and understanding. As

we emerge from an era of excessive controversy, this book is offered as one attempt among others to confirm that statement.

But it is doubtless impossible to approach any human problem with a mind free from bias. The way in which questions are put, the points of view assumed, presuppose a relativity of interest; all characteristics imply values, and every objective description, so called, implies an ethical background. Rather than attempt to conceal principles more or less definitely implied, it is better to state them openly at the beginning. This will make it unnecessary to specify on every page in just what sense one uses such words as *superior, inferior, better, worse, progress, reaction*, and the like. If we survey some of the works on woman, we note that one of the points of view most frequently adopted is that of the public good, the general interest; and one always means by this the benefit of society as one wishes it to be maintained or established. For our part, we hold that the only public good is that which assures the private good of the citizens; we shall pass judgment on institutions according to their effectiveness in giving concrete opportunities to individuals. But we do not confuse the idea of private interest with that of happiness, although that is another common point of view. Are not women of the harem more happy than women voters? Is not the housekeeper happier than the working woman? It is not too clear just what the word *happy* really means and still less what true values it may mask. There is no possibility of measuring the happiness of others, and it is always easy to describe as happy the situation in which one wishes to place them.

In particular those who are condemned to stagnation are often pronounced happy on the pretext that happiness consists in being at rest. This notion we reject, for our perspective is that of existentialist ethics. Every subject plays his part as such specifically through exploits or projects that serve as a mode of transcendence; he achieves liberty only through a continual reaching out toward other liberties. There is no justification for present existence other than its expansion into an indefinitely open future. Every time transcendence falls back into immanence, stagnation, there is a degradation of existence into the *"en-soi"* – the brutish life of subjection to given conditions – and of liberty into constraint and contingence. This downfall represents a moral fault if the subject consents to it; if it is inflicted upon him, it spells frustration and oppression. In both cases it is an absolute evil. Every individual concerned to justify his existence feels that his existence involves an undefined need to transcend himself, to engage in freely chosen projects.

Now, what peculiarly signalizes the situation of woman is that she – a free and autonomous being like all human creatures – nevertheless finds herself living in a world where men compel her to assume the status of the Other. They propose to stabilize her as object and to doom her to immanence since her transcendence is to be overshadowed and forever transcended by another ego (*conscience*) which is essential and sovereign. The drama of woman lies in this conflict between the fundamental aspirations of every subject (ego) – who always regards the self as the essential – and the compulsions of a situation in which she is the inessential. How can a human being in woman's situation attain fulfillment? What roads are open to her? Which are blocked? How can independence be recovered in a state of dependency? What circumstances limit woman's liberty and how can they be overcome? These are the fundamental questions on which I would fain throw some light. This means that I am interested in the fortunes of the individual as defined not in terms of happiness but in terms of liberty.

Quite evidently this problem would be without significance if we were to believe that woman's destiny is inevitably determined by physiological, psychological, or economic forces. Hence I shall discuss first of all the light in which woman is viewed by biology, psychoanalysis, and historical materialism. Next I shall try to show exactly how the concept of the "truly feminine" has been fashioned – why woman has been defined as the Other – and what have been the consequences from man's point of view. Then from woman's point of view I shall describe the world in which women must live; and thus we shall be able to envisage the difficulties in their way as, endeavoring to make their escape from the sphere hitherto assigned them, they aspire to full membership in the human race.

Notes

1. *Franchise*, dead today.
2. The Kinsey Report (Alfred C. Kinsey and others: *Sexual Behavior in the Human Male* (W. B. Saunders Co., 1948)) is no exception, for it is limited to describing the sexual characteristics of American men, which is quite a different matter.
3. E. Lévinas expresses this idea most explicitly in his essay *Temps et l'Autre*. "Is there not a case in which otherness, alterity [*altérité*], unquestionably marks the nature of a being, as its essence, an instance of otherness not consisting purely and simply in the opposition of two species of the same genus? I think that the feminine represents the contrary in its absolute sense, this contrariness being in no wise affected by any relation between it and its correlative and thus remaining absolutely other. Sex is not a certain specific difference . . . no more is the sexual difference a mere contradiction. . . . Nor does this difference lie in the duality of two complementary terms, for two complementary terms imply a pre-existing whole. . . . Otherness reaches its full flowering in the feminine, a term of the same rank as consciousness but of opposite meaning."

   I suppose that Lévinas does not forget that woman, too, is aware of her own consciousness, or ego. But it is striking that he deliberately takes a man's point of view, disregarding the reciprocity of subject and object. When he writes that woman is mystery, he implies that she is mystery for man. Thus his description, which is intended to be objective, is in fact an assertion of masculine privilege.
4. See C. Lévi-Strauss: *Les Structures élémentaires de la parenté*. My thanks are due to C. Lévi-Strauss for his kindness in furnishing me with the proofs of his work.
5. See *The Second Sex*, Pt II, ch. 8.
6. Or at least he thought he could.
7. A significant article on this theme by Michel Carrouges appeared in No. 292 of the *Cahiers du Sud*. He writes indignantly: "Would that there were no woman-myth at all but only a cohort of cooks, matrons, prostitutes, and bluestockings serving functions of pleasure or usefulness!" That is to say, in his view woman has no existence in and for herself; he thinks only of her *function* in the male world. Her reason for existence lies in man. But then, in fact, her poetic "function" as a myth might be more valued than any other. The real problem is precisely to find out why woman should be defined with relation to man.
8. For example, a man will say that he considers his wife in no wise degraded because she has no gainful occupation. The profession of housewife is just as lofty, and so on. But when the first quarrel comes he will exclaim: "Why, you couldn't make your living without me!"

17

One Is Not Born a Woman

Monique Wittig

A materialist feminist[1] approach to women's oppression destroys the idea that women are a "natural group": "a racial group of a special kind, a group perceived *as natural*, a group of men considered as materially specific in their bodies."[2] What the analysis accomplishes on the level of ideas, practice makes actual at the level of facts: by its very existence, lesbian society destroys the artificial (social) fact constituting women as a "natural group." A lesbian society[3] pragmatically reveals that the division from men of which women have been the object is a political one and shows that we have been ideologically rebuilt into a "natural group." In the case of women, ideology goes far since our bodies as well as our minds are the product of this manipulation. We have been compelled in our bodies and in our minds to correspond, feature by feature, with the *idea* of nature that has been established for us. Distorted to such an extent that our deformed body is what they call "natural," what is supposed to exist as such before oppression. Distorted to such an extent that in the end oppression seems to be a consequence of this "nature" within ourselves (a nature which is only an *idea*). What a materialist analysis does by reasoning, a lesbian society accomplishes practically: not only is there no natural group "women" (we lesbians are living proof of it), but as individuals as well we question "woman," which for us, as for Simone de Beauvoir, is only a myth. She said: "One is not born, but becomes a woman. No biological, psychological, or economic fate determines the figure that the human female presents in society: it is civilization as a whole that produces this creature, intermediate between male and eunuch, which is described as feminine."[4]

However, most of the feminists and lesbian-feminists in America and elsewhere still believe that the basis of women's oppression *is biological as well as* historical. Some of them even claim to find their sources in Simone de Beauvoir.[5] The belief in mother right and in a "prehistory" when women created civilization (because of a biological predisposition) while the coarse and brutal men hunted (because of a biological predisposition) is symmetrical with the biologizing interpretation of history produced up to now by the class of men. It is still the same method of finding in women and men a biological explanation of their division, outside of social facts. For me this could never constitute a lesbian approach to women's oppression, since it assumes that the basis of society or the beginning of society lies in heterosexuality. Matriarchy is no less heterosexual than patriarchy: it is only the sex of the oppressor that changes. Furthermore, not only is this conception still imprisoned in the categories of sex (woman and man), but it holds onto the idea that the capacity to give birth (biology) is what defines a woman. Although practical facts and ways of living contradict this theory in lesbian society, there are lesbians who affirm that "women and men are different species or races (the words are used interchangeably): men are biologically inferior to women; male violence is a biological inevitability . . ."[6] By doing this, by admitting that there is a "natural" division between women and men, we naturalize history, we assume that "men" and "women" have always existed and will always exist. Not only do we naturalize history, but also consequently we naturalize the social phenomena which express our oppression, making change impossible. For example, instead of seeing giving birth as a forced production, we see it as a "natural," "biological" process, forgetting that in our societies births are planned (demography), forgetting that we ourselves are programmed to produce children, while this is the only social activity "short of war"[7] that presents such a great danger of death. Thus, as long as we will be "unable to abandon by will or impulse a lifelong and centuries-old commitment to childbearing as *the* female creative act,"[8] gaining control of the production of children will mean much more than the mere control of the material means of this production: women will have to abstract themselves from the definition "woman" which is imposed upon them.

A materialist feminist approach shows that what we take for the cause or origin of oppression is in fact only the *mark*[9] imposed by the oppressor: the "myth of woman,"[10] plus its material effects and manifestations in the appropriated consciousness and bodies of women. Thus, this mark does not predate oppression: Colette Guillaumin has shown that before the socioeconomic reality of black slavery, the concept of race did not exist, at least not in its modern meaning, since it was applied to the lineage of families. However, now, race, exactly like sex, is taken as an "immediate given," a "sensible given," "physical features," belonging to a natural order. But what we believe to be a physical and direct perception is only a sophisticated and mythic construction, an "imaginary formation,"[11] which reinterprets physical features (in themselves as neutral as any others but marked by the social system) through the network of relationships in which they are perceived. (They are seen as *black*, therefore they *are* black; they are seen as *women*, therefore, they *are* women. But before being *seen* that way, they first had to be *made* that way.) Lesbians should always remember and acknowledge how "unnatural," compelling, totally oppressive, and destructive being "woman" was for us in the old days before the women's liberation movement. It was a political constraint, and those who resisted it were accused of not being "real" women. But then we were proud of it, since in the accusation there was already something like a shadow of victory: the avowal by the oppressor that "woman" is not something that goes without saying, since to be one, one has to be a "real" one. We were at the same time accused of wanting to be men. Today this double accusation has been taken up again with enthusiasm in the context of the women's liberation move-

ment by some feminists and also, alas, by some lesbians whose political goal seems somehow to be becoming more and more "feminine." To refuse to be a woman, however, does not mean that one has to become a man. Besides, if we take as an example the perfect "butch," the classic example which provokes the most horror, whom Proust would have called a woman/man, how is her alienation different from that of someone who wants to become a woman? Tweedledum and Tweedledee. At least for a woman, wanting to become a man proves that she has escaped her initial programming. But even if she would like to, with all her strength, she cannot become a man. For becoming a man would demand from a woman not only a man's external appearance but his consciousness as well, that is, the consciousness of one who disposes by right of at least two "natural" slaves during his life span. This is impossible, and one feature of lesbian oppression consists precisely of making women out of reach for us, since women belong to men. Thus a lesbian *has* to be something else, a not-woman, a not-man, a product of society, not a product of nature, for there is no nature in society.

The refusal to become (or to remain) heterosexual always meant to refuse to become a man or a woman, consciously or not. For a lesbian this goes further than the refusal of the *role* "woman." It is the refusal of the economic, ideological, and political power of a man. This, we lesbians, and nonlesbians as well, knew before the beginning of the lesbian and feminist movement. However, as Andrea Dworkin emphasizes, many lesbians recently "have increasingly tried to transform the very ideology that has enslaved us into a dynamic, religious, psychologically compelling celebration of female biological potential."[12] Thus, some avenues of the feminist and lesbian movement lead us back to the myth of woman which was created by men especially for us, and with it we sink back into a natural group. Having stood up to fight for a sexless society,[13] we now find ourselves entrapped in the familiar deadlock of "woman is wonderful." Simone de Beauvoir underlined particularly the false consciousness which consists of selecting among the features of the myth (that women are different from men) those which look good and using them as a definition for women. What the concept "woman is wonderful" accomplishes is that it retains for defining women the best features (best according to whom?) which oppression has granted us, and it does not radically question the categories "man" and "woman," which are political categories and not natural givens. It puts us in a position of fighting within the class "women" not as the other classes do, for the disappearance of our class, but for the defense of "woman" and its reenforcement. It leads us to develop with complacency "new" theories about our specificity: thus, we call our passivity "nonviolence," when the main and emergent point for us is to fight our passivity (our fear, rather, a justified one). The ambiguity of the term "feminist" sums up the whole situation. What does "feminist" mean? Feminist is formed with the word "femme," "woman," and means: someone who fights for women. For many of us it means someone who fights for women as a class and for the disappearance of this class. For many others it means someone who fights for woman and her defense – for the myth, then, and its reenforcement. But why was the word "feminist" chosen if it retains the least ambiguity? We chose to call ourselves "feminists" ten years ago, not in order to support or reenforce the myth of woman, nor to identify ourselves with the oppressor's definition of us, but rather to affirm that our movement had a history and to emphasize the political link with the old feminist movement.

It is, then, this movement that we can put in question for the meaning that it gave to feminism. It so happens that feminism in the last century could never resolve its contradictions on the subject of nature/culture, woman/society. Women started to fight for themselves as a group and rightly considered that they shared common features as a result of oppression. But for them these features were natural and biological rather than social. They went so far as to adopt the Darwinist theory of evolution. They did not believe like Darwin, however, "that women were less evolved than men, but they did believe that male and female natures had diverged in the course of evolutionary development and that society at large reflected this polarization."[14] "The failure of early feminism was that it only attacked the Darwinist charge of female inferiority, while accepting the foundations of this charge – namely, the view of woman as 'unique.' "[15] And finally it was women scholars – and not feminists – who scientifically destroyed this theory. But the early feminists had failed to regard history as a dynamic process which develops from conflicts of interests. Furthermore, they still believed as men do that the cause (origin) of their oppression lay

within themselves. And therefore after some astonishing victories the feminists of this first front found themselves at an impasse out of a lack of reasons to fight. They upheld the illogical principle of "equality in difference," an idea now being born again. They fell back into the trap which threatens us once again: the myth of woman.

Thus it is our historical task, and only ours, to define what we call oppression in materialist terms, to make it evident that women are a class, which is to say that the category "woman" as well as the category "man" are political and economic categories not eternal ones. Our fight aims to suppress men as a class, not through a genocidal, but a political struggle. Once the class "men" disappears, "women" as a class will disappear as well, for there are no slaves without masters. Our first task, it seems, is to always thoroughly dissociate "women" (the class within which we fight) and "woman," the myth. For "woman" does not exist for us: it is only an imaginary formation, while "women" is the product of a social relationship. We felt this strongly when everywhere we refused to be called a *"woman's* liberation movement." Furthermore, we have to destroy the myth inside and outside ourselves. "Woman" is not each one of us, but the political and ideological formation which negates "women" (the product of a relation of exploitation). "Woman" is there to confuse us, to hide the reality "women." In order to be aware of being a class and to become a class we first have to kill the myth of "woman" including its most seductive aspects (I think about Virginia Woolf when she said the first task of a woman writer is to kill "the angel in the house"). But to become a class we do not have to suppress our individual selves, and since no individual can be reduced to her/his oppression we are also confronted with the historical necessity of constituting ourselves as the individual subjects of our history as well. I believe this is the reason why all these attempts at "new" definitions of woman are blossoming now. What is at stake (and of course not only for women) is an individual definition as well as a class definition. For once one has acknowledged oppression, one needs to know and experience the fact that one can constitute oneself as a subject (as opposed to an object of oppression), that one can become *someone* in spite of oppression, that one has one's own identity. There is no possible fight for someone deprived of an identity, no internal motivation for fighting, since, although I can fight only with others, first I fight for myself.

The question of the individual subject is historically a difficult one for everybody. Marxism, the last avatar of materialism, the science which has politically formed us, does not want to hear anything about a "subject." Marxism has rejected the transcendental subject, the subject as constitutive of knowledge, the "pure" consciousness. All that thinks per se, before all experience, has ended up in the garbage can of history, because it claimed to exist outside matter, prior to matter, and needed God, spirit, or soul to exist in such a way. This is what is called "idealism." As for individuals, they are only the product of social relations, therefore their consciousness can only be "alienated." (Marx, in *The German Ideology*, says precisely that individuals of the dominating class are also alienated, although they are the direct producers of the ideas that alienate the classes oppressed by them. But since they draw visible advantages from their own alienation they can bear it without too much suffering.) There exists such a thing as class consciousness, but a consciousness which does not refer to a particular subject, except as participating in general conditions of exploitation at the same time as the other subjects of their class, all sharing the same consciousness. As for the practical class problems – outside of the class problems as traditionally defined – that one could encounter (for example, sexual problems), they were considered "bourgeois" problems that would disappear with the final victory of the class struggle. "Individualistic," "subjectivist," "petit bourgeois," these were the labels given to any person who had shown problems which could not be reduced to the "class struggle" itself.

Thus Marxism has denied the members of oppressed classes the attribute of being a subject. In doing this, Marxism, because of the ideological and political power this "revolutionary science" immediately exercised upon the workers' movement and all other political groups, has prevented all categories of oppressed peoples from constituting themselves historically as subjects (subjects of their struggle, for example). This means that the "masses" did not fight for themselves but for *the* party or its organizations. And when an economic transformation took place (end of private property, constitution of the socialist state), no revolutionary change took place within the new society, because the people themselves did not change.

For women, Marxism had two results. It prevented them from being aware that they are a class and therefore from constituting themselves as a

class for a very long time, by leaving the relation "women/men" outside of the social order, by turning it into a natural relation, doubtless for Marxists the only one, along with the relation of mothers to children, to be seen this way, and by hiding the class conflict between men and women behind a natural division of labor (*The German Ideology*). This concerns the theoretical (ideological) level. On the practical level, Lenin, *the* party, all the communist parties up to now, including all the most radical political groups, have always reacted to any attempt on the part of women to reflect and form groups based on their own class problem with an accusation of divisiveness. By uniting, we women are dividing the strength of the people. This means that for the Marxists women *belong* either to the bourgeois class or to the proletariat class, in other words, to the men of these classes. In addition, Marxist theory does not allow women any more than other classes of oppressed people to constitute themselves as historical subjects, because Marxism does not take into account the fact that a class also consists of individuals one by one. Class consciousness is not enough. We must try to understand philosophically (politically) these concepts of "subject" and "class consciousness" and how they work in relation to our history. When we discover that women are the objects of oppression and appropriation, at the very moment that we become able to perceive this, we become subjects in the sense of cognitive subjects, through an operation of abstraction. Consciousness of oppression is not only a reaction to (fight against) oppression. It is also the whole conceptual reevaluation of the social world, its whole reorganization with new concepts, from the point of view of oppression. It is what I would call the science of oppression created by the oppressed. This operation of understanding reality has to be undertaken by every one of us: call it a subjective, cognitive practice. The movement back and forth between the levels of reality (the conceptual reality and the material reality of oppression, which are both social realities) is accomplished through language.

It is we who historically must undertake the task of defining the individual subject in materialist terms. This certainly seems to be an impossibility since materialism and subjectivity have always been mutually exclusive. Nevertheless, and rather than despairing of ever understanding, we must recognize the *need* to reach subjectivity in the abandonment by many of us to the myth "woman" (the myth of woman being only a snare that holds us up). This real necessity for everyone to exist as an individual, as well as a member of a class, is perhaps the first condition for the accomplishment of a revolution, without which there can be no real fight or transformation. But the opposite is also true; without class and class consciousness there are no real subjects, only alienated individuals. For women to answer the question of the individual subject in materialist terms is first to show, as the lesbians and feminists did, that supposedly "subjective," "individual," "private" problems are in fact social problems, class problems; that sexuality is not for women an individual and subjective expression, but a social institution of violence. But once we have shown that all so-called personal problems are in fact class problems, we will still be left with the question of the subject of each singular woman – not the myth, but each one of us. At this point, let us say that a new personal and subjective definition for all humankind can only be found beyond the categories of sex (woman and man) and that the advent of individual subjects demands first destroying the categories of sex, ending the use of them, and rejecting all sciences which still use these categories as their fundamentals (practically all social sciences).

To destroy "woman" does not mean that we aim, short of physical destruction, to destroy lesbianism simultaneously with the categories of sex, because lesbianism provides for the moment the only social form in which we can live freely. Lesbian is the only concept I know of which is beyond the categories of sex (woman and man), because the designated subject (lesbian) is *not* a woman, either economically, or politically, or ideologically. For what makes a woman is a specific social relation to a man, a relation that we have previously called servitude,[16] a relation which implies personal and physical obligation as well as economic obligation ("forced residence,"[17] domestic corvée, conjugal duties, unlimited production of children, etc.), a relation which lesbians escape by refusing to become or to stay heterosexual. We are escapees from our class in the same way as the American runaway slaves were when escaping slavery and becoming

free. For us this is an absolute necessity; our survival demands that we contribute all our strength to the destruction of the class of women within which men appropriate women. This can be accomplished only by the destruction of heterosexuality as a social system which is based on the oppression of women by men and which produces the doctrine of the difference between the sexes to justify this oppression.

Notes

1. Christine Delphy, "Pour un féminisme matérialiste," *L'Arc* 61 (1975). Translated as "For a Materialist Feminism," *Feminist Issues* 1, no. 2 (Winter 1981).
2. Colette Guillaumin, "Race et Nature: Système des marques, idée de groupe naturel et rapports sociaux," *Pluriel*, no. 11 (1977). Translated as "Race and Nature: The System of Marks, the Idea of a Natural Group and Social Relationships," *Feminist Issues* 8, no. 2 (Fall 1988).
3. I use the word society with an extended anthropological meaning; strictly speaking, it does not refer to societies, in that lesbian societies do not exist completely autonomously from heterosexual social systems.
4. Simone de Beauvoir, *The Second Sex* (New York: Bantam, 1952), p. 249.
5. Redstockings, *Feminist Revolution* (New York: Random House, 1978), p. 18.
6. Andrea Dworkin, "Biological Superiority: The World's Most Dangerous and Deadly Idea," *Heresies* 6:46.
7. Ti-Grace Atkinson, *Amazon Odyssey* (New York: Links Books, 1974), p. 15.
8. Dworkin, "Biological Superiority."
9. Guillaumin, "Race et Nature."
10. de Beauvoir, *The Second Sex.*
11. Guillaumin, "Race et Nature."
12. Dworkin, "Biological Superiority."
13. Atkinson, *Amazon Odyssey*, p. 6: "If feminism has any logic at all, it must be working for a sexless society."
14. Rosalind Rosenberg, "In Search of Woman's Nature," *Feminist Studies* 3, no. 1/2 (1975): 144.
15. Ibid., p. 146.
16. In an article published in *L'Idiot International* (mai 1970), whose original title was "Pour un mouvement de libération des femmes" ("For a Women's Liberation Movement").
17. Christiane Rochefort, *Les Stances à Sophie* (Paris: Grasset, 1963).

18

Throwing Like a Girl: A Phenomenology of Feminine Body Comportment, Motility, and Spatiality

IRIS MARION YOUNG

In discussing the fundamental significance of lateral space, which is one of the unique spatial dimensions generated by the human upright posture, Erwin Straus pauses at "the remarkable difference in the manner of throwing of the two sexes"[1] (p. 157). Citing a study and photographs of young boys and girls, he describes the difference as follows:

> The girl of five does not make any use of lateral space. She does not stretch her arm sideward; she does not twist her trunk; she does not move her legs, which remain side by side. All she does in preparation for throwing is to lift her right arm forward to the horizontal and to bend the forearm backward in a pronate position. . . . The ball is released without force, speed, or accurate aim. . . . A boy of the same age, when preparing to throw, stretches his right arm sideward and backward; supinates the forearm; twists, turns and bends his trunk; and moves his right foot backward. From this stance, he can support his throwing almost with the full strength of his total motorium. . . . The ball leaves the hand with considerable acceleration; it moves toward its goal in a long flat curve. (pp. 157–60)[2]

Though he does not stop to trouble himself with the problem for long, Straus makes a few remarks in the attempt to explain this "remarkable differ-ence." Since the difference is observed at such an early age, he says, it seems to be "the manifestation of a biological, not an acquired, difference" (p. 157). He is somewhat at a loss, however, to specify the source of the difference. Since the feminine style of throwing is observed in young children, it cannot result from the development of the breast. Straus provides further evidence against the breast by pointing out that "it seems certain" that the Amazons, who cut off their right breasts, "threw a ball just like our Betty's, Mary's and Susan's" (p. 158). Having thus dismissed the breast, Straus considers the weaker muscle power of the girl as an explanation of the difference, but concludes that the girl should be expected to compensate for such relative weakness with the added preparation of reaching around and back. Straus explains the difference in style of throwing by referring to a "femin-ine attitude" in relation to the world and to space. The difference for him is biologically based, but he denies that it is specifically anatomical. Girls throw in a way different from boys because girls are "feminine."

What is even more amazing than this "explana-tion" is the fact that a perspective that takes body comportment and movement as definitive for the structure and meaning of human lived experience devotes no more than an incidental page to such a "remarkable difference" between masculine and feminine body comportment and style of movement, for throwing is by no means the only activity in which such a difference can be observed. If there are indeed typically "feminine" styles of body comportment and movement, this should generate for the existential phenomenologist a concern to specify such a differentiation of the modalities of the lived body. Yet Straus is by no means alone in his failure to describe the modalities, meaning, and implications of the difference between "masculine" and "feminine" body comportment and movement.

A virtue of Straus's account of the typical difference of the sexes in throwing is that he does not explain this difference on the basis of physical attributes. Straus is convinced, however, that the early age at which the difference appears shows that it is not an acquired difference, and thus he is forced back onto a mysterious "feminine essence" in order to explain it. The feminist denial that the real differences in behavior and psychology between men and woman can be attributed to some natural and eternal feminine essence is perhaps most thoroughly and systematically expressed by Beauvoir. Every human existence is defined by its *situation*; the particular existence of the female person is no less defined by the historical, cultural, social, and economic limits of her situation. We reduce women's condition simply to unintelligibility if we "explain" it by appeal to some natural and ahistorical feminine essence. In denying such a feminine essence, however, we should not fall into that "nominalism" that denies the real differences in the behavior and experiences of men and women. Even though there is no eternal feminine essence, there is "a common basis which underlies every individual female existence in the present state of education and custom."[3] The situation of women within a given sociohistorical set of circumstances, despite the individual variation in each woman's experience, opportunities, and possibilities, has a unity that can be described and made intelligible. It should be emphasized, however, that this unity is specific to a particular social formation during a particular epoch.

Beauvoir proceeds to give such an account of the situation of women with remarkable depth, clarity, and ingenuity. Yet she also, to a large extent, fails to give a place to the status and orientation of the woman's body as relating to its surroundings in living action. When Beauvoir does talk about the woman's bodily being and her physical relation to her surroundings, she tends to focus on the more evident facts of a woman's physiology. She discusses how women experience the body as a burden, how

the hormonal and physiological changes the body undergoes at puberty, during menstruation and pregnancy, are felt to be fearful and mysterious, and claims that these phenomena weigh down the woman's existence by tying her to nature, immanence, and the requirements of the species at the expense of her own individuality.[4] By largely ignoring the situatedness of the woman's actual bodily movement and orientation to its surroundings and its world, Beauvoir tends to create the impression that it is woman's anatomy and physiology *as such* that at least in part determine her unfree status.[5]

This essay seeks to begin to fill a gap that thus exists both in existential phenomenology and feminist theory. It traces in a provisional way some of the basic modalities of feminine body comportment, manner of moving, and relation in space. It brings intelligibility and significance to certain observable and rather ordinary ways in which women in our society typically comport themselves and move differently from the ways that men do. In accordance with the existentialist concern with the situatedness of human experience, I make no claim to the universality of this typicality of the bodily comportment of women and the phenomenological description based on it. The account developed here claims only to describe the modalities of feminine bodily existence for women situated in contemporary advanced industrial, urban, and commercial society. Elements of the account developed here may or may not apply to the situation of woman in other societies and other epochs, but it is not the concern of this essay to determine to which, if any, other social circumstances this account applies.

The scope of bodily existence and movement with which I am concerned here is also limited. I concentrate primarily on those sorts of bodily activities that relate to the comportment or orientation of the body as a whole, that entail gross movement, or that require the enlistment of strength and the confrontation of the body's capacities and possibilities with the resistance and malleability of things. The kind of movement I am primarily concerned with is movement in which the body aims to accomplish a definite purpose or task. There are thus many aspects of feminine bodily existence that I leave out of this account. Most notable of these is the body in its sexual being. Another aspect of bodily existence, among others, that I leave unconsidered is structured body movement that does not have a particular aim – for example, dancing. Besides reasons of space, this limitation of subject is based on the conviction, derived primarily from Merleau-Ponty, that it is the ordinary purposive orientation of the body as a whole toward things and its environment that initially defines the relation of a subject to its world. Thus a focus upon ways in which the feminine body frequently or typically conducts itself in such comportment or movement may be particularly revelatory of the structures of feminine existence.[6]

Before entering the analysis, I should clarify what I mean here by "feminine" existence. In accordance with Beauvoir's understanding, I take "femininity" to designate not a mysterious quality or essence that all women have by virtue of their being biologically female. It is, rather, a set of structures and conditions that delimit the typical *situation* of being a woman in a particular society, as well as the typical way in which this situation is lived by the women themselves. Defined as such, it is not necessary that *any* women be "feminine" – that is, it is not necessary that there be distinctive structures and behavior typical of the situation of women.[7] This understanding of "feminine" existence makes it possible to say that some women escape or transcend the typical situation and definition of women in various degrees and respects. I mention this primarily to indicate that the account offered here of the modalities of feminine bodily existence is not to be falsified by referring to some individual women to whom aspects of the account do not apply, or even to some individual men to whom they do.

The account developed here combines the insights of the theory of the lived body as expressed by Merleau-Ponty and the theory of the situation of women as developed by Beauvoir. I assume that at the most basic descriptive level, Merleau-Ponty's account of the relation of the lived body to its world, as developed in the *Phenomenology of Perception*, applies to any human existence in a general way. At a more specific level, however, there is a particular style of bodily comportment that is typical of feminine existence, and this style consists of particular *modalities* of the structures and conditions of the body's existence in the world.[8]

As a framework for developing these modalities, I rely on Beauvoir's account of woman's existence in patriarchal society as defined by a basic tension between immanence and transcendence.[9] The culture and society in which the female person dwells defines woman as Other, as the inessential correlate to man, as mere object and immanence. Woman is thereby both culturally and socially denied by the subjectivity, autonomy, and creativity that are definitive of being human and that in patriarchal society are accorded the man. At the same time, however, because she is a human existence, the female person necessarily is a subjectivity and transcendence, and she knows herself to be. The female person who enacts the existence of women in patriarchal society must therefore live a contradiction: as human she is a free subject who participates in transcendence, but her situation as a woman denies her that subjectivity and transcendence. My suggestion is that the modalities of feminine bodily comportment, motility, and spatiality exhibit this same tension between transcendence and immanence, between subjectivity and being a mere object.

Section I offers some specific observations about bodily comportment, physical engagement with things, ways of using the body in performing tasks, and bodily self-image, which I find typical of feminine existence. Section II gives a general phenomenological account of the modalities of feminine bodily comportment and motility. Section III develops these modalities further in terms of the spatiality generated by them. Finally, in Section IV, I draw out some of the implications of this account for an understanding of the oppression of women, as well as raise some further questions about feminine being in the world that require further investigation.

I

The basic difference that Straus observes between the way boys and girls throw is that girls do not bring their whole bodies into the motion as much as the boys do. They do not reach back, twist, move backward, step, and lean forward. Rather, the girls tend to remain relatively immobile except for their arms, and even the arms are not extended as far as they could be. Throwing is not the only movement in which there is a typical difference in the way men and women use their bodies. Reflection on feminine comportment and body movement in other physical activities reveals that these also are frequently characterized, much as in the throwing case, by a failure to make full use of the body's spatial and lateral potentialities.

Even in the most simple body orientations of men and women as they sit, stand, and walk, one can observe a typical difference in body style and extension. Women generally are not as open with their bodies as are men in their gait and stride. Typically, the masculine stride is longer proportional to a man's body than is the feminine stride to a woman's. The man typically swings his arms in a more open and loose fashion than does a woman and typically has more up and down rhythm in his step. Though we now wear pants more than we used to and consequently do not have to restrict our sitting postures because of dress, women still tend to sit with their legs relatively close together and their arms across their bodies. When simply standing or leaning, men tend to keep their feet farther apart than do women, and we also tend more to keep our hands and arms touching or shielding our bodies. A final indicative difference is the way each carries books or parcels; girls and women most often carry books embraced to their chests, while boys and men swing them along their sides.

The approach that people of each sex take to the performance of physical tasks that require force, strength, and muscular coordination is frequently different. There are indeed real physical differences between men and women in the kind and limit of their physical strength. Many of the observed differences between men and women in the performance of tasks requiring coordinated strength, however, are due not so much to brute muscular strength as to the way each sex *uses* the body in approaching tasks. Women often do not perceive themselves as capable of lifting and carrying heavy things, pushing and shoving with significant force, pulling, squeezing, grasping, or twisting with force. When we attempt such tasks, we frequently fail to summon the full possibilities of our muscular coordination, position, poise, and bearing. Women tend not to put their whole bodies into engagement in a physical task with the same ease and naturalness as men. For example, in attempting to lift something, women more often than men fail to plant themselves firmly and make their thighs bear the greatest proportion of the weight. Instead, we tend to concentrate our effort on those parts of the body most immediately connected to the task – the arms and shoulders – rarely bringing the power of the legs to the task at all. When turning or twisting something, to take another example, we frequently concentrate effort in the hand and wrist, not bringing to the task the power of the shoulder, which is necessary for its efficient performance.[10]

The previously cited throwing example can be extended to a great deal of athletic activity. Now,

most men are by no means superior athletes, and their sporting efforts more often display bravado than genuine skill and coordination. The relatively untrained man nevertheless engages in sport generally with more free motion and open reach than does his female counterpart. Not only is there a typical style of throwing like a girl, but there is a more or less typical style of running like a girl, climbing like a girl, swinging like a girl, hitting like a girl. They have in common first that the whole body is not put into fluid and directed motion, but rather, in swinging and hitting, for example, the motion is concentrated in one body part; and second that the woman's motion tends not to reach, extend, lean, stretch, and follow through in the direction of her intention.

For many women as they move in sport, a space surrounds us in imagination that we are not free to move beyond; the space available to our movement is a constricted space. Thus, for example, in softball or volleyball women tend to remain in one place more often than men do, neither jumping to reach nor running to approach the ball. Men more often move out toward a ball in flight and confront it with their own countermotion. Women tend to wait for and then *react* to its approach, rather than going forth to meet it. We frequently respond to the motion of a ball coming toward us as though it were coming *at* us, and our immediate bodily impulse is to flee, duck, or otherwise protect ourselves from its flight. Less often than men, moreover, do women give self-conscious direction and placement to their motion in sport. Rather than aiming at a certain place where we wish to hit a ball, for example, we tend to hit it in a "general" direction.

Women often approach a physical engagement with things with timidity, uncertainty, and hesitancy. Typically, we lack an entire trust in our bodies to carry us to our aims. There is, I suggest, a double hesitation here. On the one hand, we often lack confidence that we have the capacity to do what must be done. Many times I have slowed a hiking party in which the men bounded across a harmless stream while I stood on the other side warily testing my footing on various stones, holding on to overhanging branches. Though the others crossed with ease, I do not believe it is easy for *me*, even though once I take a committed step I am across in a flash. The other side of this tentativeness is, I suggest, a fear of getting hurt, which is greater in women than in men. Our attention is often divided between the aim to be realized in motion and the body that must accomplish it, while at the same time saving itself from harm. We often experience our bodies as a fragile encumbrance, rather than the media for the enactment of our aims. We feel as though we must have our attention directed upon our bodies to make sure they are doing what we wish them to do, rather than paying attention to what we want to do *through* our bodies.

All the above factors operate to produce in many women a greater or lesser feeling of incapacity, frustration, and self-consciousness. We have more of a tendency than men do to greatly underestimate our bodily capacity.[11] We decide beforehand – usually mistakenly – that the task is beyond us, and thus give it less than our full effort. At such a halfhearted level, of course, we cannot perform the tasks, become frustrated, and fulfill our own prophecy. In entering a task we frequently are self-conscious about appearing awkward and at the same time do not wish to appear too strong. Both worries contribute to our awkwardness and frustration. If we should finally release ourselves from this spiral and really give a physical task our best effort, we are greatly surprised indeed at what our bodies can accomplish. It has been found that women more often than men underestimate the level of achievement they have reached.[12]

None of the observations that have been made thus far about the way women typically move and comport their bodies applies to all women all of the time. Nor do those women who manifest some aspect of this typicality do so in the same degree. There is no inherent, mysterious connection between these sorts of typical comportments and being a female person. Many of them result, as will be developed later, from lack of practice in using the body and performing tasks. Even given these qualifications, one can nevertheless sensibly speak of a general feminine style of body comportment and movement. The next section will develop a specific categorical description of the modalities of the comportment and movement.

II

The three modalities of feminine motility are that feminine movement exhibits an *ambiguous transcendence*, an *inhibited intentionality*, and a *discontinuous unity* with its surroundings. A source of these contradictory modalities is the bodily self-reference of feminine comportment, which derives from the woman's experience of her body as a *thing* at the same time that she experiences it as a capacity.

1. In his *Phenomenology of Perception*,[13] Merleau-Ponty takes as his task the articulation of the primordial structures of existence, which are prior to and the ground of all reflective relation to the world. In asking how there can be a world for a subject, Merleau-Ponty reorients the entire tradition of that questioning by locating subjectivity not in mind or consciousness, but in the *body*. Merleau-Ponty gives to the lived body the ontological status that Sartre, as well as "intellectualist" thinkers before him, attribute to consciousness alone: the status of transcendence as being for itself. It is the body in its orientation toward and action upon and within its surroundings that constitutes the initial meaning-giving act (p. 121, pp. 146–7). The body is the first locus of intentionality, as pure presence to the world and openness upon its possibilities. The most primordial intentional act is the motion of the body orienting itself with respect to and moving within its surroundings. There is a world for a subject just insofar as the body has capacities by which it can approach, grasp, and appropriate its surroundings in the direction of its intentions.

While feminine bodily existence is a transcendence and openness to the world, it is an *ambiguous transcendence*, a transcendence that is at the same time laden with immanence. Now, once we take the locus of subjectivity and transcendence to be the lived body rather than pure consciousness, all transcendence is ambiguous because the body as natural and material is immanence. But it is not the ever-present possibility of any lived body to be passive, to be touched as well as touching, to be grasped as well as grasping, which I am referring to here as the ambiguity of the transcendence of the feminine lived body. The transcendence of the lived body that Merleau-Ponty describes is a transcendence that moves out from the body in its immanence in an open and unbroken directedness upon the world in action. The lived body as transcendence is pure fluid action, the continuous calling-forth of capacities that are applied to the world. Rather than simply beginning in immanence, feminine bodily existence remains in immanence or, better, is *overlaid* with immanence, even as it moves out toward the world in motions of grasping, manipulating, and so on.

In the previous section, I observed that a woman typically refrains from throwing her whole body into a motion, and rather concentrates motion in one part of the body alone, while the rest of the body remains relatively immobile. Only part of the body, that is, moves out toward a task, while the rest remains rooted in immanence. I also observed earlier that a woman frequently does not trust the capacity of her body to engage itself in physical relation to things. Consequently, she often lives her body as a burden, which must be dragged and prodded along and at the same time protected.

2.   Merleau-Ponty locates intentionality in motility (pp. 110–12); the possibilities that are opened up in the world depend on the mode and limits of the bodily "I can" (p. 137, p. 148). Feminine existence, however, often does not enter bodily relation to possibilities by its own comportment toward its surroundings in an unambiguous and confident "I can." For example, as noted earlier, women frequently tend to posit a task that would be accomplished relatively easily once attempted as beyond their capacities before they begin it. Typically, the feminine body underuses its real capacity, both as the potentiality of its physical size and strength and as the real skills and coordination that are available to it. Feminine bodily existence is an *inhibited intentionality*, which simultaneously reaches toward a projected end with an "I can" and withholds its full bodily commitment to that end in a self-imposed "I cannot."[14]

An uninhibited intentionality projects the aim to be accomplished and connects the body's motion toward that end in an unbroken directedness that organizes and unifies the body's activity. The body's capacity and motion structure its surroundings and project meaningful possibilities of movement and action, which in turn call the body's motion forth to enact them: "To understand is to experience the harmony between what we aim at and what is given, between the intention and the performance . . ." (p. 144; see also pp. 101, 131, and 132). Feminine motion often severs this mutually conditioning relation between aim and enactment. In those motions that when properly performed require the coordination and directedness of the whole body upon some definite end, women frequently move in a contradictory way. Their bodies project an aim to be enacted but at the same time stiffen against the performance of the task. In performing a physical task the woman's body does carry her toward the intended aim, often not easily and directly, but rather circuitously, with the wasted motion resulting from the effort of testing and reorienta-

tion, which is a frequent consequence of feminine hesitancy.

For any lived body, the world appears as the system of possibilities that are correlative to its intentions (p. 131). For any lived body, moreover, the world also appears to be populated with opacities and resistances correlative to its own limits and frustrations. For any bodily existence, that is, an "I cannot" may appear to set limits to the "I can." To the extent that feminine bodily existence is an inhibited intentionality, however, the same set of possibilities that appears to be correlative to its intentions also appears to be a system of frustrations correlative to its hesitancies. By repressing or withholding its own motile energy, feminine bodily existence frequently projects an "I can" and an "I cannot" with respect to the very same end. When the woman enters a task with inhibited intentionality, she projects the possibilities of that task – thus projects an "I *can*" – but projects them merely as the possibilities of "someone," and not truly *her* possibilities – and thus projects an "*I* cannot."

3.   Merleau-Ponty gives to the body the unifying and synthesizing function that Kant locates in transcendental subjectivity. By projecting an aim toward which it moves, the body brings unity to and unites itself with its surroundings; through the vectors of its projected possibilities it sets things in relation to one another and to itself. The body's movement and orientation organizes the surrounding space as a continuous extension of its own being (p. 143). Within the same act in which the body synthesizes its surroundings, moreover, it synthesizes itself. The body synthesis is immediate and primordial. "I do not bring together one by one the parts of my body; this translation and this unification are performed once and for all within me: they are my body itself" (p. 150).

The third modality of feminine bodily existence is that it stands in *discontinuous unity* with both itself and its surroundings. I remarked earlier that in many motions that require the active engagement and coordination of the body as a whole in order to be performed properly, women tend to locate their motion in part of the body only, leaving the rest of the body relatively immobile. Motion such as this is discontinuous with itself. The part of the body that is transcending toward an aim is in relative disunity from those that remain immobile. The undirected and wasted motion that is often an aspect of feminine engagement in a task also manifests this lack of body unity. The character of the inhibited intentionality whereby feminine motion severs the connection between aim and enactment, between possibility in the world and capacity in the body, itself produces this discontinuous unity.

According to Merleau-Ponty, for the body to exist as a transcendent presence to the world and the immediate enactment of intentions, it cannot exist as an *object* (p. 123). As subject, the body is referred not onto itself, but onto the world's possibilities. "In order that we may be able to move our body towards an object, the object must first exist for it, our body must not belong to the realm of the 'in-itself' " (p. 139). The three contradictory modalities of feminine bodily existence – ambiguous transcendence, inhibited intentionality, and discontinuous unity – have their root, however, in the fact that for feminine existence the body frequently is both subject and object for itself at the same time and in reference to the same act. Feminine bodily existence is frequently not a pure presence to the world because it is referred onto *itself* as well as onto possibilities in the world.[15]

Several of the observations of the previous section illustrate this self-reference. It was observed, for example, that women have a tendency to take up the motion of an object coming *toward* them as coming *at* them. I also observed that women tend to have a latent and sometimes conscious fear of getting hurt, which we bring to a motion. That is, feminine bodily existence is self-referred in that the woman takes herself to be the *object* of the motion rather than its originator. Feminine bodily existence is also self-referred to the extent that a woman is uncertain of her body's capacities and does not feel that its motions are entirely under her control. She must divide her attention between the task to be performed and the body that must be coaxed and manipulated into performing it. Finally, feminine bodily existence is self-referred to the extent that the feminine subject posits her motion as the motion that is *looked at*. In Section IV, we will explore the implications of the basic fact of the woman's social existence as the object of the gaze of another, which is a major source of her bodily self-reference.

In summary, the modalities of feminine bodily existence have their root in the fact that feminine existence experiences the body as a mere thing – a fragile thing, which must be picked up and coaxed into movement, a thing that exists as *looked at and acted upon*. To be sure, any lived body exists as a material thing as well as a transcending subject. For feminine bodily existence, however, the body is often lived as a thing that is other than it, a thing like other things in the world. To the extent that a woman lives her body as a thing, she remains rooted in immanence, is inhibited, and retains a distance from her body as transcending movement and from engagement in the world's possibilities.

III

For Merleau-Ponty there is a distinction between lived space, or phenomenal space, and objective space, the uniform space of geometry and science in which all positions are external to one another and interchangeable. Phenomenal space arises out of motility, and lived relations of space are generated by the capacities of the body's motion and the intentional relations that that motion constitutes. "It is clearly in action that the spatiality of our body is brought into being and an analysis of one's own movement should enable us to arrive at a better understanding" (p. 102, cf. pp. 148, 149, 249). In this account, if there are particular modalities of feminine bodily comportment and motility, it must follow that there are also particular modalities of feminine spatiality. Feminine existence lives space as *enclosed* or confining, as having a *dual* structure, and the woman experiences herself as *positioned* in space.

1. There is a famous study that Erik Erikson performed several years ago in which he asked several male and female preadolescents to construct a scene for an imagined movie out of some toys. He found that girls typically depicted indoor settings, with high walls and enclosures, while boys typically constructed outdoor scenes. He concluded that females tend to emphasize what he calls "inner space," or enclosed space, while males tend to emphasize what he calls "outer space," or a spatial orientation that is open and outwardly directed. Erikson's interpretation of these observations is psychoanalytical: girls depict "inner space" as the projection of the enclosed space of their wombs and vaginas; boys depict "outer space" as a projection of the phallus.[16] I find such an explanation wholly unconvincing. If girls do tend to project an enclosed space and boys to project an open and outwardly directed space, it is far more plausible to regard this as a reflection of the way members of each sex live and move their bodies in space.

In the first section, I observed that women tend not to open their bodies in their everyday movements, but tend to sit, stand, and walk with their limbs close to or closed around them. I also observed that women tend not to reach, stretch, bend, lean, or stride to the full limits of their physical capacities, even when doing so would better accomplish a task or motion. The space, that is, that is *physically* available to the feminine body is frequently of greater radius than the space that she uses and inhabits. Feminine existence appears to posit an existential enclosure between herself and the space surrounding her, in such a way that the space that belongs to her and is available to her grasp and manipulation is constricted and the space beyond is not available to her movement.[17] A further illustration of this confinement of feminine lived space is the observation already noted that in sport, for example, women tend not to move out and meet the motion of a ball, but rather tend to stay in one place and react to the ball's motion only when it has arrived within the space where she is. The timidity, immobility, and uncertainty that frequently characterize feminine movement project a limited space for the feminine "I can."

2.   In Merleau-Ponty's account, the body unity of transcending performance creates an immediate link between the body and the outlying space. "Each instant of the movement embraces its whole space, and particularly the first which, by being active and initiative, institutes the link between a here and a yonder . . ." (p. 140). In feminine existence, however, the projection of an enclosed space severs the continuity between a "here" and a "yonder." In feminine existence there is a *double spatiality*, as the space of the "here" is distinct from the space of the "yonder." A distinction between space that is "yonder" and not linked with my own body possibilities and the enclosed space that is "here," which I inhabit with my bodily possibilities, is an expression of the discontinuity between aim and capacity to realize the aim that I have articulated as the meaning of the tentativeness and uncertainty characterizing the inhibited intentionality of feminine motility. The space of the "yonder" is a space in which feminine existence projects possibilities in the sense of understanding that "someone" could move within it, but not I. Thus the space of the "yonder" exists for feminine existence, but only as that which she is looking into, rather than moving in.

3.   The third modality of feminine spatiality is that feminine existence experiences itself as *posi-tioned in* space. For Merleau-Ponty, the body is the original subject that constitutes space; there would be no space without the body (pp. 102, 142). As the origin and subject of spatial relations, the body does not occupy a position coequal and interchangeable with the positions occupied by other things (p. 143, pp. 247–9). Because the body as lived is not an *object*, it cannot be said to exist *in* space as water is *in* the glass (pp. 139–40). "The word 'here' applied to my body does not refer to a determinate position in relation to other positions or to external coordinates, but the laying down of the first coordinates, the anchoring of the active body in an object, the situation of the body in the face of its tasks" (p. 100).

Feminine spatiality is contradictory insofar as feminine bodily existence is both spatially constituted and a constituting spatial subject. Insofar as feminine existence lives the body as transcendence and intentionality, the feminine body actively constitutes space and is the original coordinate that unifies the spatial field and projects spatial relations and positions in accord with its intentions. But to the extent that feminine motility is laden with immanence and inhibited, the body's space is lived as constituted. To the extent, that is, that feminine bodily existence is self-referred and thus lives itself as an *object*, the feminine body does exist *in* space. In Section I, I observed that women frequently react to motions, even our own motions, as though we are the object of a motion that issues from an alien intention, rather than taking ourselves as the subject of motion. In its immanence and inhibition, feminine spatial existence is *positioned* by a system of coordinates that does not have its origin in her own intentional capacities. The tendency for the feminine body to remain partly immobile in the performance of a task that requires the movement of the whole body illustrates this characteristic of feminine bodily existence as rooted *in place*. Likewise does the tendency of women to wait for an object to come within their immediate bodily field, rather than move out toward it.

Merleau-Ponty devotes a great deal of attention to arguing that the diverse senses and activities of the lived body are synthetically related in such a way that each stands in a mutually conditioning relation with all the others. In particular, visual perception and motility stand in a relation of reversability; an impairment in the functioning of one, for example, leads to an impairment in the functioning of the other (pp. 133–7). If we assume that reversability of visual perception and motility, the previous account of the modalities of feminine motility and the spatiality that arises from them suggests that visual space will have its own modalities as well.

Numerous psychological studies have reported differences between the sexes in the character of spatial perception. One of the most frequently discussed of these conclusions is that females are more often "field-dependent." That is, it has been claimed that males have a greater capacity for lifting a figure out of its spatial surroundings and viewing relations in space as fluid and interchangeable, whereas females have a greater tendency to regard figures as embedded within and fixed by their surroundings.[18] The above account of feminine motility and spatiality gives some theoretical intelligibility to these findings. If feminine body spatiality is such that the woman experiences herself as rooted and enclosed, on the reversability assumption it would follow that visual space for feminine existence also has its closures of immobility and fixity. The objects in visual space do not stand in a fluid system of potentially alterable and interchangeable relations correlative to the body's various intentions and projected capacities. Rather, they too have their own *places* and are anchored in their immanence.

IV

The modalities of feminine bodily comportment, motility, and spatiality that I have described here are, I claim, common to the existence of women in contemporary society to one degree or another. They have their source, however, in neither anatomy nor physiology, and certainly not in a mysterious feminine essence. Rather, they have their source in the particular *situation* of women as conditioned by their sexist oppression in contemporary society.

Women in sexist society are physically handicapped. Insofar as we learn to live out our existence in accordance with the definition that patriarchal culture assigns to us, we are physically inhibited, confined, positioned, and objectified. As lived bodies we are not open and unambiguous transcendences that move out to master a world that belongs to us, a world constituted by our own intentions and projections. To be sure, there are actual women in contemporary society to whom all or part of the above description does not apply. Where these modalities are not manifest in or deter-

minative of the existence of a particular woman, however, they are definitive in a negative mode – as that which she has escaped, through accident or good fortune, or, more often, as that which she has had to overcome.

One of the sources of the modalities of feminine bodily existence is too obvious to dwell upon at length. For the most part, girls and women are not given the opportunity to use their full bodily capacities in free and open engagement with the world, nor are they encouraged as much as boys are to develop specific bodily skills.[19] Girls' play is often more sedentary and enclosing than the play of boys. In school and after-school activities girls are not encouraged to engage in sport, in the controlled use of their bodies in achieving well-defined goals. Girls, moreover, get little practice at "tinkering" with things and thus at developing spatial skill. Finally, girls are not often asked to perform tasks demanding physical effort and strength, while as the boys grow older they are asked to do so more and more.[20]

The modalities of feminine bodily existence are not merely privative, however, and thus their source is not merely in lack of practice, though this is certainly an important element. There is a specific positive style of feminine body comportment and movement, which is learned as the girl comes to understand that she is a girl. The young girl acquires many subtle habits of feminine body comportment – walking like a girl, tilting her head like a girl, standing and sitting like a girl, gesturing like a girl, and so on. The girl learns actively to hamper her movements. She is told that she must be careful not to get hurt, not to get dirty, not to tear her clothes, that the things she desires to do are dangerous for her. Thus she develops a bodily timidity that increases with age. In assuming herself to be a girl, she takes herself to be fragile. Studies have found that young children of both sexes categorically assert that girls are more likely to get hurt than boys are,[21] and that girls ought to remain close to home, while boys can roam and explore.[22] The more a girl assumes her status as feminine, the more she takes herself to be fragile and immobile and the more she actively enacts her own body inhibition. When I was about thirteen, I spent hours practicing a "feminine" walk, which was stiff and closed, and rotated from side to side.

Studies that record observations of sex differences in spatial perception, spatial problem-solving, and motor skills have also found that these differences tend to increase with age. While very young children show virtually no differences in motor skills, movement, spatial perception, etc., differences seem to appear in elementary school and increase with adolescence. If these findings are accurate, they would seem to support the conclusion that it is in the process of growing up as a girl that the modalities of feminine bodily comportment, motility, and spatiality make their appearance.[23]

There is, however, a further source of the modalities of feminine bodily existence that is perhaps even more profound than these. At the root of those modalities, I have stated in the previous section, is the fact that the woman lives her body as *object* as well as subject. The source of this is that patriarchal society defines woman as object, as a mere body, and that in sexist society women are in fact frequently regarded by others as objects and mere bodies. An essential part of the situation of being a woman is that of living the ever-present possibility that one will be gazed upon as a mere body, as shape and flesh that presents itself as the potential object of another subject's intentions and manipulations, rather than as a living manifestation of action and intention.[24] The source of this objectified bodily existence is in the attitude of others regarding her, but the woman herself often actively takes up her body as a mere thing. She gazes at it in the mirror, worries about how it looks to others, prunes it, shapes it, molds and decorates it.

This objectified bodily existence accounts for the self-consciousness of the feminine relation to her body and resulting distance she takes from her body. As human, she is a transcendence and subjectivity, and cannot live herself as mere bodily object. Thus, to the degree that she does live herself as mere body, she cannot be in unity with herself, but must take a distance from and exist in discontinuity with her body. The objectifying regard that "keeps her in her place" can also account for the spatial modality of being positioned and for why women frequently tend not to move openly, keeping their limbs closed around themselves. To open her body in free, active, open extension and bold outward-directedness is for a woman to invite objectification.

The threat of being seen is, however, not the only threat of objectification that the woman lives. She also lives the threat of invasion of her body space. The most extreme form of such spatial and bodily invasion is the threat of rape. But we daily are subject to the possibility of bodily invasion in many far more subtle ways as well. It is acceptable, for example, for women to be touched in ways and under circumstances that it is not acceptable for men to be touched, and by persons – i.e., men – whom it is not acceptable for them to touch.[25] I would suggest that the enclosed space that has been described as a modality of feminine spatiality is in part a defense against such invasion. Women tend to project an existential barrier closed around them and discontinuous with the "over there" in order to keep the other at a distance. The woman lives her space as confined and closed around her, at least in part as projecting some small area in which she can exist as a free subject.

This essay is a prolegomenon to the study of aspects of women's experience and situation that have not received the treatment they warrant. I would like to close with some questions that require further thought and research. This essay has concentrated its attention upon the sorts of physical tasks and body orientation that involve the whole body in gross movement. Further investigation into woman's bodily existence would require looking at activities that do not involve the whole body and finer movement. If we are going to develop an account of the woman's body experience in situation, moreover, we must reflect on the modalities of a woman's experience of her body in its sexual being, as well as upon less task-oriented body activities, such as dancing. Another question that arises is whether the description given here would apply equally well to any sort of physical task. Might the kind of task, and specifically whether it is a task or movement that is sex-typed, have some effect on the modalities of feminine bodily existence? A further question is to what degree we can develop a theoretical account of the connection between the modalities of the bodily existence of women and other aspects of our existence and experience. For example, I have an intuition that the general lack of confidence that we frequently have about our cognitive or leadership abilities is traceable in part to an original doubt of our body's capacity. None of these questions can be dealt with properly, however, without first performing the kind of guided observation and data collection that my reading has concluded, to a large degree, is yet to be performed.

Notes

This essay was first presented at a meeting of the Mid-West Division of the Society for Women in Philosophy

(SWIP) in October 1977. Versions of the essay were subsequently presented at a session sponsored by SWIP at the Western Division meetings of the American Philosophical Association, April 1978; and at the third annual Merleau-Ponty Circle meeting, Duquesne University, September 1978. Many people in discussions at those meetings contributed gratifying and helpful responses. I am particularly grateful to Professors Sandra Bartky, Claudia Card, Margaret Simons, J. Davidson Alexander, and William McBride for their criticisms and suggestions. Final revisions of the essay were completed while I was a fellow in the National Endowment for the Humanities Fellowship in Residence for College Teachers program at the University of Chicago.

1. Erwin W. Straus, "The Upright Posture," *Phenomenological Psychology* (New York: Basic Books, 1966), pp. 137–65. References to particular pages are indicated in the text.
2. Studies continue to be performed that arrive at similar observations. See, for example, Lolas E. Kalverson, Mary Ann Robertson, M. Joanne Safrit, and Thomas W. Roberts, "Effect of Guided Practice on Overhand Throw Ball Velocities of Kindergarten Children," *Research Quarterly* (American Alliance for Health, Physical Education and Recreation) 48 (May 1977); pp. 311–18. The study found that boys achieved significantly greater velocities than girls did.
    See also F. J. J. Buytendijk's remarks in *Woman: A Contemporary View* (New York: Newman Press, 1968), pp. 144–5. In raising the example of throwing, Buytendijk is concerned to stress, as am I in this essay, that the important thing to investigate is not the strictly physical phenomenon, but rather the manner in which each sex projects her or his Being-in-the-world through movement.
3. Simone de Beauvoir, *The Second Sex* (New York: Vintage Books, 1974), p. xxxv. See also Buytendijk, pp. 175–6.
4. See Beauvoir, *The Second Sex*, chapter 1, "The Data of Biology."
5. Firestone claims that Beauvoir's account served as the basis of her own thesis that the oppression of women is rooted in nature and thus requires the transcendence of nature itself to be overcome. See *The Dialectic of Sex* (New York: Bantam Books, 1970). Beauvoir would claim that Firestone is guilty of desituating woman's situation by pinning a source on nature as such. That Firestone would find inspiration for her thesis in Beauvoir, however, indicates that perhaps de Beauvoir has not steered away from causes in "nature" as much as is desirable.
6. In his discussion of the "dynamics of feminine existence," Buytendijk focuses precisely on those sorts of motions that are aimless. He claims that it is through these kinds of expressive movements – e.g., walking for the sake of walking – and not through action aimed at the accomplishment of particular purposes that the pure image of masculine or feminine existence is manifest (*Woman: A Contemporary View*, pp. 278–9). Such an approach, however, contradicts the basic existentialist assumption that Being-in-the-world consists in projecting purposes and goals that structure one's situatedness. While there is certainly something to be learned from reflecting upon feminine movement in noninstrumental activity, given that accomplishing tasks is basic to the structure of human existence, it serves as a better starting point for investigation of feminine motility. As I point out at the end of this essay, a full phenomenology of feminine existence must take account of this noninstrumental movement.
7. It is not impossible, moreover, for men to be "feminine" in at least some respects, according to the above definition.
8. On this level of specificity there also exist particular modalities of masculine motility, inasmuch as there is a particular style of movement more or less typical of men. I will not, however, be concerned with those in this essay.
9. See Beauvoir, *The Second Sex*, chapter 21, "Woman's Situation and Character."
10. It should be noted that this is probably typical only of women in advanced industrial societies, where the model of the bourgeois woman has been extended to most women. It would not apply to those societies, for example, where most people, including women, do heavy physical work. Nor does this particular observation, of course, hold true in our own society for women who do heavy physical work.
11. See A. M. Gross, "Estimated Versus Actual Physical Strength in Three Ethnic Groups," *Child Development* 39 (1968), pp. 283–90. In a test of children at several different ages, at all but the youngest age level, girls rated themselves lower than boys rated themselves on self-estimates of strength, and as the girls grow older, their self-estimates of strength become even lower.
12. See Marguerite A. Cifton and Hope M. Smith, "Comparison of Expressed Self-Concept of Highly Skilled Males and Females Concerning Motor Performance," *Perceptual and Motor Skills* 16 (1963), pp. 199–201. Women consistently underestimated their level of achievement in skills such as running and jumping far more often than men did.
13. Maurice Merleau-Ponty, *The Phenomenology of Perception*, trans., Colin Smith (New York: Humanities Press, 1962). All references to this work are noted in parentheses in the text.
14. Much of the work of Seymour Fisher on various aspects of sex differences in body image correlates suggestively with the phenomenological description developed here. It is difficult to use his conclusions

as confirmation of that description, however, because there is something of a speculative aspect to his reasoning. Nevertheless, I shall refer to some of these findings with that qualification in mind.

One of Fisher's findings is that women have a greater anxiety about their legs than men do, and he cites earlier studies with the same results. Fisher interprets such leg anxiety as being anxiety about motility itself, because in body conception and body image the legs are the body parts most associated with motility. See Fisher, *Body Experience in Fantasy and Behavior* (New York: Appleton-Century Crofts, 1970), p. 537. If his findings and his interpretation are accurate, this tends to correlate with the sort of inhibition and timidity about movement that I am claiming is an aspect of feminine body comportment.

15. Fisher finds that the most striking difference between men and women in their general body image is that women have a significantly higher degree of what he calls "body prominence," awareness of and attention to the body. He cites a number of different studies that have the same results. The explanation Fisher gives for this finding is that women are socialized to pay attention to their bodies, to prune and dress them, and to worry about how they look to others. Fisher, pp. 524–5. See also Fisher, "Sex Differences in Body Perception," *Psychological Monographs* 78 (1964) no. 14.

16. Erik H. Erikson, "Inner and Outer Space: Reflections on Womanhood," *Daedelus* 3 (1964), pp. 582–606. Erikson's interpretation of his findings is also sexist. Having in his opinion discovered a particular significance that "inner space," which he takes to be space *within* the body, holds for girls, he goes on to discuss the womanly "nature" as womb and potential mother, which must be made compatible with anything else the woman does.

17. Another of Fisher's findings is that women experience themselves as having more clearly articulated body *boundaries* than men do. More clearly than men do, they distinguish themselves from their spatial surroundings and take a distance from them. See Fisher, *Body Experience in Fantasy and Behavior*, p. 528.

18. The number of studies with these results is enormous. See Eleanor E. Maccoby and Carol N. Jacklin, *The Psychology of Sex Differences* (Palo Alto, Calif.: Stanford University Press, 1974), pp. 91–8. For a number of years psychologists used the results from tests of spatial ability to generalize about field independence in general, and from that to general "analytic" ability. Thus it was concluded that women

have less analytical ability than men do. More recently, however, such generalizations have been seriously called into question. See, for example, Julia A. Sherman, "Problems of Sex Differences in Space Perception and Aspects of Intellectual Functioning," *Psychological Review* 74 (1967), pp. 290–9. She notes that while women are consistently found to be more field-dependent in spatial tasks than men are, on nonspatial tests measuring field independence, women generally perform as well as men do.

19. Nor are girls provided with examples of girls and women being physically active. See Mary E. Duquin, "Differential Sex Role Socialization Toward Amplitude Appropriation," *Research Quarterly* (American Alliance for Health, Physical Education and Recreation) 48 (1977), pp. 188–92. A survey of textbooks for young children revealed that children are thirteen times more likely to see a vigorously active man than a vigorously active woman and three times more likely to see a relatively active man than a relatively active woman.

20. Sherman (see note 18) argues that it is the differential socialization of boys and girls in being encouraged to "tinker," explore, etc., that accounts for the difference between the two in spatial ability.

21. See L. Kolberg, "A Cognitive-Developmental Analysis of Children's Sex-Role Concepts and Attitudes," in E. E. Maccoby, ed., *The Development of Sex Differences* (Palo Alto, Calif.: Stanford University Press, 1966), p. 101.

22. Lenore J. Weitzman, "Sex Role Socialization," in Jo Freeman, ed., *Woman: A Feminist Perspective* (Palo Alto, Calif.: Mayfield Publishing Co., 1975), pp. 111–12.

23. Maccoby and Jacklin, *The Psychology of Sex Differences*, pp. 93–4.

24. The manner in which women are objectified by the gaze of the Other is not the same phenomenon as the objectification by the Other that is a condition of self-consciousness in Sartre's account. See *Being and Nothingness*, trans., Hazel E. Barnes (New York: Philosophical Library, 1956), part 3. While the basic ontological category of being for others is an objectified body for itself, the objectification that women are subject to is being regarded as a mere body in itself. On the particular dynamic of sexual objectification, see Sandra Bartky, "Psychological Oppression," in Sharon Bishop and Marjories Weinzweig, ed., *Philosophy and Women* (Belmont, Calif.: Wadsworth Publishing Co., 1979), pp. 33–41.

25. See Nancy Henley and Jo Freeman, "The Sexual Politics of Interpersonal Behavior," in Freeman, ed., *Woman: A Feminist Perspective*, pp. 391–401.

19

Mapping the Margins: Intersectionality, Identity Politics, and Violence Against Women of Color

Kimberlé Crenshaw

Introduction

Over the last two decades, women have organized against the almost routine violence that shapes their lives.[1] Drawing from the strength of shared experience, women have recognized that the political demands of millions speak more powerfully than do the pleas of a few isolated voices. This politicization in turn has transformed the way we understand violence against women. For example, battering and rape, once seen as private (family matters) and aberrational (errant sexual aggression), are now largely recognized as part of a broad-scale system of domination that affects women as a class.[2] This process of recognizing as social and systemic what was formerly perceived as isolated and individual has also characterized the identity politics of African-Americans, other people of color, and gays and lesbians, among others. For all these groups, identity-based politics has been a source of strength, community, and intellectual development.

The embrace of identity politics, however, has been in tension with dominant conceptions of social justice. Race, gender, and other identity categories are most often treated in mainstream liberal discourse as vestiges of bias or domination – that is, as intrinsically negative frameworks in which social power works to exclude or marginalize those who are different. According to this understanding, our liberatory objective should be to empty

such categories of any social significance. Yet implicit in certain strands of feminist and racial liberation movements, for example, is the view that the social power in delineating difference need not be the power of domination; it can instead be the source of social empowerment and reconstruction.

The problem with identity politics is not that it fails to transcend difference, as some critics charge, but rather the opposite – that it frequently conflates or ignores intragroup differences. In the context of violence against women, this elision of difference in identity politics is problematic, fundamentally because the violence that many women experience is often shaped by other dimensions of their identities, such as race and class. Moreover, ignoring difference *within* groups contributes to tension *among* groups, another problem of identity politics which bears on efforts to politicize violence against women. Feminist efforts to politicize experiences of women and antiracist efforts to politicize experiences of people of color have frequently proceeded as though the issues and experiences they each detail occur on mutually exclusive terrains. Although racism and sexism readily intersect in the lives of real people, they seldom do in feminist and antiracist practices. Thus, when the practices expound identity as "woman" *or* "person of color" as an either/or proposition, they relegate the identity of women of color to a location that resists telling.

My objective in this article is to advance the telling of that location by exploring the race and gender dimensions of violence against women of color. Contemporary feminist and antiracist discourses have failed to consider intersectional identities such as women of color.[3] Focusing on two dimensions of male violence against women – battering and rape – I consider how the experiences of women of color are frequently the product of intersecting patterns of racism and sexism,[4] and how these experiences tend not to be represented within the discourses either of feminism or of antiracism. Because of their intersectional identity as both women *and* of color within discourses shaped to respond to one *or* the other, women of color are marginalized within both.

In an earlier article, I used the concept of intersectionality to denote the various ways in which race and gender interact to shape the multiple dimensions of black women's employment experiences.[5] My objective there was to illustrate that many of the experiences black women face are not subsumed within the traditional boundaries of race or gender discrimination as these boundaries are currently understood, and that the intersection of racism and sexism factors into black women's lives in ways that cannot be captured wholly by looking separately at the race or gender dimensions of those experiences. I build on those observations here by exploring the various ways in which race and gender intersect in shaping structural, political, and representational aspects of violence against women of color.[6]

I should say at the outset that intersectionality is not being offered here as some new, totalizing theory of identity. Nor do I mean to suggest that violence against women of color can be explained only through the specific frameworks of race and gender considered here.[7] Indeed, factors I address only in part or not at all, such as class or sexuality, are often as critical in shaping the experiences of women of color. My focus on the intersections of race and gender only highlights the need to account for multiple grounds of identity when considering how the social world is constructed.

I have divided the issues presented in this article into three categories. In Part I, I discuss structural intersectionality, the ways in which the location of women of color at the intersection of race and gender makes our actual experience of domestic violence, rape, and remedial reform qualitatively different from that of white women. I shift the focus in Part II to political intersectionality, where I analyze how feminist and antiracist politics have both, paradoxically, often helped to marginalize the issue of violence against women of color. Finally, I address the implications of the intersectional approach within the broader scope of contemporary identity politics.

I. Structural Intersectionality

A. *Structural intersectionality and battering*

I observed the dynamics of structural intersectionality during a brief field study of battered women's shelters located in minority communities in Los Angeles. In most cases, the physical assault that leads women to these shelters is merely the most immediate manifestation of the subordination they experience. Many women who seek protection are unemployed or underemployed, and a good number of them are poor. Shelters serving these women cannot afford to address only the violence inflicted by the batterer; they must also confront the other multilayered and routinized forms of domination that often converge in these women's lives, hindering their ability to create alternatives to the abusive relationships that brought them to shelters in the first place. Many women of color, for example, are burdened by poverty, child care responsibilities, and the lack of job skills. These burdens, largely the consequence of gender and class oppression, are then compounded by the racially discriminatory employment and housing practices often faced by women of color, as well as by the disproportionately high unemployment among people of color that makes battered women of color less able to depend on the support of friends and relatives for temporary shelter.

Where systems of race, gender, and class domination converge, as they do in the experiences of battered women of color, intervention strategies based solely on the experiences of women who do not share the same class or race backgrounds will be of limited help to women who face different obstacles because of race and class. Such was the case in 1990 when Congress amended the marriage fraud provisions of the Immigration and Nationality Act to protect immigrant women who were battered or exposed to extreme cruelty by the U.S. citizens or permanent residents these women immigrated to the United States to marry. Under the marriage fraud provisions of the act, a person who immigrated to the United States in order to marry a U.S. citizen or permanent resident had to remain "properly" married for two years before even applying for permanent resident status,[8] at which time applications for the immigrant's permanent status were required of both spouses.[9] Predictably, under these circumstances, many immigrant women were reluctant to leave even the most abusive of partners for fear of being deported. When faced with the choice between protection from their batterers and protection against deportation, many immigrant women chose the latter. Reports of the tragic consequences of this double subordination put pressure on Congress to include in the Immigration Act of 1990 a provision amending the marriage fraud rules to allow for an explicit waiver for hardship caused by domestic violence.[10] Yet many immigrant women, particularly immigrant women of color, have remained vulnerable to battering because they are unable to meet the conditions established for a waiver. The evidence required to support a waiver "can include, but is not limited to, reports and affidavits from police, medical personnel, psychologists, school officials, and social service agencies."[11] For many immigrant women, limited access to these resources can make it difficult for them to obtain the evidence needed for a waiver. Cultural barriers, too, often further discourage immigrant women from reporting or escaping battering situations. Tina Shum, a family counselor at a social service agency, points out that "[t]his law sounds so easy to apply, but there are cultural complications in the Asian community that make even these requirements difficult. . . . Just to find the opportunity and courage to call us is an accomplishment for many."[12] The typical immigrant spouse, she suggests, may live "[i]n an extended family where several generations live together, there may be no privacy on the telephone, no opportunity to leave the house and no understanding of public phones."[13] As a consequence, many immigrant women are wholly dependent on their husbands as their link to the world outside their homes.

Immigrant women are also vulnerable to spousal violence because so many of them depend on their husbands for information regarding their legal status. Many women who are now permanent residents continue to suffer abuse under threats of deportation by their husbands. Even if the threats are unfounded, women who have no independent access to information will still be intimidated by such threats. Further, even though the domestic violence waiver focuses on immigrant women whose husbands are U.S. citizens or permanent residents, there are countless women married to undocumented workers (or are themselves undocumented) who suffer in silence for fear that the security of their entire families will be jeopardized should they seek help or otherwise call attention to themselves.

Language barriers present another structural problem that often limits opportunities of non-English-speaking women to take advantage of existing support services. Such barriers limit access not only to information about shelters but also to the security that shelters provide. Some shelters turn non-English-speaking women away for lack of bilingual personnel and resources.

These examples illustrate how patterns of subordination intersect in women's experience of domestic violence. Intersectional subordination need not be intentionally produced; in fact, it is frequently the consequence of the imposition of one burden interacting with pre-existing vulnerabilities to create yet another dimension of disempowerment. In the case of the marriage fraud provisions of the Immigration and Nationality Act, the imposition of a policy specifically designed to burden one class – immigrant spouses seeking permanent resident status – exacerbated the disempowerment of those already subordinated by other structures of domination. By failing to take into account immigrant spouses' vulnerability to domestic violence, Congress positioned these women to absorb the simultaneous impact of its anti-immigration policy and their spouses' abuse.

The enactment of the domestic violence waiver of the marriage fraud provisions similarly illustrates how modest attempts to respond to certain problems can be ineffective when the intersectional location of women of color is not considered in fashioning the remedy. Cultural identity and class both affect the likelihood that a battered spouse could take advantage of the waiver. Although the waiver is formally available to all women, the terms of the waiver make it inaccessible to some. Immigrant women who are socially, culturally, or economically privileged are more likely to be able to marshall the resources needed to satisfy the waiver requirements. Those immigrant women who are least able to take advantage of the waiver – women who are socially or economically the most marginal – are the ones most likely to be women of color.

II.   Political Intersectionality

The concept of political intersectionality highlights the fact that women of color are situated within at least two subordinated groups that frequently pursue conflicting political agendas. The need to split one's political energies between two sometimes-opposing groups is a dimension of intersectional disempowerment which men of color and white women seldom confront. Indeed, their specific raced *and* gendered experiences, although intersectional, often define as well as confine the interests of the entire group. For example, racism as experienced by people of color who are of a particular gender – male – tends to determine the parameters of anti-racist strategies, just as sexism as experienced by women who are of a particular race – white – tends to ground the women's movement. The problem is not simply that both discourses fail women of color by not acknowledging the "additional" issue of race or of patriarchy but, rather, that the discourses are often inadequate even to the discrete tasks of articulating the full dimensions of racism and sexism. Because women of color experience racism in ways not always the same as those experienced by men of color and sexism in ways not always parallel to experiences of white women, antiracism and feminism are limited, even on their own terms.

Among the most troubling political consequences of the failure of antiracist and feminist discourses to address the intersections of race and gender is the fact that, to the extent that they can forward the interest of "people of color" and "women," respectively, one analysis often implicitly denies the validity of the other. The failure of feminism to interrogate race means that feminism's resistance strategies will often replicate and reinforce the subordination of people of color; likewise, the failure of antiracism to interrogate patriarchy means that antiracism will frequently reproduce the subordination of women. These mutual elisions present a particularly difficult political dilemma for women of color. Adopting either analysis constitutes a denial of a fundamental dimension of our subordination and precludes the development of a political discourse that more fully empowers women of color.

A.   The politicization of domestic violence

That the political interests of women of color are obscured and sometimes jeopardized by political strategies that ignore or suppress intersectional issues is illustrated by my experiences in gathering information for this article. I attempted to review Los Angeles Police Department statistics reflecting the rate of domestic violence interventions by precinct, because such statistics can provide a rough picture of arrests by racial group, given the degree of racial segregation in Los Angeles.[14] The LAPD, however, would not release the statistics. A representative explained that the statistics were not released, in part, because domestic violence activists – both within and outside the LAPD – feared that statistics reflecting the extent of domestic violence in minority communities might be selectively interpreted and publicized in ways that would undermine long-term efforts to force the LAPD to address domestic violence as a serious problem. Activists were worried that the statistics might permit opponents to dismiss domestic violence as a minority problem and, therefore, not deserving of aggressive action.

The informant also claimed that representatives from various minority communities opposed the release of these statistics. They were concerned, apparently, that the data would unfairly represent black and brown communities as unusually violent, potentially reinforcing stereotypes that might be used in attempts to justify oppressive police tactics and other discriminatory practices. These misgivings are based on the familiar and not-unfounded premise that certain minority groups – especially black men – have already been stereotyped as uncontrollably violent. Some worry that attempts to make domestic violence an object of political action may only serve to confirm such stereotypes and undermine efforts to combat negative beliefs about the black community.

This account sharply illustrates how women of color can be erased by the strategic silences of antiracism and feminism. The political priorities of both have been defined in ways that suppress information that could facilitate attempts to confront the problem of domestic violence in communities of color.

1.   Domestic violence and antiracist politics

Within communities of color, efforts to stem the politicization of domestic violence are often grounded in attempts to maintain the integrity of the community. The articulation of this perspective takes different forms. Some critics allege that feminism has no place within communities of color, that the issues are internally divisive, and that they represent the migration of white women's concerns into a context in which they are not merely irrelevant but harmful. At its most extreme, this rhetoric denies that gender violence is a problem in the community and characterizes any effort to politicize gender subordination as itself a community problem. This is the position taken by Shahrazad Ali in her controversial book, *The Blackman's Guide to Understanding the Blackwoman*.[15] In this stridently antifeminist tract, Ali draws a positive correlation between domestic violence and the liberation of African-Americans. Ali blames the deteriorating conditions within the black community on the insubordination of black women and on the failure of black men to control them.[16] She goes so far as to advise black men to physically chastise black women when they are "disrespectful."[17] While she cautions that black men must use moderation in disciplining "their" women, she argues that they must sometimes resort to physical force to reestablish the authority over black women that racism has disrupted.

Ali's premise is that patriarchy is beneficial for the black community, and that it must be strengthened through coercive means if necessary.[18] Yet the violence that accompanies this will to control is devastating, not just for the black women who are victimized but for the entire black community.[19] The recourse to violence to resolve conflicts establishes a dangerous pattern for children raised in such environments and contributes to many other pressing problems.[20] It has been estimated that nearly 40 percent of all homeless women and children have fled violence in the home,[21] and an estimated 63 percent of young men between the ages of eleven and twenty who are imprisoned for homicide have killed their mothers' batterers.[22] Moreover, while gang violence, homicide, and other forms of black-on-black crime have increasingly been discussed within African-American politics, patriarchal ideas about gender and power preclude the recognition of domestic violence as yet another compelling form of black-on-black crime.

Efforts such as Ali's to justify violence against women in the name of black liberation are indeed extreme.[23] The more common problem is that the political or cultural interests of the community are interpreted in a way that precludes full public recognition of the problem of domestic violence. While it would be misleading to suggest that white Americans have come to terms with the degree of violence in their own homes, it is nonetheless the case

that race adds yet another dimension to sources of suppression of the problem of domestic violence within nonwhite communities. People of color often must weigh their interests in avoiding issues that might reinforce distorted public perceptions against the need to acknowledge and address intracommunity problems. Yet the cost of suppression is seldom recognized, in part because the failure to discuss the issue shapes perceptions of how serious the problem is in the first place.

The controversy over Alice Walker's novel *The Color Purple* can be understood as an intracommunity debate about the political costs of exposing gender violence within the black community. Some critics chastised Walker for portraying black men as violent brutes. One critic lambasted Walker's portrayal of Celie, the emotionally and physically abused protagonist who finally triumphs in the end; the critic contended that Walker had created in Celie a black woman whom she couldn't imagine existing in any black community she knew or could conceive of.[24]

The claim that Celie was somehow an inauthentic character might be read as a consequence of silencing discussion of intracommunity violence. Celie may be unlike any black woman we know because the real terror experienced daily by minority women is routinely concealed in a misguided (though perhaps understandable) attempt to forestall racial stereotyping. Of course, it is true that representations of black violence – whether statistical or fictional – are often written into a larger script that consistently portrays black and other minority communities as pathologically violent. The problem, however, is not so much the portrayal of violence itself as it is the absence of other narratives and images portraying a fuller range of black experience. Suppression of some of these issues in the name of antiracism imposes real costs: where information about violence in minority communities is not available, domestic violence is unlikely to be addressed as a serious issue.

The political imperatives of a narrowly focused antiracist strategy support other practices that isolate women of color. For example, activists who have attempted to provide support services to Asian- and African-American women report intense resistance from those communities. At other times, cultural and social factors contribute to suppression. Nilda Remonte, director of Everywoman's Shelter in Los Angeles, points out that in the Asian community, saving the honor of the family from shame is a priority. Unfortunately, this priority tends to be interpreted as obliging women not to scream rather than obliging men not to hit.

Race and culture contribute to the suppression of domestic violence in other ways as well. Women of color are often reluctant to call the police, a hesitancy likely due to a general unwillingness among people of color to subject their private lives to the scrutiny and control of a police force that is frequently hostile. There is also a more generalized community ethic against public intervention, the product of a desire to create a private world free from the diverse assaults on the public lives of racially subordinated people. The home is not simply a man's castle in the patriarchal sense: it may also function as a safe haven from the indignities of life in a racist society. However, but for this "safe haven" in many cases, women of color victimized by violence might otherwise seek help.

There is also a general tendency within antiracist discourse to regard the problem of violence against women of color as just another manifestation of racism. In this sense, the relevance of gender domination within the community is reconfigured as a consequence of discrimination against men. Of course, it is probably true that racism contributes to the cycle of violence, given the stress that men of color experience in dominant society; it is therefore more than reasonable to explore the links between racism and domestic violence. Yet the chain of violence is more complex and extends beyond this single link. Racism is linked to patriarchy to the extent that racism denies men of color the power and privilege that dominant men enjoy. When violence is understood as an acting-out of being denied male power in other spheres, it seems counterproductive to embrace constructs that implicitly link the solution to domestic violence to the acquisition of greater male power. The more promising political imperative is to challenge the legitimacy of such power expectations by exposing their dysfunctional and debilitating effect on families and communities of color. Moreover, while understanding links between racism and domestic violence is an important component of any effective intervention strategy, it is also clear that women of color need not await the ultimate triumph over racism before they can expect to live violence-free lives.

2. Race and the domestic violence lobby

Not only do race-based priorities function to obscure the problem of violence suffered by women of color; feminist concerns often suppress minority experiences as well. Strategies for increasing awareness of domestic violence within the white community tend to begin by citing the commonly shared assumption that battering is a minority problem. The strategy then focuses on demolishing this straw man, stressing that spousal abuse also occurs in the white community. Countless first-person stories begin with a statement like, "I was not supposed to be a battered wife." That battering occurs in families of all races and all classes seems to be an ever-present theme of antiabuse campaigns. First-person anecdotes and studies, for example, consistently assert that battering cuts across racial, ethnic, economic, educational, and religious lines. Such disclaimers seem relevant only in the presence of an initial, widely held belief that domestic violence occurs primarily in minority or poor families. Indeed, some authorities explicitly renounce the "stereotypical myths" about battered women; a few commentators have even transformed the message that battering is not *exclusively* a problem of the poor or minority communities into a claim that it *equally* affects all races and classes. Yet these comments seem less concerned with exploring domestic abuse within "stereotyped" communities than with removing the stereotype as an obstacle to exposing battering within white middle- and upper-class communities.[25]

Efforts to politicize the issue of violence against women challenge beliefs that violence occurs only in homes of Others. While it is unlikely that advocates and others who adopt this rhetorical strategy intend to exclude or ignore the needs of poor and colored women, the underlying premise of this seemingly universalistic appeal is to keep the sensibilities of dominant social groups focused on the experiences of those groups. Indeed, as subtly suggested by the opening comments of Senator David Boren (Dem.-Okla.) in support of the Violence Against Women Act of 1991, the displacement of the Other as the presumed victim of domestic violence works primarily as a political appeal to rally white elites. Boren said: "Violent crimes against women are not limited to the streets of the inner cities, but also occur in homes in the urban and rural areas across the country. Violence against women affects not only those who are actually beaten and brutalized, but indirectly affects all women. Today, our wives, mothers, daughters, sisters, and colleagues are held captive by fear generated from these violent crimes – held captive not for what they do or who they are, but solely because of gender."[26] Rather than focusing on and illuminating how violence is disregarded when the home is somehow Other, the strategy implicit in Senator Boren's remarks functions instead to politicize the problem only within the dominant community. This strategy permits white women victims to come into focus, but it does little to disrupt the patterns of neglect that permitted the problem to continue as long as it was imagined to be a minority problem. Minority women's experience of violence is ignored, except to the extent that it gains white support for domestic violence programs in the white community.

Senator Boren and his colleagues no doubt believe that they have provided legislation and resources that will address the problems of all women victimized by domestic violence. Yet despite their universalizing rhetoric of "all" women, they were able to empathize with female victims of domestic violence only by looking past the plight of Other women and by recognizing the familiar faces of their own. The strength of the appeal to "protect our women" must be its race and class specificity. After all, it has always been someone's wife, mother, sister, or daughter who has been abused, even when the violence was stereotypically black or brown, and poor. The point here is not that the Violence Against Women Act is particularistic on its own terms, but that unless the senators and other policymakers ask why violence remained insignificant as long as it was understood as a minority problem, it is unlikely that women of color will share equally in the distribution of resources and concern. It is even more unlikely, however, that those in power will be forced to confront this issue. As long as attempts to politicize domestic violence focus on convincing whites that this is not a "minority" problem but *their* problem, any authentic and sensitive attention to the experiences of black and other minority women probably will continue to be regarded as jeopardizing the movement.

While Senator Boren's statement reflects a self-consciously political presentation of domestic violence, an episode of the CBS news program *48 Hours* shows how similar patterns of othering nonwhite women are apparent in journalistic accounts of domestic violence as well.[27] The program presented seven women who were victims of abuse. Six were interviewed at some length along with their family members, friends, supporters, and even detractors. The viewer got to know something about

each of these women. These victims were humanized. Yet the seventh woman, the only nonwhite one, never came into focus. She was literally unrecognizable throughout the segment, first introduced by photographs showing her face badly beaten and later shown with her face electronically altered in the videotape of a hearing at which she was forced to testify. Other images associated with this woman included shots of a bloodstained room and blood-soaked pillows. Her boyfriend was pictured handcuffed while the camera zoomed in for a close-up of his bloodied sneakers. Of all the presentations in the episode, hers was the most graphic and impersonal. The overall point of the segment "featuring" this woman was that battering might not escalate into homicide if battered women would only cooperate with prosecutors. However, in focusing on its own agenda and failing to explore why this woman refused to cooperate, the program diminished this woman, communicating, however subtly, that she was responsible for her own victimization.

Unlike the other women, all of whom, again, were white, this black woman had no name, no family, no context. The viewer sees her only as victimized and uncooperative. She cries when shown pictures; she pleads not to be forced to view the bloodstained room and her disfigured face. The program does not help the viewer to understand her predicament. The possible reasons she did not want to testify – fear, love, or possibly both – are never suggested. Most unfortunately, she, unlike the other six, is given no epilogue. While the fates of the other women are revealed at the end of the episode, we discover nothing about the black woman. She, like the Others she represents, is simply left to herself and soon forgotten.

I offer this description to suggest that Other women are silenced as much by being relegated to the margin of experience as by total exclusion. Tokenistic, objectifying, voyeuristic inclusion is at least as disempowering as complete exclusion. The effort to politicize violence against women will do little to address black and other minority women if their images are retained simply to magnify the problem rather than to humanize their experiences. Similarly, the antiracist agenda will not be advanced significantly by forcibly suppressing the reality of battering in minority communities. As the *48 Hours* episode makes clear, the images and stereotypes we fear are indeed readily available, and they are frequently deployed in ways that do not generate sensitive understanding of the nature of domestic violence in minority communities.

3. Race and domestic violence support services

Women working in the field of domestic violence have sometimes reproduced the subordination and marginalization of women of color by adopting policies, priorities, or strategies of empowerment that either elide or wholly disregard the particular intersectional needs of women of color. While gender, race, and class intersect to create the particular context in which women of color experience violence, certain choices made by "allies" can reproduce intersectional subordination within the very resistance strategies developed to respond to the problem.

This problem is starkly illustrated by the inaccessibility of domestic violence support services for many non-English-speaking women. In a letter written to the deputy commissioner of the New York State Department of Social Services, Diana Campos, director of Human Services for Programas de Ocupaciones y Desarrollo Económico Real, Inc. (PODER), detailed the case of a Latina in crisis who was repeatedly denied accommodation at a shelter because she could not prove that she was English-proficient. The woman had fled her home with her teenaged son, believing her husband's threats to kill them both. She called the domestic violence hotline administered by PODER, seeking shelter for herself and her son. However, because most shelters would not accommodate the woman with her son, they were forced to live on the streets for two days. The hotline counselor was finally able to find an agency that would take both the mother and her son, but when the counselor told the intake coordinator at the shelter that the woman spoke limited English, the coordinator told her that they could not take anyone who was not English-proficient. When the woman in crisis called back and was told of the shelter's "rule," she replied that she could understand English if spoken to her slowly. As Campos explains, Mildred, the hotline counselor, told Wendy, the intake coordinator

that the woman said that she could communicate a little in English. Wendy told Mildred that they could not provide services to this woman because they have house rules that the woman must agree to follow. Mildred asked her, "What if the woman agrees to follow your rules? Will you still not take her?" Wendy re-

sponded that all of the women at the shelter are required to attend [a] support group and they would not be able to have her in the group if she could not communicate. Mildred mentioned the severity of this woman's case. She told Wendy that the woman had been wandering the streets at night while her husband was home, and she had been mugged twice. She also reiterated the fact that this woman was in danger of being killed by either her husband or a mugger. Mildred expressed that the woman's safety was a priority at this point, and that once in a safe place, receiving counseling in a support group could be dealt with.[28]

The intake coordinator restated the shelter's policy of taking only English-speaking women, and stated further that the woman would have to call the shelter herself for screening. If the woman could communicate with them in English, she might be accepted. When the woman called the PODER hotline later that day, she was in such a state of fear that the hotline counselor who had been working with her had difficulty understanding her in Spanish. The woman had been slipping back into her home during the day when her husband was at work. She remained in a heightened state of anxiety because he was returning shortly, and she would be forced to go back out into the streets for yet another night. Campos directly intervened at this point, calling the executive director of the shelter. A counselor called back from the shelter. As Campos reports, the counselor told her that

they did not want to take the woman in the shelter because they felt that the woman would feel isolated. I explained that the son agreed to translate for his mother during the intake process. Furthermore, that we would assist them in locating a Spanish-speaking battered women's advocate to assist in counseling her. Marie stated that utilizing the son was not an acceptable means of communication for them, *since it further victimized the victim.* In addition, she stated that they had similar experiences with women who were non-English-speaking, and that the women eventually just left because they were not able to communicate with anyone. I expressed my extreme concern for her safety and reiterated that we would assist them in providing her with the necessary services until we could get her placed someplace where they had bilingual staff.[29]

After several more calls, the shelter finally agreed to take the woman. The woman called once more during the negotiation; however, once a plan was in place, the woman never called back. Said Campos, "After so many calls, we are now left to wonder if she is alive and well, and if she will ever have enough faith in our ability to help her to call us again the next time she is in crisis."[30]

Despite this woman's desperate need, she was unable to receive the protection afforded English-speaking women, due to the shelter's rigid commitment to exclusionary policies. Perhaps even more troubling than the shelter's lack of bilingual resources was its refusal to allow a friend or relative to translate for the woman. This story illustrates the absurdity of a feminist approach that makes the ability to attend a support group without a translator a more significant consideration in the distribution of resources than the risk of physical harm on the street. The point is not that the shelter's image of empowerment is empty but, rather, that it was imposed without regard to the disempowering consequences for women who didn't match the kind of client the shelter's administrators imagined. Thus, they failed to accomplish the basic priority of the shelter movement – to get the woman out of danger.

Here the woman in crisis was made to bear the burden of the shelter's refusal to anticipate and provide for the needs of non-English-speaking women. Said Campos, "It is unfair to impose more stress on victims by placing them in the position of having to demonstrate their proficiency in English in order to receive services that are readily available to other battered women."[31] The problem is not easily dismissed as one of well-intentioned ignorance. The specific issue of monolingualism and the monistic view of women's experience that set the stage for this tragedy were not new issues in New York. Indeed, several women of color have reported that they had repeatedly struggled with the New York State Coalition Against Domestic Violence over language exclusion and other practices that marginalized the interests of women of color.[32] Yet despite repeated lobbying, the coalition did not act to incorporate the specific needs of nonwhite women into its central organizing vision.

Some critics have linked the coalition's failure to address these issues to the narrow vision of coalition that animated its interaction with women of color in the first place. The very location of the coalition's headquarters in Woodstock, New York – an area where few people of color live – seemed

to guarantee that women of color would play a limited role in formulating policy. Moreover, efforts to include women of color came, it seems, as something of an afterthought. Many were invited to participate only after the coalition was awarded a grant by the state to recruit women of color. However, as one "recruit" said, "they were not really prepared to deal with us or our issues. They thought that they could simply incorporate us into their organization without rethinking any of their beliefs or priorities and that we would be happy."[33] Even the most formal gestures of inclusion were not to be taken for granted. On one occasion when several women of color attended a meeting to discuss a special task force on women of color, the group debated all day over including the issue on the agenda.[34]

The relationship between the white women and the women of color on the board was a rocky one from beginning to end. Other conflicts developed over differing definitions of feminism. For example, the board decided to hire a Latina staff-person to manage outreach programs to the Latino community, but the white members of the hiring committee rejected candidates favored by Latina committee members who did not have recognized feminist credentials. As Campos pointed out, by measuring Latinas against their own biographies, the white members of the board failed to recognize the different circumstances under which feminist consciousness develops and manifests itself within minority communities. Many of the women who interviewed for the position were established activists and leaders within their own community, a fact in itself suggesting that these women were probably familiar with the specific gender dynamics in their communities and were accordingly better qualified to handle outreach than were other candidates with more conventional feminist credentials.[35]

The coalition ended a few months later, when the women of color walked out.[36] Many of these women returned to community-based organizations, preferring to struggle over women's issues within their communities rather than struggle over race and class issues with white middle-class women. Yet as illustrated by the case of the Latina who could find no shelter, the dominance of a particular perspective and set of priorities within the shelter community continues to marginalize the needs of women of color.

The struggle over which differences matter and which do not is neither abstract nor insignificant.

Indeed, these conflicts are about more than difference as such; they raise critical issues of power. The problem is not simply that women who dominate the antiviolence movement are different from women of color but, rather, that they frequently have the power to determine, either through material resources or rhetorical resources, whether the intersectional differences of women of color will be incorporated at all into the basic formulation of policy. Thus, the struggle over incorporating these differences is not a petty or superficial conflict about who gets to sit at the head of the table. In the context of violence, it is sometimes a deadly serious matter of who will survive – and who will not.[37]

B.   Political intersectionalities in rape

In the previous sections, I have used intersectionality to describe or frame various relationships between race and gender. I have used it as a way to articulate the interaction of racism and patriarchy generally. I have also used intersectionality to describe the location of women of color both within overlapping systems of subordination and at the margins of feminism and antiracism. When race and gender factors are examined in the context of rape, intersectionality can be used to map the ways in which racism and patriarchy have shaped conceptualizations of rape, to describe the unique vulnerability of women of color to these converging systems of domination, and to track the marginalization of women of color within antiracist and antirape discourses.[38]

1.   Racism and sexism in dominant conceptualizations of rape

Generations of critics and activists have criticized dominant conceptualizations of rape as racist and sexist. These efforts have been important in revealing the way in which representations of rape both reflect and reproduce race and gender hierarchies in American society. Black women, at once women and people of color, are situated within both groups, each of which has benefited from challenges to sexism and racism, respectively; yet the particular dynamics of gender and race relating to the rape of black women have received scant attention. Although antiracist and antisexist assaults on rape have been politically useful to black women, at some level, the monofocal antiracist and feminist critiques have also produced a political discourse that disserves black women.

Historically, the dominant conceptualization of rape as quintessentially involving a black offender and a white victim has left black men subject to legal and extralegal violence. The use of rape to legitimize efforts to control and discipline the black community is well established, and the casting of all black men as potential threats to the sanctity of white womanhood is a familiar construct that antiracists confronted and attempted to dispel over a century ago.

Feminists have attacked other dominant, essentially patriarchal, conceptions of rape, particularly as represented through law. The early emphasis of rape law on the propertylike aspect of women's chastity resulted in less solicitude for rape victims whose chastity had been in some way devalued. Some of the most insidious assumptions were written into the law, including the early common law notion that a woman alleging rape must be able to show that she resisted to the utmost in order to prove that she was raped rather than seduced. Women themselves were put on trial, as judge and jury scrutinized their lives to determine whether they were innocent victims or women who essentially got what they were asking for. Legal rules thus functioned to legitimize a good/bad woman dichotomy, and women who led sexually autonomous lives were usually the least likely to be vindicated if they were raped.

Today, long after the most egregious discriminatory laws have been eradicated, constructions of rape in popular discourse and in criminal law continue to manifest vestiges of these racist and sexist themes. As Valerie Smith notes, "a variety of cultural narratives that historically have linked sexual violence with racial oppression continue to determine the nature of public response" to interracial rapes.[39] Smith reviews the well-publicized case of a jogger who was raped in New York's Central Park to expose how the public discourse on the assault "made the story of sexual victimization inseparable from the rhetoric of racism."[40] Smith contends that in dehumanizing the rapists as "savages," "wolves," and "beasts," the press "shaped the discourse around the event in ways that inflamed pervasive fears about black men."[41] Given the chilling parallels between the media representations of the Central Park rape and the sensationalized coverage of similar allegations that in the past frequently culminated in lynchings, one could hardly be surprised when Donald Trump took out a full-page ad in four New York newspapers demanding that

New York "Bring Back the Death Penalty, Bring Back Our Police."[42]

Other media spectacles suggest that traditional gender-based stereotypes that oppress women continue to figure in the popular construction of rape. In Florida, for example, a controversy was sparked by a jury's acquittal of a man accused of a brutal rape because, in the jurors' view, the woman's attire suggested that she was asking for sex. Even the press coverage of William Kennedy Smith's rape trial involved a considerable degree of speculation regarding the sexual history of his accuser.

The racism and sexism written into the social construction of rape are merely contemporary manifestations of rape narratives emanating from a historical period when race and sex hierarchies were more explicitly policed. Yet another is the devaluation of black women and the marginalization of their sexual victimizations. This was dramatically shown in the special attention given to the rape of the Central Park jogger during a week in which twenty-eight other cases of first-degree rape or attempted rape were reported in New York. Many of these rapes were as horrific as the rape in Central Park, yet all were virtually ignored by the media. Some were gang rapes, and in a case that prosecutors described as "one of the most brutal in recent years," a woman was raped, sodomized, and thrown fifty feet off the top of a four-story building in Brooklyn. Witnesses testified that the victim "screamed as she plunged down the air shaft. . . . She suffered fractures of both ankles and legs, her pelvis was shattered and she suffered extensive internal injuries."[43] This rape survivor, like most of the other forgotten victims that week, was a woman of color.

In short, during the period when the Central Park jogger dominated the headlines, many equally horrifying rapes occurred. None, however, elicited the public expressions of horror and outrage that attended the Central Park rape. To account for these different responses, Smith suggests a sexual hierarchy in operation that holds certain female bodies in higher regard than others.[44] Statistics from prosecution of rape cases suggest that this hierarchy is at least one significant, albeit often-overlooked, factor in evaluating attitudes toward rape.[45] A study of rape dispositions in Dallas, for example, showed that the average prison term for a man convicted of raping a black woman was two years,[46] as compared to five years for the rape of a Latina and ten years for the rape of a white woman.[47] A related issue is the fact that African-American victims of rape are the least likely to be believed.[48] The Dallas study and others like it also point to a more subtle problem: neither the antirape nor the antiracist political agenda has focused on the black rape victim. This inattention stems from the way the problem of rape is conceptualized within antiracist and antirape reform discourses. Although the rhetoric of both agendas formally includes black women, racism is generally not problematized in feminism, and sexism is not problematized in antiracist discourses. Consequently, the plight of black women is relegated to a secondary importance: the primary beneficiaries of policies supported by feminists and others concerned about rape tend to be white women, and the primary beneficiaries of the black community's concern over racism and rape tend to be black men. Ultimately, the reformist and rhetorical strategies that have grown out of antiracist and feminist rape reform movements have been ineffective in politicizing the treatment of black women.

2. Race and the antirape lobby

Feminist critiques of rape have focused on the way that rape law has reflected dominant rules and expectations that tightly regulate the sexuality of women. In the context of the rape trial, the formal definition of rape as well as the evidentiary rules applicable in a rape trial discriminate against women by measuring the rape victim against a narrow norm of acceptable sexual conduct for women. Deviation from that norm tends to turn women into illegitimate rape victims, leading to rejection of their claims.

Historically, legal rules dictated, for example, that rape victims must have resisted their assailants in order for their claims to be accepted. Any abatement of struggle was interpreted as the woman's consent to the intercourse, under the logic that a real rape victim would protect her honor virtually to the death. While utmost resistance is not formally required anymore, rape law continues to weigh the credibility of women against narrow normative standards of female behavior. A woman's sexual history, for example, is frequently explored by defense attorneys as a way of suggesting that a woman who consented to sex on other occasions was likely to have consented in the case at issue. Past sexual conduct as well as the specific circumstances leading up to the rape are often used to distinguish the moral character of the "legitimate" rape victim from women who are regarded as morally debased or in some other way "responsible" for their own victimization.

This type of feminist critique of rape law has informed many of the fundamental reform measures enacted in antirape legislation, including increased penalties for convicted rapists and changes in evidentiary rules to preclude attacks on the woman's moral character. These reforms limit the tactics attorneys might use to tarnish the image of the rape victim, but they operate within preexisting social constructs that distinguish victims from nonvictims on the basis of their sexual character. Thus, these reforms, while beneficial, do not challenge the background cultural narratives that undermine the credibility of black women.

Because black women face subordination based on both race and gender, reforms of rape law and judicial procedures which are premised on narrow conceptions of gender subordination may not address the devaluation of black women. Much of the problem results from the way that certain gender expectations for women intersect with certain sexualized notions of race – notions that are deeply entrenched in American culture. Sexualized images of African-Americans go all the way back to Europeans' first engagement with Africans. Blacks have long been portrayed as more sexual, more earthy, more gratification-oriented; these sexualized images of race intersect with norms of women's sexuality, norms that are used to distinguish good women from bad, madonnas from whores. Thus, black women are essentially prepackaged as bad women in cultural narratives about good women who can be raped and bad women who cannot. The discrediting of black women's claims is the consequence of a complex intersection of a gendered sexual system, one that constructs rules appropriate for good and bad women, and a race code that provides images defining the allegedly essential nature of black women. If these sexual images form even part of the cultural imagery of black women, then the very representation of a black female body at least suggests certain narratives that may make black women's rape either less believable or less important. These narratives may explain why rapes of black women are less likely to result in convictions and long prison terms than are rapes of white women.

Rape law reform measures that do not in some way engage and challenge the narratives that are read onto black women's bodies are unlikely to affect the way that cultural beliefs oppress black women in rape trials. While the degree to which legal reform can directly challenge cultural beliefs that shape rape trials is limited, the very effort to mobilize political resources toward addressing the sexual oppression of black women can be an important first step in drawing greater attention to the problem. One obstacle to such an effort has been the failure of most antirape activists to analyze specifically the consequences of racism in the context of rape. In the absence of a direct attempt to address the racial dimensions of rape, black women are simply presumed to be represented in and benefited by prevailing feminist critiques.

3. *Antiracism and rape*

Antiracist critiques of rape law focus on how the law operates primarily to condemn rapes of white women by black men. While the heightened concern with protecting white women against black men has been primarily criticized as a form of discrimination against black men, it just as surely reflects devaluation of black women; this disregard for black women results from an exclusive focus on the consequences of the problem for black men.[49] Of course, rape accusations historically have provided a justification for white terrorism against the black community, generating a legitimating power of such strength that it created a veil virtually impenetrable to appeals based on either humanity or fact. Ironically, while the fear of the black rapist was exploited to legitimate the practice of lynching, rape was not even alleged in most cases. The well-developed fear of black sexuality served primarily to increase white tolerance for racial terrorism as a prophylactic measure to keep blacks under control. Within the African-American community, cases involving race-based accusations against black men have stood as hallmarks of racial injustice. The prosecution of the Scottsboro boys and the Emmett Till tragedy, for example, triggered African-American resistance to the rigid social codes of white supremacy. To the extent that rape of black women is thought to dramatize racism, it is usually cast as an assault on black manhood, demonstrating his inability to protect black women. The direct assault on black womanhood is less frequently seen as an assault on the black community.

The sexual politics that this limited reading of racism and rape engenders continues to play out today, as illustrated by the Mike Tyson rape trial. The use of antiracist rhetoric to mobilize support for Tyson represented an ongoing practice of viewing with considerable suspicion rape accusations against black men and interpreting sexual racism through a male-centered frame. The historical experience of black men has so completely occupied the dominant conceptions of racism and rape that there is little room to squeeze in the experiences of black women. Consequently, racial solidarity was continually raised as a rallying point on behalf of Tyson, but never on behalf of Desiree Washington, Tyson's black accuser. Leaders ranging from Benjamin Hooks to Louis Farrakhan expressed their support for Tyson, yet no established black leader voiced any concern for Washington. Thus, the fact that black men have often been falsely accused of raping white women underlies the antiracist defense of black men accused of rape even when the accuser herself is a black woman.

As a result of this continual emphasis on black male sexuality as the core issue in antiracist critiques of rape, black women who raise claims of rape against black men are not only disregarded but also sometimes vilified within the African-American community. One can only imagine the alienation experienced by a black rape survivor such as Desiree Washington when the accused rapist is embraced and defended as a victim of racism while she is, at best, disregarded and, at worst, ostracized and ridiculed. In contrast, Tyson was the beneficiary of the long-standing practice of using antiracist rhetoric to deflect the injury suffered by black women victimized by black men. Some defended the support given to Tyson on the ground that all African-Americans can readily imagine their sons, fathers, brothers or uncles being wrongly accused of rape; yet daughters, mothers, sisters, and aunts also deserve at least a similar concern, since statistics show that black women are more likely to be raped than black men are to be falsely accused of it. Given the magnitude of black women's vulnerability to sexual violence, it is not unreasonable to expect as much concern for black women who are raped as is expressed for the men who are accused of raping them.

Black leaders are not alone in their failure to empathize with or rally around black rape victims. Indeed, some black women were among Tyson's staunchest supporters and Washington's harshest critics.[50] The media widely noted the lack of sympathy black women had for Washington; Barbara Walters used the observation as a way of challenging Washington's credibility, going so far as to press her for a reaction.[51] The most troubling revelation was that many of the women who did not support

Washington also doubted Tyson's story. These women did not sympathize with Washington because they believed that she had no business being in Tyson's hotel room at 2:00 A.M. A typical response was offered by one young black woman who stated, "She asked for it, she got it, it's not fair to cry rape."

Indeed, some of the women who expressed their disdain for Washington acknowledged that they encountered the threat of sexual assault almost daily.[52] Yet it may be precisely this threat – along with the relative absence of rhetorical strategies challenging the sexual subordination of black women – that animated their harsh criticism. In this regard, black women who condemned Washington were quite like all other women who seek to distance themselves from rape victims as a way of denying their own vulnerability. Prosecutors who handle sexual assault cases acknowledge that they often exclude women as potential jurors because women tend to empathize least with the victim.[53] To identify too closely with victimization may reveal their own vulnerability.[54] Consequently, women often look for evidence that the victim brought the rape on herself, usually by breaking social rules that are generally held applicable only to women. And when the rules classify women as dumb, loose, or weak, on the one hand, and smart, discriminating, and strong, on the other, it is not surprising that women who cannot step outside the rules to critique them would attempt to validate themselves within them. The position of most black women on this issue is particularly problematic, first, because of the extent to which they are consistently reminded that they are the group most vulnerable to sexual victimization, and, second, because most black women share the African-American community's general resistance to explicitly feminist analysis when it appears to run up against long-standing narratives that construct black men as the primary victims of sexual racism.

C.   Rape and intersectionality in social science

The marginalization of black women's experiences within the antiracist and feminist critiques of rape law are facilitated by social science studies that fail to examine the ways in which racism and sexism converge. Gary LaFree's *Rape and Criminal Justice: The Social Construction of Sexual Assault* is a classic example.[55] Through a study of rape prosecutions in Minneapolis, LaFree attempts to determine the validity of two prevailing claims regarding rape prosecutions. The first claim is that black defendants face significant racial discrimination;[56] the second is that rape laws serve to regulate the sexual conduct of women by withholding from rape victims the ability to invoke sexual assault law when they have engaged in nontraditional behavior.[57] LaFree's compelling study concludes that law constructs rape in ways that continue to manifest both racial and gender domination.[58] Although black women are positioned as victims of both the racism and the sexism that LaFree so persuasively details, his analysis is less illuminating than might be expected, because black women fall through the cracks of his dichotomized theoretical framework.

1. Racial domination and rape

LaFree confirms the findings of earlier studies which show that race is a significant determinant in the ultimate disposition of rape cases. He finds that black men accused of raping white women were treated most harshly, while black offenders accused of raping black women were treated most leniently.[59] These effects held true even after controlling for other factors such as injury to the victim and acquaintance between victim and assailant: "Compared to other defendants, blacks who were suspected of assaulting white women received more serious charges, were more likely to have their cases filed as felonies, were more likely to receive prison sentences if convicted, were more likely to be incarcerated in the state penitentiary (as opposed to a jail or minimum-security facility), and received longer sentences on the average."[60]

LaFree's conclusions that black men are differentially punished depending on the race of the victim do not, however, contribute much to understanding the plight of black rape victims. Part of the problem lies in the author's use of "sexual stratification" theory, which posits both that women are differently valued according to their race and that there are certain "rules of sexual access" governing who may have sexual contact with whom in this sexually stratified market.[61] According to the theory, black men are discriminated against in that their forced "access" to white women is more harshly penalized than their forced "access" to black women.[62] LaFree's analysis focuses on the harsh regulation of access by black men to white women, but is silent about the relative subordination of black women to white women. The emphasis on differential access to women is consistent with analytical perspectives that view racism primarily in terms of the inequality between men. From this prevailing viewpoint, the problem of discrimination is that white men can rape black women with relative impunity while black men cannot do the same with white women.[63] Black women are considered victims of discrimination only to the extent that white men can rape them without fear of significant punishment. Rather than being viewed as victims of discrimination in their own right, they become merely the means by which discrimination against black men can be recognized. The inevitable result of this orientation is that efforts to fight discrimination tend to ignore the particularly vulnerable position of black women, who must both confront racial bias *and* challenge their status as instruments, rather than beneficiaries, of the civil rights struggle.

Where racial discrimination is framed by LaFree primarily in terms of a contest between black and white men over women, the racism experienced by black women will only be seen in terms of white male access to them. When rape of black women by white men is eliminated as a factor in the analysis, whether for statistical or other reasons, racial discrimination against black women no longer matters, since LaFree's analysis involves comparing the "access" of white and black men to white women. Yet discrimination against black women does not result simply from white men raping them with little sanction and being punished less than black men who rape white women, nor from white men raping them but not being punished as white men who rape white women would be. Black women are also discriminated against because intraracial rape of white women is treated more seriously than is intraracial rape of black women. However, the differential protection that black and white women receive against intraracial rape is not seen as racist because intraracial rape does not involve a contest between black and white men. In other words, the way the criminal justice system treats rapes of black women by black men and rapes of white women by white men is not seen as raising issues of racism, because black and white men are not involved with each other's women.

In sum, black women who are raped are racially discriminated against because their rapists, whether black or white, are less likely to be charged with rape; and, when charged and convicted, their rapists are less likely to receive significant jail time than are the rapists of white women. While sexual stratification theory does posit that women are stratified sexually by race, most applications of the theory focus on the inequality of male agents of rape rather than on the inequality of rape victims, thus marginalizing the racist treatment of black women by consistently portraying racism in terms of the relative power of black and white men.

In order to understand and treat the victimization of black women as a consequence of racism and of sexism, it is necessary to shift the analysis away from the differential access of men, and more toward the differential protection of women. Throughout his analysis, LaFree fails to do so. His sexual stratification thesis – in particular, its focus on the comparative power of male agents of rape – illustrates how the marginalization of black women in antiracist politics is replicated in social science research. Indeed, the thesis leaves unproblematized the racist subordination of less valuable objects (black women) to more valuable objects (white women), and it perpetuates the sexist treatment of women as property extensions of "their" men.

2. *Rape and gender subordination*

Although LaFree does attempt to address gender-related concerns of women in his discussion of rape and the social control of women, his theory of sexual stratification fails to focus sufficiently on the effects of stratification on women.[64] LaFree quite explicitly uses a framework that treats race and gender as separate categories, but he gives no indication that he understands how black women may fall between categories, or within both. The problem with LaFree's analysis lies not in its individual observations, which can be insightful and accurate, but rather in his failure to connect them and to develop a broader, deeper perspective. His two-track framework makes for a narrow interpretation of the data because it leaves untouched the possibility that these two tracks may intersect. Further, it is those who exist at the intersection of gender and race discrimination – black women – who suffer from this fundamental oversight.

LaFree attempts to test the feminist hypothesis that "the application of law to nonconformist women in rape cases may serve to control the behavior of all women."[65] This inquiry is important, he explains, because "if women who violate traditional sex roles and are raped are unable to obtain justice through the legal system, then the law may be interpreted as an institutional arrangement for reinforcing women's gender-role conformity."[66] He finds that "acquittals were more common and final

sentences were shorter when nontraditional victim behavior was alleged."[67] Thus, LaFree concludes, the victim's moral character was more important than victim injury – indeed, was second only to the defendant's character. Overall, 82.3 percent of the traditional victim cases resulted in convictions and average sentences of 43.38 months; only 50 percent of nontraditional victim cases led to convictions, with an average term of 27.83 months. The effects of traditional and nontraditional behavior by black women are difficult to determine from the information given and must be inferred from LaFree's passing comments. For example, he notes that black victims were evenly divided between traditional and nontraditional gender roles. This observation, together with the lower rate of conviction for men accused of raping blacks, suggests that gender-role behavior was not as significant in determining case disposition as it was in cases involving white victims. Indeed, LaFree explicitly notes that "the victim's *race* was . . . [a]n important predictor of jurors' case evaluations."[68]

> Jurors were less likely to believe in a defendant's guilt when the victim was black. Our interviews with jurors suggested that part of the explanation for this effect was that jurors . . . [w]ere influenced by stereotypes of black women as more likely to consent to sex or as more sexually experienced and hence less harmed by the assault. In a case involving the rape of a young black girl, one juror argued for acquittal on the grounds that a girl her age from "that kind of neighborhood" probably wasn't a virgin anyway.[69]

LaFree also notes that "[o]ther jurors were simply less willing to believe the testimony of black complainants."[70] One white juror is quoted as saying: "Negroes have a way of not telling the truth. They've a knack for coloring the story. So you know you can't believe everything they say."[71]

Despite explicit evidence that the race of the victim is significant in determining the disposition of rape cases, LaFree concludes that rape law functions to penalize nontraditional behavior in women. LaFree fails to note that racial identification may in some cases serve as a proxy for nontraditional behavior. That is, rape law serves not only to penalize actual examples of nontraditional behavior but also to diminish and devalue women who belong to groups in which nontraditional behavior is perceived

as common. For the black rape victim, the disposition of her case may often turn less on her behavior
than on her identity. LaFree misses the point that
although white and black women have shared interests in resisting the madonna/whore dichotomy
altogether, they nevertheless experience its oppressive power differently. Black women continue to
be judged by who they are, not by what they do.

3.   Compounding the marginalizations of rape
LaFree offers clear evidence that racial and sexual
hierarchies subordinate black women to white
women, as well as to men – both black and white.
However, the different effects of rape law on black
women are scarcely mentioned in LaFree's conclusions. In a final section, LaFree treats the devaluation of black women as an aside – one without
apparent ramifications for rape law. He concludes:
"The more severe treatment of black offenders who
rape white women (*or, for that matter, the milder
treatment of black offenders who rape black women*)
is probably best explained in terms of racial discrimination within a broader context of continuing
social and physical segregation between blacks and
whites."[72] Implicit throughout LaFree's study is
the assumption that blacks who are subjected to
social control are black *men*. Moreover, the social
control to which he refers is limited to securing the
boundaries between black males and white females.
His conclusion that race differentials are best understood within the context of social segregation as
well as his emphasis on the interracial implications
of boundary enforcement overlook the intraracial
dynamics of race and gender subordination. When
black men are leniently punished for raping black
women, the problem is *not* "best explained" in terms
of social segregation, but in terms of both the race-
and gender-based devaluation of black women. By
failing to examine the sexist roots of such lenient
punishment, LaFree and other writers sensitive to
racism ironically repeat the mistakes of those who
ignore race as a factor in such cases. Both groups
fail to consider directly the situation of black women.
   Studies like LaFree's do little to illuminate how
the interaction of race, class, and nontraditional
behavior affects the disposition of rape cases involving black women. Such an oversight is especially
troubling given evidence that many cases involving
black women are dismissed outright. Over 20 percent of rape complaints were recently dismissed as
"unfounded" by the Oakland Police Department,
which did not even interview many, if not most, of

the women involved.[73] Not coincidentally, the vast
majority of the complainants were black and poor;
many of them were substance abusers or prostitutes.
Explaining their failure to pursue these complaints,
the police remarked that "those cases were hopelessly
tainted by women who are transient, uncooperative,
untruthful or not credible as witnesses in court."[74]
   The effort to politicize violence against women
will do little to address the experiences of black
and other nonwhite women until the ramifications
of racial stratification among women are acknowledged. At the same time, the antiracist agenda
will not be furthered by suppressing the reality
of intraracial violence against women of color. The
effect of both these marginalizations is that women
of color have no ready means to link their experiences with those of other women. This sense of
isolation compounds efforts to politicize sexual violence within communities of color and perpetuates
the deadly silence surrounding these issues.

D.   Implications

With respect to the rape of black women, race and
gender converge in ways that are only vaguely
understood. Unfortunately, the analytical frameworks that have traditionally informed both antirape
and antiracist agendas tend to focus only on single
issues. They are thus incapable of developing solutions to the compound marginalization of black
women victims, who, yet again, fall into the void
between concerns about women's issues and concerns about racism. This dilemma is complicated
by the role that cultural images play in the treatment of black women victims. That is, the most
critical aspects of these problems may revolve less
around the political agendas of separate race- and
gender-sensitive groups, and more around the
social and cultural devaluation of women of color.
The stories our culture tells about the experience
of women of color present another challenge – and
a further opportunity – to apply and evaluate the
usefulness of the intersectional critique.

III.   Conclusion

This article has presented intersectionality as a way
of framing the various interactions of race and gender in the context of violence against women of color.
Yet intersectionality might be more broadly useful
as a way of mediating the tension between assertions

of multiple identity and the ongoing necessity of group politics. It is helpful in this regard to distinguish intersectionality from the closely related perspective of antiessentialism, from which women of color have critically engaged white feminism for the absence of women of color, on the one hand, and for speaking for women of color, on the other. One rendition of this antiessentialist critique – that feminism essentializes the category "woman" – owes a great deal to the postmodernist idea that categories we consider natural or merely representational are actually socially constructed in a linguistic economy of difference. While the descriptive project of postmodernism – questioning the ways in which meaning is socially constructed – is generally sound, this critique sometimes misreads the meaning of social construction and distorts its political relevance.

One version of antiessentialism, embodying what might be called the vulgarized social construction thesis, is that since all categories are socially constructed, there is no such thing as, say, blacks or women, and thus it makes no sense to continue reproducing those categories by organizing around them.[75] Even the Supreme Court has gotten into this act. In *Metro Broadcasting, Inc.* v. *FCC*,[76] the court conservatives, in rhetoric that oozes vulgar constructionist smugness, proclaimed that any setaside designed to increase the voices of minorities on the airwaves was itself based on a racist assumption that skin color is in some way connected to the likely content of one's broadcast.[77]

To say that a category such as race or gender is socially constructed is not to say that that category has no significance in our world. On the contrary, a large and continuing project for subordinated people – and indeed, one of the projects for which postmodern theories have been very helpful – is thinking about the way in which power has clustered around certain categories and is exercised against others. This project attempts to unveil the processes of subordination and the various ways in which those processes are experienced by people who are subordinated and people who are privileged by them. It is, then, a project that presumes that categories have meaning and consequences. This project's most pressing problem, in many if not most cases, is not the existence of the categories but, rather, the particular values attached to them and the way those values foster and create social hierarchies.

This is not to deny that the process of categorization is itself an exercise of power; the story is much more complicated and nuanced than that. First, the process of categorizing – or, in identity terms, naming – is not unilateral. Subordinated people can and do participate, sometimes even subverting the naming process in empowering ways. One need only think about the historical subversion of the category "black" or the current transformation of "queer" to understand that categorization is not a one-way street. Clearly, there is unequal power, but there is nonetheless some degree of agency that people can and do exert in the politics of naming. Moreover, it is important to note that identity continues to be a site of resistance for members of different subordinated groups. We all can recognize the distinction between the claims "I am black" and the claim "I am a person who happens to be black." "I am black" takes the socially imposed identity and empowers it as an anchor of subjectivity; "I am black" becomes not simply a statement of resistance but also a positive discourse of self-identification, intimately linked to celebratory statements like the black nationalist "black is beautiful." "I am a person who happens to be black," on the other hand, achieves self-identification by straining for a certain universality (in effect, "I am first a person") and for a concomitant dismissal of the imposed category ("black") as contingent, circumstantial, nondeterminant. There is truth in both characterizations, of course, but they function quite differently, depending on the political context. At this point in history, a strong case can be made that the most critical resistance strategy for disempowered groups is to occupy and defend a politics of social location rather than to vacate and destroy it.

Vulgar constructionism thus distorts the possibilities for meaningful identity politics by conflating at least two separate but closely linked manifestations of power. One is the power exercised simply through the process of categorization; the other, the power to cause that categorization to have social and material consequences. While the former power facilitates the latter, the political implications of challenging one over the other matter greatly. We can look at debates over racial subordination throughout history and see that, in each instance, there was a possibility of challenging either the construction of identity or the system of subordination based on that identity. Consider, for example, the segregation system in *Plessy* v. *Ferguson*.[78] At issue were multiple dimensions of domination, including categorization, the sign of race, and the subordination of those so labeled. There were at least two targets for Plessy to challenge: the construction of identity ("What is a black?"), and the system of subordination based on that identity ("Can blacks and whites sit together on a train?"). Plessy actually made both arguments, one against the coherence of race as a category, the other against the subordination of those deemed to be black. In his attack on the former, Plessy argued that the segregation statute's application to him, given his mixed race status, was inappropriate. The court refused to see this as an attack on the coherence of the race system and instead responded in a way that simply reproduced the black/white dichotomy that Plessy was challenging. As we know, Plessy's challenge to the segregation system was not successful either. In evaluating various resistance strategies today, it is useful to ask which of Plessy's challenges would have been best for him to have won – the challenge against the coherence of the racial categorization system or the challenge to the practice of segregation?

The same question can be posed for *Brown* v. *Board of Education*.[79] Which of two possible arguments was politically more empowering – that segregation was unconstitutional because the racial categorization system on which it was based was incoherent, or that segregation was unconstitutional because it was injurious to black children and oppressive to their communities? While it might strike some as a difficult question, for the most part, the dimension of racial domination that has been most vexing to African-Americans has not been the social categorization as such but, rather, the myriad ways in which those of us so defined have been systematically subordinated. With particular regard to problems confronting women of color, when identity politics fail us, as they frequently do, it is not primarily because those politics take as natural certain categories that are socially constructed – instead, it is because the descriptive content of those categories and the narratives on which they are based have privileged some experiences and excluded others.

Along these lines, consider the controversy involving Clarence Thomas and Anita Hill. During the Senate hearings for the confirmation of Clarence Thomas to the Supreme Court, Anita Hill, in bringing allegations of sexual harassment against Thomas, was rhetorically disempowered in part because she fell between the dominant interpretations of feminism and antiracism. Caught between the competing narrative tropes of rape (advanced by feminists), on the one hand, and lynching (advanced by Thomas and his antiracist supporters), on the other, the race and gender dimensions of her position could not be told. This dilemma could be described as the consequence of antiracism's having essentialized blackness and feminism's having essentialized womanhood. However, recognizing as much does not take us far enough, for the problem is not simply linguistic or philosophical in nature; rather, it is specifically political: the narratives of gender are based on the experience of white, middle-class women, and the narratives of race are based on the experience of black men. The solution does not merely entail arguing for the multiplicity of identities or challenging essentialism generally. Instead, in Hill's case, for example, it would have been necessary to assert those crucial aspects of her location which were erased, even by many of her advocates – that is, to state what difference her difference made.

If, as this analysis asserts, history and context determine the utility of identity politics, how then do we understand identity politics today, especially in light of our recognition of multiple dimensions of identity? More specifically, what does it mean to argue that gender identities have been obscured in antiracist discourses, just as race identities have been obscured in feminist discourses? Does that mean we cannot talk about identity? Or instead, that any discourse about identity has to acknowledge how our identities are constructed through the intersection of multiple dimensions? A beginning response to these questions requires us first to recognize that the organized identity groups in which we find ourselves are in fact coalitions, or at least potential coalitions waiting to be formed.

In the context of antiracism, recognizing the ways in which the intersectional experiences of women of color are marginalized in prevailing conceptions of identity politics does not require that we give up attempts to organize as communities of color. Rather, intersectionality provides a basis for reconceptualizing race as a coalition between men and women of color. For example, in the area of rape, intersectionality provides a way of explaining why women of color must abandon the general argument that the interests of the community require the suppression of any confrontation around intraracial rape. Intersectionality may provide the means for dealing with other marginalizations as well. For example, race can also be a coalition of straight and gay people of color, and thus serve as a basis for critique of churches and other cultural institutions that reproduce heterosexism.

With identity thus reconceptualized, it may be easier to understand the need for – and to summon – the courage to challenge groups that are after all, in one sense, "home" to us, in the name of the parts of us that are not made at home. This takes a great deal of energy and arouses intense anxiety. The most one could expect is that we will dare to speak against internal exclusions and marginalizations, that we might call attention to how the identity of "the group" has been centered on the intersectional identities of a few. Recognizing that identity politics takes place at the site where categories intersect thus seems more fruitful than challenging the possibility of talking about categories at all. Through an awareness of intersectionality, we can better acknowledge and ground the differences among us and negotiate the means by which these differences will find expression in constructing group politics.

Notes

1. Feminist academics and activists have played a central role in forwarding an ideological and institutional challenge to the practices that condone and perpetuate violence against women. See generally S. Brownmiller, *Against Our Will: Men, Women and Rape* (1975); L. M. G. Clark and D. J. Lewis, *Rape: The Price of Coercive Sexuality* (1977); R. E. Dobash and R. Dobash, *Violence against Wives: A Case against the Patriarchy* (1979); N. Gager and C. Schurr, *Sexual Assault: Confronting Rape in America* (1976); D. E. H. Russell, *The Politics of Rape: The Victim's Perspective* (1974); E. A. Stanko, *Intimate Intrusions: Women's Experience of Male Violence* (1985); L. E. Walker, *Terrifying Love: Why Battered Women Kill and How Society Responds* (1989); L. E. Walker, *The Battered Woman Syndrome* (1984); L. E. Walker, *The Battered Woman* (1979).

2. See, for example, S. Schechter, *Women and Male Violence: The Visions and Struggles of the Battered Women's Movement* (1982) (arguing that battering is a means of maintaining women's subordinate position); S. Brownmiller, see note 1 (arguing that rape is a patriarchal practice that subordinates women to men); E. Schneider, "The Violence of Privacy," 23 *Conn. L. Rev.*, 973, 974 (1991) (discussing how "concepts of privacy permit, encourage and reinforce violence against women"); S. Estrich, "Rape," 95 *Yale L. J.* 1087 (1986) (analyzing rape law as one illustration of sexism in criminal law); see also C. A. Mackinnon, *Sexual Harassment of Working Women: A Case of Sex Discrimination*, 143–213 (1979) (arguing that sexual harassment should be redefined as sexual discrimination actionable under Title VII, rather than viewed as misplaced sexuality in the workplace).

3. Although the objective of this article is to describe the intersectional location of women of color and their marginalization within dominant resistance discourses, I do not mean to imply that the disempowerment of women of color is singularly or even primarily caused by feminist and antiracist theorists or activists. Indeed, I hope to dispel any such simplistic interpretations by capturing, at least in part, the way that prevailing structures of domination shape various discourses of resistance. As I have noted elsewhere, "People can only demand change in ways that reflect the logic of the institutions they are challenging. Demands for change that do not reflect . . . dominant ideology . . . will probably be ineffective"; Crenshaw, *Race, Reform, and Retrenchment: Transformation and Legitimation in Antidiscrimination Law*, at 1367. Although there are significant political and conceptual obstacles to moving against structures of domination with an intersectional sensibility, my point is that the effort to do so should be a central theoretical and political objective of both antiracism and feminism.

4. Although this article deals with violent assault perpetrated by men against women, women are also subject to violent assault by women. Violence among lesbians is a hidden but significant problem. One expert reported in a study of 90 lesbian couples that roughly 46 percent of lesbians have been physically abused by their partners; J. Garcia, "The Cost of Escaping Domestic Violence: Fear of Treatment in a Largely Homophobic Society May Keep Lesbian Abuse Victims from Calling for Help," *Los Angeles Times* (May 6, 1991), 2; see also K. Lobel, ed., *Naming the Violence: Speaking Out about Lesbian Battering* (1986); R. Robson, "Lavender Bruises: Intralesbian Violence, Law and Lesbian Legal Theory," 20 *Golden Gate U. L. Rev.*, 567 (1990). There are clear parallels between violence against women in the lesbian community and violence against women in communities of color. Lesbian violence is often shrouded in secrecy for reasons similar to those which have suppressed the exposure of heterosexual violence in communities of color – fear of embarrassing other members of the community, which is already stereotyped as deviant, and fear of being ostracized from the community. Despite these similarities, there are nonetheless distinctions between male abuse of women and female abuse of women that, in the context of patriarchy, racism, and homophobia, warrant more focused analysis than is possible here.

5. K. Crenshaw, "Demarginalizing the Intersection of Race and Sex," *U. Chi. Legal F.*, 139 (1989).

6. I explicitly adopt a black feminist stance in this survey of violence against women of color. I do this

cognizant of several tensions that such a position entails. The most significant one stems from the criticism that while feminism purports to speak for women of color through its invocation of the term "woman," the feminist perspective excludes women of color because it is based upon the experiences and interests of a certain subset of women. On the other hand, when white feminists attempt to include other women, they often add our experiences into an otherwise unaltered framework. It is important to name the perspective from which one constructs her analysis; and for me, that is as a black feminist. Moreover, it is important to acknowledge that the materials that I incorporate in my analysis are drawn heavily from research on black women. On the other hand, I see my own work as part of a broader collective effort among feminists of color to expand feminism to include analyses of race and other factors such as class, sexuality, and age. I have attempted therefore to offer my sense of the tentative connections between my analysis of the intersectional experiences of black women and the intersectional experiences of other women of color. I stress that this analysis is not intended to include falsely nor to exclude unnecessarily other women of color.

7. I consider intersectionality a provisional concept linking contemporary politics with postmodern theory. In mapping the intersections of race and gender, the concept does engage dominant assumptions that race and gender are essentially separate categories. By tracing the categories to their intersections, I hope to suggest a methodology that will ultimately disrupt the tendencies to see race and gender as exclusive or separable. While the primary intersections that I explore here are between race and gender, the concept can and should be expanded by factoring in issues such as class, sexual orientation, age, and color.

8. 8 U.S.C. § 1186a (1988). The marriage fraud amendments provide that an alien spouse "shall be considered, at the time of obtaining the status of an alien lawfully admitted for permanent residence, to have obtained such status on a conditional basis subject to the provisions of this section"; § 1186a(a)(1). An alien spouse with permanent resident status under this conditional basis may have her status terminated if the attorney general finds that the marriage was "improper" (§ 1186a(b)(1)), or if she fails to file a petition or fails to appear at the personal interview (§ 1186a(c)(2)(A)).

9. The marriage fraud amendments provided that for the conditional resident status to be removed "the alien spouse and the petitioning spouse (if not deceased) *jointly* must submit to the Attorney General . . . a petition which requests the removal of such conditional basis and which states, under penalty of perjury, the facts and information";

§ 1186a(b)(1)(A) (emphasis added). The amendments provided for a waiver, at the attorney general's discretion, if the alien spouse was able to demonstrate that deportation would result in extreme hardship, or that the qualifying marriage was terminated for good cause; § 1186a(c)(4). However, the terms of this hardship waiver have not adequately protected battered spouses. For example, the requirement that the marriage be terminated for good cause may be difficult to satisfy in states with no-fault divorces; E. P. Lynsky, "Immigration Marriage Fraud Amendments of 1986: Till Congress Do Us Part," 41 *U. Miami L. Rev.*, 1087, 1095 n. 47 (1987) (student author) (citing J. B. Ingber and R. L. Prischet, "The Marriage Fraud Amendments," in S. Mailman, ed., *The New Simpson-Rodino Immigration Law of 1986*, 564–5 (1986).

10. Immigration Act of 1990, Pub. L. No. 101–649, 104 Stat. 4978. The act, introduced by Rep. Louise Slaughter (Dem.–N.Y.), provides that a battered spouse who has conditional permanent resident status can be granted a waiver for failure to meet the requirements if she can show that "the marriage was entered into in good faith and that after the marriage the alien spouse was battered by or was subjected to extreme mental cruelty by the U.S. citizen or permanent resident spouse"; H.R. Rep. No. 723(1), 101st Cong., 2d Sess. 78 (1990), reprinted in 1990 U.S.C.C.A.N. 6710, 6758; see also 8 C.F.R. § 216.5(3) (1992) (regulations for application for waiver based on claim of having been battered or subjected to extreme mental cruelty).

11. H.R. Rep. No. 723(1), see note 10, at 79, reprinted in 1990 U.S.C.C.A.N. 6710, 6759.

12. D. Hodgin, "'Mail-Order' Brides Marry Pain to Get Green Cards," *Washington Post*, October 16, 1990, at E5.

13. Ibid.

14. Most crime statistics are classified by sex or race but none are classified by sex and race. Because we know that most rape victims are women, the racial breakdown reveals, at best, rape rates for black women. Yet even given this head start, rates for other nonwhite women are difficult to collect. While there are some statistics for Latinas, statistics for Asian and Native American women are virtually nonexistent; cf. G. Chezia Carraway, "Violence Against Women of Color," 43 *Stan. L. Rev.*, 1301 (1993).

15. S. Ali, *The Blackman's Guide to Understanding the Blackwoman* (1989). Ali's book sold quite well for an independently published title, an accomplishment no doubt due in part to her appearances on the Phil Donahue, Oprah Winfrey, and Sally Jesse Raphael television talk shows. For public and press reaction, see D. Gillism, "Sick, Distorted Thinking," *Washington Post* (Oct. 11, 1990), D3; L.

Williams, "Black Woman's Book Starts a Predict-able Storm," *New York Times* (Oct. 2, 1990), C11; see also P. Cleacue, *Mad at Miles: A Black Woman's Guide to Truth* (1990). The title clearly styled after Ali's, *Mad at Miles* responds not only to issues raised by Ali's book, but also to Miles Davis's admission in his autobiography, *Miles: The Autobiography* (1989), that he had physically abused, among other women, his former wife, actress Cicely Tyson.

16. Ali suggests that the Blackwoman "certainly does not believe that her disrespect for the Blackman is destructive, nor that her opposition to him has deteriorated the Black nation"; S. Ali, *The Blackman's Guide*, at viii. Blaming the problems of the commun-ity on the failure of the black woman to accept her "real definition," Ali explains that "[n]o nation can rise when the natural order of the behavior of the male and the female have been altered against their wishes by force. No species can survive if the female of the genus disturbs the balance of her nature by acting other than herself"; ibid. at 76.

17. Ali advises the Blackman to hit the Blackwoman in the mouth, "[b]ecause it is from that hole, in the lower part of her face, that all her rebellion culmin-ates into words. Her unbridled tongue is a main reason she cannot get along with the Blackman. She often needs a reminder"; ibid. at 161. Ali warns that "if [the Blackwoman] ignores the authority and superiority of the Blackman, there is a penalty. When she crosses this line and becomes viciously insulting it is time for the Blackman to soundly slap her in the mouth"; ibid.

18. In this regard, Ali's arguments bear much in com-mon with those of neoconservatives who attribute many of the social ills plaguing black America to the breakdown of patriarchal family values; see, for example, W. Raspberry, "If We Are to Rescue Amer-ican Families, We Have to Save the Boys," *Chicago Tribune* (July 19, 1989), C15; G. F. Will, "Voting Rights Won't Fix It," *Washington Post* (Jan. 23, 1986), A23; G. F. Will, "'White Racism' Doesn't Make Blacks Mere Victims of Fate," *Milwaukee Journal* (Feb. 21, 1986), 9. Ali's argument shares remarkable similarities to the controversial "Moyni-han Report" on the black family, so called because its principal author was now-Senator Daniel P. Moynihan (Dem.–N.Y.). In the infamous chapter entitled "The Tangle of Pathology," Moynihan argued that "the Negro community has been forced into a matriarchal structure which, because it is so out of line with the rest of American society, ser-iously retards the progress of the group as a whole, and imposes a crushing burden on the Negro male and, in consequence, on a great many Negro women as well"; Office of Policy Planning and Research, U.S. Department of Labor, *The Negro Family: The Case for National Action*, 29 (1965), reprinted in

L. Rainwater and W. L. Yancey, *The Moynihan Report and the Politics of Controversy* 75 (1967). A storm of controversy developed over the book, although few commentators challenged the patriarchal discourse embedded in the analysis. Bill Moyers, then a young minister and speechwriter for President Lyndon B. Johnson, firmly believed that the criticism directed at Moynihan was unfair. Some twenty years later, Moyers resurrected the Moynihan thesis in a spe-cial television program, *The Vanishing Family: Cri-sis in Black America* (CBS television broadcast, Jan. 25, 1986). The show first aired in January 1986 and featured several African-American men and women who had become parents but were unwilling to marry. See A. Linger, "Hardhitting Special About Black Families," *Christian Science Monitor* (Jan. 23, 1986), 23. Many saw the Moyers show as a vindica-tion of Moynihan. President Reagan took the opportunity to introduce an initiative to revamp the welfare system a week after the program aired; M. Barone, "Poor Children and Politics," *Washington Post* (Feb. 10, 1986), A1. Said one official, "Bill Moyers has made it safe for people to talk about this issue, the disintegrating black family structure"; R. Pear, "President Reported Ready to Propose Overhaul of Social Welfare System," *New York Times* (Feb. 1, 1986), A12. Critics of the Moynihan/Moyers thesis have argued that it scapegoats the black family generally and black women in particu-lar. For a series of responses, see "Scapegoating the Black Family," *The Nation* (July 24, 1989) (special issue, edited by Jewel Handy Gresham and Margaret B. Wilkerson, with contributions from Margaret Burnham, Constance Clayton, Dorothy Height, Faye Wattleton, and Marian Wright Edelman). For an analysis of the media's endorsement of the Moynihan/Moyers thesis, see C. Ginsburg, *Race and Media: The Enduring Life of the Moynihan Report* (1989).

19. Domestic violence relates directly to issues that even those who subscribe to Ali's position must also be concerned about. The socioeconomic condition of black males has been one such central concern. Recent statistics estimate that 25 percent of black males in their twenties are involved in the criminal justice systems; see D. G. Savage, "Young Black Males in Jail or in Court Control Study Says," *Los Angeles Times* (Feb. 27, 1990), A1; *Newsday* (Feb. 27, 1990), 15; "Study Shows Racial Imbalance in Penal System," *New York Times* (Feb. 27, 1990), A18. One would think that the linkages between violence in the home and the violence on the streets would alone persuade those like Ali to conclude that the African-American community cannot afford domestic violence and the patriarchal values that support it.

20. A pressing problem is the way domestic violence reproduces itself in subsequent generations. It is

estimated that boys who witness violence against women are ten times more likely to batter female partners as adults; *Women and Violence: Hearings before the Senate Comm. on the Judiciary on Legislation to Reduce the Growing Problem of Violent Crime against Women*, 101st Cong., 2d Sess., pt. 2, at 89 (1991) (testimony of Charlotte Fedders). Other associated problems for boys who witness violence against women include higher rates of suicide, violent assault, sexual assault, and alcohol and drug use; ibid., pt. 2, at 131 (statement of Sarah M. Buel, assistant district attorney, Massachusetts, and supervisor, Harvard Law School Battered Women's Advocacy Project).

21. Ibid. at 142 (statement of Susan Kelly-Dreiss, discussing several studies in Pennsylvania linking homelessness to domestic violence).

22. Ibid. at 143 (statement of Susan Kelly-Dreiss).

23. Another historical example includes Eldridge Cleaver, who argued that he raped white women as an assault upon the white community. Cleaver "practiced" on black women first; E. Cleaver, *Soul on Ice*, 14–15 (1968). Despite the appearance of misogyny in both works, each professes to worship black women as "queens" of the black community. This "queenly subservience" parallels closely the image of the "woman on a pedestal" against which white feminists have railed. Because black women have been denied pedestal status within dominant society, the image of the African queen has some appeal to many African-American women. Although it is not a feminist position, there are significant ways in which the promulgation of the image directly counters the intersectional effects of racism and sexism that have denied African-American women a perch in the "gilded cage."

24. T. Harris, "On *The Color Purple*, Stereotypes, and Silence," 18 *Black Am. Lit. F.*, 155 (1984).

25. On January 14, 1991, Sen. Joseph Biden (Dem.–Del.) introduced Senate Bill 15, the Violence Against Women Act of 1991, comprehensive legislation addressing violent crime confronting women; S. 15, 102d Cong., 1st Sess. (1991). The bill consists of several measures designed to create safe streets, safe homes, and safe campuses for women. More specifically, Title III of the bill creates a civil rights remedy for crimes of violence motivated by the victim's gender; ibid. § 01. Among the findings supporting the bill were "(1) crimes motivated by the victim's gender constitute bias crimes in violation of the victim's right to be free from discrimination on the basis of gender," and "(2) current law [does not provide a civil rights remedy] for gender crimes committed on the street or in the home"; S. Rep. No. 197, 102d Cong., 1st Sess. 27 (1991).

26. 137 Cong. Rec. S611 (daily ed. Jan. 14, 1991) (statement of Senator Boren). Sen. William Cohen

(Dem.–Me.) followed with a similar statement, noting "that rapes and domestic assaults are not limited to the streets of our inner cities or to those few highly publicized cases that we read about in the newspapers or see on the evening news. Women throughout the country, in our nation's urban areas and rural communities, are being beaten and brutalized in the streets and in their homes. It is our mothers, wives, daughters, sisters, friends, neighbors, and coworkers who are being victimized; and in many cases, they are being victimized by family members, friends, and acquaintances"; ibid. (statement of Senator Cohen).

27. *48 Hours*, "Till Death Do Us Part" (CBS television broadcast, Feb. 6, 1991).

28. Letter of Diana M. Campos, director of Human Services, PODER, to Joseph Semidei, deputy commissioner, New York State Department of Social Services (Mar. 26, 1992).

29. Ibid. (emphasis added).

30. Ibid.

31. Ibid.

32. Roundtable Discussion on Racism and the Domestic Violence Movement (April 2, 1992) (transcript on file with the *Stanford Law Review*). The participants in the discussion – Diana Campos, director, Bilingual Outreach Project of the New York State Coalition Against Domestic Violence; Elsa A. Rios, project director, Victim Intervention Project (a community-based project in East Harlem, New York, serving battered women); and Haydee Rosario, a social worker with the East Harlem Council for Human Services and a Victim Intervention Project volunteer – recounted conflicts relating to race and culture during their association with the New York State Coalition Against Domestic Violence, a state oversight group that distributed resources to battered women's shelters throughout the state and generally set policy priorities for the shelters that were part of the coalition.

33. Ibid.

34. Ibid.

35. Ibid.

36. Ironically, the specific dispute that led to the walkout concerned the housing of the Spanish-language domestic violence hotline. The hotline was initially housed at the coalition's headquarters, but languished after a succession of coordinators left the organization. Latinas on the coalition board argued that the hotline should be housed at one of the community service agencies, while the board insisted on maintaining control of it. The hotline is now housed at PODER; ibid.

37. Said Campos, "It would be a shame that in New York state a battered woman's life or death were dependent upon her English language skills"; D. M. Campos, see note 28.

38. The discussion in the following section focuses rather narrowly on the dynamics of a black-white sexual hierarchy. I specify African-Americans in part because, given the centrality of sexuality as a site of racial domination of African-Americans, any generalizations that might be drawn from this history seem least applicable to other racial groups. To be sure, the specific dynamics of racial oppression experienced by other racial groups are likely to have a sexual component as well. Indeed, the repertoire of racist imagery that is commonly associated with different racial groups each contain a sexual stereotype as well. These images probably influence the way that rapes involving other minority groups are perceived both internally and in society at large, but they are likely to function in different ways.

39. V. Smith, "Split Affinities: The Case of Interracial Rape," in M. Hirsch and E. F. Keller, eds., *Conflicts in Feminism*, 271, 274 (1990).

40. Ibid. at 276–8.

41. Smith cites the use of animal images to characterize the accused black rapists, including descriptions such as: " 'a wolfpack of more than a dozen young teenagers' and '[t]here was a full moon Wednesday night. A suitable backdrop for the howling of wolves. A vicious pack ran rampant through Central Park. . . . This was bestial brutality.' " An editorial in the *New York Times* was entitled "The Jogger and the Wolf Pack"; ibid. at 277 (citations omitted).

    Evidence of the ongoing link between rape and racism in American culture is by no means unique to media coverage of the Central Park jogger case. In December 1990, the George Washington University student newspaper, *The Hatchet*, printed a story in which a white student alleged that she had been raped at knifepoint by two black men on or near the campus; the story caused considerable racial tension. Shortly after the report appeared, the woman's attorney informed the campus police that his client had fabricated the attack. After the hoax was uncovered, the woman said that she hoped the story "would highlight the problems of safety for women"; F. Banger, "False Rape Report Upsetting Campus," *New York Times* (Dec. 12, 1990), A2; see also L. Payne, "A Rape Hoax Stirs Up Hate," *New York Newsday* (Dec. 16, 1990), 6.

42. W. C. Troft, "Deadly Donald," UP (Apr. 30, 1989). Donald Trump explained that he spent $85,000 to take out these ads because "I want to hate these muggers and murderers. They should be forced to suffer and, when they kill, they should be executed for their crimes"; "Trump Calls for Death to Muggers," *Los Angeles Times* (May 1, 1989), A2. But cf. "Leaders Fear 'Lynch' Hysteria in Response to Trump Ads," UPI (May 6, 1989) (community leaders feared that Trump's ads would fan "the flames of racial polarization and hatred"); C. Fuchs

Epstein, "Cost of Full Page Ad Could Help Fight Causes of Urban Violence," *New York Times* (May 15, 1989), A18 ("Mr. Trump's proposal could well lead to further violence").

43. R. D. McFadden, "2 Men Get 6 to 18 Years for Rape in Brooklyn," *New York Times* (Oct. 2, 1990), B2. The woman "lay half naked, moaning and crying for help until a neighbor heard her" in the air shaft; "Community Rallies to Support Victim of Brutal Brooklyn Rape," *New York Daily News* (June 26, 1989), 6. The victim "suffered such extensive injuries that she had to learn to walk again. . . . She faces years of psychological counseling"; McFadden, ibid.

44. Smith points out that "[t]he relative invisibility of black women victims of rape also reflects the differential value of women's bodies in capitalist societies. To the extent that rape is constructed as a crime against the property of privileged white men, crimes against less valuable women – women of color, working-class women, and lesbians, for example – mean less or mean differently than those against white women from the middle and upper classes"; Smith, "Split Affinities," at 275–6.

45. "Cases involving black offenders and black victims were treated the least seriously"; G. D. LaFree, *Rape and Criminal Justice: The Social Construction of Sexual Assault* (1989). LaFree also notes, however, that "the race composition of the victim-offender dyad" was not the only predictor of case dispositions; ibid. at 219–20.

46. "Race Tilts the Scales of Justice. Study: Dallas Punishes Attacks on Whites More Harshly," *Dallas Times Herald* (Aug. 19, 1990), A1. A study of 1988 cases in Dallas County's criminal justice system concluded that rapists whose victims were white were punished more severely than those whose victims were black or Hispanic. The *Dallas Times Herald*, which had commissioned the study, reported that "[t]he punishment almost doubled when the attacker and victim were of different races. Except for such interracial crime, sentencing disparities were much less pronounced"; ibid.

47. Ibid. Two criminal law experts, Iowa law professor David Baldus and Carnegie-Mellon University professor Alfred Blumstein, "said that the racial inequities might be even worse than the figures suggest"; ibid.

48. See G. LaFree, *Rape and Criminal Justice*, at 219–20 (quoting jurors who doubted the credibility of black rape survivors); see also H. Field and L. Bienen, *Jurors and Rape: A Study in Psychology and Law* 141 (1980), at 117–18.

49. The statistic that 89 percent of all men executed for rape in this country were black is a familiar one. *Furman* v. *Georgia*, 408 U.S. 238, 364 (1972) (Marshall, J., concurring). Unfortunately, the dominant analysis of racial discrimination in rape

prosecutions generally does not discuss whether any of the rape *victims* in these cases were black; see J. Wriggins, "Rape, Racism, and the Law," 6 *Harv. Women's L. J.*, 103, 113 (1983) (student author).

50. See M. Rosenfeld, "After the Verdict, the Doubts: Black Women Show Little Sympathy for Tyson's Accuser," *Washington Post* (Feb. 13, 1992), D1; A. Johnson, "Tyson Rape Case Strikes a Nerve Among Blacks," *Chicago Tribune* (Mar. 29, 1992), C1; S. P. Kelly, "Black Women Wrestle with Abuse Issue: Many Say Choosing Racial over Gender Loyalty Is Too Great a Sacrifice," *Chicago Star Tribune* (Feb. 18, 1992), A1.

51. *20/20* (ABC television broadcast, Feb. 21, 1992).

52. According to a study by the Bureau of Justice, black women are significantly more likely to be raped than white women, and women in the 16–24 age group are two to three times more likely to be victims of rape or attempted rape than women in any other age group; see R. J. Ostrow, "Typical Rape Victim Called Poor, Young," *Los Angeles Times* (Mar. 25, 1985), 8.

53. See P. Tyre, "What Experts Say About Rape Jurors," *New York Newsday* (May 19, 1991), 10 (reporting that "researchers had determined that jurors in criminal trials side with the complainant or defendant whose ethnic, economic and religious background most closely resembles their own. The exception to the rule . . . is the way women jurors judge victims of rape and sexual assault"). Linda Fairstein, a Manhattan prosecutor, states, "too often women tend to be very critical of the conduct of other women, and they often are not good jurors in acquaintance-rape cases"; M. Carlson, "The Trials of Convicting Rapists," *Time* (Oct. 14, 1991), 11.

54. As sex crimes prosecutor Barbara Eganhauser notes, even young women with contemporary lifestyles often reject a woman's rape accusation out of fear. "To call another woman the victim of rape is to acknowledge the vulnerability in yourself. They go out at night, they date, they go to bars, and walk alone. To deny it is to say at the trial that women are not victims"; Tyre, see note 53.

55. G. LaFree, *Rape and Criminal Justice*.

56. Ibid. at 49–50.

57. Ibid. at 50–1.

58. Ibid. at 237–40.

59. LaFree concludes that recent studies finding no discriminatory effect were inconclusive because they analyzed the effects of the defendant's race independently of the race of the victim. The differential race effects in sentencing are often concealed by combining the harsher sentences given to black men accused of raping white women with the more lenient treatment of black men accused of raping black women; ibid. at 117, 140. Similar results were found in another study: see A. Walsh, "The Sexual Strati-

fication Hypothesis and Sexual Assault in Light of the Changing Conceptions of Race," 25 *Criminology*, 153, 170 (1987) ("sentence severity mean for blacks who assaulted whites, which was significantly in excess of mean for whites who assaulted whites, was masked by the lenient sentence severity mean for blacks who assaulted blacks").

60. G. LaFree, *Rape and Criminal Justice*, at 139–40.

61. Sexual stratification, according to LaFree, refers to the differential valuation of women according to their race and to the creation of "rules of sexual access" governing who may have contact with whom. Sexual stratification also dictates what the penalty will be for breaking these rules: the rape of a white woman by a black man is seen as a trespass on the valuable property rights of white men and is punished most severely; ibid. at 48–9. The fundamental propositions of the sexual stratification thesis have been summarized as follows: (1) Women are viewed as the valued and scarce property of the men of their own race. (2) White women, by virtue of membership in the dominant race, are more valuable than black women. (3) The sexual assault of a white by a black threatens both the white man's "property rights" and his dominant social position. This dual threat accounts for the strength of the taboo attached to interracial sexual assault. (4) A sexual assault by a male of any race upon members of the less valued black race is perceived as nonthreatening to the status quo and therefore less serious. (5) White men predominate as agents of social control. Therefore, they have the power to sanction differentially according to the perceived threat to their favored social position; Walsh, "Sexual Stratification Hypothesis," at 155.

62. I use the term "access" guardedly because it is an inapt euphemism for rape. On the other hand, rape is conceptualized differently depending on whether certain race-specific rules of sexual access are violated. Although violence is not explicitly written into the sexual stratification theory, it does work itself into the rules, in that sexual intercourse which violates the racial access rules is presumed to be coercive rather than voluntary; see, for example, *Sims* v. *Balkam*, 136 S.E. 2d 766, 769 (Ga. 1964) (describing the rape of a white woman by a black man as "a crime more horrible than death"); *Story* v. *State*, 59 So. 480 (Ala. 1912) ("The consensus of public opinion, unrestricted to either race, is that a white woman prostitute is yet, though lost of virtue, above the even greater sacrifice of the voluntary submission of her person to the embraces of the other race"); Wriggins, "Rape, Racism, and the Law," at 125, 127.

63. This traditional approach places black women in a position of denying their own victimization, requiring them to argue that it is racist to punish black

men more harshly for raping white women than for raping black women. However, in the wake of the Mike Tyson trial, it seems that many black women are prepared to do just that; see notes 50–2 above and accompanying text.

64. G. LaFree, *Rape and Criminal Justice*, at 148. LaFree's transition between race and gender suggests that the shift might not loosen the frame enough to permit discussion of the combined effects of race and gender subordination on black women. LaFree repeatedly separates race from gender, treating them as wholly distinguishable issues; see, for example, ibid. at 147.

65. Ibid.

66. Ibid. at 151. LaFree interprets nontraditional behavior to include drinking, drug use, extramarital sex, illegitimate children, and "having a reputation as a 'partier,' a 'pleasure seeker' or someone who stays out late at night"; ibid. at 201.

67. Ibid. at 204.

68. Ibid. at 219 (emphasis added). While there is little direct evidence that prosecutors are influenced by the race of the victim, it is not unreasonable to assume that since race is an important predictor of conviction, prosecutors determined to maintain a high conviction rate might be less likely to pursue a case involving a black victim than a white one. This calculus is probably reinforced when juries fail to convict in strong cases involving black victims. For example, the acquittal of three white St. John's University athletes for the gang rape of a Jamaican schoolmate was interpreted by many as racially influenced. Witnesses testified that the woman was incapacitated during much of the ordeal, having ingested a mixture of alcohol given to her by a classmate who subsequently initiated the assault. The jurors insisted that race played no role in their decision to acquit. "There was no race, we all agreed to it," said one juror; "They were trying to make it racial but it wasn't," said another; "Jurors: 'It Wasn't Racial,'" *New York Newsday* (July 25, 1991), at 4. Yet it is possible that race did influence on some level their belief that the woman consented to what, by all accounts, amounted to dehumanizing conduct; see, for example, C. Agus, "Whatever Happened to 'The Rules,'" *New York Newsday* (July 28, 1991), 11 (citing testimony that at least two of the assailants hit the victim in the head with their penises). The jury nonetheless thought, in the words of its foreman, that the defendants' behavior was "obnoxious" but not criminal; see S. H. Schanberg, "Those 'Obnoxious' St. John's Athletes," *New York Newsday* (July 30, 1991), 79. One can imagine a different outcome had the races of the parties only been reversed. Rep. Charles Rangel (Dem.–N.Y.) called the verdict "a rerun of what used to happen in the South"; J. M. Brodie, "The St. John's Rape Acquittal: Old Wounds That Just Won't Go Away," *Black Issues in Higher Educ.* (Aug. 15, 1991), 18. Denise Snyder, executive director of the D.C. Rape Crisis Center, commented: "It's a historical precedent that white men can assault black women and get away with it. Woe be to the black man who assaults white women. All the prejudices that existed a hundred years ago are dormant and not so dormant, and they rear their ugly heads in situations like this. Contrast this with the Central Park jogger who was an upper-class white woman"; J. Mann, "New Age, Old Myths," *Washington Post* (July 26, 1991), C3 (quoting Snyder); see K. Bumiller, "Rape as a Legal Symbol: An Essay on Sexual Violence and Racism," 42 *U. Miami L. Rev.*, 75, 88 ("The cultural meaning of rape is rooted in a symbiosis of racism and sexism that has tolerated the acting out of male aggression against women and, in particular, black women").

69. Ibid. at 219–20 (citations omitted). Anecdotal evidence suggests that this attitude exists among some who are responsible for processing rape cases. Fran Weinman, a student in my seminar on race, gender, and the law, conducted a field study at the Rosa Parks Rape Crisis Center. During her study, she counseled and accompanied a twelve-year-old black rape survivor who became pregnant as a result of the rape. The girl was afraid to tell her parents, who discovered the rape after she became depressed and began to slip in school. Police were initially reluctant to interview the girl. Only after the girl's father threatened to take matters into his own hands did the police department send an investigator to the girl's house. The city prosecutor indicated that the case wasn't a serious one, and was reluctant to prosecute the defendant for statutory rape even though the girl was underage; the prosecutor reasoned, "After all, she looks sixteen." After many frustrations, the girl's family ultimately decided not to pressure the prosecutor any further and the case was dropped; see F. Weinman, "Racism and the Enforcement of Rape Law," 13–30 (1990) (unpublished manuscript) (on file with the *Stanford Law Review*).

70. G. LaFree, *Rape and Criminal Justice*, at 220.

71. Ibid.

72. Ibid. at 239 (emphasis added). The lower conviction rates for those who rape black women may be analogous to the low conviction rates for acquaintance rape. The central issue in many rape cases is proving that the victim did not consent. The basic presumption in the absence of explicit evidence of lack of consent is that consent exists. Certain evidence is sufficient to disprove that presumption, and the quantum of evidence necessary to prove nonconsent increases as the presumptions warranting an inference of consent increase. Some

women – based on their character, identity, or dress – are viewed as more likely to consent than other women. Perhaps it is the combination of the sexual stereotypes about black people along with the greater degree of familiarity presumed to exist between black men and black women that leads to the conceptualization of such rapes as existing somewhere between acquaintance rape and stranger rape.

73. C. Cooper, "Nowhere to Turn for Rape Victims: High Proportion of Cases Tossed Aside by Oakland Police," *S. F. Examiner*, Sept. 16, 1990, at A10.

74. Ibid. Advocates point out that because investigators work from a profile of the kind of case likely to get a conviction, people left out of that profile are people of color, prostitutes, drug users, and people raped by acquaintances. This exclusion results in "a whole class of women . . . systematically being denied justice. Poor women suffer the most"; ibid.

75. I do not mean to imply that all theorists who have made antiessentialist critiques have lapsed into vulgar constructionism. Indeed, antiessentialists avoid making these troubling moves and would no doubt be receptive to much of the critique set forth herein. I use the phrase "vulgar constructionism" to distinguish between those antiessentialist critiques that leave room for identity politics and those that do not.

76. 110 S. Ct. 2997 (1990).

77. The FCC's choice to employ a racial criterion embodies the related notions that a particular and distinct viewpoint inheres in certain racial groups and that a particular applicant, by virtue of race or ethnicity alone, is more valued than other applicants because the applicant is "likely to provide [that] distinct perspective." The policies directly equate race with belief and behavior, for they establish race as a necessary and sufficient condition of securing the preference. . . . The policies impermissibly value individuals because they presume that persons think in a manner associated with their race; ibid. at 3037 (O'Connor, J., joined by Rehnquist, C. J., and Scalia and Kennedy, J. J., dissenting) (internal citations omitted).

78. 163 U.S. 537 (1896).

79. 397 U.S. 483 (1954).

20

Gender Trouble, Feminist Theory, and Psychoanalytic Discourse

Judith Butler

Within the terms of feminist theory, it has been quite important to refer to the category of "women" and to know what it is we mean. We tend to agree that women have been written out of the histories of culture and literature that men have written, that women have been silenced or distorted in the texts of philosophy, biology, and physics, and that there is a group of embodied beings socially positioned as "women" who now, under the name of feminism, have something quite different to say. Yet, this question of being a woman is more difficult than it perhaps originally appeared, for we refer not only to women as a social category but also as a felt sense of self, a culturally conditioned or constructed subjective identity. The descriptions of women's oppression, their historical situation or cultural perspective has seemed, to some, to require that women themselves will not only recognize the rightness of feminist claims made in their behalf, but that, together, they will discover a common identity, whether in their relational attitudes, in their embodied resistance to abstract and object-ifying modes of thought and experience, their felt sense of their bodies, their capacity for maternal identification or maternal thinking, the nonlinear directionality of their pleasures or the elliptical and plurivocal possibilities of their writing.

But does feminist theory need to rely on a notion of what it is fundamentally or distinctively to be a "woman"? The question becomes a crucial one when we try to answer what it is that characterizes the world of women that is marginalized, distorted, or negated within various masculinist practices. Is there a specific femininity or a specific set of values that have been written out of various histories and descriptions that can be associated with women as

a group? Does the category of woman maintain a meaning separate from the conditions of oppression against which it has been formulated?

For the most part, feminist theory has taken the category of women to be foundational to any further political claims without realizing that the category effects a political closure on the kinds of experiences articulable as part of a feminist discourse. When the category is understood as representing a set of values or dispositions, it becomes normative in character and, hence, exclusionary in principle. This move has created a problem both theoretical and political, namely, that a variety of women from various cultural positions have refused to recognize themselves as "women" in the terms articulated by feminist theory with the result that these women fall outside the category and are left to conclude that (1) either they are not women as they have perhaps previously assumed or (2) the category reflects the restricted location of its theoreticians and, hence, fails to recognize the intersection of gender with race, class, ethnicity, age, sexuality, and other currents which contribute to the formation of cultural (non)identity. In response to the radical exclusion of the category of women from hegemonic cultural formations on the one hand and the internal critique of the exclusionary effects of the category from within feminist discourse on the other, feminist theorists are now confronted with the problem of either redefining and expanding the category of women itself to become more inclusive (which requires also the political matter of settling who gets to make the designation and in the name of whom) or to challenge the place of the category as a part of a feminist normative discourse. Gayatri Spivak has argued that feminists need to rely on an operational essentialism, a false ontology of women as a universal in order to advance a feminist political program.[1] She concedes that the category of women is not fully expressive, that the multiplicity and discontinuity of the signified rebels against the univocity of the sign, but she suggests that we need to use it for strategic purposes. Julia Kristeva suggests something similar, I think, when she recommends that feminists use the category of women as a political tool without attributing ontological integrity to the term, and she adds that, strictly speaking, women cannot be said to exist.[2]

But is it the presumption of ontological integrity that needs to be dispelled, or does the practical redeployment of the category without any ontological commitments also effect a political consolidation of its semantic integrity with serious exclusionary implications? Is there another normative point of departure for feminist theory that does not require the reconstruction or rendering visible of a female subject who fails to represent, much less emancipate, the array of embodied beings culturally positioned as women?

Psychoanalytic theory has occupied an ambiguous position in the feminist quandary over whether the category of women has a rightful place within feminist political discourse. On the one hand, psychoanalysis has sought to identify the developmental moments in which gendered identity is acquired. Yet, those feminist positions which take their departure from the work of Jacques Lacan have sought to underscore the unconscious as the tenuous ground of any and all claims to identity. A work that makes both arguments, Juliet Mitchell's *Psycho-analysis and Feminism* (1974), sought not only to show that gender is constructed rather than biologically necessitated but to identify the precise developmental moments of that construction in the history of gendered subjects. Mitchell further argues on structuralist grounds that the narrative of infantile development enjoyed relative universality and that psychoanalytic theory seemed, therefore, to offer feminists a way to describe a psychological and cultural ground of shared gender identification.[3] In a similar position, Jacqueline Rose asserts: "The force of psychoanalysis is therefore precisely that it gives an account of patriarchal culture as a trans-historical and cross-cultural force. It therefore conforms to the feminist demand for a theory which can explain women's subordination across specific cultures and different historical moments."[4]

As much as psychoanalytic theory provided feminist theory with a way to identify and fix gender difference through a metanarrative of shared infantile development, it also helped feminists show how the very notion of the subject is a masculine prerogative within the terms of culture. The paternal law which Lacanian psychoanalysis takes to be the ground of all kinship and all cultural relations not only sanctions male subjects but institutes their very possibility through the denial of the feminine. Hence, far from being subjects, women are, variously, the Other, a mysterious and unknowable lack, a sign of the forbidden and irrecoverable maternal body, or some unsavory mixture of the above.

Elaborating on Lacanian theory, but making significant departures from its presumptions of universal patriarchy, Luce Irigaray maintains that the very construct of an autonomous subject is a masculine cultural prerogative from which women have been excluded. She further claims that the subject is always already masculine, that it bespeaks a refusal of dependency required of male acculturation, understood originally as dependency on the mother, and that its "autonomy" is founded on a repression of its early and true helplessness, need, sexual desire for the mother, even identification with the maternal body. The subject thus becomes a fantasy of autogenesis, the refusal of maternal foundations and, in generalized form, a repudiation of the feminine. For Irigaray, then, it would make no sense to refer to a female subject or to women as subjects, for it is precisely the construct of the subject that necessitates relations of hierarchy, exclusion, and domination. In a word, there can be no subject without an Other.[5]

Psychoanalytic criticism of the epistemological point of departure, beginning with Freud's criticism of Enlightenment views of "man" as a rational being and later echoed in Lacan's critique of Cartesianism, has offered feminist theorists a way of criticizing the disembodied pretensions of the masculine knower and exposing the strategy of domination implicit in that disingenuous epistemological gesture. The destabilization of the subject within feminist criticism becomes a tactic in the exposure of masculine power and, in some French feminist contexts, the death of the subject spells the release or emancipation of the suppressed feminine sphere, the specific libidinal economy of women, the condition of *écriture féminine*.

But clearly, this set of moves raises a political problem: If it is not a female subject who provides the normative model for a feminist emancipatory politics, then what does? If we fail to recuperate the subject in feminist terms, are we not depriving feminist theory of a notion of agency that casts doubt on the viability of feminism as a normative model? Without a unified concept of woman or, minimally, a family resemblance among gender-related terms, it appears that feminist politics has lost the categorial basis of its own normative claims. What constitutes the "who," the subject, for whom feminism seeks emancipation? If there is no subject, who is left to emancipate?

The feminist resistance to the critique of the subject shares some concerns with other critical and emancipatory discourses: If oppression is to be defined in terms of a loss of autonomy by the oppressed, as well as a fragmentation or alienation within the psyche of the oppressed, then a theory which insists upon the inevitable fragmentation of the subject appears to reproduce and valorize the very oppression that must be overcome. We need perhaps to think about a typology of fragmentations or, at least, answer the question of whether oppression ought to be defined in terms of the fragmentation of identity and whether fragmentation *per se* is oppressive. Clearly, the category of women is internally fragmented by class, color, age, and ethnic lines, to name but a few; in this sense, honoring the diversity of the category and insisting upon its definitional nonclosure appears to be a necessary safeguard against substituting a reification of women's experience for the diversity that exists.[6] But how do we know what exists prior to its discursive articulation? Further, the critique of the subject means more than the rehabilitation of a multiple subject whose various "parts" are interrelated within an overriding unity, a coalitional subject, or an internal polity of pluralistically related points of view. Indeed, the political critique of the subject questions whether making a conception of identity into the ground of politics, however internally complicated, prematurely forecloses the possible cultural articulations of the subject-position that a new politics might well generate.

This kind of political position is clearly not in line with the humanist presuppositions of either feminism or related theories on the Left. At least since Marx's *Early Manuscripts*, the normative model of an integrated and unified self has served emancipatory discourses. Socialist feminism has clearly reformulated the doctrine of the integrated subject in opposition to the split between public and private spheres which has concealed domestic exploitation and generally failed to acknowledge the value of women's work, as well as the specific moral and cultural values which originate or are sustained within the private sphere. In a further challenge to the public/private distinction in moral life, Carol Gilligan and others have called for a reintegration of conventional feminine virtues, such as care and other relational attitudes, into conventional moral postures of distance and abstraction, a kind of reintegration of the human personality, conceived as a lost unity in need of restoration. Feminist psychoanalytic theory based in object-relations has similarly called for a restructuring of child-rearing practices which would narrow the schism between gender differences produced by the predominating presence of the mother in the nurturing role. Again, the integration of nurturance and dependency into the masculine sphere and the concomitant assimilation of autonomy into the feminine sphere suggests a normative model of a unified self which tends toward the androgynous solution. Others insist on the deep-seated specificity of the feminine rooted in a primary maternal identification which grounds an alternative feminine subject, who defines herself relationally and contextually and who fails to exhibit the inculcated masculine fear of dependency at the core of the repudiation of the maternal and, subsequently, of the feminine. In this case, the unified self reappears not in the figure of the androgyne but as a specifically feminine subject organized by a founding maternal identification.

The differences between Lacanian and post-Lacanian feminist psychoanalytic theories on the one hand and those steeped in the tradition of object-relations and ego psychology on the other center on the conception of the subject or the ego and its ostensible integrity. Lacanian feminists such as Jacqueline Rose argue that object-relations theorists fail to account for the unconscious and for the radical discontinuities which characterize the psyche prior to the formation of the ego and a distinct and separate sense of self. By claiming certain kinds of identifications are primary, object-relations theorists make the relational life of the infant primary to psychic development itself, conflating the psyche with the ego and relegating the unconscious to a less significant role. Lacanian theorists insist upon the unconscious as a source of discontinuous and chaotic drives or significations, and they claim that the ego is a perpetually unstable phenomenon, resting upon a primary repression of unconscious drives which return perpetually to haunt and undermine the ostensible unity of the ego.[7]

Although these theories tend to destabilize the subject as a construct of coherence, they nevertheless institute gender coherence through the stabilizing metanarrative of infantile development. According to Rose and to Juliet Mitchell, the unconscious is an open libidinal/linguistic field of discontinuities which contest the rigid and hierarchizing codes of sexual difference encoded in language, regulating cultural life. Although the unconscious thus becomes a locus of subversion, it remains unclear what changes the unconscious can provide considering the rigid synchronicity of the structuralist frame. The rules constituting and regulating sexual difference within Lacanian terms evince an immutability which seriously challenges their usefulness for any theory of social and cultural transformation. The failure to historicize the account of the rules governing sexual difference inevitably institutes that difference as the reified foundation of all intelligible culture, with the result that the paternal law becomes the invariant condition of intelligibility, and the variety of contestations not only can never undo that law but, in fact, require the abiding efficacy of that law in order to maintain any meaning at all.

In both sets of psychoanalytic analyses, a narrative of infantile development is constructed which assumes the existence of a primary identification (object-relations) or a primary repression (the *Ürverdrangung* which founds the Lacanian male subject and marks off the feminine through exclusion) which instantiates gender specificity and subsequently informs, organizes, and unifies identity. We hear time and again about *the* boy and *the* girl, a tactical distancing from spatial and temporal locations which elevates the narrative to the mythic tense of a reified history. Although object-relations poses an alternative version of the subject based in relational attitudes characteristically feminine and Lacanian (or anti-Lacanian) theories maintain the instability of the subject based in the disruptive potential of the unconscious manifest at the tentative boundaries of the ego; they each offer story lines about gender acquisition which effect a narrative closure on gender experience and a false stabilization of the category of woman. Whether as a linguistic and cultural law which makes itself known as the inevitable organizing principle of sexual difference or as the identity forged through a primary identification that the Oedipal complex requires, gender meanings are circumscribed within a narrative frame which both unifies certain legitimate sexual subjects and excludes from intelligibility sexual identities and discontinuities which challenge the narrative beginnings and closures offered by these competing psychoanalytic explanations.

Whether one begins with Freud's postulation of primary bisexuality (Juliet Mitchell and Jacqueline Rose) or with the primacy of object-relations (Chodorow, Benjamin), one tells a story that constructs a discrete gender identity and discursive location which remains relatively fixed. Such theories do not need to be explicitly essentialist in their arguments in order to be effectively essentialist in their narrative strategies. Indeed, most psychoanalytic feminist theories maintain that gender is constructed, and they view themselves (and Freud) as debunking the claims of essential femininity or essential masculinity. Indeed, this seems to be the case when we consider Freud's claim, for instance, in *The Three Essays on the Theory of Sexuality* that heterosexuality is not a given of biological life but a developmental accomplishment,[8] his theory of primary bisexuality,[9] and his further claim in *New Introductory Lectures on Psychoanalysis* that to become a woman is a laborious construction which takes the repression of primary bisexuality as its premise.[10]

At its most general level of narrative development, the object-relations and Lacanian versions of gender development offer (1) a utopian postulation of an originally predifferentiated state of the sexes which (2) also preexists the postulation of hierarchy, and (3) gets ruined either by the sudden and swift action of the paternal law (Lacanian) or the anthropologically less ambitious Oedipal injunction to repudiate and devalue the mother (object-relations). In both cases, an originally undifferentiated state of the sexes suffers the process of differentiation and hierarchization through the advent of a repressive law. "In the beginning" is sexuality without power, then power arrives to create both culturally relevant sexual distinction (gender) and, along with that, gender hierarchy and dominance.

The Lacanian position proves problematic when we consider that the state prior to the law is, by definition, prior to language and yet, within the confines of language, we are said somehow to have access to it. The circularity of the reasoning becomes all the more dizzying when we realize that prior to language we had a diffuse and full pleasure which, unfortunately, we cannot remember, but which disrupts our speech and haunts our dreams. The object-relations postulation of an original identification and subsequent repudiation constructs the terms of a coherent narrative of infantile development which works to exclude all kinds of developmental histories in which the nurturing presence of the nuclear family cannot be presupposed.

By grounding the metanarratives in a myth of the origin, the psychoanalytic description of gender identity confers a false sense of legitimacy and universality to a culturally specific and, in some contexts, culturally oppressive version of gender identity. By claiming that some identifications are more primary than others, the complexity of the latter set of identifications is effectively assimilated into the primary one, and the "unity" of the identifications is preserved. Hence, because within object-relations the girl-mother identification is "founding," the girl-brother and girl-father identifications are easily assimilated under the already firmly established gender identification with women. Without the assumption of an orderly temporal development of identifications in which the first identifications serve to unify the latter ones, we would not be able to explain which identifications get assimilated into which others; in other words, we would lose the unifying thread of the narrative. Indeed, it is important to note that primary identifications establish gender in a substantive mode, and secondary identifications thus serve as attributes. Hence, we witness the discursive emergence of "feminine men" or "masculine women," or the meaningful redundancy of a "masculine man." Without the temporal prioritization of primary identifications, it would be unclear which characterizations were to serve as substance and which as attributes, and in the case in which that temporal ordering were fully contested, we would have, I suppose, the gender equivalent of an interplay of attributes without an abiding or unifying substance. I will suggest what I take to be the subversive possibilities of such a gender arrangement toward the end of my remarks.

Even within the psychoanalytic frame, however, we might press the question of identification and desire to a further limit. The primary identification in which gender becomes "fixed" forms a history of identifications in which the secondary ones revise and reform the primary one but in no way contest its structural primacy. Gender identities emerge and sexual desires shift and vary so that different "identifications" come into play depending upon the availability of legitimating cultural norms and opportunities. It is not always possible to relate those shifts back to a primary identification which is suddenly manifest. Within the terms of psychoanalytic theory, then, it is quite possible to understand gendered subjectivity as a history of identifications, parts of which can be brought into play in given contexts and which, precisely because they encode the contingencies of personal history, do not always point back to an internal coherence of any kind.

Of course, it is important to distinguish between two very different ways in which psychoanalysis and narrative theory work together. Within psychoanalytic literary criticism, and within feminist psychoanalytic criticism in particular, the operation of the unconscious makes all narrative coherence suspect; indeed, the defenders of that critical enterprise tend to argue that the narrative capacity is seriously undermined by that which is necessarily excluded or repressed in the manifest text and that a serious effort to admit the unconscious, whether conceived in terms of a repressed set of drives (Kristeva) or as an excluded field of metonymic associations (Rose), into the text disrupts and inverts the linear assumptions of coherent narrativity. In this sense, the text always exceeds the narrative; as the field of excluded meanings, it returns, invariably, to contest and subvert the explicitly attempted narrative coherence of the text.

The multiplication of narrative standpoints within the literary text corresponds to an internally fragmented psyche which can achieve no final, integrated understanding or "mastery" of its component parts. Hence, the literary work offers a textual means of dramatizing Freud's topographical model of mind in motion. The nonliterary use of psychoanalysis, however, as a psychological explanatory model for the acquisition and consolidation of gender identification and, hence, identity generally fails to take account of itself as a narrative. Subject to the feminist aim to delimit and define a shared femininity, these narratives attempt to construct a coherent female subject. As a result, psychoanalysis as feminist metatheory reproduces that false coherence in the form of a story line about infantile development where it ought to investigate genealogically the exclusionary practices which condition that particular narrative of identity formation. Although Rose, Mitchell, and other Lacanian feminists insist that identity is always a tenuous and unstable affair, they nevertheless fix the terms of that instability with respect to a paternal law which is culturally invariant. The result is a narrativized myth of origins in which primary bisexuality is arduously rendered into a melancholic heterosexuality through the inexorable force of the law.

Juliet Mitchell claims that it is only possible to be in one position or the other in a sexual relation and never in both at once. But the binary disjunction implicit to this gendered law of noncontradiction suggests that desire functions through a gender difference instituted at the level of the symbolic that necessarily represses whatever unconscious multiplications of positions might be at work. Kristeva argues similarly that the requirements of intelligible culture imply that female homosexuality is a contradiction in terms, with the consequence that this particular cultural manifestation is, even within culture, outside it, in the mode of psychosis. The only intelligible female homosexuality within Kristeva's frame is in the prohibited incestuous love between daughter and mother, one that can only be resolved through a maternal identification and the quite literal process of becoming a mother.[11]

Within these appropriations of psychoanalytic theory, gender identity and sexual orientation are accomplished at once. Although the story of sexual development is complicated and quite different for *the* girl than *the* boy, it appeals in both contexts to an operative disjunction that remains stable throughout: one identifies with one sex and, in so doing, desires the other, that desire being the elaboration of that identity, the mode by which it creates its opposite and defines itself in that opposition. But what about primary bisexuality, the source of disruption and discontinuity that Rose locates as the subversive potential of the unconscious? A close examination of what precisely Freud means by bisexuality, however, turns out to be a kind of bisexedness of libidinal dispositions. In other words, there are male and female libidinal dispositions in every psyche which are directed heterosexually toward opposite sexes. When bisexuality is relieved of its basis in the drive theory, it reduces, finally, to the coincidence of two heterosexual desires, each proceeding from oppositional identifications or dispositions, depending on the theory, so that desire, strictly speaking, can issue only from a male-

identification to a female object or from a female-identification to a male object. Granted, it may well be a woman, male-identified, who desires another woman, or a man, female-identified, who desires another man, and it may also be a woman, male-identified, who desires a man, female-identified, or similarly, a man, female-identified, who desires a woman, male-identified. One either identifies with a sex or desires it, but only those two relations are possible.

But is identification always restricted within the binary disjunction in which it has been framed so far? Clearly, within psychoanalytic theory, another set of possibilities emerges whereby identifications work not to consolidate identity but to condition the interplay and the subversive recombination of gender meanings. Consider that in the previous sketch, identifications exist in a mutually exclusive binary matrix conditioned by the cultural necessity of occupying one position to the exclusion of the other. But in fantasy, a variety of positions can be entertained even though they may not constitute culturally intelligible possibilities. Hence, for Kristeva, for instance, the semiotic designates precisely those sets of unconscious fantasies and wishes that exceed the legitimating bounds of paternally organized culture; the semiotic domain, the body's subversive eruption into language, becomes the transcription of the unconscious from the topographical model into a structuralist discourse. The tenuousness of all identity is exposed through the proliferation of fantasies that exceed and contest the "identity" that forms the conscious sense of self. But are identity and fantasy as mutually exclusive as the previous explanation suggests? Consider the claim, integral to much psychoanalytic theory, that identifications and, hence, identity are in fact *constituted* by fantasy.

Roy Schafer argues in *A New Language for Psychoanalysis* that when identifications are understood as internalizations, they imply a trope of inner psychic space that is ontologically insupportable. He further suggests that internalization is understood better not as a process but as a fantasy.[12] As a result, it is not possible to attribute some kind of ontological meaning to the spatial internality of internalizations, for they are only fantasied as internal. I would further argue that this very fantasy internal psychic space is essentially conditioned and mediated by a language that regularly figures interior psychic locations of various kinds, a language, in other words, that not only produces that fantasy but then redescribes that figuration within an uncritically accepted topographical discourse. Fantasies themselves are often imagined as mental contents somehow projected onto an interior screen, a conception conditioned by a cinematic metaphorics of the psyche. However, identifications are not merely fantasies of internally located objects or features, but they stand in a transfigurative relation to the very objects they purport to internalize. In other words, within psychoanalytic theory, to identify with a figure from the past is to figure that figure within the configuration of interior psychic space. Identification is never simply mimetic but involves a strategy of wish fulfillment; one identifies not with an empirical person but with a fantasy, the mother one wishes one had, the father one thought one had but didn't, with the posture of the parent or sibling which seems to ward off a perceived threat from some other, or with the posture of some imagined relation whom one also imagines to be the recipient of love. We take up identifications not only to receive love but also to deflect from it and its dangers; we also take up identifications in order to facilitate or prohibit our own desires. In each case of identification, there is an interpretation at work, a wish and/or a fear as well, the effect of a prohibition, and a strategy of resolution.

What is commonly called an introject is, thus, a fantasied figure within a fantasied locale, a double imagining that produces the effect of the empirical other fixed in an interior topos. As figurative productions, these identifications constitute impossible desires that figure the body, active principles of incorporation, modes of structuring and signifying the enactment of the lived body in social space. Hence, the gender fantasies constitutive of identifications are not part of the set of properties that a subject might be said to have, but they constitute the genealogy of that embodied/psychic identity, the mechanism of its construction. One does not have the fantasies, and neither is there a one who lives them, but the fantasies condition and construct the specificity of the gendered subject with the enormously important qualification that these fantasies are themselves disciplinary productions of grounding cultural sanctions and taboos – a theme to which I will momentarily turn. If gender is constituted by identification and identification is invariably a fantasy within a fantasy, a double figuration, then gender is precisely the fantasy enacted by and through the corporeal styles that constitute bodily significations.

In a separate context, Michel Foucault challenges the language of internalization as it operates in the service of the repressive hypothesis. In *Discipline and Punish*, Foucault rewrites the doctrine of internalization found in Nietzsche's *On the Genealogy of Morals* through the language of *inscription*. In the context of prisoners, Foucault writes, the strategy has not been to enforce a repression of their desires but to compel their bodies to signify the prohibitive law as their ownmost essence, style, necessity. That law is not internalized, but it is incorporated, with the consequence that bodies are produced which signify that law as the essence of their selves, the meaning of their soul, their conscience, the law of their desire. In effect, the law is at once fully manifest and fully latent, for it never appears as external to the bodies it subjects and subjectivates. "It would be wrong", Foucault writes, "to say that the soul is an illusion, or an ideological effect. On the contrary, it exists, it has a reality, it is produced permanently around, on, within, the body by the functioning of a power that is exercised on those that are punished. . . ."[13] The figure of the interior soul understood as "within" the body is signified through its inscription *on* the body, even though its primary mode of signification is through its very absence, its potent invisibility, for it is through that invisibility that the effect of a structuring inner space is produced. The soul is precisely what the body lacks; hence, that lack produces the body as its other and as its means of expression. In this sense, then, the soul is a surface signification that contests and displaces the inner/outer distinction itself, a figure of interior psychic space inscribed on the body as a social signification that perpetually renounces itself as such. In Foucault's terms, the soul is not imprisoned by the body, as some Christian imagery would suggest, but "the body becomes a prisoner of the soul."[14]

The redescription of intrapsychic processes in terms of the surface politics of the body implies a corollary redescription of gender as the disciplinary production of the figures of gender fantasy through the play of presence and absence in the body's surface, the construction of the gendered body through a series of exclusions and denials, signifying absences.

But what determines the manifest and latent text of the body politic? What is the prohibitive law that generates the corporeal stylization of gender, the fantasied and fantastic figuration of the gendered body? Clearly, Freud points to the incest taboo and the prior taboo against homosexuality as the generative moments of gender identity, the moments in which gender becomes fixed (meaning both immobilized and, in some sense, repaired). The acquisition of gender identity is thus simultaneous with the accomplishment of coherent heterosexuality. The taboo against incest, which presupposes and includes the taboo against homosexuality, works to sanction and produce identity at the same time that it is said to repress the very identity it produces. This disciplinary production of gender effects a false stabilization of gender in the interests of the heterosexual construction and regulation of sexuality. That the model seeks to produce and sustain coherent identities and that it requires a heterosexual construction of sexuality in no way implies that practising heterosexuals embody or exemplify this model with any kind of regularity. Indeed, I would argue that in principle no one can embody this regulatory ideal at the same time that the compulsion to embody the fiction, to figure the body in accord with its requirements, is everywhere. This is a fiction that operates within discourse, and which, discursively and institutionally sustained, wields enormous power.

I noted earlier the kinds of coherences instituted through some feminist appropriations of psychoanalysis but would now suggest further that the localization of identity in an interior psychic space characteristic of these theories implies an expressive model of gender whereby identity is first fixed internally and only subsequently manifest in some exterior way. When gender identity is understood as causally or mimetically related to sex, then the order of appearance that governs gendered subjectivity is understood as one in which sex conditions gender, and gender determines sexuality and desire; although both psychoanalytic and feminist theory tend to disjoin sex from gender, the restriction of gender within a binary relation suggests a relation of residual mimeticism between sex, conceived as binary[15] and gender. Indeed, the view of sex, gender, and desire that presupposes a metaphysics of substance suggests that gender and desire are understood as attributes that refer back to the substance of sex and make sense only as its reflection.

I am not arguing that psychoanalytic theory is a form of such substantive theorizing, but I would suggest that the lines that establish coherence between sex, gender, and desire, where they exist, tend to reenforce that conceptualization and to constitute its contemporary legacy. The construction of coherence conceals the gender discontinuities that run rampant within heterosexual, bisexual, and gay and lesbian contexts in which gender does not necessarily follow from sex, and desire, or sexuality generally, does not seem to follow from gender; indeed, where none of these dimensions of significant corporeality "express" or reflect one another. When the disorganization and disaggregation of the field of bodies disrupts the regulatory fiction of heterosexual coherence, it seems that the expressive model loses its descriptive force, and that regulatory ideal is exposed as a norm and a fiction that disguises itself as a developmental law that regulates the sexual field that it purports to describe.

According to the understanding of identification as fantasy, however, it is clear that coherence is desired, wished for, idealized, and that this idealization is an effect of a corporeal signification. In other words, acts, gestures, and desire produce the effect of an internal core or substance, but produce this on the surface of the body, through the play of signifying absences that suggest, but never reveal, the organizing principle of identity as a cause. Such acts, gestures, enactments, generally construed, are performative in the sense that the essence of identity that they otherwise purport to express becomes a *fabrication* manufactured and sustained through corporeal signs and other discursive means. That the gendered body is performative suggests that it has no ontological status apart from the various acts which constitute its reality, and if that reality is fabricated as an interior essence, that very interiority is a function of a decidedly public and social discourse, the public regulation of fantasy through the surface politics of the body. In other words, acts and gestures articulate and enacted desires create the illusion of an interior and organizing gender core, an illusion discursively maintained for the purposes of the regulation of sexuality within the obligatory frame of reproductive heterosexuality. If the "cause" of desire, gesture, and act can be localized within the "self" of the actor, then the political regulations and disciplinary practices which produce that ostensibly coherent gender are effectively displaced from view. The displacement of a political and discursive origin of gender identity onto a psychological "core" precludes an analysis of the political constitution of the gendered subject and its fabricated notions about the ineffable interiority of its sex or of its true identity.

If the inner truth of gender is a fabrication and if a true gender is a fantasy instituted and inscribed on the surface of bodies, then it seems that genders can be neither true nor false but are only produced as the truth effects of a discourse of primary and stable identity.

In *Mother Camp: Female Impersonators in America*, anthropologist Esther Newton suggests that the structure of impersonation reveals one of the key fabricating mechanisms through which the social construction of gender takes place. I would suggest as well that drag fully subverts the distinction between inner and outer psychic space and effectively mocks both the expressive model of gender and of the notion of a true gender identity. "At its most complex," Newton writes, "[drag] is a double inversion that says, 'appearance is an illusion.' Drag says [Newton's curious personification], my 'outside' appearance is feminine, but my essence 'inside' {the body} is masculine." At the same time it symbolizes the opposite inversion: "my appearance 'outside' {my body, my gender} is masculine but my essence 'inside' myself is feminine."[16] Both claims to truth contradict one another and so displace the entire enactment of gender significations from the discourse of truth and falsity.

The notion of an original or primary gender identity is often parodied within the cultural practices of drag, cross-dressing, and the sexual stylization of butch/femme identities. Within feminist theory, such parodic identities have been understood to be either degrading to women, in the case of drag and cross-dressing, or an uncritical appropriation of sex-role stereotyping from within the practice of heterosexuality, especially in the case of butch/femme lesbian identities. But the relation between the "imitation" and the "original" is, I think, more complicated than that critique generally allows. Moreover, it gives us a clue to the way in which the relationship between primary identification, that is, the original meanings accorded to gender, and subsequent gender experience might be reframed.

The performance of drag plays upon the distinction between the anatomy of the performer and the gender that is being performed. But we are actually in the presence of three separate dimensions of significant corporeality: anatomical sex, gender identity and gender performance. If the anatomy of the performer is already distinct from the gender of the performer, and both of those distinct from the gender of the performance, then the performance suggests a dissonance not only between sex and performance but between sex and gender, and gender and performance. As much as drag creates a unified picture of "woman" (what its critics often oppose), it also reveals the distinctness of those aspects of gendered experience which are falsely naturalized as a unity through the regulatory fiction of heterosexual coherence. In imitating gender, drag implicitly reveals the imitative structure of gender itself – as well as its contingency. Indeed, part of the pleasure, the giddiness of the performance is in the recognition of a radical contingency in the relation between sex and gender in the face of cultural configurations of causal unities that are regularly assumed to be natural and necessary. In the place of the law of heterosexual coherence, we see sex and gender denaturalized by means of a performance which avows their distinctness and dramatizes the cultural mechanism of their fabricated unity.

The notion of gender parody defended here does not assume that there is an original which such parodic identities imitate. Indeed, the parody is *of* the very notion of an original; just as the psychoanalytic notion of gender identification is constituted by a fantasy of a fantasy, the transfiguration of an other who is always already a "figure" in that double sense, so gender parody reveals that the original identity after which gender fashions itself is itself an imitation without an origin. To be more precise, it is a production which, in effect, that is, in its effect, postures as an imitation. This perpetual displacement constitutes a fluidity of identities that suggests an openness to resignification and recontextualization, and it deprives hegemonic culture and its critics of the claim to essentialist accounts of gender identity. Although the gender meanings which are taken up in these parodic styles are clearly part of hegemonic, misogynist culture, they are nevertheless denaturalized and mobilized through their parodic recontextualization. As imitations which effectively displace the meaning of the original, they imitate the myth of originality itself. In the place of an original identification which serves as a determining cause, gender identity might be reconceived as a personal/cultural history of received meanings subject to a set of imitative practices which refer laterally to other imitations, and which, jointly, construct the illusion of a primary and interior gendered self or which parody the mechanism of that construction.

Inasmuch as the construct of women presupposes a specificity and coherence that differentiates it from that of men, the categories of gender appear as an unproblematic point of departure for feminist politics. But if we take the critique of Monique Wittig seriously, namely, that "sex" itself is a category produced in the interests of the heterosexual contract,[17] or if we consider Foucault's suggestion that "sex" designates an artificial unity that works to maintain and amplify the regulation of sexuality within the reproductive domain, then it seems that gender coherence operates in much the same way, not as a ground of politics but as its effect. The political task that emerges in the wake of this critique requires that we understand not only the "interests" that a given cultural identity has, but, more importantly, the interests and the power relations that establish that identity in its reified mode to begin with. The proliferation of gender style and identity, if that word still makes sense, implicitly contests the always already political binary distinction between genders that is often taken for granted. The loss of that reification of gender relations ought not to be lamented as the failure of a feminist political theory, but, rather, affirmed as the promise of the possibility of complex and generative subject-positions as well as coalitional strategies that neither presuppose nor fix their constitutive subjects in their place.

The fixity of gender identification, its presumed cultural invariance, its status as an interior and hidden cause may well serve the goals of the feminist project to establish a transhistorical commonality between us, but the "us" who gets joined through such a narration is a construction built upon the denial of a decidedly more complex cultural identity – or non-identity, as the case may be. The psychological language which purports to describe the interior fixity of our identities as men or women works to enforce a certain coherence and to foreclose convergences of gender identity and all manner of gender dissonance – or, where that exists, to relegate it to the early stages of a developmental and, hence, normative history. It may be that standards of narrative coherence must be radically revised and that narrative strategies for locating and articulating gender identity ought to admit to a greater complexity or it may be that performance may preempt narrative as the scene of gender production. In either case, it seems crucial to resist the myth of interior origins, understood either as naturalized or culturally fixed. Only then, gender coherence might be understood as the regulatory fiction it is – rather than the common point of our liberation.

Notes

My genuine thanks to Joan W. Scott for giving thoughtful response to many versions of this piece. I am grateful to the American Council of Learned Societies and to the Institute for Advanced Study in Princeton for sponsoring this work.

1. Remarks, Center for the Humanities, Wesleyan University, Spring 1985.
2. Julia Kristeva, "Woman Can Never Be Defined," *New French Feminisms*, ed. Elaine Marks and Isabelle de Courtivron (New York: Schocken, 1984).
3. Juliet Mitchell, *Psycho-analysis and Feminism* (New York: Vintage, 1975), p. 377.
4. Jacqueline Rose, "Femininity and its Discontents," *Sexuality in the Field of Vision* (London: Verso, 1987), p. 90.
5. Luce Irigaray, "Any Theory of the Subject Has Already Been Appropriated by the Masculine," *Speculum of the Other Woman*, trans. Gillian Gill (Ithaca, NY: Cornell University Press, 1985), p. 140. See also "Is the Subject of Science Sexed?," *Cultural Critique*, vol. 1, Fall 1985, p. 11.
6. For an interesting discussion of the political desirability of keeping the feminist subject incoherent, see Sandra Harding, "The Instability of the Analytical Categories of Feminist Theory," *Sex and Scientific Inquiry*, ed. Sandra Harding and Jean F. O'Barr (Chicago: University of Chicago Press, 1987).
7. See Jacqueline Rose's argument in "Femininity and its Discontents," *Sexuality in the Field of Vision*, pp. 90–4.
8. Sigmund Freud, *Three Essays on the Theory of Sexuality*, trans. James Strachey (New York: Basic Books, 1975), p. 1.
9. Freud, *Three Essays*, p. 7; see also "The Ego and the Superego," *The Ego and the Id*, trans. Joan Riviere (New York: Norton, 1960), pp. 22–3.
10. See Freud, Chapter 33, "Femininity," *New Introductory Lectures*, trans. James Strachey (New York: Norton, 1965), p. 116.
11. For a fuller exposition of Kristeva's positions, see my article "The Body Politics of Julia Kristeva" in the French Feminism issue of *Hypatia: A Journal of Feminist Philosophy*, vol. 3, no. 3, pp. 104–8.
12. Roy Schafer, *A New Language for Psychoanalysis* (New Haven, CT: Yale University Press, 1976), p. 177.
13. Michel Foucault, *Discipline and Punish* (New York: Pantheon, 1977), p. 29.
14. Foucault, *Discipline and Punish*, p. 30.
15. The assumption of binary sex is in no sense stable. For an interesting article on the complicated "sexes" of some female athletes and the medicolegal disputes about how and whether to render their sex decidable, see Jerold M. Loewenstein, "The Conundrum of

Gender Identification, Two Sexes Are Not Enough," *Pacific Discovery*, vol. 40, no. 2, 1987, pp. 38–9. See also Michel Foucault's *The History of Sexuality, Volume I: An Introduction*, trans. Robert Hurley (New York: Vintage, 1980), pp. 154–5, and *Herculine Barbin, Being the Recently Discovered Memoirs of a Nineteenth-Century French Hermaphrodite*, trans. Richard McDougall (New York: Pantheon, 1986), pp. vii–xvii. For a feminist analysis of recent research into "the sex gene," a DNA sequence which is alleged to "decide" the sex of otherwise ambiguous bodies, see Anne Fausto-Sterling, "Recent Trends in Developmental Biology: A Feminist Perspective" (Departments of Biology and Medicine, Brown University).

16. Esther Newton, *Mother Camp: Female Impersonators in America* (Chicago: University of Chicago Press, 1972), p. 103.

17. Monique Wittig, "The Category of Sex," *Feminist Issues*, vol. 2, p. 2.

21

Revolutions, Universals, and Sexual Categories

JOHN BOSWELL

One of the revolutions in the study of history in the twentieth century might be called "minority history": the effort to recover the histories of groups previously overlooked or excluded from mainstream historiography. Minority history has provoked predictable skepticism on the part of some traditional historians, partly because of its novelty – which will, of course, inevitably wear off – and partly because the attitudes that previously induced neglect or distortion of minority history still prevail in many quarters. The most reasonable criticism of minority history (aside from the objection that it is sometimes very poor scholarship, against which no discipline is proof) is that it lends itself to political use, which may distort scholarly integrity. As a point about minority history as a genre this is not cogent: Since the exclusion of minorities from much historiography prior to the twentieth century was related to or caused by concerns other than purely scholarly interest, their inclusion now, even for purely political ends, not only corrects a previous "political" distortion but also provides a more complete data base for judgments about the historical issues involved. Such truth as is yielded by historical analysis generally emerges from the broadest possible synthesis of the greatest number of viewpoints and vantages: The addition of minority history and viewpoints to twentieth-century historiography is a net gain for all concerned.

But at a more particular level political struggles can cause serious problems for scholars, and a curious debate now taking place among those interested in the history of gay people provides a relevant and timely example of a type of difficulty that could subvert minority history altogether if not addressed intelligently. To avoid contributing further to the undue political freight the issue has lately been forced to bear, I propose to approach it by way of another historical controversy, one that was – in its day – no less heated or urgent, but that is now sufficiently distant to be viewed with dispassion by all sides.

The conflict in question is as old as Plato and as modern as cladism, and although the most violent struggles over it took place in the twelfth and thirteenth centuries, the arguments of the ancients on the subject are still in use today. Stated as briefly and baldly as possible, the issues are these: Do categories exist because humans recognize real distinctions in the world around them, or are categories arbitrary conventions, simply names for things that have categorical force because humans agree to use them in certain ways? The two traditional sides in this controversy, which is called "the problem of universals," are "realists" and "nominalists." Realists consider categories to be the footprints of reality ("universals"): They exist because humans perceive a real order in the universe and name it. The order is present without human observation, according to realists; the human contribution is simply the naming and describing of it. Most scientists operate – tacitly – in a realist mode, on the assumption that they are discovering, not inventing, the relationships within the physical world. The scientific method is, in fact, predicated on realist attitudes. On the other hand, the philosophical structure of the modern West is closer to nominalism: the belief that categories are only the names (Latin: *nomina*) of things agreed upon by humans, and that the "order" people see is their creation rather than their perception. Most modern philosophy and language theory is essentially nominalist, and even the more theoretical sciences are nominalist to some degree: In biology, for example, taxonomists disagree strongly about whether they are discovering (realists) or inventing (nominalists) distinctions among phyla, genera, species, etc. (When, for example, a biologist announces that bats, being mammals, are "more closely related to" humans than to birds, is he expressing some real relationship, present in nature and detected by humans, or is he employing an arbitrary convention, something that helps humans organize and sort information but that bears no "truth" or significance beyond this utility?)

This seemingly arcane struggle now underlies an epistemological controversy raging among those studying the history of gay people. The "universals" in this case are categories of sexual preference or orientation (the difference is crucial). Nominalists ("social constructionists" in the current debate) in the matter aver that categories of sexual preference and behavior are created by humans and human societies. Whatever reality they have is the consequence of the power they exert in those societies and the socialization processes that make them seem real to persons influenced by them. People consider themselves "homosexual" or "heterosexual" because they are induced to believe that humans are either "homosexual" or "heterosexual." Left to their own devices, without such processes of socialization, people would simply be sexual. The category "heterosexuality," in other words, does not so much describe a pattern of behavior inherent in human beings as it creates and establishes it.

Realists ("essentialists") hold that this is not the case. Humans are, they insist, differentiated sexually. Many categories might be devised to characterize human sexual taxonomy, some more or less apt than others, but the accuracy of human perceptions does not affect reality. The heterosexual/homosexual dichotomy exists in speech and thought because it exists in reality: It was not invented by sexual taxonomists, but observed by them.[1]

Neither of these positions is usually held absolutely: Most nominalists would be willing to admit that some aspects of sexuality are present, and might be distinguished, without direction from society. And most realists are happy to admit that the same real phenomenon might be described by various systems of categorization, some more accurate and helpful than others. One might suppose that "moderate nominalists" and "moderate realists" could therefore engage in a useful dialogue on those areas

where they agree and, by careful analysis of their differences, promote discussion and understanding of these issues.

Political ramifications hinder this. Realism has historically been viewed by the nominalist camp as conservative, if not reactionary, in its implicit recognition of the value and/or immutability of the status quo; and nominalism has generally been regarded by realists as an obscurantist radical ideology designed more to undercut and subvert human values than to clarify them. Precisely these political overtones can be seen to operate today in scholarly debate over issues of sexuality. The efforts of sociobiology to demonstrate an evolutionary etiology of homosexuality have been vehemently denounced by many who regard the enterprise as reactionary realism, an effort to persuade people that social categories are fixed and unchangeable, while on the other side, psychiatric "cures" of homosexuality are bitterly resented by many as the cynical folly of nominalist pseudoscience: Convince someone he shouldn't want to be a homosexual, persuade him to think of himself as a "heterosexual," and – presto! – he is a heterosexual. The category is the person.

Whether or not there are "homosexual" and "heterosexual" persons, as opposed to persons called "homosexual" or "heterosexual" by society, is obviously a matter of substantial import to the gay community, since it brings into question the nature and even the existence of such a community. It is, moreover, of substantial epistemological urgency to nearly all of society,[2] and the gravity and extent of this can be seen in the case of the problems it creates for history and historians.

The history of minorities poses ferocious difficulties: censorship and distortion, absence or destruction of records, the difficulty of writing about essentially personal and private aspects of human feelings and behavior, problems of definition, political dangers attendant on choosing certain subjects, etc. But if the nominalists are correct and the realists wrong, the problems in regard to the history of gay people are of an entirely different order: If the categories "homosexual/heterosexual" and "gay/straight" are the inventions of particular societies rather than real aspects of the human psyche, there is no gay history.[3] If "homosexuality" exists only when and where people are persuaded to believe in it, "homosexual" persons will have a "history" only in those particular societies and cultures.

In its most extreme form, this nominalist view has argued that only early modern and contemporary industrial societies have produced "homosexuality," and it is futile and misguided to look for "homosexuality" in earlier human history.

> What we call "homosexuality" (in the sense of the distinguishing traits of "homosexuals"), for example, was not considered a unified set of acts, much less a set of qualities defining particular persons, in pre-capitalist societies. . . . Heterosexuals and homosexuals are involved in social "roles" and attitudes which pertain to a particular society, modern capitalism.[4]

If this position is sustained, it will permanently alter, for better or worse, the nature and extent of minority history.

Clearly it has much to recommend it. No characteristics interact with the society around them uniformly through time. Perceptions of, reactions to, and social response regarding blackness, blindness, left-handedness, Jewishness, or any other distinguishing (or distinguished) aspect of persons or peoples must necessarily vary as widely as the social circumstances in which they occur, and for this reason alone it could be reasonably argued that being Jewish, black, blind, left-handed, etc., is essentially different from one age and place to another. In some cultures, for example, Jews are categorized chiefly as an ethnic minority; in others they are not or are not perceived to be ethnically distinct from the peoples around them, and are distinguished solely by their religious beliefs. Similarly, in some societies anyone darker than average is considered "black"; in others, a complex and highly technical system of racial categorization classes some persons as black even when they are lighter in color than many "whites." In both cases, moreover, the differences in attitudes held by the majority must affect profoundly the self-perception of the minority itself, and its patterns of life and behavior are in all probability notably different from those of "black" or "Jewish" people in other circumstances.

There can be no question that if minority history is to merit respect it must carefully weigh such fundamental subtleties of context: Merely cataloguing references to "Jews" or to "Blacks" may distort more than it reveals of human history if due attention is not paid to the meaning, in their historical setting, of such words and the concepts to which they apply. Do such reservations, on the other hand, uphold the claim that categories

such as "Jew," "black," or "gay" are not diachronic and can not, even with apposite qualification, be applied to ages and times other than those in which the terms themselves were used in precisely their modern sense? Extreme realists, without posing the question, have assumed the answer was no; extreme nominalists seem to be saying yes.

The question can not be addressed intelligently without first noting three points. First, the positions are not in fact as clearly separable as this schema implies. It could be well argued, for example, that Padgug, Weeks, et al., are in fact extreme *realists* in assuming that *modern* homosexuality is not simply one of a series of conventions designated under the same rubric, but is instead a "real" phenomenon that has no "real" antecedent in human history. Demonstrate to us the "reality" of this homosexuality, their opponents might legitimately demand, and prove to us that it has a unity and cohesiveness that justifies your considering it a single, unparalleled entity rather than a loose congeries of behaviors. Modern scientific literature increasingly assumes that what is at issue is not "homosexuality" but "homosexualities"; if these disparate patterns of sexuality can be grouped together under a single heading in the present, why make such a fuss about a diachronic grouping?

Second, adherents of both schools fall prey to anachronism. Nearly all of the most prominent nominalists are historians of the modern U.S., modern Britain, or modern Europe, and it is difficult to eschew the suspicion that they are concentrating their search where the light is best rather than where the answers are to be found, and formulating a theoretical position to justify their approach. On the other hand, nominalist objections are in part a response to an extreme realist position that has been predicated on the unquestioned, unproven, and overwhelmingly unlikely assumption that exactly the same categories and patterns of sexuality have always existed, pure and unchanged by the systems of thought and behavior in which they were enmeshed.

Third, both extremes appear to be paralyzed by words. The nominalists are determined that the same word can not apply to a wide range of meaning and still be used productively in scholarly discourse: In order to have meaning, "gay," for example, must be applied only as the speaker would apply it, with all the precise ramifications he associates with it. This insistence follows understandably from the implicit assumption that the speaker is generating the category himself, or in concert with certain contemporaries, rather than receiving it from a human experience of great longevity and adjusting it to fit his own understanding. Realist extremists, conversely, assume that lexical equivalence betokens experiential equality, and that the occurrence of a word that "means" "homosexual" demonstrates the existence of "homosexuality," as the modern realist understands it, at the time the text was composed.

It is my aim to circumvent these difficulties as far as possible in the following remarks, and my hope that in so doing I may reduce the rhetorical struggle over "universals" in these matters and promote thereby more useful dialogue among the partisans. Let it be agreed at the outset that something can be discussed, by modern historians or ancient writers, without being named or defined. (Ten people in a room might argue endlessly about proper definitions of "blue" and "red," but could probably agree instantly whether a given object was one or the other [or a combination of both].) "Gravity" offers a useful historical example. A nominalist position would be that gravity did not exist before Newton invented it, and a nominalist historian might be able to mount a convincing case that there is no mention of gravity in any texts before Newton. "Nonsense," realists would object. "The Latin *gravitas*, which is common in Roman literature, describes the very properties of matter Newton called 'gravity.' Of course gravity existed before Newton discovered it."

Both, of course, are wrong. Lack of attention to something in historical sources can in no wise be taken as evidence of its nonexistence, and discovery can not be equated with creation or invention. But *gravitas* does not mean "gravity"; it means "heaviness," and the two are not at all the same thing. Noting that objects have heaviness is entirely different from understanding the nature and operations of gravity. For adherents of these two positions to understand each other each would have to abandon specific nomenclature, and agree instead on questions to be asked of the sources. If the proper questions were addressed, the nominalist could easily be persuaded that the sources prove that gravity existed before Newton, in the sense that the operations of the force now designated gravity are well chronicled in nearly all ancient literature. And the realist could be persuaded that despite this fact the nature of gravity was not clearly articulated – whether or not it was apprehended – before Newton.

The problem is rendered more difficult in the present case by the fact that the equivalent of gravity has not yet been discovered: There is still no essential agreement in the scientific community about the nature of human sexuality. Whether humans are "homosexual" or "heterosexual" or "bisexual" by birth, by training, by choice, or at all is still an open question.[5] Neither realists nor nominalists can, therefore, establish any clear correlation – positive or negative – between modern sexuality and its ancient counterparts. But it is still possible to discuss whether modern conceptualizations of sexuality are novel and completely socially relative, or correspond to constants of human epistemology which can be documented in the past.

To simplify discussion, three broad types of sexual taxonomy are abbreviated here as Types A, B, and C. According to Type A theories, all humans are polymorphously sexual, i.e., capable of erotic and sexual interaction with either gender. External accidents, such as social pressure, legal sanctions, religious beliefs, historical or personal circumstances, determine the actual expression of each person's sexual feelings. Type B theories posit two or more sexual categories, usually but not always based on sexual object choice, to which all humans belong, though external pressures or circumstance may induce individuals in a given society to pretend (or even to believe) that they belong to a category other than their native one. The most common form of Type B taxonomy assumes that humans are heterosexual, homosexual, and bisexual, but that not all societies allow expression of all varieties of erotic disposition. Subsets or other versions of Type B categorize on the basis of other characteristics, e.g., a predilection for a particular role in intercourse. Type C theories consider one type of sexual response normal (or "natural" or "moral" or all three) and all other variants abnormal ("unnatural," "immoral").

It will be seen that Type A theories are nominalist to the extent that they regard categorizations like "homosexual" and "heterosexual" as arbitrary conventions applied to a sexual reality that is at bottom undifferentiated. Type B theories are conversely realist in predicating categories that underlie human sexual experience even when obscured by social constraints or particular circumstances. Type C theories are essentially normative rather than epistemological, but borrow from both sides of the universals question in assuming, by and large, that people are born into the normal category but become members of a deviant grouping by an act of the will, although some Type C adherents regard "deviants" as inculpably belonging to an "abnormal" category through mental or physical illness or defect.

That no two social structures are identical should require no proof; and since sexual categories are inevitably conditioned by social structure, no two systems of sexual taxonomy should be expected to be identical. A slight chronological or geographical shift would render one Type A system quite different from another one. But to state this is not to demonstrate that there are no constants in human sexual epistemology. The frequency with which these theories or variations on them appear in Western history is striking.

The apparent gender blindness of the ancient world has often been adduced as proof that Type B theories were unknown before comparatively recent times. In Plutarch's *Dialogue on Love* it is asserted that

> the noble lover of beauty engages in love wherever he sees excellence and splendid natural endowment without regard for any difference in physiological detail. The lover of human beauty [will] be fairly and equally disposed toward both sexes, instead of supposing that males and females are as different in the matter of love as they are in their clothes.[6]

Such statements are commonplaces of ancient lore about love and eroticism, to the extent that one is inclined to believe that much of the ancient world was completely unaware of differentiation among humans in sexual object choice, as I have myself pointed out at length elsewhere.[7] But my statements and the evidence on which they rest can easily be misapprehended. Their purport is that ancient *societies* did not distinguish heterosexuality from homosexuality, not that all, or even most, individuals failed to make such a distinction.

A distinction can be present and generally recognized in a society without forming any part of its social structure. In some cultures skin color is a major determinant of social status; in others it is irrelevant. But it would be fatuous to assume that societies that did not "discriminate on the basis of" [i.e., make invidious distinctions concerning] skin color could not "discriminate" [distinguish] such differences. This same paranomastic subtlety must

be understood in regard to ancient views of sexuality: City-states of the ancient world did not, for the most part, discriminate on the basis of sexual orientation, and, as societies, appear to have been blind to the issue of sexual object choice, but it is not clear that individuals were unaware of distinctions in the matter.

It should be obvious, for instance, that in the passage cited above Plutarch is arguing against precisely that notion that Padgug claims had not existed in precapitalist societies, i.e., Type B theories. Plutarch believes that a normal human being is susceptible to attraction to either gender, but his comments are manifestly directed against the contrary view. Which attitude was more common in his day is not apparent, but it is clearly inaccurate to use his comments as demonstration that there was only one view. The polemical tone of his remarks, in fact, seems good evidence that the position he opposes was of considerable importance. The whole genre of debates about the types of love of which this dialogue is a representative[8] cuts both ways on the issue: On the one hand, arguing about the matter and adducing reasons for preferring one gender to the other suggests a kind of polymorphous sexuality that is not predirected by heredity or experience toward one gender or the other. On the other, in each of the debates there are factions that are clearly on one side or the other of the dichotomy not supposed to have existed before modern times: Some disputants argue for attraction to males only; some for attraction to females only. Each side derogates the preference of the other side as distasteful. Sometimes bisexuality is admitted, but as a third preference, not as the general nature of human sexuality:

> Zeus came as an eagle to god-like Ganymede,
> as a swan came he to the fair-haired mother of Helen.
> So there is no comparison between the two things: one person likes one, another likes the other; I like both.[9]

This formulation of the range of human sexuality is almost identical to popular modern conceptions of Type B: Some people prefer their own gender; some the opposite; some both. Similar distinctions abound in ancient literature. The myth of Aristophanes in Plato's *Symposium* is perhaps the most familiar example: Its manifest and stated purpose is to explain why humans are divided into groups of predominantly homosexual or heterosexual interest. It is strongly implied that these interests are both exclusive and innate; that is stated outright by Longus, who describes a character as "homosexual by nature [*physei*]."[10]

It is true that there were no terms in common use in Greece or Rome to describe categories of sexual preference, but it does not follow that such terms were wholly unknown: Plato, Athenaeus, and other writers who dealt with the subject at length developed terms to describe predominant or exclusive interest in the apposite gender.[11] Many writers, moreover, found it possible to characterize homosexuality as a distinct mode of erotic expression without naming it. Plautus, for example, characterized homosexual activity as the "mores of Marseilles," suggesting that he considered it a variant on ordinary human sexuality.[12] Martial found it possible to describe an exclusively heterosexual male, even though he had no terminology available to do so and was himself apparently interested in both genders.[13]

One even finds expressions of solidarity among adherents of one preference or another in ancient literature, as when Clodius Albinus, noted for his exclusively heterosexual interest, persecutes those involved in homosexual behavior,[14] or when a character who has spoken on behalf of love between men in one of the debates bursts out, "We are like strangers cut off in a foreign land . . . ; nevertheless, we shall not be overcome by fear and betray the truth,"[15] or when Propertius writes, "Let him who would be our enemy love girls; he who would be our friend enjoy boys."[16] That there is a jocular tone to some of these statements, especially the last, is certainly attributable to the fact that the distinctions involved in no way affected the well-being, happiness, or social status of the individuals, owing to the extreme sexual tolerance of ancient societies; but it does not cast doubt on the existence of the distinctions. Even when preferences are attributed ironically, as is likely the case in Plato's placing the myth of sexual etiology in the mouth of Aristophanes, the joke depends on the familiarity of the distinction.

Subtler indications of Type B taxonomies can also be found. In the *Ephesiaca*, a Hellenistic love novel by Xenophon of Ephesus, sexual categories are never discussed, and are clearly not absolute, but they do seem to be well understood and constitute an organizing principle of individual lives. Habrocomes is involved throughout only with

women, and when, after his long separation from his true love Anthia, she desires to know if he has been faithful to her, she inquires only if he has slept with other women, although she knows that men have been interested in him, and it is clear that sex with a man would also constitute infidelity (as with Corymbus). It seems clear that Habrocomes is, in fact, heterosexual, at least in Anthia's opinion. Another character, Hippothoos, had been married to an older woman and attracted to Anthia, but is apparently mostly gay: The two great loves of his life are males (Hyperanthes and Habrocomes); he left all to follow each of these, and at the end of the story he erects a statue to the former and establishes his residence near that of the latter. The author tidies up all the couples at the end by reuniting Anthia and Habrocomes and introducing a new male lover (Clisthenes) for Hippothoos. This entire scenario corresponds almost exactly to modern conceptualizations: Some people are heterosexual, some homosexual, some bisexual; the categories are not absolute, but they are important and make a substantial difference in people's lives.

Almost the very same constellation of opinions can be found in many other preindustrial societies. In medieval Islam one encounters an even more overwhelming emphasis on homosexual eroticism than in classical Greek or Roman writing. It is probably fair to say that most premodern Arabic poetry is ostensibly homosexual, and it is clear that this is more than a literary convention. When Saadia Gaon, a Jew living in Muslim society in the tenth century, discusses the desirability of "passionate love,"[17] he apparently refers only to homosexual passion. There is the sort of love men have for their wives, which is good but not passionate; and there is the sort of love men have for each other, which is passionate but not good. (And what of the wives' loves? We are not told.) That Saadia assumes the ubiquity of homosexual passion is the more striking because he is familiar with Plato's discussion of homosexual and heterosexual varieties of love in the *Symposium*.[18]

Does this mean that classical Islamic society uniformly entertained Type A theories of human sexuality and regarded eroticism as inherently pansexual? No. There is much evidence in Arabic literature for the very same Type B dichotomies known in other cultures. Saadia himself cites various theories about the determination of particular erotic interests (e.g., astrological lore),[19] and in the ninth century Jahiz wrote a debate involving partisans of homosexual and heterosexual desire, in which each disputant, like his Hellenistic counterpart, expresses distaste for the preference of the other.[20] Three debates of this sort occur in the *Thousand and One Nights*, a classic of Arabic popular literature.[21] "Homosexuals" are frequently (and neutrally) mentioned in classical Arabic writings as a distinct type of human being. That the "type" referred to involves predominant or exclusive preference is often suggested: In tale 142 of the *Nights*, for example, it is mentioned as noteworthy that a male homosexual does not dislike women; in Night 419 a woman observes a man staring longingly at some boys and remarks to him, "I perceive that you are among those who prefer men to women."

A ninth-century text of human psychology by Qustā ibn Luqā treats twenty areas in which humans may be distinguished psychologically.[22] One area is sexual object-choice: Some men, Qustā explains, are "disposed towards" [*yamīlu ilā*] women, some toward other men, and some toward both.[23] Qustā has no terminology at hand for these categories; indeed, for the second category he employs the euphemism that such men are disposed toward "sexual partners other than women":[24] obviously lack of terminology for the homosexual/heterosexual dichotomy should not be taken as a sign of ignorance of it. Qustā, in fact, believed that homosexuality was often inherited, as did ar-Razi and many other Muslim scientific writers.[25]

It has been claimed that "homosexuality" was viewed in medieval Europe "not as a particular attribute of a certain type of person but as a potential in all sinful creatures."[26] It is certainly true that some medieval writers evinced Type A attitudes of this sort: Patristic authors often address to their audiences warnings concerning homosexual attraction predicated on the assumption that any male might be attracted to another.[27] The Anglo-Saxon life of Saint Eufrasia[28] recounts the saint's efforts to live in a monastery disguised as a monk and the turmoil that ensued: The other monks were greatly attracted by Agapitus (the name she took as a monk), and reproached the abbot for bringing "so beautiful a man into their minster" ["forþam swa wlitigne man into heora mynstre gelædde," p. 344]. Although it is in fact a woman to whom the monks are drawn, the account evinces no surprise on anyone's part that the monks should experience intense sexual attraction toward a person ostensibly of their own gender.

Some theologians clearly regarded homosexual activity as a vice open to all rather than as the peculiar sexual outlet of a portion of the population, but this attitude was not universal and was often ambiguously or inconsistently held even by those who did most to promulgate it. Albertus Magnus and Thomas Aquinas both wrote of homosexual acts as sins that presumably anyone might commit, but both also recognized that it was somewhat more complex than this: Aquinas, following Aristotle, believed that some men were "naturally inclined" to desire sexual relations with other men – clearly a theory of Type B – and Albertus Magnus considered homosexual desire to be a manifestation of a contagious disease, particularly common among the wealthy, and curable through the application of medicine.[29] This attitude is highly reminiscent of psychiatric opinion in late Victorian times, and a far cry from categorizing homosexuality simply as a vice.

"Sodomy" was defined by many clerics as the improper emission of semen – the gender of the parties and their sexual appetites being irrelevant – but many others understood *sodomita* to apply specifically to men who preferred sexual contact with other men, generally or exclusively, and *sodomia* to apply only to the sexual acts performed in this context.[30]

Medieval literature abounds in suggestions that there is something special about homosexuality, that it is not simply an ordinary sin. Many writers view it as the special characteristic of certain peoples; others argue that it is completely unknown among their own kind. There are constant associations of homosexual preference with certain occupations or social positions, clearly indicating that it is linked in some way to personality or experience. The modern association of homosexuality with the arts had as its medieval counterpart a regular link with the religious life: When Bernard of Clairvaux was asked to restore life to the dead son of a Marquess of Burgundy he had the boy taken to a private room and lay down upon him. No cure transpired; the boy remained lifeless. The chronicler, who had been present, nonetheless found humor in the incident and remarked, "That was the unhappiest monk of all. For I've never heard of any monk who lay down upon a boy that did not straightaway rise up after him. The abbot blushed and they went out as many laughed."[31]

Chaucer's pardoner, also a cleric, appears to be innately sexually atypical, and his association with the hare has led many to suppose that it is homosexuality that distinguishes him.[32] Even non-Christians linked the Christian clergy with homosexuality.[33]

Much of the literature of the High Middle Ages that deals with sexual-object choice assumes distinct dispositions, most often exclusive. A long passage in the *Roman d'Énéas* characterizes homosexual males as devoid of interest in women and notable in regard to dress, habits, decorum, and behavior.[34] Debates of the period characterize homosexual preference as innate or God-given, and in the well-known poem "Ganymede and Helen" it is made pellucidly clear that Ganymede is exclusively gay (before the intervention of the gods): It is Helen's frustration at his inability to respond properly to her advances that prompts the debate.[35] In a similar poem, "Ganymede and Hebe," homosexual relations are characterized as "decreed by fate," suggesting something quite different from an occasional vice.[36] Indeed, the mere existence of debates of this sort suggests very strongly a general conceptualization of sexuality as bifurcated into two camps distinguished by sexual object-choice. Popular terminology of the period corroborates this: as opposed to words like *sodomita*, which might designate indulgence in a specific activity by any human, writers of the High Middle Ages were inclined to use designations like "Ganymede," whose associations were exclusively homosexual, and to draw analogies with animals like the hare and the hyena, which were thought to be naturally inclined to sexual relations with their own gender.

Allain of Lille invokes precisely the taxonomy of sexual orientation used in the modern West in writing about sexuality among his twelfth-century contemporaries: "Of those men who employ the grammar of Venus there are some who embrace the masculine, others who embrace the feminine, and some who embrace both. . . ."[37]

Clearly all three types of taxonomy were known in Western Europe and the Middle East before the advent of modern capitalist societies. It is, on the other hand, equally clear that in different times and places one type of theory has often predominated over the others, and for long periods in many areas one or two of the three may have been quite rare. Does the prevalence of one theory over another in given times and places reveal something about human sexuality? Possibly, but many factors other than sexuality itself may influence, deform, alter, or transform conceptualizations of sexuality among peoples and individuals, and much attention must be devoted to analyzing such factors and their effects before it will be possible to use them effectively in analyzing the bedrock of sexuality beneath them.

Nearly all societies, for example, regulate sexual behavior in some way; most sophisticated cultures articulate rationalizations for their restrictions. The nature of such rationalizations will inevitably affect sexual taxonomy. If "the good" in matters sexual is equated with procreation, homosexual relations may be categorically distinguished from heterosexual ones as necessarily excluding the chief good of sexuality. Such a moral taxonomy might create a homosexual/heterosexual dichotomy in and of itself, independent of underlying personal attitudes. This appears, in fact, to have played some role in the Christian West. That some heterosexual relations also exclude procreation is less significant (though much heterosexual eroticism has been restricted in the West), because there is not an easily demonstrable *generic* incompatibility with procreative purpose. (Compare the association of chest hair with maleness: Not all men have hairy chests, but only men have chest hair; hence, chest hair is thought of as essentially masculine; though not all heterosexual couplings are procreative, only heterosexual acts could be procreative, so heterosexuality seems essentially procreative and homosexuality essentially not.)

In a society where pleasure or the enjoyment of beauty are recognized as legitimate aims of sexual activity, this dichotomy should seem less urgent. And in the Hellenistic and Islamic worlds, where sexuality has traditionally been restricted on the basis of standards of decorum and propriety[38] rather than procreative purpose, the homosexual/heterosexual dichotomy has been largely absent from public discourse. Just as the presence of the dichotomy might be traceable to aspects of social organization unrelated to sexual preference, however, its absence must likewise be seen as a moot datum: As has been shown, individual Greek and Muslim writers were often acutely conscious of such a taxonomy. The prevalence of either Type A or Type B concepts at the social level, in other words, may be related more to other social structures than to personal perceptions of or beliefs about the nature of sexuality.

Another factor, wholly overlooked in previous literature on this subject, is the triangular relationship of mediated desire, beauty, and sexual stereotypes. It seems safe enough to assume that most humans are influenced to some degree by the values of the society in which they live. Many desires are "mediated" by the valorization accorded things by surrounding society, rather than generated exclusively by the desiring individual. If one posits for the sake of argument two opposed sets of social values regarding beauty and sex roles, it is easy to see how conceptualizations of sexual desire might be transformed to fit "mediated desire" resulting from either pole. At one extreme, beauty is conceived as a male attribute: Standards and ideals of beauty are predicated on male models, art emphasizes male beauty, and males take pride in their own physical attractions. Greece and the Muslim world approach this extreme: Greek legend abounds in examples of males pursued for their beauty, standards of beauty are often predicated on male archetypes (Adonis, Apollo, Ganymede, Antinous), and beauty in males is considered a major good, for the individual and for his society. Likewise, in the Muslim world, archetypes of beauty are more often seen in masculine than in feminine terms, beauty is thought to be a great asset to a man, and the universal archetype of beauty, to which even beautiful women are compared, is Joseph.

This pole can be contrasted with societies in which "maleness" and beauty are thought unrelated or even contradictory, and beauty is generally predicated only of females. In such societies "maleness" is generally idealized in terms of social roles, as comprising, for example, forcefulness, strength, the exercise of power, aggression, etc. In the latter type of society, which the modern West approaches, "beauty" would generally seem inappropriate, perhaps even embarrassing in males, and males possessing it would be regarded as "effeminate" or sexually suspect to some degree.

In nearly all cultures some linkage is expressed between eroticism and beauty, and it should not therefore be surprising that in societies of the former type there will be greater emphasis on males as sex objects than in those of the latter type. Since beauty is conceptualized as a good, and since it is recognized to subsist on a large scale – perhaps even primarily – among men, men can be admired even by other men for their beauty, and this admiration is often indistinguishable (at the literary level, if not in reality) from erotic interest. In cultures of the latter type, however, men are not admired for their beauty; sexual interest is generally imagined to be applied by men (who are strong, forceful,

powerful, etc., but not beautiful) to women, whose beauty may be considered their chief – or even sole – asset. In the latter case, expressions of admiration for male beauty will be rare, even among women, who will prize other attributes in men they desire.

These descriptions are deliberate oversimplifications to make a point: In fact, no society is exclusively one or the other, and elements of both are present in all Western cultures. But it would be easy to show that many societies tend more toward one extreme than the other, and it is not hard to see how this might affect the prominence of the homosexual/heterosexual dichotomy: In a culture where male beauty was generally a source of admiration, the dividing line between what some taxonomies would define as homosexual and heterosexual interest would be considerably blurred by common usage and expression. Expressions of admiration and even attraction to male beauty would be so familiar that they would not provoke surprise or require designation as a peculiar category. Persons in such a society might be uninterested in genital interaction with persons of their own sex, might even disapprove of it, but they would tend not to see romantic interest in male beauty – by males or females – as bizarre or odd or as necessitating special categorization.

In cultures that deemphasize male beauty, however, expressions of interest in it by men or women might be suspect. In a society that has established no place for such interest in its esthetic structures, mere admiration for a man's physical attraction, without genital acts, could be sharply stigmatized, and a strict division between homosexual and heterosexual desire would be easy to promulgate and maintain.

Female roles would also be affected by such differences: If women are thought of as moved by beauty, even if it is chiefly male beauty, the adoption of the role of admirer by a woman will not seem odd or peculiar. If women are viewed, however, as the beautiful but passive objects of a sexual interest largely limited to men, their expressing sexual interest – in men or women – may be disapproved.[39] George Chauncey has documented precisely this sort of disapproval in Victorian medical literature on "homosexuality": At the outset sexual deviance is perceived only in women who violate the sex role expected of them by playing an active part in a female-female romantic relationship. The "passive" female, who does not violate expectations of sex role by receiving, as females are thought naturally to do, the attentions of her "husband," is not considered abnormal. Gradually, as attitudes and the needs of society to define more precisely the limits of approved sexuality change, attention is transferred from the role the female "husband" plays to the sexual object choice of both women, and both come to be categorized as "homosexual" on the basis of the gender to which they are attracted.[40]

Shifts of this sort, relating to conceptions of beauty, rationalization of sexual limitations, etc., are supported, affected, and overlaid by more specific elements of social organization. These include patterns of sexual interaction (between men and women, the old and young, the rich and the poor, etc.), specific sexual taboos, and what might be called "secondary" sexual behavior. Close attention must be devoted to such factors in their historical context in assessing sexual conceptualizations of any type.

Ancient "pederasty," for example, seems to many to constitute a form of sexual organization entirely unrelated to modern homosexuality. Possibly this is so, but the differences seem much less pronounced when one takes into account the sexual context in which "pederasty" occurs. The age differential idealized in descriptions of relations between the "lover" and the "beloved" is less than the disparity in age between heterosexual lovers as recommended, for example, by Aristotle (nineteen years). "Pederasty" may often represent no more than the homosexual side of a general pattern of cross-generation romance.[41] Issues of subordination and power likewise offer parallel structures that must be collated before any arguments about ancient "homosexuality" or "heterosexuality" can be mounted. Artemidorus Daldianus aptly encapsulates the conflation of sexual and social roles of his contemporaries in the second century AD in his discussion of the significance of sexual dreams: "For a man to be penetrated [in a dream] by a richer and older man is good: for it is customary to receive from such men. To be penetrated by a younger and poorer is bad: for it is the custom to give to such persons. It signifies the same [i.e., is bad] if the penetrator is older and poor."[42] Note that these comments do not presuppose either Type A or Type B theories: They might be applied to persons who regard either gender as sexually apposite, or to persons who feel a predisposition to one or the other. But they do suggest the social matrix of a system of sexual distinctions that might override, alter, or disguise other taxonomies.

The special position of passive homosexual behavior, involving the most common premodern form of Type C theory, deserves a separate study, but it might be noted briefly that its effect on sexual taxonomies is related not only to status considerations about penetration, as indicated above, but also to specific sexual taboos that may be highly culturally variable. Among Romans, for instance, two roles were decorous for a free adult male, expressed by the verbs *irrumo*, to offer the penis for sucking, and *futuo*, to penetrate a female, or *pedico*, to penetrate a male.[43] Indecorous roles for citizen males, permissible for anyone else, were expressed in particular by the verbs *fello*, to fellate, and *ceveo*, not translatable into English.[44] The distinction between roles approved for male citizens and others appears to center on the giving of seed (as opposed to the receiving of it) rather than on the more familiar modern active/passive division. (American prison slang expresses a similar dichotomy with the terms "catchers" and "pitchers.") It will be seen that this division obviates to a large degree both the active/passive split – since both the *irrumator* and the *fellator* are conceptually active[45] – and the homosexual/heterosexual one, since individuals are categorized not according to the gender to which they are drawn but to the role they play in activities that could take place between persons of either gender. It is not clear that Romans had no interest in the gender of sexual partners, only that the division of labor, as it were, was a more pressing concern and attracted more analytical attention.

Artemidorus, on the other hand, considered both "active" and "passive" fellatio to be categorically distinct from other forms of sexuality. He divided his treatment of sexuality into three sections – the natural and legal, the illegal, and the unnatural – and he placed fellatio, in any form, among illegal activities, along with incest. In the ninth-century translation of his work by Hunain ibn Ishaq (the major transmitter of Aristotelian learning to the West), a further shift is evident: Hunain created a separate chapter for fellatio, which he called "that vileness of which it is not decent even to speak."[46]

In both the Greek and the Arabic versions of this work the fellatio that is objurgated is both homosexual and heterosexual, and in both, anal intercourse between men is spoken of with indifference or approval. Yet in the Christian West the most hostile legislation regarding sexual behavior has been directed specifically against homosexual anal intercourse: Fellatio has generally received milder treatment. Is this because fellatio is more widely practiced among heterosexuals in the West, and therefore seems less bizarre (i.e., less distinctly homosexual)? Or is it because passivity and the adoption of what seems a female role in anal intercourse is particularly objectionable in societies dominated by rigid ideals of "masculine" behavior? It may be revealing, in this context, that many modern languages, including English, have skewed the donor/recipient dichotomy by introducing a chiastic active/passive division: The recipient (i.e., of semen) in anal intercourse is "passive"; in oral intercourse he is "active." Could the blurring of the active/passive division in the case of fellatio render it less obnoxious to legislative sensibilities?

Beliefs about sexual categories in the modern West vary widely, from the notion that sexual behavior is entirely a matter of conscious choice to the conviction that all sexual behavior is determined by heredity or environment. The same individual may, in fact, entertain with apparent equanimity contradictory ideas on the subject. It is striking that many ardent proponents of Type C etiological theories who regard homosexual behavior as pathological and/or depraved nonetheless imply in their statements about the necessity for legal repression of homosexual behavior that it is potentially ubiquitous in the human population, and that if legal sanctions are not maintained everyone may suddenly become homosexual.

Humans of previous ages were probably not, as a whole, more logical or consistent than their modern descendants. To pretend that a single system of sexual categorization obtained at any previous moment in Western history is to maintain the unlikely in the face of substantial evidence to the contrary. Most of the current spectrum of belief appears to have been represented in previous societies. What that spectrum reveals about the inner nature of human sexuality remains, for the time being, moot and susceptible of many divergent interpretations. But if the revolution in modern historical writing – and the recovery of whatever past the "gay community" may be said to have – is not to be stillborn, the problem of universals must be sidestepped or at least approached with fewer doctrinaire assumptions. Both realists and nominalists must lower their voices. Reconstructing the monuments of the past from the rubble of the present requires quiet concentration.

Postscript

This essay was written five years ago [1982], and several of the points it raises now require clarification or revision. I would no longer characterize the constructionist-essentialist controversy as a "debate" in any strict sense: One of its ironies is that no one involved in it actually identifies him- or herself as an "essentialist," although constructionists (of whom, in contrast, there are many)[47] sometimes so label other writers. Even when applied by its opponents the label seems to fit extremely few contemporary scholars.[48] This fact is revealing, and provides a basis for understanding the controversy more accurately not as a dialogue between two schools of thought, but as a revisionist (and largely one-sided) critique of assumptions believed to underlie traditional historiography. This understanding is not unrelated to my nominalist/realist analogy: One might describe constructionism (with some oversimplification) as a nominalist rejection of a tendency to "realism" in the traditional historiography of sexuality. The latter treated "homosexuality" as a diachronic, empirical entity (not quite a "universal," but "real" apart from social structures bearing on it); constructionists regard it as a culturally dependent phenomenon or, as some would have it, not a "real" phenomenon at all. It is not, nonetheless, a debate, since no current historians consciously defend an essentialist point of view.

Second, although it is probably still accurate to say that "most" constructionists are historians of the nineteenth and twentieth centuries, a number of classicists have now added their perspective to constructionist theory. This has broadened and deepened the discussion, although, strikingly, few if any historians of periods between Periclean Athens and the late nineteenth century articulate constructionist views.[49]

Third, my own position, perhaps never well understood, has changed. In my book *Christianity, Social Tolerance and Homosexuality* I defined "gay persons"[50] as those "conscious of erotic inclination toward their own gender as a distinguishing characteristic" (p. 44). It was the supposition of the book that such persons have been widely and identifiably present in Western society at least since Greco-Roman times, and this prompted many constructionists to label the work "essentialist." I would now define "gay persons" more simply as those whose erotic interest is predominantly directed toward their own gender (i.e., regardless of how conscious they are of this as a distinguishing characteristic). This is the sense in which, I believe, it is used by most American speakers, and although experts in a field may well wish to employ specialized language, when communicating with the public it seems to me counterproductive to use common words in senses different from or opposed to their ordinary meanings.

In this sense, I would still argue that there have been "gay persons" in most Western societies. It is not clear to me that this is an "essentialist" position. Even if societies formulate or create "sexualities" that are highly particular in some ways, it might happen that different societies would construct similar ones, as they often construct political or class structures similar enough to be subsumed under the same rubric (democracy, oligarchy, proletariat, aristocracy, etc. – all of which are both particular and general).[51]

Most constructionist arguments assume that essentialist positions necessarily entail a further supposition: that society does not create erotic feelings, but only acts on them. Some other force – genes, psychological forces, etc. – creates "sexuality," which is essentially independent of culture. This was not a working hypothesis of *Christianity, Social Tolerance and Homosexuality*. I was and remain agnostic about the origins and etiology of human sexuality.

Notes

This essay originally appeared in somewhat different form in *Salmagundi*, No. 58–9, Fall 1982–Winter 1983, 89–113.

1. For particularly articulate examples of "nominalist" history, see Robert A. Padgug, "Sexual Matters: On Conceptualizing Sexuality in History," *Radical History Review* 20 (1979): 3–33; and Jeffrey Weeks, *Coming Out: Homosexual Politics in Britain from the Nineteenth Century to the Present* (London, 1977). Most older studies of homosexuality in the past are essentially realist; see bibliography in John Boswell, *Christianity, Social Tolerance and Homosexuality* (Chicago, 1980), p. 4, n. 3.
2. It is of substantial import to several moral traditions, e.g., whether or not homosexuality is a "condition" – an essentially "realist" position – or a "lifestyle" – basically a "nominalist" point of view. For a summary of shifting attitudes on these points within the Christian tradition, see Peter Coleman, *Christian Attitudes to Homosexuality* (London, 1980),

or Edward Batchelor, *Homosexuality and Ethics* (New York, 1980).
3. Note that at this level the debate is to some extent concerned with the degree of convention that can be sustained without loss of accuracy. It is conventional, for instance, to include in a history of the United States treatment of the period before the inauguration of the system of government that bears that title, and even to speak of the "colonial U.S.," although while they were colonies they were not the United States. A history of Greece would likewise, by convention, concern itself with all the states that would someday constitute what is today called "Greece," although those states may have recognized no connection with each other (or even have been at war) at various points in the past. It is difficult to see why such conventions should not be allowed in the case of minority histories, so long as sufficient indication is provided as to the actual relationship of earlier forms to later ones.
4. Padgug, "Sexual Matters," p. 59.
5. For the variety of etiological explanations to date see the brief bibliography in Boswell, *Christianity*, p. 9, n. 9. To this list should now be added (in addition to many articles) three studies: Alan Bell and M. S. Weinberg, *Homosexualities: A Study of Diversity Among Men and Women* (New York, 1978); idem, *Sexual Preference: Its Development in Men and Women* (Bloomington, Indiana, 1981); and James Weinrich, *Sexual Landscapes* (New York, 1987). An ingenious and highly revealing approach to the development of modern medical literature on the subject of homosexuality is proposed by George Chauncey Jr., "From Sexual Inversion to Homosexuality: Medicine and the Changing Conceptualization of Female Deviance," *Salmagundi*, no. 58–9 (Fall 1982–Winter 1983): 114–46.
6. Moralia 767: *Amatorius*, trans. W. C. Helmhold (Cambridge, Mass., 1961), p. 415.
7. Boswell, *Christianity*, Part I *passim*, esp. pp. 50–9.
8. See Boswell, *Christianity*, pp. 125–7.
9. *Greek Anthology*, trans. W. R. Paton (Cambridge, Mass., 1918) 1.65.
10. Daphnis and Chloe, 4.11. The term *paiderastēs* here can not be understood as a reference to what is now called paedophilia, since Daphnis – the object of Gnatho's interest – is full grown and on the point of marriage. It is obviously a conventional term for "homosexual."

   Among many complex aspects of Aristophanes' speech in the *Symposium* as an indication of contemporary sexual constructs, two are especially notable. (1) Although it is the sole Attic reference to lesbianism as a concept, male homosexuality is of much greater concern as an erotic disposition in the discussion than either female homosexuality or heterosexuality. (2) It is this, in my view, which accounts for the additional subtlety of age distinctions in male-male relations, suggesting a general pattern of older *erastes* and younger *eromenonos*. Age differential was unquestionably a part of the construct of sexuality among elements of the population in Athens, but it can easily be given more weight than it deserves. "Romantic love" of any sort was thought to be provoked by and directed toward the young, as is clearly demonstrated in Agathon's speech a little further on, where he uses the greater beauty of young males and females interchangeably to prove that Love is a young god. In fact, most Athenian males married women considerably younger than themselves, but since marriage was not imagined to follow upon romantic attachment, this discrepancy does not appear in dialogues on *eros*.

David Halperin argues in "Sex Before Sexuality" (in Martin Duberman, Martha Vicinus, and George Chauncey, Jr., *Hidden From History* (New York, 1990) [see also this volume, ch. 22]) that the speech does not indicate a taxonomy comparable to modern ones, chiefly because of the age differential, although in fact the creatures described by Aristophanes must have been seeking a partner of the same age, since, joined at birth, they were coeval. What is clear is that Aristophanes does not imagine a populace undifferentiated in experience or desire, responding circumstantially to individuals of either gender, but persons with lifelong preferences arising from innate character (or a mythic prehistory).

11. For Plato and Pollianus, see Boswell, *Christianity*, p. 30, n. 56; Athenaeus uses *philomeirax* of Sophocles and *philogynēs* of Euripides, apparently intending to indicate that the former was predominantly (if not exclusively) interested in males and the latter in females. Cf. *Scriptores physiognomici*, ed. R. Foerster (Leipzig, 1893), 1:29, p. 36, where the word *philogynaioi*, "woman lover," occurs.

12. Casina, V.4.957.

13. Epigrams, 2.47.

14. Capitolinus, 11.7.

15. Boswell, *Christianity*, p. 127.

16. 2.4: "Hostis si quis erit nobis, amet ille puellas: / gaudeat in puero si quis amicus erit."

17. Saadia Gaon, *Kitāb al-'Amanāt wa'l-I 'tikhadāt*, ed. S. Landauer (Leyden, 1880), 10.7, pp. 294–7 (English translation by S. Rosenblatt in *Yale Judaica Series*, vol. 1: *The Book of Beliefs and Opinions*).

18. *Kitāb*, p. 295.

19. Ibid.

20. *Kitāb mufākharāt al-jawārī wa'l-ghilmān*, ed. Charles Pellat (Beirut, 1957).

21. See discussion in Boswell, *Christianity*, pp. 257–8.

22. "Le Livre des caractères de Qostâ ibn Loûqâ," ed. and trans. Paul Sbath, *Bulletin de l'Institut d'Egypte* 23 (1940–1): 103–39. Sbath's translation is loose and misleading, and must be read with caution.

23. Ibid., p. 112.

24. "... waminhim man yamīlu īlā ghairihinna mini 'Ighilmāni ... ," ibid. A treatment of the fascinating term *ghulām* (pl. *ghilmān*), whose meanings range from "son" to "sexual partner," is beyond the scope of this essay.

25. Qustā discusses this at some length, pp. 133–6. Cf. F. Rosenthal, "ar-Râzî on the Hidden Illness," *Bulletin of the History of Medicine* 52, no. 1 (1978): 45–60, and the authorities cited there. Treating "passive sexual behavior" (i.e., the reception of semen in anal intercourse) in men as a hereditary condition generally implies a conflation of Types A and C taxonomies in which the role of insertor with either men or women is thought "normal," but the position of the "insertee" is regarded as bizarre or even pathological. Attitudes toward *ubnah* should be taken as a special aspect of Muslim sexual taxonomy rather than as indicative of attitudes toward "homosexuality." A comparable case is that of Caelius Aurelianus: see Boswell, *Christianity*, p. 53; cf. remarks on Roman sexual taboos, below.

26. Weeks, *Coming Out*, p. 12.

27. See Boswell, *Christianity*, pp. 159–61.

28. *Aelfric's Lives of Saints*, ed. and trans. W. W. Skeat (London, 1881), p. 33.

29. Discussed in Boswell, *Christianity*, pp. 316ff.

30. "Sodomia" and "sodomita" are used so often and in so many competing senses in the High Middle Ages that a separate study would be required to present even a summary of this material. Note that in the modern West the term still has overlapping senses, even in law: In some American states "sodomy" applies to any inherently nonprocreative sex act (fellatio between husband and wife, e.g.), in others to all homosexual behavior, and in still others only to anal intercourse. Several "sodomy" statutes have in fact been overturned on grounds of unconstitutional vagueness. See, in addition to the material cited in Boswell, *Christianity*, pp. 52, 183–4; Giraldus Cambrensis, *Descriptio Cambriae*, 2.7; J. J. Tierney, "The Celtic Ethnography of Posidonius," *Proceedings of the Royal Irish Academy* 60 (1960): 252; and *Carmina Burana: Die Lieder der Benediktbeurer Handschrift. Zweisprachige Ausgabe* (Munich, 1979), 95.4, p. 334 ("Pura semper ab hac infamia/nostra fuit minor Britannia"; the ms. has *Bricciavia*).

31. Walter Map, *De nugis curialium* 1.23, trans. John Mundy, *Europe in the High Middle Ages, 1150–1309* (New York, 1973), p. 302. Cf. discussion of this theme in Boswell, *Christianity*, chapter 8.

32. Prologue, 669ss. Of several works on this issue now in print see especially Monica McAlpine, "The Pardoner's Homosexuality and How it Matters," *PMLA*, January 1980, pp. 8–22; and Edward Schweitzer, "Chaucer's Pardoner and the Hare,"

English Language Notes 4, no. 4 (1967): 247–50 (not cited by McAlpine).

33. See Boswell, *Christianity*, p. 233.
34. 8565ss; cf. *Roman de la Rose* 2169–74, and Gerald Herman, "The 'Sin Against Nature' and its Echoes in Medieval French Literature," *Annuale Mediaevale* 17 (1976): 70–87.
35. "Altercatio Ganimedis et Helene: Kritische Edition mit Kommentar," ed. Rolf Lenzen, *Mittellateinisches Jahrbuch* 7 (1972): 161–86; English translation in Boswell, *Christianity*, pp. 381–9.
36. Boswell, *Christianity*, pp. 392–8.
37. *The Anglo-Latin Satirical Poets and Epigrammatists*, ed. Thomas Wright (London, 1872), 2:463.
38. The relationship between the words "propriety" and "property" is not coincidental, and in this connection is highly revealing. Although social attitudes toward sexual propriety in pre-Christian Europe are often touted as more humane and liberal than those which followed upon the triumph of the Christian religion, it is often overlooked that the comparative sexual freedom of adult free males in the ancient world stemmed largely from the fact that all the members of their household were either legally or effectively their *property*, and hence could be used by them as they saw fit. For other members of society what has seemed to some in the modern West to have been sexual "freedom" might be more aptly viewed as "abuse" or "exploitation," although it is of course silly to assume that the ability to coerce necessarily results in coercion.
39. Lesbianism is often regarded as peculiar or even pathological in cultures which accept male homosexuality with equanimity. In the largely gay romance *Affairs of the Heart* (see Boswell, *Christianity*, pp. 126–7) lesbianism is characterized as "the tribadic disease" [tēs tribakēs aselgeias] (s. 28). A detailed analysis of the relationship of attitudes toward male and female homosexuality will comprise a portion of a study I am preparing on the phenomenology of homosexual behavior in ancient and medieval Europe.
40. Cf. n. 5, above.
41. Since the publication of my remarks on this issue in *Christianity*, pp. 28–30, several detailed studies of Greek homosexuality have appeared, most notably those of Félix Buffière, *Eros adolescent: la pédérastie dans la Grèce antique* (Paris, 1980); and K. J. Dover, *Greek Homosexuality* (Cambridge, Mass., 1978). Neither work has persuaded me to revise my estimate of the degree to which Greek fascination with "youth" was more than a romantic convention. A detailed assessment of both works and their relation to my own findings will appear in the study mentioned above, no. 39.
42. Artemidorus Daldianus, *Onirocriticon libri quinque*, ed. R. Park (Leipzig, 1963) 1.78, pp. 88–9. (An

English translation of this work is available: *The Interpretation of Dreams*, trans. R. J. White [Park Ridge, N.J., 1975].)
43. "Non est pedico maritus: / quae faciat duo sunt: irrumat aut futuit" Martial 2:47 (cf. n. 14, above: *pedico* is apparently Martial's own coinage).
44. *Ceveo* is, that is, to *futuo* or *pedico* what *fello* is to *irrumo*: It describes the activity of the party being entered. The vulgar English "put out" may be the closest equivalent, but nothing in English captures the actual meaning of the Latin.
45. *Futuo/pedico* and *ceveo* are likewise both active.
46. Hunayn ibn Ishāq, trans., *Kitāb Taʿbīr ar-Ruʾyā*, ed. Toufic Fahd (Damascus, 1964), pp. 175–6.
47. For an overview of this literature since the material cited in note 1, see most recently Steven Epstein, "Gay Politics, Ethnic Identity: The Limits of Social Constructionism," *Socialist Review* 93/94 (1987): 9–54; also John D'Emilio, *Sexual Politics, Sexual Communities: The Making of a Homosexual Minority in the United States, 1940–1970* (Chicago, 1983); and the essays in Kenneth Plummer, ed., *The Making of the Modern Homosexual* (London, 1981). See also note 48.
48. Three recent writers on the controversy (Steven Murray, "Homosexual Categorization in Cross-Cultural Perspective," in Murray, *Social Theory, Homosexual Realities* [Gai Saber Monograph, 3] [New York, 1984]; Epstein, "Gay Politics"; and David Halperin, "Sex before Sexuality: Pederasty, Politics, and Power in Classical Athens" [see ch. 22 this volume] identify among them a dozen or more "constructionist" historians, but Murray and Halperin adduce only a single historian (me) as an example of modern "essentialist" historiography; Epstein, the most sophisticated of the three, can add to this only Adrienne Rich, not usually thought of as a historian. As to whether my views are actually "essentialist" or not, see further.
49. See, for example, Halperin, "Sex before Sexuality." Much of the controversy is conducted through scholarly papers: at a conference on "Homosexuality in History and Culture" held at Brown University in February 1987, of six presentations four were explicitly constructionist; two of these were by classicists. On the other hand, the standard volume on Attic homosexuality, K. J. Dover, *Greek Homosexuality* (New York, 1985), defies easy classification, but falls closer to an "essentialist" point of view than a "constructionist" one, and Keith DeVries's *Homosexuality and Athenian Society*, when it appears, will be a nonconstructionist survey of great subtlety and sophistication. See also David Cohen, "Law, Society and Homosexuality in Classical Athens," *Past and Present* 117 (1987): 3–21. For the (relatively few) recent studies of periods between Athens and the late nineteenth century, see Saara

Lilja, *Homosexuality in Republican and Augustan Rome* (Helsinki, 1983) (Societas Scientiarum Fennica, Commentationes Humanarum Litterarum, 74); Alan Bray, *Homosexuality in Renaissance England* (London, 1982); James Saslow, *Ganymede in the Renaissance: Homosexuality in Art and Society* (New Haven, 1986); Guido Ruggiero, *The Boundaries of Eros: Sex, Crime and Sexuality in Renaissance Venice* (New York, 1985); Claude Courouve, *Vocabulaire de l'homosexualité masculine* (Paris, 1985).

50. An expression I use to include both women and men.

51. Of course, if a constructionist position holds that "gay person" refers only to one particular modern identity, it is then, tautologically, not applicable to the past.

22

Sex Before Sexuality: Pederasty, Politics, and Power in Classical Athens

DAVID M. HALPERIN

I

In 1992, when the patriots among us will be celebrating the five hundredth anniversary of the discovery of America by Christopher Columbus, our cultural historians may wish to mark the centenary of an intellectual landfall of almost equal importance for the conceptual geography of the human sciences: the invention of homosexuality by Charles Gilbert Chaddock. Though he may never rank with Columbus in the annals of individual achievement, Chaddock would hardly seem to merit the obscurity that has surrounded him throughout the past hundred years. An early translator of Krafft-Ebing's *Psychopathia sexualis*, Chaddock is credited by the *Oxford English Dictionary*[1] with having introduced "homo-sexuality" into the English language in 1892, in order to render a German cognate twenty years its senior.[2] Homosexuality, for better or for worse, has been with us ever since.

Before 1892 there was no homosexuality, only sexual inversion. But, as George Chauncey, Jr., has demonstrated:

> Sexual inversion, the term used most commonly in the nineteenth century, did not denote the same conceptual phenomenon as homosexuality. "Sexual inversion" referred to a broad range of deviant gender behavior, of which homosexual desire was only a logical but indistinct aspect, while "homosexuality" focused on the narrower issue of sexual object choice. The differentiation of homosexual desire from "deviant"

gender behavior at the turn of the century reflects a major reconceptualization of the nature of human sexuality, its relation to gender, and its role in one's social definition.[3]

Throughout the nineteenth century, in other words, sexual preference for a person of one's own sex was not clearly distinguished from other sorts of nonconformity to one's culturally defined sex role: Deviant object-choice was viewed as merely one of a number of pathological symptoms exhibited by those who reversed, or "inverted," their proper sex roles by adopting a masculine or a feminine style at variance with what was deemed natural and appropriate to their anatomical sex. Political aspirations in women and (at least according to one expert writing as late as 1920) a fondness for cats in men were manifestations of a pathological condition, a kind of psychological hermaphroditism tellingly but not essentially expressed by the preference for a "normal" member of one's own sex as a sexual partner.[4]

This outlook on the matter seems to have been shared by the scientists and by their unfortunate subjects alike: Inversion was not merely a medical rubric, then, but a category of lived experience. Karl Heinrich Ulrichs, for example, an outspoken advocate for the freedom of sexual choice and the founder, as early as 1862, of the cult of Uranism (based on Pausanias's praise of Uranian, or "heavenly," pederasty in Plato's *Symposium*), described his own condition as that of an *anima muliebris virili corpore inclusa* – a woman's soul confined by a man's body. That sexual object-choice might be wholly independent of such "secondary" characteristics as masculinity or femininity never seems to have occurred to anyone until Havelock Ellis waged a campaign to isolate object-choice from role-playing and, concurrently, Freud, in his classic analysis of a drive in the *Three Essays* (1905), clearly distinguished in the case of the libido between the sexual "object" and the sexual "aim."[5]

The conceptual isolation of sexuality per se from questions of masculinity and femininity made possible a new taxonomy of sexual behaviors and psychologies based entirely on the anatomical sex of the persons engaged in a sexual act (same sex vs. different sex); it thereby obliterated a number of distinctions that had traditionally operated within earlier discourses pertaining to same-sex sexual contacts and that had radically differentiated active from passive sexual partners, normal from abnormal (or conventional from unconventional) sexual roles, masculine from feminine styles, and pederasty from lesbianism: All such behaviors were now to be classed alike and placed under the same heading.[6] Sexual identity was thus polarized around a central opposition defined by the binary play of sameness and difference in the sexes of the sexual partners; people belonged henceforward to one or the other of two exclusive categories, and much ingenuity was lavished on the multiplication of techniques for deciphering what a person's sexual orientation "really" was – independent, that is, of beguiling appearances.[7] Founded on positive, ascertainable, and objective behavioral phenomena – on the facts of who had sex with whom – the new sexual taxonomy could lay claim to a descriptive, trans-historical validity. And so it crossed the "threshold of scientificity"[8] and was enshrined as a working concept in the social sciences.[9]

A scientific advance of such magnitude naturally demanded to be crowned by the creation of a new technical vocabulary, but, unfortunately, no objective, value-free words readily lent themselves to the enterprise. In 1891, just one year before the inauguration of "homosexuality," John Addington Symonds could still complain that "The accomplished languages of Europe in the nineteenth century supply no terms for this persistent feature of human psychology, without importing some implication of disgust, disgrace, vituperation."[10] A number of linguistic candidates were quickly put forward to make good this lack, and "homosexuality" (despite scattered protests over the years) gradu-

ally managed to fix its social-scientistic signature upon the new conceptual dispensation. The word itself, as Havelock Ellis noted, is a barbarous neologism sprung from a monstrous mingling of Greek and Latin stock;[11] as such, it belongs to a rapidly growing lexical breed most prominently represented by the hybrid names given to other recent inventions – names whose mere enumeration suffices to conjure up the precise historical era responsible for producing them: e.g., "automobile," "television."

Unlike the language of technology, however, the new terminology for describing sexual behavior was slow to take root in the culture at large. In his posthumous autobiographical memoir, *My Father and Myself* (1968), J. R. Ackerley recalls how mystified he was when, about 1918, a Swiss friend asked him, "Are you homo or hetero?": "I had never heard either term before," he writes. Similarly, T. C. Worsley observes in his own memoir, *Flannelled Fool* (1966), that in 1929 "The word [homosexual], in any case, was not in general use, as it is now. Then it was still a technical term, the implications of which I was not entirely aware of."[12] These two memoirists, moreover, were not intellectually deficient men: At the respective times of their recorded bewilderment, Ackerley was shortly about to be, and Worsley already had been, educated at Cambridge. Nor was such innocence limited – in this one instance, at least – to the holders of university degrees: The British sociologist John Marshall, whose survey presumably draws on more popular sources, testifies that "a number of the elderly men I interviewed had never heard the term 'homosexual' until the 1950s."[13] The *Oxford English Dictionary*, originally published in 1933, is also ignorant of (if not willfully blind to) "homosexuality"; the word appears for the first time in the *OED*'s 1976 three-volume Supplement.[14]

It is not exactly my intention to argue that homosexuality, as we commonly understand it today, didn't exist before 1892. How, indeed, could it have failed to exist? The very word displays a most workmanlike and scientific indifference to cultural and environmental factors, looking only to the sexes of the persons engaged in the sexual act. Moreover, if homosexuality didn't exist before 1892, heterosexuality couldn't have existed either (it came into being, in fact, like Eve from Adam's rib, eight years later),[15] and without heterosexuality, where would all of us be right now?

The comparatively recent genesis of heterosexuality – strictly speaking, a twentieth-century affair

– should provide a clue to the profundity of the cultural issues over which, hitherto, I have been so lightly skating. How is it possible that until the year 1900 there was not a precise, value-free, scientific term available to speakers of the English language for designating what we would now regard, in retrospect, as the mode of sexual behavior favored by the vast majority of people in our culture? Any answer to that question – which, in its broadest dimensions, I shall leave for the intellectual heirs of Michel Foucault to settle – must direct our attention to the inescapable historicity of even the most innocent, unassuming, and seemingly objective of cultural representations. Although a blandly descriptive, rigorously clinical term like "homosexuality" would appear to be unobjectionable as a taxonomic device, it carries with it a heavy complement of ideological baggage and has, in fact, proved a significant obstacle to understanding the distinctive features of sexual life in the ancient world.[16] It may well be that homosexuality properly speaking has no history of its own much before the beginning of our century. For, as John Boswell remarks, "If the categories 'homosexual/heterosexual' and 'gay/straight' are the inventions of particular societies rather than real aspects of the human psyche, there is no gay history."[17]

II

Of course, if we are to believe Foucault, there are basic historical and cultural factors that prohibit the easy application of the concept of homosexuality to persons living in premodern societies. For homosexuality presupposes sexuality: It implies the existence of a separate, sexual domain within the larger field of man's psychophysical nature and it requires the conceptual demarcation and isolation of that domain from other, more traditional, territories of personal and social life that cut across it, such as carnality, venery, libertinism, virility, passion, amorousness, eroticism, intimacy, love, affection, appetite, and desire – to name but a few. The invention of homosexuality therefore had to await, in the first place, the eighteenth-century discovery and definition of sexuality as the total ensemble of physiological and psychological mechanisms governing the individual's genital functions and the concomitant identification of that ensemble with a specially developed part of the brain and nervous system; it had also to await, in the second place,

the early-nineteenth-century interpretation of sexuality as a singular "instinct" or "drive," a mute force that shapes our conscious life according to its own unassailable logic and thereby determines, at least in part, the character and personality of each one of us.[18]

Before the scientific construction of "sexuality" as a positive, distinct, and constitutive feature of individual human beings – an autonomous system within the physiological and psychological economy of the human organism – a person's sexual *acts* could be individually evaluated and categorized, but there was no conceptual apparatus available for identifying a person's fixed and determinate sexual *orientation*, much less for assessing and classifying it.[19] That human beings differ, often markedly, from one another in their sexual tastes in a great variety of ways (of which the liking for a sexual partner of a specific sex is only one, and not necessarily the most significant one) is an unexceptionable and, indeed, an ancient observation;[20] but it is not immediately evident that differences in sexual preference are by their very nature more revealing about the temperament of individual human beings, more significant determinants of personal identity, than, for example, differences in dietary preference.[21] And yet, it would never occur to us to refer a person's dietary object-choice to some innate, characterological disposition or to see in his or her strongly expressed and even unvarying preference for the white meat of chicken the symptom of a profound psychophysical orientation, leading us to identify him or her in contexts quite removed from that of the eating of food as, say, a "pectoriphage" or a "stethovore" (to continue the practice of combining Greek and Latin roots); nor would we be likely to inquire further, making nicer discriminations according to whether an individual's predilection for chicken breasts expressed itself in a tendency to eat them quickly or slowly, seldom or often, alone or in company, under normal circumstances or only in periods of great stress, with a clear or a guilty conscience ("ego-dystonic pectoriphagia"), beginning in earliest childhood or originating with a gastronomic trauma suffered in adolescence.[22] If such questions did occur to us, moreover, I very much doubt whether we would turn to the academic disciplines of anatomy, neurology, clinical psychology, or genetics in the hope of obtaining a clear causal solution to them. That is because (1) we regard the liking for certain foods as a matter of taste; (2) we currently lack a theory of taste; and (3) in the absence of a theory we do not normally subject our behavior to intense scientific or etiological scrutiny.

In the same way, it never occurred to premodern cultures to ascribe a person's sexual tastes to some positive, structural, or constitutive feature of his or her personality. Just as we tend to assume that human beings are not individuated at the level of dietary preference and that we all, despite many pronounced and frankly acknowledged differences from one another in dietary habits, share the same fundamental set of alimentary appetites, and hence the same "dieticity" or "edility," so most premodern and non-Western cultures, despite an awareness of the range of possible variations in human sexual behavior, refuse to individuate human beings at the level of sexual preference and assume, instead, that we all share the same fundamental set of sexual appetites, the same "sexuality." For most of the world's inhabitants, in other words, "sexuality" is no more a fact of life than "dieticity." Far from being a necessary or intrinsic constituent of the eternal grammar of human subjectivity, "sexuality" seems to be a uniquely modern, Western, even bourgeois production – one of those cultural fictions that in every society give human beings access to themselves as meaningful actors in their world, and that are thereby objectivated.

At any rate, positivism dies hard, and sexual essentialism (the belief in fixed sexual essences) dies even harder. Not everyone will welcome a neohistoricist critique of "sexuality." John Boswell, for example, has argued reasonably enough that any debate over the existence of universals in human culture must distinguish between the respective modes of being proper to words, concepts, and experiences: According to this line of reasoning, the ancients experienced gravity even though they lacked both the term and the concept; similarly, Boswell claims that the "manifest and stated purpose" of Aristophanes' famous myth in Plato's *Symposium* "is to explain why humans are divided into groups of predominantly homosexual or heterosexual interest," and so this text, along with a number of others, vouches for the existence of homosexuality as an ancient (if not a universal) category of human experience – however newfangled the word for it may be.[23] Now the speech of Plato's Aristophanes would seem indeed to be a *locus classicus* for the differentiation of homo from heterosexuality, because Aristophanes' taxonomy of human beings features a distinction between those who desire a sexual partner of the same sex as themselves and those who desire a sexual partner of a different sex. The Platonic passage alone, then, would seem to offer sufficient warrant for positing an ancient concept, if not an ancient experience, of homosexuality. But closer examination reveals that Aristophanes stops short of deriving a distinction between homo- and heterosexuality from his own myth just when the logic of his analysis would seem to have driven him ineluctably to it. That omission is telling – and it is worth considering in greater detail.

According to Aristophanes, human beings were originally round, eight-limbed creatures, with two faces and two sets of genitals – both front and back – and three sexes (male, female, and androgyne). These ancestors of ours were powerful and ambitious; in order to put them in their place, Zeus had them cut in two, their skin stretched over the exposed flesh and tied at the navel, and their heads rotated so as to keep that physical reminder of their daring and its consequences constantly before their eyes. The severed halves of each former individual, once reunited, clung to one another so desperately and concerned themselves so little with their survival as separate entities that they began to perish for lack of sustenance; those who outlived their mates sought out persons belonging to the same sex as their lost complements and repeated their embraces in a foredoomed attempt to recover their original unity. Zeus at length took pity on them, moved their genitals to the side their bodies now faced, and invented sexual intercourse, so that the bereaved creatures might at least put a temporary terminus to their longing and devote their attention to other, more important (if less pressing) matters. Aristophanes extracts from this story a genetic explanation of observable differences among human beings with respect to sexual object-choice and preferred style of life: males who desire females are descended from an original androgyne (adulterers come from this species), whereas males descended from an original male "pursue their own kind, and would prefer to remain single and spend their entire lives with one another, since by nature they have no interest in marriage and procreation but are compelled to engage in them by social custom" (191e–192b, quoted selectively). Boswell, understandably, interprets this to mean that, according to Plato's Aristophanes, homosexual and heterosexual interests are "both exclusive and innate."[24]

But that, significantly, is not quite the way Aristophanes sees it. The conclusions that he draws from his own myth help to illustrate the lengths to which classical Athenians were willing to go in order to avoid conceptualizing sexual behaviors according to a binary opposition between different- and same-sex sexual contacts. First of all, Aristophanes' myth generates not two but at least three distinct "sexualities" (males attracted to males, females attracted to females, and – consigned alike to a single classification, evidently – males attracted to females as well as females attracted to males). Moreover, there is not the slightest suggestion in anything Aristophanes says that the sexual acts or preferences of persons descended from an original female are in any way similar to, let alone congruent or isomorphic with, the sexual acts or preferences of those descended from an original male;[25] hence, nothing in the text allows us to suspect the existence of even an implicit category to which males who desire males and females who desire females *both* belong in contradistinction to some *other* category containing males and females who desire one another.[26] On the contrary, one consequence of the myth is to make the sexual desire of every human being *formally identical* to that of every other: We are all looking for the same thing in a sexual partner, according to Plato's Aristophanes – namely, a symbolic substitute for an originary object once loved and subsequently lost in an archaic trauma. In that respect we all share the same "sexuality" – which is to say that, despite the differences in our personal preferences or tastes, we are not individuated at the level of our sexual being.

Second, and equally important, Aristophanes' account features a crucial distinction *within* the category of males who are attracted to males, an infrastructural detail missing from his description of each of the other two categories: "while they are still boys [i.e., pubescent or preadult],[27] they are fond of men, and enjoy lying down together with them and twining their limbs about them, . . . but when they become men they are lovers of boys. . . . Such a man is a pederast and philerast [i.e., fond of or responsive to adult male lovers]"[28] at *different stages of his life* (*Symposium* 191e–192b, quoted selectively). Contrary to the clear implications of the myth, in other words, and unlike the people comprehended by the first two categories, those descended from an original male are *not* attracted to one another *without qualification*; rather, they desire boys when they are men and they take a certain (nonsexual) pleasure in physical contact with men when they are boys.[29] Now since – as the foregoing passage suggests – the classical Athenians sharply distinguished the roles of pederast and philerast, relegating them not only to different age-classes but virtually to different "sexualities,"[30] what Aristophanes is describing here is not a single, homogeneous sexual orientation common to all those who descend from an original male but rather a set of distinct and incommensurable behaviors that such persons exhibit in different periods of their lives; although his genetic explanation of the diversity of sexual object-choice among human beings would seem to require that there be some adult males who are sexually attracted to other adult males, Aristophanes appears to be wholly unaware of such a possibility, and in any case he has left no room for it in his taxonomic scheme.[31] That omission is all the more unexpected because, as Boswell himself has pointed out (in response to the present argument), the archetypal pairs of lovers from whom all homoerotically inclined males are supposed to descend must themselves have been the same age as one another, inasmuch as they were originally halves of the same being.[32] No age-matched couples figure among their latter-day offspring, however: The social reality described by Aristophanes features an erotic asymmetry absent from the mythical paradigm used to generate it. In the world of contemporary Athenian actuality – at least, as Aristophanes portrays it – reciprocal erotic desire among males is unknown.[33] Those who descend from an original male are not defined as male homosexuals but as willing boys when they are young and as lovers of youths when they are old. Contrary to Boswell's reading of the passage, then, neither the concept nor the experience of "homosexuality" is known to Plato's Aristophanes.

A similar conclusion can be drawn from careful examination of the other document from antiquity that might seem to vouch for the existence both of homosexuality as an indigenous category and of homosexuals as a native species. Unlike the myth of Plato's Aristophanes, a famous and much-excerpted passage from a classic work of Greek prose, the document to which I refer is little known and almost entirely neglected by modern historians of "sexuality";[34] its date is late, its text is corrupt, and, far from being a self-conscious literary artifact, it forms part of a Roman technical treatise. But despite its distance from Plato in time, in style, in language, and in intent, it displays the same remarkable innocence of modern sexual categories, and I have chosen to discuss it here partly in order to show what can be learned about the ancient world from texts that lie outside the received canon of classical authors. Let us turn, then, to the ninth chapter in the Fourth Book of *De morbis chronicis*, a mid-fifth-century AD Latin translation and adaptation by the African writer Caelius Aurelianus of a now largely lost work on chronic diseases by the Greek physician Soranus, who practiced and taught in Rome during the early part of the second century AD.

The topic of this chapter is *molles* (*malthakoi* in Greek) – that is, "soft" or unmasculine men who depart from the cultural norm of manliness insofar as they actively desire to be subjected by other men to a "feminine" (i.e., receptive) role in sexual intercourse. Caelius begins with an implicit defense of his own unimpeachable masculinity by noting how difficult it is to believe that such people actually exist;[35] he then goes on to observe that the cause of their affliction is not natural (that is, organic) but is rather their own excessive desire, which – in a desperate and foredoomed attempt to satisfy itself – drives out their sense of shame and forcibly converts parts of their bodies to sexual uses not intended by nature. These men willingly adopt the dress, gait, and other characteristics of women, thereby confirming that they suffer not from a bodily disease but from a mental (or moral) defect. After some further arguments in support of that point, Caelius draws an interesting comparison: "For just as the women called *tribades* [in Greek], because they practise both kinds of sex, are more eager to have sexual intercourse with women than with men and pursue women with an almost masculine jealousy . . . so they too [i.e., the *molles*] are afflicted by a mental disease" (132–3). The mental disease in question, which strikes both men and women alike and is defined as a perversion of sexual desire, would certainly seem to be nothing other than homosexuality as it is often understood today.

Several considerations combine to prohibit that interpretation, however. First of all, what Caelius treats as a pathological phenomenon is not the desire on the part of either men or women for sexual contact with a person of the same sex; quite the contrary: Elsewhere, in discussing the treatment of satyriasis (a state of abnormally elevated sexual desire accompanied by itching or tension in the genitals), he issues the following advice to people who suffer from it (*De morbis acutis*, 3.18.180–1).[36]

Do not admit visitors and particularly young women and boys. For the attractiveness of such visitors would again kindle the feeling of desire in the patient. Indeed, *even healthy persons*, seeing them, would in many cases seek sexual gratification, stimulated by the tension produced in the parts [i.e., in their own genitals].[37]

There is nothing medically problematical, then, about a desire on the part of males to obtain sexual pleasure from contact with males; what is of concern to Caelius,[38] as well as to other ancient moralists,[39] is the male desire to be sexually penetrated by males, for such a desire represents the voluntary abandonment of a "masculine" identity in favor of a "feminine" one. It is sex-role reversal, or *gender deviance*, that is problematized here and that also furnishes part of the basis for Caelius's comparison of *molles* to *tribades*, who assume a "masculine" role in their relations with other women and actively "pursue women with an almost *masculine* jealousy." Indeed, the "soft" – that is, sexually submissive – man, possessed of a shocking and paradoxical desire to surrender his masculine autonomy and precedence, is monstrous precisely because he seems to have "a woman's soul confined by a man's body" and thus to violate the deeply felt and somewhat anxiously defended sense of congruence on the part of the ancients between gender, sexual practices, and social identity.[40]

Second, the ground of the similitude between Caelius's *molles* and *tribades* is not that they are both homosexual but rather that they are both *bi*-sexual (in our terms). The *tribades* "are *more* eager to have sexual intercourse with women *than with men*" and "practise both kinds of sex" – that is, they have sex with both men and women.[41] As for the *molles*, Caelius's earlier remarks about their extraordinarily intense sexual desire implies that they turn to receptive sex because, although they try, they are not able to satisfy themselves by means of more conventionally masculine sorts of sexual activity, including insertive sex with women;[42] far from having desires that are structured differently from those of normal folk, these gender-deviants desire sexual pleasure just as most people do, but they have such strong and intense desires that they are driven to devise some unusual and disreputable (though ultimately futile) means of gratifying them. That diagnosis becomes explicit at the conclusion of the chapter when Caelius explains why the disease responsible for turning men into *molles* is the only chronic disease that becomes stronger as the body grows older (137).

> For in other years when the body is still strong and can perform the normal functions of love, the sexual desire [of these persons] assumes a dual aspect, in which the soul is excited sometimes while playing a passive and sometimes while playing an active role. But in the case of old men who have lost their virile powers, all their sexual desire is turned in the opposite direction and consequently exerts a stronger demand for the feminine role in love. In fact, many infer that this is the reason why boys too are victims of this affliction. For, like old men, they do not possess virile powers; that is, they have not yet attained those powers which have already deserted the aged.[43]

"Soft" or unmasculine men, far from being a fixed and determinate sexual species, are evidently either men who once experienced an orthodoxly masculine sexual desire in the past or who will eventually experience such a desire in the future. They may well be men with a constitutional tendency to gender-deviance, according to Caelius, but they are not homosexuals. Moreover, all the other ancient texts known to me that place in the same category both males who enjoy sexual contact with males and females who enjoy sexual contact with females display one or the other of the two taxonomic strategies employed by Caelius Aurelianus: If such men and women are classified alike, it is either because they are both held to *reverse* their proper sex roles and to adopt the sexual styles, postures, and modes of copulation conventionally associated with the opposite sex or because they are both held to *alternate* between the personal characteristics and sexual practices proper, respectively, to men and to women.[44] No category of homosexuality, defined in such a way as to contain men and women alike, is indigenous to the ancient world.

No scruple need prevent *us*, to be sure, from qualifying as "homosexual" any person who seeks sexual contact with another person of the same sex, whether male or female. But the issue before us isn't whether or not we can accurately apply our concept of homosexuality to the ancients – whether or not, that is, we can discover in the historical record of classical antiquity evidence of behaviors or psychologies that are amenable to classification in our own terms (obviously, we can, given the supposedly descriptive and trans-historical nature of those terms); the issue isn't even whether or not the ancients were able to express within the terms provided by their own conceptual schemes an experience of something approximating to homosexuality as we understand it today.[45] The real issue confronting any cultural historian of antiquity, and any critic of contemporary culture, is, first of all, how to recover the terms in which the experiences of individuals belonging to past societies were actually constituted and, second, how to measure and assess the differences between those terms and the ones we currently employ. For, as this very controversy over the scope and applicability of sexual categories illustrates, concepts in the human sciences – unlike in this respect, perhaps, concepts in the natural sciences (such as gravity) – do not merely describe reality but, at least partly, constitute it.[46] What this implies about the issue before us may sound paradoxical, but it is, I believe, profound – or, at least, worth pondering: Although there have been, in many different times and places (including classical Athens), persons who sought sexual contact with other persons of the same sex as themselves, it is only within the last hundred years or so that such persons (or some portion of them) have been homosexuals.

Instead of attempting to trace the history of "homosexuality" as if it were a *thing*, therefore, we might more profitably analyze how the significance of same-sex sexual contacts has been variously constructed over time by members of human living groups. Such an analysis will probably lead us into a plurality of only partly overlapping social and conceptual territories, a series of cultural formations that vary as their constituents change, combine in different sequences, or compose new patterns. In the following paragraphs I shall attempt to draw a very crude outline of the cultural formation underlying the classical Athenian institution of pederasty, an outline whose details will have to be filled in at some later point if this aspect of ancient Greek social relations is ever to be understood historically.

III

The attitudes and behaviors publicly displayed by the citizens of Athens (to whom the surviving evidence for the classical period effectively restricts our power to generalize) tend to portray sex not as a collective enterprise in which two or more persons jointly engage but rather as an action performed by one person upon another. The foregoing statement does not purport to describe positively what the experience of sex was "really" like for all members of Athenian society but to indicate how sex is *represented* by those utterances and actions of free adult males that were intended to be overheard and witnessed by other free adult males.[47] Sex, as it is constituted by this public, masculine discourse, is either act or impact: It is not knit up in a web of mutuality, not something one invariably has *with* someone. Even the verb *aphrodisiazein*, meaning "to have sex" or "to take active sexual pleasure," is carefully differentiated into an active and a passive form; the active form occurs, tellingly, in a late antique list (that we nonetheless have good reason to consider representative for ancient Mediterranean culture, rather than eccentric to it)[48] of acts that "do not regard one's neighbors but only the subjects themselves and are not done in regard to or through others: namely, speaking, singing, dancing, fist-fighting, competing, hanging oneself, dying, being crucified, diving, finding a treasure, having sex, vomiting, moving one's bowels, sleeping, laughing, crying, talking to the gods, and the like."[49] As John J. Winkler, in a commentary on this passage, observes, "It is not that second parties are not present at some of these events (speaking, boxing, competing, having sex, being crucified, flattering one's favorite divinity), but that their successful achievement does not depend on the cooperation, much less the benefit, of a second party."[50]

Not only is sex in classical Athens not intrinsically relational or collaborative in character; it is, further, a deeply polarizing experience: It serves to divide, to classify, and to distribute its participants into distinct and radically dissimilar categories. Sex possesses this valence, apparently, because it is conceived to center essentially on, and to define itself around, an asymmetrical gesture, that of the penetration of the body of one person by the body – and, specifically, by the phallus[51] – of another. Phallic penetration, moreover, is construed as sexual "activity"; even if a sexual act does not involve physical penetration, it still remains polarized by the distribution of phallic pleasure: The partner whose pleasure is promoted is considered "active," while the partner who puts his or her body *at the service* of another's pleasure is deemed "passive" – read "penetrated," in the culture's unself-conscious ideological shorthand. Sexual penetration, and

sexual "activity" in general, are, in other words, thematized as domination: The relation between the "active" and the "passive" sexual partner is thought of as the same kind of relation as that obtaining between social superior and social inferior, between master and servant.[52] "Active" and "passive" sexual roles are therefore necessarily isomorphic with superordinate and subordinate social status; hence, an adult, male citizen of Athens can have legitimate sexual relations only with statutory minors (his inferiors not in age but in social and political status): The proper targets of his sexual desire include, specifically, women, boys, foreigners, and slaves – all of them persons who do not enjoy the same legal and political rights and privileges that he does.[53] Furthermore, what a citizen does in bed reflects the differential in status that distinguishes him from his sexual partner: The citizen's superior prestige and authority express themselves by his sexual precedence – by his power to initiate a sexual act, his right to obtain pleasure from it, and his assumption of an "active" sexual role. What Paul Veyne has said about the Romans can apply equally well to the classical Athenians: They were indeed puritans when it came to sex, but (unlike modern bourgeois Westerners) they were not puritans about conjugality and reproduction; rather, like many Mediterranean peoples, they were puritans about virility.[54]

The very enterprise of inquiring into ancient Greek "sexuality," then, necessarily obscures the nature of the phenomenon it is designed to elucidate because it effectively isolates sexual norms from social practices and thereby conceals the strict sociological correspondences between them. In classical Athens sex, as we have seen, was not simply a private quest for mutual pleasure that absorbed, if only temporarily, the social identities of its participants. Sex was a manifestation of public status, a declaration of social identity; it did not so much express an individual's unique "sexuality" as it served to position social actors in the places assigned to them (by virtue of their political standing) in the hierarchical structure of the Athenian polity. Instead of reflecting the peculiar sexual orientation of individual Athenians, the sexual protocols of classical Athens reflected a marked division in the social organization of the city-state between a superordinate group, composed of citizens, and a subordinate group, composed of noncitizens; sex between members of the first group was practically inconceivable, whereas sex between a member of the first group and a member of the second group mirrored in the minute details of its hierarchical arrangement the relation of structured inequality that governed their wider social interaction. Far from being interpreted as an expression of commonality, as a sign of some shared sexual status or orientation, sex between social superordinate and subordinate served, at least in part, to articulate the social distance between them. To assimilate both the senior and the junior partner in a pederastic relationship to the same "sexuality," for example, would therefore have struck a classical Athenian as no less bizarre than to classify a burglar as an "active criminal," his victim as a "passive criminal," and the two of them alike as partners in crime[55] (burglary – like sex, as the Greeks understood it – is, after all, a "nonrelational" act). The sexual identities of the ancient Greeks – their experiences of themselves as sexual actors and as desiring human beings – were hardly autonomous; quite the contrary: They were inseparable from, if not determined by, their social identities, their outward, public standing. Indeed, the classical Greek record strongly supports the conclusion drawn (from a quite different body of evidence) by the French anthropologist Maurice Godelier: "It is not sexuality which haunts society, but society which haunts the body's sexuality."[56]

In classical Athens, then, sexual partners came in two different kinds – not male and female but active and passive, dominant and submissive.[57] The relevant features of a sexual object were not so much determined by a physical typology of genders as by the social articulation of power. That is why the currently fashionable distinction between homosexuality and heterosexuality had no meaning for the classical Athenians: There were not, so far as they knew, two different kinds of "sexuality," two differently structured psychosexual states or modes of affective orientation, but a single form of sexual experience, which all free adult males shared – making due allowance for variations in individual tastes, as one might make for individual palates. Thus, in the Third Dithyramb by the classical poet Bacchylides, the Athenian hero Theseus, voyaging to Crete among the seven youths and seven maidens destined for the Minotaur and defending one of the maidens from the sexual advances of the libidinous Cretan commander, warns him vehemently against molesting *any one* of the Athenian youths (*tin' êitheôn:* 43) – that is, any girl *or boy*. Conversely, the antiquarian *littérateur* Athenaeus,

writing six or seven hundred years later, is amazed that Polycrates, the tyrant of Samos in the sixth century BC, did not send for any boys *or women* along with the other luxury articles he imported to Samos for his personal use during his reign, "despite his passion for relations with males" (12.540c–e).[58] Now *both* the notion that an act of heterosexual aggression in itself makes the aggressor suspect of homosexual tendencies *and* the mirror-opposite notion that a person with marked homosexual tendencies is bound to hanker after heterosexual contacts are nonsensical to us, associating as we do sexual object-choice with a determinate kind of "sexuality," a fixed sexual nature, but it would be a monumental task indeed to enumerate all the ancient documents in which the alternative "boy or woman" occurs with perfect nonchalance in an erotic context, as if the two were functionally interchangeable.[59] Scholars sometimes describe this cultural formation as a bisexuality of penetration[60] or as a heterosexuality indifferent to its object,[61] but I think it would be more accurate to describe it as a single, undifferentiated phallic "sexuality" of penetration and domination, a socio-sexual discourse whose basic terms are phallus and non-phallus.[62]

If there is a lesson that historians should draw from this picture of ancient sexual attitudes and behaviors, it is that we need to de-center *sexuality* from the focus of the interpretation of sexual experience. Just because modern bourgeois Westerners are so obsessed with sexuality, so convinced that it holds the key to the hermeneutics of the self (and hence to social psychology as an object of historical study), we ought not therefore to conclude that everyone has always considered sexuality a basic and irreducible element in, or a central feature of, human life. On the contrary, if the sketch I have offered is accurate, it seems that many ancients conceived of "sexuality" in nonsexual terms: What was fundamental to their experience of sex was not anything *we* would regard as essentially sexual; rather, it was something essentially social – namely, the modality of power relations that informed and structured the sexual act. Instead of viewing public and political life as a dramatization of individual sexual psychology, as we often tend to do, they saw sexual behavior as an expression of the dominant themes in contemporary social relations. When Artemidorus, a master dream analyst who lived and wrote in the second century AD, came to address the meaning of sexual dreams, for example, he almost never presumed that such dreams were *really* about sex: They were about the rise and fall of the dreamer's public fortunes, the vicissitudes of his domestic economy.[63] If a man dreams of having sex with his mother, according to Artemidorus, his dream signifies nothing in particular about his own sexual psychology, his fantasy life, or the history of his relations with his parents; it may signify – depending on the family's circumstances at the time, the sexual postures of the partners in the dream, and the mode of penetration – that the dreamer will be successful in politics, that he will go into exile or return from exile, that he will win his lawsuit, obtain a rich harvest from his lands, or change professions, among many other things (1.79). Artemidorus' system of dream interpretation begs to be compared to the indigenous dream lore of certain Amazonian tribes, equally innocent of "sexuality," who (despite their quite different socio-sexual systems) also believe in the predictive value of dreams and similarly reverse what modern bourgeois Westerners take to be the natural flow of signification in dreams (i.e., from what is public and social to what is private and sexual): in both Kagwahiv and Mehinaku culture, for example, dreaming about the female genitalia portends a wound; dreamt wounds do not symbolize the female genitalia.[64]

To discover and to write the history of sexuality has long seemed to many a sufficiently radical undertaking in itself, inasmuch as its effect (if not the intention behind it) is to call into question the very naturalness of what we currently take to be essential to our individual natures. But in the course of implementing that ostensibly radical project many historians of sexuality seem to have reversed – perhaps unwittingly – its radical design: By preserving "sexuality" as a stable category of historical analysis not only have they not denaturalized it but, on the contrary, they have newly idealized it.[65] To the extent, in fact, that histories of "sexuality" succeed in concerning themselves with *sexuality*, to just that extent are they doomed to fail as *histories* (Foucault himself taught us that much), unless they also include as an integral part of their proper enterprise the task of demonstrating the historicity, conditions of emergence, modes of construction, and ideological contingencies of the very categories of analysis that undergird their own practice.[66] Instead of concentrating our attention specifically on the history of sexuality, then, we need to define and refine a new, and radical, historical sociology of psychology, an intellectual discipline designed to analyze the cultural poetics of desire, by which I mean the processes whereby sexual desires are constructed, mass-produced, and distributed among the various members of human living-groups.[67] We must train ourselves to recognize conventions of feeling as well as conventions of behavior and to interpret the intricate texture of personal life as an artefact, as the determinate outcome, of a complex and arbitrary constellation of cultural processes. We must, in short, be willing to admit that what seem to be our most inward, authentic, and private experiences are actually, in Adrienne Rich's admirable phrase, "shared, unnecessary/and political."[68]

Notes

An earlier version of this paper, taking the form of an extended book review of Harald Patzer's *Die griechische Knabenliebe* (Wiesbaden, 1982), appeared under the title "One Hundred Years of Homosexuality" in *The Mêtis of the Greeks*, ed. Milad Doueihi = *Diacritics*, 16, no. 2 (Summer 1986): 34–45. The present essay is closely based on this earlier work; it was first recast for delivery at a conference on "Homosexuality in History and Culture, and the University Curriculum," held at Brown University on 20–1 February 1987, and was later given as a public lecture at Duke University on 20 April 1987. For these more recent occasions I have eliminated the review format (and, hence, omitted consideration of Patzer's monograph), removed some of the documentation, supplemented the discussion of ancient sources, and translated into English citations from works in modern foreign languages. The most complete version of the essay will be found in my collection, *One Hundred Years of Homosexuality and Other Essays on Greek Love* (New York: Routledge, 1989).

The writing and revising of this paper have been generously supported by two fellowships, both funded by the Andrew W. Mellon Foundation, from the National Humanities Center and the Stanford Humanities Center, respectively. I am very grateful to Martha Nussbaum, for having invited me to speak at Brown, and to Peter Burian, for having invited me to speak at Duke, as well as to the audiences at both universities, for their sympathetic but rigorous scrutiny. I also wish to thank Barry D. Adam, Judith M. Bennett, Mary T. Boatwright, Elizabeth A. Clark, Kostas Demelis, Judith Ferster, Ernestine Friedl, Maud W. Gleason, Madelyn Gutwirth, Jean H. Hagstrum, Glenn W. Most, Cynthia B. Patterson, Daniel A. Pollock, Marilyn B. Skinner, Emery J. Snyder, Gregory Vlastos, and John J. Winkler for much friendly help and advice.

1. Wrongly, no doubt: The same entry in the *OED* records the use of the word by J. A. Symonds in a

letter of the same year, and so it is most unlikely that Chaddock alone is responsible for its English coinage. See R. W. Burchfield, ed., *A Supplement to the Oxford English Dictionary* (Oxford, 1976), 2:136, s.v. homosexuality.

2. The terms "homosexual" and "homosexuality" appeared in print for the first time in 1869 in two anonymous pamphlets published in Leipzig and composed, apparently, by Karl Maria Kertbeny. Kertbeny (né Benkert) was an Austro-Hungarian translator and *littérateur* of Bavarian extraction, not a physician (as Magnus Hirschfeld and Havelock Ellis – misled by false clues planted in those pamphlets by Kertbeny himself – maintained); he wrote in German under his acquired Hungarian surname and claimed (rather unconvincingly) in the second of the two tracts under discussion not to share the sexual tastes denominated by his own ingenious neologism. For the most reliable accounts of Kertbeny and his invention, see Manfred Herzer, "Kertbeny and the Nameless Love," *Journal of Homosexuality*, 12.1 (1985): 1–26, and, now, Hubert Kennedy, *Ulrichs: The Life and Works of Karl Henrich Ulrichs, Pioneer of the Modern Gay Movement* (Boston, 1988), pp. 149–56. See also John Lauritsen and David Thorstad, *The Early Homosexual Rights Movement (1864–1935)* (New York: Times Change Press, 1974), pp. 6–8; Jean-Claude Féray, "Une histoire critique du mot homosexualité," *Arcadie* 28, nos. 325–8 (1981): 11–21, 115–24, 171–81, 246–58; Wayne Dynes, *Homolexis: A Historical and Cultural Lexicon of Homosexuality*, Gai Saber Monograph No. 4 (New York: Gay Academic Union, 1985), p. 67, who notes that Kertbeny's term "might have gone unnoticed had not [Kertbeny's friend] Gustav Jaeger popularized it in the second edition of his *Entdeckung der Seele* (1880)." The earlier of Kertbeny's two pamphlets is reprinted in the *Jahrbuch für sexuelle Zwischenstufen* 7 (1905): 1–66.

3. George Chauncey, Jr., "From Sexual Inversion to Homosexuality: Medicine and the Changing Conceptualization of Female Deviance," in *Homosexuality: Sacrilege, Vision, Politics*, ed. Robert Boyers and George Steiner = *Salmagundi* 58–9 (1982–3): 114–46 (quotation on p. 116). Cf. Michel Foucault, *The History of Sexuality, Volume I: An Introduction*, trans. Robert Hurley (New York, 1978), pp. 37–8; Féray, "Une histoire," esp. pp. 16–17, 246–56; Jeffrey Weeks, "Discourse, Desire and Sexual Deviance: Some Problems in a History of Homosexuality," in *The Making of the Modern Homosexual*, ed. Kenneth Plummer (London: Hutchinson, 1981), pp. 76–111, esp. 82ff.; John Marshall, "Pansies, Perverts and Macho Men: Changing Conceptions of Male Homosexuality," in *The Making of the Modern Homosexual*, pp. 133–54; Arnold I. Davidson, "Closing Up the Corpses: Diseases of Sexuality and the Emergence

of the Psychiatric Style of Reasoning," in *Reason, Language and Method: Essays in Honour of Hilary Putnam*, ed. George Boolos (Cambridge, forthcoming). To be sure, the formal introduction of "inversion" as a clinical term (by Arrigo Tamassia, "Sull' inversione dell' istinto sessuale," *Rivista sperimentale di freniatria e di medicina legale* 4 [1878]: 97–117: the earliest published use of "inversion" that Havelock Ellis, *Sexual Inversion = Studies in the Psychology of Sex*, vol. 2, 3d ed. [Philadelphia, 1922]: 3, was able to discover) occurred a decade *after* Kertbeny's coinage of "homosexuality," but Ellis suspected the word of being considerably older: It seems to have been well established by the 1870s, at any rate, and it was certainly a common designation throughout the 1880s. "Homosexuality," by contrast, did not begin to achieve currency in Europe until the Eulenburg affair of 1907–8 (see Féray, "Une histoire," pp. 116–22), and even thereafter it was slow in gaining ascendancy. The main point, in any case, is that "inversion," defined as it is by reference to gender deviance, represents an age-old outlook, whereas "homosexuality" marks a sharp break with traditional ways of thinking.

4. Chauncey, "From Sexual Inversion to Homosexuality," esp. pp. 117–22, citing W. C. Rivers, "A New Male Homosexual Trait (?)," *Alienist and Neurologist* 41 (1920): 22–7; the persistence of this outlook in the United States, along with some of its practical (military, legal, and ecclesiastical) applications, has now been documented by Chauncey, "Christian Brotherhood or Sexual Perversion? Homosexual Identities and the Construction of Sexual Boundaries in the World War One Era," *Journal of Social History* 19 (1985): 189–211, in a study of the role-specific morality that once governed sexual attitudes and practices among members of the United States Navy. For even more recent expressions of the traditional outlook in Great Britain, see the citations discussed by Marshall, "Pansies, Perverts, and Macho Men," pp. 149–52. Cf., also, Albert J. Reiss, Jr., "The Social Integration of Queers and Peers," *Social Problems* 9 (1961/62): 102–20, with references to earlier work; John H. Gagnon and William Simon, *Sexual Conduct: The Social Sources of Human Sexuality* (Chicago, 1973), pp. 240–51; and, esp., Jack H. Abbott, "On 'Women,' " *New York Review of Books*, 28, no. 10 (June 11, 1981): 17. The classic statement of the "inversion" thesis is the opening chapter of Proust's *Sodom and Gomorrah*: see Marcel Proust, *À la recherche du temps perdu*, ed. Pierre Clarac and André Ferré (Paris, 1954), 2: 601–32, esp. 614–15, 620–2; *Remembrance of Things Past*, trans. C. K. Scott Moncrieff and Terence Kilmartin (New York, 1981), 2: 623–56, esp. 637–8, 643–5.

5. See Chauncey, "From Sexual Inversion to Homosexuality," pp. 122–5; Marshall, "Pansies, Perverts

and Macho Men," pp. 137–53; Arnold I. Davidson, "How to Do the History of Psychoanalysis: A Reading of Freud's *Three Essays on the Theory of Sexuality*," in *The Trial(s) of Psychoanalysis*, ed. Françoise Meltzer, *Critical Inquiry* 13 (1986/87): 252–77, esp. 258–71; Jerome Neu, "Freud and Perversion," in *Sexuality and Medicine*, ed. Earl E. Shelp, Philosophy and Medicine, 22–3 (D. Reidel: Dordrecht, 1987), 1: 153–84, esp. 153ff. For the modern distinction between "inversion" (i.e., sex-role reversal) and "homosexuality," see C. A. Tripp, *The Homosexual Matrix* (New York, 1975), pp. 22–35.

6. For the lack of congruence between traditional and modern sexual categories, cf. Gilbert H. Herdt, ed., *Ritualized Homosexuality in Melanesia* (Berkeley, 1984), pp. viii–x; Gianni De Martino and Arno Schmitt, *Kleine Schriften zu zwischenmännlicher Sexualität und Erotik in der muslimischen Gesellschaft* (Berlin: author, 1985), esp. pp. 3–10. The new scientific conceptualization of homosexuality reflects, to be sure, a much older habit of mind, distinctive to northern and northwestern Europe since the Renaissance, whereby sexual acts are categorized not according to the modality of sexual or social roles assumed by the sexual partners but rather according to the anatomical sex of the persons engaged in them: see Randolph Trumbach, "London's Sodomites: Homosexual Behavior and Western Culture in the 18th Century," *Journal of Social History* 11 (1977): 1–33, esp. 2–9, with notes. This habit of mind seems to have been shaped, in its turn, by the same aggregate of cultural factors responsible for the much older division, accentuated during the Renaissance, between European and Mediterranean marriage-patterns; northern and northwestern Europe typically exhibits a pattern of marriage between mature coevals, a bilateral kinship system, neolocal marriage, and a mobile labor force, whereas Mediterranean societies are characterized by late male and early female marriage, patrilineal kinship organization, patrivirilocal marriage, and inhibited circulation of labor: see R. M. Smith, " 'The People of Tuscany and their Families in the Fifteenth Century: Medieval or Mediterranean?' " *Journal of Family History* 6 (1981): 107–28; recent work has produced evidence for the antiquity of the Mediterranean marriage-pattern: see M. K. Hopkins, "The Age of Roman Girls at Marriage," *Population Studies* 18 (1964/65): 309–27; Richard P. Saller, "Men's Age at Marriage and Its Consequences in the Roman Family," *Classical Philology* 82 (1987): 21–34, esp. 30; Martha T. Roth, "Age at Marriage and the Household: A Study of Neo-Babylonian and Neo-Assyrian Forms," *Comparative Studies in Society and History* 29 (1987): 715–47.

7. E.g., K. Freund, "A Laboratory Method for Diagnosing Predominance of Homo- or Hetero-Erotic Interest in the Male," *Behavior Research and Therapy* 1 (1963–64): 85–93; N. McConaghy, "Penile Volume Change to Moving Pictures of Male and Female Nudes in Heterosexual and Homosexual Males," *Behavior Research and Therapy* 5 (1967): 43–8. For a partial, and critical, review of the literature on testing procedures, see Bernard F. Riess, "Psychological Tests in Homosexuality," in *Homosexual Behavior: A Modern Reappraisal*, ed. Judd Marmor (New York, 1981), pp. 296–311. Compare the parallel tendency in the same period to determine the "true sex" of hermaphrodites: see Michel Foucault's introduction to *Herculine Barbin, Being the Recently Discovered Memoirs of a Nineteenth-Century French Hermaphrodite*, trans. Richard McDougall (New York, 1980), esp. pp. vii–xi.

8. See Foucault, *The Archaeology of Knowledge and the Discourse on Language*, trans. A. M. Sheridan Smith (New York, 1972), p. 190, for the introduction of this concept; for its application to the history of sexual categories, see Arnold I. Davidson, "Sex and the Emergence of Sexuality," *Critical Inquiry* 14 (1987/88): 16–48, esp. 48.

9. On the emergence of the concept of homosexuality, see Jeffrey Weeks, " 'Sins and Diseases': Some Notes on Homosexuality in the Nineteenth Century," *History Workshop* 1 (1976): 211–19, and *Sex, Politics and Society: The Regulation of Sexuality since 1800* (London, 1981), esp. pp. 96–121; also, Marshall, "Pansies, Perverts and Macho Men." For a lucid discussion of the sociological implications, see Mary McIntosh, "The Homosexual Role," *Social Problems* 16 (1968/69): 182–92, who also examines some of the quasi-theological refinements ("bisexuality," "latent homosexuality," "pseudo-homosexuality") that have been added to this intellectual structure in order to buttress its central concept.

10. *A Problem in Modern Ethics*, quoted by Jeffrey Weeks, *Coming Out: Homosexual Politics in Britain, from the Nineteenth Century to the Present* (London, 1977), p. 1.

11. While condemning "homosexuality" as "a bastard term compounded of Greek and Latin elements" (p. 2), Ellis acknowledged that its classical etymology facilitated its diffusion throughout the European languages; moreover, by consenting to employ it himself, Ellis helped further to popularize it. On the philological advantages and disadvantages of "homosexuality," see Féray, "Une histoire," pp. 174–6.

12. This passage, along with others in a similar vein, has been well discussed by Marshall.

13. Marshall, "Pansies, Perverts and Macho Men," p. 148, who goes on to quote the following passage from the preface to a recent survey by D. J. West, *Homosexuality Reassessed* (London, 1977), p. vii: "A generation ago the word homosexuality was best avoided in polite conversation, or referred to in

muted terms appropriate to a dreaded and scarcely mentionable disease. Even some well-educated people were hazy about exactly what it meant." Note, however, that Edward Westermarck, writing for a scholarly audience in *The Origin and Development of the Moral Ideas*, could allude to "what is nowadays commonly called homosexual love" (2: 456) as early as 1908. Westermarck's testimony has escaped the *OED* Supplement, which simply records that in 1914 George Bernard Shaw felt free to use the word "homosexual" adjectivally in the *New Statesman* without further explanations and that the adjective reappears in *Blackwood's Magazine* in 1921 as well as in Robert Graves's *Good-bye to All That* in 1929. The French version of "homosexuality," by contrast, showed up in the *Larousse mensuel illustré* as early as December 1907 (according to Féray, "Une histoire," p. 172).

14. The earliest literary occurrence of the German loan-word "homosexualist," of which the *OED* is similarly ignorant, took place only in 1925, to the best of my knowledge, and it illustrates the novelty that evidently still attached to the term: In Aldous Huxley's *Those Barren Leaves* we find the following exchange between a thoroughly modern aunt and her up-to-date niece, who are discussing a mutual acquaintance.

> "I sometimes doubt," [Aunt Lilian] said, "whether he takes any interest in women at all. Fundamentally, unconsciously, I believe he's a homosexualist."
>
> "Perhaps," said Irene gravely. She knew her Havelock Ellis. [Part III, Chapter 11]

(The earliest occurrence of "homosexualist" cited in the *OED* Supplement dates from 1931.)

15. According, once again, to the dubious testimony of the *OED*'s 1976 Supplement, 2:85, s.v. heterosexuality. (Note that Kertbeny, the coiner of the term "homosexual," opposed it not to "heterosexual" but to *normalsexual*: Féray, "Une histoire," p. 171.) On the dependence of "heterosexuality" on "homosexuality," see ibid., pp. 171–2; Harold Beaver, "Homosexual Signs (*In Memory of Roland Barthes*)," *Critical Inquiry* 8 (1981/82): 99–119, esp. 115–16.

16. Some doubts about the applicability of the modern concept of homosexuality to ancient varieties of sexual experience have been voiced by George Devereux, "Greek Pseudo-Homosexuality and the 'Greek Miracle,'" *Symbolae Osloenses* 42 (1968): 60–92, esp. 71–6; W. Thomas MacCary, *Childlike Achilles: Ontogeny and Phylogeny in the ILIAD* (New York, 1982), pp. 178–85; Bernard Sergent, *Homosexuality in Greek Myth*, trans. Arthur Goldhammer (Boston, 1986), pp. 46–7.

17. John Boswell, "Revolutions, Universals and Sexual Categories," *Salmagundi* 58–9 (1982–3): 89–113 [see

ch. 21 this volume]. Boswell himself, however, argues for the contrary position, which has been most baldly stated by Vern L. Bullough, *Homosexuality: A History* (New York, 1979), pp. 2, 62: "Homosexuality has always been with us; it has been a constant in history, and its presence is clear." Opponents of the view advocated by Boswell and Bullough can be found in Guy Hocquenghem, *Homosexual Desire*, trans. Daniella Dangoor (London, 1978), esp. pp. 36–7; Paul Veyne, "La famille et l'amour sous le Haut-Empire romain," *Annales (E.S.C.)* 33 (1978): 35–63, esp. 52; Robert A. Padgug, "Sexual Matters: On Conceptualizing Sexuality in History," *Radical History Review* 20 (1979): 3–23; Weeks, *Sex, Politics and Society*, esp. pp. 96–121; Alan Bray, *Homosexuality in Renaissance England* (London: Gay Men's Press, 1982), esp. pp. 8–9, 13–32; Gayle Rubin, "Thinking Sex: Notes for a Radical Theory of the Politics of Sexuality," in *Pleasure and Danger: Exploring Female Sexuality*, ed. Carole S. Vance (Boston, 1984), pp. 267–319, esp. 285–6; De Martino and Schmitt, *Kleine Schriften*; Davidson, "Sex and the Emergence of Sexuality"; and, most pertinently, the essays collected in Plummer, ed., *The Making of the Modern Homosexual*. Additional fuel for the fires of historicism can be found in the writings of those who attempt to relate the rise of homosexuality to the rise of capitalism: see Hocquenghem; Jeffrey Weeks, "Capitalism and the Organisation of Sex," in *Homosexuality: Power & Politics*, ed. Gay Left Collective (London, 1980), pp. 11–20; Dennis Altman, *The Homosexualization of America* (New York, 1982), esp. pp. 79–107; John D'Emilio, "Capitalism and Gay Identity," in *Powers of Desire: The Politics of Sexuality*, ed. Ann Snitow, Christine Stansell, and Sharon Thompson (New York, 1983), pp. 100–13; Barry D. Adam, "Structural Foundations of the Gay World," *Comparative Studies in Society and History* 27 (1985): 658–71.

18. See Foucault, *The History of Sexuality*, pp. 68–9, and *The Use of Pleasure*, The History of Sexuality, vol. 2., trans. Robert Hurley (New York, 1985), pp. 35–52; Weeks, "Capitalism and the Organisation of Sex," p. 13 (paraphrasing Foucault): "Our culture has developed a notion of sexuality linked to reproduction and genitality and to 'deviations' from these. . . ."; Féray, "Une histoire," pp. 247–51; Davidson, "How to Do the History of Psychoanalysis," pp. 258–62; Thomas Laqueur, "Orgasm, Generation, and the Politics of Reproductive Biology," in *Sexuality and the Social Body in the Nineteenth Century*, ed. Catherine Gallagher and Thomas Laqueur, *Representations* 14 (Spring 1986): 1–41. The biological conceptualization of "sexuality" as an instinct is neatly disposed of by Tripp, *The Homosexual Matrix*, pp. 10–21.

19. See Foucault, *The History of Sexuality*, p. 43: "As defined by the ancient civil or canonical codes, sodomy was a category of forbidden acts; their perpetrator was nothing more than the juridical subject of them. The nineteenth-century homosexual became a personage, a past, a case history, and a childhood, in addition to being a type of life, a life form, and a morphology, with an indiscreet anatomy and possibly a mysterious physiology. Nothing that went into his total composition was unaffected by his sexuality. It was everywhere present in him: at the root of all his actions because it was their insidious and indefinitely active principle; written immodestly on his face and body because it was a secret that always gave itself away. It was consubstantial with him, less as a habitual sin than as a singular nature." Cf. Trumbach, "London's Sodomites," p. 9; Weeks, *Coming Out*, p. 12; Richard Sennett, *The Fall of Public Man* (New York, 1977), pp. 6–8; Padgug, "Sexual Matters," pp. 59–60; Féray, "Une histoire," pp. 246–7; Alain Schnapp, "Une autre image de l'homosexualité en Grèce ancienne," *Le Débat* 10 (March 1981): 107–17, esp. 116 (speaking of Attic vase-paintings): "One does not paint acts that characterize persons so much as behaviors that distinguish groups"; Pierre J. Payer, *Sex and the Penitentials: The Development of a Sexual Code 550–1150* (Toronto, 1984), pp. 40–4, esp. 40–1: "There is no word in general usage in the penitentials for homosexuality as a category. . . . Furthermore, the distinction between homosexual acts and people who might be called homosexuals does not seem to be operative in these manuals. . . ."

20. For ancient expressions by males of a sexual preference for males, see, e.g., Theognis, 1367–8; Euripides, *Cyclops* 583–4; Xenophon, *Anabasis* 7.4.7–8; Aeschines, *Against Timarchus* 41, 195; the fragment of Seleucus quoted by Athenaeus, 15.697de (= J. U. Powell, ed., *Collectanea Alexandrina* [Oxford, 1925], p. 176); an anonymous dramatic fragment cited by Plutarch, *Amatorius* 766f–767a (= August Nauck, ed., *Tragicorum Graecorum Fragmenta*, 2d ed. [Leipzig, 1926], p. 906, #355 [also in Kock, *Com. Att. Fr.*, 3:467, #360]); Athenaeus, 12.540e, 13.601e and ff.; Achilles Tatius, 2.35.2–3; pseudo-Lucian *Erôtes* 9–10; Airmicus Maternus, *Mathesis* 7.15.1–2; and a number of epigrams by various hands contained in the *Palatine Anthology*: V, 19, 65, 116, 208, 277, 278; XI, 216; XII, 7, 17, 87, 145, 192, 198, and *passim*. See, generally, K. J. Dover, *Greek Homosexuality* (London, 1978), pp. 62–3; Boswell, "Revolutions, Universals, and Sexual Categories," pp. 98–101; John J. Winkler, "Unnatural Acts: Erotic Protocols in Artemidorus' Dream Analysis," in *The Constraints of Desire: The Anthropology of Sex and Gender in Ancient Greece* (New York, 1989).

21. Foucault, *The Use of Pleasure*, pp. 51–2, remarks that it would be interesting to determine exactly when in the evolving course of Western cultural history sex became more morally problematic than eating; he seems to think that sex won out only at the turn of the eighteenth century, after a long period of relative equilibrium during the middle ages: see, also, *The Use of Pleasure*, p. 10; "On the Genealogy of Ethics: An Overview of Work in Progress," in Hubert L. Dreyfus and Paul Rabinow, *Michel Foucault: Beyond Structuralism and Hermeneutics*, 2d ed. (Chicago, 1983), pp. 229–52, esp. 229; *The Care of the Self*, The History of Sexuality, vol. 3, trans. Robert Hurley (New York, 1986), p. 143. For a discussion of Foucault's approach to "the history of sexuality," see my review of the original French edition of *The Use of Pleasure*: "Sexual Ethics and Technologies of the Self in Classical Greece," *American Journal of Philology* 107 (1986): 274–86, where I observe that the evidence newly assembled by Caroline Walker Bynum, *Holy Feast and Holy Fast: The Religious Significance of Food to Medieval Women* (Berkeley, 1987) suggests that moral evolution may not have been quite such a continuously linear affair as Foucault appears to imagine. (See, also, note 22.)

22. See, however, Stephen Nissenbaum, *Sex, Diet, and Debility in Jacksonian America: Sylvester Graham and Health Reform*, Contributions in Medical History, vol. 4 (Westport, Conn.: 1980), for an example from relatively recent history of the possible linkage between sexual and dietary morality. Hilary Putnam, *Reason, Truth and History* (Cambridge, 1981), pp. 150–5, in the course of analyzing the various criteria by which we judge matters of taste to be "subjective," argues that we are right to consider sexual preferences more thoroughly constitutive of the human personality than dietary preferences, but his argument remains circumscribed, as Putnam himself emphasizes, by highly culture-specific assumptions about sex, food, and personhood.

23. Boswell, "Revolutions, Universals, and Sexual Categories," pp. 21–7. Bullough, *Homosexuality*, p. 3, similarly appeals to Aristophanes' myth as "one of the earliest explanations" of homosexuality.

24. Boswell, "Revolutions, Universals, and Sexual Categories," p. 25; cf. Auguste Valensin, "Platon et la théorie de l'amour," *Études* 281 (1954): 32–45, esp. 37.

25. Something like this point is implicit in Luc Brisson, "Bisexualité et médiation en Grèce ancienne," *Nouvelle revue de psychanalyse* 7 (1973): 27–48, esp. 42–3; see also Neu, "Freud and Perversions," p. 177, n. 1. My own (somewhat different) reading of Aristophanes' speech is set forth in greater detail in "Platonic *Erôs* and What Men Call Love," *Ancient Philosophy* 5 (1985): 161–204, esp. 167–70; I have reproduced some of my earlier formulations here.

26. To be sure, a certain symmetry does obtain between the groups composed, respectively, of those making a homosexual and those making a heterosexual object-choice: Each of them is constituted by Aristophanes in such a way as to contain both males and females in their dual capacities as subjects and objects of erotic desire. Aristophanes does nothing to highlight this symmetry, however, and it may be doubted whether it should figure in our interpretation of the passage.

27. The term "boy" (*pais* in Greek) refers by convention to the junior partner in a pederastic relationship, or to one who plays that role, regardless of his actual age; youths are customarily supposed to be desirable between the onset of puberty and the arrival of the beard: see Dover, *Greek Homosexuality*, pp. 16, 85–7; Félix Buffière, *Eros adolescent: la pédérastie dans la Grèce antique* (Paris, 1980), pp. 605–14; N. M. Kay, *Martial Book XI: A Commentary* (London, 1985), pp. 120–1.

28. On the meaning of the term "philerast," see Elaine Fantham, "*Zêlotypia:* A Brief Excursion into Sex, Violence, and Literary History," *Phoenix* 40 (1986): 45–57, esp. 48, n. 10.

29. For an explication of what is meant by "a certain (nonsexual) pleasure in physical contact with men," see note 33.

30. See Dover, *Greek Homosexuality*, esp. pp. 73–109; a general survey of this issue together with the scholarship on it can be found in my essay, "Plato and Erotic Reciprocity," *Classical Antiquity* 5 (1986): 60–80.

31. Nor does Aristophanes make any allowance in his myth for what was perhaps the most widely shared sexual taste among his fellow Athenian citizens – namely, an undifferentiated liking for good-looking women and boys (that is, a sexual preference not defined by an exclusively gender-specific sexual object-choice). Such a lacuna should warn us not to treat Aristophanes' myth as a simple description or reflection of contemporary experience.

32. Public lecture delivered at Brown University, 21 February 1987.

33. In "Plato and Erotic Reciprocity," I have argued that – in this one respect, at least – the picture drawn by Plato's Aristophanes, *if* taken to represent *the moral conventions* governing sexual behavior in classical Athens rather than the reality of sexual behavior itself – is historically accurate. To be sure, the pederastic ethos of classical Athens did not prohibit a willing boy from responding enthusiastically to his lover's physical attentions: Aristophanes himself maintains that a philerast both "enjoys" and "welcomes" (*khairein, aspazesthai*: 191e–192b) his lover's embraces. But that ethos did stipulate that whatever enthusiasm a boy exhibited for sexual contact with his lover sprang from sources other than sexual desire. The distinction between "welcom-

ing" and "desiring" a lover's caresses, as it applies to the motives for a boy's willingness, spelled the difference between decency and degeneracy; that distinction is worth emphasizing here because the failure of modern interpreters to observe it has led to considerable misunderstanding (as when historians of sexuality, for example, misreading the frequent depictions on Attic black-figure pottery of a boy leaping into his lover's arms, take those paintings to be evidence for the strength of the junior partner's sexual desire). A very few Greek documents seem truly ambiguous on this point, and I have reviewed their testimony in some detail in the notes to "Plato and Erotic Reciprocity": see esp. p. 64, nn. 10 and 11; p. 66, n. 14.

34. The notable exceptions are Bullough, *Homosexuality*, pp. 3–5, who cites it as evidence for the supposed universality of homosexuality in human history, and John Boswell, *Christianity, Social Tolerance, and Homosexuality: Gay People in Western Europe from the Beginning of the Christian Era to the Fourteenth Century* (Chicago, 1980), pp. 53n, 75n.

35. See P. H. Schrijvers, *Eine medizinische Erklärung der männlichen Homosexualität aus der Antike (Caelius Aurelianus DE MORBIS CHRONICIS IV 9)* (Amsterdam: B. R. Grüner, 1985), p. 11.

36. I have borrowed this entire argument from Schrijvers, pp. 7–8; the same point had been made earlier by Boswell, p. 53, n. 33.

37. Translation, with emphasis added, by I. E. Drabkin, ed. and trans., *Caelius Aurelianus: ON ACUTE DISEASES and ON CHRONIC DISEASES* (Chicago, 1950), p. 413.

38. As the chapter title, "De mollibus *sive subactis*," implies.

39. See, esp., the pseudo-Aristotelian *Problemata* 4.26, well discussed by Dover, *Greek Homosexuality*, pp. 168–70; by Boswell, *Christianity*, p. 53; and by Winkler, "Unnatural Acts"; generally, Foucault, *The Use of Pleasure*, pp. 204–14.

40. Compare Aeschines, *Against Timarchus* 185: Timarchus is "a man who is male in body but has committed a woman's transgressions" and has thereby "outraged himself contrary to nature" (discussed by Dover, *Greek Homosexuality*, pp. 60–8). On the ancient figure of the *kinaidos*, or *cinaedus*, the man who actively desires to submit himself passively to the sexual uses of other men, see the essays by John J. Winkler and by Maud W. Gleason in *Before Sexuality: The Construction of Erotic Experience in the Ancient Greek World*, ed. Halperin, Winkler, and Froma I. Zeitlin (Princeton, 1989). Davidson, "Sex and the Emergence of Sexuality," p. 22, is therefore quite wrong to claim that "Before the second half of the nineteenth century persons of a determinate anatomical sex could not be thought to be really, that is, psychologically, of the opposite sex."

41. The Latin phrase *quod utranque Venerem exerceant* is so interpreted by Drabkin, *Caelius Aurelianus*, p. 901n., and by Schrijvers, *Eine medizinische Erklärung*, 32–3, who secures this reading by citing Ovid, *Metamorphoses* 3.323, where Teiresias, who had been both a man and a woman, is described as being learned in the field of *Venus utraque*. Compare Petronius, *Satyricon* 43.8: *omnis minervae homo*.

42. I follow, once again, the insightful commentary by Schrijvers, p. 15.

43. I quote from the translation by Drabkin, p. 905, which is based on his plausible, but nonetheless speculative, reconstruction (accepted by Schrijvers, p. 50) of a desperately corrupt text.

44. Anon., *De physiognomonia* 85 (vol. ii, p. 114.5–14 Förster); Vettius Valens, 2.16 (p. 76.3–8 Kroll); Clement of Alexandria, *Paedagogus* 3.21.3; Firmicus Maternus, *Mathesis* 6.30.15–16 and 7.25.3–23 (esp. 7.25.5).

45. Thus, Boswell, "Revolutions, Universals, and Sexual Categories," argues that the term "pederast," at least as it is applied to Gnathon by Longus in *Daphnis and Chloe* 4.11, is "obviously a conventional term for 'homosexual' " (p. 478 n. 10) and he would presumably place a similar construction on *paiderastês* and *philerastês* in the myth of Plato's Aristophanes, dismissing my interpretation as a terminological quibble or as a misguided attempt to reify lexical entities into categories of experience.

46. For a philosophical defense and qualification of this claim (and of other, similarly "constructionist," claims), see Ian Hacking, "Making Up People," in *Reconstructing Individualism: Autonomy, Individuality, and the Self in Western Thought*, ed. Thomas C. Heller, Morton Sosna, and David E. Wellbery, with Arnold I. Davidson, Ann Swidler, and Ian Watt (Stanford, 1986), pp. 222–36, 347–8.

47. On the characteristic failure of "culturally dominant ideologies" actually to dominate all sectors of a society, and for a demonstration of their greater pertinence to the dominant than to the dominated classes, see Nicholas Abercrombie, Stephen Hill, and Bryan S. Turner, *The Dominant Ideology Thesis* (London, 1980), esp. pp. 70–127.

48. See Winkler, "Unnatural Acts."

49. Artemidorus, *Oneirocritica* 1.2 (pp. 8.21–9.4 Pack).

50. Winkler, "Unnatural Acts."

51. I say "phallus" rather than "penis" because (1) what qualifies as a phallus in this discursive system does not always turn out to be a penis (see note 62) and (2) even when phallus and penis have the same extension, or reference, they still do not have the same intention, or meaning: "Phallus" betokens not a specific item of the male anatomy *simpliciter* but that same item *taken under the description* of a cultural signifier; (3) hence, the meaning of "phallus" is ultimately determined by its function in the larger socio-sexual discourse: i.e., it is that which penetrates, that which enables its possessor to play an "active" sexual role, and so forth: see Gayle Rubin, "The Traffic in Women: Notes on the 'Political Economy' of Sex," in *Toward an Anthropology of Women*, ed. Rayna R. Reiter (New York, 1975), pp. 157–210, esp. 190–2.

52. Foucault, *The Use of Pleasure*, p. 215.

53. In order to avoid misunderstanding, I should emphasize that by calling all persons belonging to these four groups "statutory minors," I do not wish either to suggest that they enjoyed the *same* status as one another or to obscure the many differences in status that could obtain between members of a single group – e.g., between a wife and a courtesan – differences that may not have been perfectly isomorphic with the legitimate modes of their sexual use. Nonetheless, what is striking about Athenian social usage is the tendency to collapse such distinctions as did indeed obtain between different categories of social subordinates and to create a single opposition between them all, *en masse*, and the class of adult male citizens. On this point, see Mark Golden, *"Pais*, 'Child' and 'Slave,' " *L'Antiquité classique* 54 (1985): 91–104, esp. 101 and 102, n. 38.

54. Veyne, "La famille et l'amour," p. 55, and "Homosexuality in Ancient Rome," in *Western Sexuality: Practice and Precept in Past and Present Times*, ed. Philippe Ariès and André Béjin, trans. Anthony Forster (Oxford, 1985), pp. 26–35. Cf. Alan Dundes, Jerry W. Leach, and Bora Özkök, "The Strategy of Turkish Boys' Verbal Dueling Rhymes," *Journal of American Folklore* 83 (1970): 325–49, supplemented and qualified by Mark Glazer, "On Verbal Dueling Among Turkish Boys," *Journal of American Folklore* 89 (1976): 87–9; J. M. Carrier, "Mexican Male Bisexuality," in *Bisexualities: Theory and Research*, ed. Fritz Klein and Timothy J. Wolf = *Journal of Homosexuality* 11.1–2 (1985): 75–85; De Martino and Schmitt, *Kleine Schriften*, esp. pp. 3–22; Michael Herzfeld, *The Poetics of Manhood: Contest and Identity in a Cretan Mountain Village* (Princeton, 1985).

55. I have borrowed this analogy from Arno Schmitt, who uses it to convey what the modern sexual categories would look like from a traditional Islamic perspective: see De Martino and Schmitt, *Kleine Schriften*, p. 19.

56. Maurice Godelier, "The Origins of Male Domination," *New Left Review* 127 (May–June 1981): 3–17 (quotation on p. 17); see, also, Godelier, "Le sexe comme fondement ultime de l'ordre social et cosmique chez les Baruya de Nouvelle-Guinée. Mythe et réalité," in *Sexualité et pouvoir*, ed. Armando Verdiglione (Paris, 1976), pp. 268–306, esp. 295–6.

57. The same point is made, in the course of an otherwise unenlightening (from the specialist's point of

view) survey of Greek social relations, by Bernard I. Murstein, *Love, Sex, and Marriage through the Ages* (New York, 1974), p. 58.

58. Cf. Padgug, "Sexual Matters," p. 3.

59. See Dover, *Greek Homosexuality*, pp. 63–7, for an extensive, but partial, list.

60. "Une bisexualité de sabrage": Veyne, "La famille et l'amour," pp. 50–5; cf. the critique by Ramsay MacMullen, "Roman Attitudes to Greek Love," *Historia* 32 (1983): 484–502. Other scholars who describe the ancient behavioral phenomenon as "bisexuality" include Brisson, "Bisexualité"; Schnapp, "Une autre image," esp. pp. 116–17; Hans Kelsen, "Platonic Love," trans. George B. Wilbur, *American Imago* 3 (1942): 3–110, esp. 40–1; Lawrence Stone, "Sex in the West," *The New Republic*, July 8, 1985, pp. 25–37, esp. 30–2 (with doubts). *Contra*, Padgug, "Sexual Matters," p. 59: "to speak, as is common, of the Greeks as 'bisexual' is illegitimate as well, since that merely adds a new, intermediate category, whereas it was precisely the categories themselves which had no meaning in antiquity."

61. Cf. T. M. Robinson, review of Dover, *Greek Homosexuality*, in *Phoenix* 35 (1981): 160–3, esp. 162: "The reason why a heterosexual majority might have looked with a tolerant eye on 'active' homosexual practice among the minority, and even in some measure within their own group [!], . . . is predictably a sexist one: to the heterosexual majority, to whom (in a man's universe) the 'good' woman is *kata physin* [i.e., naturally] passive, obedient, and submissive, the 'role' of the 'active' homosexual will be tolerable precisely because his goings-on can, without too much difficulty, be equated with the 'role' of the male *hetero*sexual, i.e., to dominate and subdue; what the two have in common is greater than what divides them." But this seems to me to beg the very question that the distinction between heterosexuality and homosexuality is supposedly designed to solve.

62. By "phallus" I mean a culturally constructed signifier of social power: for the terminology, see note 51. I call Greek sexuality phallic because (1) sexual contacts are polarized around phallic action – i.e., they are defined by who has the phallus and by what is done with it; (2) sexual pleasures other than phallic pleasures do not count in categorizing sexual contacts; (3) in order for a contact to qualify as sexual, one – and no more than one – of the two partners is required to have a phallus (boys are treated in pederastic contexts as essentially un-phallused [see Martial, 11.22; but cf. *Palatine Anthology* XII: 3, 7, 197, 207, 216, 222, 242] and tend to be assimilated to women; in the case of sex between women, one partner – the "tribad" – is assumed to possess a phallus-equivalent [an over-developed clitoris] and to penetrate the other: Sources for the ancient conceptualization of the tribad – no complete modern

study of this fascinating and long-lived fictional type, which survived into the early decades of the twentieth century, is known to me – have been assembled by Friedrich Karl Forberg, *Manual of Classical Erotology*, trans. Julian Smithson [Manchester, 1884; repr. New York, 1966], 2:108–67; Gaston Vorberg, *Glossarium eroticum* [Hanau, 1965], pp. 654–5; Werner A. Krenkel, "Masturbation in der Antike," *Wissenschaftliche Zeitschrift der Wilhelm-Pieck-Universität Rostock* 28 [1979]: 159–78, esp. 171; see, now, Judith P. Hallett, "Female Homoeroticism and the Denial of Roman Reality in Latin Literature," *Yale Journal of Criticism*, 3.1 [1989]).

63. Foucault, *The Care of the Self*, pp. 3–36, esp. 26–34; S. R. F. Price, "The Future of Dreams: From Freud to Artemidorus," *Past and Present* 113 (November, 1986): 3–37, abridged in *Before Sexuality*.

64. See Waud H. Kracke, "Dreaming in Kagwahiv: Dream Beliefs and Their Psychic Uses in an Amazonian Indian Culture," *The Psychoanalytic Study of Society* 8 (1979): 119–71, esp. 130–2, 163 (on the predictive value of dreams) and 130–1, 142–5, 163–4, 168 (on the reversal of the Freudian direction of signification – which Kracke takes to be a culturally constituted defense mechanism and which he accordingly undervalues); Thomas Gregor, " 'Far, Far Away My Shadow Wandered . . .': The Dream Symbolism and Dream Theories of the Mehinaku Indians of Brazil," *American Ethnologist* 8 (1981): 709–20, esp. 712–13 (on predictive value) and 714 (on the reversal of signification), largely recapitulated in Thomas Gregor, *Anxious Pleasures: The Sexual Lives of an Amazonian People* (Chicago, 1985), pp. 152–61, esp. 153.

65. Cf. Davidson, "Sex and the Emergence of Sexuality," p. 16.

66. Cf. Padgug, "Sexual Matters," p. 55: "In any approach that takes as predetermined and universal the categories of sexuality, real history disappears."

67. My conclusion coincides exactly with that of Jeffrey Weeks, "Discourse, Desire and Sexual Deviance," p. 111: "Social processes construct subjectivities not just as 'categories' but at the level of individual desires. This perception . . . should be the starting point for future social and historical studies of 'homosexuality' and indeed of 'sexuality' in general." Stephen Greenblatt, "Fiction and Friction," in *Reconstructing Individualism*, ed. Heller, Sosna, and Wellbury, pp. 30–52, 329–32, esp. 34, makes a similar point; arguing that "a culture's sexual discourse plays a critical role in shaping individuality," he goes on to say, "it does so by helping to implant in each person an internalized set of dispositions and orientations that governs individual improvisations."

68. "Translations" (1972), lines 32–3, in Adrienne Rich, *Diving into the Wreck: Poems 1971–1972* (New York, 1973), pp. 40–1 (quotation on p. 41).

23

Sexual Indifference and Lesbian Representation

Teresa de Lauretis

> If it were not lesbian, this text would make no sense
>
> Nicole Brossard, *L'Amèr*

There is a sense in which lesbian identity could be assumed, spoken, and articulated conceptually as political through feminism – and, current debates to wit, *against* feminism; in particular through and against the feminist critique of the Western discourse on love and sexuality, and therefore, to begin with, the rereading of psychoanalysis as a theory of sexuality and sexual difference. If the first feminist emphasis on sexual difference as gender (woman's difference from man) has rightly come under attack for obscuring the effects of other differences in women's psychosocial oppression, nevertheless that emphasis on sexual difference did open up a critical space – a conceptual, representational, and erotic space – in which women could address themselves to women. And in the very act of assuming and speaking from the position of subject, a woman could concurrently recognize women as subjects *and* as objects of female desire.

It is in such a space, hard-won and daily threatened by social disapprobation, censure, and denial, a space of contradiction requiring constant reaffirmation and painful renegotiation, that the very notion of sexual difference could then be put into question, and its limitations be assessed, both *vis-à-vis* the claims of other, not strictly sexual, differences, and with regard to sexuality itself. It thus appears that "sexual difference" is the term of a conceptual paradox corresponding to what is in effect a real contradiction in women's lives: the term, at once, of a sexual *difference* (women are, or want, something different from men) and of a sexual *indifference* (women are, or want, the same as men). And it seems to me that the racist and class-biased practices legitimated in the notion of "separate but equal" reveal a very similar paradox in the liberal ideology of pluralism, where social difference is also, at the same time, social indifference.

The psychoanalytic discourse on female sexuality, wrote Luce Irigaray in 1975, outlining the terms of what here I will call sexual (in)difference, tells "that *the feminine occurs only within models and laws devised by male subjects.* Which implies that there are not really two sexes, but only one. A single practice and representation of the sexual."[1] Within the conceptual frame of that *sexual indifference*, female desire for the self-same, an other female self, cannot be recognized. "That a woman might desire a woman 'like' herself, someone of the 'same' sex, that she might also have auto- and homosexual appetites, is simply incomprehensible" in the phallic regime of an asserted sexual difference between man and woman which is predicated on the contrary, on a complete indifference for the "other" sex, woman's. Consequently, Irigaray continues, Freud was at a loss with his homosexual female patients, and his analyses of them were really about male homosexuality. "The object choice of the homosexual woman is [understood to be] determined by a *masculine* desire and tropism" – that is, precisely, the turn of so-called sexual difference into sexual indifference, a single practice and representation of the sexual.

So there will be no female homosexuality, just a hommo-sexuality in which woman will be involved in the process of specularizing the phallus, begged to maintain the desire for the same that man has, and will ensure at the same time, elsewhere and in complementary and contradictory fashion, the perpetuation in the couple of the pole of "matter."[2]

With the term *hommo-sexuality* [*hommo-sexualité*] – at times also written *hom(m)osexuality* [*hom(m)osexualité*] – Irigaray puns on the French word for man, *homme*, from the Latin *homo* (meaning "man"), and the Greek *homo* (meaning "same"). In taking up her distinction between homosexuality (or homo-sexuality) and "hommosexuality" (or "hom(m)osexuality"), I want to re-mark the conceptual distance between the former term, homosexuality, by which I mean lesbian (or gay) sexuality, and the diacritically marked hommo-sexuality, which is the term of sexual indifference, the term (in fact) of heterosexuality; I want to re-mark both the incommensurable distance between them and the conceptual ambiguity that is conveyed by the two almost identical acoustic images. Another paradox – or is it perhaps the same?

There is no validation for sodomy found in the teaching of the ancient Greek philosophers Plato or Aristotle.
Michael Bowers, Petitioner's Brief in
Bowers v. *Hardwick*

To attempt to answer that question, I turn to a very interesting reading of Plato's *Symposium* by David Halperin which (1) richly resonates with Irigaray's notion of sexual indifference (see also her reading of "Plato's Hystera" in *Speculum*), (2) emphasizes the embarrassing ignorance of the present Attorney General of the State of Georgia in matters of classical scholarship, which he nevertheless invokes,[3] and (3) traces the roots of the paradoxes here in question to the very philosophical foundation of what is called Western civilization, Plato's dialogues. For in those master texts of hommo-sexuality, as Halperin proposes, it is the female, reproductive body that paradoxically guarantees true eros between men, or as Plato calls it, "proper paederasty."[4]

"Why Is Diotima a Woman?," Halperin argues, is a question that has been answered only tautologically: because she is not or cannot be a man. It would have been indecorous to imply that Socrates owed his knowledge of erotic desire to a former paederastic lover. But there is a reason more stringent than decorum why Socrates's teacher should have been a woman. Plato wanted to prescribe a

new homoerotic ethos and a model of "proper paederasty" based on the reciprocity of erotic desire and a mutual access to pleasure for both partners, a reciprocity of eros whose philosophical import found ultimate expression in the dialogue form. His project, however, ran against the homoerotic sexual ethos and practices of the citizens of classical Athens, "locked as they were into an aggressive, phallic sexuality of domination – and, consequently, into a rigid hierarchy of sexual roles in their relations with males and females alike." For an adult male citizen of Athens could have legitimate sexual relations only with his social inferiors: boys, women, foreigners, and slaves. Plato repudiated such erotic asymmetry in relations between men and boys and, through the teaching of Socrates/Diotima, sought to erase "the distinction between the active and the passive partner – according to Socrates, both members of the relationship become active, desiring lovers; neither remains a merely passive object of desire."

Hence the intellectual and mythopoetic function of Diotima: her discourse on erotic desire, unlike a man's, could appear directly grounded in the experiential knowledge of a non-hierarchical, mutualistic and reproductive sexuality, i.e., female sexuality as the Greeks construed it. It is indeed so grounded in the text, both rhetorically (Diotima's language systematically conflates sexual pleasure with the reproductive or generative function) and narratively, in the presumed experience of a female character, since to the Greeks female sexuality differed from male sexuality precisely in that sexual pleasure for women was intimately bound up with procreation. Halperin cites many sources from Plato's *Timaeus* to various ritual practices which represented, for example, "the relation of man to wife as a domestic form of cultivation homologous to agriculture whereby women are tamed, mastered, and made fruitful. . . . [I]n the absence of men, women's sexual functioning is aimless and unproductive, merely a form of rottenness and decay, but by the application of male pharmacy it becomes at once orderly and fruitful."

After remarking on the similarity between the Greek construction and the contemporary gynaecological discourses on female eroticism, Halperin raises the question of Plato's politics of gender, noting that "the interdependence of sexual and reproductive capacities is in fact a feature of male, not female, physiology," and that male sexuality is the one in which "sexual pleasure and reproductive function cannot be separated (to the chagrin of

Augustine and others)." His hypothesis is worth quoting at length:

> Plato, then, would seem to be interpreting as feminine and allocating to men a form of sexuality which is masculine to begin with and which men had previously alienated from themselves by constructing it as feminine. In other words, it looks as if what lies behind Plato's doctrine is a double movement whereby men project their own sexuality onto women only to reabsorb it themselves in the guise of a feminine character. This is particularly intriguing because it suggests that in order to facilitate their own appropriation of the feminine men have initially constructed femininity according to a male paradigm while creating a social and political ideal of masculinity defined by the ability to isolate what only women can *actually* isolate – namely, sexuality and reproduction, recreative and procreative sex.

Let me restate the significance of Halperin's analysis for my own argument here. Plato's repudiation of asymmetrical paederasty and of the subordinate position in which that placed *citizen* boys, who, after all, were the future rulers of Athens, had the effect of elevating the status of all male *citizens* and thus of consolidating *male citizen* rule. It certainly was no favor done to women or to any "others" (male and female foreigners, male and female slaves). But his move was yet more masterful: the appropriation of the feminine for the erotic ethos of a male social and intellectual elite (an ethos that would endure well into the twentieth century, if in the guise of "heretical ethics" or in the femininity ["*devenir-femme*"] claimed by his most deconstructive critics)[5] had the effect not only of securing the millenary exclusion of women from philosophical dialogue, and the absolute excision of non-reproductive sexuality from the Western discourse on love. The construction and appropriation of femininity in Western erotic ethos has also had the effect of securing the heterosexual social contract by which all sexualities, all bodies, and all "others" are bonded to an ideal/ ideological hierarchy of males.[6]

The intimate relationship of sexual (in)difference with social (in)difference, whereby, for instance, the defense of the mother country and of (white) womanhood has served to bolster colonial conquest and racist violence throughout Western history, is nowhere more evident than in "the teaching of the ancient Greek philosophers," *pace* the Attorney General. Hence the ironic rewriting of history, in a female-only world of mothers and amazons, by Monique Wittig and Sande Zeig in *Lesbian Peoples: Material for a Dictionary*.[7] And hence, as well, the crucial emphasis in current feminist theory on articulating, specifying, and historicizing the position of the female social subject in the intricate experiential nexus of (often contradictory) heterogeneous differences, across discourses of race, gender, cultural, and sexual identity, and the political working through those differences toward a new, global, yet historically specific and even local, understanding of community.[8]

> Pardon me, I must be going!
> Djuna Barnes, *The Ladies' Almanack*

Lesbian representation, or rather, its condition of possibility, depends on separating out the two contrary undertows that constitute the paradox of sexual (in)difference, on isolating but maintaining the two senses of homosexuality and hommo-sexuality. Thus the critical effort to dislodge the erotic from the discourse of gender, with its indissoluble knot of sexuality and reproduction, is concurrent and interdependent with a rethinking of what, in most cultural discourses and sociosexual practices, is still, nevertheless, a gendered sexuality. In the pages that follow, I will attempt to work through these paradoxes by considering how lesbian writers and artists have sought variously to escape gender, to deny it, transcend it, or perform it in excess, and to inscribe the erotic in cryptic, allegorical, realistic, camp, or other modes of representation, pursuing diverse strategies of writing and of reading the intransitive and yet obdurate relation of reference to meaning, of flesh to language.

Gertrude Stein, for example, "encrypted" her experience of the body in obscure coding, her "somagrams" are neither sexually explicit or conventionally erotic, nor "radically visceral or visual," Catharine Stimpson argues.[9] Stein's effort was, rather, to develop a distinguished "anti-language" in which to describe sexual activity, her "delight in the female body" (38) or her ambivalence about it, as an abstract though intimate relationship where "the body fuses with writing itself" (36), an act "at once richly pleasurable and violent" (38). But if Stein does belong to the history of women writers, claims Stimpson, who also claims her for the history of lesbian writers, it is not because she wrote out of femaleness "as an elemental condition, inseparable from the body" (40), the way some radical feminist critics would like to think; nor because her writing sprung from a preoedipal, maternal body, as others would have it. Her language was not "female" but quite the contrary, "as genderless as an atom of platinum" (42), and strove to obliterate the boundaries of gender identity.

Djuna Barnes's *Nightwood*, which Stimpson calls a "parable of damnation,"[10] is read by others as an affirmation of inversion as homosexual difference. In her "Writing Toward *Nightwood*: Djuna Barnes's Seduction Stories," Carolyn Allen reads Barnes's "little girl" stories as sketches or earlier trials of the sustained meditation on inversion that was to yield in the novel the most suggestive portrait of the invert, the third sex.

> In that portrait we recognize the boy in the girl, the girl in the Prince, not a mixing of gendered behaviors, but the creation of a new gender, "neither one and half the other". . . . In their love of the same sex [Matthew, Nora and Robin] admire their non-conformity, their sexual difference from the rest of the world.[11]

That difference, which for the lesbian includes a relation to the self-same ("a woman is yourself caught as you turn in panic; on her mouth you kiss your own," says Nora), also includes her relation to the child, the "ambivalence about mothering one's lover," the difficult and inescapable ties of female sexuality with nurture and with violence. In this light, Allen suggests, may we read Barnes's personal denial of lesbianism and her aloofness from female admirers as a refusal to accept and to live by the homophobic categories promoted by sexology: man and woman, with their respective deviant forms, the effeminate man and the mannish woman – a refusal that in the terms of my argument could be seen as a rejection of the hommo-sexual categories of gender, a refusal of sexual (in)difference.

Thus the highly metaphoric, oblique, allusive language of Barnes's fiction, her "heavily embedded and often appositional" syntax, her use of the passive voice, indirect style, and interior monologue techniques in narrative descriptions, which Allen admirably analyzes in another essay, are motivated less by the modernist's pleasure in formal experimentation than by her resistance to what *Nightwood* both thematizes and demonstrates, the failure of language to represent, grasp, and convey her subjects: "The violation [of reader's expectation] and the appositional structure permit Barnes to suggest that the naming power of language is insufficient to make Nora's love for Robin perceivable to the reader."[12]

> "Dr. Knox," Edward began, "my problem this week is chiefly concerning restrooms."
>
> Judy Grahn, "The Psychoanalysis of Edward the Dyke"

Ironically, since one way of escaping gender is to so disguise erotic and sexual experience as to suppress any representation of its specificity, another avenue of escape leads the lesbian writer fully to embrace gender, if by replacing femaleness with masculinity, as in the case of Stephen Gordon in *The Well of Loneliness*, and so risk to collapse lesbian homosexuality into hommo-sexuality. However, representation is related to experience by codes that change historically and, significantly, reach in both directions: the writer struggles to inscribe experience in historically available forms of representation, the reader accedes to representation through her own historical and experiential context; each reading is a rewriting of the text, each writing a rereading of (one's) experience. The contrasting readings of Radclyffe Hall's novel by lesbian feminist critics show that each critic reads from a particular position, experiential but also historically available to her, and, moreover, a position chosen, or even politically assumed, from the spectrum of contemporary discourses on the relationship of feminism to lesbianism. The contrast of interpretations also shows to what extent the paradox of sexual (in)difference operates as a semiotic mechanism to produce contradictory meaning effects.

The point of contention in the reception of a novel that by general agreement was the single most popular representation of lesbianism in fiction, from its obscenity trial in 1928 to the 1970s, is the figure of its protagonist Stephen Gordon, the "mythic mannish lesbian" of the title of Esther Newton's essay, and the prototype of her more recent incarnation, the working-class butch.[13] Newton's impassioned defense of the novel rests on the significance of that figure for lesbian self-definition, not only in the 1920s and 1930s, when the social gains in gender independence attained by the New Woman were being reappropriated via sexological discourses within the institutional practices of heterosexuality, but also in the 1970s and 1980s, when female sexuality has been redefined by a women's movement "that swears it is the enemy of traditional gender categories and yet validates lesbianism as the ultimate form of femaleness" (558).

Newton argues historically, taking into account the then available discourses on sexuality which asserted that "normal" women had at best a reactive heterosexual desire, while female sexual deviancy articulated itself in ascending categories of inversion marked by increasing masculinization, from deviant – but rectifiable – sexual orientation (or "homosexuality" proper, for Havelock Ellis) to congenital inversion. Gender crossing was at once a symptom and a sign of sexual degeneracy.[14] In the terms of the cultural representations available to the novelist, since there was no image of female sexual desire apart from the male, Newton asks, "Just how was Hall to make the woman-loving New Woman a sexual being? . . . To become avowedly sexual, the New Woman had to enter the male world, either as a heterosexual on male terms (a flapper) or as – or with – a lesbian in male body drag (a butch)" (572–3). Gender reversal in the mannish lesbian, then, was not merely a claim to male social privilege or a sad pretense to male sexual behavior, but represented what may be called, in Foucault's phrase, a "reverse discourse": an assertion of sexual agency and feelings, but autonomous from men, a reclaiming of erotic drives directed toward women, of a desire for women that is not to be confused with woman identification.

While other lesbian critics of *The Well of Loneliness* read it as an espousal of Ellis's views, couched in religious romantic imagery and marred by a self-defeating pessimism, aristocratic self-pity, and inevitable damnation, what Newton reads in Stephen Gordon and in Radclyffe Hall's text is the unsuccessful attempt to represent a female desire not determined by "masculine tropism," in Irigaray's words, or, in my own, a female desire not hommosexual but homosexual. If Radclyffe Hall herself could not envision homosexuality as part of an autonomous female sexuality (a notion that has emerged much later, with the feminist critique of patriarchy as phallic symbolic order), and if she therefore did not succeed in escaping the hommosexual categories of gender ("Unlike Orlando, Stephen is trapped in history; she cannot declare gender an irrelevant game," as Newton remarks [570]), nevertheless the figure of the mannish female invert

continues to stand as the representation of lesbian desire against both the discourse of hommosexuality and the feminist account of lesbianism as woman identification. The context of Newton's reading is the current debate on the relationship of lesbianism to feminism and the reassertion, on the one hand, of the historical and political importance of gender roles (e.g., butch-femme) in lesbian self-definition and representation, and on the other, of the demand for a separate understanding of sex and gender as distinct areas of social practice.

The latter issue has been pushed to the top of the theoretical agenda by the polarization of opinions around the two adverse and widely popularized positions on the issue of pornography taken by Women Against Pornography (WAP) and by S/M lesbians (Samois). In "Thinking Sex," a revision of her earlier and very influential "The Traffic in Women," Gayle Rubin wants to challenge the assumption that feminism can contribute very much to a theory of sexuality, for "feminist thought simply lacks angles of vision which can encompass the social organization of sexuality."[15] While acknowledging some (though hardly enough) diversity among feminists on the issue of sex, and praising "pro-sex" feminists such as "lesbian sadomasochists and butch-femme dykes," adherents of "classic radical feminism," and "unapologetic heterosexuals" for not conforming to "movement standards of purity" (303), Rubin nonetheless believes that a "theory and politics specific to sexuality" must be developed apart from the theory of gender oppression, that is feminism. Thus she goes back over her earlier feminist critique of Lacan and Lévi-Strauss and readjusts the angle of vision:

> "The Traffic in Women" was inspired by the literature on kin-based systems of social organization. It appeared to me at the time that gender and desire were systematically intertwined in such social formations. This may or may not be an accurate assessment of the relationship between sex and gender *in tribal organizations.* But it is surely not an adequate formulation for sexuality *in Western industrial societies.* (307, emphasis added)

In spite of Rubin's rhetorical emphasis (which I underscore graphically in the above passage), her earlier article also had to do with gender and sexuality in Western industrial societies, where indeed Rubin and several other feminists were articulating the critique of a theory of symbolic signification that elaborated the very notion of desire (from psychoanalysis) in relation to gender as symbolic construct (from anthropology) – a critique that has been crucial to the development of feminist theory. But whereas "The Traffic in Women" (a title directly borrowed from Emma Goldman) was focused on women, here her interest has shifted toward a non-gendered notion of sexuality concerned, in Foucault's terms, "with the sensations of the body, the quality of pleasures, and the nature of impressions."[16]

Accordingly, the specificity of either female or lesbian eroticism is no longer a question to be asked in "Thinking Sex," where the term "homosexual" is used to refer to both women and men (thus sliding inexorably, it seems, into its uncanny hommo-sexual double), and which concludes by advocating a politics of "theoretical as well as sexual pluralism" (309). At the opposite pole of the debate, Catharine MacKinnon argues:

> If heterosexuality is the dominant gendered form of sexuality in a society where gender oppresses women through sex, sexuality and heterosexuality are essentially the same thing. This does not erase homosexuality, it merely means that sexuality in that form may be no less gendered.[17]

I suggest that, despite or possibly because of their stark mutual opposition and common reductivism, both Rubin and MacKinnon collapse the tension of ambiguity, the semantic duplicity, that I have tried to sort out in the two terms homosexual and hommo-sexual, and thus remain caught in the paradox of sexual (in)difference even as they both, undoubtedly, very much want to escape it, one by denying gender, the other by categorically asserting it. As it was, in another sense, with Radclyffe Hall, Newton's suggestive reading notwithstanding. I will return to her suggestions later on.

A theory in the flesh
Cherríe Moraga, *This Bridge Called My Back*

It is certain, however, as Rubin notes, that "lesbians are *also* oppressed as queers and perverts" (308, emphasis added), not only as women; and it is equally certain that some lesbians are also oppressed as queers and perverts, and *also* as women of color. What cannot be elided in a politically responsible theory of sexuality, of gender, or of culture is the

critical value of that "also," which is neither simply additive nor exclusive but signals the nexus, the mode of operation of *interlocking* systems of gender, sexual, racial, class, and other, more local categories of social stratification.[18] Just a few lines from *Zami*, Audre Lorde's "biomythography," will make the point, better than I can.

> But the fact of our Blackness was an issue that Felicia and I talked about only between ourselves. Even Muriel seemed to believe that as lesbians, we were all outsiders and all equal in our outsiderhood. "We're all niggers," she used to say, and I hated to hear her say it. It was wishful thinking based on little fact; the ways in which it was true languished in the shadow of those many ways in which it would always be false.
>
> . . .
>
> It was hard enough to be Black, to be Black and female, to be Black, female, and gay. To be Black, female, gay, and out of the closet in a white environment, even to the extent of dancing in the Bagatelle, was considered by many Black lesbians to be simply suicidal. And if you were fool enough to do it, you'd better come on so tough that nobody messed with you. I often felt put down by their sophistication, their clothes, their manners, their cars, and their femmes.[19]

If the black/white divide is even less permeable than the gay/straight one, it does not alone suffice to self-definition: "Being Black dykes together was not enough. We were different. . . . Self-preservation warned some of us that we could not afford to settle for one easy definition, one narrow individuation of self" (226). Neither race nor gender nor homosexual difference alone can constitute individual identity or the basis for a theory and a politics of social change. What Lorde suggests is a more complex image of the psycho-socio-sexual subject ("our place was the very house of difference rather [than] the security of any one particular difference") which does not deny gender or sex but transcends them. Read together with the writings of other lesbians of color or those committed to antiracism (see note 8 above), Lorde's image of the house of difference points to a conception of community not pluralistic but at once global and local – global in its inclusive and macro-political strategies, and local in its specific, micro-political practices.

I want to propose that, among the latter, not the least is the practice of writing, particularly in that form which the *québecoise* feminist writer Nicole Brossard has called "*une fiction théorique*," fiction/ theory: a formally experimental, critical and lyrical, autobiographical and theoretically conscious, practice of writing-in-the-feminine that crosses genre boundaries (poetry and prose, verbal and visual modes, narrative and cultural criticism), and instates new correlations between signs and meanings, inciting other discursive mediations between the symbolic and the real, language and flesh.[20] And for all its specific cultural, historical, and linguistic variation – say between francophone and anglophone contemporary Canadian writers, or between writers such as Gloria Anzaldúa, Michelle Cliff, Cherríe Moraga, Joanna Russ, Monique Wittig, or even the Virginia Woolf of *Three Guineas* and *A Room of One's Own* – the concept of fiction/theory does make the transfer across borderlines and covers a significant range of practices of lesbian (self-)representation.

Lesbians are not women
Monique Wittig, "The Straight Mind"

In a superb essay tracing the intertextual weave of a lesbian imagination throughout French literature, the kind of essay that changes the landscape of both literature and reading irreversibly, Elaine Marks proposes that to undomesticate the female body one must dare reinscribe it in excess – as excess – in provocative counterimages sufficiently outrageous, passionate, verbally violent and formally complex to both destroy the male discourse on love and redesign the universe.[21] The undomesticated female body that was first *concretely* imaged in Sappho's poetry ("she is suggesting equivalences between the physical symptoms of desire and the physical symptoms of death, not between Eros and Thanatos," Marks writes [372]) has been read and effectively recontained within the male poetic tradition – with the very move described by Halperin above – as phallic or maternal body. Thereafter, Marks states, no "sufficiently challenging counter-images" were produced in French literature until the advent of feminism and the writing of a lesbian feminist, Monique Wittig.

"Only the women's movement," concurred the writer in her preface to the 1975 English edition of *The Lesbian Body*, "has proved capable of producing lesbian texts in a context of total rupture with

masculine culture, texts written by women exclusively for women, careless of male approval."[22] If there is reason to believe that Wittig would no longer accept the designation lesbian-feminist in the 1980s (her latest published novel in English, *Across the Acheron*, more than suggests as much), Marks's critical assessment of *The Lesbian Body* remains, to my way of seeing, correct:

> In *Le corps lesbien* Monique Wittig has created, through the incessant use of hyperbole and a refusal to employ traditional body codes, images sufficiently blatant to withstand reabsorption into male literary culture. . . . The J/e of *Le corps lesbien* is the most powerful lesbian in literature because as a lesbian-feminist she reexamines and redesigns the universe. (375–6)

Like Djuna Barnes's, Wittig's struggle is with language, to transcend gender. Barnes, as Wittig reads her, succeeds in "universalizing the feminine" because she "cancels out the genders by making them obsolete. I find it necessary to suppress them. That is the point of view of a lesbian."[23] And indeed, from the impersonal *on* [one] in *L'Opoponax*, to the feminine plural *elles* [they] replacing the generic masculine *ils* [they] in *Les guérillères*, to the divided, linguistically impossible *j/e* [*I*], lover and writing subject of *The Lesbian Body*, Wittig's personal pronouns work to "lesbianize" language as impudently as her recastings of both classical and Christian myth and Western literary genres (the Homeric heroes and Christ, *The Divine Comedy* and *Don Quixote*, the epic, the lyric, the *Bildungsroman*, the encyclopaedic dictionary) do to literary history.[24] What will not do, for her purposes, is a "feminine writing" [*écriture féminine*] which, for Wittig, is no more than "the naturalizing metaphor of the brutal political fact of the domination of women" (63) and so complicit in the reproduction of femininity and of the female body as Nature.

Thus, as I read it, it is in the garbage dump of femininity, "In this dark adored adorned gehenna," that the odyssey of Wittig's *j/e-tu* in *The Lesbian Body* begins: "Fais tes adieux m/a très belle," "say your farewells m/y very beautiful . . . strong . . . indomitable . . . learned . . . ferocious . . . gentle . . . best beloved to what they call affection tenderness or gracious abandon. No one is unaware of what takes place here, it has no name as yet."[25] Here where? – in this book, this journey into the body of Western culture, this season in hell. And what takes place here? – the dismemberment and slow decomposition of the *female* body limb by limb, organ by organ, secretion by secretion. No one will be able to stand the sight of it, no one will come to aid in this awesome, excruciating and exhilarating labor of love: dis-membering and re-membering, reconstituting the body in a new erotic economy, relearning to know it ("it has no name as yet") by another semiotics, reinscribing it with invert/ inward desire, rewriting it otherwise, other-wise: a *lesbian* body.

The project, the conceptual originality and radical import of Wittig's lesbian as subject of a "cognitive practice" that enables the reconceptualization of the social and of knowledge itself from a position eccentric to the heterosexual institution, are all there in the first page of *Le corps lesbien*.[26] A "subjective cognitive practice" and a practice of writing as consciousness of contradiction ("the language you speak is made up of words that are killing you," she wrote in *Les guérillères*); a consciousness of writing, living, feeling, and desiring in the noncoincidence of experience and language, in the interstices of representation, "in the intervals that your masters have not been able to fill with their words of proprietors."[27] Thus, the struggle with language to rewrite the body beyond its precoded, conventional representations is not and cannot be a reappropriation of the female body as it is, domesticated, maternal, oedipally or preoedipally en-gendered, but is a struggle to transcend both gender and "sex" and recreate the body other-wise: to see it perhaps as monstrous, or grotesque, or mortal, or violent, and certainly also sexual, but with a material and sensual specificity that will resist phallic idealization and render it accessible to women in another sociosexual economy. In short, if it were not lesbian, this body would make no sense.

Replacing the Lacanian slash with a lesbian bar Sue-Ellen Case, "Towards a Butch-Femme Aesthetic"

At first sight, the reader of *The Lesbian Body* might find in its linguistically impossible subject pronoun several theoretically possible valences that go from the more conservative (the slash in *j/e* represents the division of the Lacanian subject) to the less conservative (*j/e* can be expressed by writing but not by speech, representing Derridean *différance*), and to the radical feminist ("*j/e* is the symbol of

the lived, rending experience which is *m/y* writing, of this cutting in two which throughout literature is the exercise of a language which does not constitute m/e as subject," as Wittig is reported to have said in Margaret Crosland's introduction to the Beacon paperback edition I own). Another reader, especially if a reader of science fiction, might think of Joanna Russ's brilliant lesbian-feminist novel, *The Female Man*, whose protagonist is a female genotype articulated across four spacetime probabilities in four characters whose names all begin with J – Janet, Jeannine, Jael, Joanna – and whose sociosexual practices cover the spectrum from celibacy and "politically correct" monogamy to live toys and the 1970s equivalent of s/m.[28] What Wittig actually said in one of her essays in the 1980s is perhaps even more extreme:

> The bar in the *j/e* of *The Lesbian Body* is a sign of excess. A sign that helps to imagine an excess of "I," an "I" exalted. "I" has become so powerful in *The Lesbian Body* that it can attack the order of heterosexuality in texts and assault the so-called love, the heroes of love, and lesbianize them, lesbianize the symbols, lesbianize the gods and the goddesses, lesbianize the men and the women. This "I" can be destroyed in the attempt and resuscitated. Nothing resists this "I" (or this *tu* [you], which is its name, its love), which spreads itself in the whole world of the book, like a lava flow that nothing can stop.[29]

Excess, an exaltation of the "I" through costume, performance, *mise-en-scène*, irony, and utter manipulation of appearance, is what Sue-Ellen Case sees in the discourse of camp. If it is deplorable that the lesbian working-class bar culture of the 1950s "went into the feminist closet" during the 1970s, when organizations such as the Daughters of Bilitis encouraged lesbian identification with the more legitimate feminist dress codes and upwardly mobile lifestyles, writes Case, "yet the closet, or the bars, with their hothouse atmosphere [have] given us camp – the style, the discourse, the *mise-en-scène* of butch-femme roles." In these roles, "recuperating the space of seduction,"

> the butch-femme couple inhabit the subject position together. . . . These are not split subjects, suffering the torments of dominant ideology. They are coupled ones that do not impale themselves on the poles of sexual difference or

metaphysical values, but constantly seduce the sign system, through flirtation and inconstancy into the light fondle of artifice, replacing the Lacanian slash with a lesbian bar.[30]

The question of address, of who produces cultural representations and for whom (in any medium, genre, or semiotic system, from writing to performance), and of who receives them and in what contexts, has been a major concern of feminism and other critical theories of cultural marginality. In the visual arts, that concern has focused on the notion of spectatorship, which has been central to the feminist critique of representation and the production of different images of difference, for example in women's cinema.[31] Recent work in both film and performance theory has been elaborating the film-theoretical notion of spectatorship with regard to what may be the specific relations of homosexual subjectivity, in several directions. Elizabeth Ellsworth, for one, surveying the reception of *Personal Best* (1982), a commercial man-made film about a lesbian relationship between athletes, found that lesbian feminist reviews of the film adopted interpretive strategies which rejected or altered the meaning carried by conventional (Hollywood) codes of narrative representation. For example, they redefined who was the film's protagonist or "object of desire," ignored the sections focused on heterosexual romance, disregarded the actual ending and speculated, instead, on a possible extratextual future for the characters beyond the ending. Moreover, "some reviewers named and illicitly eroticized moments of the film's 'inadvertent lesbian verisimilitude' [in Patrice Donnelly's performance] ... codes of body language, facial expression, use of voice, structuring and expression of desire and assertion of strength in the face of male domination and prerogative."[32]

While recognizing limits to this "oppositional appropriation" of dominant representation, Ellsworth argues that the struggle over interpretation is a constitutive process for marginal subjectivities, as well as an important form of resistance. But when the marginal community is directly addressed, in the context of out-lesbian performance such as the WOW Cafe or the Split Britches productions, the appropriation seems to have no limits, to be directly "subversive," to yield not merely a site of interpretive work and resistance but a representation that requires no interpretive effort and is immediately, univocally legible, signalling "the creation of new imagery, new metaphors, and new conventions that can be read, or given new meaning, by a very specific spectator."[33]

The assumption behind this view, as stated by Kate Davy, is that such lesbian performance "undercut[s] the heterosexual model by implying a spectator that is not the generic, universal male, not the cultural construction 'woman,' but lesbian – a subject defined in terms of sexual similarity ... whose desire lies outside the fundamental model or underpinnings of sexual difference" (47). Somehow, this seems too easy a solution to the problem of spectatorship, and even less convincing as a representation of "lesbian desire." For, if sexual similarity could so unproblematically replace sexual difference, why would the new lesbian theatre need to insist on gender, if only as "the residue of sexual difference" that is, as Davy herself insists, worn in the "stance, gesture, movement, mannerisms, voice, and dress" (48) of the butch-femme play? Why would lesbian camp be taken up in theatrical performance, as Case suggests, to recuperate that space of seduction which historically has been the lesbian bar, and the Left Bank salon before it – spaces of daily-life performance, masquerade, cross-dressing, and practices constitutive of both community and subjectivity?

In an essay on "The Dynamics of Desire" in performance and pornography, Jill Dolan asserts that the reappropriation of pornography in lesbian magazines ("a visual space meant at least theoretically to be free of male subordination") offers "liberative fantasies" and "representations of one kind of sexuality based in lesbian desire," adding that the "male forms" of pornographic representation "acquire new meanings when they are used to communicate desire for readers of a different gender and sexual orientation."[34] Again, as in Davy, the question of lesbian desire is begged; and again the ways in which the new context would produce new meanings or "disrupt traditional meanings" (173) appear to be dependent on the presumption of a unified lesbian viewer/reader, gifted with undivided and non-contradictory subjectivity, and every bit as generalized and universal as the female spectator both Dolan and Davy impute (and rightly so) to the anti-pornography feminist performance art. For, if all lesbians had one and the same definition of "lesbian desire," there would hardly be any debate among us, or any struggle over interpretations of cultural images, especially the ones we produce.

What is meant by a term so crucial to the specificity and originality claimed for these performances and strategies of representation is not an inappropriate question, then. When she addresses it at the end of her essay, Dolan writes: "Desire is not necessarily a fixed, male-owned commodity, but can be exchanged, with a much different meaning, between women" (173). Unless it can be taken as the ultimate camp representation, this notion of lesbian desire as commodity exchange is rather disturbing. For, unfortunately – or fortunately, as the case may be – commodity exchange does have the same meaning "between women" as between men, by definition – that is, by Marx's definition of the structure of capital. And so, if the "aesthetic differences between cultural feminist and lesbian performance art" are to be determined by the presence or absence of pornography, and to depend on a "new meaning" of commodity exchange, it is no wonder that we seem unable to get it off (our backs) even as we attempt to take it on.

The king does not count lesbians
        Marilyn Frye, *The Politics of Reality*

The difficulty in defining an autonomous form of female sexuality and desire in the wake of a cultural tradition still Platonic, still grounded in sexual (in)difference, still caught in the tropism of hommosexuality, is not to be overlooked or wilfully bypassed. It is perhaps even greater than the difficulty in devising strategies of representation which will, in turn, alter the standard of vision, the frame of reference of visibility, of *what can be seen*. For, undoubtedly, that is the project of lesbian performance, theatre and film, a project that has already achieved a significant measure of success, not only at the WOW Cafe but also, to mention just a few examples, in Cherríe Moraga's *teatro Giving Up the Ghost* (1986), Sally Potter's film *The Gold Diggers* (1983), or Sheila McLaughlin's *She Must Be Seeing Things* (1987). My point here is that redefining the conditions of vision, as well as the modes of representing, cannot be predicated on a single, undivided identity of performer and audience (whether as "lesbians" or "women" or "people of color" or any other single category constructed in opposition to its dominant other, "heterosexual women," "men," "whites," and so forth).

Consider Marilyn Frye's suggestive Brechtian parable about our culture's conceptual reality ("phallocratic reality") as a conventional stage play, where the actors – those committed to the performance/maintenance of the Play, "the phallocratic loyalists" – visibly occupy the foreground, while stagehands – who provide the necessary labor and framework for the material (re)production of the Play – remain invisible in the background. What happens, she speculates, when the stagehands (women, feminists) begin thinking of themselves as actors and try to participate visibly in the performance, attracting attention to their activities and their own role in the play? The loyalists cannot conceive that anyone in the audience may see or focus their attention on the stagehands' projects in the background, and thus become "disloyal" to the Play, or, as Adrienne Rich has put it, "disloyal to civilization."[35] Well, Frye suggests, there are some people in the audience who do see what the conceptual system of heterosexuality, the Play's performance, attempts to keep invisible. These are lesbian people, who can see it because their own reality is not represented or even surmised in the Play, and who therefore reorient their attention toward the background, the spaces, activities and figures of women elided by the performance. But "attention is a kind of passion" that "fixes and directs the application of one's physical and emotional work":

> If the lesbian sees the woman, the woman may see the lesbian seeing her. With this, there is a flowering of possibilities. The woman, feeling herself seen, may learn that she *can be* seen; she may also be able to know that a woman can see, that is, can author perception. . . . The lesbian's seeing undercuts the mechanism by which the production and constant reproduction of heterosexuality for women was to be rendered *automatic*. (172)

And this is where we are now, as the critical reconsideration of lesbian history past and present is doing for feminist theory what Pirandello, Brecht, and others did for the bourgeois theatre conventions, and avant-garde filmmakers have done for Hollywood cinema; the latter, however, have not just disappeared, much as one would wish they had. So, too, have the conventions of seeing, and the relations of desire and meaning in spectatorship, remained partially anchored or contained by a frame of visibility that is still heterosexual, or hommosexual, and just as persistently color blind.

For instance, what are the "things" the Black/Latina protagonist of McLaughlin's film imagines seeing, in her jealous fantasies about her white lover (although she does not "really" see them), if not those very images which our cultural imaginary and the whole history of cinema have constructed as the visible, what can *be seen*, and eroticized? The originality of *She Must Be Seeing Things* is in its representing *the question of* lesbian desire in these terms, as it engages the contradictions and complicities that have emerged subculturally, in both discourses and practices, through the feminist-lesbian debates on sex-radical imagery as a political issue of representation, as well as real life. It may be interestingly contrasted with a formally conventional film like Donna Deitch's *Desert Hearts* (1986), where heterosexuality remains off screen, in the diegetic background (in the character's past), but is actively present nonetheless in the spectatorial expectations set up by the genre (the love story) and the visual pleasure procured by conventional casting, cinematic narrative procedures, and commercial distribution. In sum, one film works *with and against* the institutions of heterosexuality and cinema, the other works *with* them. A similar point could be made about certain films with respect to the novels they derive from, such as *The Color Purple* or *Kiss of the Spider Woman*, where the critical and formal work of the novels against the social and sexual indifference built into the institution of heterosexuality is altogether suppressed and rendered invisible by the films' compliance with the apparatus of commercial cinema and its institutional drive to, precisely, commodity exchange.

So what *can* be seen? Even in feminist film theory, the current "impasse regarding female spectatorship is related to the blind spot of lesbianism," Patricia White suggests in her reading of Ulrike Ottinger's film *Madame X: An Absolute Ruler* (1977).[36] That film, she argues, on the contrary, displaces the assumption "that feminism finds its audience 'naturally' " (95); it does so by addressing the female spectator through specific scenarios and "figures of spectatorial desire" and "trans-sex identification," through figures of transvestism and masquerade. And the position the film thus constructs for its spectator is not one of essential femininity or impossible masculinization (as proposed by Mary Ann Doane and Laura Mulvey, respectively), but rather a position of marginality or "deviance" *vis-à-vis* the normative heterosexual frame of vision.[37]

Once again, what *can* be seen? "When I go into a store, people see a black person and only incidentally a woman," writes Jewelle Gomez, a writer of science fiction and author of at least one vampire story about a black lesbian blues singer named Gilda. "In an Upper West Side apartment building late at night when a white woman refuses to get on an elevator with me, it's because I am black. She sees a mugger as described on the late night news, not another woman as nervous to be out alone as she is."[38] If my suspicion that social and sexual indifference are never far behind one from the other is not just an effect of paranoia, it is quite possible that, in the second setting, the elevator at night, what a white woman sees superimposed on the black image of the mugger is the male image of the dyke, and both of these together are what prevents the white woman from seeing the other one like herself. Nevertheless, Gomez points out, "I can pass as straight, if by some bizarre turn of events I should want to . . . but I cannot pass as white in this society." Clearly, the very issue of passing, across any boundary of social division, is related quite closely to the frame of vision and the conditions of representation.

"Passing demands quiet. And from that quiet – silence," writes Michelle Cliff.[39] It is "a dual masquerade – passing straight/passing lesbian [that] enervates and contributes to speechlessness – to speak might be to reveal."[40] However, and paradoxically again, speechlessness can only be overcome, and her "journey into speech" begin, by "claiming an identity they taught me to despise"; that is, by passing black "against a history of forced fluency," a history of passing white.[41] The dual masquerade, her writing suggests, is at once the condition of speechlessness and of overcoming speechlessness, for the latter occurs by recognizing and representing the division in the self, the difference and the displacement from which any identity that needs to be claimed derives, and hence can be claimed only, in Lorde's words, as "the very house of difference."

Those divisions and displacements in history, memory, and desire are the "ghost" that Moraga's characters want to but cannot altogether give up. The division of the Chicana lesbian Marisa/Corky from the Mexican Amalia, whose desire cannot be redefined outside the heterosexual imaginary of her culture, is also the division of Marisa/Corky from herself, the split produced in the girl Corky by sexual and social indifference, and by her internalization of a notion of hommo-sexuality which Marisa now lives as a wound, an infinite distance between her female body and her desire for women. If "the realization of shared oppression on the basis of being women and Chicanas holds the promise of a community of Chicanas, both lesbians and heterosexual," Yvonne Yarbro-Bejarano states, nevertheless "the structure of the play does not move neatly from pain to promise," and the divisions within them remain unresolved.[42] The character Marisa, however, I would add, has moved away from the hommo-sexuality of Corky (her younger self at age 11 and 17); and with the ambiguous character of Amalia, who loved a man almost as if he were a woman and who can love Marisa only when she (Amalia) is no longer one, the play itself has moved away from any simple opposition of "lesbian" to "heterosexual" and into the conceptual and experiential continuum of a female, Chicana subjectivity from where the question of lesbian desire must finally be posed. The play ends with that question – which is at once its outcome and its achievement, its *éxito*.

What to do with the feminine invert?
Esther Newton, "The Mythic
Mannish Lesbian"

Surveying the classic literature on inversion, Newton notes that Radclyffe Hall's "vision of lesbianism as sexual difference and as masculinity," and her "conviction that sexual desire must be male," both assented to and sought to counter the sociomedical discourses of the early twentieth century. "The notion of a feminine lesbian contradicted the congenital theory that many homosexuals in Hall's era espoused to counter the demands that they undergo punishing 'therapies' " (575). Perhaps that counter-demand led the novelist further to reduce the typology of female inversion (initially put forth by Krafft-Ebing as comprised of four types, then reduced to three by Havelock Ellis) to two: the invert and the "normal" woman who misguidedly falls in love with her. Hence the novel's emphasis on Stephen, while her lover Mary is a "forgettable and inconsistent" character who in the end gets turned over to a man. However, unlike Mary, Radclyffe Hall's real-life lover Una Troubridge "did not go back to heterosexuality even when Hall, late in her life, took a second lover," Newton points out. Una would then represent what *The Well of Loneliness* elided, the third type of female invert, and the most troublesome for Ellis: the "womanly" women "to whom the actively inverted woman is most attracted. These women differ in the first

place from normal or average women in that . . . they seem to possess a genuine, though not precisely sexual, preference for women over men."[43] Therefore, Newton concludes, "Mary's real story has yet to be told" (575), and a footnote after this sentence refers us to "two impressive beginnings" of what could be Mary's real story, told from the perspective of a self-identified, contemporary femme.[44]

The discourses, demands, and counter-demands that inform lesbian identity and representation in the 1980s are more diverse and socially heterogeneous than those of the first half of the century. They include, most notably, the political concepts of oppression and agency developed in the struggles of social movements such as the women's movement, the gay liberation movement, and third world feminism, as well as an awareness of the importance of developing a theory of sexuality that takes into account the working of unconscious processes in the construction of female subjectivity. But, as I have tried to argue, the discourses, demands, and counter-demands that inform lesbian representation are still unwittingly caught in the paradox of sociosexual (in)difference, often unable to think homosexuality and hommo-sexuality at once separately *and* together. Even today, in most representational contexts, Mary would be either passing lesbian or passing straight, her (homo)sexuality being in the last instance what can not be seen. Unless, as Newton and others suggest, she enter the frame of vision *as or with* a lesbian in male body drag.[45]

Notes

1. Luce Irigaray, "*Così fan tutti*," in *This Sex Which Is Not One*, trans. Catherine Porter (Ithaca: Cornell University Press, 1985), 86. The phrase "sexual indifference" actually appeared in Luce Irigaray, *Speculum of the Other Woman* [1974], trans. Gillian C. Gill (Ithaca: Cornell University Press, 1985), 28.
2. Irigaray, *Speculum*, 101–3.
3. See Petitioner's Brief in *Bowers v. Hardwick*, cited by Mary Dunlap, "Brief *Amicus Curiae* for the Lesbian Rights Project et al.," *Review of Law and Social Change* 14 (1986): 960.
4. David M. Halperin, "Why Is Diotima a Woman?," in Halperin, *One Hundred Years of Homosexuality and Other Essays on Greek Love* (New York: Routledge, 1989 [still forthcoming when de Lauretis wrote this essay]); subsequent references to this work, which is still in manuscript form, will have no page number. See also Halperin, "Plato and Erotic Reciprocity," *Classical Antiquity* 5:1 (1986): 60–80.

5. I am thinking in particular of Julia Kristeva, "Stabat Mater" (originally published as "Héréthique de l'amour") in *Tales of Love*, trans. Leon Roudiez (New York: Columbia University Press, 1987), and Jacques Derrida, *Spurs: Nietzsche's Styles*, trans. Barbara Harlow (Chicago: University of Chicago Press, 1979).

6. For a related reading of Aristotle and theatre, see Sue-Ellen Case, "Classic Drag: The Greek Creation of Female Parts," *Theatre Journal* 37:3 (1985): 317–27. I have developed the notion of heterosexual contract (originally suggested in Monique Wittig, "The Straight Mind," *Feminist Issues* 1:1 [1980]: 103–11) in my "The Female Body and Heterosexual Presumption," *Semiotica* 67:3/4 (1987): 259–79.

7. Monique Wittig and Sande Zeig, *Lesbian Peoples: Material for a Dictionary* (New York: Avon Books, 1979).

8. See Biddy Martin and Chandra Mohanty, "Feminist Politics: What's Home Got to Do with It," in *Feminist Studies/Critical Studies*, ed. Teresa de Lauretis (Bloomington: Indiana University Press, 1986), 191–212, and Teresa de Lauretis, "Eccentric Subjects: Feminist Theory and Historical Consciousness," forthcoming in *Poetics Today*.

9. Catharine R. Stimpson, "The Somagrams of Gertrude Stein," in *The Female Body in Western Culture: Contemporary Perspectives*, ed. Susan Suleiman (Cambridge: Harvard University Press, 1986), 34.

10. Catharine R. Stimpson, "Zero Degree Deviancy: The Lesbian Novel in English," *Critical Inquiry* 8:2 (1981): 369.

11. Carolyn Allen, "Writing Toward *Nightwood*: Djuna Barnes' Seduction Stories," in *Silence and Power: A Reevaluation of Djuna Barnes*, ed. M. L. Broe (Carbondale: Southern Illinois University Press, 1987).

12. Carolyn Allen, " 'Dressing the Unknowable in the Garments of the Known': The Style of Djuna Barnes' *Nightwood*," in *Women's Language and Style*, ed. Butturft and Epstein (Akron: L&S Books, 1978), 116.

13. Esther Newton, "The Mythic Mannish Lesbian: Radclyffe Hall and the New Woman," *Signs* 9:4 (1984): 557–75. See also Madeline Davis and Elizabeth Lapovsky Kennedy, "Oral History and the Study of Sexuality in the Lesbian Community: Buffalo, New York, 1940–1960," *Feminist Studies* 12:1 (1986): 7–26; and Joan Nestle, "Butch-Fem Relationships: Sexual Courage in the 1950s," *Heresies* 12 (1981): 21–4, now reprinted in Joan Nestle, *A Restricted Country* (Ithaca: Firebrand Books, 1987), 100–9.

14. See the discussion of Krafft-Ebing, Ellis, and others in George Chauncey, Jr., "From Sexual Inversion to Homosexuality: Medicine and the Changing Conceptualization of Female Deviance," *Salmagundi* 58–9 (1982–3): 114–46, and in Carroll Smith-Rosenberg, "The New Woman as Androgyne," in *Disorderly Conduct: Visions of Gender in Victorian America* (New York: Oxford University Press, 1985), 245–349.

15. Gayle Rubin, "Thinking Sex: Notes for a Radical Theory of the Politics of Sexuality," in *Pleasure and Danger: Exploring Female Sexuality*, ed. Carole S. Vance (Boston: Routledge & Kegan Paul, 1984), 309; "The Traffic in Women: Notes on the 'Political Economy' of Sex," in *Toward an Anthropology of Women*, ed. Rayna R. Reiter (New York: Monthly Review Press, 1975), 157–210. On the feminist "sex wars" of the 1970s and 1980s, see B. Ruby Rich, "Feminism and Sexuality in the 1980s," *Feminist Studies* 12:3 (1986): 525–61. On the relationship of feminism to lesbianism, see also Wendy Clark, "The Dyke, the Feminist and the Devil," in *Sexuality: A Reader*, ed. *Feminist Review* (London: Virago, 1987), 201–15.

16. Michel Foucault, *The History of Sexuality* (New York: Pantheon, 1978), 106, cited by Rubin, "Thinking Sex," 307. For a critical reading of the relevance and limitations of Foucault's views with regard to female sexuality, see Biddy Martin, "Feminism, Criticism, and Foucault," *New German Critique* 27 (1982): 3–30, and Teresa de Lauretis, *Technologies of Gender: Essays on Theory, Film, and Fiction* (Bloomington: Indiana University Press, 1987), chapters 1 and 2.

17. Catharine A. MacKinnon, *Feminism Unmodified: Discourses on Life and Law* (Cambridge: Harvard University Press, 1987), 60.

18. Combahee River Collective, "A Black Feminist Statement," in *This Bridge Called My Back: Writings by Radical Women of Color*, ed. Cherríe Moraga and Gloria Anzaldúa (New York: Kitchen Table: Women of Color Press, 1983), 210.

19. Audre Lorde, *Zami: A New Spelling of My Name* (Trumansburg, New York: The Crossing Press, 1982), 203 and 224.

20. "Writing. It's work. Changing the relationship with language. . . . Women's fictions raise theoretical issues: women's theorizing appears as/in fiction. Women's writing disturbs our usual understanding of the terms fiction and theory which assign value to discourses. . . . Fiction/theory has been the dominant mode of feminist writing in Québec for more than a decade," states Barbara Godard for the editorial collective of *Tessera* no. 3, a Canadian feminist, dual-language publication that has appeared annually as a special issue of an already established magazine ("Fiction/Theory: Editorial," *Canadian Fiction Magazine* 57 [1986]: 3–4). See Nicole Brossard, *L'Amèr ou Le Chapitre effrité* (Montréal:

Quinze, 1977) and *These Our Mothers Or: The Disintegrating Chapter*, trans. Barbara Godard (Toronto: Coach House, 1983). On Brossard and other Canadian writers of fiction/theory, see Shirley Neuman, "Importing Difference," and other essays in *A Mazing Space: Writing Canadian Women Writing*, ed. Shirley Neuman and Smaro Kamboureli (Edmonton: Longspoon Press and NeWest Press, 1986).

21. Elaine Marks, "Lesbian Intertextuality," in *Homosexualities and French Literature*, ed. George Stambolian and Elaine Marks (Ithaca: Cornell University Press, 1979), 353–77.

22. Monique Wittig, *The Lesbian Body*, trans. David LeVay (New York: William Morrow, 1975), 9, cited by Marks, 373.

23. Monique Wittig, "The Point of View: Universal or Particular," *Feminist Issues* 3:2 (1983): 64.

24. See Hélène Vivienne Wenzel, "The Text as Body/Politics: An Appreciation of Monique Wittig's Writings in Context," *Feminist Studies* 7:2 (1981): 264–87, and Namascar Shaktini, "Displacing the Phallic Subject: Wittig's Lesbian Writing," *Signs* 8:1 (1982): 29–44, who writes: "Wittig's reorganization of metaphor around the lesbian body represents an epistemological shift from what seemed until recently the absolute, central metaphor – the phallus" (29).

25. Monique Wittig, *Le corps lesbien* (Paris: Minuit, 1973), 7. I have revised the English translation that appears in *The Lesbian Body*, 15.

26. The concept of "subjective, cognitive practice" is elaborated in Wittig, "One Is Not Born a Woman," *Feminist Issues* 1:2 (1981): 47–54. I discuss it at some length in my "Eccentric Subjects" (note 8 above).

27. Monique Wittig, *Les Guérillères*, trans. David LeVay (Boston: Beacon Press, 1985), 114.

28. Joanna Russ, *The Female Man* (New York: Bantam, 1975). See also Catherine L. McClenahan, "Textual Politics: The Uses of Imagination in Joanna Russ's *The Female Man*," *Transactions of the Wisconsin Academy of Sciences, Arts and Letters* 70 (1982): 114–25.

29. Monique Wittig, "The Mark of Gender," *Feminist Issues* 5:2 (1985): 71.

30. Sue-Ellen Case, "Towards a Butch-Femme Aesthetic," in *Feminist Perspectives on Contemporary Women's Drama*, ed. Lynda Hart (Ann Arbor: University of Michigan Press, forthcoming). The butch-femme couple, like Wittig's *j/e-tu* and like the s/m lesbian couple – all of whom, in their respective self-definitions, are one the name and the love of the other – propose a dual subject that brings to mind again Irigaray's *This Sex Which Is Not One*, though they all would adamantly deny the latter's suggestion that a non-phallic eroticism may be traced to the preoedipal relation to the mother. One has to wonder, however, whether the denial has more to do with the committedly heterosexual bias of neo-Freudian psychoanalysis and object relations theory, with their inability to work through the paradox of sexual (in)difference on which they are founded but perhaps not destined to, or with our rejection of the maternal body which phallic representation has utterly alienated from women's love, from our desire for the self-same, by colonizing it as the "dark continent" and so rendering it at once powerless and inaccessible to us and to all "others."

31. See, for example, Judith Mayne, "The Woman at the Keyhole: Women's Cinema and Feminist Criticism," and B. Ruby Rich, "From Repressive Tolerance to Erotic Liberation: *Maedchen in Uniform*," in *Re-vision: Essays in Feminist Film Criticism*, ed. Mary Ann Doane, Patricia Mellencamp, and Linda Williams (Frederick, Md.: University Publications of America and the American Film Institute, 1984), 49–66 and 100–30; and Teresa de Lauretis, "Rethinking Women's Cinema: Aesthetics and Feminist Theory," in *Technologies of Gender*, 127–48.

32. Elizabeth Ellsworth, "Illicit Pleasures: Feminist Spectators and *Personal Best*," *Wide Angle* 8:2 (1986): 54.

33. Kate Davy, "Constructing the Spectator: Reception, Context, and Address in Lesbian Performance," *Performing Arts Journal* 10:2 (1986): 49.

34. Jill Dolan, "The Dynamics of Desire: Sexuality and Gender in Pornography and Performance," *Theatre Journal* 39:2 (1987): 171.

35. "To Be and Be Seen," in Marilyn Frye, *The Politics of Reality: Essays in Feminist Theory* (Trumansburg, New York: The Crossing Press, 1983), 166–73; Adrienne Rich, "Disloyal to Civilization: Feminism, Racism, Gynephobia," in *On Lies, Secrets, and Silence: Selected Prose 1966–1978* (New York: Norton, 1979), 275–310.

36. Patricia White, "Madame X of the China Seas," *Screen* 28:4 (1987): 82.

37. The two essays discussed are Mary Ann Doane, "Film and the Masquerade: Theorising the Female Spectator," *Screen* 23:3–4 (1982): 74–87, and Laura Mulvey, "Afterthoughts on 'Visual Pleasure and Narrative Cinema' Inspired by *Duel in the Sun*," *Framework* 15/16/17 (1981): 12–15. Another interesting discussion of the notion of masquerade in lesbian representation may be found in Sue-Ellen Case, "Toward a Butch-Femme Aesthetic."

38. Jewelle Gomez, "Repeat After Me: We Are Different. We Are the Same," *Review of Law and Social Change* 14:4 (1986): 939. Her vampire story is "No Day Too Long," in *Worlds Apart: An Anthology of Lesbian and Gay Science Fiction and Fantasy*, ed. Camilla Decarnin, Eric Garber, and Lyn Paleo (Boston: Alyson Publications, 1986), 215–23.

39. "Passing," in Michelle Cliff, *The Land of Look Behind* (Ithaca: Firebrand Books, 1985), 22.

40. Michelle Cliff, "Notes on Speechlessness," *Sinister Wisdom* 5 (1978): 7.

41. Michelle Cliff, "A Journey into Speech" and "Claiming an Identity They Taught Me to Despise," both in *The Land of Look Behind*, 11–17 and 40–7; see also her novel *No Telephone To Heaven* (New York: E. P. Dutton, 1987).

42. Yvonne Yarbro-Bejarano, "Cherríe Moraga's *Giving up the Ghost*: The Representation of Female Desire," *Third Woman* 3: 1–2 (1986): 118–19. See also Cherríe Moraga, *Giving Up the Ghost: Teatro in Two Acts* (Los Angeles: West End Press, 1986).

43. Havelock Ellis, "Sexual Inversion in Women," *Alienist and Neurologist* 16 (1895): 141–58, cited by Newton, "The Mythic Mannish Lesbian," 567.

44. Joan Nestle, "Butch-Fem Relationships" (see note 13 above) and Amber Hollibaugh and Cherríe Moraga, "What We're Rollin' Around in Bed With," both in *Heresies* 12 (1981): 21–4 and 58–62.

45. For many of the ideas developed in this essay, I am indebted to the other participants of the student-directed seminar on Lesbian History and Theory sponsored by the Board in Studies in History of Consciousness at the University of California, Santa Cruz in Fall 1987. For support of various kinds, personal and professional, I thank Kirstie McClure, Donna Haraway, and Michael Cowan, Dean of Humanities and Arts.

24

Transsexual Discourses and Languages of Identification

Jason Cromwell

Language . . . can be extraordinarily ambiguous and inaccurate, especially when describing feelings.

Blacking 1977: 9

Transsexual discourses are those created by medico-psychological practitioners who "diagnose, classify, regulate, and produce transsexed bodies" and the supposed truths about their lives and experiences (Hale 1995: 2). These discourses are a "moral discourse" (Mageo 1995: 285) that assumes that trans-behaviors of any kind are abnormal. Consequently, those who engage in these behaviors need to be cured. That assumption is reflected in the language used to speak about transpeople. Furthermore, these discourses were developed by practitioners who "treated" male-to-female transsexuals and then blithely applied the same discourses to female-bodied transpeople (cf. Hale 1995: 2). Such language, touted as being "scientific and neutral" (Birke 1982: 77) or merely descriptive, is stigmatizing and seldom descriptive (e.g., gender dysphoria, "wrong body," and "afflicted" or "suffering" transsexuals).

The discussion over whether to spell the word *transsexual* with one *s* or two is, in part, a creation of "strategic discourse" (Mageo 1995: 289), which inverts and reframes stigmatized words and meanings. Strategic discourse is a step toward the creation of transdiscourses adapted out of (or created from) trans experiences (chapter 10). Transdiscourses are nonmedical, nonpathological, and noncolonizing. They are affirming, empowering, positive, and reflective of trans experiences and the lives people choose to live. The development of an alternate discourse is necessary because the transcommunity is, as Stryker has astutely observed, "something more, and something other than the creatures our makers [i.e., therapists, endocrinologists, and surgeons] intended us to be" (cited in Hale 1995: 20).

For some, the use of the single *s* spelling of the word *transsexual* is one step toward ending complicity with transsexual discourses.

Words Spoken about Transsexuals

The words aren't just about identity, or positive and negative value judgments. The words are about danger.

Christina 1997: 34

By clinical definition, a transvestite is a heterosexual male who dresses in women's clothing and is erotically and/or sexually aroused by doing so (Benjamin 1969: 2; Blanchard 1985: 231; Stoller 1975: 143; Stoller 1982: 100). Within the limitations of that definition such behavior is considered to be extremely rare in females (cf. Stoller 1968, 1975); nonetheless, female transvestites do exist. Just as the clinical definition excludes females, it also excludes males who cross-dress for other reasons.

The third edition of the *Diagnostic and Statistical Manual of Mental Disorders* defines transsexualism as a gender identity "disorder" in which the individual experiences "a persistent sense of discomfort and inappropriateness about one's anatomic sex and a persistent wish to be rid of one's genitals and to live as a member of the opposite sex" (American Psychiatric Association 1987: 74, sec. 302.50). By its fourth edition, however, the manual had dropped the term *transsexual* as a diagnostic category and replaced it with "Gender Identity Disorder." The criteria remain the same (Bradley et al. 1991; Levine et al. 1991). Although the term did not originate with Benjamin, he has defined transsexuals as individuals who believe they belong to, want to be, and function as the "other" sex (1977[1966]: 27).[1] "Transsexual" is used in two ways: first, to describe someone who is in the process of becoming (transitioning) a man (and vice versa); and, second, to describe someone who has completed sex reassignment surgery. As Lynn points out, many postoperative transsexuals no longer consider themselves to be transsexual (1988: 30).[2]

From a clinical perspective it is believed that the transsexual's goal is to have sex reassignment surgery (SRS) and ultimately live as a heterosexual woman or man. Rather than "sex reassignment," some transpeople prefer "gender assignment," or "sex confirmation," or "gender confirmation," or "genital reassignment" surgery. Others, however, like myself, do not believe they are changing or confirming genders, nor that changing or confirming sex is possible. For some transpeople, a more appropriate terminology might be "sex and/or gender congruence surgery" (i.e., making gender congruent with sex as much as is possible given current medical technology). Regardless of the terminology, the goal for many transsexuals embedded in the ideology of the Euro-American sex and gender system is surgeries that will result in legally being seen as nontranssexual men or women.

Although transgender has begun to emerge in medico-psychological discourses (Bockting 1997; Cole 1998; Cole and Meyer 1998), it still is not recognized as a diagnostic category. Frequently these discourses read as if "transgender" is the same as "transsexual." An early example is that of Docter, a psychologist, who defines transgender in his own terms without regard to its origins or its definition by transgendered people themselves (1988: 21–2). He restricts the usage of the term to those who go "back and forth from one gender role to the other. Without such oscillations, the full-time cross-gender living would qualify in our definition as transsexual behavior. We prefer the term, *preoperative transsexual*, simply to indicate that reassignment procedures are anticipated" (22, emphasis in the original).

The Beginnings of Transdiscourses

More broadly defined, a transvestite is any person, regardless of sex or gender, who cross-dresses

(Feinbloom 1977: 16) for social presentations. The term itself was coined by Hirschfeld in 1910 (Karlen 1971: 213), who noted that it was derived "from 'trans' 'across' and 'vestitus' 'clothed' "; furthermore, he "readily admit[ted] that this name indicates only the most obvious aspect" of such behavior (Hirschfeld 1966[1938]: 187).[3] Some of the transcommunity objects to the term because of its clinical designation as compulsive and sexual behavior and the fact that, by implication, it connotes a perversion.

> It is in itself an innocent term, but it is very easy to understand why so many people who cross-dress do not want to be identified with that word. The initials "TV" for some reason do not carry the same negative connotations the word "transvestite" does. Many people who absolutely abhor the word "transvestite" have no qualms whatever with being called a "TV." . . . Also, the initials "TV" are convenient to use, and readily identifiable.
>
> The only difference between "cross-dresser" and "transvestite" is that "transvestite" implies a psychological condition (compulsion), while "cross-dresser" implies voluntary behavior. Most people who cross-dress would rather be identified with the word "cross-dresser" than "transvestite." (Lynn 1988: 28)

In a similar vein, Prince, considered by many male-bodied transpeople as the "grandmother" of the transcommunity, has noted (1992: 20) that the term *transvestite* has come "into disfavor because it has a medical and thus 'abnormal' and pejorative flavor to it. Thus crossdresser, or CD (which simply substitutes English for Latin), has come into common use." Regardless of individual preferences, "transvestite" and "cross-dresser" mean someone who wears the clothing and takes on the behaviors, socially constructed as the proper domain, of the other biological sex: males who present themselves as women (male transvestites) and females who present themselves as men (female transvestites).

Although most people in US society do not recognize three or more sexes and genders, some individuals identify as other than men or women. They may identify as transvestites, transsexuals, transgenderists (Bolin 1994), or "somethingelse."[4] Bolin (1988) discusses the identity shift of male-to-female transsexuals (MTFs) as they make the transition from men to women. Initially, they identify as transsexuals, which gradually gives way to a femin-ine identity as they learn to be, and become, com-fortable as women in society. During Bolin's study the only option available to MTFs/transwomen was to become as physically female as possible. Since the early 1990s, however, another category has emerged: Some individuals label themselves as "transgender-ists." They neither want nor desire sex reassign-ment surgery, and their gender diversity is not limited to periodic episodes of cross-dressing. They live the majority of their lives in a gender that opposes their biological sex. They may or may not identify as men or women, and they may identify as either/or, neither/nor, or both/and (Bolin 1994).

Some who define themselves as transgendered may go back and forth between gender roles.[5] Docter fails, however, to recognize that some define them-selves as transgenderists yet have no intention of having genital surgeries. Furthermore, he does not recognize that many individuals are content to be – and have purposely chosen – an intermediate category. Transgenderists are all too aware of the term *preoperative transsexual* but have rejected it because it does not describe them. Individuals who define themselves as transsexual but have not yet had genital surgery (yet anticipate doing so) often use "preoperative transsexual (pre-op)." Trans-genderists who have no intention of having surgery do not view themselves as transsexuals, preoperative transsexuals, or transvestites.

Notwithstanding the emergence of "transgender" in the humanities and social sciences literature (Rubin 1992; Weston 1993), the term and its derivatives arose out of the transvestite and trans-sexual community (Lynn 1984, 1988).[6] Within that community it is used in two ways. First, it desig-nates individuals who do not fit into the categories of transvestite and transsexual. Transgendered iden-tification offers a more specific reference to people who live as social men or as social women but neither desire nor have sex reassignment surgery. Transgender is viewed as a "viable option *between* crossdresser [transvestite] and transsexual" (Holly 1991: 31, emphasis in the original). Second, "trans-gender" is used as an encompassing term for trans-vestites and transsexuals as well as for those who do not fit neatly into either category. Bolin asserts that the transgender community

is in the process of creating not just a third gender, but the possibility of numerous genders and multiple social identities. As such, they chal-lenge the dominant American gender paradigm with its emphasis on reproduction and the bio-logical social body as the *sine qua non* of gender identity and role. As a political movement the transgender community views gender and sex systems as relativistic structures imposed by society and by the privileged controllers of individual bodies, the medical professions. The transgenderist is disquieting to the established gender system and unsettles the boundaries of bipolarity and opposition in the gender schema by suggesting a continuum of masculinity and femininity, renouncing gender as aligned with genitals, body, social status and/or role. Trans-genderism reiterates what the cross-cultural record reveals, the independence of gender traits embodied in a Western bio-centric model of sex. (1994: 447–8)

Transgender is a move away from a physically based definition (sex of body), and the sexual con-notations implied by "transsexual," toward a social definition (gender or gender identity) (Holly 1991: 31; Lynn 1984: 61; Lynn 1988: 30). Many within the transgender community have adopted the terms *transsexual, transgender, transgenderist,* and *cross-dresser* intentionally to distance themselves from the medico-psychiatry and subsequent stigmatization attached to the terms *transsexual, pre-operative trans-sexual,* and *transvestite.* Consequently, members of the transgendered community are individuals of any sex who are incompatible with and/or beyond specific gender assignments or are preoperative or postoperative transsexuals, cross-dressers, trans-vestites, and transgenderists.

There are important differences in the use of some terminology. For female-bodied transpeople, for example, terminology such as "the operation," "pre-op," and "post-op" are inadequate (cf. Hale 1995: 26). There are no clearcut pre- and post-op statuses for FTMs or transmen. Those who have surgery must have more than one operation. Is an FTM or transman who has had chest reconstruc-tion still pre-op? Would he be post-op if chest reconstruction were his only surgery? Is he pre-op or post-op if, in addition to chest reconstruction, he has surgery to remove female reproductive organs? Or is he only considered post-op if he has chest reconstruction, a hysterectomy (the removal of the uterus), and phalloplasty (the construction of a penis) and/or metoidioplasty (the surgical release of the posthormonally enlarged clitoris)?

Untying the Tongues of Transpeople

Language produces the reality it names.
                                    Lazreg 1990: 331

The vocabulary is only now developing to speak of the experiences of transpeople who do not fit neatly within existing categories. Butler has noted that language constrains what "constitutes the imaginable" (1990: 9). In order for people to be coherent and congruent they must fall within "socially instituted and maintained norms." Those who do not are no longer intelligible and thus supposedly cannot exist (Butler 1990: 17). If they are found to exist, they are either rendered invisible or considered pathological and labeled as gender failures (gender-confused or disoriented, gender-misidentified, gender-disordered or a gender aberration, and gender-dysphoric).[7]

Transpeople are developing other terminologies, including "transperson," "transpeople," "transmen," "transwomen," and "trans community." They have also devised a number of acronyms: FTM (female-to-male) or F2M; MTM (male-to-men, based on some FTMs'/transmen's belief that they have always been men in spite of being born with female bodies); and (for male-to-females) MTF (M2F) and FTF (with the opposite meaning and belief basis as for MTM). These are "native," insider, or emic terms.

Although the definitions of some terms and their appropriateness for general usage are often the topics of debate, it is important to use the language – trans discourse – to write and speak about the transcommunity. The terms are more accurate descriptors of how people self-identify, and they enable self-recognition. Furthermore, the transsexual discourses that medico-psychological practitioners have made available are too frequently applicable only to a small minority and are agenda-laden. Most practitioners continue to attempt to regulate what transsexuals and transvestites are and are not, regardless of whether they fit within the narrow definitions of those terms. Many practitioners, for example, exclude gay-identified female-bodied transpeople, individuals who flexibly shift from one gender role to another, and those not obsessed with having genital surgeries.

Many female-bodied people do not and have never felt like "a man trapped in a woman's body" or as though they have "the wrong body." Nor have they felt gender-dysphoric (i.e., disassociated or disconnected from their gender). It is inconsistent to feel trapped in a category – woman – when one has never felt like others in that category. Many have expressed confusion over the whole notion of "wrong body." I, for example, have asked on more than one occasion, "If I have the wrong body, whose body do I have and where is my body?" Many female-bodied transpeople have never experienced gender dysphoria yet have felt stigmatized by others' discomfort concerning gender expressions. "Gender dysphoria" is "a term used by nontransexual shrinks who write surgery letters" (Wilchins 1997: 225). Many transpeople believe that it is nontranspeople who have gender dysphoria.

Because transpeople are in the process of developing the language to speak of their identities and lives, terms are still under development. Some, such as the various forms of FTM (F2M, FtM, F-t-M), are viewed as being either politically correct or incorrect. In general, although I only have anecdotal evidence, it is male-bodied transpeople who find the term politically incorrect.

I once became embroiled in a heated discussion with Wilchins, who insisted that I was a MTM (male-to-male or male-to-man) transsexual. She insisted that she could not think of me (and others she mentioned by name) as ever having been females – I think she used "women" – and that FTM was derived from the medical and colonizing term *female-to-male transsexual*. I argued passionately that I had every right to turn a medical term into a shorthand that I found descriptive and useful. I asserted, and still maintain, my right to recognize and acknowledge that a personal history includes a female body and its incumbent socialization. Most important, I argued that neither she nor anyone else could label me in a way I found inappropriate. For her to do so is no less restricting than the actions of the medico-psychological people against whom she railed.

Being trans-anything is a self-diagnosis. Female-bodied transpeople identify in varying degrees with masculinity and maleness and with the category labeled "men." Individuals have every right to use whatever terms they wish. Some refer to themselves as transsexuals, others as transgendered, and others as something else. A new discourse is being created by those who articulate their transsubjectivity differently than medico-psychological discourses have allowed.[8] They are, in a real sense, untying their tongues.

Nicholson proposes thinking of the "meaning of woman" in a manner similar to Wittgenstein's use of the word *game*: "We see a complicated network of similarities overlapping and criss-crossing: sometimes overall similarities, sometimes similarities of detail" (Wittgenstein, cited in Nicholson 1994: 100). Therefore, the meaning of woman "is not found through the elucidation of some specific characteristic but is found through the elaboration of a complex network of characteristics." Doing so, Nicholson suggests, first acknowledges that for extended periods some characteristics (e.g., "possessing a vagina and being over a certain age") may have been present within a particular network; second permits the use of the word in some contexts in which particular "characteristics are not present" (e.g., transwomen who do not have vaginas but identify as women); and third provides a framework for "all those words into which *woman* is translatable" (100–1, emphasis in the original). Seeing "woman" as encompassing many meanings indicates that the meaning has changed and is changing and recognizes that there are many ways of being a woman. Consequently, the meaning can be a map that illustrates the intersection of similarities and differences (101).

I suggest that we think of words regarding transpeople in the same ways. Whether transexuals or transsexuals, transvestites, transgenderists, butch women, "nelly" men, or other gender nonconformers, transpeople still have characteristics that may be present in some contexts and not in others but have existed in different historical epochs and cultures. Moreover, the prefix *trans* has several meanings, both singular and multiple. According to the *Oxford English Dictionary* it indicates, but is not limited to, outside of; a change from one place, state, or form to another; to pass across or go beyond; to exceed the limits of; to go against; and to be brief. Some transpeople may use these meanings interchangeably, others may use only one, and still others may use them all.

Seeing *trans* as meaning more than one thing allows for acknowledging multiple terms that express transidentities: transgender (TG), transexual, or transsexual; FTM, trans or tranny man, boy, fag, and gay (for MTFs replaced by woman, girl, dyke, and lesbian); masculine or male-identified woman, lesbian man, dyke daddy, drag king and queen, new woman, new man, baby butch, soft butch, butch dyke, tryke, boy chick, and boy dyke; transfaghag, gender-bender or blender, gender fuck,

gender outlaw, and gender queer; transqueer, queer, cross-dresser, androgynous, transhuman, transfolk, transpeople, man or woman of transgendered or transsexual experience, and, finally, people.

In every regard such ways of expressing trans-identities are "the creation of a new transgender language" (Hemmings 1996: 38, n. 3); they are the creation of transdiscourse. Yet some terms may have different meanings, depending on the communities in which they are used. A transgendered lesbian is a butch dyke in lesbian communities, for example, whereas in transcommunities the same term means being a MTF transsexual and a lesbian.

Butches, FTMs, and Transmen

> Female-to-male transsexuals appear to share many similarities with lesbian butches.
> Newton 1994: 574, n. 41

Outside of surgical contexts it is sometimes difficult to understand the differences among butches, FTMs, and transmen.[9] Jamison Green, a leader of the FTM/transmen community, notes that "many people assume that FTMs are lesbians" (1994b: 2). Complicating matters is the fact that many FTMs and transmen have lived as, or attempted to live as, lesbians and have found lesbian communities to be relatively tolerant of masculine identities and behaviors. Some may have even identified as lesbians for a time; Green, for example, "identified as a lesbian for twenty-two years" (2). Most rarely felt that they truly fit in or belonged, however. Their masculinity was often regarded with suspicion and may have been allowed expression only in androgynous ways (Green 1994b: 1).

To further complicate matters, several "scientific" studies have compared lesbians and FTMs/transmen (Blanchard and Freund 1983; Ehrhardt, Grisanti, and McCauley 1979; Lyons 1986; McCauley and Ehrhardt 1978; Strassberg et al. 1979) with respect to childhood and adolescent development and behaviors, parental and sibling relationships, mental abilities, sexual functioning and fantasy/desire, and life-style.[10] These studies inevitably conclude that there are similarities as well as differences between FTMs/transmen and lesbians. Paramount is the fact that many butch lesbians have masculine gender identities, but, unlike FTMs and transmen, they do not identify as men. Nonetheless, "Many butches have partially male gender identities. Others border on being, and some are, female-to-male transsexuals (FTMs), although many lesbians *and* FTMs find the areas of overlap disturbing. Saying many butches identify as masculine to some degree does not mean that all, even most, butches 'want to be men,' although some undoubtedly do. Most butches enjoy combining expressions of masculinity with a female body" (Rubin 1992: 468, emphasis in the original).

FTM and transman identities are not necessarily clear-cut either, and there are gray areas between trans- and butch identities. Among a minority of butches and FTM/transmen these gray areas have given rise to what Halberstam (1998) and Hale (1998) term butch-FTM "border wars." In part, those who perpetuate border wars operate from places of misunderstanding; neither side clearly understands the other's perspective. From some FTM/transmen's perspectives, butches are transsexuals in denial; from some butches' perspectives, FTM/transmen are misguided lesbians. It is not always possible to make clear distinctions.

Intersections on a Transmap

More pertinent to this discussion are the differing but also overlapping ways in which the terms *FTM* and *transmen* are used.[11] "FTM" is used in at least two ways: female-to-male and female-toward-male (as in having surgery) or female-toward-man/masculine (as in gender or gender identity). In the first instance FTMs are those individuals who pursue genital surgeries and disappear into society as men. Those who use the term in this sense do so to designate a temporary status and as a transitional definition of the process they are going through. Once through the process (no matter what surgeries they ultimately have), their identities shift from FTM to that of males/men. In a personal communication with me in 1998 Gary Bowen referred to these individuals as "hardcore FTMs." They are also referred to as "stealth" or as "woodworkers." They may already be living as men. Often when (and if) they contact a support group or other support network they do not maintain that contact for long. They tend to obtain the information or resources they need and then disappear again into the woodwork. Some may resurface after five, ten, even twenty years to seek new information and connect with others like themselves. In the second instance, FTMs may retain the label in order to

acknowledge their female socialization and history. Some prefer this terminology because they are moving toward male and may not think of themselves as men. Some may prefer the term *FTM* because they identify as female men. Those who use it in this sense may or may not take testosterone and may not have surgeries that would alter their bodies.

In its original coinage, "transman" was intended to be an encompassing term that included anyone assigned female at birth but who identifies somewhere on the so-called continuum between male/female and man/woman. They may or may not take testosterone and may or may not have body-altering surgeries but live either some or all of the time as men (Bowen 1998, personal communication). Some transmen still use "FTM" as a way to reinforce the fact that they have a female socialization and history. Others may use "transman" instead to distance themselves from anything that connotes female or feminine. Still others use the term to distance themselves from their transsexual status.

Transmen and FTMs may also use any number of the other transidentity terms to name themselves. In essence, the terms *transman* and *FTM* are interchangeable. That may be because there is always, at some physical level, an awareness of having a history as female, if for no other reason than being assigned such at birth. Sex reassignment surgeries (in particular, genital surgeries) are inadequate no matter what techniques are used. Depending upon the technique and the surgeon's skill there is at least one or more physical reminder of once being female in body: scars, an inability to have spontaneous erections, and (for most) a lack of sensation in the penile shaft, the insertion of a prosthetic device for intercourse, and an inability to urinate through the penis.

Nonetheless, some transmen and FTMs who have these surgeries may deny ever being female. But some among both those who do not have genital surgery and those who do may retain a label of trans. That label may be retained, in part, because testosterone does change the shape, yet the genitalia are anatomically still female. Some FTMs and transmen may never identify as transsexuals, contact a support group, or have sex reassignment surgeries yet live out their lives as men. Some who do contact medico-psychological practitioners may only have chest surgery and/or a hysterectomy/salpingo-oophorectomy (the removal of the ovaries and fallopian tubes) yet still identify as men.[12] Regardless of what steps are taken, most FTMs and transmen live out their lives as men.

To encompass all manifestations of transness, I prefer the term *transpeople*. My intention is to move away from "transsexual" because the label implies female/feminine identity (Bolin 1988: 77). Transpeople is a change from the sexed connotations of transsexual, which only heightens the confusion between sexual behavior and gender identity. When a distinction is necessary between female-to-male and male-to-female, I have prefaced the term *transpeople* with "female-bodied" and "male-bodied," respectively.

The conceptualization of the term *female-bodied* resulted from conversations with female-bodied transpeople. "Female-bodied man" is akin to but not the same as "man with a vagina," nor is it meant to imply women who became men. Rather "female-bodied" recognizes that the individual was assigned as female or had a female body. Biologically, the individual's genitalia, chromosomes, and phenotype (although that varies from person to person) are those of a female. Many may have medical interventions that reconstruct their bodies to be more congruent with their identities, yet they never, contrary to what some may believe, have male bodies in the same sense that those born male, phenotypically and genotypically, do. Instead they have transbodies or transsexed bodies, which is not to insinuate that they are imprisoned by or limited in phenotype or genotype. After all, if they were, testosterone would not have the effects it does nor would they be able to live as men.

The designation *man* recognizes that the individual lived (or is living) as a man. Female-bodied men or female-bodied transpeople are also those individuals who acknowledge that their bodies are those of biological females but may or may not identify as either a female transvestite or a female-to-male transsexual. By making that distinction I am signifying female-bodied transpeople's differences from male-bodied transpeople. I intend this signification as a move away from generalizations and toward specificity and the equal marking of females and males.[13]

I use "FTM" and "transmen" as identities, recognizing that not all people who use the label *transsexual* have an identity as FTM or as transmen. One misunderstanding that occurs in the FTM/transmen community centers around the issue of retaining trans terms whatever they may be and

identifying as trans. On one hand, many see being transsexual as a temporary status, and many do not understand why transmen and FTMs want to be, in their estimation, anything other than men. On the other hand, many have trouble understanding why some want to deny so vehemently (in many cases) that they were born female and socialized as women. Perhaps part of the misunderstanding is in not making a distinction between an adjective and a noun. "FTM" and whatever "trans" prefix is used are descriptors (adjectives) of the process of going from being seen as female to being seen as men. For the majority of FTMs and transmen, being transidentified is not the sum of all existence any more than being transsexual is for others.

Rather than engage in turf wars, it is important to recognize and acknowledge overall similarities as well as those of detail. Overall similarities occur among female-bodied transpeople, such as being socialized – although in varying degrees – as girls who presumably grow up to be women yet identify as men or with masculinity. There are also similarities of detail, such as whether to live as men and pursue or reject medical interventions. In the former, the similarities intersect on a transmap. In the latter, the differences result in the choice of different paths. Failing to recognize and, accordingly, acknowledge similarities as well as differences and diversity among transmen and FTMs has a coercive and regulatory effect (Bohan 1993: 8; Butler 1990).

Notes

1. David O. Cauldwell is credited with coining the term *transsexual* in 1949 (275–80). Hirschfeld (1991) used the term as early as 1910, however. Regardless of its coinage, it did not come into general use until the 1950s following Christine Jorgensen's return to the United States after her "sex change" surgery in 1953. Cauldwell, in a commentary on Jorgensen, did not use the term *transsexual*. He stated unequivocally that only hermaphrodites ("true" and "pseudo") can change their sexes (1953: 494–503). Thus it is ironic that Cauldwell's case of "psychopathia transexualis" involved a female-bodied individual who was not a hermaphrodite.

2. Jon Meyer, a psychiatrist, prefers the latter usage (1974: 276). He is, however, adamantly opposed to transpeople receiving body-altering surgeries and was one of the people behind the closing of the Johns Hopkins Gender Identity Clinic in 1979.

3. Although Hirschfeld is credited with coining the term *transvestite*, according to the *Oxford English Dictionary* the first use of "transvest" was in 1652 in *Camus' National Paradox*, translated by J. Wright: "Has often did shee please her fancy with the imagination of *transvesting* herself, and by the help of a Man's disguise deceiving the eyes of those that watched her deportments?" If, as Friedli asserts, "the word transvestite originally meant a woman who wore men's clothes" (1991: 4), then it is more than ironic that the term is now considered exclusively applicable to male-bodied people. The etymology of the term lends credence to her claim.

4. Devin Hathaway explained his coinage of this term in a personal communication (March 12, 1998): "Some people may reject the labels 'girl' and 'woman' and also not rush to embrace the default choices, 'boy,' 'man,' 'butch,' etc." That is especially true for "folks who have not transitioned yet and/or do not pass all the time." After transition some people may "begin to self-identify as men (with the twist that they are men with unusual sexual anatomy or history)." The term is meant to be "open on the point of self-identity."

5. Many of these individuals define themselves as *bigendered*, signifying their belief that they are both male/men/masculine and female/women/feminine and also rejecting the terms *transvestite* and *crossdresser*.

6. Transpeople refer to the community in at least three ways: "gender community," "transgendered community," and "transcommunity" (which I use throughout).

7. Examples of these terms can be found in Benjamin (1969; 1977[1966]); Pauly (1974a, b); Steiner, ed. (1985); and Stoller (1975).

8. By subjectivity I mean the sense of self, conscious and also unconscious, and how individuals understand themselves as persons. Transsubjectivity is the sense of self and understanding of the self as a transperson.

9. My appreciation to Carolyn Allen for re-posing this dilemma and to Sue-Ellen Jacobs, Evelyn Blackwood, Jeff Dickemann, Rena Davis Phoenix, and Spencer Bergstedt for many discussions concerning the differences between butches, mannish lesbians, mannish women, and female-bodied transpeople. See Burana, Roxxie, and Due (1994); Kennedy and Davis (1993); Nestle, ed. (1992); and Newton (1993).

10. Most of these studies operate from several premises: (1) all lesbians and FTMs/transmen have masculine gender identities (based on masculinity/femininity measurements); (2) both lesbians' and transmen/FTMs' sexualities (desire and behavior) are abnormal; (3) these identities and sexualities are defective and as a result (4) both FTMs/transmen and lesbians are maladjusted; and (5) an etiology

must be determined to explain these defective identities and abnormal sexualities.

11. My sincere appreciation to Jackal, Spencer Bergstedt, Rena Davis Phoenix, Jamison Green, Max Fuhrmann, Stephen Whittle, C. Jacob Hale, Gary Bowen, and Mike Hernandez for their comments and suggestions on terminology.

12. A hysterectomy and a bilateral salpingo-oophorectomy are the surgical methods of removing all female reproductive organs: the uterus, ovaries, and fallopian tubes.

13. Bowen points out in a personal communication (1998) that this terminology is not inclusive of intersexed people. It is not my intent to be exclusive; however, as Bowen also notes, intersexed people are not diagnosed as transsexuals according to the *Diagnostic and Statistical Manual of Mental Disorders* (American Psychiatric Association 1987). I agree that intersexed people have unresolved needs and issues because of being excluded from the diagnostic category. To my knowledge, no intersexed people have been a part of my research, and thus I feel unqualified to specifically include them.

References

American Psychiatric Association. 1987. *Diagnostic and Statistical Manual of Mental Disorders.* 3d edn. Washington: American Psychiatric Association.

Benjamin, Harry. 1969. "Introduction." In *Transsexualism and Sex Reassignment*, ed. Richard Green and John Money, 1–11. Baltimore: Johns Hopkins University Press.

Benjamin, Harry. 1977 [1966]. *The Transsexual Phenomenon.* New York: Warner Books.

Birke, Lynda I. A. 1982. "From Sin to Sickness: Hormonal Theories of Lesbianism." In *Biological Woman: The Convenient Myth*, ed. Ruth Hubbard, Mary Sue Henifin, and Barbara Fried, 71–90. Cambridge: Schenkman Publishing.

Blanchard, Ray. 1985. "Research Methods for the Typological Study of Gender Disorders in Males." In *Gender Dysphoria: Development, Research, Management*, ed. Betty Steiner, 227–57. New York: Plenum Press.

Blanchard, Ray, and Kurt Freund. 1983. "Measuring Masculine Gender Identity in Females." *Journal of Consulting and Clinical Psychology* 51 (2): 205–14.

Bockting, Walter. 1997. "Transgender Coming Out: Implications for the Clinical Management of Gender Dysphoria." In *Gender Blending*, ed. Bonnie Bullough, Vern Bullough, and James Elias, 48–53. Amherst: Prometheus Books.

Bohan, Janis S. 1993. "Regarding Gender: Essentialism, Constructionism, and Feminist Psychology." *Psychology of Women Quarterly* 17 (1): 5–21.

Bolin, Anne. 1988. *In Search of Eve: Transsexual Rites of Passage.* South Hadley: Bergin and Garvey.

Bolin, Anne. 1994. "Transcending and Transgendering: Male-to-Female Transsexuals, Dichotomy, and Diversity." In *Third Sex, Third Gender: Beyond Sexual Dimorphism in Culture and History*, ed. Gilbert Herdt, 447–85. Chicago: University of Chicago Press.

Bradley, Susan J., Ray Blanchard, Susan Coates, Richard Green, Stephen B. Levine, Heino Meyer-Bahlburg, Ira Pauly, and Kenneth Zucker. 1991. "Interim Report of the DSM-IV Subcommittee on Gender Identity Disorders." *Archives of Sexual Behavior* 20 (4): 333–43.

Burana, Lily, Roxxie, and Linnea Due. 1994. *Dagger: On Butch Women.* San Francisco: Cleis Press.

Butler, Judith. 1990. *Gender Trouble: Feminism and The Subversion of Identity.* New York: Routledge.

Cauldwell, David O. 1949. "Psychopathia Transexualis." *Sexology Magazine*, Dec: 275–80.

Cauldwell, David O. 1953. "Man Becomes Woman." *Sexology Magazine*, March: 494–503.

Cole, Collier M., and Walter J. Meyer III. 1998. "Transgender Behavior and the DSM IV." In *Current Concepts in Transgender Identity*, ed. Dallas Denny, 227–36. New York: Garland.

Cole, Sandra S. 1998. "The Female Experience of the Femme." In *Current Concepts in Transgender Identity*, ed. Dallas Denny, 373–90. New York: Garland.

Docter, Richard. 1988. *Transvestites and Transsexuals: Toward a Theory of Cross-Gender Behavior.* New York: Plenum Press.

Ehrhardt, Anke A., Gudrun Grisanti, and Elizabeth McCauley. 1979. "Female-to-Male Transsexuals Compared to Lesbians: Behavioral Patterns of Childhood and Adolescent Development." *Archives of Sexual Behavior* 8 (6): 481–90.

Feinbloom, Deborah. 1977. *Transvestites and Transsexuals: Mixed Views.* New York: Delta Books.

Friedli, Lynne. 1991. "In Male Disguise." *Connexions* 37: 4–5, 30.

Green, James. 1994b. "Inside the TS Closet." Unpublished ms., Emeryville, Calif.

Halberstam, Judith. 1998. "Transgender Butch: Butch/FTM Border Wars and the Masculine Continuum." *GLQ: A Journal of Lesbian and Gay Studies* 4 (2): 287–310.

Hale, C. Jacob. 1995. "Transgendered Strategies for Refusing Gender." Presented at the Society for Women in Philosophy, Pacific Division, May 20, Los Angeles.

Hale, C. Jacob. 1998. "Consuming the Living, Dis(re)membering the Dead in the Butch/FTM Borderlands." *GLQ: A Journal of Lesbian and Gay Studies* 4 (2): 311–48.

Hemmings, Clare. 1996. "From Lesbian Nation to Transgender Liberation: A Bisexual Feminist Perspective." *Journal of Gay, Lesbian, and Bisexual History* 1 (1): 37–59.

Hirschfeld, Magnus. 1966 [1938]. *Sexual Anomalies and Perversions.* London: Encyclopedic Press.

Hirschfeld, Magnus. 1991. *Transvestites: The Erotic Drive to Cross Dress.* Trans. Michael A. Lombardi-Nash. Buffalo: Prometheus Books.

Holly. 1991. "The Transgender Alternative." *TV/TS Tapestry Journal*, no. 59: 31–3.

Karlen, Arno. 1971. *Sexuality and Homosexuality: A New View.* New York: W. W. Norton.

Kennedy, Elizabeth Lapovsky, and Madeline D. Davis. 1994. *Boots of Leather, Slippers Of Gold: The History of a Lesbian Community.* New York: Penguin.

Levine, Steven, Heino Meyer-Bahlburg, Ira Pauly, and Kenneth Zucker. 1991. "Interim Report of the DSM-IV Subcommittee on Gender Identity Disorder." *Archives of Sexual Behavior* 20 (4): 333–43.

Lynn, Merissa Sherrill. 1984. "Definitions Follow-Up." *TV/TS Tapestry Journal*, no. 44: 60–1.

Lynn, Merissa Sherrill. 1988. "Definitions of Terms Commonly Used in the Transvestite-Transsexual Community." *TV/TS Tapestry Journal*, no. 51: 19–31.

Lyons, Terrie. 1986. "Gender Identity and Internalized Object Relations: A Comparison of Female-to-Male Transsexuals, Lesbians and Heterosexual Women." Ph.D. diss., Wright Institute Graduate School.

Mageo, Jeannette. 1995. "The Reconfiguring Self." *American Anthropologist* 97 (2): 282–96.

McCauley, Elizabeth, and Anke Ehrhardt. 1978. "Role Expectations and Definitions: A Comparison of Female Transsexuals and Lesbians." *Journal of Homosexuality* 3 (2): 137–47.

Meyer, Jon K. 1974. "Psychiatric Considerations in the Sexual Reassignment of Non-Intersex Individuals." *Clinics in Plastic Surgery* 1 (2): 275–83.

Nestle, Joan, ed. 1992. *The Persistent Desire: A Butch-Femme Reader.* Boston: Alyson Publications.

Newton, Esther. 1993. *Cherry Grove, Fire Island: Sixty Years in America's First Gay and Lesbian Town.* Boston: Beacon Press.

Nicholson, Linda. 1994. "Interpreting Gender." *Signs* 20 (1): 79–105.

Pauly, Ira. 1974a. "Female Transsexualism: Part I." *Archives of Sexual Behavior* 3 (6): 487–507.

Pauly, Ira. 1974b. "Female Transsexualism: Part II." *Archives of Sexual Behavior* 3 (6): 509–26.

Prince, Virginia. 1992. "Rose by Any Other Name." *TV/TS Tapestry Journal*, no. 60: 20–1.

Rubin, Gayle. 1992. "Of Catamites and Kings: Reflections on Butch, Gender, and Boundaries." In *The Persistent Desire: A Femme-Butch Reader*, ed. Joan Nestle, 466–82. Boston: Alyson Publications.

Steiner, Betty, ed. 1985. *Gender Dysphoria: Development, Research, Management.* New York: Plenum Press.

Stoller, Robert. 1968. *Sex and Gender, Volume I.* London: Hogarth Press.

Stoller, Robert. 1975. *Sex and Gender.* Vol. 2: *The Transsexual Experiment.* New York: Jason Aronson.

Stoller, Robert. 1982. "Transvestism in Women." *Archives of Sexual Behavior* 11 (2): 99–115.

Strassberg, Donald, Howard Roback, Jean Cunningham, Embry McKee, and Paul Larson. 1979. "Psychopathology in Self-Identified Female-to-Male Transsexuals, Homosexuals, and Heterosexuals." *Archives of Sexual Behavior* 8 (6): 491–6.

Weston, Kath. 1993. "Lesbian/Gay Studies in the House of Anthropology." *Annual Review of Anthropology* 22: 339–67.

Wilchins, Riki Anne. 1997. *Read My Lips: Sexual Subversion and the End of Gender.* Ithaca: Firebrand.

Part V
National/Transnational Identities

25

National Identity and Citizenship

ROSS POOLE

National Identity

To be an African is not a choice, it is a
condition . . . To be [an African] is not through
lack of being integrated in Europe . . . neither is
it from regret of the crimes perpetrated by "my
people" . . . No, it is simply the only opening
I have for making use of all my senses and
capabilities . . . The [African] earth was the
first to speak. I have been pronounced once
and for all.

(Breyten Breytenbach)[1]

For the past two centuries or more, a good deal of
rhetoric and a not inconsiderable amount of blood
have been expended to demonstrate that our national identity is the primary form of identity available to us, that it underlies and informs all our
other identities, and that in case of conflict it should
take priority over them. Many people have been
prepared to sacrifice, not only themselves but those
dear to them, and have put the claims of the nation
ahead of the demands of religion, political commitment and morality. We now need to ask: What is it
about national identity which has rendered these
claims and sacrifices so terribly plausible?

The beginnings of an answer to this question
were provided by one of the very first theorists
of nationalism, Johann Gottlieb Herder.[2] Herder
argued that a nation is constituted through its language and culture. He emphasised the significance
of the practices, customs and rituals of everyday
life, and of the stories, folk beliefs and myths in
terms of which people make sense of their lives –
indeed, he can claim to be one of the first theorists
of what we now call "popular culture". The most

fundamental constituent of a culture was the language in which these stories, beliefs and myths find
expression. Language and culture were not, Herder
argued, merely aspects of the social environment
within which people made their lives; they were
constitutive of their very identity. For Herder – as
for Charles Taylor who explicitly follows Herder
in this respect – human identity exists only in a
framework of interpretation. The basic framework
is provided by the language and cultural symbols
in terms of which we become aware of ourselves
and of others. Though our native language is not
part of our natural equipment, it becomes a second
nature. It provides the taken for granted and inescapable framework within which we think, experience, imagine and dream. It provides us with a
primary form of self- and other-consciousness. It is
most intimately involved in the ways in which we
perceive the world, the forms in which we think,
and even in the manner in which we experience
our feelings and emotions. But as it enters into our
most intimate sense of self, at the same time it
defines a special relationship with those other selves
who share the same world, think in the same way,
and experience the same emotions.

Cultural identity does not always take the form
of national identity. It is plausible to think that, for
most of human history, the cultural and linguistic
horizons of the vast majority of people were limited to the small rural communities in which they
lived. Those who ruled over them did not think of
themselves as sharing a common culture with their
subjects, and certainly did not claim political legitimacy on this basis. Part of the secret of national
identity lies in the emergence of vernacular print
languages, their spread through large numbers of

the population, and their coming to play a privileged role in public and private life. As these languages formed the identities of those who lived in a particular region, they provided the foundation for a shared sense of belonging to the same community. But a common language is not the whole story. On its own, this would only create an extended network of mutual recognition. The users of a specific language might well recognise other users of that language; but they need not form the concept of a *community* of which they are all members. In this respect they might be like participants who will recognise other participants (potential buyers and sellers), but need not form the concept of a market to which all buyers and sellers belong. Or, to take an example nearer at hand, they might be like persons who recognise other persons (i.e. other bearers of rights and duties), but who do not form the concept of a moral community to which they all belong. So the other aspect of the story of national identity was the mobilisation of linguistic and other cultural resources to create a representation of the *nation* to which those who shared a language and a culture belonged. A nation – like all "imagined communities" – is not merely an extended web of relationships between those who share a certain identity; it also involves a conception of the community to which the members of the nation belong.[3]

A major source of the strength of national identity has been in its inescapability. For much of the modern world, the nation has appropriated to itself the linguistic and cultural means necessary for the articulation of the sense of self of its members. The fusion of language, culture and polity defined by the nation has so entered our conception of ourselves that it becomes difficult to address the question of who we are except in terms which presuppose that we already have a national identity. As we come to have a sense of who we were, we form a conception of ourselves as belonging to a particular nation. As we speak, we find ourselves spoken for. We are, in Breytenbach's words, "pronounced, once and for all". The strength and inescapability of the feelings and commitments associated with national identity has tempted some theorists to see them as evidence of deep and primordial attachments.[4] There is no need to take this route. The language and cultural symbols through which we now understand who we are may be relatively recent phenomena, but for most of us they have come to provide an inescapable structure of experience.

Another aspect of the strength of a national identity lies in the richness of the cultural resources which are employed in forming the conception of national community. This identity provides us with a land in which we are at home, a history which is ours, and a privileged access to a vast heritage of culture and creativity. It not only provides us with the means to understand this heritage; it also assures us that it is *ours*. If on occasion the nation may require that we endure losses and hardships on its behalf, it also makes available a fund of meanings, pleasures and rewards beyond anything that we are likely to find in our individual lives. Where it asks us to make sacrifices, even to the extent of giving up our lives for the sake of the nation, the voluntary act of renunciation exemplifies an identity which transcends the limitations of our own particular and limited concerns. Paradoxically, the greater the sacrifice, the more significant the values embodied in the nation. By its capacity to demand sacrifices, the nation provides its members with a share in a life which transcends their own.[5]

Like other identities, a national identity provides us with a specific *moral* agenda. Indeed, it has been suspicion about the content of this agenda which has led many to be wary of the claims of nationalism. Our national identity, for example, is often used as an argument for the existence of special obligations. It is suggested that I have a responsibility to my compatriots that I do not have to other – perhaps equally deserving – foreigners. That one's fellow nationals are morally privileged in this way has seemed to many as one of the most problematic features of nationalism.[6] What moral reason do I, as a member of a relatively affluent country, have to give preference to someone merely because he or she happens to be a fellow citizen, when there are many who are vastly more in need of assistance? There is a genuine issue here. Too often, national identity has served as a reason to ignore morally more urgent demands outside the borders of one's own nation. Still, we need to recognise that the nation is not the only moral community which privileges mutual responsibilities between members over those from outside the group. To be a member of a family, a group of friends, or even a university, for example, means that one has greater responsibilities to some than one has to others. To enter into certain kinds of human relationship simply *is* to acknowledge that the concerns of those who are also involved in those relationships will, in certain respects, take priority over the concerns of others. These relations are, in part, constituted by a framework of special responsibilities. They could not exist except on this basis.[7] The point is not to object to preferential treatment *per se*. We should rather ask whether the relationship and communities which require preferential treatment are inescapable or desirable features of human life, and whether they contribute to larger human goals. No doubt the extent of the preferential treatment licensed by the nation – and by the family for that matter – should be limited by considerations of equality and justice. But that preferences should be limited does not mean that they should not exist.[8] Indeed, as David Miller has argued, there is good reason to suppose that the nation has provided its members with a stronger motivation to extend their concerns to the needs of a larger community than has the appeal to universal principle.[9]

It is also important to recognise that the existence of special obligations between members of a nation does not exhaust the moral content of national identity. The moral agenda defined by the nation is more complex than this. For example, if I have special responsibilities *to* my co-nationals, e.g. to provide assistance when they need it, to provide for their welfare through the taxation system, etc., it is also the case that I have a special involvement in what they do.[10] This aspect of the moral agenda of national identity is most apparent in those cases where we take pride in the achievements of our co-nationals, for example, in the sporting triumphs of athletes or the discoveries of scientists. This is not a pride in what I as an individual achieved, nor even in what I imagine myself to have achieved. The emotion of pride attests to the belief that I share an identity with the athlete or scientist, and their achievement belongs to all who share that identity. On the other hand, we sometimes find ourselves implicated in the failings of our compatriots. This involvement may be minimal: I feel a twinge of embarrassment at the boorish behaviour of Australian tourists overseas. But it may involve much more than this: I may well feel some responsibility to make amends for what has been done by compatriots, especially if it is done in the name of the nation to which I belong. As with the case of pride, the embarrassment or feeling of responsibility attests to a shared identity.[11]

The moral agenda of national identity overlaps with that of persons, but is not identical with it. As a person, I feel pride or guilt at what I as an indi-

vidual have done or failed to do. If what I have done is especially meritorious, I may deserve to be rewarded; if it is especially bad, I may deserve to be punished. In each case, the moral responsibility is sheeted home to me as an individual.[12] Guilt, and the sense of pride in which it is the contrary of guilt, belongs within an individualist model agenda. On the other hand, when I am embarrassed at the behaviour of my fellow nationals, the emotion I feel is that of *shame*. Guilt would only be appropriate if I felt that I was somehow responsible for their poor behaviour (perhaps I gave them too much to drink). And when I am proud of my compatriots' achievements, it is not the pride of individual responsibility, but of collective identity. It is not I who should be punished or rewarded; but the individuals concerned.[13]

It is useful to contrast the moral world of persons with that of national identity in terms of their different relations to the past. Part of the process of my becoming a person is learning to take responsibility for my past and carry out the commitments incurred in the past. Acquiring the "right to make promises" is a crucial part of the moral education of persons. When I discover that I have done things in the past which I have forgotten or repressed, I must recognise that I now must take responsibility for them. Unless special circumstances obtain, the credit or blame which was mine remains. Acquiring a national identity also involves learning to take responsibility for past events. As I become conscious of myself as a member of a nation, I become aware of a certain past – the history of my nation – and I learn to appropriate it as a past which is mine – though one I share with many others. This may be a source of pleasure and pride, or perhaps of shame; in either case, it is a past in which I am morally implicated. I may have been brought up with the idea that my nation had a heroic imperial past; but I am then told that it was one of exploitation and oppression. I may resist this account. But if I am persuaded to accept it, I must also accept that this national repressed past is one for which I must now take some responsibility. What was a source of pride is now a source of shame.

It is this moral involvement in the past which fuels the controversies about the meaning of national histories, for example, of the involvement of the United States in slavery, of postcolonial countries in the expropriation and genocide of their indigenous peoples, of Germany in the Holocaust, and so on, which have been familiar items in recent public debate. These are not matters of mere scholarly interest; they concern the self-conception of the nation, and often define its present responsibilities. It has been suggested by many, even by such sympathetic interpreters of nationalism as Ernest Renan and David Miller, that there is an inevitable element of myth in the stories which nations tell themselves.[14] No doubt this is true. But it should not be exaggerated. Celebratory national histories are subject to public debate and criticism; and it is not inevitable that the forces of historical self-justification and glorification will win out. The long and painful debates about national histories, in the United States, Germany, Canada and Australia, would be pointless unless there was some commitment to establishing the truth about the national past.

If the moral agenda associated with national identity includes an involvement with the national past, it may well carry with it a responsibility to make reparation for what was done in the past.[15] To many this has seemed unjust. Why should people living now be held to share responsibility for acts which were performed (in some cases) many years before they were born? While this is not the place to explore this issue in depth (I will say something more about it in the next section), it is important to distinguish the different ways in which the issue of "collective responsibility" arises in the moral world of persons and in other spheres. As persons, we can only be held responsible for the consequences of acts which we as individuals have performed. We have a general responsibility to respect the rights of other persons, but, after that, our responsibilities are up to us. But of course we are not just persons, and this is not the only moral world we inhabit. As I have already noted, as members of a family, we may find that we have responsibilities – and also sources of pleasure and pride – which are not consequent upon anything that we as an individual have done. As a member of a nation we are in a similar position. Our national identity carries with it a moral involvement in our nation's past and its future, an involvement which may bring with it special sources of joy and happiness, but also special responsibilities to compensate, make reparation, or to remember.

In certain circumstances, governments inherit the obligation to make reparation for what was done in the past. For example, the postwar Federal Republic of Germany acknowledged its responsibility to make reparations for crimes committed against Jews by its predecessor. There is an institutional imperative here. There must be a mechanism which establishes a continuity of commitment between one government and its successor. However, underlying this mechanism, even in the case of institutional continuity but especially where one form of State power replaces another (as in the German case), is the idea that it is the nation which inherits the responsibilities – as well as the glories – of its past.

For most of us, our national identity was not chosen, but determined by the contingencies of birth and upbringing. It is this very contingency which makes this identity seem morally suspect. How can something so arbitrary, over which I have had such little control, determine a significant part of my moral agenda? Part of the answer lies in the fact that these contingencies have become pervasive and inescapable features of our lives. They come to us in the language we speak, the culture we identify with, and the political responsibilities we may evade but which we cannot escape. If, from a more global perspective, they are local and particular, they have come to form an essential part of identity. As such, they bring with them commitments and responsibilities which we may evade, but we cannot deny.[16] The contours of national identity are often most apparent to the expatriate, most poignantly perhaps to the political exile. That the experience of exile is one of loss, even of tragedy; and the fact that the political allegiances of so many exiles still lie with the destiny of their nation attests to the centrality of national identity in our lives. Even those who think of themselves in transnational or cosmopolitan terms still find themselves morally implicated by what has been done in the name of their nation, as Australians are implicated in the expropriation and genocide of the Aboriginal population, Americans in slavery, Germans in the Holocaust, English in Ireland, and so on. The moral reach of national identity remains present, even in the thoughts and emotions of those who would reject the claims of nationalism.

[. . .]

Citizenship and National Identity

Hegel was well aware of the emergence of political, cultural and intellectual nationalism in the early nineteenth century and he was contemptuous of it.

For Hegel, nationalism substituted emotion for reason, and particularity for the universal.[17] But there is little doubt that the doctrine of national identity was to have much greater presence in later history than Hegel's own project of rational reconciliation. If we are to accept the judgement of the past 200 years of world history – and Hegel could hardly object to the choice of tribunal – then it is not the rational identification of the individual with the political structure but national identity which has provided the moral resources for modern citizenship.

There is a *Bildung* involved in the formation of national identity. However, it is not the narrative towards mature citizenship described by Hegel. It begins in the family. As Hegel's compatriot, Johann Gottlieb Herder, recognised, we begin to acquire our national identity literally on our mother's knee. We discover our nation – as we discover ourselves – in the bed-time stories we are told, the songs which put us to sleep, the games we play as children, the heroes we are taught to admire and the enemies we come to fear and detest. Our national identity comes to us in the language in which we learn to articulate our most primitive demands. As we learn to speak, we find ourselves already spoken for. If, in our later life, the market and its associated institutions contribute to our sense of national identity, this is not because of their character as rational economic activity, but because the transactions are performed in the language, the cultural forms and modes of interaction characteristic of the nation. Even the currency in which we are paid for our endeavours will bear its imprint. But the rewards which accrue to our national belonging are not, or not merely, financial. We are provided with access to a store of cultural achievement, a history of triumph and tragedy, and a land, all of which go well beyond the possibilities of our individual or local aspirations but which are nevertheless defined as ours. Our national identity – any identity, for that matter – would not be able to demand sacrifices of us if it did not also provide us with pleasures and satisfactions.

National identity is never fully available to the rational reflection and reappropriation which was such a central part of Hegel's presentation of life in the modern State. In part this is because the conceptions of reason which are available to us are as much cultural products as the language we speak. Reason may be universal in aspiration, but the forms in which it actually exists are almost as diverse as

their host cultures. It does not provide an external vantage point from which claims of a specific national culture may be assessed. And if it did, it would *for that reason* be inadequate to the task. The resources which are necessary to understand national identity are those provided by the language, history, literature, music and other cultural traditions which form the national narrative. If reflection attempts to occupy a place outside the nation's narrative, it will deny itself the resources fully to understand it. Esperanto – or French – is not the language in which to appreciate the plays of Shakespeare nor the poetry of Pushkin. A good deal of the strength of a culture is only fully available to those who are within it. This is not only because those whose culture it is are more likely to have the resources to understand. In principle, these resources are available to the anthropologically inclined outsider. It is also because it is *their* culture. As Yael Tamir has emphasised, my nation – like my family – has a particular claim on me, not merely because it is different from others, nor because it can from some vantage point be judged to be superior to others. Its claim lies in the fact that it is mine.[18] For me to step outside that web of relationships in order to discover its sufficient reason would be to repudiate the very particularity which constitutes its moral force.

This does not mean that national identity is unreflective. All national cultures provide resources for internal criticism and are open to external influence. Every national culture is subject to development and change. Reflection is not the prerogative of the philosopher, nor is it only a matter of reason; it is part of the day to day business of politics and culture. Philosophy should seek both to understand what is at stake in these debates and also to contribute to them. But the very universality which is the ambition and the occasional achievement of philosophy places certain barriers in the way of both these projects. In searching for a form of reason adequate to evaluate the claims of a national culture, philosophical reflection risks overlooking the call of particularity. We must also recognise that other cultural forms – including literature, art, sport and music – have a role to play in contributing to the process by which a nation reflects on what it has been and what it ought to be. The role of reason is not, as Hegel imagined, to comprehend the whole; but to understand what it can, and also to understand the limits of that understanding. Philosophy too should recognise its own limitations.

There is a certain hubris in the pretensions of philosophy to occupy a privileged position in the debates about national belonging.

It is difficult to trace the genealogy of national identity in seventeenth- and eighteenth-century political thought, not least because the new identity was being formulated in the language of the old. Rousseau and his Jacobin followers employed the rhetoric of citizenship in their attempts to conceive and construct a political community. Both Walzer and Constant treat this as an unsuccessful attempt to revive classical conceptions in the changed conditions of modern life. Perhaps this corresponds to Rousseau's own conception of his project. But, on a close reading, it is clear that, combined with a republican discourse about the nature of the State, political obligation and the like, Rousseau was employing another rhetoric about identity, culture, land, history and belonging. Rousseau is as much part of the story of modern nationalism as he is a late episode in classical republicanism.[19] Herder, on the other hand, is recognised to be a nationalist (though he had some very uncharacteristic ideas about political sovereignty); what is not so often noted is that he was also a republican.[20] The entanglement of citizenship with what we can now recognise as national identity is symptomatic of later developments. For modern citizenship has always relied for its moral force on its association with national identity, and national identity has always aspired to citizenship. The French Revolutionary appeal to citizenship, the *levée en masse*, the politics of mass involvement, not to mention its educational policies and the destruction of regional languages and cultures, were not the anachronistic revivals of a past practice of citizenship, but harbingers of the new politics of nationalism and identity. Indeed, once the fusion of culture and politics is established, then it is possible to wonder whether some form of cultural identity was not presupposed in earlier classical models of citizenship.[21]

When I act according to my national identity, I express what I, in some essential sense, have come to be. In this respect the concept of national identity is analogous to that of classical citizenship. Freedom is the expression of a pre-given essence. But there are major differences. Classical citizenship was appropriate for the politically active élite in societies where most of the population were allowed no political role. It was sustained by activity: each citizen was engaged in politics, and this engagement could plausibly be conceived in terms of self-rule. Politics was not merely about the exercise of power and the distribution of benefits, but was a way of life with its own pleasures and rewards. Citizenship needed to be demonstrated by participation in that life; in principle at least, it was this participation which formed the culture of the State. National identity, on the other hand, is characteristic of large-scale, anonymous societies. It provides the accent and the tone in which everyday life is carried on, but it rarely provides its central focus or content. It is an aspect of our lives, a latent quality available to be mobilised as and when necessary. The key difference between the republican and the national conceptions of citizenship lies in the relationship of the individual to the political realm. For the republican, the relationship is ideally one of *agency*: citizens *form* the State through their political activity. For the nationalist, the relationship is one of *mimesis*: citizens *recognise* themselves in the State. National subjects find their identity affirmed in the political realm, and for this reason make themselves available to its demands.

In practice, the difference between republicanism and nationalism is one of degree. Different political communities encourage more or less participation by citizens in political affairs. In one notable case, the United States of America, certain republican ideals have found their way into significant constitutional documents and have a significant place in the national culture.[22] As we have seen, a healthy political life requires a degree of political participation, so there is good reason to encourage a greater level of political participation in all countries, and to the extent that this becomes an aspect of a national culture, then there will be partial fusion of the two doctrines. However, it is important to recognise that, in the social and political conditions which have obtained in the modern world, there must always be a significant gap between the activities and concerns of the citizen and the realm of politics, and that every state will rely on cultural *mimesis* to fill that gap. The citizen's relationship with the State – the nation-state – is constituted by his or her national identity. It is this which provides the commitment, both to one's fellow citizens and to the political institutions, necessary for public life. It also provides the motivation for some level of participation. Even though modern citizenship is largely a passive affair, as we have seen, it is never completely so. It still requires a certain minimal level of civic engagement in everyday life, as well as the more extreme commitments demanded in times of crisis. It involves a measure of identification with the political community to which one belongs, and a readiness to override one's more private and local concerns in order to act on behalf of that community. In the modern world, it has been the nation which has provided the requisite identity and motivation. Becoming a citizen has involved acquiring the appropriate cultural identity. In certain cases, citizenship may be a matter of choice, as in voluntary migration, and a choice which may be made for purely self-interested reasons. But the responsibilities incurred go beyond the purview of the original decision. Ultimately, it is a responsibility to acquire a new identity, one which is not experienced as a matter of choice.[23]

The rhetoric of national liberation has been a familiar part of world politics for some hundred years now. However, political theorists and philosophers have paid little attention to the notion of freedom involved, perhaps because they have judged it to be both confused and dangerous. No doubt there is good reason for caution here. It is all too easy to catalogue the instances where appeals to national liberation have justified oppression and worse. Still, there is a legitimate thread to the rhetoric and it is important to draw it out. Clearly, it is not equivalent to the liberal notion of freedom of choice, even though the way of nationalism has been chosen by many. As I have already noted, it is closer to the conception of freedom associated with classical citizenship: when I act according to my national identity I express my essential nature. But it goes beyond this. The freedom – "liberation" – sought by the nationalist is that of living in a political and social world which corresponds to one's nature. It is the freedom of living with one's fellow countrymen, those who share one's culture and thus one's identity, and of making one's life within institutions and practices which sustain one's own conception of oneself. We have already had occasion to note this conception of freedom in Hegel, and it may well be that it is implicit in the republican tradition. But the nationalist recognises, as the republican did not, the primary role of culture in forming the relationship between the individual and his or her environment. The freedom of modern citizens is not that of making the political order to which they are subject; it is rather that of making and remaking the cultural world which sustains their own identity. To borrow a metaphor that

Marx used to describe the relationship between humans and the natural world, there is a "metabolism" between socially formed individuals and the culture in which they live.[24] The culture provides the necessary support for their identity, and, as they live, they reproduce that culture.

If national identity is not the negative freedom of choice valued by liberals, it does provide the context in which that freedom is exercised. As Will Kymlicka has argued, we do not exercise our freedom of choice in a void. Choosing, especially where the choices concern the kind of life we intend to lead, presupposes the existence of a framework within which various options may be evaluated. It is:

> only through having a rich and secure cultural structure that people can become aware, in a vivid way, of the options available to them, and intelligently examine their value.[25]

This is not a matter of the national culture providing a set of criteria by which options may be ranked against each other. It is rather that it provides the language in which the choices are articulated, the symbols which give significance to various alternatives, and the sense of belonging which sets the boundaries of the choices which one might make. There is, of course, no a priori necessity that this role is played by our *national* culture. In other historical situations it might be played by a religion, a tribal community, or even a form of political activity of the kind envisaged by republicans. However, in the modern world it has been national cultures which have played this role.

National cultures could not provide the context in which freedom of choice is exercised if they did not also restrict that freedom, any more than the nation-state can provide the legal and political conditions necessary for freedom of choice without also restricting it. One way of expressing this is to say that negative freedom cannot exist without negative *un*freedom. But a more perspicuous mode of expression is that negative freedom requires its positive counterpart. For the recognition of the need for these limitations means that they might in principle be accepted – indeed, willed – as conditions of one's freedom.

The sense of freedom appealed to here is not unique to national identity. It arises in all areas in which a deep commitment is experienced as essential to one's conception of what one is. For example, my commitments to my partner, my friends and my children are not as such experienced as matters of choice. Or it may be that I have a commitment to a certain way of life, perhaps through vocation, as on a romantic conception of the artist, or perhaps through habituation. Choice is involved in *how* I fulfil these commitments, not in *whether* I do so. Indeed, when I begin to experience them as matters of choice, this is likely to be a symptom of the waning of the commitment. On some occasions, I acquire these commitments through an act of choice. For example, I get married or choose to have children. Sometimes, however, I incur the commitment in ways which I could not have chosen. For example, the responsibilities I have to my parents or other members of my family. When I act to fulfil these commitments, I do so not because I choose the action from a range of alternatives, but because I feel I must. Of course, in many cases the choice is "objectively" available: there is no law or even very much social pressure compelling me to act in a certain way. But it is not "subjectively" present: the alternative is not a presence in my conception of what I might do. That the alternative is objectively available may not be important to us. Indeed, in certain cases we undertake formal commitments which do constrain our future choices just in order to make public the depth of our commitment. To conceive of these as matters of choice is not so much an indication of the high value placed on freedom as a symptom of a lack of depth.

Of course, commitments are subject to change: artists become accountants, devoted spouses form new attachments, and migrants seek to better themselves in foreign lands. It is important – and this is a significant truth in liberalism – that such changes be possible. But it would be superficial to bring these under the rubric of freedom of choice. They involve a change in the determinants of choice – the standards we bring to bear, the aspirations we seek to further, and the meaning we assign to our life as a whole. For the individuals concerned, such transitions do not involve a choice between clearly understood alternatives, but a step – or a leap – from a present which has become unsatisfactory to a murky future. Such transitions are not and *ought not* to be easy. Where we enter legally enforceable commitments we do so partly in order to make future changes difficult. In the case of national identity, for most of us the transition is almost impossible to make completely: our national culture has

inescapably formed our voice and our vision. Though here too we may (and certainly ought to) allow the possibility of change, we do not feel that it should be too lightly made.

The role of deep commitments – of *identities* – is analogous to that of constitutions in political life. Normally, the constitution provides the framework for political debate and decision; it is not itself the subject of debate and decision. But in certain situations, it may – and should – become subject to the political process, and the constitution itself should make provision for this. But it will do so in a way which recognises that the changes envisaged are more fundamental than others, and will require more consideration and (perhaps) a greater burden of proof. In other words, there is a distinction between the political change enabled by the constitution and the politics of constitutional change. In an analogous way, our national identity provides one of the contexts in which we exercise our freedom of choice. For this reason, it is not itself subject to that freedom. But this does not mean that it is not subject to change. Debate about the meaning of a nation's past, about the nature of commitments involved in membership of a nation, and about the criteria of membership, are all part of a healthy national culture. The content of a national identity will change as a result of these debates. But these changes are not a matter of individual choice, however much individuals may contribute to them. What an individual may choose to do – a matter of radical choice – is to give up membership of one nation in favour of another. But this is not an easy matter. For most, it is impossible to make the transition completely (though one's children, and children's children may do so); nor is it always possible to leave behind the commitments and responsibilities which go with a national identity. In extreme cases, we have the concept of a *traitor* to remind us of the peculiarly inescapable nature of the responsibilities which go with national identity.

However we construe the notion of freedom involved with national identity, choice is not central to it. Indeed, that it is not usually a matter of choice is what this kind of freedom is about. It is just because our national identity is a nearly inescapable condition of our life that it provides the freedom, not of choice, but of necessity: of acting as we must. But it also promises another form of freedom: that of living in a political and social world which we can identify as our own. When we are free in this sense, we are at home in our world, in a community with others who speak the same language, experience the same emotions, and experience the world in the same terms. It is this sense of individual freedom which underlies the familiar appeal of nationalism – the claim of each nation to be its own State. The force of this appeal lies in the aspiration of members of the national community to live in a society which expresses and sustains their fundamental sense of self. When this aspiration is fulfilled, the social and political environment is not experienced as a constraint on the individual's interests and concerns, but a condition of a worthwhile and satisfying life.

Notes

1. Breyten Breytenbach, *Return to Paradise* (New York, Harcourt Brace, 1992), quoted in J. M. Coetzee, "Resisters", *New York Review of Books* (2 December 1993), pp. 3–6.
2. J. G. Herder, *J. G. Herder on Social and Political Culture*, translated and edited by J. G. Barnard (Cambridge, Cambridge University Press, 1969). It should be noted here that Herder seemed not to have envisaged a political role for the nation.
3. See the discussion in R. Poole, *Nation and Identity* (New York, Routledge, 1999), ch. 1, in the section entitled "The nation: imagination and culture".
4. It is not hard to discern this as an implicit presence in Anthony D. Smith's argument for the ethnic core of modern nations. See *The Ethnic Origins of Nations* (Oxford, Blackwell, 1986), and *National Identity* (London, Penguin, 1991).
5. See Anderson, *Imagined Communities* (London and New York, Verso, 1983), especially ch. 1, on this theme. However, we need to emphasise – as Anderson does not – that what is provided is not survival in any very strong sense. If it were, then giving up one's life could hardly count as sacrifice.
6. See, for example, Robert Goodin, "What is so special about our fellow countrymen?", *Ethics* vol. 98 (1988), pp. 663–86. Goodin notes that at least sometimes we have more stringent obligations to aliens, e.g. to respect their rights, than we have to compatriots.
7. This point is emphasised by Samuel Scheffler in an important series of papers on (his terminology) "special responsibilities". See "Individual responsibility in a global age", *Social Philosophy and Policy* vol. 12 (1995), pp. 219–36; *Families, Nations and Strangers*, The Lindley Lecture (Lawrence, University of Kansas, 1995); and "Relationships and responsibilities", *Philosophy and Public Affairs* vol. 26 (1997), pp. 189–209.
8. I return to this issue in *Nation and Identity*, ch. 5.
9. See Miller, *On Nationality* (Oxford, Clarendon Press, 1995), ch. 3, where Miller provides a powerful defence of "the ethics of nationality" against universalistic criticisms.
10. It is a weakness of Miller's defence of nationalist ethics that he focusses on our special responsibilities to attend to the needs of our co-nationals, and all but ignores the responsibility for what they do.
11. See Yael Tamir, *Liberal Nationalism* (Princeton, Princeton University Press, 1993), pp. 97–8.
12. As Hannah Arendt comments, we properly feel guilt about something that we as individuals have done or failed to do: "Guilt, unlike responsibility, always singles out; it is strictly personal." Arendt's use of the adjective "personal" in this context is significant. See Hannah Arendt, "Collective responsibility", in *Amor Mundi: Explorations in the Faith and Thought of Hannah Arendt*, ed. James W. Bernauer (Boston, Martin Nijhoff, 1987), p. 43.
13. The distinction between guilt and shame deserves much more discussion than I can provide here. For a key recent discussion, see Bernard Williams, *Shame and Necessity* (Berkeley, Los Angeles and London, University of California Press, 1994), especially ch. IV and Endnote 1. Williams does not however explore the extent to which one can appropriately feel shame, but not guilt, for what others have done. This distinction has been pressed in Australia in the context of indigenous issues by Raimond Gaita; see especially "Not right", in Peter Craven (ed.), *Best Australian Essays 1998* (Melbourne, Bookman Press, 1998). See also Desmond Manderson, "Unutterable shame/unuttered guilt: Semantics, Aporia and the possibility of Mabo", *Law, Text, Culture* vol. 4.1, Special Issue: *In the Wake of Terra Nullius* (ed. Colin Perrin), pp. 234–44.
14. Renan, "What is a nation?", first published 1882, repr. in part in Louis L. Snyder (ed.), *The Dynamics of Nationalism* (Princeton, Van Nostrand, 1964) and in full in Momi Bhabha (ed.), *Nations and Narration* (London and New York, Routledge, 1990), and Miller, *On Nationality*, pp. 34–42.
15. I return to this issue in *Nation and Identity*, ch. 4, when I will be specifically concerned with the responsibility of postcolonial nations such as Australia, Canada and the United States, to come to terms with the expropriation of their indigenous people.
16. Yael Tamir presents a persuasive case for the importance of identity and (what she calls) "connectedness". See *Liberal Nationalism*, especially ch. 5.
17. It is therefore deeply ironic that Hegel's political philosophy is sometimes interpreted as an apologia for nationalism. For a – surely definitive – refutation of this legend, see Shlomo Avineri, "Hegel and nationalism", in Walter Kaufmann (ed.), *Hegel's Political Philosophy* (New York, Atherton Press, 1970).

18. Yael Tamir, *Liberal Nationalism*, especially ch. 5.

19. The key texts here are *Considerations on the Government of Poland* and *Constitutional Project for Corsica*, both in Rousseau, *Political Writings*, ed. Frederick Watkins. For an account of the reception and influence of Rousseau in pre-Revolutionary France, see Simon Schama, *Citizens: A Chronicle of the French Revolution* (London, Penguin Books, 1989), Part I, ch. 4. The title of the chapter, "The cultural construction of a citizen", sums up my theme very nicely.

20. See the extract from *Ideas for a Philosophy of History* in *J. G. Herder on Social and Political Culture*, pp. 317–26; see also the discussion in F. M. Barnard (ed.), *Herder's Social and Political Thought* (Cambridge, Cambridge University Press, 1969), pp. 80–1.

21. As suggested by Barry Hindess, "Multiculturalism and citizenship", in Chandran Kukathas (ed.), *Multicultural Citizens* (St Leonards, NSW, Centre for Independent Studies, 1993). It is significant in this context to recall Walzer's suggestion that Roman citizenship became a more formal matter of entitlement not of participation, as it was extended to culturally distinct peoples.

22. See Michael Sandel, *Democracy's Discontent: America in Search of a Public Philosophy* (Cambridge, MA and London, Harvard University Press, 1996). Sandel argues that a liberal understanding of American national culture has displaced a previously dominant republican understanding.

23. I discuss immigration and the acquisition of citizenship in *Nation and Identity*, ch. 4.

24. See Marx, *Capital* vol. 1 (Harmondsworth, Penguin, 1976), ch. 7, p. 283.

25. Will Kymlicka, *Liberalism, Community and Culture* (Oxford, Clarendon Press, 1989), p. 165. It should be noted that Kymlicka does not identify the "rich and secure cultural structure" with a specifically *national* culture.

26

On the Making of Transnational Identities in the Age of Globalization: The US Latina/o–"Latin" American Case

Daniel Mato

"...
Oye latino, oye hermano, oye amigo
nunca vendas tu destino
por el oro y la comodidad
nunca descanses, pues nos falta andar bastante"
. . .
"...
Orgulloso de su herencia, de ser latina
de una raza unida, la que Bolívar soñó.
Siembra:
Panamá,
Puerto Rico,
México,
Venezuela,
Perú,
República Dominicana,
Cuba,
Costa Rica,
Colombia,
Honduras,
Ecuador,
Bolivia,
Argentina,
Nicaragua sin Somoza,
el barrio,
la esquina."[1]

(Rubén Blades, excerpts from his song "Plástico")

What is the united race invoked in this song by Rubén Blades, produced and recorded in the United States, which contains other lyrics alluding to US Latinas/os, and which is included in an album also containing other lyrics referring to US Latinas/os?

Who are those constituting the united race ("raza unida") *community* that Blades both visualizes himself and would stimulate us to visualize?

Have you noticed that through the lyrics of the quote, and others like them, he simultaneously appeals to and proposes the existence of a *transnational community* that binds together so-called US Latinas/os, whole "Latin" American countries, and specific urban communities like "el barrio"?[2] Have you also noticed that the expression "el barrio" has two meanings? Depending on the context of interpretation it may be a particular New York "Latino" neighbourhood, and more in general each and every *barrio* – the generic Spanish word for neighbourhood, and more particularly for "popular" neighbourhoods – in every "Latin" American city where his song is heard?

Blades' lyrics are a way of interpreting and representing certain social experiences, and, in doing this, they also stimulate our feelings and imaginations. They both express feelings and build meaning. The circulation of these representations and their appropriation by diverse social agents take part in larger social processes of both visualizing and developing a transnational community.

But these lyrics do not operate in a vacuum. This "Latina/o united race" transnational community is not the exclusive reference of Blades' lyrics. It is also the subject of, or at least it is embedded in, the discourses of a significative number of social actors throughout the American continent. In this way, Blades' lyrics also constitute a significant hint to larger ongoing transnational social processes.

These lyrics, as other similar representations, are indicative of the existence of significant ties linking, if not the daily practices, at least the souls, imaginations and feelings of diverse populations spanning from one end to the other of this continental mass called America. Do Blades' lyrics include all of them? Are there not any exclusions or significant reductive homogenizations? These are key questions that underlie this article's discussion.

As I said, Blades is not alone. Nor has his expression reached us through several kinds of media just by chance. His expression overlaps with those of a whole list of several kinds of artists made up not only of poets and singers, but also of writers, musicians, visual artists, and video, television, cinema and theatre creators who increasingly and diversely appeal to our consciousness and subconsciousness with different representations of that more or less same *imagined transnational community*. I have to state clearly that beyond any possible debates regarding the interpretation of Anderson's idea of *imagined community* (1991), I am not using the adjective "imagined" as opposite to "real", but

to emphasize the existence and importance of a mental image of such a proposed community. In a certain way, assuming that any specific group of people constitutes a community always involves a mental image of that group which emphasizes the importance of certain common factors over others that may comprise references of differences among them, or us – depending on whether or not we are part of the community in question. In this sense any community would be imagined, but in the particular case of this transnational community the importance of such a mental image is perhaps even greater because of the immensity of the proposed community.

The issue is that those producers of influential representations of such a transnational community are not lonely spirits dreaming in a vacuum. Their works reach us through specific means: books, magazines and newspapers, films, television, performances, compact discs and tapes, festivals, exhibitions, multimedia events, etc. The production of these concrete means involves the creative initiatives, and the voluntary and/or waged energy, that is the work of many individuals. All this also involves capital expenditures in producing, promoting and making these creators' images available to different audiences, readerships and viewerships. With this in mind, our list of producers of representations of this transnational community must be enriched by adding to it other key players such as entrepreneurs, corporate managers, advertising campaign creators and organizers, actors and actresses, models, etc. In addition, in making this enhanced listing of producers of images of that *imagined community* we cannot ignore the roles played by scholars, intellectuals, social leaders, politicians and state agencies from different countries. Moreover, we have to take into account that these images are also diversely supported, enjoyed, co-imagined, and – in certain ways – co-produced by millions of individuals who at the same time constitute the audiences, readerships, viewerships, followers or clients of those makers of *public images*, among whom also exist diverse kinds of mutual or complementary relations.

All this means that the different representations of such an imagined community, *"una raza unida"*, elaborated and advanced by all these particularly influential kinds of public image-makers resonate – in diverse ways – in the souls, heads and bodies (questionable partitions of the selves, but suggestive for the present purposes) of several million people. This does not mean that all the incumbent representations and associated social, political, cultural and economic practices traversing the continent – as well as some latitudes beyond – are alike, but that there are significant resonances among them.

The former reflexive (and also self-reflexive) description is to call our attention to the fact that numerous social actors are advancing representations of peoplehood that would bind large populations throughout the American continent, spanning countries' borders. This is to say that representations of a *transnational US Latina/o–"Latin" American identity* are being produced and circulated by multiple social actors.

The development of representations of this transnational identity is not good or bad in itself. It does not have any particular pre-assigned meaning. But it is taking place. Speculations about whether it may result in being more or less strategically beneficial are also taking place; but "for whom?" and "how?" become the obvious questions.

As an intellectual who feels part of these ongoing historical social processes, I consider it necessary to contribute to its development by producing and encouraging both conscious critical reflection and open dialogue.

The overall argument I will present below may be briefly summarized as follows. Identities are not legacies passively received but representations socially produced, and – in this sense – matters of social dispute. The case under discussion presents particular dimensions in connection with both a certain historical macrocontext, the present age of globalization, and the histories of the US and the different "Latin" American countries. Every and each collective identity representation highlights assumed similarities while obscuring presumed differences that at times may become more or less significant. Current representations of a US Latina/o identity as well as of a "Latin" American identity and an all-encompassing transnational US Latina/o–"Latin" American identity entail images that, according to several social actors' representations, obscure differences that are significant.

I do not believe that the existence of certain significant assertions of difference may invalidate *per se* any social practices which are based upon or promote representations of a US Latina/o–"Latin" American identity, but I do think that the existence of these assertions of difference makes it unavoidable to think these identity representations by means of those representations of difference. Explicitly, I state that it is necessary to think representations of a US Latina/o–"Latin" American identity by means of significant representations of difference, and to adopt a conscious posture towards avoiding homogenizing traps. I am conscious that perhaps this position is not shared by other people. I do not know how acceptable such a position would be from, for example, the perspective of marketing campaigns' producers, whose main interest seems to be to expand the scope of the category "Latinos", or sometimes "Hispanos" (*sic*, and even taking the masculine forms as paradigmatic), as much as possible, as a way of reaching the widest possible audiences with their campaigns. But, I think that, if one is to develop a social practice that in any way embodies representations of such an all-encompassing identity, and – at the same time – is aimed at lessening social, political and economic injustices, one cannot avoid thinking of such an identity by means of those assertions of differences, be they related to race, ethnicity, class or socioeconomic status, gender, sexual orientation, local experiences, international and transnational relations of domination, or any other relations of power.

Before expanding on the Latina/o–"Latin" American case, I will present a few preliminary theoretical remarks that will enhance our discussion of the case. They are related to three specific issues: the idea of globalization, the social processes of identity-making, and the social processes of identity-making in the present age of globalization.

On the Idea of Globalization

The use of the word *globalization* has become a widespread phenomenon these days. I think that this fact is revealing of the worldwide development of something that we may call a *consciousness of globalization*. It does not matter at this moment how differently globalization is represented by the many and various narratives of the phenomenon we may find throughout the planet. But the point is that forms of a consciousness of globalization are currently being developed throughout the world. An important consequence of the development of this consciousness is that it informs the social practices and representations of numerous social actors everywhere (not just economic agents, but also political, cultural, etc.).

This consciousness is a relatively new phenomenon. An indication of its newness may be that the word *globalization* was included in the *Webster Dictionary* only in 1961. Nevertheless, I would say that globalization is not a recent phenomenon, which would be just a consequence of certain business practices, communication technologies and neoliberal macroeconomics, as it is often portrayed. Globalization may be more fruitfully analysed as a long-standing historical tendency towards the worldwide interconnection of the peoples of the planet, their cultures and institutions, resulting from many different social processes. These social processes produce – among other things – forms of tendential worldwide interconnection, and because of this they may be called *globalizing processes*, or *globalization processes*.

In view of widely assumed misconceptions, it is particularly important to highlight that the keyword to explain globalization is worldwide interconnections, and not homogenization. The diverse ongoing processes of globalization have different outcomes: while some may be said to produce homogenization, others foster differentiation, and still others have combined effects. This is a matter that we do not have space to discuss here, but that I have addressed in previous writings (Mato, 1995, 1996a).

Although globalization is an old phenomenon, there are good reasons to characterize our present times as the age of globalization. This present age of globalization exhibits three significant characteristics that are particularly relevant to our discussion. The first is the already mentioned worldwide development of a consciousness of globalization. The second is that because of different historical circumstances those previously mentioned interconnections have – for the first time – acquired nearly a worldwide scope. Interconnections are not just flows of ideas, symbols and commodities, but of permanent relationships among social agents (this concept, of course, includes economic agents but is not limited to them). Striking among the historical circumstances that have made possible that interconnections became almost fully planetarian have been: (1) the development of an almost planetarian system of production and exchange of goods and services; (2) the growing diffusion of communication technologies; (3) the dissolution of the old colonial empires and the (quasi) end of the cold war and the associated barriers to direct relations between social agents in certain regions of the planet; and (4) the development of numerous international and transnational organizations and institutions whose very rationale is global linking. I believe that

this latter circumstance, the development of numerous international and transnational organizations, is at the same time the third significant characteristic of this age of globalization.

As we will see below, these three characteristics of the age of globalization are crucial in discussing current identity-making processes worldwide.

On the Social Processes of Identity-making

A good number of recent case studies illustrate how cultural identities, as other social representations, are socially produced and not passively inherited legacies. Representations of identities are continuously produced by individual and collective social actors who constitute and transform themselves through both these very symbolic practices, and their relations (alliance, competition, struggle, negotiation, etc.) with other social actors. It may be said that the work of producing symbolic representations is permanent and that it may include, at least in theory, cases ranging from fully unconscious-making to fully intentional constructions – this latter sometimes named "inventions". Although not always explicitly differentiating between so-called "invention" and "construction", and beyond diverse theoretical differences, numerous studies may be cited as presenting examples that illustrate this argument (e.g. Anderson, 1991; Fox, 1990; García-Canclini, 1989; Habermas, 1989; Handler, 1988; Herzfeld, 1982; Hobsbawm, 1983; Linnekin, 1992; Mato, 1994a, 1995, 1996b, 1996c, 1997, 1998a, 1998b; Rogers, 1996; Wagner, 1981).

The constructed character of identities is not asserted here as opposed to something presumably more "real". From my point of view, the proposed dilemmas "real vs. imagined", "authentic vs. false", or "genuine vs. spurious" are simply not pertinent. Asserting that identities are socially constructed does not imply that they are false or arbitrary, but that identities are not things, but matters of social dispute.[3]

Collective social actors form and transform themselves through identity-making processes. Social actors take part in identity-making processes in a wide range of social collectivities, like so-called ethnic, local, regional and national societies. They participate in these processes, advancing and transforming their own representations – whether consciously or unconsciously elaborated. In the present age of globalization identities – as other representations – are socially produced in contexts that are increasingly interconnected, both internationally and transnationally.

On the Social Processes of Identity-making in the Age of Globalization

In the present age of globalization there are practically no fully isolated social units. Although some exceptions may exist, most social aggregates, or at least some social actors within them, are in one way or another internationally and/or transnationally linked.

According to the scope of their practices social actors may be classified in local, regional, national, international, transnational and global. Limits are of course difficult to assert with precision but this differentiation may be helpful in explaining differences in the representations and orientations of practices among several actors participating in any given process. Global social actors like the multilateral banks, US and Western European countries' governmental agencies, non-governmental organizations based in these same countries act tendentially almost everywhere, and do this by advancing their own representations of, for example, democracy, citizenship, justice, race, gender, etc. This implies that not only the media – as often recognized – but also this wide diversity of social actors take part in varied ways in identity-making processes throughout the world.

A brief example may be illustrative. In these days Amazon indigenous peoples' identity-making processes take place in the context of the complex and varied relations they maintain not only with neighbouring ethnic groups and mestizo populations, state and country governmental agencies, non-governmental organizations and professionals, but also with distant indigenous peoples with whom they interact in an increasingly complex system of transnational meetings. But our list of meaningful interrelations cannot end here. It must also include conservationist and indigenous peoples' advocacy organizations, anthropologists, environmentalists, journalists, cinema producers, agents of oil, timber, pharmacological, biochemical corporations, bilateral development agencies, the World Bank and the Inter-America Development Bank, etc. However different these agents may be, all of them – through their relations – advance their own representations

of self and other, and some of them even promote and/or finance projects that encourage the development of certain representations to the detriment of others. It is in this sense that I say that all identities are nowadays made in transnationally and internationally linked social fields. This does not imply any assumption regarding the possible shapes and meanings of these identities and other representations. In other words this does not imply that local identities are shaped or influenced by global agents, but rather that they are made by local actors in social fields directly and indirectly (for example, through the media) exposed to the practices and representations of global agents.

If the previous description based on my and others' research (e.g. Amodio, 1996; Brysk, 1994; Chirif et al., 1991; Conklin and Graham, 1995; Gnerre and Botasso, 1985; Jackson, 1995; Mato, 1992, 1996c, 1997, 1998a, 1998b) on the cases of Amazonian and other South American indigenous peoples makes it meaningful to understand how identity-making processes of supposedly remote and isolated peoples are affected by transnational and international relations, it may also be at least suggestive to understanding identity-making processes in a wide variety of local, regional and national societies more openly – although not necessarily more intensely – interconnected.

To finish this preliminary theoretical consideration I must explain both the distinctions I am pointing out through using the adjectives "transnational" and "international" applied to relations, and the distinctions I will be indicating between transnational and pan-national when talking of identities in the next section.

According to current usage among some international relations literature, I call "international relations" those maintained among states, or state agencies, or among them and intergovernmental organizations. I call "transnational relations" those maintained between agents from two or more states, when at least one of these agents is not a governmental agent (Keohane and Nye, 1971). Consistent with the implicit meaning of the word "nation" in this usage, I call "pan-national identities" those encompassing the dominant representations of national identities of significant groups of countries, and "transnational identities" those proposed as binding segments of populations of two or more countries across international borders.

I have decided to adhere to this usage of the word "nation" in order to avoid complicating the presentation of my arguments through the incorporation of too many *ad hoc* categories. Nevertheless, there are some problems with this terminology that in the context of a discussion on the making of identities and other representations – like the present – must at least be mentioned. This whole set of categories carries implicit the assumption that the word "nation" is an equivalent of the words "country" and "nation state". I have to make explicit that these equivalencies have been criticized from at least two perspectives that are relevant to our present discussion. First, because they imply that states are equivalent to nations, and to the extent to which no further specifications are made, they also imply that governments and states actually represent whole nations, or whole country populations, as if these populations were practically homogeneous. Second, because of the ethnic dimension of the word "nation", which in the "Latin" American context has motivated a number of indigenous peoples' organizations to argue that it tends to delegitimize their own claims of being nations.

International and Transnational Relations in the Making of "Latin" American Identities

As it already emerged when discussing the word "nation", words, or at least some words, are not neutral. They carry particular meanings, some of which are highly political and/or become politicized over time. As I said before, these sorts of questions cannot be avoided when discussing matters of social representations. To make matters more difficult, some words evoke quite different meanings for different audiences. I therefore have to make it explicit that I use the word "America" to name the whole continental mass, the word "United States" or its abbreviated expression "the US", to name this particular country, and the abbreviated adjective "US" to identify individuals, institutions or phenomena based on or taking place in this country. This usage is not personally mine, but well extended in "Latin" America. This is not the time to explore the different meanings that the word "America" has for US and "Latin" American readerships, but it is necessary to mention the point to communicate the following ideas more clearly.

While I use the term "Latin America", I find it problematic too, and this naming problem is central to the present discussion. The expression is problematic in various respects, but for the moment I would like to draw your attention to only the first of them, which is related to the word "Latin" in this name. This word recalls a long-term process of the making of social identities and differences and still serves as a subtle legitimating device for certain social groups, and simultaneously legitimate discriminations against other population groups in America – that is, in the continent.

Nineteenth-century *Latinoamericanismo* may be characterized as a nationalist ideology advancing the idea of a quasi-continental "nation" (Zea, 1986). Its roots – not the expression itself – come from the period of the anticolonial movements. As with almost any nationalist ideology it advanced representations of cultural homogeneity that contributed to obscuring social differences and legitimating social discrimination along the lines of those differences.

At that time, white and mestizo elites began building new nation states upon the system of exclusions of the colonial period. Those elites assumed that they, not the so-called *indios*, nor the imported African slaves and their descendants, were "the people". The alliances developed during the quasi-continental anticolonial war were the origin of the making of the interdependent system of national identities and interstate-crafted representations of what later came to be called "Latin American culture".

Nevertheless, it must be noted that the expression "Latin America" did not exist in the lexicon of the independence movements of the end of the eighteenth and beginning of the nineteenth century. At that time the names for the whole region that lies south of the United States and which today is called "Latin America" were *Nuevo Mundo, América, América del Sur, América Meridional*. The portion under Spanish colonial rule was also called *América Española* and *Hispanoamérica*. The idea of *Latinness* and its application as an adjective to this region was crafted by the French intellectual Michel Chevalier in 1836. On the other hand, "Latin America" as a compound name first appeared in writing in a book by the Colombian intellectual José María Torres Caicedo in 1865 (Ardao, 1980). Interestingly, as Arturo Ardao has pointed out in his documented study on the genesis of the name Latin America, to understand this name it is necessary to place it in the context of the ideas and historical facts that made it emerge as one of the two elements of "the antithesis Saxon [*sic*] America-Latin America". As he said, this terminological creation was the result of very complex historical circumstances, "the dominant of which came to be the annexation of Texas, the invasion and dismembering of Mexico, and the Central American incursions of William Walker. All this in the context of the intense ethno-cultural speculation of romantic historicism" (1980: 8; my translation).

This genealogical reference of the use of the expression "Latin America" cannot be ignored in our present discussion because it reminds us of at least three meaningful circumstances. First, that the name "Latin America" has itself emerged from complex international and transnational circumstances. Second, that it emerged in oppositional terms to that which was regarded as a different part of America, the United States. And third, that since that very period, since 1848, when Northern Mexico became the US Southwest, and a large Mexican population became foreign, or estranged, in its own homeland, a stateless people within the United States, since that very moment the United States became incurably pregnant of Mexicanness, and potentially of Latinness. As we will see below, this latter element is crucial in discussing the making of a Latina/o identity in the US.

Let us for the moment go back to so-called "Latin" America. The interdependent making of both national identities and a Latin American all-encompassing pan-national identity did not cease in the nineteenth century. "Latin" American political ruling groups controlling state apparatuses are also nowadays involved in different international systems of mutual support and legitimation for their participation in the social processes of constructing culture and power in their home countries.

Cultural, educational and political relations and the coordination of policies are cultivated in the name of – and mutually reinforce – the idea that a language (or a pair of related romance languages) and a colonial and postcolonial history are the common and distinctive features shared by the millions of inhabitants of so-called "Latin" American countries. State bureaucracy and ruling group discourses assume and address these millions of people as "*latinoamericanos*" as if they (we) were a sort of extended ethnic group, homogeneous crowd, undifferentiated in terms of class, gender or race, "*la raza cósmica*". Such a pretended extended ethnic group has its own mythology of origin, which has long been crafted through educational systems and other social institutions. Such a mythology begins with the arrival of Columbus, yearly celebrated in "*el Día de la Raza*" or "*Día del Descubrimiento de América*", and the subsequent process of "*mestizaje*". School books and thousands of statues constantly remind us of this founding myth. The European root has been overemphasized everywhere, while the American and African roots – not to mention some specific others – have been practically ignored in "Latin" American states' practices and discourses. This "mestizo" identity has been crucial in providing meaning and legitimating diverse social, cultural and economic mechanisms that have historically undermined the situation of both indigenous peoples and diverse populations constituted by the descendants of the African slaves within these national societies, including forms of open exclusion (Agostinho et al., 1972; Fernándes, 1959; Klor de Alva, 1992; Stavenhagen, 1988; Wright, 1990).

Apart from their long-standing regional networking and construction of what I would call an "official interstate 'Latin' American identity", mutually supportive with the related "national identities", these 'Latin' American states have recently been participating in other international systems of relations. Significantly, most of them also take part in the construction of a supposed "Latin" identity at a planetary level, which is advanced by the "Unión Latina", an intergovernmental body, mainly promoted by French diplomacy in which are represented about twenty-five nation states in which the official language is a Romance language. It seems interesting, however, to point out that the Unión Latina has recently confronted dilemmas in accepting the demands for incorporation made by some ex-colonial African states in which Romance languages are the official language. On the other hand, as the Quincentenary was approaching, another version of such European root-centred cultural representations became notorious, a postulated Ibero-American identity, which has been celebrated as binding the peoples of "Latin" America and those of the Iberian peninsula. This identity has been the subject of intensive interstate networking in recent years. Related discourses and actions were deployed during not only the celebration of the Columbus Quincentenary but also in its preparation, including the associated series of Ibero-American Presidential Summits, as well as numerous cultural and educational activities, long-term programmes and permanent mechanisms for policy-making coordination.

Paradoxically, the Quincentenary has been a benchmark in the history of the conflicts around the making of an extended socio-symbolic representation of the peoples of so-called "Latin" America and the associated system of "national identities". Even those less concerned about these matters noticed that the Quincentenary was commemorated not only by official celebrations but also by numerous critical or alternative events and demonstrations. On the very day, 12 October 1992, different groups publicly voiced their alternate points of view in most capital cities of the region, as well as in many other regional and extra-regional localities. While most of these groups were Amerindian, some were Afro-American groups (remember that I use this denomination in relation to the whole continent). Such a coordinated display was not incidental; it was the public emergence of the transnational practices of numerous non-governmental agents of diverse kinds. Nor was this display purely circumstantial and exclusively related to the Quincentenary. There are many public evidences that this display was just one coordinated action, among many others, emerging from the transnational relations maintained by a large number of social agents engaged in the making of transnational and related local identities in the region (Mato, 1994b, 1996c, 1998a, 1998b).

In constructing both national identities and a "Latin" American identity, states' policies and practices regarding Amerindian and Afro-American peoples have not been totally homogeneous. They have varied with countries' peculiarities and with historical circumstances. Even in the same country and period they have differed according to varying constructions of ethnic and racial identities of these populations. Nevertheless, in one way or another, these peoples have been subject either to systematic discrimination or to paternalistic policies of integration and "modernization".

The case is that in response to both of these long-term issues and the problems and opportunities that the globalization process entails for them, the social and political organizations of these excluded groups – particularly of the indigenous peoples – have begun to develop diverse transnational practices as well as to construct local and related transnational identities. These identity-making processes are meaningfully interconnected with other ongoing transnational phenomena, and must be analysed in the context of these interconnections. Three interconnected phenomena have been par-

ticularly striking in this regard. One has been the increasing importance of the practices of transnational corporations of diverse sectors, including, among others, those in the mass media and entertainment industries. Another has been the increasing importance of transnational migration movements, which have been related to diverse political and economic factors, not a few of them related to global phenomena like civil wars that have been nurtured by cold war schemes, and/or the application of structural adjustment programmes. Yet another has been the increasing importance of the practices of a diversity of international and transnational organizations that have in different ways promoted linkages among social movements and non-governmental organizations throughout the continent.

In connection with all this, "Latin" America has become the locus of various processes of construction of transnational identities and related social movements, as well as of local identities diversely associated to them. There are diverse kinds of transnational identities, and it is worthwhile to differentiate between them. Chronologically speaking, the first transnational cultures and identities were those which we would call "border ethnic transnational identities". They were a consequence of the new international borders that modernist nation states set up across the former territories of particular ethnic groups. Cases of this kind remain numerous and culturally and politically relevant. Two significant examples would be the cases of the Aymaras (Argentina, Bolivia, Chile and Peru), and the Mayas (Mexico, Belize, Guatemala and Honduras), but there exist many others. Discussing this conceptual sub-class of transnational identities is not the subject of this text. Nevertheless, this class has to be mentioned for two reasons. First, to avoid projecting a partial image of the category "transnational identity" as if it were the whole. Second, because some of these ethnic transnational identities are significant in discussing the Latina/o–"Latin" American case, as I will illustrate below. A different kind of transnational identity in border regions began to develop later and was not necessarily centred around indigenous peoples' ethnicities. These more recent border identities acquired new characteristics and importance in connection with the activities of transnational corporations and free trade regional agreements (NAFTA and Mercosur). The US–Mexico border case is not only a notable example in this regard, but also meaningful to our present discussion because it is interwoven with the US Latina/o case.

Other kinds of transnational identities are those constructed in connection with the practices of transmigrants and their organizations (Basch et al., 1993). This conceptual class has probably been the most studied, to the point that it is sometimes the only case that comes to mind when discussing transnational identities. Various significant transnational identities of this class have been advanced by diverse social actors throughout the continent and several of them are also significantly interwoven with the Latina/o–"Latin" American case that we are discussing. It is interesting to note that many of these cases may be said to have "national identities" as their symbolic referential axis, such as, for example, the Mexican, Puerto Rican, Cuban, Dominican and Colombian cases in the US. Instead, other cases have a particular local community or an ethnic identity as their reference, like the case of US residents from specific Mexican localities, or the Mixteco and Zapoteco identities which constitute the reference of transnational identities currently advanced by US residents of Mixteco, or Zapoteco, indigenous origin in connection with their ethnic fellow individuals and organizations in Oaxaca, Mexico (e.g. Georges, 1990; Kearney, 1992; Smith, 1992).

Finally, another class of transnational identities could be called "extended racial transnational identities", and would include three currently significant cases: Afro-American, Amerindian and Latina/o–"Latin" American. Note that this latter transnational identity, which is the focus of our present discussion, is mainly advanced by a wide range of non-governmental subjects and should not be confused with the "pan-national" case promoted by "Latin" American governments, although both have their common roots in nineteenth-century *Latinoamericanismo*, and overlapping and mutual influences among them must also be recognized. The making of these three extended transnational racial identities involves social actors throughout "Latin" America and even beyond its currently assumed borders, including related groups in the United States and Canada. Some of them are interwoven in different ways not only with processes of identity-making at local and national level, but also with cases of transmigrant and transnational border identities (Mato, 1994b, 1995). For the present discussion, the relevant issue regarding these extended identity-making processes is that these constructions of identity inform and legitimize the practices of organizations and individuals that are important producers and disseminators of public representations as well as producers of political agendas (for example, certain social movements, non-governmental organizations, civil leaders, artists, intellectuals, etc.).

Transnational Relations and the US Latina/o–"Latin" American Connection

On 19 September 1993, the famous *salsa* singer and – at the time – Panamanian presidential candidate Rubén Blades gave a concert in San Antonio, Texas. This concert, which was organized by the Guadalupe Cultural Arts Center of San Antonio, may be significant in various respects. First of all, the concert was in part a "progressively" oriented politicized meeting. Some Panamanians were present, waving Panamanian flags and voicing their support for Blades' campaign. They were echoed by non-Panamanian people as well. The exchanges between the public and the singer mainly expressed rejection of corrupt politicians, military governments and paramilitary actions; and the hope for freedom, redemption and progress towards a "united Latin America", most of these expressions also constituting themes poetically elaborated in Blades' and others' *salsa* compositions. Second, and more significantly for this article, the concert was an example of the ongoing making of what some Latina/o intellectuals called a "Latino unity" (Padilla, 1989) in the United States. In the audience there were Chicanos, Puerto Ricans, Panamanians and Peruvians, who made public their national affiliation in various ways, but, based upon the research I conducted during as well as before and after the event, I can say that there were also other Central Americans and South Americans of diverse national origins, as well as what in the US would be considered diverse "colours". Such a mix partially represents what Rubén Blades' lyric calls "the united race dreamed by Simón Bolívar" (the quasi-continental anti-colonial leader) (my translation of Blades' lyrics).

While the song's lyrics merit discussion themselves, what I consider more significant is their appropriation by social actors. These and other lyrics of key cultural political meaning were first disseminated as such in an album released in 1978. Since then they have been constantly echoed by grass-roots cultural and political activists throughout the region, as well as sung by concert audiences and groups of people at private and public *fiestas*. These and other politicized *salsa* lyrics, as well as others less and non-politicized, have achieved an amazing dissemination through live concerts and recorded productions. What is significant about them is that they have been taken, re-sung and even transformed by the public in an extended "Latin" America, one that in this system of representations explicitly includes "Latina/o" populations in the United States. From my own participation in diverse cultural and intellectual circles in various "Latin" American countries as well as from interviews with participants in others, I can attest that these lyrics have acquired a sort of emblematic status.

One simplistic interpretation of *salsa*'s success is to assume that it is just a commercial musical phenomenon produced by the record industry. It would also be simplistic to attribute *salsa*'s success exclusively to the lyrics' mix of political and romantic content. But the reality seems to be more complex than these one-dimensional interpretations. While we need specific studies of the subject, it seems reasonable to assume provisionally that on the one hand the record industry and the media pursue their profitable business, while on the other hand that business is possible because large groups of people far away from each other feel certain connections related to both such a powerful musical fusion and those progressively politicized lyrics. It is also likely that such a convergence of feelings happens because – among other reasons – some other connections do exist between such audiences. Unfortunately, my limited knowledge does not allow me to discuss the significance of the music itself, which in this case constitutes a powerful element. Nevertheless, I can at least mention that *salsa* brings together elements borrowed from several Puerto Rican and Cuban popular rhythms which already combined elements of African and Spanish musical traditions, and reworks them with an important influence of jazz. However, let me briefly note a few thought-provoking facts in relation to those connections throughout involved audiences.

I once heard that for us so-called Latin Americans, "Latin" America became a reality because of the multiple exiles and economic migrations in the 1970s that came together in Mexico and Venezuela "Latin" Americans from diverse latitudes. I have

personally experienced this phenomenon. Reflection on it was pervasive among groups of exiled or simply migrated "Latin" Americans in Venezuela, where I have lived since I left Argentina, where I grew up. I have more recently become acquainted with the argument of some Latina/o intellectuals that *salsa* is an expression of the "Latinos" amalgamating experience in the United States – closely associated to their common experiences of racism – and of their permanent relations with their countries of origin (Padilla, 1989). The making of such a "Latino" identity in the United States has not been a process free of differences and conflicts. It has sometimes been contested and at other times helped by the making of more particularistic identities and social movements, most notably those of Chicanos and Puerto Ricans.

This is not the time to attempt a comprehensive theorizing on these social processes. Nevertheless, it seems that significant moments and events have been: the transformation of Northern Mexico into the US Southwest since 1848 and the associated incorporation of a Mexican population within the US; the later trans-border movement of both family linked and non-linked Mexicans; the war between the US and Spain and the quasi-colonial incorporation of Puerto Rico to the US since 1898; the increasing migrations of populations from other and diverse "Latin" American countries; the experiences with racial discrimination of these populations; the civil rights movement; the creation of the Hispanic label by the US government, its incorporation into numerous public policies and practices, and thus the exposure of populations to the term in highly racialized social contexts. The point I want to make here is that these historical references contribute to an understanding of the multiple discourses of identity through difference that some Latina/o intellectuals advance (Acosta-Belén and Santiago, 1995; Flores, 1993; Flores and Yudice, 1990; Giménez, 1992; Oboler, 1992).

Beyond the particularities of these developments in the US and different "Latin" American sites, it seems that quasi-continental and criss-crossed networks of diverse kinds of individuals and organizations have developed throughout the continent. It also seems that at least some of these networks create overlapped spaces of political activism, cultural production and consumption, and a panoply of related business. These criss-crossing networks play significant roles in the ongoing making of this transnational culture and particularly in the production, marketing and consumption of certain common cultural products. I have learned from personal experience and fieldwork that political subjects, literary readerships, film, theatre and musical audiences, as well as other groups of cultural consumers and producers, create overlapped realities in particular neighbourhoods – for example, Mount Pleasant in Washington, DC, the so-called Harlem Latino or Hispano in New York City – and in diverse kinds of spaces in certain cities in the United States, Mexico and Venezuela – for example, bookstores, cultural centres, academic institutions and social clubs. The Guadalupe Cultural Arts Center in San Antonio, which hosted Rubén Blades' concert, is just one example of this kind of organization.

I noted that the Rubén Blades concert was organized by the Guadalupe Cultural Arts Center. Let me now say that Rubén Blades did not request – nor did he receive – any honorarium for his performance. It was a generous contribution on his part to the work of the cultural centre. Due to its geographical location and constituency, the Guadalupe Cultural Center is mainly a Chicano centre, but it is open to other streams of the "Latino"/"Hispanic" world. It annually organizes an International Latino Film and Video Exhibition. During its sixteenth festival, US Latino productions of diverse backgrounds were presented alongside productions from Argentina, Brazil, Cuba, Ecuador, Mexico, Nicaragua, Puerto Rico and Venezuela. Similarly, the Guadalupe Cultural Arts Center, among other activities involving artists from "Latin" America, hosted a concert of the famous Argentine politically progressive folk singer Mercedes Sosa.

At the time of Rubén Blades' concert, the Guadalupe Center's director was also the second chairperson on the board of the National Association of Latino Arts and Culture (NALAC), a recently created arts service association that coordinates the activities of several important US Latino cultural organizations. NALAC's agenda explicitly includes the development of international relations with the "communities of historic origin" of participant organizations. The Caribbean Cultural Center of New York is one of those organizations. On 20 to 23 October 1993, it held a conference that it presented as the third biannual international gathering of scholars, artists and "culturalists" who actively promote "cultural rights" and "social equity". Among the cultural groups participating in this conference were three so-called traditional music groups representing "Latinoamerica Negra" "direct" from Cuba, Mexico and Venezuela. Among the sponsoring agencies were the Guadalupe Cultural Arts Center and the National Association of Latino Arts and Culture. Among the participant scholars was a member of the Centro de Estudios Puertorriqueños (CUNY–Hunter College). At that time, this centre was also hosting a fellowship-in-residence programme entitled "Claiming Social Equity and Cultural Rights", which – according to its brochure – encourages comparative studies to "help to build alliances and construct social visions of the future". This centre maintains active relations with Puerto Rico, Mexico, Cuba and the Dominican Republic, and constantly receives expressions of interest in developing collaborative relations from academic institutions and advocacy groups throughout "Latin" America and the Caribbean. The fellowship programme of the Centro de Estudios Puertorriqueños was supported by the Rockefeller Foundation. Other activities of the Center dealing with questions of equity and cultural rights receive support from the Rockefeller and Ford foundations, among others. These two foundations were also founders of the conference at the Caribbean Cultural Center. The National Association of Latino Arts and Culture has already received a grant from the Rockefeller Foundation. The Guadalupe Cultural Arts Center has received support from the National Endowment for the Arts, the Rockefeller Foundation and the Ford Foundation, among other major supporters.

The interconnected practices of all these organizations around that set of events is not an isolated case. It is just one significant example of the kinds of practices of some transnational organizations, which I earlier pointed out as characteristic of this age of globalization. It is also revealing of ways in which transnational identities are constructed in our historical time, and it is also suggestive of how some representations of this particular transnational identity are advanced. But there are several different circuits, which do not necessarily advance the same kind of representations of this imagined community.

As I said, Rubén Blades is just one case. The activities and productions of other individuals and organizations are also echoed, announced and disseminated by local "Latino"/"Hispanic" radio stations, journals and newspapers in the United States. Some musical and audiovisual productions also reach mainstream markets, and in some cases, like that of Rubén Blades, they are even televised. In connection with this, let me mention that Univisión, a television corporation co-owned by US investors Televisa of Mexico, and Venevisión of Venezuela, is watched in eighteen "Latin" American countries and reaches "91 percent of all US Hispanic households through 36 broadcast affiliates and more than 600 cable affiliates" (Subervi-Vélez, 1994: 349). The interesting point here is that this television corporation is simultaneously exposing US "Latinos" to soap operas, news and other productions from "Latin" America, and "Latin" American audiences to news and other programmes that allow them to learn about the lives of "Hispanos" in the US. Through several programmes it celebrates the national independence days of many "Latin" American countries, as well as diverse elements of their national identities. It also maintains very good coverage of significant political news in these countries as well as for Hispanos in the US. Both audiences are becoming familiar with each other's daily lives, and both are directly addressed as "Hispanos", through some editorial programmes like Noticias Univision, and as Hispanos or Latinos through different programming. From what I have observed personally, these representations have become familiar among, and partially incorporated in the vocabulary of, members of viewerships in at least Argentina, Bolivia, Peru and Venezuela. In this way, Univision is participating as a major player in the making and dissemination of representations of a large transnational community that is relatively new in the minds of many "Latin" Americans. It incorporates thirty million new brothers and sisters from the US – whose existence many had ignored until quite recently – into the already large transnational community that others have been proposing. This imagined transnational community as represented by Univision speaks Spanish, and therefore does not include the numerous US Latinos who only speak English, nor does it include Brazilians, and again it leaves aside at least those indigenous populations who do not speak Spanish.

Final Remarks

As I said at the beginning of this article, current representations of a US Latina/o identity as well as of a "Latin" American identity and of an all-encompassing transnational US Latina/o–"Latin" American identity encircle images that according to several social actors' representations obscure differences that are significant.

In order to stimulate reflection and debate I would like to conclude this article by restating something that I already said above: I do not believe that the existence of certain significant assertions of difference may invalidate *per se* any social practices which are based upon or promote representations of a US Latina/o–"Latin" American identity. However, I do think that the existence of these assertions of difference make it unavoidable to think of these identity representations by means of difference. Explicitly, I state that it is necessary to think of representations of US Latina/o–"Latin" American identity by means of significant representations of difference, and to adopt a conscious posture towards avoiding homogenizing traps. I am conscious that perhaps this position is not shared by other people, for example, those involved in marketing campaigns who represent these populations as undifferentiated. However, I think that, if one develops a social practice that in any way embodies representations of such an all-encompassing identity, and – at the same time – is aimed at lessening social, political and economic injustices, one cannot avoid thinking such an identity through those assertions of differences, be they related to race, class or socioeconomic status, gender, sexual orientation, local experiences, international and transnational relations of domination, or any other relations of power.

Notes

This article is a revised version of the text I prepared as a basis for my lecture as the E. L. Tinker visiting professor at the Institute of Latin American and Iberian Studies at Columbia University, in the summer semester of 1996. This version has benefited from the discussion following that presentation, as well as from the comments and suggestions that some friends and colleagues have made on former presentations of some of the ideas offered in this text. They are Olivia Cadaval, Juan Flores, Nestor García-Canclini, Nina Glick-Schiller, Lawrence Grossberg, Richard Handler, Michael Kearney, Agustín Lao, Alberto Moreiras, Marvette Pérez, Federico Subervi-Vélez, George Yúdice and Patricia Zavella – of course, they are not responsible for my opinions and mistakes.

1. "Listen Latino, listen brother, listen friend / never sell your destiny / for gold or comfort / never rest, for we have a long way to go." "Proud of his heritage, of being Latino / of being a united race, as Bolívar

dreamt / Sow: Panama, Puerto Rico . . . Nicaragua without Somoza, *el barrio*, the corner."
2. "El Barrio" is the name colloquially given by its inhabitants – and many others – to a sector of East Harlem (New York City) predominantly inhabited by Spanish-speaking people. References to "el Barrio", literally "the neighbourhood", are also made in a number of *salsa* compositions.
3. I have discussed the ideas of invention and social construction in more detail in Mato (1994a, 1995, 1996b).

References

Acosta-Belén, Edna and Santiago, Carlos E. (1995) "Merging borders: the remapping of America". *The Latino Review of Books*, 1(1): 2–11.

Agostinho, P. et al. (1972) *La Situación del Indígena en América del Sur*. Montevideo: Tierra Nueva.

Amodio, Emanuel (1996) "Los Indios metropolitanos". In D. Mato, M. Montero and E. Amodio (eds), *América Latina en Tiempos de Globalización*. Caracas: UNESCO-ALAS-UCV.

Anderson, Benedict (1991) *Imagined Communities*. London, New York: Verso.

Ardao, Arturo (1980) *Génesis de la idea y el nombre de América Latina*. Caracas: CELARG.

Basch, Linda N., Schiller, Glick and Blanc, C. Szanton (1993) *Nations Unbound*. Langhorne: Gordon and Breach.

Brysk, Alison (1994) "Acting globally: Indian rights and international politics in Latin America". In Donna Lee Van Cott (ed.), *Indigenous Peoples and Democracy in Latin America*. New York: St Martin's Press, 29–54.

Chirif, Alberto, García, P. and Smith, R. (1991) *El Indígena y su territorio*. Lima: COICA and Oxfam-America.

Conklin, Beth and Graham, Laura (1995) "The shifting middle ground: Amazonian Indians and eco-politics". *American Anthropologist*, 97(4): 695–710.

Fernándes, Florestán (1959) *Brancos e negros em Sao Paulo*. Sao Paulo: Companhia Editora Nacional.

Flores, Juan (1993) " 'Qué assimilated, brother, yo soy asimilao': the structuring of Puerto Rican identity". In his *Divided Borders*. Houston: Arte Público Press, 182–95.

Flores, Juan and Yúdice, George (1990) "Buscando América: languages of Latino self-formation". *Social Text*, 24: 57–84.

Fox, Richard (ed.) (1990) *Nationalist Ideologies and the Production of National Cultures*. Washington, DC: American Ethnological Society.

García-Canclini, Nestor (1989) *Culturas Híbridas: Estrategias para Entrar y Salir de la Modernidad*. Mexico: Grijalbo.

Georges, Eugenia (1990) *The Making of a Transnational Community: Migration, Development, and Cultural Change in the Dominican Republic*. New York: Columbia University Press.

Giménez, Martha E. (1992) "U.S. ethnic politics: implications for Latin Americans". *Latin American Perspectives*, 19(4): 7–17.

Gnerre, Mauricio and Botasso, Juan (1985) "Del indigenismo a las organizaciones indígenas". In AA.VV. (*sic*) (ed.), *Del Indigenismo a las Organizaciones Indígenas*. Quito: Abya-Yala, 7–29.

Habermas, Jürgen (1989) *The Structural Transformation of the Public Sphere: An Inquiry into a Category of Bourgeois Society*, trans. Thomas Burger. Cambridge, MA: MIT Press.

Handler, Richard (1988) *Nationalism and the Politics of Culture in Quebec*. Madison: University of Wisconsin Press.

Herzfeld, Michael (1982) *Ours Once More: Folklore, Ideology, and the Making of Modern Greece*. Austin: University of Texas Press.

Hobsbawm, Eric (1983) "Introduction: inventing traditions". In E. Hobsbawm and T. Ranger (eds), *The Invention of Tradition*. Cambridge: Cambridge University Press, 1–14.

Jackson, Jean (1995) "Culture, genuine and spurious: the politics of Indianness in the Vaupes, Colombia". *American Ethnologist*, 22(1): 3–27.

Kearney, Michael (1992) "Beyond the limits of the nation-state: popular organizations of transnational Mixtec and Zapotec migrants". Paper presented at the 91st Annual Meeting of the American Anthropological Association, San Francisco, 2–6 December.

Keohane, Robert O. and Nye, Joseph S. (eds) (1971) *Transnational Relations and World Politics*. Cambridge, MA: Harvard University Press.

Klor de Alva, Jorge (1992) "La invención de los orígenes etnicos y la negociación de la identidad Latina". In Manuel Gutiérrez Estévez et al. (eds), *De Palabra y Obra en el Nuevo Mundo*. Madrid: Siglo XXI, Vol. 2: 457–88.

Linnekin, Jocelin (1992) "On the theory and politics of cultural construction in the Pacific". *Oceania*, 62(4): 249–63.

Mato, Daniel (1992) "Disputas en la construcción de identidades y 'literaturas orales' en comunidades indígenas de Venezuela: conflictos entre narradores y papel de investigadores y editoriales". In *Revista de Investigaciones Folklóricas* (Universidad de Buenos Aires) 7: 40–7.

Mato, Daniel (1994a) "Teoría y política de la construcción de identidades y diferencias". In his (ed.), *Teoría y Política de la Construcción de Identidades y Diferencias en América Latina y el Caribe*. Caracas: UNESCO-Nueva Sociedad, 13–29.

Mato, Daniel (1994b) "Procesos de construcción de identidades en América 'Latina' en tiempos de globalización". In his (ed.), *Teoría y Política de la*

Construcción de Identidades y Diferencias en América Latina y el Caribe. Caracas: UNESCO-Nueva Sociedad, 251–61.

Mato, Daniel (1995) *Crítica de la Modernidad, Globalización y Construcción de Identidades.* Caracas: Universidad Central de Venezuela.

Mato, Daniel (1996a) "Globalización, procesos culturales y cambios sociopolíticos en América Latina". In D. Mato, M. Montero and E. Amodio (eds), *América Latina en Tiempos de Globalización.* Caracas: UNESCO-Asociación Latinoamericana de Sociología-UCV.

Mato, Daniel (1996b) "On the theory, epistemology, and politics of the social construction of 'cultural identities' in the age of globalization". *Identities*, 3(1–2): 205–18.

Mato, Daniel (1996c) "International and transnational relations, the struggles for the rights of indigenous peoples in 'Latin' America and the transformation of encompassing societies". *Sociotam*, 6(2): 45–79.

Mato, Daniel (1997) "Culturas indígenas y populares en tiempos de globalización". *Nueva Sociedad*, 149 (May–June): 100–15.

Mato, Daniel (1998a) "The transnational making of representations of gender, ethnicity and culture: indigenous peoples' organizations at the Smithsonian Institution's festival". *Cultural Studies*, 12(2): 193–209.

Mato, Daniel (1998b) "On global agents, transnational relations, and the social making of transnational identities and associated agendas in 'Latin' America". *Identities*, 4(2): 167–212.

Oboler, Suzanne (1992) "The politics of labeling: Latino/a cultural identities of self and others". *Latin American Perspectives*, 19(4): 18–36.

Padilla, Félix (1989) "Salsa music as a cultural expression of Latino consciousness and unity". *Hispanic Journal of Behavioral Sciences,* 11(1): 28–45.

Rogers, Mark (1996) "Beyond authenticity: conservation, tourism, and the politics of representation in the Ecuadorian Amazon". In Jeremy Beckett and Daniel Mato (eds), *Indigenous Peoples/Global Terrains*, special issue of *Identities*, 3(1–2): 73–126.

Smith, Robert (1992) " 'Los ausentes siempre presentes': the imagining, making, and politics of a transnational community between New York City and Ticuani, Puebla". *Working Papers on Latin America*. Institute of Latin American and Iberian Studies, Columbia University.

Stavenhagen, Rodolfo (1988) *Derecho Indígena y Derechos Humanos en América Latina.* Mexico: El Colegio de México.

Subervi-Vélez, Federico et al. (1994) "Mass communication and Hispanics". In Félix Padilla (ed.), *Handbook of Hispanic Cultures in the United States.* Houston, TX: Arte Público Press, 304–57.

Wagner, Roy (1981) *The Invention of Culture.* Chicago, Ill: The University of Chicago Press (originally published 1975 by Prentice Hall).

Wright, Winthrop (1990) *Café con Leche: Race, Class, and National Image in Venezuela.* Austin: University of Texas Press.

Zea, Leopoldo (ed.) (1986) *América Latina en sus ideas.* Mexico DF: Siglo XXI.

27

Globalization as a Problem

ROLAND ROBERTSON

The Crystallization of a Concept and a Problem

Globalization as a concept refers both to the compression of the world and the intensification of consciousness of the world as a whole. The processes and actions to which the concept of globalization now refers have been proceeding, with some interruptions, for many centuries, but the main focus of the discussion of globalization is on relatively recent times. In so far as that discussion is closely linked to the contours and nature of modernity, globalization refers quite clearly to recent developments. In the present book globalization is conceived in much broader terms than that, but its main empirical focus is in line with the increasing acceleration in both concrete global interdependence and consciousness of the global whole in the twentieth century. But it is necessary to emphasize that globalization is not equated with or seen as a direct consequence of an amorphously conceived modernity.

Use of the noun "globalization" has developed quite recently. Certainly in academic circles it was not recognized as a significant concept, in spite of diffuse and intermittent usage prior to that, until the early, or even middle, 1980s. During the second half of the 1980s its use increased enormously, so much so that it is virtually impossible to trace the patterns of its contemporary diffusion across a large number of areas of contemporary life in different parts of the world. By now, even though the term is often used very loosely and, indeed, in contradictory ways, it has *itself* become part of "global consciousness," an aspect of the remarkable proliferation of terms centered upon "global." Although

the latter adjective has been in use for a long time (meaning, strongly, worldwide; or, more loosely, "the whole"), it is indicative of our contemporary concern with globalization that the *Oxford Dictionary of New Words* (1991: 133) actually includes "global" as a *new* word, focusing specifically, but misleadingly, on its use in "environmental jargon." That same *Dictionary* also defines "global consciousness" as "receptiveness to (and understanding) of cultures other than one's own, often as part of an appreciation of world socio-economic and ecological issues." It maintains that such a use has been much influenced by Marshall McLuhan's idea of "the global village," introduced in his book *Explorations in Communication* (1960). The notion of compression, or "shrinking," is indeed present in that influential book about the shared simultaneity of media, particularly televisual, experience in our time. There can be little doubt that McLuhan both reflected and shaped media trends, so much so that in time we have come to witness (self-serving) media attempts to consolidate the idea of the global *community*. On the other hand the media fully acknowledge the "nationality" of particular media systems, and report at length on the tough realities of international relations, wars and so on. Such realities are far from the communal connotations which some have read into McLuhan's imagery. In the same period when McLuhan's notion of the global village was becoming influential there occurred the "expressive revolution" of the 1960s (Parsons, 1978: 300–24). That was, to put it very simply, a "revolution" in consciousness among the young in numerous parts of the world, centered upon such themes as liberation and love, in both individual and collective terms. In fact the *Oxford*

Dictionary of New Words maintains that the current term "global consciousness . . . draws on the fashion for *consciousness-raising* in the sixties" (1991: 133).

Undoubtedly the 1960s "revolution" in consciousness had an important effect in many parts of the world, in its sharpening of the sense of what was supposedly common to all in an increasingly tight-knit world. Yet, as we will see more fully, this sense of global interdependence has rapidly become recognized in numerous other, relatively independent, domains and fora. World wars, particularly World War II with its "humanity-shaking" events and its aftermath, the rise of what became known as the Third World, the proliferation of international, transnational and supranational institutions and the attempts to coordinate what has become known as the global economy have played crucial parts in the twofold process of "objective" and "subjective" "globalization." And surely McLuhan's own Catholic-tinged observations concerning the media-centered "global village" were partly shaped by such developments (Miller, 1973).

Some of these considerations will be further explored in subsequent chapters. I have tried both to bring these and other considerations into some overall shape and to connect them to my primary discipline of sociology. At the same time, I have some ambivalence about whether what I am doing is "sociology," an expanded or revised version of sociology, or much more than can be captured by such a designation. In the current, but increasingly contested and complex, climate of "interdisciplinarity" it may not really matter. But on the whole I feel that present discussions of globalization constitute an extension and refocusing of sociological work, work which enables sociology and more generally social theory to transcend the limitation of the conditions of its own maturation in the so-called classical period of the discipline. Although there are various "global openings" in the work of the classical sociologists, sociology's "official" role has been to address societal, or comparative-societal, issues. In any case, discussion of globalization touches just about every aspect of the academic disciplines, including their moral foundations and implications. The position I adopt with respect to these moral issues is that matters concerning the global complexity induced by globalization must be confronted on their own terms, that "critical" and moral concerns must to some extent depend on an appreciative understanding of what is "going on" in the world as a whole. At the same time I fully recognize that sociologists and others who are seeking to analyze and comprehend contemporary global complexity are participants in projects of globalization, reglobalization and, even, deglobalization.

Mention of the idea of deglobalization – loosely speaking, attempts to undo the compression of the world – should remind us again that what we currently call globalization has been a very long, uneven and complicated process. In the immediate context we should be aware that movements, institutions and individuals have not merely been implicated in actions that have propelled the overall globalization process but that quite frequently there has been resistance to this. In the contemporary world the use of the term "globalism" as a *negative* comment on what has with equal pejorativeness been described in ideological terms as "one-worldism" or "cosmopolitanism" is not uncommon in political and other campaigns; and of course there is a quite long genealogy of such terms. But we have to be very conscious of the fact that negative gestures, gestures of opposition, are typically expressed in contemporary terms and in reference to contemporary circumstances. I will try to show that just as ostensibly anti-modern gestures are inevitably in a sense modern, so are anti-global gestures encapsulated within the discourse of globality. In *that* particular sense there can be no foreseeable retreat from globalization and globality.

Leaving on one side for the moment the quite important question of anticipations of the study of the global "system," it can be said that the contemporary sociological analysis of "the world" in its relatively mundane sense began explicitly in the 1960s. At that time a number of attempts were made to discuss the topic of the modernization of Third World societies – that is, the manner in and the degree to which nationally organized societies achieve "maturity" – within the context of the overall pattern of *relations* among all nations conceived as a system of *international stratification* (Lagos, 1963). Applying models which had previously been applied only to *intra*-societal structures to relations between societies was a novel idea in the early 1960s (even though in its French origin the idea of the Third World already implied stratification, in the sense of the "third estate"). Some of this work was connected to "peace studies," particularly in the writings of Johan Galtung (1966), while another connection was pursued in terms of the ways in which orientations to the processes of modernization were positively or negatively established on the part of political elites in a fluidly conceived international system (Nettl and Robertson, 1966; Nettl and Robertson, 1968; Robertson and Tudor, 1968). Other ideas concerning the increasing necessity for a "global sociology" (Moore, 1966), the study of "war and peace" in broadly sociological terms (Aron, 1966; Robertson, 1968), and the non-power dimensions of relations between national societies (Etzioni, 1965), and so on, flowered in the same decade. Needless to say, some specialists in international relations and other fields were moving in roughly the same direction.

To the extent that the discussion of the currently popular theme of modernity arose in those developments of the 1960s it was largely in terms of the conventional sociological analysis of the move from *Gemeinschaft* ("community") to *Gesellschaft* ("society"). While that and related stage-images of the "old" and the "new" had originally been developed in the context of primarily European debates about the diffusely conceived pros and cons of modern life in late nineteenth- and early twentieth-century Europe and, to a lesser extent, North America, its translation to the poor and underprivileged societies of the Third World involved in the main thrust of modernization theory (or at least in terms of the stereotypes of the latter with which we now, for the most part, operate) a considerable truncation of the original question. In much of societal modernization theory and the individual modernization theory (Inkeles and Smith, 1974) which followed in its trail, "modernization" referred most frequently to objectively measurable attributes – such as education, occupation, literacy, income and wealth. There was little attention to subjective, interpretive aspects of modernization. In so far as culture was invoked it was largely in terms of the functional significance of "the Protestant ethic" in having supposedly stimulated a disciplined orientation to work, political participation, and so on.

At the same time there developed an interest arising out of modernization theory which had little to do, on the face of it, with a "world system." I speak of the debate about convergence and divergence. Put simply, advocates of the convergence position argued that all, or nearly all, societies were, at different speeds, moving towards the same point, mainly as the result of the overriding emergence of "industrial man" (Kerr et al., 1960), while adherents to the divergence stance emphasized the idea

of there being different paths to and forms of "modernity" (rather narrowly conceived) and that in that sense there was not convergence but divergence. Needless to say this debate has been revived in the light of the collapse of communism in much of the world by the early 1990s and the wave of societal democratization that swept across the continents in the late 1980s and the early 1990s (notwithstanding resistance in China, parts of the territory of the old Soviet Union, the Middle East, and elsewhere). Aspects of the convergence–divergence debate pointed, in a few cases strongly (Inkeles, 1981), to crystallization of what was at least implied in the convergence framework as a homogenized "world system." In discussing and assessing the convergence–divergence debate, Baum (1974, 1980) was to add an important concept to those of convergence and divergence: invariance. Baum claimed that societies are converging in some respects (mainly economic and technological), diverging in others (mainly social relational) *and*, in a special sense, staying the same in yet others. In other words, Baum firmly injected the issue of *societal* continuity into the debate. Unfortunately few have taken up this important question, centered on matters concerning the links between identity and authority (although see Lechner, 1990). Baum did not in any case locate his argument within a conception of the "global system." Questions of the degree to which globalization encourages or involves homogenization, as opposed to heterogenization, and universalization, as opposed to particularization, are crucial, as well as complex.

It should be noted that in the course of debate about modernization in the late 1950s and the first half of the 1960s the issue of postmodernity, or postmodernization, was diffusely raised. That, in turn, was to feed into the developing debate about post-industrial society, which has become part of the modernity-and-postmodernity debate of recent years. However, we need note here only that the question of postmodernity arose in the debate about modernization (in its narrow sense) primarily in terms of the relatively simple notion that there must be "something after" modernity (as it was conceived in the rather narrow terms previously indicated). In my work with Nettl (Nettl and Robertson, 1966, 1968) we attempted, *inter alia*, to transcend this simplistic perspective by emphasizing that "modernization" (or "progress" in the version taken over from the West by some communist regimes) was much more fluid and "subjective," as well as cultural, than the "objective" approach of many mainstream modernization theorists. This in large part arose because of what we regarded as the essentially reflexive character of modernization. Using the examples of Meiji Japan and the Russia of Peter the Great, we tried to show that "late-comers" to the project of modernization (conceived somewhat more broadly than in mainstream modernization theory) were particularly prone to various dilemmas as to which images of modernity should guide them and from where, in relation to the important issue of national identity, they should select the pieces of such images. We could equally well have spoken of many other societies confronting such predicaments, in other parts of Asia or in Latin America, for example. Our extended discussion of what we called "the inheritance situation" in newly independent societies of the Third World was closely linked to this general emphasis on reflexive modernization (Nettl and Robertson, 1968: 63–128). We argued that not merely latecomers but all societies implicated in projects of modernization are also involved in processes of interactive comparison with other societies. In that perspective "modernization" has been an ongoing problem for virtually *all* societies. While the explicit focus of our work was upon the "macro" problem of politically structured relations between societies in the international system, that work was greatly informed by a comparative-international approach inspired by symbolic interactionism (and, less explicitly, pragmatism). The reflexive nature of contemporary modernization is well illustrated by the way in which Japan is currently attempting to impose "higher" standards of "society" on the USA, to which the latter must in some way respond.

In the early 1970s a strong, effective and quickly very influential challenge to narrowly conceived modernization theory arose, one which had some of its roots in basically Marxist ideas about the impossibility of "socialism in one country." The historically detailed world-systems theory of Immanuel Wallerstein (initially stated at length in Wallerstein, 1974) grew out of his own dissatisfaction with narrowly conceived modernization theory, which considered societies only *comparatively*, with Western societies as the major reference points, as opposed to seeing them as parts of a *systematic pattern of relations* among societies. It is to the question of the crystallization and expansion of that system that Wallerstein and his numerous followers have devoted their attention since the early

1970s, the primary emphasis being upon the expanding "world" conceived as a capitalist system of exchange. Wallerstein's very important, but I believe one-sided, work on the world-system has overlapped, sometimes in contentious ways, with other forms of "world-system" theory and "world history" which have emphasized economic factors and processes in the making of the modern global circumstance. It is important to note that some of the issues that led to Wallerstein's critique of modernization theory paralleled those which Nettl and I advanced in the second half of the 1960s, in spite of obvious differences. On both sides there was a firm intention to bring the countries of the Third World firmly into the overall picture (Simpson, 1991). Rather than seeing those countries as merely problematic newcomers to or laggards within the world or international system, both positions involved the view that much more had to be said about the *formation* of the present world as a whole, the ways in which different societies had been, so to say, inserted into that system. In both cases there was, then, a definite commitment to seeing, in one way or another, the world as exhibiting systemic properties. The differences should be equally apparent. I have continued to develop the theme of societal reflexiveness and do not consider the world to be exhausted by its systemic characteristics, whereas what is usually called world-systems theory continues to pursue the theme of systemicity, looking to a world-socialist *future* for the time when men and women can make history "voluntarily." Yet there is a tendency to share the view that the old *Gemeinschaft-to-Gesellschaft* problematic, which plagued old-style modernization theory, much of sociological theory and research before and after the latter, and which now underlies much of "the theory of modernity," has been misconceived.

The strong view advanced by Wallerstein is that the *Gemeinschaft* problem was largely produced by an increasingly worldwide, capitalist *Gesellschaft* and that obsession with the basically internal-societal problem of the transition from *Gemeinschaft* to *Gesellschaft* set the social sciences off on an entirely wrong foot (Wallerstein, 1991). I have some sympathy with that view, although on different grounds and not quite to the same degree. The general basis of my agreement may be indicated via Wallerstein's orientation to the theme of what he has called "timespace realities" (1991a: 135–48). Whereas it is my view and Wallerstein's that the matter of negotiated and contested categories of time and space has been intimately bound up over many centuries with the asymmetrical "creation" of the world (in a secular sense), Giddens tends to think of "time-space distantiation" as a product of relatively free-floating and ahistorical "structuration" (Urry, 1991). (Giddens has in some of his most recent writing attempted to join the idea of the disembedding of action from "local" contexts, as an aspect of the move into "modernity" and then "high" modernity, to the interpretation and analysis of globalization. This is discussed in Robertson, 1994: ch. 9.) Nonetheless, my own approach differs substantially from that of Wallerstein. I do not, for example, assume that one can or should, so to say, wipe out the significance of the *Gemeinschaft*-to-*Gesellschaft* problematic by sheer analytical reasoning. That problematic and its contemporary expression in terms of ideas such as the project of modernity has not simply been an analytical issue. For better or for worse, it has in one way or another greatly informed the reality of the world we study and the theories we form about it. I think something like a middle ground should be established between those who emphasize world systemicity and those who tend to think of current trends towards world unicity as having issued from a particular set of societies, as an outgrowth of the shift from the "traditional" to the "modern" and the theorization thereof.

It is in reference to the first issue, that of world systemicity, that the debate about globalization has the most continuity. While the particular debate about globality and modernity in its broad sense, as well as about postmodernity, is certainly of importance, the fact remains that the explicit attempt to "map" the world as a whole is older. One must make a rough, certainly not a hard and fast, distinction between those attempts – which have been greatly caricatured by Giddens (1990) – and the way in which "globalization" has been theorized within recent and relatively mainstream debates in general social theory. Another complication must be added. Wallerstein and the numerous other system-theorists are by no means of one mind in their analysis of global formation (Chase-Dunn, 1989). At least in the present context, the most interesting general pattern of variation within the overall world-systems group concerns the issue of the terms in which the contemporary world-system has actually been formed. In part this is a question of historical length as well as depth. Indeed one of the points of disagreement and contestation, not only within Wallersteinian world-systems theory but also, per-

haps even more importantly, in rival schools of basically economic explanations of the origins of the world-system, concerns the age of the world-system, or systems. The latter use of the plural is necessary because, strictly speaking, the term "world" does not necessarily, in world-systems theory, apply to the *entire* world. Needless to say, the latter is the main focus of the present book. Thus Wallerstein himself has been concerned almost exclusively with the making of the modern world since the fifteenth century (in the sense of the current worldwide system). Nevertheless there are disputes over the extent to which the making of this *capitalist* world system was framed and/or preceded by previous developments, as well as over applications of the work of Wallerstein to "premodern," i.e. pre-sixteenth century, circumstances. In world-systems theory the whole question of what is normally understood by the idea of modernity is relativized and diminished by the claims of increasingly worldwide *system* formation. In Wallerstein's perspective capitalism becomes stronger as the system develops; and societies increasingly come to play roles in the worldwide system as a consequence of their positions in the world-systemic division of labor. Political and military relations flow along the lines indicated by these more basic economic relations, while culture, including religion, is largely epiphenomenal. Culture is not, however, unimportant in Wallerstein's own work, for it serves, often in subtle ways, to support and sustain the increasingly worldwide system.

As I have said, I regard this scheme as one-sided. That objection has been made by various other critics of world-systems theory. However, those critics have not, for the most part, presented an alternative conception of what Wallerstein calls, I think misleadingly, the contemporary world-system. The way in which I speak of globalization *is*, on the other hand, centered on such a conception, which involves the attempt to take the notion of globality very seriously. While it may be convenient for certain purposes to speak of a world or global *system*, much of the thrust of my own thinking centers on my attempt to depict the main general contours of the world as a whole. Thus the concept of globalization as used in this book is specific, yet much more wide-ranging, open and fluid than Wallerstein's conception of the world-system. Even though they have a few important things in common, globalization analysis and world-systems analysis are rival perspectives.

Sociology and the Problem of Globalization

Nineteenth-century social theorists and sociologists, such as Comte, Saint-Simon and Marx, made what many now call globalization central to their analytical (as well as their political) work. During the later period of so-called classical sociology the situation became particularly complex on the sociological front, mainly because of the hardening and expansion of the apparatus of the nation state and the strengthening of nationalism. So the classical sociologists were faced with the Janus-faced problem of the simultaneity of "nationalization" and "globalization." In a sense, modern sociology was born from this dilemma; it may in fact be regarded as partly a victim of the dilemma. Let us then inspect briefly the history of sociology in this light. In doing so we will find that in the most crucial founding stages of sociology there were both openings to the theorization of globalization and closures which have constituted impediments to such theorization.

Although there is much in the writings of Emile Durkheim, Max Weber, Georg Simmel and their contemporaries that suggests a definite interest in globalization and its ramifications, for the most part they (although Simmel is a "peculiar" case) concentrated on the problems of "societality," at least as far as their contemporary times were concerned. In that regard the large issue of what we now, more explicitly, call modernity received much attention, most clearly in the writings of Weber. Working within the parameters of classical sociology has misleadingly involved concentration on the basically internal affairs of "modern societies," a perspective which was, to a large extent, consolidated by the rise, during the period of "high" classical sociology, of the discipline of international relations (the new "dismal science"). Thus sociology (as well as anthropology) came to deal, often *comparatively*, with societies; while international relations (and portions of political science) dealt with them *interactively*, with relations between nations. Certain aspects and consequences of this division are dealt with in the following chapters.

Slowly at first, in recent years more rapidly, the division between the internal and the external has been destabilized. Out of that destabilization has been born the present and growing interest in globalization, in which new academic areas such as communication and cultural studies have played

significant roles. Interest in the phenomenon of globalization is multifaceted. A growing number of movements, organizations and interest groups have their own perspective on, as well as interests in, globalization; while "analysts," who certainly cannot be simplistically separated from "participants," have different interests in that issue. "Globalization" has also become a significant ingredient of advertising. It has, as well, become a matter of great concern in considerations of the curriculum in many educational systems, along with an often competing interest in multicultural – indeed "postmodern" – education.

Albrow (1990: 6–8) has argued that we can identify five stages in the history of sociology, considering the latter from within the current concern with globalization: *universalism; national sociologies; internationalism; indigenization;* and *globalization.* Although I have some reservations about this scheme it is, on the whole, a helpful way of considering the history of sociology in relation to the theme of globalization.

In referring to what he calls the stage of *universalism* Albrow (1990: 6) points to the aspiration of early sociology "to provide a science of, and for, humanity based on timeless principles and verified laws." The universalistic stage of sociology had roots in strands of the Enlightenment which stressed such ideas as humanity, fraternity and, indeed, universalism. It reached its strongest point in the philosophy and sociology of Saint-Simon and Comte, on the one hand, and Marx, on the other. It was, says Albrow, a sociology greatly inspired by the natural sciences; although it should be added that unlike the natural sciences there was in the minds of two of its most well-known practitioners, Saint-Simon and Comte, a strong practical component in that both sought, although in different ways, to expand the very empirical conditions to which their cognitive schemes could be applied. Thus the allegedly positive stage of scientific thought was not fully guaranteed even in "rationalistic" West European societies, let alone the rest of the world, without additional practical effort. Paradoxically, a new kind of religion was thought to be necessary, not merely to provide a sense of order and commitment to "real life" but also to sustain and expand the scientific commitment to a universal, foundational analysis of humanity. Saint-Simon drew up a program for the reorganization of European society "which was in fact a forerunner, suited to its period, of future world government" (Merle,

1987: 7). His ideas were elaborated in a review which was called the *Globe*, whose reach can be demonstrated in the words of one of his disciples, who wrote that "the era of universal politics which is opening up is that of contact with Africans and Asians, Christians and Moslems" (Merle, 1987: 7). Another disciple wrote that "there is in fact only one great branch of knowledge, that of humanity, which includes everything and epitomizes everything" (Merle, 1987: 7). Moreover, Saint-Simon's followers were actually involved in large projects for "world" organization, including the cutting of the Suez Canal and the colonization of Algeria.

As Turner (1990: 344–8) has argued, Saint-Simon saw a close relationship between a new form of social science, or rather the establishment of the study of society on a scientific basis, on the one hand, and the coming of "globalism," on the other. Saint-Simon basically thought that a science of society was impossible without the unification of humanity and vice versa. This general thrust of Saint-Simon's thought was at the core of Comte's simultaneous advocacy of a *positivistic* science of society, which he called sociology, and a "religion of humanity." The programs of Saint-Simon and Comte were, from our point of view, marked by a mixture of scientism and utopianism; although Saint-Simon should be called a utopian only to the extent that, as Durkheim (1962: 222) put it, "one would apply the same term to his industrialism." For Saint-Simon believed that it was industrialism which promoted cosmopolitanism and internationalism. Marx's approach was, of course, different, although he was influenced by Saint-Simon. In general terms Marx agreed that the combination of labor and industry on a global scale would result in "peace." But his image of the path to this was much more sophisticated than that of Saint-Simon. Capitalism as a determining mode of production would provide the grounds for universalization on a global scale. The proletariat, as an exploited but potentially global class within expanding capitalism, would eventually develop and install a genuine global universalism.

In speaking of the stage of *national sociologies* Albrow (1990: 6) is concerned with "the foundation of sociology on a professional basis in the academies of the Western world, especially in Germany, France, and the United States, but also in Italy, Britain, Spain and non-Western countries, such as Japan." While he argues that the "universal aspirations" were not given up, he maintains that "the

intellectual products . . . took on striking characteristics of the national culture" and professional contacts became largely confined by national boundaries. Thus the fusion of national sociologies with "the residues of universalism" produced a quest for "exclusive intellectual hegemony which was not so remote from the imperial territorial ambitions of the nation-states associated with the parent culture." There is much to agree with in this characterization, but I think that Albrow exaggerates the difference between the first and second stages. The universalistic stage was undoubtedly concerned directly with humanity as a whole, *as if* it made no difference where "the universalistic message" came from, but Saint-Simon and Comte did nonetheless project a distinctively French view of that whole. Within the stage of so-called national sociologies we see in Durkheim's work a continuation of a nineteenth-century tendency – to be found, for example, in the writings of John Stuart Mill and Karl Marx – to try to establish a "universal" theory by weaving together central themes from what were perceived to be the "higher" Western traditions. So Durkheim in his social epistemology sought to synthesize German idealism and British empiricism. But the result of the synthesis was in fact – and Durkheim openly proclaimed his epistemology in this way – a *French-rational* synthesis. Thus although Durkheim operated within the national frame of reference, he was concerned with the theme of "universalism." I will return to this later.

The stage which Albrow (1990: 6) calls *internationalism* started, he says, after World War II with the collapse of national sociologies and the general disaster of the two world wars. Internationalism in science "was taken for granted." However, it was basically divided in ways that roughly corresponded to Cold War divisions, between "an all-embracing modernization thesis, especially in the American Parsons version" and the "internationalism" propounded by Marxist proletarianism. Albrow provides no stage, however transitional, between the phase of national sociologies, the collapse of which he surely exaggerates, and the phase of internationalism – which would make the national-sociologies phase stretch all the way from the late nineteenth century to the post-1945 period. This is unconvincing, because it was during the 1920s and, even more so, the 1930s that the problem of *relativism* first became thoroughly thematized in sociology and anthropology. In sociology we find the attempts of Max Scheler and Karl Mannheim to deal directly with the issue of the relativism – or, which is not exactly the same, the relativity – of perspectives. To be sure, Simmel had made relativity a central ingredient of his interpretation of modernity, but he did not confront the problem of *global* relativism or relativity, as Scheler did (Stark, 1958). And while Mannheim's pragmatic sociology of knowledge was ostensibly directed at intra-societal relativism and relativity there can be little doubt that in a general sense his concern to overcome or resolve those problems was a manifestation of a more widespread and diffuse concern with the theme of commensurability. This was also the period of the rise of relativistic anthropological perspectives, contrasting with the evolutionism, historicism or diffusionism of previous anthropology. In sum, the lack of ostensible "internationalism" should not lead us to conclude that concern with *problems* arising from globalization was not present. The rising concern with relativism can thus be regarded as a manifestation of the problems raised by increased global compression, as well as by the crystallization of distinctive ideologies of world order. Those ideologies – such as German fascism, Japanese neo-fascism, communism and Woodrow Wilson's "self-determinationism" – themselves arose in relationship to the great acceleration of the globalization process which had begun in the late nineteenth century. Again, this is a point which I will take up later.

Albrow does make an important point about the bifurcated internationalism of the post-1945 period. I would add only two, closely related, points. First, it is ironic that Albrow should single out Talcott Parsons as the representative of an extreme position with respect to "the increasing worldwide penetration of Western rationality" expressed as "an all-embracing modernization thesis." In fact, Parsons spent his entire career striving to resist sociologies based upon instrumental rationality (which was in any case a distinctively Germanic *Problemstellung*). Second, tempted as he may have been by "modernization theory" and in spite of having often been designated as a leading proponent of it, he always insisted that the Cold War would be ended by the democratization of communist countries and the generalization of their *internationalism* (Parsons, 1964). He also maintained that it was through *a convergence* of communism's collectivism and capitalism's individualism that we would reach beyond the Cold War. That this would be an asymmetrical convergence (in favor of the

West) is not particularly relevant in the present context, nor are certain weaknesses in his projections. What is of relevance is that of the people to blame for promoting a one-sided view in a bifurcated field of "internationalism" Albrow has not chosen a good candidate. However, the general idea that the thrust of modernization theory in the 1950s and 1960s constituted the prevalent form of Western "internationalism" is accurate. I would add only two things. First, modernization theory has deeper roots than Albrow claims. Quite apart from its embeddedness in the *Gemeinschaft–Gesellschaft* problems, it had a more immediate grounding in the "applied sociology" which was encouraged during World War II in the USA. Indeed sociology in the USA came of age through its mixture of professionalism and patriotism in the early 1940s (and Parsons played a significant role in that respect). Specifically, the immediate origins of 1950s and early 1960s modernization theory lay in the Allied, but particularly the American, attempt to force democracy on (West) Germany and Japan. It was in the 1940s setting of World War II that we find, in a very interesting way, a context in which the idea of "modernization" was nurtured. Second, the idea of the Third World had some of its highly problematic origins in American President Woodrow Wilson's model for a "self-determined world," presented in Paris at the conclusion of World War I. At the same time the Wilson Principles constituted one of the grounds of the fissures in twentieth-century "world politics." From another point of view, Wilson sought a universalistic entitlement to particularism.

The phase of *indigenization*, according to Albrow (1990: 7), was centered upon the crystallization of the Third World. Albrow rightly says that this phase has to be distinguished from the phase of national sociologies – but he does not provide entirely convincing accounts of its difference. In attempting to improve on his typification of this period, I would say that it was, and to a large extent still is, one in which practitioners of "national sociologies" have attempted for the most part to *insert* their perceived "traditional sociologies" into a worldwide sociology. It is obvious that such an attempt requires continuity with a "universal language" (Archer, 1990). It makes no sense to produce an entirely idiosyncratic point of view, unless one simply wants to *retreat* from the world. Even then the terms in which the retreat takes place are likely to be constrained by contemporary discourse. However, much of the point of "indigenization" in sociology is to enlarge and revise the prevailing discourse so as to make "local" sociology definitely present on the global scene.

Albrow maintains that there are two leading characteristics of Third World indigenization as it developed in the 1970s: opposition to external, particularly Western, terminology and methods and a stress on the perceived national-cultural tradition, although there has been a strong tendency to lean on Marxist models. In any case, one can delineate the general indigenization movement into relatively distinct tendencies. One such tendency is to be found in Latin American contexts (which Albrow does not discuss), where it has not so much been the case that foreign theories, methods and substantive themes as such have been rejected, but rather that particular ways of "Western" thinking – mainly Hegelian and Marxist, but recently postmodernist – have been invoked in order to account for "dependency" and to produce a form of praxis with respect to the surmounting of deprivation. So the primary targets of such tendencies have been – at least until quite recently – theories of societal modernization which, according to their critics, propose that "development" can occur only along a US trajectory, in terms of a definite pattern of differentiation, and on a society-by-society basis. The recent importation of and enthusiasm about ideas concerning postmodernity have enhanced this view, but this time as part of a worldwide "cultural turn" in the social sciences. Specifically, the idea of postmodernity in Latin American societies seems to fit a relatively autochthonous genre of literary expression, namely magical realism, and, from a more distinctively sociological standpoint, provides a kind of solution to the question of whether Latin America is moving from premodernity to modernity. The idea of postmodernity confirms the view that the question of modernity can be transcended. Postmodernism is seen as legitimizing *mixtures* of the traditional and the modern. There is much to be said for the argument that Latin America is the importer of "alien" ideas *par excellence* and that it does not seriously fall into the category of indigenization. But although the first part of that view may be persuasive, the second does not follow from the first. The point is that imported themes have been syncretized into unique constellations of ideas with certain elements of autochthony constraining receptivity to some ideas rather than others. The notion of indigenization is relevant

because the syncretic bundles are for very "domestic" purposes.[1]

In coming to what Albrow (1990: 7–8) calls the present, but not necessarily the last, phase, he speaks of the *globalization* of sociology. Globalization, he says, is directly the result of the interaction of "nationalism" and internationalism, and indirectly of all the preceding stages. The principle of globalization "results from the freedom individual sociologists have to work with other individuals anywhere on the globe and to appreciate the worldwide processes within which and on which they work" (Albrow, 1990: 7). "A universal discourse has arisen with multiple interlocutors based on different regions and cultures," says Albrow. And he goes on to remark that globalization does not only mean that sociologists can communicate openly but, first, that they are "confronted with the full diversity . . . of sociological dialects and special visions" and, second, that they are constrained to focus on globalization as "a process at a new level of social reality." Albrow adds that that new reality is best described by the term "global society."

Albrow's outline of the history of sociology in relation to globalization becomes increasingly concerned with relations between sociologists on a worldwide basis, rather than with the issue of the analysis of the global circumstance as such. As he moves through the stages which he has identified in the history of sociology Albrow shifts his attention from sociological *ideas* to the scope of *relationships* among sociologists and he tends, with respect to the more recent stages, to conflate the two. The second issue is certainly not unimportant; it is indeed relevant to the consideration of globalization. But the globalization of sociology must not be confused with the sociology of globalization. The second is my concern. It is the theorization of the world which is my immediate interest. So let us turn directly to that theme.

Openings to Globalization in Mature Classical Sociology

In spite of my observations about the relative lack of attention on the part of sociologists of the period 1890 to 1920 to what we would now consider crucial aspects of a particularly acute period of globalization, we can see that in that period ideas were produced which have a strong bearing on that theme. For example, in the works of both Simmel and Durkheim we find definite concerns with the category of humanity, which in the scheme that I will articulate shortly relates to a particular aspect of the overall delineation of the global circumstance.[2]

Writing in reference to Kant's notion of basic human presuppositions and Nietzsche's advocacy of autonomous human action, as opposed to action heteronomously guided by cultural, societal or religious constraints, Simmel became interested in two closely connected aspects of the problem of humanity. On the one hand, he made the point, in revision of Nietzsche, that looking at human experience in the frame of "humanity" was but one of four forms of apprehension or analysis, the other three being culture, society and individual. From Simmel's perspective, Nietzsche had chosen but one way of considering human experience. It was equally valid to consider experience in, for example, the frame of society. Simmel thus relativized Nietzsche's position. He argued that Nietzsche had somewhat arbitrarily selected one frame of analysis, claiming that it was the only appropriate one. On the other hand, Simmel maintained that Nietzsche's way of thinking was, in significant part, a refraction of empirical changes (Simmel, 1986). The latter point indicated Simmel's tendency to focus not merely on the analytical categories of human experience as such, but also on the empirical circumstances which led to the intellectual production of one-sided theories, a strategy he also employed in relation to Marx (Simmel, 1978).

Simmel argued that what he called the "values of human existence" differ profoundly from social values, in that the latter rest primarily upon the effects of individuals, whereas human values involve the "immediate existence of man." Following Nietzsche, Simmel (1950: 63) insisted that it is the "qualitative being of the personality which marks the stage that the development of mankind has reached." It is thus not only in a quantitative sense that mankind is more than society.

> Mankind is not merely the sum of all societies: it is an entirely different synthesis of the same elements that in other syntheses result in societies. . . . Society requires the individual to differentiate himself from the humanly general, but forbids him to stand out from the socially general. . . . In recent historical periods [the] conflicts into which [the individual] falls with his political group, with his family . . . etc., have eventually become sublimated in the abstract

need . . . for individual freedom. This is the general category that came to cover what was common in the various complaints . . . of the individual against society. (Simmel, 1950: 63–4)

Durkheim approached a similar problem, but from a very different angle. The primary difference pivots on Durkheim's insistence that the fully developed individual is a social being, in contrast to Simmel's view that the individual is increasingly an extra-societal entity. Durkheim claimed that we would soon as individuals have little in common but our humanity. In fact, Durkheim appeared to think that the diversification of individuals to the point where they had nothing much in common as members of specific groups would constitute a consummation of men and women's sociality. In other words, for Durkheim the diversification of individuals occurred directly in terms of a general trend within modern societies (a view which clearly does not involve direct consideration of migration and the formation of what Balibar (1991) has usefully called "world spaces"). The long-term result of processes of (social) individuation was a pluralistic assimilation by individuals of what might be called essential sociality. Individuals become the bearers of "deep sociality." Here, of course, is a remnant of Comte's thinking, in the sense that when Comte tried to establish a program for the institutionalized celebration of society, he labeled that form of celebration the "religion of humanity." There seems to have been a tendency within the early French sociological tradition to equate that which is most basically social (or societal) with the notion of humanity. Striking confirmation of this is to be found in a comparison of maxims drawn respectively from Kant and Durkheim, and the use of Kantian ideas by Simmel in his discussion of the category of humanity. Kant argued that although a man is profane, the mankind in him is sacred; while Durkheim (1974: 34) maintained that if the individual is spiritual, "society" is hyperspiritual. The fact that Simmel, as well as Durkheim, invoked Kant's original maxim in order to make somewhat different points is of considerable interest in relation to the issue in question.

On the other hand, we find that Durkheim (1961: 463–96) spoke of the transcendence of concrete, national societies in reference to what he called "international life," in such a way as to imply that there would arise in the twentieth century a category of concern, which by conventional socio-logical standards does not, strictly speaking, belong at the societal but at the civilizational or extra-national level (Durkheim and Mauss, 1971). Additional substance can be provided by pointing to Durkheim's claim that, in the modern world, categories of thought become increasingly released from their social or societal moorings and, as he put it, take on a life of their own. In this, and many other areas of Durkheim's *oeuvre*, we encounter a generalized interest in the relationship between particularism and universalism, one crucial aspect having to do with the relationship between what has sometimes been called Durkheim's moral relativism – morality as being societally specific and bound up with the social realities of each society – and his humanity-oriented moral universalism, which, in effect, relativized societal relativism.

In dealing with Max Weber the situation is much more complex. Weber was very skeptical about the modern concern with what has come to be called human rights. It would appear that he thought that in the modern world concern with matters which we now address in terms such as "humanity" could in extreme form derive from a kind of charismatic fanaticism (Weber, 1978: 6). And yet there is a strand of Weber's work which indicates, according to Nelson (1969), a world-historical trend in the direction of "universal otherhood." That trend was, of course, in continuous rivalry with the counter-trend of "tribal brotherhood." In any case, there is little doubt that Weber knew well that there were trends in the modern world which raised acutely the problem of the degree to which one could sensibly assign the individual to the simple status of member-of-society. Nothing displays this trend in Weber's thought better than the two famous essays, "Politics as a Vocation" and "Science as a Vocation" (Gerth and Mills, 1948: 77–158). Particularly in the former, Weber raised what might be called the modern Lutheran problem concerning the link between the ultimate concerns of individuals and the functional operation of societies. Notwithstanding the nature of Weber's own "intra-societal" attitude toward that predicament, it is clear that he, as a social scientist, acknowledged the tension between the demands of purely societal membership and the demands of what Simmel, following Nietzsche, called the state of one's being.

One of Weber's leading interests was, of course, in the making of the "iron cage" of modern life. The major challenge was how one should live in

relation to it. Weber resisted all arguments and practices which involved or implied absolute rejection of the alleged iron cage. He was equally adamant in denying that the charismatic glorification of reason had helped to create definitely modern forms of economic and political individualism. Weber argued against Rousseauesque ideas concerning the social celebratory origins of modern ideas about democracy, emphasizing instead the contribution of Puritanical asceticism. However, as cogent as Weber's arguments in these respects may be, the fact remains that he left relatively unattended the consequences and implications of his image of a dualistic condition in which the "non-societal" domain is constituted by a mass of discrete individual-personal values. In the perspective of his great concern with Germany's future and "fate," Weber found the kinds of ideas which I have identified in the writings of both Simmel and Durkheim distinctly uncongenial. For Weber the world as a whole was basically to be seen as an arena of struggle between nations. Of course, in so far as Weber saw that struggle as occurring in an increasingly singular world economy (Collins, 1986: 19–44) he can be said to have had a partial image of a compressed world, in fact a one-sided view of what is now called globalization. Moreover, in that he argued that struggles between nations were in part about the preservation and enrichment of societal values he certainly, but only in a negative sense, saw that culture is an important ingredient of the global field. In these ways Weber was almost certainly reacting to and attempting to reshape the global and the universal thrust in the writings of Kant, Hegel and Marx, by employing Nietzsche's ideas on the "polytheism" of values to relationships between nations. While inheriting much of Hegel's conceptual apparatus in his work on religion, Weber was eager to promote what has sometimes been called a comparative-differential and concretely historical perspective on "universal history," rather than the abstract, "spiritual" or "utopian" views of his great German predecessors (Robertson, 1985).

One might well say that Durkheim's and Simmel's views were, in their different ways, also one-sided. But in Durkheim's case there was more openness generally to what is now called globalization, in spite of his neglect of many of what we see to have been obvious concrete manifestations of globalization in his lifetime. In the case of Simmel we can see that his relative detachment from societal matters *per se* (although he clearly expressed his commitment to "the European ideal") in the frame of his concern with forms of life in general led to the production of ideas which are relevant in theoretical terms to the concept of globalization.

Coming to Terms with the World as a Whole

In my initial attempt to develop a flexible model of the global whole, a paper by Dumont (1979) played a significant part. It is interesting to note that in his own effort to deal with the problem of totality (a notion which was also important in the formative years of Wallerstein's (1974) world-systems theory), Dumont spoke as a philosophically minded social anthropologist – one who had sought to comprehend "the West" by approaching it from *outside* (Dumont, 1977, 1983). Moreover, in tackling the problem of totality Dumont credited a central member of the Durkheimian school, Marcel Mauss, with having been a source of inspiration. Dumont argued that the discipline of anthropology was committed simultaneously to the rival ideas of the "unity" of mankind and the uniqueness of individual societies. He attempted to resolve this contradiction by arguing that the world as a whole, the world in its totality, should be regarded as consisting in a set of globewide *relationships between societies*, on the one hand, and of *self-contained*, "*windowless monads*," on the other. Whatever the limitations of Dumont's attempt to deal with the epistemological problem of allowing for both uniqueness and discontinuity, and wholeness and continuity, his particular focus is important.

It has been the question of the relationship between the epistemological terms in which it is possible to think of the world and the primary "objects" which appear to exist in the world that has formed a central part of my thinking about globalization. I have sought to lay bare the quintessential features of the terms in which it is possible to conceive of the world, taking into account the empirical constituents of the world of relatively recent times. My model of what, in the most flexible terms, may be called the global field is centered on the way(s) in which we think about globality in relation to the basic makeup of that field. My formulation is more multifaceted than that of Dumont, in that I think in terms of four major aspects, or reference points, rather than two. These are *national societies*; *individuals*, or more basically, *selves*; *relationships between national societies*, or *the world system of societies*; and, in the generic sense, *mankind*, which, to avoid misunderstanding, I frequently call *humankind*. To repeat, this model or image is based upon both epistemic and empirical observations. Sparked by "Dumont's question," the attempt to set out the basic features of the global field involves a mixture of intuition and historical investigation concerning the terms in which the world as a whole is conceived to be, in a special sense, *possible*. (See Robertson, 1994: ch. 3.)

In the broadest sense I am concerned with the way(s) in which the world is ordered. Whereas I am setting out this model of order in what may appear to be formal terms, the intent which actually guides it is to inject *flexibility* into our considerations of "totality." In so far as we think about the world as a whole, we are inevitably involved in a certain kind of what is sometimes pejoratively called totalistic analysis.[3] But even though my scheme does involve a "totalizing" tendency, it does so partly in order to comprehend *different* kinds of orientation to the global circumstance. It will be seen that movements, individuals and other actors perceive and construct the order (or disorder) of the world in a number of different ways (see Robertson, 1994: ch. 4). In *that* sense what my model does is to facilitate interpretation and analysis of such variation. So there is a crucial difference between imposing a model of the global field on all the present and potential actors in that field and setting out a model which facilitates comprehension of variation in that field. The latter is an important consideration. My interest is in how order is, so to speak, *done*; including order that is "done" by those seeking explicitly to establish legal principles for the ordering of the world (Lechner, 1991). To put it yet another way, my model is conceived as an attempt to make analytical and interpretive sense of how quotidian actors, collective or individual, go about the business of conceiving of the world, including attempts to *deny* that the world is one.

Nevertheless, in spite of my acknowledgment of certain denials of global wholeness, I maintain that the trends towards the unicity of the world are, when all is said and done, inexorable. For example, the trends towards economic protectionism in the early 1990s (paralleled by a certain kind of "fundamentalism" concerning identity and tradition) are in one sense negative reactions to increasing compression of the entire world, but they are also

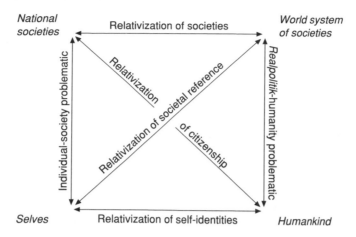

Figure 1 *The global field*

reactions that are, however tortuously, reflexively monitored (Giddens, 1987). Compared to the older protectionisms and autarkies of the eighteenth and the nineteenth centuries (Moravcsik, 1991) the new ones are more self-consciously situated within a globewide system of global rules and regulations concerning economic trade and a consciousness of the global economy as a whole. This certainly does not mean that protectionism will be overcome by such factors, but it does mean that relevant parties, including "average citizens," are increasingly constrained to think in terms, not necessarily favorable terms, of the world as a whole, more specifically the global economy.

It must also be emphasized that although in this chapter I set out what I call a flexible model of globality in *sychronic* terms, as a one-shot, basically contemporary image of what is involved in thinking about the "theory-and-practice" of globality, the model is in fact applied *diachronically*. It is intended to take strongly into account changes in each of the four major components (societies, individuals, international relations, and humankind) in tandem with shifts in the relations between them. Such considerations are dealt with intermittently in Robertson, 1994. Globalization as a process is closely bound up with this diachronic perspective. Yet it should be clear that my model of the global circumstance is both multidimensional and much more global than is usually meant by social-scientific and other connotations of that word. [. . .] Multidimensionality refers in the present context to a mode of grasping the basics of what I sometimes

call the global-human condition, basics which at one and the same time take into account the most general features of *life* in relatively recent history and the growing concern with the connections between different conceptions thereof. We can again see that globalization involves *comparative interaction* of different forms of life.

Globalization refers in this particular sense to the coming into, often problematic, conjunction of different forms of life. This cannot be accurately captured in the simple proposition that globalization is "a consequence of modernity" (Giddens, 1990), which I consider specifically in Robertson, 1994. Present concern with globality and globalization cannot be comprehensively considered simply as an aspect of outcome of the Western "project" of modernity or, except in very broad terms, enlightenment. In an increasingly globalized world there is a heightening of civilizational, societal, ethnic, regional and, indeed, individual self-consciousness. There are constraints on social entities to locate themselves within world history and the global future. Yet globalization in and of itself also involves the diffusion of the *expectation* of such identity declarations.

This model, which is presented diagrammatically in Figure 1, gives the basic outline of what I here call the global field but which for other purposes I call the global-human condition. The figure indicates the four major components, or reference points, of the conception of globality, the basic way in which we are able as empirically informed analysts to "make sense" of globality, as well as the form in terms of which globalization has in the last few centuries actually proceeded. (Discussion of different, or alternative, forms in terms of which globalization *might* have occurred or, indeed, did partially occur are discussed in Robertson, 1994: esp. ch. 3.) To provide an example at this stage, it is clear that Islam historically has had a general "globalizing" thrust; but had that potential form of globalization succeeded we would now almost certainly comprehend contemporary "globality" differently. There would be a need for a different kind of model.

The model is presented in primary reference to twentieth-century developments. In that it partly summarizes such developments it draws attention to increasing, interrelated thematizations of societies, individual selves, international relations and humankind. At the same time, it opens the way to the discussion and study of the ways in which the general pattern came historically to prevail. It also allows for different, indeed conflicting, empirical emphases within "the field" (discussed in Robertson, 1994). (Discussion of what I call the phases of the increasingly dominant form of globalization, occurs specifically in ibid. ch. 3, and with respect to phases since the middle of the nineteenth century in later chapters.) A number of other points should be stressed.

First, while I have emphasized that my perspective allows for empirical variation with respect to what [elsewhere] I call images of world order and that my primary task in analyzing globalization is to lay bare and open up relatively neglected aspects of that theme, there are clearly moral and critical dimensions of my approach to globalization. I will only mention the most general here. There is certainly a sense in which I am trying to tackle directly the problem of *global complexity*, a point which becomes even clearer towards the end of Robertson, 1994, when I address the question of the shifting contents of the four major components of my model. It will, I hope, also become clear that I am arguing for the moral acceptance of that complexity. In other words, complexity becomes something like a moral issue in its own right (Robertson, 1989). Specifically, the way in which I tackle the issues of globality and globalization suggests that in order for one to have a "realistic" view of the world as a whole one must, at least in the contemporary circumstance, accept in principle the relative autonomy of each of the four main components and that, by the same token, one should acknowledge that each of the four is in one way or another constrained by

the other three. In one sense, then, overemphasis on one to the expense of attention to the other three constitutes a form of "fundamentalism." Simply put, one cannot and should not wish away the reality of one or more aspects of the terms in which globalization has been proceeding. This certainly does not exhaust the issue of the extent to which my approach to globalization is moral and critical. But it must suffice for the moment.

Second, there is the issue of the processes which bring about globalization – the "causal mechanisms" or the "driving forces." What happens here to arguments about the dynamics of capitalism and the forces of imperialism which have undoubtedly played a large part in bringing the world into an increasingly compressed condition? In arguing that mine is a cultural perspective on globalization I do not wish to convey the idea that I consider the matter of "the forces" or "the mechanisms" of globalization unimportant. However, I am well aware that that is well-trodden ground. The spread of Western capitalism and the part played by imperialism have been addressed at great length, as has the increasingly complex crystallization of the contemporary global economy. In contrast, the discussion of the disputed terms in which globalization has occurred and is occurring has been greatly neglected. It is that and directly related issues which form the main concern of this book, and it is hoped that such a cultural focus will place work in the more traditional vein in a new light. While the use of the term "culture" here is certainly not as broad and all-embracing as is to be found in some tendencies within the relatively new field of cultural studies, it is employed much more fluidly and adventurously than in conventional sociological work. In particular, my approach is used to demonstrate discontinuities and differences, rather than the traditional sociological view of culture as integrating. It is also meant to indicate a particular way of doing sociology, rather than a sociology that concentrates on culture as such.

Third, in my representation of the global field I have emphasized a number of processes of *relativization*. That term is meant to indicate the ways in which, as globalization proceeds, challenges are increasingly presented to the stability of particular perspectives on, and collective and individual participation in, the overall globalization process. As I have said, this picture of the global field has been produced in primary reference to contemporary globality and globalization. It is an ideal-typical representation of what is meant here by global complexity. In one important respect it indicates overall processes of differentiation in so far as global complexity is concerned. Broadly speaking, application of the model involves the view that processes of differentiation of the main spheres of globality increase over time. Thus differentiation between the spheres was much lower in earlier phases of globalization; while the effects of such differentiation have been encountered unevenly and with different responses in different parts of the world. Clearly these processes of differentiation have definite, and problematic, implications for socialization in the contemporary world (Turner, 1992). An important aspect of this has to do with the ways in which school, college and university curricula are currently being revised in some societies along "international" and/or "multicultural" lines.

There are numerous ramifications of the adoption of a fully global approach to the world, ramifications which are not exhausted by a concentration on the recent and contemporary form of globalization as such. While exploration of the latter is a particular concern of this book, that is not its only concern. In concluding this introductory chapter I should like to consider briefly one of these larger issues: the theme of world history.[4] Books and essays about world history have proliferated in recent times, this development constituting something of a revival of a genre which was intellectually popular during what I call the take-off phase of modern globalization that peaked at the beginning of the twentieth century. This can be attributed to two closely related sets of circumstances. On the one hand, the fact and the consciousness of rapidly increasing interdependence across the world has sharpened the concern with an understandable trajectory of the whole of humanity. On the other hand, whereas earlier writing in that vein consisted, and to some extent still consists, in variations on one "grand narrative" depicting the rise and the "triumph" of the West, there has been an increasing tendency for world history to be written with respect to heretofore unheard "voices." Current controversies about the teaching canon are thus significant manifestations of globalization, not least because in the contemporary phase of globalization the concept of the homogeneous national society is breaking down, in spite of the reassertion of nationalism in certain parts of the world. At the same time those controversies themselves generate new conceptions of world history.

A good example of a fairly recent attempt to develop an alternative to the grand-narrative approach is that of Eric Wolf, who writes that his "central assertion is that the world of humankind constitutes a manifold, a totality of interconnected processes, and inquiries that disassemble this totality into bits and then fail to reassemble it falsify reality" (Wolf, 1982: 3). Like Wallerstein, Wolf believes that the modern tendency to endow "nations, societies, or cultures with the qualities of internally homogeneous and externally distinctive and bounded objects" leads to the creation of "a model of the world as a global pool hall in which the entities spin off each other like so many hard and rounded billiard balls" (Wolf, 1982: 6). Also like Wallerstein, Wolf contends that this situation was largely produced by the intellectual division of labor among the nascent social sciences in the middle of the nineteenth century. While I have great sympathy for this general view, such an approach – which in Wolf's case leads to a fascinating empirical study of "the connectedness of human aggregates" (Wolf, 1982: 387) across a vast portion of the world since 1400 – involves a diminution of the importance of studying the actual trajectory and form of contemporary globalization.

We need to recognize both Wolf's "totality of interconnected processes" *and* the form of totality which has developed in recent centuries. That social science has both consolidated and refracted what from Wolf's standpoint are essentially denials of real, empirical "totality" is a refreshing proposition. But even though normal social science may well have turned "names into things" (Wolf, 1982: 6) and produced an image of a world of sharp boundaries between societies, it has not been entirely responsible for that situation. Social science, and here we are particularly concerned with sociology, developed *in the wake of* national-societal boundary setting. That it was unreflexive in that respect and *contributed to* the prevalent way of thinking in terms of discontinuities between the "internal" and the "external" is undoubtedly the case. But to go to the other extreme and deny the reality of "things" is unwarranted. In this book I attempt to find a bridge between the view that Wolf seeks to sustain and the reality of the world in which we now live. This does involve me in an attempt to transcend the divisions of which Wolf speaks, but not by trying to wipe them out. Thus "world history" is conceived on two levels. On the one hand, world history is to be done in terms of the formation of the world along the lines which I am indicating. On the other, it must be done in due recognition of the ways in which different, indeed an increasing number of, "entities" in the contemporary world are making and remaking their histories in terms of the constraints of the current phase of globalization. "Modernity" has undoubtedly enhanced this kind of reflexivity, which itself has *also* helped to produce a certain kind of wilful nostalgia. But "modernity" should not, in my view, be employed as the essential *explanans*.

Of course, we are all in a certain way contestants in this "postmodern game" of making histories and inventing traditions. The world as a whole is, in a sense, a world of reflexive interlocutors. One of the major tasks of the contemporary sociologist is to make sense of this vast array of interlocutions, in which he or she is at the same time one of the interlocutors.

Notes

1. For an excellent discussion of nostalgic interpretation on the part of Latin Americanists, see Merquior (1991).
2. A few of the remaining pages of this chapter rely a lot upon Robertson and Chirico (1985). An early version of the latter was presented at a conference of the International Society for the Comparative Study of Civilizations (US), Syracuse University, 1980. Over the years the model of what I now often call "the global field" has been altered in significant ways, in a more emphatically global and processual direction. I am grateful to JoAnn Chirico for her contributions to my early thinking about the themes of humanity and humankind. The delay in the publication of this paper was due largely to the fact that it was scheduled to appear in a collection (edited by another academic) which came to naught. In its published form of 1985 it is centered empirically on the simultaneous occurrence of religious "fundamentalisms" and church–state tensions in a variety of societies in the late 1970s and early 1980s (Robertson, 1981), but that was not a feature of the original 1980 paper. Revised versions of the formulation first stated in 1980 have informed much of my work on globalization since the early 1980s.
3. For a well-argued case against "totalizing theory" see Poster (1990). Arguments opposing such theories are particularly popular among "poststructuralists." Fraser (1989: 13), while arguing against "ahistorical philosophical 'metanarratives'," expresses her approval of what she calls "big empirical narratives." By and large I agree with that distinction and, moreover,

would claim that my form of globalization analysis approximates the latter.

4. A particularly good example of historical sociology in the broad tradition of world history is Mann (1986). For an acute discussion of the properties of Western societies which make them "extensive," as well as "intensive," see Meyer (1989).

References

Albrow, M. 1990. "Globalization, knowledge and society," in M. Albrow and E. King (eds.), *Globalization, Knowledge and Society*. London: Sage.

Archer, M. S. 1990. "Foreword," in M. Albrow and E. King (eds.), *Globalization, Knowledge and Society*. London: Sage.

Aron, R. 1966. *Peace and War: A Theory of International Relations*. London: Weidenfeld & Nicolson.

Balibar, E. 1991. "Es gibt keinen Staat in Europa: racism and politics in Europe today." *New Left Review* (March/April).

Baum, R. C. 1974. "Beyond convergence: toward theoretical relevance in quantitative modernization research." *Sociological Inquiry* 44 (4).

Baum, R. C. 1980. "Authority and identity: the case for evolutionary invariance," in R. Robertson and B. Holzner (eds.), *Identity and Authority Explorations in the Theory of Society*. Oxford: Basil Blackwell.

Chase-Dunn, C. 1989. *Global Formation*. Oxford: Basil Blackwell.

Collins, R. 1986. *Weberian Sociological Theory*. Cambridge: Cambridge University Press.

Dumont, L. 1977. *From Mandeville to Marx*. Chicago: Chicago University Press.

Dumont, L. 1979. "The anthropological community and ideology." *Social Science Information* 18 (6): 785–817.

Dumont, L. 1983. *Essais sur l'individualisme*. Paris: Editions du Seuil.

Durkheim, E. 1962. *Socialism*. New York: Collier Books.

Durkheim, E. 1974. *Sociology and Philosophy*. New York: Free Press.

Durkheim, E. and Mauss, M. 1971. "A note on the notion of civilization." *Social Research* 38 (4): 808–13.

Etzione, A. 1965. *Political Unification: A Comparative Study of Leaders and Forces*. New York: Holt, Rinehart & Winston.

Fraser, N. 1989. *Unruly Practices*. Minneapolis: University of Minnesota Press.

Galtung, J. 1966. "Rank and social integration: a multidimensional approach," in J. Berger (ed.), *Sociological Theories of Progress*. Boston: Houghton Mifflin.

Gerth, H. H. and Mills, C. W. 1948. *From Max Weber*. London: Routledge & Kegan Paul.

Giddens, A. 1987. *The Nation-State and Violence*. Berkeley: University of California Press.

Giddens, A. 1990. *The Consequences of Modernity*. Stanford: Stanford University Press.

Inkeles, A. 1981. "Convergence and divergence in industrial societies," in M. O. Attit, B. Holzner, and Z. Suda (eds.), *Directions of Change*. Boulder, CO: Westview Press.

Lagos, G. 1963. *International Stratification and Underdeveloped Countries*. Chapel Hill: University of North Carolina Press.

Lechner, F. J. 1990. "Fundamentalism and sociocultural revitalization: on the logic of dedifferentiation," in J. C. Alexander and P. Colomy (eds.), *Differentiation Theory and Social Change*. New York: Columbia University Press.

Lechner, F. J. 1991. "Religion, law, and global order," in R. Robertson and W. R. Garrett (eds.), *Religion and Global Order*. New York: Paragon House.

Mann, M. 1986. *The Sources of Social Power: Volume 1, A History of Power from the Beginning to AD 1760*. Cambridge: Cambridge University Press.

McLuhan, M. 1960. *Explorations in Communication*, ed. E. S. Carpenter. Boston: Beacon Press.

Merle, M. 1987. *The Sociology of International Relations*. New York: Berg.

Merquior, J. G. 1991. "The other West: on the historical position of Latin America." *International Sociology* 6 (2): 149–64.

Meyer, J. W. 1989. "Conceptions of Christendom: notes on the distinctiveness of the West," in M. L. Kohn (ed.), *Cross-National Research in Sociology*. Newbury Park, CA: Sage.

Miller, J. 1973. *Marshall McLuhan*. New York: Viking Press.

Moore, W. E. 1966. "Global sociology: the world as a singular system." *American Journal of Sociology* 71 (5).

Moravcski, A. 1991. "Arms and autarky in modern European history." *Daedalus* 120 (4).

Nelson, B. 1969. *The Idea of Usury From Tribal Brotherhood to Universal Otherhood*. Chicago: University of Chicago Press.

Nettl, J. P. and Robertson, R. 1966. "Industrialization, development of modernization." *British Journal of Sociology* 17 (3): 274–87.

Nettl, J. P. and Robertson, R. 1968. *International Systems and the Modernization of Societies: The Formation of National Goals and Attitudes*. New York: Basic Books.

Oxford Dictionary of New Words. 1991. Compiled by Sara Tulloch. Oxford: Oxford University Press.

Parsons, T. 1964. "Communism and the West: the sociology of conflict," in A. Etzioni and E. Etzioni (eds.), *Social Change: Sources, Patterns and Consequences*. New York: Basic Books.

Parsons, T. 1978. *Action Theory and the Human Condition*. New York: Free Press.

Poster, M. 1990. *The Mode of Information: Poststructuralism and Social Context*. Cambridge: Polity.

Robertson, R. 1968. "Strategic relations between national societies: a sociological analysis." *Journal of Conflict Resolution* 12 (1): 16–33.

Robertson, R. 1981. "Considerations from within the American context on the significance of church–state tension." *Sociological Analysis* 42 (3): 193–208.

Robertson, R. 1985. "Max Weber and German sociology of religion," in N. Smart, J. Clayton, P. Sherry and S. T. Katz (eds.), *Nineteeth-Century Religious Thought in the West*, vol. III. Cambridge: Cambridge University Press.

Robertson, R. 1989. "A new perspective on religion and secularization in the global context," in J. K. Hadden and A. Shupe (eds.), *Secularization and Fundamentalism Reconsidered*. New York: Paragon House.

Robertson, R. 1994. *Globalization: Social Theory and Global Culture*. London: Sage Publications.

Robertson, R. and Chirico, J. 1985. "Humanity, globalization and worldwide religious resurgence: a theoretical exploration." *Sociological Analysis* 46 (3): 219–42.

Robertson, R. and Tudor, A. 1968. "The Third World and international stratification: theoretical considerations and research finding." *Sociology* 2 (1): 47–64.

Simmel, G. 1950. *The Sociology of Georg Simmel*, ed. K. Wolf. New York: Free Press.

Simmel, G. 1978. *The Philosophy of Money*. London: Routledge & Kegan Paul.

Simmel, G. 1986. *Schopenhauer and Nietzsche*. Amherst: University of Massachusetts Press.

Simpson, J. H. 1991. "Globalization and religion: themes and prospects," in R. Robertson and W. R. Garrett (eds.), *Religion and Global Order*. New York: Paragon House.

Stark, W. 1958. *The Sociology of Knowledge*. London: Routledge & Kegan Paul.

Turner, B. S. 1990. "The two faces of sociology: global or national?" in M. Featherstone (ed.), *Global Culture: Nationalism, Globalization and Modernity*. London: Sage.

Turner, B. S. 1992. "The concept of 'the world' in sociology: a commentary on Roland Robertson's theory of globalization." *Journal for the Scientific Study of Religion* 31 (Sept): 311–18.

Urry, J. 1991. "Time and Space in Giddens' social theory," in C. G. Bryant and D. Jary (eds.), *Giddens' Theory of Structuration*. London: Routledge.

Wallerstein, I. 1974. "The rise and future demise of the world capitalist system: concepts for comparative analysis." *Comparative Studies in Society and History*, 16.

Wallerstein, I. 1991. *Unthinking Social Science: The Limits of Nineteenth-Century Paradigms*. Cambridge: Polity.

Weber, M. 1978. *Economy and Society*. Berkeley: University of California Press.

Wolf, E. R. 1982. *Europe and the People without History*. Berkeley: University of California Press.

28

Postcoloniality and the Boundaries of Identity

R. RADHAKRISHNAN

Why is it that the term "postcoloniality" has found such urgent currency in the first world but is in fact hardly ever used within the formerly colonized worlds of South Asia and Africa?[1] What is the secret behind the academic formation called "postcoloniality" and its complicity with certain forms of avant-garde Eurocentric cultural theory? Is the entire world "postcolonial," and if so, can every world citizen lay claim to an "equal postcoloniality," that is, without any historical reference to the asymmetries that govern the relationship between the worlds of the former colonizers and the colonized? Is "postcoloniality" (notice the ontological-nominalist form of the category) a general state of being, a powerful shorthand for an intense but traveling human condition, or is it a more discrete and circumstantial experience taking place within specific geopolitical boundaries? In general, how is postcoloniality as allegory a response to postcoloniality as a historical phenomenon? These are some of the questions that I wish to elaborate interconnectedly in this essay, and perhaps I might end up making certain suggestions, making certain preferences. But at any rate, "postcoloniality" is in need of a rigorous and situated unpacking before it gets canonized as a universal constant by the imperatives of metropolitan theory.

First of all, it is important to historicize the term with reference to its site of production, namely, the first world in general and, more specifically, the intellectual-theoretical-academic-cultural field within the first world. In other words, we need to contextualize the term both as "project" and as "formation," both macro- and micropolitically.[2] The first world conjuncture within which "postcoloniality" is taking shape is one of unmixed triumph and celebration. The first world or the West[3] is caught up in its own successful contemporaneity (experienced almost as epiphany), which more than ever before has a synchronic stranglehold over the rest of the world. Exhilarated by its many recent victories, the first world is in a state of countermnemonic innocence, freely and unilaterally choosing what to remember and what not to remember from the pages of history. We heard President Bush proudly declare that the memories of Vietnam have been effectively and legitimately buried in the sands of the Gulf War. There is the prevalent understanding that "we" somehow ended up winning the cold war and are therefore in a position of absolute ethico-political authority in relation to the rest of the world. "We" have earned the privilege of initiating a new world order on behalf of everybody else. If in the past, interventions in other spaces and histories had to be justified after the event, the current global situation lies in the form of a carte blanche for the ethico-political as well as epistemic signature of the first world. The entire world has been deterritorialized in anticipation of a democratic-capitalist takeover by the free world.[4] In short, the joyous countermemory of the first world has succeeded in putting to rest the troubling and ongoing histories of colonialism, neocolonialism, and imperialism.[5] Within the indeterminate spatiality of the "post-" the first world finds no problem or contradiction or experiences no sense of shame or guilt while it insists on a dominant role for itself in projects of identity reconstruction the world over. Unwilling to accept a nonleaderlike role, much less exclusion from third world projects, the first world mandates a seamless methodological universalism to legitimate its centrality the world over.[6] Clearly, this strategy is full of "betrayals within," in particular, the duplicitous take on nationalism and a protectionist attitude to American and/or Western identity.[7]

These very tensions, it turns out, occupy center stage when we consider "postcoloniality" in its theoretical-academic formation. The articulation of postcoloniality has gone hand in hand with the development of cultural theory and studies. If anything, postcoloniality is being invested in as the cutting edge of cultural studies. Now what can this mean? Is this a legitimation or a depoliticization of postcoloniality as constituency? The important thing to notice here is the overall *culturalist* mode of operation: in other words, we are not talking about postcolonial economies, histories, or politics. The obsessive focus is on postcoloniality as a cultural conjuncture. The implication is that whatever distances, differences, and boundaries cannot be transcended or broken down politically can in fact be deconstructed through the universalist agency of culture and cultural theory. Indians, Nigerians, Kenyans, Pakistanis, Somalians, Zimbabweans, Bangladeshis, and so on, however resistant they may be otherwise, are available to metropolitan theory in their cultural manifestations. Culture is set up as a nonorganic, free-floating ambience that frees intellectuals and theorists from their solidarities to their regional modes of being.[8] It is within this transcendent space that postcoloniality is actively cultivated as the cutting edge of cultural theory. This sacrifice of postcoloniality as potential politics or activism at the altar of postcoloniality as metropolitan epistemology is an effect inscribed in the very semantics of the term "post-," a point that Ella Shohat makes with telling effect in her essay, "Notes on the 'Post-Colonial' ":

Echoing "post-modernity," "postcoloniality" marks a contemporary state, situation, condition or epoch. The prefix "post," then aligns "postcolonialism" with a series of other "posts" – "post-structuralism," "post-modernism," "post-marxism", "post-feminism," "post-deconstructionism" – all sharing the notion of a movement beyond. Yet while these "posts" refer largely to the supercession of outmoded philosophical, aesthetic and political theories, the "post-colonial" implies both going beyond anti-colonial nationalist theory as well as a movement beyond a specific point in history, that of

colonialism and Third World nationalist struggle. (101)

Shohat in this passage, as well as in the general trend of her essay, demonstrates how the theoretical metaphorics of the "post" conflates politics with epistemology, history with theory, and operates as the master code of *transcendence as such*. "Posthaste," states of historical being are left behind, and the seemingly nameless modality of the "post" shores up for itself an overarching second-order jurisdiction over a variety of heterogeneous and often unrelated constituencies. She also points out how the term "postcolonial" suggests a form of benign acquiescence as against the political activism and oppositionality available to the term "third world" (111). Although I agree with Shohat that the transcendence or "going beyond" implicit in the avant-garde use of the "post" is indeed in bad faith, I wish to argue that distinctions need to be made, based on historical and empirical criteria, between politically relevant and necessary acts of transcendence and mere gestures of transcendence.[9] Thus, a genuine and substantive transcendence of nationalism needs to be differentiated from an elitist transnationalist configuration, and a subaltern interrogation of the nationalist regime (an interrogation often premised on the notion of a "return")[10] must be read differently from a putative capitalist deterritorialization of the nation-state. Similarly, diasporic deconstructions of identity have to be understood differently from "indigenous" divestments from nationalist identity. But for us to be able to do this, the spatiality of the "post" has to be simultaneously critiqued and endorsed, that is, when the endorsement is in opposition to what Homi Bhabha calls "the pedagogical plenitude" of a unilinear historicism ("Dissemination," 291–322). I would like to add that in this instance the critique and the endorsement may not add up to a unified politics of constituency, for the critique of the "post" and the endorsement of the "post" are operating in two discontinuous but related spaces. Shohat's essay does not get into this problematic mainly because, given its immediate polemical concern, it overlooks the discourse of space altogether.[11] My point is that the chronotope of the "post" can be studied with reference to the "time-space" after colonialism without necessarily privileging the "post" as a free-floating signifier. For, in a real sense, aren't "we" all looking for a genuine "time-place" – that is, *after* colonialism, a chronotope that has made a break from the *longue durée* of colonialism? The challenging and complex question is how to enable a mutually accountable dialogue among the many locations that have something important to say about "the after" of postcoloniality.

The phrase "boundaries of identity" in this chapter's title suggests boundedness in a plural form. At the very outset the objection might be made that identities are monolithic and nonhyphenated by nature and therefore can have only single boundaries, each identity entrenched within its own single time. My point here is to multiply time by spaces to suggest (1) that the concept of identity is in fact a normative measure that totalizes heterogeneous "selves" and "subjectivities" and (2) that the normative citizenship of any identity within its own legitimate time or history is an ideological effect that secures the regime of a full and undivided identity. And in our own times, whether we like it or not, the dominant paradigm of identity has been "the imagined community" of nationalism. To backtrack a little, the theme of spaces times time is particularly appropriate in the context of peoples who have had colonialism forced on them. Before colonialism, these peoples lived in their own spaces with their own different senses of history. I am not suggesting that there were not other conquests or that there was pure undifferentiated indigeny before colonialism, but rather that colonialism is a very special and effective instance of intervention and takeover. In the case of India, for example, before the colonialist invasion, there were all kinds of battles, skirmishes, conquests for territories, and negotiations among the Moghul emperors and Hindu and Rajput kings and chieftains, and there was a different set of affairs among the peninsular kings of south India. But there was no real attempt at *unification* for purposes of effective administration. When the East India Company aggressively expanded its role into one of empire building, it also became a task of nation building on behalf of the "native" people.[12] Consequently, and in pursuit of this mandate, local times and spaces and modes of self-governance were dismantled and/or destroyed, and the British invented a tradition on behalf of the Indians and presented it to them so that, in their very act of self-understanding, they could acquiesce in the moral and epistemic legitimacy of British sovereignty.[13] This political gerrymandering of a heterogeneous people into nation-state identification for purposes of control and domination unfortunately creates long-term disturbances that last well into the postcolonialist/nationalist phase.

I am rehearsing this familiar thesis of the postcolonial predicament by way of arguing that heterogeneity or even hybridity is written into the postcolonial experience and that there is a relationship of historical continuity, however problematic, between colonialism and nationalism and between nationalism and its significant Other, the diaspora.

Let us consider the phenomenon of hybridity, a theme so dear to post-structuralist theories of deferral, difference (differance), and dissemination. The crucial difference that one discerns between metropolitan versions of hybridity and "postcolonial" versions is that, whereas the former are characterized by an intransitive and immanent sense of *jouissance*, the latter are expressions of extreme pain and agonizing dislocations. Again, whereas metropolitan hybridity is ensconced comfortably in the heartland of both national and transnational citizenship, postcolonial hybridity is in a frustrating search for constituency and a legitimate political identity. It is important to the postcolonial hybrid to compile a laborious "inventory of one's self"[14] and, on the basis of that complex genealogical process, to produce her own version of hybridity and find political legitimacy for that version. I say this in a Gramscian vein to insist on a fundamental difference between hybridity as a comfortably given state of being and hybridity as an excruciating act of self-production by and through multiple traces. When metropolitan hybridity begins to speak for postcolonial hybridity, it inevitably depoliticizes the latter and renders its rebellion virtually causeless. Let me explain further with reference to Salman Rushdie and *The Satanic Verses*. My general contention is that, although avant-garde theories of hybridity would have us believe that hybridity is "subjectless," that is, that it represents the decapitation of the subject and the permanent retirement of identitarian forms of thinking and belonging, in reality, hidden within the figurality of hybridity is the subject of the dominant West. All hybridities are not equal, and furthermore hybridity does carry with it an ideological tacit nominal qualifier, such as in *Western* or *European* hybridity. Although, theoretically speaking, it would seem that hybridity functions as the ultimate decentering of all identity regimes, in fact and in history, hybridity is valorized on the basis of a stable identity, such as European hybridity, French hybridity, American hybridity, and so on. So which hybridity are we talking about? It would be most disingenuous to use "hybridity" as a theoretical sleight of hand to exorcise the reality of unequal histories and identities.

In the case of Salman Rushdie, a book, intentionally a singing celebration of hybridity, got caught up in codes of identity, and the many scholars, writers, intellectuals, politicians, and religious leaders who responded polemically to the affair did so not from "hybridity's own point of view," but each from the point of view of a certain axiology, ideology, or "bottom line." And what is significant is that the putatively free and liberal Western scholars, with their First Amendment hang-ups, were no exception to this rule.[15] My simple point here is that every point of view on this issue was heavily and deeply identity-based, and the more each point of view encountered resistance from other perspectives, the more it receded into its own home of identity: Western secularism-freedom and the separation of church and state, or Islamic "fundamentalism" that seemed to deny to literature its own relative autonomy and mode of articulation. So, where was hybridity in all this, when the entire polemical pattern was a reminder of the Crusades? The integrity of the West was as much at stake as the rectitude of an authoritarian Islam. It would appear, then, that, in the act of responding to or evaluating a hybrid work, the critic/intellectual (secular or religious, that is, unless "the secular" as a Western norm is made to operate naturally and therefore namelessly) is compelled to step back from hybridity itself in the act of evaluating it. The problem has to do not with hybridity per se, but rather with specific *attitudes to hybridity*.

Next, the juridicolegal battle had to do with the following question: which of the many attitudes to hybridity got it right? But how could this question be adjudicated for lack of a common hermeneutic ground? The irony is that, once the text was internalized and reproposed by each interpretive code in its own way, the hybrid text as objective material was thoroughly derealized.[16] It really did not (and in a way, should not) matter that Western-trained aesthetes of literary detail and nuance went on and on about the "dream scenes" and about intrinsic textual problems concerning the locatability of the author's intention, and so on, for, from another and a different ideological perspective, no such distinction could be made between author and persona, between reality and figuration, or between performative and constative utterances. It then becomes a matter of brute interpretive authority:

which authority is more powerful globally? Ironically, the *fatwa* (horrendous as it is) is in fact the protest symbol of the weak and much maligned-exploited-stereotyped-racialized-othered East trying to stand up to the unquestioned global jurisdiction of Western secular interpretive norms. Lest I be misunderstood, I am wholehearted in my condemnation of the *fatwa* and in my solidarity with Rushdie the individual, but that should not come in the way of a geopolitical (as against a merely individual) understanding of the entire affair. To code it all as exclusively individual versus society, or as the freedom of the artist versus political dictatorship, only simplifies, from a single point of view, the many valences of the issue.

To get back to the theme of hybridity, hybridity was exposed for its semantic insufficiency. In other words, Rushdie was being asked: In what identitarian mode or "as who" are you a hybrid? Obviously, the self-styling of hybridity from its own point of view left too much unexplained. Was Rushdie hybrid as a Muslim, or as an Indian, or as a Westerner, or as a Londoner, or as a metropolitan intellectual-artist? And even if one were to hyphenate all of these identities, one still has to face the question of unequal mediation. Among the many selves that constitute one's identity, there exists a relationship of unevenness and asymmetry, since each of these selves stems from a history that is transcendent of individual intentionality. And again, the canonization of individuality as a first principle is a Western and not a universal phenomenon. Let us also not forget the many vagaries and contradictions of Rushdie's own situation vis-à-vis a racist and ethnicity-busting contemporary England. There were real questions concerning whether or not his "internal politics" were worth defending; it was much easier to value his stand against the Islamic clerisy, but not so his many critiques of the racism and the ethnocentrism "within."

My argument here is that he was being protected as a Western individual with a prerogative to hybridity. When Rushdie got called upon to make "a critical inventory" of himself and furthermore make clear his representational stance, all hell broke loose. What had seemed a hybrid and post-representational expression of personal being was now being forced into the realms of representational cultural geopolitics. Who is Rushdie, and when his hybrid self speaks, who is being spoken for? How and in what direction does Rushdie's hybridity add up? And clearly, this is a question that any responsible reader of Rushdie does ask: one does not have to be an Islamic *ayatollah* to register some form of unease with the radical indeterminacies of Rushdie's *écriture* (Sangari, 216–45). There had been earlier contestations about *Shame* and *Midnight's Children*, and these arguments had to do with Rushdie's sense of perspectival location in relation to India, Pakistan, and South Asian nationalism. The hybrid articulation in all its hyphenated immanence was called upon to account for its representational truth claims. I am focusing strongly on the issue of representation so as to connect this discussion with issues concerning "constituency" and "transgression." For example, why is it more fashionable and/or acceptable to transgress Islam toward a secular constituency rather than the other way around? Why do Islamic forms of hybridity, such as women wearing veils and attending Western schools (here again I am not defending the veils, but I hope my readers will see that I am making a different point here) encounter resistance and ridicule? Why is it that the targets of "ethnic cleansing" are people who see their identities as coextensive with a religion? Why are Gypsies being persecuted the world over? I would argue that it is only in a philosophic-bohemian sense that Occidental hybridity is the victim, but historically speaking, the victims are those groups of people who are striving for any kind of collective identity other than the forms of sovereignty prescribed by Western secularism. In Rushdie's own case, victim though he is, undeniably and tragically, in another sense he is indeed a privileged figure whose perils have mobilized the entire West.

To sum up my argument, metropolitan hybridity is underwritten by the stable regime of Western secular identity and the authenticity that goes with it, whereas postcolonial hybridity has no such guarantees: neither identity nor authenticity. And strange and outrageous as it may sound to secular ears, secularism is one of the chief obstacles on the postcolonial way to self-identification and self-authentication (Chatterjee, *Nationalist Thought*). The question of authenticity has to do not just with identity but with a certain attitude to identity. In other words, authentic identity is a matter of choice, relevance, and a feeling of rightness. In other words, authentication also means ruling out certain options as incorrect or inappropriate. It needs to be stated here that the term "authenticity" deserves more sympathetic attention than it has been getting of late. I do agree that certain ways of theorizing

authenticity have indeed veered dangerously toward blood-and-guts fundamentalism, mystical and primordial essentialism, or forms of divisive separatism. But what I mean by "authenticity" here is that critical search for a third space that is complicitous neither with the deracinating imperatives of Westernization nor with theories of a static, natural, and single-minded autochthony.[17] The authenticity I have in mind here is an invention with enough room for multiple rootedness; in other words, there need be no theoretical or epistemological opposition between authenticity and historical contingency, between authenticity and hybridity,[18] between authenticity and invention.

The postcolonial search for identity in the third world is beset primarily with the problem of location. Within what macropolitical parameters should such a narrative search take place? Given the reality of nonsynchronous histories within the so-called one nation, how are any blueprints to be drawn up towards authentic Indian identity? As Partha Chatterjee has shown us, the very project of nationalism, liberating though it may have been, has been proven to be flawed and ineffective after independence. Chatterjee goes on to demonstrate that, in the case of India, there had always been serious incompatibilities between the visions for the future thought up by Mohandas Gandhi and those championed by Jawaharlal Nehru (*Nationalist Thought*, 131–66). While Nehru was passionately persuaded by "the comity of nation-states" and the promise of a science-reason-technology-based internationalism (based on the unilinear chronology of developmental time), Gandhi's rural plans of decentralization and non-Western modes of organization had nothing whatever to do with nationalism or internationalism. It must be remembered that Gandhi was that early deconstructive thinker who proposed that the Indian Congress should dissolve itself after independence (and this never happened; if anything, the party got a stranglehold over electoral politics to the extent that the party virtually "became" the country), but he was totally marginalized by his own protégé, Nehru, after independence.

Nehru's insistence on heavy industries and progress as Westernization exacerbated the existing problem of nonsynchronous development. In philosophical terms, it was as if Nehru had conceded that India was indeed the third world and therefore should do everything it could to catch up with and be part of the first world. The flight of critical intelligentsia from India to lands overseas and the general problem of "brain drain" can be attributed to the uncritical haste with which Nehru yoked India's political destiny to a thoroughly Western epistemology.[19] It is not surprising that Nehru's career right now is being submitted to a rigorously harsh revisionism. The problem with the internationally oriented Nehru was that he did not make some all-important distinctions between Indian "subjecthood" and Indian "agency," whereas to Gandhi "agency" was of paramount importance. From Gandhi's point of view, an Indian subject who could not speak for India or a definition of India that brought about a serious rupture between "agency" and "subjectivity" was seriously flawed and actually not worth the effort. Whereas "subjectivity" represents a theoretical mode of self-consciousness that does not explicitly raise the issue of representation, "agency" is unthinkable except in terms of representation. "Subjectivity" all too often consents to remain an effect of an alien form of representation, whereas "agency" is an attempt to realize subjectivity as an effect of an authentic act of self-representation that one can call one's own.

Equally at stake is the category "constituency" and how it gets spoken for. If India is a constituency made up of other and smaller constituencies, how should it be represented: through unification or through decentralization? Where lies authenticity? Whereas to Nehru "constituency" meant the transgression of existing identifications toward Westernization, to Gandhi India already existed as a vibrant collection of constituencies. There was no need to abandon, disband, or rename these constituencies in the name of nation building. What comes to mind here is Gandhi's comparison of a free India to a house with open windows all around so that breezes may blow in from every possible side, but there is a constraint: that the house itself not be blown away by the force of the winds from without.[20] There are two important implications here. First, there is the need for a stable identity base for the assimilation of heterogeneous ideas. Second, the whole enterprise of international influence, global eclecticism, and the hybridization as well as the heterogenization of identity requires the specification of actual and historical parameters, alas, with all the inside/outside differentiations that parameters inevitably entail. To state it differently, the crosscurrents of international and eclectic exchange do not by themselves constitute a real-

historical place. We need to have a prior sense of place, which then gets acted upon by the winds of change, for only then can we raise such significant questions as whether India is amenable to capitalism or computerization is good for the Nigerian economy. No place is a pure tabula rasa for inscriptions of arbitrary change, and it is important to build into the notion of change the possibility that certain forms of change may not be desirable for a particular people.[21] These resistances become virtually unthinkable (just as the Gandhian program by now has become "The Road Not Taken") once we accept the thesis of "pure subjectless change." And as we have already seen, the so-called pure change is nothing but the universal travel of Western modes of dominance.[22]

In a sense all that we have been talking about concerns the geopolitical coordination of postcolonial peoples. What are some of the better modes of postcolonial identification? What forms of collective organization as a people are authentic? What affiliations are real and which ones are merely virtual? In the context of postcoloniality, the significant signpost happens to be that of nationalism. Should postcoloniality be expressed through nationalism, or should it be antinationalistic? Is antinationalism the same thing as postnationalism? Are the "posts" in "postcoloniality" and "postnationalism" the same?[23] By and large, most of the options are premised upon the historical reality of nationalism. The significant alternatives are the following: (1) Historicize postcoloniality through nationalism with a full and untroubled faith in the ethicopolitical and epistemological agenda of nationalism. (2) Cultivate nationalism strategically, that is, use it politically without necessarily accepting its entire mandate.[24] (3) Attempt a return to one's own indigenous past in spite of the intervening colonialist-nationalist epoch. This return itself could be coded in two ways: (a) embark on the return as though colonialism-nationalism had not happened at all; and (b) retrace the histories of colonialism-nationalism in a spirit of revisionism – read these histories "against the grain" – as a necessary precondition for one's own authentic emergence.[25] (4) Envision the diaspora as an effective way of disseminating the legitimacy of the nationalist form itself.

I am not particularly persuaded by the first two options. Accepting nationalism wholesale at the present global conjuncture seems unwise and quite risky. Let us remind ourselves that the postcolonial

predicament is being played out during an anoma-
lous historical period when nationalisms are back
with a vengeance all over the world. But it is strange
that this should be happening at a time when
nationalism stands discredited theoretically and
epistemologically. How does the political need for
nationalism coexist with the intellectual deconstruction of nationalism? I would argue that the only,
and the inescapably compelling, rationale for the
legitimacy of nationalism is the plight of the Palestinian people: a people without a sovereign home.
For the rest of the world both to enjoy nationalism
and at the same time to spout a deconstructive
rhetoric about nationalism in the face of Palestinian homelessness is downright perfidious and unconscionable.[26] But that apart, looking around the
world, it is not immediately clear how the nationalist urge is functioning in different arenas. Although
there is a general trend of secession, separatism,
and, in the Eastern European context, Balkanization,
it is not obvious if these are majoritarian or minoritarian movements. Is nationalism being rejected
as an agent of repressive unification, or is it being
upheld along racial and ethnic lines? Clearly, there
is a fierce and passionate return to prenationalist
allegiances, and the burden of the thesis is that for
all these years nationalist unity has been a mere
veneer, a thin lid trying to conceal the long-
suppressed violence and resentment within.[27] In
many instances, it is ironic that even the term "nationalism" should be used, as in "ethnic nationalism."[28] One would imagine that, if anything,
"ethnicity" would be a powerful counterstatement
to the modernist discourse of nationalism. But on
the contrary, what we are finding is that even movements that are pitted against nationalism are using
the language of nationalism in their very act of
resistance. We thus have ethnic nationalism squar-
ing off against nationalism; what is left untouched
is the morphology of nationalism. This is clearly an
indication of the extent to which nationalism has
dominated the political scene for the last two
hundred years or so. It has reached a point where
projects of legitimation have become unthinkable
except in nationalist terms: nationalism has become
the absolute standard for the political as such. As a
result, even the most ferocious counterhegemonic
collective practices are forced to take on the discredited form of nationalism.

The second scenario where nationalism is to
be practiced strategically for purposes of political
legitimation falls very much under the same trap.

The very idea of espousing nationalism for public-
political causes perpetuates an already existing
inner-outer split into a chronic schizophrenia.[29] As
Partha Chatterjee has argued, in such a situation
nationalism becomes a male preserve and "women"
are punished into becoming the vehicles of a pure
interiority that takes the form of a double deprivation ("Nationalist Resolution," 238–9). Women are
effectively excluded both from the history of the
"outside" and that of the "inside" – yet another
instance of women being used as pawns in a male
game of paranoia.[30] Moreover, such an internalized Manichaean doubleness eventually celebrates
the symptom itself as the cure. The cure (within
nationalist terms) becomes viable only if we accept
the distinction that Fanon makes between an official nationalism presided over by the indigenous
elite and a genuine populist national consciousness.[31] But the Fanonian hope, when viewed through
Partha Chatterjee's lenses, sounds naive precisely
because it does not identify the very epistemic form
of nationalism as part of the problem.

The politics of the "return" and of the diaspora,
however, are full of possibilities. Although there
are significant overlaps between these two alternatives, I will take them up one at a time. The very
necessity of the "return" is posited on a prior
premise: the realization that to be a postcolonial is
to live in a state of alienation, alienation from one's
true being, history, and heritage. The "return" takes
the form of a cure, or remedy, for the present ills
of postcoloniality. The "return" also raises the
important issue of "false consciousness" and the
problem of "real-historical consciousness" versus
"virtual historical consciousness." Postcolonial subjectivity is made to choose between its contemporary hybridity as sedimented by the violent history
of colonialism and an indigenous genealogy as it
existed prior to the colonialist chapter. The mandate
of the return is based on the following diagnosis:
the modern-nationalist postcolonial identity is erroneous, inauthentic, not one's own; hence the need for
correction and redirection. I would caution against
facilely dismissing this option as "fundamentalist"
or nostalgic. The return does not have to be based
on either notions of ontological or epistemological
purity. The return is a matter of political choice
by a people on behalf of their own authenticity,
and there is nothing regressive or atavistic about
people revisiting the past with the intention of
reclaiming it.[32] The problem comes up when
revisionist identities are held up as primordial and

transcendentally sanctioned and not as historically produced. As I have already indicated, the "returns" that I am talking about are all the results of narrative invention. The dilemma then is not between two pure identities (Western or indigenous), but between two different narratives and their intended teleologies. The dilemma is this: in which narrative should the postcolonial subject be launched on its way to identity? But before the launching can be initiated, there is a prior methodological problem to be resolved: how to deal with present history and its immediate prehistory? Should the location of present history be invested in critically, or should it be strategically bypassed and neglected?

We are faced with two kinds of postcolonial returns: the subaltern route that revisits colonialist-nationalist historiographies oppositionally and non-identically[33] and the indigenous path, with its strong countermemory or forgetfulness of matters colonialist and nationalist.[34] What is interesting to observe is the extent to which the originary assumptions of each project determine, by way of a theoretical apriorism, what is possible within the project. Subaltern historiographies as undertaken by Ranajit Guha, Dipesh Chakraborty, and others are in keeping with the classic subaltern program as enunciated by Antonio Gramsci. The six-phase program acknowledges that subalternity is necessarily mixed up with the historiographies of the dominant mode and that the production of subaltern identity has to go through (albeit critically and adversarially) dominant discourses before it can seize its agency as its own. The subaltern path to self-recovery lies through histories of negative identification where the subaltern consciousness identifies itself in terms of "what it is not." Its alienation from its self comes to an end when it succeeds in articulating its own hegemonic identity.[35]

Although this is not my present concern here, I would like to mention in passing that the epistemological status of "alienation" is double-coded. As Gayatri Chakravorty Spivak has contended powerfully, alienation is both a political and a philosophical phenomenon. In the political–Marxian sense, alienation is a negative state corrigible through revolutions. But alienation in a philosophic sense (and this is something that Spivak develops in her work[36] as she reads the subaltern project "against the grain" and, in doing so, submits the project of alienation-remediation, in the political sense, to interrogation by poststructuralist readings of alienation in a philosophical sense, that is, alienation as

incorrigible) when understood deconstructively admits of no final correction. Hence Spivak's insistence that the political project of subalternity undertaken in the scrupulosity of political interest must be interrupted by the radical theme of "cognitive failure." Will the subaltern subject ever arrive at its true identity, or is its narrative fated to eternal deferral? What is the point at all in undertaking the subaltern political project when it cannot be philosophically validated? What indeed is the gain if the subaltern project, too, is predetermined to failure and its failure is nothing but an allegorical instantiation of the thesis of "cognitive failure"?

Theorists of indigeny would point out that subalternity is not an inherent state of being or a historically objective condition, but very much a matter of narrative production.[37] In other words, the alignment of postcoloniality with subalternity is not natural. A so-called subaltern text may well be an indigenous text that warrants a different historiography. We are now back to questions of interpretive authority and widely divergent narrative epistemologies. Even the grand thesis of philosophic alienation, viewed from this perspective, sounds suspect, for after all, why should the philosophical valence of alienation be allowed to contain and dominate the political semantics of alienation? Moreover, why should the epistemological project be "radically other" and therefore heterogeneous with the realities of the political program? What is at stake in privileging the epistemological as the ultimate pedagogical deconstructor of political naïveté? And even more pertinently, the indigenous theorist might well ask: why does the general-philosophical question get narrativized through Hegel-Marx-Derrida (Spivak, *In Other Worlds*, 202–15)? Isn't it more than likely that the indigenous political project is quite capable of articulating its own philosophy, its own epistemology of the "subject"? As we can see, we have come back to the same old issues: the separation of theories of knowledge from acts of political independence, and the specificity of parameters of solidarity. The danger with subaltern theory refracted through poststructuralist perspectives is that it, too, privileges Western theory and therefore insists that radical deconstructive critiques have no place for solidarity or constituency unless solidarity itself is conceptualized as a congeries of traveling interruptions and transgressions, that is, as perennial transactional readings among vastly different subject positions. Committed to the utopianism of high theory, these readings privilege perennial crisis as the appropriate historical content of postcoloniality. A further objection that could be raised by advocates of indigeny is the following, and this very much concerns the statements that Spivak makes in one of her interviews that there can be no such thing as indigenous theory: how is one to know if and when the subaltern project has succeeded in subverting dominant historiographies and has ushered in its own hegemony (*Postcolonial Critic*, 69)? Where is the guarantee that subalternity will not be totally lost in complicity with the dominant historiographies, especially given (and this is true not of the Gramscian program but of poststructuralist versions of Gramsci) the overdetermination of the political by the philosophical? Also, the claim that "there is no indigenous theory" makes no particular sense except within the subject-positional conjuncture from which it is made.

Perhaps the problem here is twofold: (1) the nature and the politics of location and (2) (this brings us back to my critique of culturalism early on in the essay) the "intellectual/critical" nature of the whole enterprise. Drawing on the work of Michel Foucault, Spivak cautions us against using the term "subject position" romantically as a surrogate term for the freedom of the self. If anything, subject positions are "assigned" and not freely chosen. It is de rigueur for any kind of subject-positional politics to take its own positionality as constitutive of the politics: in other words, the variations or inflections brought about by one's specific positionality as an academic intellectual are not epiphenomenal to some primary originary politics. To put this in Gramscian-Foucauldian terms, the very organicity of one's politics is subtended and professionally produced by one's specific positionality. Even more broadly speaking, there can be no access to macropolitics except through micropolitical mediations. By this logic, a postcolonial critic-academic-intellectual's sense of constituency is split, crosshatched, anything but unitary. Invested as she is in academic-disciplinary practices, the postcolonial intellectual would be dishonest to seek a direct cathexis with postcolonial identity politics in abeyance of her specific subject-positional location.

Is this way of accounting for one's subject position politically progressive, or is it in fact an admission and perhaps even an ironic glorification of the powerlessness of specific intellectuals beyond their immediate specialist domain?[38] With the

worldliness of macropolitics "always already" mediated and spoken for by their professionalism, the postcolonial-specific intellectuals have little else to do except invest in their subject positions self-reflexively and autocritically.

In an essay that addresses the political production of knowledge in universities, Jacques Derrida calls for "protocols of vigilance and radical self-reflexivity" by way of politicizing the university (3–20). Derrida's assumption here is that the academic site of knowledge, by producing a critical second-order or metatopical awareness of itself, will have become political. While I do applaud this move of locating politics in professionalism, I still find Derrida's formulation inadequate. What is missing in this formulation is a sense of the university's relationality with other sites. For Derrida's (and by extension, Spivak's) formulation to work, the disinterested autonomy of the university as a site has to be endorsed as a first principle. Thus, when Derrida expresses the desire for producing a radical "other" critique that will be truly heterogeneous with the object of the critique, he is in fact utterly privileging the academic mode of labor.[39] There is an unwarranted confidence that somehow the ability of the critique "to think thought itself" will result in the emergence of a different cultural politics. The simple questions are these: How could anything have changed when the site remains the same? How can an intrainstitutional revolution connect with anything "outside" when the "outside" itself is conceptualized as the result of an institutional mode of production? There is a narcissistic circularity to the whole process, and the result is the glorification of the institution's accountability to itself, although in this instance the accountability is of the deconstructive persuasion. The object of my critique here is a certain poststructuralist smugness about autocritiques and rigorous protocols of self-reflexivity. The purpose of self-reflexivity should be persuasion, and persuasion should result in change, and change is too significant to be adjudicated by merely institutional-professional norms. Unless autocritiques succeed in establishing a different relationality with "the world," they are exercises in a vacuum, sans cause, sans constituency. Such a single-minded dedication to one's professional formation in fact belies what is most promising in the politics of location: that locations can recoordinate themselves macropolitically through persuasion and in response to the imperatives of other locations. For example, the formation known as African studies may and can rethink or modify its project in response to Latin American critiques of colonialism. But this dialogue cannot take place if the emphasis is merely on methodologies and protocols. In aligning "location" obsessively with the micropolitical discourses of professional knowledge, Derrida and Spivak in fact end up immobilizing locations and subject positions. And paradoxically, the professional site, in not traveling, becomes the home of a methodological universalism.[40]

In much of the work on postcoloniality, the emphasis is on the postcolonial critic and the postcolonial intellectual. I have no problem with this provided the terms "critic" and "intellectual" are problematized. As I have tried to demonstrate in the last few pages, the mediation of the intellectual-critic becomes the master mediation with a mandate of its own. Well might one ask why other positions and locations such as "being a taxpayer," "being a union leader/social activist," or "being a parent" are denied the dignity of being mediations in their own right. What about forms of knowledge produced from other sites? In addition to the culturalism tacit in "intellectuality" and "criticism," these terms, when understood as poststructuralist coinages, pose a different kind of problem. The critic-intellectual is divorced from the politics of solidarity and constituency. The critic is forever looking for that radical "elsewhere" that will validate "perennial readings against the grain," and the intellectual is busy planning multiple transgressions to avoid being located ideologically and/or macropolitically.[41] In this particular context postcoloniality as constituency, when pressured by metropolitan theory and its professionalism, is allegorized too easily and is made to forget "the return" aspect of its teleology. From an indigenous perspective, this "return" is doomed from the start. How is a "return" possible when the critic's allegiance to the *detour* is more compelling than her commitment to the return? The teleologically minded (or ends-oriented) indigenous theorist would insist that the "return" requires a different path altogether, a path that does not recuperate the historical realities of colonialism and Westernization. The difference between the two returns lies in their very different readings of the means and ends of the project. Each of the returns is underwritten by a different telos.

It is quite clear that there cannot be any one normative articulation of postcoloniality that is nation-centered or centered around the return or the diaspora. Postcoloniality at best is a problematic

field where heated debates and contestations are bound to take place for quite a while to come. My point here is that whoever joins the polemical dialogue should do so with a critical-sensitive awareness of the legitimacies of several other perspectives on the issue. In other words, it would be quite futile and divisive in the long run for any one perspective, such as the diasporic, the indigenous, or the orthodox Marxist, to begin with the brazen assumption that it alone has the ethicopolitical right to speak representatively on behalf of "postcoloniality." Such an assumption can only take the form of a pedagogical arrogance that is interested more in correcting other points of view than in engaging with them in a spirit of reciprocity. No one historical angle can have a monopolistic hold over the possible elaborations of the "postcolony," especially during times when master discourses in general – for example, modernity, nationalism, or international Communism/Marxism – are deservedly in disarray.[42] Although this may sound a little too irresponsibly allegorical, I would venture to say that "postcoloniality" as a field could well be the arena where inequalities, imbalances, and asymmetries could historicize themselves "relationally," an arena where dominant historiographies could be made accountable to the ethicopolitical authority of emerging histories.[43] The kind of noncoercive and justice-based universalism that Samir Amin envisions in his book, *Eurocentrism*, may well call for a versatile and multivalent postcoloniality rooted differently in different histories (136–52).

Among the many heated dialogues that are taking place under the tentative aegis of postcoloniality, there is none more frustrating than the exchange between "diasporic" and "resident" voices. The exchange invariably centers around questions of authenticity and perceptions of "insideness" and "outsideness." Who has got it right, the insider or the outsider? Who speaks for the majority, the insider or the outsider? Unfortunately, what could develop into a productive dialogue often never goes beyond the preliminary moves of self-authentication and credentials presentation. It would seem at first glance that the "resident" position is representative and representational, that is, that it speaks for and on behalf of the majority of Indians or Pakistanis or Nigerians, for example, who live within their respective nation-states, whereas the diasporic voices by virtue of their travel and/or deracinatedness are postrepresentational: they do not add up to a viable constituency. There are a number of problems here. First, there is an untested assumption that majoritarianism equals moral-political authority, that minoritarian voices are either exceptional or elitist. In our own times, such knee-jerk adjudications of right and wrong will just not do: if anything, what is challenging in the present historical conjuncture is the very task of differentiating authentic hegemony from mere dominance. There are regional situations where the majority is dominant-repressive and other situations where the minority represents top-down oppression. A programmatic position that associates minorities with virtue and moral outrage and majorities with tyranny, or vice versa, is insensitive to the actual nuance of history. The complex critical task is to analyze the various processes of majority and minority interpellations as they occur in different geopolitical locations (Appadurai, 5–17).

Second, the claim that "insiders" are more representative is a specious claim. There are several "insides" within any given postcolonial nation-state, and any monolithic use of the "inside" as authentic space is dangerous. Besides, the equation of the insider with the political correctness of the majority is a gross ideological falsification, for it would have us believe that a hegemonic totality has indeed been produced through political processes, a totality that has earned the right to speak for the plenitude of the nation-state. But as Homi Bhabha and others have argued, nationalisms in general are a compelling symptom of the noncoincidence of the "performative" with the "pedagogical" ("Dissemination"). An unproblematic use of geopolitical space as either "in" or "out" also authorizes a facile forgiveness of insider elitisms and oppressions. "Differences within" are consequently not acknowledged as forms of political being.

Finally (and this to me is quite serious), almost by fiat, certain positions vis-à-vis the sovereignty of the nation-state are preemptively identified as erroneous and/or inappropriate. This is indeed a deadly formal procedure that ensures that certain articulations will not even be read as "historical contents" because they arise from positions that are inherently incorrect. Thus the diasporic takes on nationalism are virtually depoliticized and dehistoricized in one fell epistemological edict. To put it colloquially, "I will not listen to you because of where you come from." Such die-hardism is hardly helpful when diasporas and nationalisms are engaged the world over in the task of reciprocal constitution and invention. Is the diaspora the tail that wags "nationalism," or is "nationalism" the primary body that wags the diaspora? That is a question that cannot be answered through recourse to unilateral declarations of authority and privilege.

Lest I be perceived as a diasporic zealot, let me add in explanation that what I am arguing for is a mutual politicization. Just as much as I have been contending against the morphology of national identity as basic or primary and the diasporic as secondary or epiphenomenal, I will also assert that the diaspora does not constitute a pure heterotopia informed by a radical countermemory. The politics of diasporic spaces is indeed contradictory and multi-accentual. I will begin, then, with specific critiques of the diaspora before I offer my preferred versions of the politics of the diaspora. First, within the intellectual-culturalist contexts that define the production of discourses like the present essay, there is the temptation to read the diaspora as a convenient metaphorical/tropological code for the unpacking of certain elitist intellectual agendas. The diaspora, for example, offers exciting possibilities for the intellectual who has always dreamed of pure spaces of thought disjunct from ideological interpellations and identity regimes. The diaspora as the radical nonname of a nonplace empowers the intellectual to seek transcendence through exile and an epiphanic escape from the pressures of history. As such, the diaspora holds possibilities of a "virtual theoretical consciousness" sundered from the realities of a historical consciousness. This virtual consciousness may well be a form of uncorrected false consciousness. What could I mean by "false consciousness"? Let me explain: the context of the diaspora has the capacity to exacerbate the disharmony between utopian realities available exclusively through theory and agential predicaments experienced in history. Thus, given the alienated spatiality of the diaspora, one can both belong and not belong to either one of two worlds at the same time. To the diasporic sensibility, it is easy to practice a perennial politics of transgression in radical postponement of the politics of constituency. To put it differently, traveling or peripatetic transgressions in and by themselves begin to constitute a politics of difference or postrepresentation. Belonging nowhere and everywhere at the same time, the diasporic subject may well attempt to proclaim a heterogeneous "elsewhere" as its actual epistemological home.[44]

Now I would argue that such a self-understanding on the part of the diasporic subject is purely mythical and allegorical. In history, the conditions of the diasporic subject are indeed quite "other." The hyperrealization of the diaspora as a pure countermnemonic politics of its own is admissible only if we concede without qualification (1) that poststructuralist theories of "dissemination" are the natural expressions of diasporic subjectivity whereby the epistemology of poststructuralism and the politics of the diaspora become "one" without any mediation, and (2) that the historiographies of difference have effected a break from identitarian productions of historical consciousness. Neither of these claims is defensible. The poststructuralist appropriation of the diaspora aestheticizes it as an avant-garde lifestyle based on deterritorialization (hence, the frequent offensive and unconscionable use of the Palestinian diaspora as pure allegory), and poststructuralist historiographers of the diaspora are indeed guilty of mendacity, for their celebration of "difference" is completely at odds with the actual experience of difference as undergone by diasporic peoples in their countries of residence.[45] My diagnostic reading is that in these instances, high metropolitan theory creates a virtual consciousness as a form of blindness to historical realities. The metropolitan theory of the diaspora is in fact a form of false consciousness that has to be demystified before the diasporic condition can be historicized as a condition of pain and double alienation.

To consider, then, the diaspora as "the history of the present" within the *longue durée* of colonialism-nationalism: if nationalism in a deep structural sense is the flip side of colonialism, and if the diaspora is "nationalism's significant Other," how is the diaspora related to colonialism? This question takes on even greater complexity when we consider the fact that the diasporas we are talking about are "metropolitan diasporas," that is, diasporas that have found a home away from home in the very heartland of former colonialism. And this home away from home is full of lies and duplicities. A diasporic citizen may very likely find economic betterment in the new home, but this very often is allied with a sense of political-cultural loss. If the diasporic self is forever marked by a double consciousness,[46] then its entry as legitimate citizen into the adopted home is also necessarily double. Thus in the American context (the so-called nation of nations context, as Walt Whitman saw it) of ethnic hyphenation, the passage into citizenship is also a passage into minoritization. The African-American in her very citizenship is "different" and thus rendered a target of hyphenation in pain and in alienation. The utopian response to this predicament (one favored by Homi Bhabha) would be to privilege the moment of passage as a perennial moment of crisis, as though crisis were a constituency by itself. Arguing against Bhabha, I would maintain that the ethnic diasporic self is in fact seeking validation as a constituency. As I have elaborated elsewhere, there is a place for "postethnicity," but such a place cannot be disjunct from ethnic spaces or their polemical negotiations with the putative mainstream identity. The ethnic cannot be transcended or postponed unless and until ethnicity has been legitimated, both within and without, as historiography.[47] The perennial crisis mode plays too easily into "dominant traps" and their attempts to undo and deny ethnicity. Furthermore, as Jesse Jackson reminded Michael Dukakis (that although they may now be on the same boat, they have come to the United States on different ships), there are ethnicities and ethnicities, and the difference often is the racial line of color.[48]

I agree that the diasporic location is by no means that harmonious representational space characterized by a one-to-one correspondence between self and constituency, between experienced worldliness and cognitive worldview. As Maxine Hong Kingston and many others have demonstrated, the diasporic/ethnic location is a "ghostly" location where the political unreality of one's present home is to be surpassed only by the ontological unreality of one's place of origin.[49] This location is also one of painful, incommensurable simultaneity: the Chinese/Indian past as countermemory and memory (depending upon one's actual generational remove from one's "native" land) coexists with the modern or the postmodern present within a relationship that promises neither transcendence nor return. Does this mean that the diasporic location marks an epochal spot that announces the end of representation? Does the diaspora express a liminal, phantasmal, borderline[50] phenomenology inexpressible within the representational grid? I would respond, most certainly not. Sure enough, diasporan realities do show up the poverty of conventional modes of representation with their insistence on single-rooted, nontraveling, natural origins. But this calls for multidirectional, heterogeneous modes of representation and not the premature claim that "representation no longer exists." I do not see how representation "can no longer exist" until the political "no longer exists," and I for one must admit

324

R. Radhakrishnan

that I do not know what "the postpolitical" is all about. The much-vaunted obsolescence of representation also oversimplifies the phenomenon of the diaspora by equating it with that of metropolitan deracination. There is a strange signifying system of equivalence operating here in the name of theory: diaspora = metropolitan deracination = loss of "where one came from" = loss of historical perspectivism = the removal of "interestedness" from the realm of the "political" and, finally, the realization of politics as a kind of unsituated anarchism. Needless to say, what is shored up as the immutable transcendent signified through this play of signifiers is the metropolitan will to meaning as effected by metropolitan avant-garde theories and methodologies. But in actuality, the diasporic self acquires a different historicity and a different sense of duration within its new location that is neither home nor not-home.[51] Rather than glorify the immigrant moment as a mode of perennial liminality, the diasporic self seeks to reterritorialize itself and thereby acquire a name.

I believe that there is something to be gained in naming the diasporic self or subject as the ethnic self. Whereas the term "diaspora" indicates a desire to historicize the moment of departure as a moment of pure rupture both from "the natural home" and "the place of residence," the ethnic mandate is to live "within the hyphen" and yet be able to speak. Whereas the pure diasporic objective is to "blow the hyphen out of the continuum of history," the ethnic program is to bear historical witness to the agonizing tension between two histories (Benjamin). Informed exclusively, almost obsessively, by "the countermemory" and the utopian urge to focus only on second-order or metatopical revolutions, metropolitan theories of the diaspora tend to make light of the tension between "past history" and "present history." I would even go so far as to say that "disseminative" articulations of the diasporic predicament are an attempt to realize theory as an allegorical prescription for the ills of history.

The repoliticization of the diaspora has to be accomplished in two directions simultaneously. First of all, and this is in accordance with the requirements of the politics of location, diasporic communities need to make a difference within their places/nations/cultures of residence. This cannot be achieved unless and until the metropolitan location itself is understood as problematic and, in some sense, quite hostile to "ethnicity." The use of

location by diasporic/ethnic (I am using the two terms interchangeably in light of my earlier recommendation that the diasporic be named as the "ethnic") communities has to be "oppositional." In other words, "mainstreaming" is not the answer at all.[52] If "ethnicity" is to be realized both as an "itself" and as a powerful factor in the negotiation of the putative mainstream identity, it must necessarily be rooted in more than one history: that of the present location and that of its past. I am not suggesting for a moment that the ethnic self indulge in uncritical nostalgia or valorize a mythic past at the expense of the all-too-real present, but rather that it engage in the critical task of reciprocal invention. Particularly, in the American context, it is of the utmost importance that a variety of emerging postcolonial-diasporic ethnicities (Asian-American, Latina, Chinese-American, Chicano, and so forth) establish themselves "relationally" with the twin purpose of affirming themselves and demystifying the so-called mainstream. But this task is unthinkable unless ethnicity is coordinated as a "critical elsewhere" in active relationship with the status quo. These "emerging relational ethnicities" may be said to be interpellated in more than one direction: there is (1) the affirmation of "identity politics" inherent in each historically discrete ethnicity; (2) the relational cultivation of each ethnicity in response to other coeval ethnicities;[53] (3) achieving common (and not identical) cause with those deconstructive metropolitan identity productions that stem from within the dominant histories; and (4) opposing perennially dominant historiographies that resist change and ethicopolitical persuasion.

I can anticipate a vociferous objection here, namely, "Is it appropriate to use one's origins (such as Indian, Korean, Chinese, or Zimbabwean) in a purely strategic way? For example, isn't the "Africa" in "African-American" different from the "African" in "African"? Doesn't an ethnic awareness of "Africanness" within the American context somehow distort and misrepresent "Africanness" as understood as an "inside" reality within Africa? Is "ethnicity," then, a mere invention, whereas "native realities" are natural? How then do we decide which is the real India, the real Nigeria, and so on? I have a number of responses. First of all, it is not at all clear that African or Indian or Nigerian reality even within its "native place" is undifferentiated or indivisible. Second, the fortuitous coincidence of a historical reality with the place of its origin does not make that "reality" any more "natural" than other realities that have traveled or been displaced through demographic movements. Reality from within is as much a production or invention as realities that straddle two or more spaces. Third, the invention of realities is the result of perspectival imaginings, and each perspective is implicated in the polemics of its own positionality.[54] Fourth, diasporas are too real and historically dense in our own times to be dismissed as aberrations. Finally, any discussions of nation-centered formations without reference to diasporic movements and vice versa are really not worthwhile: a more rewarding task would be to read the two versions relationally and to locate and identify intersections of both consent and strong dissent, for neither version has the authority to speak for the other or to speak for nationalism or postcoloniality.

In conclusion, I would like to return to the politics of the "post." Much as I critique the use of "postcoloniality" as a floating signifier, in the final analysis my own take on the term is "double" since I do wish to retain for it a sense of open spatiality for the occurrence of coalitional transformations. This may not be a "big deal" in the home country, but to me and many others in the diaspora, the politics of solidarity with other minorities and diasporic ethnicities is as important and primary as the politics of the "representations of origins." It is in this sense, then, that I am in favor of the allegorization of the "postcolonial condition": that the allegory be made available as that relational space to be spoken for heterogeneously but relationally by diverse subaltern/oppressed/minority subject positions in their attempts to seek justice and reparation for centuries of unevenness and inequality.[55] Diasporic communities do not want to be rendered discrete or separate from other diasporic communities, for that way lies co-optation and depoliticization.[56] To authenticate their awareness of themselves as a form of political knowledge, these communities need to share worldviews, theories, values, and strategies so that none of them will be "divided and ruled" by the racism of the dominant historiography.

I cannot end this essay without reference to the other "p.c.," that is, the much publicized "political correctness," for the two "p.c.'s" are indeed interconnected in the public imagination. "Postcoloniality" (and here I am talking about it as an academic formation in a certain relationship to cultural studies) is often presented as a haven for terrorists and tenured radicals who are out to destroy Western civilization itself. Laughable and unconscionable as this charge is (much like the nonexistent phenomenon of "reverse discrimination"), postcolonial intellectuals should respond to it firmly and aggressively. This response is not even thinkable unless we think of postcoloniality as everyone's concern, its ethicopolitical authority a matter for general concern and awareness and not the mere resentment of a ghetto.[57] It is important for postcolonials of the diaspora to reject patronage, containment, and ghettoization and to insist rigorously that their internal perspective is equally an intervention in the general scheme of things. To put it in terms that might best appeal to academic departments of Western literature, teaching Conrad without teaching Chinua Achebe is as much bad faith as it is bad scholarship.

Notes

1. For a sustained discussion of the term "postcoloniality" from several different perspectives, see *Social Text* 31/32 (1992), a special issue on postcoloniality.
2. I am using the terms "project" and "formation" as elaborated by Raymond Williams in his posthumously published *The Politics of Modernism*.
3. I may be perceived here as guilty of using the term "West" in a monolithic way. Although I admit that the West itself is full of "differences within," I would insist that the West as a global political effect on the non-West has indeed been the result of colonialist-imperialist orchestration, that is, it has spoken with one voice.
4. For a critique of glib celebrations of democratic-capitalist triumphalism, see essays by Neil Larsen, Barbara Foley, and R. Radhakrishnan in the "remarx" section, *Rethinking Marxism* 5, no. 2 (Summer 1992): 109–40.
5. For probing analyses of postcoloniality in the context of imperialism, colonialism and neocolonialism, see *Social Text* 31/32 (1992), the special issue on postcoloniality – in particular, essays by Gyan Prakash, Ella Shohat, Anne McClintock, and Madhava Prasad. See also Aijaz Ahmed, *In Theory*, for a number of provocative position statements on theory, Marxism, nationalism, cultural elitism, and the diasporic intellectual.
6. Chandra Talpade Mohanty discusses the issue of "methodological universalism" and other related issues concerning subject positionality in her essay "Under Western Eyes," in *Third World Women and the Politics of Feminism*, ed. Mohanty, Russo, and Torres, 51–80.

7. It is ironic that in recent years American trade policy statements call for the deterritorializations of national spaces by the flow of capital and, at the same time, bemoan the surrender of American jobs to cheap labor overseas. On the theme of "denials within the West," see Akhil Gupta, "The Reincarnation of Souls and the Rebirth of Commodities."

8. For a sustained discussion of the organicity or the lack thereof of intellectuals, in the context of Antonio Gramsci and Michel Foucault, see Radhakrishnan's *Diasporic Mediation*, chapter 2.

9. Transcendence usually suggests some sort of cartographic reconfiguration and liberation. For two very different uses of cartography, the one imperialist-colonialist and the other postcolonial, see Joseph Conrad's *Heart of Darkness* and Amitav Ghosh's *The Shadow Lines*. See also Nuruddin Farah's *Maps*.

10. For a discussion of the "return" and its relationship to the "postcolonial *detour*," see Vivek Dhareshwar.

11. For rich and politically suggestive uses of space in post-Marxist geography, refer to the works of Edward Soja and Neil Smith.

12. For an original reading of the relationship between nationalism and imperialism, see Gauri Viswanathan's "Raymond Williams and British Colonialism" and her book *The Masks of Conquest*.

13. I refer here to the growing body of work of such postcolonial/subaltern scholars as Partha Chatterjee, Ashis Nandy, Vandana Shiva, and Dipesh Chakraborty, each of whom, in her own way, problematizes received historiographies. Also see *The Invention of Tradition*, ed. Hobsbawm and Ranger.

14. This idea of a critical inventory is elaborated brilliantly by Antonio Gramsci, *The Modern Prince and Other Writings*, 59.

15. Among the many publications on the Rushdie affair, I would single out the following essays: "Editors' Comments: On Fictionalizing the Real"; Sara Suleri; Gayatri Chakravorty Spivak, "Reading *The Satanic Verses*"; Tim Brennan; and Aamir Mufti. For general information on the many global receptions of *The Satanic Verses*, see Lisa Appignanesi and Sara Maitland, eds., *The Rushdie File*.

16. On the question of the objectivity of the text and the interpretive authority of different reading communities, see Stanley Fish.

17. This search for the third space is characteristic of so much contemporary ethnic and postmodern fiction: Maxine Hong Kingston, Toni Morrison, Jamaica Kincaid, and others.

18. Amitav Ghosh's *The Shadow Lines* effectively thematizes notions of "authenticity" and "invention" in a way that accounts for political agency without at the same time resorting to doctrines of epistemological and/or ontological purity.

19. For a radical critique of Western science and reason in the context of Indian life and culture, see *Science,*

Hegemony and Violence: A Requiem for Modernity, ed. Ashis Nandy, in particular, essays by Claude Alvares, Shiv Visvanathan, Vandana Shiva, and Jatinder K. Bajaj.

20. There is a hymn from the *Rig Veda* that captures a similar idea: "Let noble thoughts come to us from every side."

21. Edward W. Said's "Traveling Theory" takes up this vital question of the modification of theory through travel from one geopolitical location to another.

22. See chapter 7, "Cultural Theory and the Politics of Location," in Radhakrishnan's *Diasporic Mediations*.

23. For a historically sensitive analysis of the locationality of the "post," see Anthony Appiah, "Is the 'Post' in Postcoloniality the Same as the 'Post' in Post-Modernism?"

24. For a powerful critique of a developmental nationalism, see Madhava Prasad's essay in *Social Text* 31/32 (1992).

25. See Dhareshwar for an interesting elaboration of a postcolonial detour by way of poststructuralist epistemology.

26. Edward Said's numerous recent essays on the Palestinian intifada remind us of the pitfalls of a purely allegorical mode of thinking that is divorced from geopolitical realities. See, for example, "An Ideology of Difference," *Critical Inquiry* 12 (Autumn 1985): 38–58; "On Palestinian Identity: A Conversation with Salman Rushdie," *New Left Review* 160 (November–December 1986); "Intifada and Independence," *Social Text* 22 (Spring 1989); and "Representing the Colonized: Anthropology's Interlocutors," *Critical Inquiry* 15 (Winter 1989): 205–25.

27. For a rigorous and brilliant analysis of the many reconstituted forms of nationalism, see Arjun Appadurai, "Disjuncture and Difference in the Global Cultural Economy."

28. Ernest Gellner's book on nationalism is a useful guide to the many kinds of nationalism that have been active during this century.

29. See Partha Chatterjee, "The Nationalist Resolution of the Woman's Question"; see also chapter 9, "Nationalism, Gender, and the Narrative of Identity," in Radhakrishnan's *Diasporic Mediations*.

30. For an in-depth study of the manner in which the woman's question in the context of *sati* is marginalized, see Lata Mani, "Contentious Traditions." For a global sense of women's issues in a third world context, see Chandra Talpade Mohanty's introduction to *Third World Women and the Politics of Feminism*, 1–47.

31. See Frantz Fanon's *The Wretched of the Earth* for an optimistic articulation of national consciousness. See also Neil Lazarus, *Resistance in Postcolonial African Fiction*, and Mowitt, "Algerian Nation: Fanon's Fetish."

32. Toni Morrison's *Beloved* and Gayl Jones's *Corregidora* are two powerful and moving fictional attempts at "the return" to one's own history.

33. The entire subaltern project initiated by Ranajit Guha poses this question of the subaltern's "own identity" in complex historiographic terms.

34. Friedrich Nietzsche's *The Use and Abuse of History* is a seminal text that deals with questions of historical forgetting and remembering. See also Michel Foucault, "Nietzsche, Genealogy, History."

35. Antonio Gramsci's formulation of the subaltern agenda is absolutely fundamental in this regard. For a simultaneously postcolonial and poststructuralist take on the subaltern, see Spivak, "Subaltern Studies: Deconstructing Historiography."

36. For further discussion of Spivak's work, see Lazarus, *Hating Tradition Properly*, and my book *Theory in an Uneven World*.

37. For an interesting understanding of the nature of the subaltern text, see Poonam Pillai.

38. Edward Said's notion of worldliness, which permeates his book *The World, the Text, the Critic*, is an attempt to call into question the narcissistic arrogance of specialist knowledges.

39. In significant opposition to Derrida, Foucault would question the adequacy of institutional-scientific productions of knowledge. See Foucault, *Power/Knowledge*.

40. For further discussions of intellectuality in a worldly context, see Bruce Robbins, ed.

41. In contrast to this notion of "criticism against the grain," indigenous Indian (Sanskrit *rasa*) aesthetic theory stresses the importance of the critic's empathy/*sahridaya* with the text.

42. Aijaz Ahmed's *In Theory* is an attempt, unsuccessful in my reading, to reestablish the claims of a dogmatic Marxism in the area of developmental nationalism.

43. For a sustained, historically responsible and brilliant discussion of historiography, see Ranajit Guha, "Dominance without Hegemony and Its Historiography."

44. Ghosh's *The Shadow Lines* is an interesting study of the location and its bearing on one's worldview. Ghosh also raises the question of "imagined reality" in relationship to inhabited realities.

45. The journal *Diaspora* is a recently established magazine whose primary focus is the cultural politics of various diasporas in relation to themselves and their "home" cultures.

46. For example, Maxine Hong Kingston's *The Woman Warrior*, with its double-conscious narrative, refers to both "American ghosts" and "Chinese ghosts" in the context of immigration and naturalization.

47. For an early, memorable account of the boundaries of ethnicity, see Ralph Ellison's *Invisible Man*.

48. W. E. B. Du Bois astutely remarked that race indeed has been the dividing line in our own times. Recent happenings in this country and elsewhere testify to the truth of his statement. See also Anthony Appiah's essay on Du Bois in *Race, Writing and Difference*.

49. For a thought-provoking discussion of diasporic reality vis-à-vis the reality of the place of origin, see Rey Chow. The fiction of Amy Tan also dramatizes this issue.

50. See Gloria Anzaldúa's *Borderlines/La Frontera*.

51. For notions of "home" in the context of the postcolony, see *Public Culture* 4, no. 2 (Spring 1992) and 5, no. 1 (Fall 1992).

52. See Mohanty, "On Race and Voice . . ."; also see Henry A. Giroux, "Post-Colonial Ruptures and Democratic Possibilities."

53. For the concept of coevalness, see Johannes Fabian, *Time and the Other: How Anthropology Makes Its Object*.

54. See my essay "Postmodernism and the Rest of the World," *Organization* 1, no. 2 (October 1994): 305–40. See also Julie Stephens, "Feminist Fictions: A Critique of the Category 'Non-Western Woman' in Feminist Writings on India," and Susie Tharu, "Response to Julie Stephens," both in *Subaltern Studies VI*, ed. Guha, 92–125 and 126–31.

55. Samir Amin and Neil Smith, among others, have theorized the notion of unevenness in geopolitical relationships.

56. A case in point here is the ethnic predicament in the United Kingdom: during Thatcher's rule, ethnicity was successfully minoritized and ghettoized. See Stuart Hall, *The Hard Road to Renewal*.

57. Kumkum Sangari and Sudesh Vaid, in their introduction to *Recasting Women*, quite astutely claim for feminist historiography both a "special interest" and a general or total valence.

References

Ahmed, Aijaz. *In Theory*. London: Verso, 1992.

Amin, Samir. *Eurocentrism*. New York: Monthly Review Press, 1989.

Anzaldúa, Gloria. *Borderlands/La Frontera: The New Mestiza*. San Francisco: Spinster/Aunt Lute, 1987.

Appadurai, Arjun. "Disjuncture and Difference in the Global Cultural Economy." *Public Culture* 2, no. 2 (Spring 1990): 1–24.

Appiah, Anthony. "Is the 'Post' in Postcoloniality the Same as the 'Post' in Post-Modernism?" *Critical Inquiry* 17 (Winter 1991): 336–57.

——. "The Uncompleted Argument: Du Bois and the Illusion of Race." In *Race, Writing and Difference*, ed. H. L. Gates, 21–37. Chicago: University of Chicago Press, 1986.

Appignanesi, Lisa, and Sara Maitland, eds. *The Rushdie File*. Syracuse, N.Y.: Syracuse University Press, 1990.

Benjamin, Walter. "Theses on the Philosophy of History." In *Illuminations*, ed. and intro. Hannah Arendt, trans. Harry Zohn, 253–64. New York: Harcourt, Brace and World, 1968.

Bhabha, Homi K. "Dissemination: Time, Narrative, and the Margins of the Modern Nation." In *Nation and Narration*, ed. Homi K. Bhabha, 291–322. New York: Routledge, 1990.

Brennan, Tim. "Rushdie, Islam and Postcolonial Criticism." *Social Text* 31/32 (1992): 271–6.

Chatterjee, Partha. "The Nationalist Resolution of the Woman's Question." In *Recasting Women: Essays in Colonial History*, ed. Kumkum Sangari and Sudesh Vaid, 233–53. New Brunswick, N.J.: Rutgers University Press, 1990.

——. *Nationalist Thought and the Colonial World*. London: Zed, 1986; Minneapolis: University of Minnesota Press, 1993.

Chow, Rey. *Woman and Chinese Modernity*. Minneapolis: University of Minnesota Press, 1991.

Conrad, Joseph. *Heart of Darkness*. Oxford and New York: Oxford University Press, 1984.

Derrida, Jacques. "The Principle of Reason: The University on the Eye of Its Pupils." *Diacritics* 13 (Fall 1983): 3–20.

Dhareshwar, Vivek. "Toward a Narrative Epistemology of the Postcolonial Predicament." *Inscriptions* 5 (1989): 135–57.

Dworkin, Dennis L., and Leslie G. Roman, eds. *Views beyond the Border Country: Raymond Williams and Cultural Politics*. New York: Routledge, 1993.

"Editors' Comments: On Fictionalizing the Real." *Public Culture* 2 (Spring 1989): i–v.

Ellison, Ralph. *The Invisible Man*. New York: Random House, 1952.

Fabian, Johannes. *Time and the Other: How Anthropology Makes Its Object*. New York: Columbia University Press, 1983.

Fanon, Frantz. *The Wretched of the Earth*. Trans. Constance Farrington. New York: Grove Press, 1968.

Farah, Nuruddin. *Maps*. London: Pan Books, 1986.

Fish, Stanley. *Is There a Text in This Class?: The Authority of Interpretive Communities*. Cambridge, Mass.: Harvard University Press, 1980.

Foley, Barbara, Neil Larsen, and R. Radhakrishnan. "Remarx." *Rethinking Marxism* 5, no. 2 (Summer 1992): 109–40.

Foucault, Michel. "Nietzsche, Genealogy, History." In *Language, Counter-Memory, Practice: Selected Essays and Interviews*, ed. and intro. Donald F. Bouchard, trans. Donald F. Bouchard and Sherry Simon, 139–64. Ithaca, N.Y.: Cornell University Press, 1980.

——. *Power/Knowledge: Selected Interviews and Other Writings*, ed. and trans. Colin Gordon. New York: Pantheon Books, 1980.

Gellner, Ernest. *Nations and Nationalism*. Oxford: Blackwell, 1983.

Ghosh, Amitav. *The Shadow Lines*. London: Bloomsbury, 1988.

Giroux, Henry A. "Post-Colonial Ruptures and Democratic Possibilities." *Cultural Critique* 21 (Spring 1992): 5–39.

Gramsci, Antonio. *The Modern Prince and Other Writings*. Trans. and intro. Louis Marks. New York: International Publishers, 1968.

Guha, Ranajit. "Dominance without Hegemony and Its Historiography." In *Subaltern Studies VI*, ed. Ranajit Guha, 210–39. Oxford: Oxford University Press, 1989.

Gupta, Akhil. "The Reincarnation of Souls and the Rebirth of Commodities: Representations of Time in 'East' and 'West.'" *Cultural Critique* 22 (Fall 1992): 187–211.

Hall, Stuart. *The Hard Road to Renewal*. London: Verso, 1988.

Hobsbawm, E., and T. Ranger, eds. *The Invention of Tradition*. Cambridge and New York: Cambridge University Press, 1983.

Jones, Gayl. *Corregidora*. New York: Random House, 1975.

Kingston, Maxine Hong. *The Woman Warrior*. New York: Knopf, distrib. Random House, 1976.

Lazarus, Neil. *Hating Tradition Properly*. Forthcoming.

——. *Resistance in Postcolonial African Fiction*. Yale University Press, 1990.

Mani, Lata. "Contentious Traditions: The Debate on Sati in Colonial India, 1790–1833." Ph.D. diss., University of California, 1989.

Mohanty, Chandra Talpade. "On Race and Voice: Challenges for Liberal Education in the 1990's." *Cultural Critique* 14 (Winter 1989–90): 179–208.

Mohanty, Chandra Talpade, A. Russo, and L. Torres, eds. *Third World Women and the Politics of Feminism*. Bloomington: Indiana University Press, 1991.

Morrison, Toni. *Beloved*. New York: Knopf, distrib. Random House, 1987.

Mowitt, John. "Algerian Nation: Fanon's Fetish." *Cultural Critique* 22 (Fall 1992): 165–86.

Mufti, Aamir. "Reading the Rushdie Affair: An Essay on Islam and Politics." *Social Text* 29 (1992): 95–116.

Nandy, Ashis, ed. *Science, Hegemony and Violence: A Requiem for Modernity*. Tokyo: United Nations University; Delhi: Oxford University Press, 1990.

Nietzsche, Friedrich. *The Use and Abuse of History*. Indianapolis: Bobbs-Merrill, 1949.

Pillai, Poonam. "Theorizing the Margins." Ph.D. diss., University of Massachusetts at Amherst, 1993.

Prasad, Madhava. "On the Question of a Theory of (Third World) Literature." *Social Text* 31/32 (1992): 57–83.

Public Culture 4, no. 2 (Spring 1992).

Public Culture 5, no. 1 (Fall 1992).

Radhakrishnan, R. "Postmodernism and the Rest of the World." *Organization* 1, no. 2 (October 1994): 305–40.

——. *Theory in an Uneven World*. Oxford: Blackwell, forthcoming.

———. *Diasporic Mediations: Between Home and Location.* Minneapolis: University of Minnesota Press, 1996.

Rig-Veda Sanhita. Trans. H. H. Wilson. New Delhi: Cosmo, 1977.

Robbins, Bruce, ed. *Intellectuals: Aesthetics, Politics, Academics.* Minneapolis: University of Minnesota Press, 1990.

Said, Edward W. "Traveling Theory." In *The World, the Text, the Critic,* 226–47. Cambridge, Mass.: Harvard University Press, 1983.

Sangari, Kumkum. "The Politics of the Possible." In *The Nature and Context of Minority Discourse,* ed. David Lloyd and Abdul JanMohamed, 216–45. Oxford: Oxford University Press, 1990.

Shohat, Ella. "Notes on the 'Post-Colonial.' " *Social Text* 31/32 (1992): 99–113.

Smith, Neil. *Uneven Development.* Oxford: Blackwell, 1984.

Social Text 31/32 (1992). Special issue on "postcoloniality."

Soja, Edward W. *Postmodern Geographies: The Reassertion of Space in Critical Social Theory.* London: Verso, 1989.

Spivak, Gayatri Chakravorty. *The Post-Colonial Critic: Interviews, Strategies, Dialogues.* Ed. Sarah Harasym. New York: Routledge, 1990.

———. "Reading the Satanic Verses." *Public Culture* 21 (Fall 1989): 79–99.

———. "Subaltern Studies: Deconstructing Historiography." In *In Other Worlds: Essays in Cultural Politics,* 197–221. New York: Methuen, 1987.

Suleri, Sara. "Whither Rushdie." *Transition* 51 (1991): 198–212.

Viswanathan, Gauri. *The Masks of Conquest.* New York: Columbia University Press, 1989.

———. "Raymond Williams and British Colonialism: The Limits of Metropolitan Cultural Theory." In *Views beyond the Border Country,* ed. Dworkin and Roman, 217–30, 336–9.

Williams, Raymond. *The Politics of Modernism: Against the New Conformists.* London and New York: Verso, 1989.

Part VI
Reconfigurations

29

The Clash of Definitions

EDWARD W. SAID

The language of group identity makes a particularly strident appearance from the middle to the end of the nineteenth century as the culmination of decades of international competition between the great European and American powers for territories in Africa and Asia. In the battle for the empty spaces of Africa – the dark continent – France and Britain as well as Germany and Belgium resort not only to force but to a whole slew of theories and rhetorics for justifying their plunder. Perhaps the most famous of such devices is the French concept of civilizing mission, *la mission civilisatrice*, an underlying notion of which is the idea that some races and cultures have a higher aim in life than others; this gives the more powerful, more developed, more civilized the right therefore to colonize others, not in the name of brute force or raw plunder, both of which are standard components of the exercise, but in the name of a noble ideal. Joseph Conrad's most famous story, *Heart of Darkness*, is an ironic, even terrifying enactment of this thesis, that – as his narrator Marlow puts it – "the conquest of the earth, which mostly means the taking it away from those who have a different complexion or slightly flatter noses than ourselves, is not a pretty thing when you look into it too much. What redeems it is the idea only. An idea at the back of it, not a sentimental pretence but an idea; and an unselfish belief in the idea – something you can set up, and bow down before, and offer a sacrifice to."

In response to this sort of logic, two things occur. One is that competing powers invent their own theory of cultural or civilizational destiny in order to justify their actions abroad. Britain had such a theory, Germany had one, Belgium had one, and of course in the concept of manifest des-

tiny, the United States had one, too. These redeeming ideas dignify the practice of competition and clash, whose real purpose, as Conrad quite accurately saw, was self-aggrandizement, power, conquest, treasure, and unrestrained self-pride. I would go so far as to say that what we today call the rhetoric of identity, by which a member of one ethnic or religious or national or cultural group puts that group at the center of the world, derives from that period of imperial competition at the end of the nineteenth century. And this in turn provokes the concept of "worlds at war" that quite obviously is at the heart of Huntington's article. It received its most frightening futuristic application in H. G. Wells's fable *The War of the Worlds*, which, recall, expands the concept to include a battle between this world and a distant, interplanetary one. In the related fields of political economy, geography, anthropology, and historiography, the theory that each "world" is self-enclosed, has its own boundaries and special territory, is applied to the world map, to the structure of civilizations, to the notion that each race has a special destiny, psychology, ethos, and so on. All these ideas, almost without exception, are based not on the harmony but on the conflict, or clash, between worlds. It is evident in the works of Gustave LeBon (cf. *The World in Revolt*) and in such relatively forgotten works as F. S. Marvin's *Western Races and the World* (1922) and George Henry Lane-Fox Pitt Rivers's *The Clash of Culture and the Contact of Races* (1927).

The second thing that happens is that, as Huntington himself concedes, the lesser peoples, the objects of the imperial gaze, so to speak, respond by resisting their forcible manipulation and settlement. We now know that active primary resistance to the white man began the moment he set foot in places like Algeria, East Africa, India, and elsewhere. Later, primary resistance was succeeded by secondary resistance, the organization of political and cultural movements determined to achieve independence and liberation from imperial control. At precisely the moment in the nineteenth century that a rhetoric of civilizational self-justification begins to be widespread among the European and American powers, a responding rhetoric among the colonized peoples develops, one that speaks in terms of African or Asian or Arab unity, independence, self-determination. In India, for example, the Congress party was organized in 1880 and by the turn of the century had convinced the Indian elite that only by supporting *Indian* languages, industry, and commerce could political freedom come; these are ours and ours alone, runs the argument, and only by supporting our world against *theirs* – note the us-versus-them construction here – can we finally stand on our own. One finds a similar logic at work during the Meiji period in modern Japan. Something like this rhetoric of belonging is also lodged at the heart of each independence movement's nationalism, and shortly after World War Two it achieved the result not only of dismantling the classical empires, but of winning independence for dozens and dozens of countries thereafter. India, Indonesia, most of the Arab countries, Indochina, Algeria, Kenya, and so on: all these emerged onto the world scene sometimes peacefully, sometimes as the effect of internal developments (as in the Japanese instance), ugly colonial wars, or wars of national liberation.

In both the colonial and the post-colonial context, therefore, rhetorics of general cultural or civilizational specificity went in two potential directions, one a utopian line that insisted on an overall pattern of integration and harmony among all peoples, the other a line which suggested that all civilizations were so specific and jealous, monotheistic, in effect, as to reject and war against all others. Among instances of the first are the language and institutions of the United Nations, founded in the aftermath of World War Two, and the subsequent development out of the U.N. of various attempts at world government predicated on coexistence, voluntary limitations of sovereignty, and the harmonious integration of peoples and cultures. Among the second are the theory and practice of the Cold War and, more recently, the idea that the clash of civilizations is, if not a necessity for a world of so

many different parts, then a certainty. According to this view, cultures and civilizations are basically *separated* from each other. I do not want to be invidious here. In the Islamic world there has been a resurgence of rhetorics and movements stressing the inimicability of Islam with the West, just as in Africa, Europe, Asia, and elsewhere, movements have appeared that stress the need for excluding designated others as undesirable. White apartheid in South Africa was such a movement, as is the current interest in Afrocentrism and a totally independent Western civilization to be found in Africa and the United States respectively.

The point of this short cultural history of the idea of the clash of civilizations is that people like Huntington are products of that history, and are shaped in their writing by it. Moreover, the language describing the clash is laced with considerations of power: the powerful use it to protect what they have and what they do, the powerless or less powerful use it to achieve parity, independence, or a comparative advantage with regard to the dominant power. Thus to build a conceptual framework around the notion of us-versus-them is in effect to pretend that the principal consideration is epistemological and natural – our civilization is known and accepted, theirs is different and strange – whereas in fact the framework separating us from them is belligerent, constructed, and situational. Within each civilizational camp, we will notice, there are official representatives of that culture or civilization who make themselves into its mouthpiece, who assign themselves the role of articulating "our" (or for that matter "their") essence. This always necessitates a fair amount of compression, reduction, and exaggeration. So on the first and most immediate level, then, statements about what "our" culture or civilization is, or ought to be, necessarily involve a contest over the definition. This is certainly true of Huntington, who writes his essay at a time in U.S. history when a great deal of turmoil has surrounded the very definition of Western civilization. Recall that in the United States many college campuses have been shaken during the past couple of decades over what the canon of Western civilization is, which books should be taught, which ones read or not read, included, or otherwise given attention. Places like Stanford and Columbia debated the issue not simply because it was a matter of habitual academic concern but because the definition of the West and consequently of America was at stake.

Anyone who has the slightest understanding of how cultures work knows that defining a culture, saying what it is for members of the culture, is always a major and, even in undemocratic societies, a democratic contest. There are canonical authorities to be selected and regularly revised, debated, re-selected, or dismissed. There are ideas of good and evil, belonging or not belonging (the same and the different), hierarchies of value to be specified, discussed, re-discussed, and settled or not, as the case may be. Moreover, each culture defines its enemies, what stands beyond it and threatens it. For the Greeks beginning with Herodotus, anyone who did not speak Greek was automatically a barbarian, an Other to be despised and fought against. An excellent recent book by the French classicist François Hartog, *The Mirror of Herodotus*, shows how deliberately and painstakingly Herodotus sets about constructing an image of a barbarian Other in the case of the Scythians, more even than in the case of the Persians.

The official culture is that of priests, academies, and the state. It provides definitions of patriotism, loyalty, boundaries, and what I have called belonging. It is this official culture that speaks in the name of the whole, that tries to express the general will, the general ethos and idea which inclusively holds in the official past, the founding fathers and texts, the pantheon of heroes and villains, and so on, and excludes what is foreign or different or undesirable in the past. From it come the definitions of what may or may not be said, those prohibitions and proscriptions that are necessary to any culture if it is to have authority.

It is also true that in addition to the mainstream, official, or canonical culture there are dissenting or alternative unorthodox, heterodox cultures that contain many anti-authoritarian strains that compete with the official culture. These can be called the counter-culture, an ensemble of practices associated with various kinds of outsiders – the poor, the immigrants, artistic bohemians, workers, rebels, artists. From the counter-culture comes the critique of authority and attacks on what is official and orthodox. The great contemporary Arab poet Adonis has written a massive account of the relationship between orthodoxy and heterodoxy in Arabic culture and has shown the constant dialectic and tension between them. No culture is understandable without some sense of this ever-present source of creative provocation from the unofficial to the official; to disregard this sense of restlessness within each culture, and to assume that there is complete homogeneity between culture and identity, is to miss what is vital and fecund.

30

Cultural Citizenship, Inequality, and Multiculturalism

Renato Rosaldo

The cultural citizenship project involves research teams that have worked in California, Texas, and New York. The project's central focus has been a set of social processes that we have chosen to call cultural citizenship. In defining cultural citizenship, a phrase that yokes together terms usually kept apart, I should like to begin with reflections on the component "citizenship" and then discuss the implications of "cultural."

Citizenship

Citizenship is often understood as a universal concept. In this view, all citizens of a particular nation state are equal before the law. A background assumption of our work, by contrast, is that one needs to distinguish the formal level of theoretical universality from the substantive level of exclusionary and marginalizing practices. Even in its late-eighteenth-century Enlightenment origins, citizenship in the republic differentiated men of privilege from the rest: second-class citizens and noncitizens.

In France the people who gathered in public squares were putatively all equal. They were *les citoyens*, the citizens. Certain contemporary thinkers propose that we should return to the model of the public square, to the situation of the citoyens who were supposedly all equal. The public square, they argue, was the democratic space par excellence, and it should be adopted as the model for the late-twentieth-century civil society.

Such thinkers thus affirm that there were no distinctions among citizens who gathered in public squares. These gatherings were a significant step

forward in the process of democratization, no doubt, particularly in comparison with the tyranny of excessive social distinctions that reigned during the regime dominated by the monarchy and the aristocracy. One cannot but agree, at least to a point, that the universal notion of citizen was a significant step toward democracy in relation to the ancien régime that preceded it. Nonetheless, at least from the present standpoint, the public square is not the final goal, but only a point of departure for democratization.

In this respect, I differ with commentaries that stress the central importance of developing urban spaces where people may form face-to-face civil societies in sites of public gathering. Such spaces appear to certain thinkers as a solution to problems of contemporary urban life where corporate takeovers and the Foucauldian disciplining of subject populations have replaced what was once relatively unregulated social life in parks and public squares. In this view, the very notion of the public in late-twentieth-century urban spaces begins to shrink as stadiums replace parks and shopping malls replace public squares.

Consider, however, the inequalities that operated in the public squares of the romanticized past. Begin with differences of gender. Can women disguise their gender in the public sphere? If they must appear as women, and not as universal unmarked citizens, then one can ask, who has the right to speak in public debates conducted in the square? Are men or women more likely to be interrupted with greater frequency? Are men or women more likely to be referred to as having had a good idea in these discussions? As much recent sociolinguistic and feminist research has shown, one must consider much more than whether or not certain categories of persons are present in the public square. One must consider categories that are visibly inscribed on the body, such as gender and race, and their consequences for full democratic participation. The moment a woman or a person of color enters the public square both difference and inequality come to the surface. It is difficult to conceal differences of gender and race, and given the prejudiced norms under which we still live, inequities will come to the surface.

Following Enlightenment ideals, the language of the U.S. Constitution granted universal rights to its citizens. It declared that all citizens are equal (implicitly assuming, of course, that the condition of their equality is their sameness in relation to language and culture). In this sense the question of citizenship is bipolar and simple: either one is a citizen or one is not, and that is that.

In the beginning the U.S. Constitution declared that citizens were white men of property. And indeed, as has often been remarked, the stipulation can be read the other way around: that is, the Constitution disenfranchised men without property, women, and people of color. These exclusions derive from discrimination based on class, gender, and race. In the long run, these forms of discrimination defined the parameters of dissident traditions that have endured into the present. The dissident traditions so engendered have involved struggles to be full citizens in ways that were set in motion by the Constitution's original exclusions.

The dissident traditions of struggle for first-class citizenship have achieved a great deal, even if much remains to be achieved. The struggle for women's suffrage (which did not succeed until 1920) was the first step in a historical process whose present phase is contemporary feminism. Issues of women's rights have moved beyond the vote to sets of practices where, in spite of formal equality, one notices such forms of marginalization as systemic differences in pay and subtle mechanisms for not attending to what women say. Similarly, the legacy of antislavery movements has moved through civil rights to the new social movements that encompass African Americans, Asian Americans, Native Americans, and Latinos.

The long history and the success of these dissident traditions of struggle grants a certain depth and legitimacy to their successors in the present. Slavery and formally disenfranchised women are obsolete as social institutions in the late-twentieth-century United States. Debates about race and gender today often invoke that history of abolition and suffrage.

While emphasizing the continuity of dissident traditions in the United States from the nineteenth century to the present, social analysts such as Stuart Hall and David Held (1990) have discussed the new politics of citizenship in the 1990s. They assert that "from the ancient world to the present day, citizenship has entailed a discussion, and a struggle over, the meaning and scope of membership of the community in which one lives" (1990: 175). For them, the key innovation has been an expansion of the definition of citizenship and the base upon which rights are demanded:

> A contemporary "politics of citizenship" must take into account the role which the social movements have played in *expanding* the claims to right and entitlements to new areas. It must address not only issues of class and inequality, but also questions of membership posed by feminism, the black and ethnic movements, ecology (including the moral claims of the animal species and of Nature itself) and vulnerable minorities, like children. (1990: 176)

The new social movements have expanded the emphasis on citizens' rights from questions of class to issues of gender, race, sexuality, ecology, and age. In effect, new citizens have come into being as new categories of persons who make claims on both their fellow citizens and the state. For Hall and Held, the rights of citizenship have expanded in a quantitative sense, but I should like to note that the shift is also qualitative.

In this qualitative shift one can identify two dimensions of change. First, one can think of the redistribution of resources. This dimension refers, above all, to class and the struggle for economic democracy. The second dimension of change could be called recognition and responsiveness. For example, one can consider gay and lesbian rights as an area where issues of the redistribution of resources may be less central than issues of recognition and unbiased treatment in the workplace and other institutional contexts. Such issues range from blatant to subtle matters of second-class citizenship. If issues of class and the equitable distribution of resources were resolved, matters of recognition and fair treatment in the face of bias regarding sexuality, gender, and race would still remain.

A case in point for the politics of recognition would be the current situation of Latinos in the United States. A significant number of people in the United States, for example, have come to question the citizenship of Latinos by declaring undocumented workers to be "alien" or "illegal." By a psychological and cultural mechanism of association all Latinos are thus declared to have a blemish that brands us with the stigma of being outside the law. We always live with that mark indicating that whether or not we belong in this country is always in question. The distortions here are twofold.

First, the term "illegal" misleads because it suggests that undocumented workers are illegal in the sense of failing to obey and living outside the law. On the contrary, they obey the law more punctiliously than most citizens because they know that the punishment for the slightest infraction is deportation. In this respect, they tend to be more law-abiding than citizens with legal documents. Undocumented workers deserve to be treated in accord with universal human rights.

Second, the icon of the Latino illegal alien suggests, again obliquely but powerfully, that all Latinos in the United States are immigrants, most of whom came under questionable circumstances. A young Chicana poet expressed the real situation succinctly when she said, *"No crucé la frontera, la frontera me cruzó a mí"* (I did not cross the border, the border crossed me). After the War of 1848, Mexican territory became part of the United States and Mexican citizens in that territory found that the border crossed them as it moved from north to south. In other words, many Chicanos lived within the present territorial borders of the United States before the first northern European settlements were established in the New World, certainly well before Jamestown. These early settlements contained Spaniards, Indians, and Africans. Increasingly the mestizo and mulatto blends became evident. Far from being newcomers, Latinos are oldtimers in the New World. It is not difficult to document the continuous presence of Chicanos within the present territorial boundaries of the United States.

The mass media often present sensational views of Latinos as new immigrant communities with the consequence, intended or not, of questioning our citizenship and hardening racialized relations of dominance and subordination. Cynical politicians have used such ideological maneuvers to secure the approval of such legislation as Proposition 187. The tactic divides the Latino community against itself and separates Latinos from dominant white groups.

Culture

By way of moving on to the question of how culture intersects crucially with citizenship today, I now should like to make some themes concrete through a series of examples.

Public and private

In his memoir *Hunger of Memory* Richard Rodríguez asserts that Spanish is a domestic language; it is, he says, fine for expressing feelings, but it is no good for thinking. It is good for family life, but it has no place in school, politics, and the workplace. He thus opposes public bilingualism. In other words, he claims that racialized ethnic culture can thrive only within the domestic rather than the public sphere. Rodríguez is no doubt being true to his experience, but I would argue that he ignores the social and ideological factors that have structured his experience.

Rodríguez's perceptions do not, I think, belong to him alone. This is a case where ideology colors personal insights about culture. The segregationist ideology of white supremacy is speaking through Rodríguez, and one should not blame either the author or the Spanish language. A day in Mexico, elsewhere in Latin America, or Spain should suffice to make it clear that the linguistic limitations Rodríguez experiences are built into social arrangements, not the language. If the United States has placed a taboo on the use of Spanish in public life, it derives from prejudice manifest in legal and informal arrangements and not because of the language. In Mexico and Puerto Rico Spanish is the language of both the heart and the mind, domestic and public life.

Border theater, border violence

The U.S.–Mexico border has become theater, and border theater has become social violence. Actual violence has become inseparable from symbolic ritual on the border – crossings, invasions, lines of defense, high-tech surveillance, and more. Social scientists often think of public rituals as events that resemble formal rituals separated from daily life in time and space and marked by repeated formal structures. In contrast the violence and high-tech weaponry of border theater is at once symbolic and material. Social analysts need to recognize the centrality of actual violence and the symbolics that shape that violence.

The new technologies of violence were tested in the Gulf War and in the staged television coverage of smart missiles and precision mayhem. These technologies are now directed at unarmed Mexicans as they enter the United States in search of work. The risk they run is real; the threat of death can readily be delivered. For North American politicians, however, the key element is theatrical, a cynical work of lethal art that they offer to their voters with an invocation of previous wars, not only the Gulf War but also the Vietnam War (thus the U.S.–Mexico border becomes a DMZ, a Demilitarized Zone). They attempt to stage the vulnerability of North American citizens who are at risk because of the "illegals" (read: outlaws) invading their land. They of course add that the government is using all means at its disposal to protect citizens from the brown invaders from the south.

Voting

The vote is the citizen's most sacred right/rite. Yet in California statewide initiatives provide citizens with an occasion for voting their prejudices. Proposition 187 was arguably in large measure an expression of white supremacy. Proposition 209, the so-called California Civil Rights Initiative (CCRI) that appeared on the November 1996 ballot, actually dismantles affirmative action programs and thus opposes civil rights in a manner manipulated by self-serving politicians in order to deepen racial cleavages in the state. The CCRI was explicitly designed to be a "wedge" issue that would divide Democrats and increase the chances of Republican presidential candidate Robert Dole. Indeed because of its popular referenda California has become a testing ground for hot-button conservative political issues at the national level.

The study of voter behavior requires analysis at the symbolic cultural level. Arguably, such referenda manifest legal-juridical violence against Latinos, African Americans, Asian Americans, Native Americans, and women. The workings of such electoral violence cry out for an understanding of a voting subject who is quite unlike the rational choice-maker who is favored by political

scientists who regard voter behavior as if it were the same as the consumer's market behavior. The people who voted for Proposition 187 and the CCRI are engaged less in a rational calculus than in expressing their inner prejudices and fears.

Quetzalcóatl in San Jose

My final example concerns the unveiling of a statue of Quetzalcóatl, the Aztec divinity of urban civilization, about a year ago in San Jose, California. The unveiling was marred by controversy and by protests from anti-abortion activist Evangelical Christians. The Evangelical groups inspired fear because they had been involved in militant actions at abortion clinics. For the eve of the unveiling I had been asked to give a talk at the San Jose Museum of Art on the cultural and historical significance of Quetzalcóatl. As I prepared to leave my house to go and give the talk, I felt anxious because I feared the worst, particularly from the Evangelical groups. Just before I left the house my daughter Olivia wrote and gave me the following poem, called "Remember," which she dedicated "To Dad and Quetzalcóatl":

> Remember
> who, how,
> Remember who you are.
> How did I get here?
> Remember your descendents.
> Remember your language.
> Remember who you are
> even where there's prejudice
> of who
> and what you are.
> Remember.

What I did not know as I left was that I would find, in addition to the Evangelicals I feared, an audience composed of public officials, militant Chicano brown berets, and Native American and Chicano costumed dancers from as far away as Mexico City, Texas, and New Mexico. Once I arrived and scanned the audience I felt secure and confident. I was present as a cultural interpreter at an event that had clear political as well as cultural meanings.

The examples just discussed – Rodríguez's view of Spanish as a domestic (not a public) language, border technology as cultural theater, referenda as expressions of prejudice, and the community event surrounding the unveiling of the Quetzalcóatl statue – are all instances of how we need to understand the way citizenship is informed by culture, the way that claims to citizenship are reinforced or subverted by cultural assumptions and practices. In addition, each of the four cases contains a methodological principle critical to studies in cultural citizenship.

Rodríguez's example stands as a methodological caution against relying uncritically and exclusively on personal testimony, and as a reminder of the impact of larger structural factors on local situations. He sees English as the only language of citizenship in contrast with Spanish, which he sees as the language of the heart and of domestic life. He is true to his experience but, in a way made classic by the phrase internalized oppression, he studiously pays no heed to how his experience has been structured by larger forces of domination and white supremacy.

The U.S.–Mexico border theater underscores the tenet that all human conduct is culturally mediated and that cultural citizenship studies, in everyday life, forms of exclusion, marginalization, and enfranchisement in modes that require joining together cultural meanings and material life. The way force is deployed at the border expresses dominant Anglo cultural views of limited Latino rights to full U.S. citizenship. The physical border has become a line of demarcation enforced by staged high-tech violence that is no less violent for being symbolic and vice versa – no less suffused with cultural meanings for being lethal and material.

The referenda of recent California politics underscore the way that cultural citizenship research seeks out cases that have become sites of contestation, negotiation, and struggle over cultural meaning and social violence. California referenda can productively be understood as ways of voting prejudices and fears. Unarmed Mexicans working in the United States have, for many voters, become objects of fear and hatred that require exceptional legislative action. This example emphasizes the psychological mechanism of projection, whereby people attribute their own feelings of hatred to somebody else and then in turn fear their own projected feelings.

For the Latino community of San Jose, the events surrounding the unveiling of the Quetzalcóatl statue were a classic act of cultural citizenship, using cultural expression to claim public rights and recognition, and highlighting the interaction between citizenship and culture. The artistic and cultural event of the unveiling was clearly seen as an important public statement both by the Evangelicals and by a number of distinct elements of the Latino community. In this struggle over the placement and meanings of public art, more was at stake than "culture" in a narrow sense. The Evangelical community clearly saw the cultural expression as a claim to rights in the public square.

My own reactions to the evening reflected the larger dynamic. I went as cultural interpreter, but initially felt disenfranchised as a citizen by the prospect of potential violence. When I saw the remarkable and varied Chicano community presence at the rally – costumes and traditional dance reinforcing the group ties – my own sense of isolation evaporated. I found myself transformed from voiceless vulnerable individual to full-fledged citizen.

Cultural citizenship operates in an uneven field of structural inequalities where the dominant claims of universal citizenship assume a propertied white male subject and usually blind themselves to their exclusions and marginalizations of people who differ in gender, race, sexuality, and age. Cultural citizenship attends, not only to dominant exclusions and marginalizations, but also to subordinate aspirations for and definitions of enfranchisement. In her book on writing, Anne Lamott has eloquently described the hopes of cultural citizenship as virtually universal in the United States:

> Writing can be a pretty desperate endeavor, because it is about some of our deepest needs: our need to be visible, to be heard, our need to make sense of our lives, to wake up and grow and belong. (1994: 19)

The universality of cultural citizenship aspirations most probably reflects the historical experience of civil rights and suffrage struggles. In this vein, our research has found that Latinos are conscious and articulate about their needs to be visible, to be heard, and to belong.

The notion of cultural citizenship challenges social analysts to attend with care to the point of view from which they conduct their studies. Too often social thought anchors its research in the vantage point of the dominant social group and thus reproduces dominant ideology by studying subordinate groups as a "problem" rather than as people with agency – with goals, perceptions, and purposes of their own.

Inequality and social position are critical to studies of cultural citizenship. Social position is a reminder that people in different and often unequal subject positions have different understandings of a given situation and that as they make claims to proper first-class treatment they operate with distinct definitions of such treatment. Chicana poet Lorna Dee Cervantes (1981) sums this insight up in her poem entitled "Poem for the Young White Man Who Asked Me How I, an Intelligent, Well-Read Person, Could Believe in the War Between the Races." The young man sees peace and prosperity in his land; the poet sees a war being inflicted on her people in the "same" land. Cervantes derives this difference of perceptions from the stark fact that those conducting the race war are shooting at her, not him.

Cultural citizenship thus argues that analysts need to anchor their studies in the aspirations and perceptions of people who occupy subordinate social positions. This research demands studies of vernacular notions of citizenship. In this collection the term *respeto* (respect) has appeared frequently as a requirement of full citizenship for Latinos in the United States. Bridging the discourses of the state and everyday life, of citizenship and culture, the demand for *respeto* is a defining demand of cultural citizenship. It is an ongoing, contested, and – for the participants – urgent process.

References

Cervantes, Lorna Dee. 1981. *Emplumada*. Pittsburgh: University of Pittsburgh Press.

Hall, Stuart and Held, David. 1990. "Citizens and Citizenship." In Stuart Hall and Martin Jacques (eds.), *New Times: The Changing Face of Politics in the 1990s.* London: Verso, pp. 173–88.

Lamott, Anne. 1994. *Bird by Bird: Some Instructions on Writing and Life*. New York: Anchor.

31

Localism, Globalism and Cultural Identity

MIKE FEATHERSTONE

To live in one land, is captivitie.
(John Donne, "Change", 1593–8)

There is a third world in every first world and vice-versa.
(Trinh T. Minh-ha, 1989)

To know who you are means to know where you are.
(James Clifford, 1989)

One of the problems in attempting to formulate a theory of globalization is of adopting a totalizing logic and assuming some master process of global integration is under way which is making the world more unified and homogeneous. From this perspective the intensification of global time-space compression through the universalizing processes of the new communications technology, the power of the flows of information, finance and commodities, means that local cultures inevitably give way. Our experiences and means of orientation necessarily become divorced from the physical locations in which we live and work. The fate of our places of residence and work is seen as in the hands of unknown agencies in other parts of the world. Localism and a sense of place gives way to the anonymity of "no place spaces", or simulated environments in which we are unable to feel an adequate sense of being at home.

There is also the sense that such monological accounts, which equate the success of the globalization process with the extension of modernity, that "globalization is basically modernity writ large", miss not only the cultural variability of non-Western nation-states and civilizations, but the specificity of the cultural complex of Western modernity. It is insufficient to assume that other non-Western cultures will simply give way to the logic of modernity and adopt Western forms, or to regard their formulations of national particularity as merely reactions to Western modernity.

Rather, the globalization process should be regarded as opening up the sense that now the world is a single place with increased contact becoming unavoidable, we necessarily have greater dialogue between various nation-states, blocs and civilizations: a dialogical space in which we can expect a good deal of disagreement, clashing of perspectives and conflict, not just working together and consensus. Not that participating nation-states and other agents should be regarded as equal partners to the dialogue. They are bound together in increasing webs of interdependencies and power balances, which partly through their complexity and sensitivity to change, and capacity to transmit information about shifts in fortune, means that it is more difficult to retain lasting and oversimplified images of others. The difficulty of handling increasing levels of cultural complexity, and the doubts and anxieties these often engender, are reasons why "localism", or the desire to remain in a bounded locality or return to some notion of "home", becomes an important theme. It can also be ventured that this is regardless of whether the home is real or imaginary, or whether it is temporary and syncretized or a simulation, or whether it is manifest in a fascination with the sense of belonging, affiliation and community which are attributed to the homes of others, such as tribal people. What does seem clear is that it is not helpful to regard the global and local as dichotomies separated in space or time; it would seem that the processes of globalization and localization are inextricably bound together in the current phase.

Localism and Symbolic Communities

Within the sociological tradition the term *local* and its derivatives *locality*, and *localism*, have generally been associated with the notion of a particular bounded space with its set of close-knit social relationships based upon strong kinship ties and length of residence.[1] There is usually the assumption of a stable homogeneous and integrated cultural identity which is both enduring and unique. In this sense it was often assumed that members of a locality formed a distinctive community with its own unique culture – something which turns the location of their day-to-day interactions from a physical space into a "place". Much of the research on localities which developed within urban sociology and community studies was influenced by two main assumptions.

The first derived from nineteenth-century models of social change in which the past was regarded as entailing simpler, more direct, strongly bonded social relationships, as we find in the paired oppositions: status and contract (Maine), mechanical and organic solidarity (Durkheim), and community and association (Tönnies). The latter terms, drawn from the ideal types delineated in Tönnies's (1955) influential *Gemeinschaft und Gesellschaft*, have been used to emphasize the historical and spatial continuum between small relatively isolated integrated communities based upon primary relationships and strong emotional bonding and the more anonymous and instrumental secondary associations of the modern metropolis. The work of Tönnies and other German theorists has helped sanction over-romantic and nostalgic depictions of "the world we have lost" to the relentless march of modernization.

The second, deriving from anthropology, emphasized the need to provide ethnographically rich descriptions of the particularity of relatively isolated small towns or villages. We have, for example, studies of small rural communities in the west of Ireland (Arensberg, 1968; Arensberg and Kimball, 1940) or North Wales (Frankenberg, 1966). Yet here and in other community studies

researchers soon became preoccupied with the problems of delineating the boundaries of the locality. It soon became clear that the most isolated community in Britain or the United States was firmly plugged into national societies. The illusion of spatial isolation which drew researchers into focusing upon the rich particularity of local traditions soon gave way to an acceptance that the "small town was *in* mass society", to paraphrase the title of one of the American studies of the 1950s (Vidich and Bensman, 1958). The intention here, and in earlier influential studies such as those of Middletown (Lynd and Lynd, 1929, 1937) and Yankee City (Warner and Lunt, 1941), was to examine the ways in which local communities were being transformed by industrialization, urbanization and bureaucratization. These modernizing processes were perceived to be all-pervasive and heralded "the eclipse of community", to use the title of a book by Maurice Stein (1960) which discussed this literature.

In Britain there were also a number of studies of localities, some of which provided rich descriptions of the particularities of working-class life. In studies such as *Coal is Our Life* (Dennis et al., 1956), *Working Class Community* (Jackson, 1968) and *Class, Culture and Community* (Williamson, 1982) we get a strong sense of a distinctive working-class way of life with its occupational homogeneity and strictly segregated gender roles, with male group ties and the "mateship" code of loyalty predominant in both work and leisure (drinking, gambling, sport) – women were largely confined to the separate home sphere. The classic account of this culture which captures the fullness of everyday working-class life was provided by Richard Hoggart's account of his Leeds childhood in *The Uses of Literacy* (1957). Hoggart (1957: esp. Ch. 5 "The Full Rich Life") documented the sayings, songs, the sentimentality and generous indulgences of working-class life (the Sunday afternoon big meat tea, the Saturday night "knees-up" and singing in the pub, the charabanc seaside outings at which all the saved-up money had to be squandered, the belly-laugh survival humour and vulgarity, the larger-than-life characters and general emotional warmth and group support, the gossip and knowledge of family histories and local institutions).

As has been pointed out, there is a danger of taking this picture of working-class life as the definitive one, the real working-class community, and missing its particular location in time and space – the northern working-class towns of the 1930s

(Critcher, 1979). The same era produced working-class film star heroes, Gracie Fields and George Formby, who epitomized the working-class sense of fun and capacity to mock and deflate pretentiousness. They had a strong sense of community and loyalty to place, and the retention of a local accent showed their unwillingness to lose their roots, and reinforced their apparent "naturalness", which made them forever seem a Lancashire lad and lass at heart. Here we think of Gracie Fields in films such as *Looking on the Bright Side* (1932), *Sing as We Go* (1934), *Keep Smiling* (1938) and *The Show Goes On* (1937) (see Richards, 1984: Ch. 10). George Formby likewise maintained an irrepressible cheerfulness: the "cheeky chappie", the little man forever playing the fool, yet possessing local knowledge with which to outsmart the upper-class "toffs" in films such as *Off the Dole* (1935), *Keep Fit* (1938) and *No Limit* (1935) (see Richards, 1984: Ch. 11). The films of both Fields and Formby showed Britain very much as a class-divided society, and both achieved fame through their ability to poke fun at middle- and upper-class decorum and the respectability, formality and reserve which the BBC typified.

The films were important in their attempt to present society from the bottom up, and their capacity to install a sense of pride in working-class localism. They presented a contrast to the accounts of working-class life provided by the middle and upper classes. For some in the upper echelons of society the working class was akin to an exotic tribe. Frances Donaldson, for example, remarks that the upper and middle classes regarded the working class as quasi-foreign, and when they moved amongst them with a view to improving their lot "they did so as anthropologists . . . or missionaries visiting a tribe more primitive than themselves" (Donaldson, 1975, quoted in Fussell, 1980: 74). George Orwell's famous *The Road to Wigan Pier* (1937) was written in this style: he had received an upper-class public school education at Eton which provided him with a keen sense of social distinctions.[2]

One memorable passage that sticks in the mind, and that epitomized Orwell's frequent discomfort with aspects of working-class life, was the uneasiness with which he received his daily breakfast slice of bread and dripping. Each time it was put on his plate it contained a black thumbprint, left by the coal miner he was lodging with who always cut the bread after lighting the coal fire and slopping out the chamber-pots. Here we have an example of what Elias (1978) refers to as the "disgust function", the feeling of revulsion which those who have developed more refined taste and bodily controls can experience when they encounter the habits of common people (see also Bourdieu, 1984; Featherstone, 1991: Ch. 9). In this type of writing, in which all is revealed about "darkest England", we frequently get swings from emotional identification, the desire for the immersion in the directness, warmth and spontaneity of the local community, to revulsion, disgust and the desire for distance.

The audience for accounts of working-class life has a long history, going back to Engels and Charles Booth in the nineteenth century. It is still evident in the dramatic exposé style of many of the accounts written by "one of us" about "the people of the abyss", to mention the title of one of Jack London's books. This sense of an anthropologist parachuted into the alien depths of deepest working-class England was still to be found in the 1950s in the publicity for Richard Hoggart's *The Uses of Literacy*: the inside cover of the first Penguin edition suggested that the book sought "to remedy our ignorance" about "how the other half lives" (Laing, 1986: 47).

Hoggart's book, as has been suggested, is noticeable for its sympathetic descriptions of traditional working-class life; but it also presents this life as threatened by modernization in the form of the mass media and commercialization. Many of these negative influences were seen as originating in the United States. Hoggart has little time for television, milk bars, jukebox boys and other elements of the "candy-floss world" of mass culture. The tensions which developed within working-class culture as it encountered the forces of the affluent society, consumerism and mass culture were captured in a series of novels of the late 1950s and 1960s many of which were made into films. Here we think of Alan Sillitoe's *Saturday Night and Sunday Morning* (1958), Stan Barstow's *A Kind of Loving* (1960), David Storey's *This Sporting Life* (1960) and Ken Loach's films of Nell Dunn's *Up the Junction* (1965), *Poor Cow* (1967), and Barry Hine's *Kes* (1967) which explored the earthiness and richness of life within the closed working-class community with occasional glimpses of the modernizing processes (see Laing, 1986; Stead, 1989). Notable here is the central character in the much-acclaimed film version of *Saturday Night and Sunday Morning*, Arthur Seaton, a working-class hero if there ever was one, played by Albert Finney, who although he finally is entrapped into marriage, in the last moments of the film defiantly casts a stone at the newly built modern suburban housing estate which is to be his future.

As Bernice Martin (1981: 71) reminds us, many of the accounts of working-class life focus upon its directness and simplicity of emotional expression. To the middle-class observer it is too often the "immediate gratification", the ritual swearing and the aggression, sexuality, drinking and violence which attract attention. Yet these features are actually liminal moments of working-class life, a part which is too often mistaken for a whole. The moments of brotherhood and "communitas" are necessarily limited moments of "framed liminality", moments of "anti-structure" (Turner, 1969) in which celebration and taboo-breaking are planned for, in stark contrast to the careful budgeting, time management and concern for reputation and respectability in routine everyday life. It is the representations of these liminal moments which provide a rich repertoire of images. Here one thinks of, for example, Ridley Scott's "Hovis Bread" commercial which is packed with nostalgic images of a nineteenth-century northern English working-class town set to a mournful refrain from Dvořák's *New World Symphony* played by a brass band. Or the former British Prime Minister Harold Macmillan reminiscing about the people in his northern working-class constituency of Stockton-on-Tees: "Wonderful people, the finest people in the world", he remarked in a television interview, in a voice heavy with emotion and a tear in the corner of his eye, which almost had us convinced he regarded the Stockton working class as his only true organic community.

Many of these images of working-class community help to foster myths of belonging, warmth and togetherness which suggest the mythical security of a childhood long relinquished. There is nothing so powerful as the image of an integrated organic community in the childhood one has left behind (Hall, 1991: 46). Geoffrey Pearson (1985) has provided an important account of the ways in which successive generations always have recourse to the myth of "the good old days", the existence of a less violent, more law-abiding and harmonious community in the past of their childhood or parents' times. As one goes further and further back into history one finds successive displacements of this golden age back to the 1950s, 1930s, 1900s, 1870s

and so on. Successive generations have invested in a form of nostalgia in which the past is viewed as the epitome of coherence and order, something which was more simple and emotionally fulfilling, with more direct and integrated relationships. The assumption, here, is that one's identity and those of one's significant others are anchored in a specific locale, a physical space which becomes emotionally invested and sedimented with symbolic associations so that it becomes a place. As Bryan Turner (1987) remarks, nostalgia, or the loss of a sense of home, is a potent sentiment in the modern world, particularly so for those groups who are ambivalent about modernity and retain the strong image of the alleged greater integration and simplicity of a more integrated culture in the past.

When we speak of a locality, then, we should be careful not to presume an integrated community. There are problems with establishing the extent to which localities were integrated in the past. We have to be aware of the location in time-space and social space of those who make such pronouncements and that they might be painting a nostalgic and over-unified picture. It is also important that we do not operate with the view that localities are able to change only through the working out of a one-way modernization process entailing the eclipse of community and the local culture.

Usually when we think of a locality we have in mind a relatively small place in which everyone can know everyone else; that is, social life is based upon face-to-face relations. It is assumed that the intensity of the day-to-day contacts will generate a common stock of knowledge at hand which makes misunderstandings less frequent. It is the regularity and frequency of contacts with a group of significant others which are held to sustain a common culture. While the existence of such an integrated set of "core values" or common assumptions rooted in everyday practices may be overstated at both local and national levels (see Featherstone, 1991a: Ch. 9) there is a further dimension of cultural integration which must be referred to. This is the generation of powerful emotionally sustaining rituals, ceremonies and collective memories.

Durkheim (1961), in his *The Elementary Forms of the Religious Life*, placed particular emphasis upon the way in which a sense of the sacred was generated in emotionally bonding periods of "collective effervescence". Over time the intense sense of involvement and excitement which bound people together tends to diminish; the use of commemorative rituals and ceremonies can be understood as acting like batteries which store and recharge the sense of communality. Outside the regular calendar of ceremonies which reinforce our family, local and national sense of collective identity, it is also possible to draw on collective memories. As Halbwachs (1992) reminds us, collective memories refer to group contexts in the past which are periodically reinforced through contact with others who shared the initial experience (see also Middleton and Edwards, 1990).

Nations as Communities

Yet are there limits to the size of the group and place to be considered a local community? Could a nation be considered a local community? If we examine the origins of the term it refers not only to the modern nation-state, but also draws on the meaning of *natio*, a local community, domicile family condition of belonging (Brennan, 1990: 45). There is often a clear reluctance to accept that the nation could ever embody the type of bonding typically attributed to the local community, especially from Marxists with internationalist sympathies. Hence Raymond Williams remarks:

> "Nation" as a term is radically connected with "native." We are *born* into relationships which are typically settled in a place. This form of primary and "placeable" bonding is of quite fundamental human and natural importance. Yet the jump from that to anything like the modern nation-state is entirely artificial. (Williams, 1983: 180, quoted in Brennan, 1990: 45)

This contrasts with the position of Benedict Anderson (1991: 6), who argues that "all communities larger than the primordial village of face-to-face contact (and perhaps even these) are imagined. Communities are to be distinguished not by their falseness/genuineness, but by the style in which they are imagined." In this sense a nation may be considered as an imagined community because it provides a quasi-religious sense of belonging and fellowship which is attached to those who are taken to share a particular symbolic place. The place is symbolic in that it can be a geographically bounded space which is sedimented with symbolic sentiments; the configuration of the landscape, buildings and people have been invested with collective

memories which have sufficient emotional power to generate a sense of communality. Certain places may be enshrined with a particular emblematic status as national monuments and used to represent a form of symbolic bonding which overrides and embodies the various local affiliations people possess.

Indeed, this is an essential part of the nation-building process in which the nation-state actively encourages the cultivation and elaboration of the *ethnie*, or ethnic core (Smith, 1990). In this sense the creation of a national community is invented, but it is not invented out of nothing. Anthony Smith emphasizes the need for a common repository of myths, heroes, events, landscapes and memories which are organized and made to assume a primordial quality. In the eighteenth century with the birth of nationalism in Europe there was a deliberate attempt by cultural specialists (or proto-intellectuals) to discover and record the vernacular customs and practices, legends and myths, the culture of the people, which it was assumed was fast disappearing (see Burke, 1978). In effect, the expanding strata of the indigenous intelligentsia sought to pull together and weave into a coherent form this body of popular cultural sources which could be used to give the past a sense of direction and construct a national identity.

This can be linked to what Gellner (1983), Anderson (1991) and others regard as a crucial factor in the construction of nationalism: the availability of a print culture which can interconnect people over time and space. The possibility of the nation therefore depends upon the development of the book and the newspaper alongside a literate reading public capable of using these sources throughout the territorial area and thus able to imagine themselves as a community. The development of the film industry facilitates this process even better, as film provides a sense of instanciation and immediacy which is relatively independent of the long learning process and institutional and other supports necessary to be able to assimilate knowledge through books (S. F. Moore, 1989; Higson, 1989).

The nation, therefore, becomes represented through a set of more or less coherent images and memories which deal with the crucial questions of the origins, difference and distinctiveness of a people. In this sense it has a quasi-religious basis, as it is able to answer some of the questions of theodicy in a world which is subject to processes of secularization. The sacrifice and suffering people are willing to undergo for the nation must in part be understood with respect to the capacity of the discourses, images and practices which sustain the nation to provide a sense of overarching significance which transcends death, or renders death meaningful through subsuming the individual under a sacred totality. Yet the fact that a national culture is constituted as a unique particularity points to the situation of the rise of the European nation-states which were locked into power struggles and elimination contests in which the mobilization of the population by the idea of the distinctiveness of the nation through its difference from its neighbours attained significance.

The external pressures of the figuration of significant others to which the nation-state belongs and the escalating power struggles can make the construction of an identity for the nation more important. It has been argued that conflicts heighten the sense of the boundary between the "in-group" and the "out-group". Hence Georg Simmel, who had written at length about the capacity of external conflicts to unify the internal structure of a group, remarked on the way in which the German reaction to the First World War resulted in a strong wave of social ecstasy and intensification of social bonds which unified the nation (Watier, 1991).

Simmel's writings are important because he gives us a sense of the multidimensional and relational nature of social life. A local culture may have a common set of work and kinship relationships that reinforce the practical everyday lived culture which is sedimented into taken-for-granted knowledge and beliefs. Yet the articulation of these beliefs and sense of the particularity of the local place will tend to become sharpened and more well defined when the locality becomes locked into power struggles and elimination contests with its neighbours. In such situations we can see the formation of a local culture in which the particularity of its own identity is emphasized. In this case the locality presents an oversimplified unified image of itself to outsiders. This image, to use a metaphor of Cohen (1985), can be likened to the local community's face, or mask. This does not mean that inside the locality social differentiation has been eliminated and relationships are necessarily more egalitarian, simple and homogeneous; rather, its internal differences and discourses may very well be complex. Internally we may be able to consider the community as incorporating all sorts of independencies, rivalries, power struggles and conflicts. Many community

studies document these conflicts: here one thinks of Elias and Scotson's (1994) account of the struggles between the established and the outsiders. Yet under certain circumstances such struggles may be forgotten, as, for example, when the locality is brought into conflict with another locality, or the region is involved in inter-regional disputes. In such situations one's own particularity is subsumed into some larger collectivity and appropriate cultural work is undertaken to develop an acceptable public face for it. This process entails the mobilization of the repertoire of communal symbols, sentiments and collective memories.

The shifts in the interdependencies and power balances increase the local people's consciousness of the symbolic boundary between themselves and others which is aided by the mobilization and re-constitution of symbolic repertoires with which the community can think and formulate a unified image of its difference from the opposite party (Cohen, 1985). It is the capacity to shift the frame, and move between a varying range of foci, the capacity to handle a range of symbolic material out of which various identities can be formed and reformed in different situations, which is relevant in the contemporary global situation. Here we have the sense that the contemporary world has not seen a cultural impoverishment, an attenuation of cultural resources. Rather there has been an extension of cultural repertoires and an enhancement of the resourcefulness of various groups to create new symbolic modes of affiliation and belonging, as well as struggling to rework and reshape the meaning of existing signs, to undermine existing symbolic hierarchies, for their own particular purposes in ways that become difficult for those in the dominant cultural centres to ignore. This shift has been aided and abetted by various sets of cultural specialists and intermediaries with sympathies for the local.

The sense of the strength of the sentiments which become embodied in the nation and their resilience over time, it has been argued, have been underestimated by some theorists who miss the role of the nation in the nation-state and assume that the national sentiments were merely a by-product of the modernization process devised to facilitate the integration of the nation-state. These sentiments have subsequently been proved redundant and undermined by the modernizing process (Arnason, 1990). In addition, there are often tendencies to underestimate the ways in which the formation of the nation and nationalism draw upon cultural resources which have yet to be modernized, such as the cultural memories, symbols, myths and sentiment surrounding the ethnic core (Smith, 1990). This suggests that the stock sociological contrast between tradition and modernity may not be that useful. This is noticeable in the case of nation-states such as Japan which, it is argued, cannot easily be fitted into the assumed developmental logic of modernization (Sakai, 1989; Mitsuhiro, 1989). In effect Japan managed to impose a restrictive and particularistic project of modernity and was able to protect it against universalistic challenges (Maruyama, 1969; Arnason, 1987a, 1987b). This would point to the continuing importance of cultural factors in the development of nation-states and in their relations with other nation-states.

The bilateral interactions that occur between nation-states, especially those which involve increasing competition and conflict, can have the effect of unifying the self-image of the nation: the image or national face which is presented to the other. A growth in the regularity and intensity of contacts as nation-states become bound up in regional figurations (their reference group of significant others) can intensify the pressures to form a distinctive and coherent identity. It is important to emphasize that this is a process which, in addition to the external presentation of the national face, also has an internal dimension and depends upon the power resources particular groups possess to mobilize the ethnic core. They will endeavour to mobilize different aspects of the ethnic core to suit their own particular interests and aspirations; in effect the process of cultural formation of a national identity always entails a part being represented as a whole: a particular representation of the nation is presented as unanimous and consensual.

Here one thinks of Margaret Thatcher's Downing Street statement on news of victory in the Falklands War in 1982: "We are one nation tonight." Such statements also point to the fragility of particular formulations of national identity: while to be legitimate they have to draw upon a finite and recognizable repository of the ethnic core, they are also subjected to a continuous process of struggle to develop and impose alternative formulations. The fragility and volatility of the emotional sentiments embodied in the nation, and the struggle over the legitimacy of the representation, therefore suggest that we should consider national cultures in processual terms. When we consider processes of the formation and deformation of national identity we

should also be clear that it is easier to identify a common ethnic core where there has been a long-term process of national formation in European nations, as is the case in Britain and France. That we should be wary of taking their individual cases as the model for nation formation is evident when we consider newer nations, especially those endeavouring to construct a multicultural sense of identity. The case of Australia is interesting in this context and there are now a number of studies about the attempts to generate a unified national identity: to "invent Australia", through the cultivation of representations of particular places such as Ayers Rock or Bondi Beach, and historical events such as Gallipoli (see White, 1981; Fiske et al., 1987; Game, 1990).

The images that are constructed through television and the cinema are a necessary part in the process of the formation of a nation, especially in their capacity to bridge the public and the private. A nation is an abstract collectivity which is far too big to be directly experienced by people. Hence it is not only the existence of civic rituals such as Remembrance Day that provide the sense of the sacred which binds the nation together; increasingly it is the representation of these events which is crucial (Chaney, 1986). For people whose knowledge of these events is restricted to viewing television in their living room, television does not merely represent such events, but also constructs them. Yet it is not just a question of a passive audience taking in the event, as Dyan and Katz (1988) have argued; it is also possible for individuals and families to reconstitute the ceremonial space in the home by observing rituals, dressing up and "participating", in the knowledge that countless others are doing the very same thing. Hence an "atomized" audience can occasionally be united via television media events.

Yet it is insufficient to see the process of imagining the nation as purely the product of internal factors. In the Second World War the British film industry played an important part in mobilizing a nation identity through the production of representations of the common foe (Higson, 1989). We should not consider cultures in isolation, but endeavour to locate them in the relational matrix of their significant others (c.f. Gupta and Ferguson, 1992). It is not the isolation of the nation which is the crucial factor in developing an image of itself as a unique and integrated national culture. Rather, it is the need to mobilize a particular representation of national identity, as part of the series of unavoidable contacts, interdependencies and power struggles which nation-states become locked into with their significant others.

This means we should not just focus on bilateral relations between nation-states. Nation-states do not just interact; they form a *world*. That is, increasingly their interactions take place within a global context: a context which has seen the development of its own body of formal and taken-for-granted procedures based upon processes and modes of integration which cannot simply be reduced to the interests and control of individual nation-states (see Arnason, 1990). The gradual development of diplomatic conventions and procedures, such as international law which emerged alongside and independent from nation-states to form a nexus of underpinning ground-rules for international conflicts, are one set of examples (Bergesen, 1990). Another would be the independent power of multinational corporations to act independently to weaken the integrity of national culture through their capacity to direct a range of flows of cultural goods and information from the dominant economic centres to the peripheries – the cultural imperialism thesis would be a strong case of this type of argument. The perception and extent of these processes can increase nation-states' sensitivity to the need to preserve the integrity of their own national traditions and can be used to promote counter- or deglobalizing and fundamentalist reactions.

One effect, then, of the globalization process – the increasing contact and sense of the finitude of the world, the consciousness that the world is one place – is to lead to a clashing of a plurality of different interpretations of the meaning of the world formulated from the perspective of different national and civilizational traditions. The density and multidirectionality of the talk which takes place on the global stage necessarily demands that nation-states take up a position as they increasingly find it impossible to silence the other voices or consider opting out. Hence we have a plurality of national responses to the process of globalization which cannot be conceived as reducible to the ideas generated by Western modernity. One of the problems entailed in mapping the contemporary global condition is this range of different national cultural responses which continue to deform and reform, blend, syncretize and transform, in various ways, the alleged master processes of modernity.

With respect to theories of modernity there is often the assumption that modernization necessarily entails the eclipse of the national tradition and cultural identity. Yet theories of modernity that emphasize a relentless process of instrumental rationalization which effectively "empties out" a society's repository of cultural traditions and meanings are misconceived. Weber's notion of the imposition of an "iron cage", a new bureaucratized serfdom or "Egyptification" of life, and the related arguments about the progressive commodification, rationalization and disenchantment of the world by critical theorists such as Habermas, would seem to be difficult to substantiate (see Haferkamp, 1987; Knorr-Cetina, 1994).[3]

Knorr-Cetina (1994), for example, argues that if we examine everyday practices closely we find that they "testify to the presence of 'meaning', and 'tradition', of 'the body', of 'intimacy', 'local knowledge' and everything else that is often thought to have been bred out of 'abstract systems.' " In effect the everyday practices of participants, even if they work within highly technicized organizations, operate with and by means of fictions. Hence if we observe the practices in local environments we find that the shared, deeply cherished classifications people use are a form of the sacred. Modernity has not meant a loss of magic and enchantment, or the fictional use of symbolic classifications in local institutions.

Globalization and Cultural Identity

If globalization refers to the process whereby the world increasingly becomes seen as "one place" and the ways in which we are made conscious of this process (Robertson, 1992a) then the cultural changes which are thematized under the banner of the postmodern seem to point in the opposite direction by directing us to consider the local. Yet this is to misunderstand the nature of the process of globalization. It should not be taken to imply that there is, or will be, a unified world society or culture – something akin to the social structure of a nation-state and its national culture, only writ large. Such an outcome may have been the ambition of particular nation-states at various points of their history, and the possibility of a renewed world state formation process cannot be discounted in the future. In the present phase it is possible to refer to the development of a global culture in a less totalistic sense by referring to two aspects of the process of globalization.

First, we can point to the existence of a global culture in the restricted sense of "third cultures": sets of practices, bodies of knowledge, conventions and lifestyles that have developed in ways which have become increasingly independent of nation-states. In effect there are a number of trans-societal institutions, cultures and cultural producers who cannot be understood as merely agents and representatives of their nation-states. Second, we can talk about a global culture in the Simmelian sense of a cultural form: the sense that the globe is a finite, knowable bounded space, a field into which all nation-states and collectivities will inevitably be drawn. Here the globe, the planet earth, acts both as a limit and as the common bounded space on which our encounters and practices are inevitably grounded. In this second sense the result of the growing intensity of contact and communication between nation-states and other agencies is to produce a clashing of cultures, which can lead to heightened attempts to draw the boundaries between the self and others. From this perspective the changes which are taking place as a result of the current phase of intensified globalization can be understood as provoking reactions that seek to rediscover particularity, localism and difference which generate a sense of the limits of the culturally unifying, ordering and integrating projects associated with Western modernity. So in one sense it can be argued that globalization produces postmodernism.

If we examine the first aspect of the globalization process, it is evident that the problems of intercultural communication in fields such as law have led to the development of mediating "third cultures" (Gessner and Schade, 1990). These were initially designed to deal with the practical problems of intercultural legal disputes, but as with the development of the European Court of Justice and other institutions and protocols in international law, they can achieve autonomy and function beyond the manipulation of individual nation-states. In addition we can point to the further integrating effects of the internationalization of the world financial markets following the move to 24-hour trading after the "Big Bang" of October 1986 (Dezalay, 1990). The process of deregulation encouraged the demonopolization of national legal systems and a more meritocratic market ethos in which international lawyers became part of a group of new professionals, which includes corporate tax accountants,

financial advisers, management consultants and "design professionals".

The deregulation of markets and capital flows can be seen to produce a degree of homogenization in procedures, working practices and organizational cultures. In addition there are some convergences in the lifestyle, habitus and demeanour of these various sets of professionals. There are also similarities in the quarters of the cities they live and work in. Yet it should be emphasized that such groups are not to be found in every city, or even national capital. They are concentrated in various world cities such as New York, Tokyo, London, Paris, Los Angeles, São Paulo (King, 1990; Sassen, 1991; Zukin, 1991). It is the integration of the particular services located in particular quarters of these world cities which produces transnational sets of social relations, practices and cultures. The process of globalization is therefore uneven, and if one aspect of it is the consciousness of the world as a single place, then it is in these select quarters of world cities that we find people working in environments which rely upon advanced means of communications which overcome time-space separation. Here we find the most striking examples of the effects of time-space compression, as new means of communication effectively make possible simultaneous transactions which sustain "deterritorialized cultures".

It is when we take the next step and assume that such areas are the prototypes for the future and that the international economy and communications networks will produce similar homogenizing effects in other areas of national societies that we run into problems. Here some would make the mistake of assuming that the extension of various social and cultural forms to different parts of the world is necessarily producing a homogenization of content. That is, the globalization process is seen as producing a unified and integrated common culture. Hence we find that theories of cultural imperialism and media imperialism assume that local cultures are necessarily battered out of existence by the proliferation of consumer goods, advertising and media programmes stemming from the West (largely the United States).

Such theories share with theories of mass culture a strong view of the manipulability of mass audiences by a monolithic system and an assumption of the negative cultural effects of the media as self-evident, with little empirical evidence about how goods and information are adapted and used in everyday practices (Tomlinson, 1991). Of course it is possible to point to the availability of Western consumer goods, especially major brands of food, drink, cigarettes and clothing, following the business and tourist trails to the remotest part of the world. It is also clear that certain images – the tough guy hero fighting against innumerable odds – have a strong appeal in many cultures. Hence we find Rambo movies played throughout southern and eastern Asia so that "remote villagers in rural Burma could now applaud Rambo's larger-than-life heroics only days after they hit the screens of Wisconsin" (Iyer, 1989: 12). To take a second example, one of the major contemporary travel writers, Paul Theroux (1992: 178), in his book *The Happy Islands of Oceania* recounts how in the remotest parts of the Pacific Islands he found men coming up to him to tell him about the latest developments in the Gulf War they had heard on the radio. In addition he found that in the tiny island of Savo in the Solomon Islands group, Rambo was a big folk hero. The one generator on the island had no use except as a source of power for showing videos. One can surmise that it may not be too long before Savo has its satellite TV receiver or personal computers which link it into the worldwide "net". Such accounts are by now legion – yet how are we to read them?

One possibility is to attempt to outline some of the absorption/assimilation/resistance strategies which peripheral cultures can adopt towards the mass and consumer culture images and goods originating from metropolitan centres (Hannerz, 1991). In the first place it is apparent that once we investigate actual cases the situation is exceedingly complex. It is not just a question of the everyday practical culture of local inhabitants giving way to globally marketed products. Such market culture/ local culture interactions are usually mediated by the nation-state, which in the process of creating a national identity will educate and employ its own range of cultural specialists and intermediaries. Some of these may well have been educated in world cities and have retained strong networks and lifestyle identifications with other transnational "design professionals", managers and intellectuals and para-intellectuals. Some of these may even be official "cultural animateurs" employed by the ministry of culture, in some cases perhaps with one eye on national cultural integration and one eye on the international tourist trade.

Hence, depending on the priority it gives to the nation-forming project and the power resources that the nation-state possesses, it can reinvent memories, traditions and practices with which to resist, channel or control market penetration. Some nation-states, for example, will invest in locally produced film and television programmes. Yet as we have previously mentioned, such experiments in cultural engineering are by no means certain to succeed unless they can find a base to ground themselves in local forms of life and practices. Hence the scenario of "cultural dumping" of obsolete American television programmes on a powerless nation-state on the periphery is only one possibility from a range of responses. It has to be set alongside the activities of cultural gatekeepers, brokers and entrepreneurs within the major cities of the nation-state in conjunction with colleagues abroad in the world cities collaborating in deciding what aspects of the local popular culture – music, food, dress, crafts, etc. – can be packaged and marketed in the metropolitan centres and elsewhere. In many cases it may be that various forms of hybridization and creolization emerge in which the meanings of externally originating goods, information and images are reworked, syncretized and blended with existing cultural traditions and forms of life.

In the case of the effects of global television it is important to move beyond oversimplified oppositionally conceived formulations which stress either the manipulation, or the resistance, of audiences. In recent years the pendulum has swung towards the latter populist direction and it is claimed that a new cultural studies orthodoxy has emerged around the assumption of the creativity and skilfulness of active audiences and consumers (Morris, 1990). Television and the new communications technology are frequently presented as producing both manipulation and resistance, and the homogenization and fragmentation of contemporary culture (Morley, 1991).

The new communications technology is presented as producing a global *Gemeinschaft* which transcends physical place through bringing together disparate groups who unite around the common experience of television to form new communities (Meyrowitz, 1985). This means that the locality is no longer the prime referent of our experiences. Rather, we can be immediately united with distant others with whom we can form a "psychological neighbourhood" or "personal community" through telephone or the shared experience of the news of the "generalized elsewhere" we get from watching television. Hence as Morley (1991: 8) remarks, "Thus, it seems, locality is not simply subsumed in a national or global sphere: rather, it is increasingly bypassed in both directions; experience is both unified beyond localities and fragmented within them." Yet this is not to suggest that the fragmentation of experience within localities is random or unstructured. Access to power resources creates important differentials. Just as there are "information rich" nations on a global level there are also "information poor" ones. Within localities there are clear differentials, with the wealthy and well-educated most likely to have access to the new forms of information and communications technology through possession of the necessary economic and cultural capital (Morley, 1991: 10). Here we can also point to Mary Douglas and Baron Isherwood's (1980) concept of "informational goods", goods which require a good deal of background knowledge to make their consumption meaningful and strategically useful, as is the case with personal computers.

On the other hand it is the sense of instanciation and immediacy that television presents which appears to make its messages unproblematically accessible. American soap operas, Italian football or the Olympic games all have an apparent immediacy and intelligibility which could be misunderstood as producing a homogeneous response. Yet these global resources are often indigenized and syncretized to produce particular blends and identifications which sustain the sense of the local (see Canevacci, 1992).[4]

A further problem with the homogenization thesis is that it misses the ways in which transnational corporations increasingly direct advertising towards various parts of the globe which is increasingly tailored to specific differentiated audiences and markets. Hence the global and the local cannot be neatly separated, as we find in the statement by Coca-Cola: "We are not a multi-national, we are a multi-local" (quoted in Morley, 1991: 15). Here we can usefully refer to the term "glocal", the fusion of the terms global and local to make a blend. Apparently the term is modelled on the Japanese *dochaku*, which derives from the agricultural principle of adapting one's farming techniques to local conditions, and which was taken up by Japanese business interests in the 1980s (Robertson, 1995; see also Luke, 1995).

The various combinations, blends and fusions of seemingly opposed and incompatible processes such as homogenization and fragmentation, globalization and localization, universalism and particularism,

indicate the problems entailed in attempts to conceive the global in terms of a singular integrated and unified conceptual scheme. Appadurai (1990) has rejected such attempts at theoretical integration to argue that the global order must be understood as "a complex, overlapping, disjunctive order". It can be best conceived as involving sets of non-isomorphic flows of people, technology, finance, media images and information, and ideas. Individual nation-states may attempt to promote, channel or block flows with varying degrees of success depending upon the power resources they possess and the constraints of the configuration of interdependencies they are locked into.

It is, of course, important that we examine the evidence from systematic studies which focus upon specific localities to examine the effects of these flows on groups of people. One important site where the various flows of people, goods, technology, information and images cross and intermingle is the world city. World cities are the sites in which we find the juxtaposition of the rich and the poor, the new middle-class professionals and the homeless, and a variety of other ethnic, class and traditional identifications, as people from the centre and periphery are brought together to face each other within the same spatial location (Berner and Korff, 1992). The socio-spatial redevelopment of the inner areas and docklands of some large Western cities in the 1980s have been regarded by some as examples of "postmodernization" (Cooke, 1988; Zukin, 1988).

Yet, many of the cultural factors associated with this process – the postmodern emphasis upon the mixing of codes, pastiche, fragmentation, incoherence, disjunction and syncretism – were characteristics of cities in colonial societies decades or even centuries before they appeared in the West (King, 1995). From this perspective the first multicultural city was not London or Los Angeles but probably Rio de Janeiro or Calcutta, or Singapore. At the very least this points to some of the problems involved in defining the modern and the postmodern and their family of associated terms. A more nuanced and elaborated notion of cultural modernity which goes beyond Eurocentric notions of the homogenizing effects of industrialization, urbanization and bureaucratization is needed. A global conception of the modern is required, which rather than being preoccupied with the historical sequences of transitions from tradition to modernity and postmodernity, instead focuses upon the spatial dimension, the geographical relationship between the centre and the periphery in which the first multi-racial and multi-cultural societies were on the periphery not the core. Cultural diversity, syncretism and dislocation occurred there first. The inter-dependencies and power balances which developed between Western nation-states such as England and France and colonial societies clearly form an important, yet neglected aspect of modernity; an aspect which is noticeably absent from those accounts which derive from those working in the classic tradition deriving from French and German theorists (see also Bhabha, 1991). (These themes will be discussed more fully in Featherstone, 1995; see also Featherstone and Lash, 1995).

It is the very process of intensified flows of people from the ex-colonial countries to the Western metropolitan centres in the postwar era that has made us increasingly conscious of this colonial aspect of the development of modernity and the question of cultural identity. The inward movement of people, as well as images and information, from places which for many in the West were constructed through oversimplified racist and exotic stereotypes of "the Other", means that new levels of complexity are introduced to the formulation of notions of identity, cultural tradition, community and nation. This challenges the notion of one-way flows from the centre to the peripheries, as the dominant centres in the West become not only importers of raw materials and goods, but of people too.[5] The visibility and vociferousness of "the rest in the West" (Hall, 1992) means that cultural differences once maintained between societies now exist within them. The unwillingness of migrants to passively absorb the dominant cultural mythology of the nation or locality raises issues of multiculturalism and the fragmentation of identity.

In some cases this has provoked intensified and extremist nationalist reactions, as has occurred in France (the racist campaigns of Le Pen) and Britain (the 1980s Falklands War and its associated "little Englanderism"). This can lead to a complex series of reactions on the part of immigrants. For some ethnic groups this entails a retreat into the culture of origin (in Britain a re-identification with the Caribbean, Pakistan, India or Bangladesh); or a retreat into fundamentalist religions from the home country. For others this may entail the construction of complex counter-ethnicities as with young second-generation Afro-Caribbeans who have de-veloped identities around the symbols and mytho-logies of Rastafarianism (Hall, 1992: 308). For yet others the prospect of a unified single identity may be impossible and illusory as they move between various identities. Some third-generation young blacks in Britain constantly shift between British, Caribbean, black, subcultural and various gender identifications. For example, the film *My Beautiful Laundrette* (1981), by Stephen Frears and Hanif Kureishi, has central characters, who are two gay men, one white, one brown, with the latter's Pakistani landlord uncle throwing black people out on to the street: characters who do not present positive unified identity images and who are consequently not easy to identify with (Hall, 1991: 60).

The problems involved in trying to live with multiple identities helps to generate endless discourses about the process of finding or constructing a coherent identity (see Marcus, 1992, on multiple and dispersed identities; also Gupta and Ferguson, 1992, on cultural dislocation). Yet in contrast to those arguments which assume that the logic of modernity is to produce an increasingly narrow individualism, a narcissistic preoccupation with individual identity which was common in the 1970s, today we find arguments which emphasize the search for a strong collective identity, some new form of community, within modern societies.

Maffesoli (1995), for example, sees the process of development from modernity to postmodernity as entailing a movement from individualism to collectivism, from rationality to emotionality. In this sense postmodernity is seen as sharing with its premodern antecedents an emphasis on emotionality, the cultivation of intense feelings and sensory experiences such as were found in the spectacles of the baroque. Here Maffesoli speaks of post-modernity as bringing about a new tribalism, the emergence of ephemeral postmodern *tribes*, which are to be found especially amongst young people in large cities such as Paris. These groupings provide a strong sense of localism and emotional identification (*Einfühlung*) through the tactile embodied sense of being together. They are regarded as *neo*-tribes because they exist in an urban world where relationships are transitory, hence their identifications are temporary as people will necessarily move on and through the endless flow of sociality to make new attachments (see also discussions in Bauman, 1991, 1992). The subject of tribalism, both in its traditional sense of exclusive membership of a group based upon kin-ties and strong identification with a locality or region, and in the sense of the emergence of more transitory neo-tribes, has recently attracted a good deal of public interest (see Maybury-Lewis, 1992a, 1992b).

This interest too has been subjected to the process of global marketing by various arms of the tourist industry, which it has been predicted will become the world's leading industry by 1996 (Urry, 1992). Of course for many tourists the ease with which they can now travel to the more exotic and remote parts of the world amounts to a step into a tourist reservation in which they enjoy "home plus". In effect, they are locals whose contact with another set of locals in the tourist location is highly regulated and ritualized. It has been argued that this particular set of tourists is being replaced by more sophisticated post-tourists who seek a whole range of experiences and direct encounters with locals. Some of those post-tourists are not at all worried that what they are presented with is a simulation of a local culture; they are interested in the whole paraphernalia of the "behind the scenes" and the construction of the performance and set (Urry, 1990). Such staged simulations of localities can vary from reassuring clear cartoon-style parodies (the Jungle Cruise in the Magic Kingdom), to small-scale "walk-in, see and touch" simulations of the key buildings and icons which in the popular imagination are taken to represent a national culture (the World Showcase at EPCOT [the Experimental Prototype Community of Tomorrow]), to the whole heritage industry efforts to preserve and restore full-scale living and working examples of "the past" (for discussion of Walt Disney World see Fjellman, 1992). Some would see this as part of a wider shift away from the imposition of abstraction and uniformity through modernist architecture to a postmodern struggle for place, to reinvent place and rehumanize urban space (Ley, 1989).

In yet other situations it is the locals themselves who are asked to take part in staged authenticity for tourists. Here the tourists are granted the privilege of moving around the living working locality in which the real inhabitants perform for them. Hence McCannell (1992: Ch. 8) discusses the case of Locke, California, a company town, the home of the last surviving Chinese farm labourers. The whole town was sold to tourist developers in 1977 who marketed it as "the only intact rural Chinatown in the United States". Here the inhabitants along with the town became museumified, presented as

the last living examples of "a way of life which no longer exists".

McCannell (1992: 18) also discusses examples of "enacted or staged savagery", such as the deal struck between MCI Incorporated and the Masai of Kenya covering wage rates, admission fees, television and movie rights, etc. which could allow the Masai to earn a living by perpetually *acting Masai*. Also interesting in this context is Dennis O'Rourke's film *Cannibal Tours* (1987) which follows a group of wealthy European and North American tourists up the Sepik River in Papua New Guinea aboard a luxury cruise ship (see the interview with O'Rourke by Lutkehaus, 1989; the review by Bruner, 1989; and discussion in McCannell, 1992). Such situations vary a great deal in both the objectives of the tourists and the relative power of the parties involved. In the case of New Guinea the tribespeople were well aware of the unequal exchange and of the hard bargains which the wealthy tourists invariably strike, and that the middle-men and local representatives of the tourist agencies had creamed off the money. The tribespeople here did not have sufficient power resources to manipulate the degree of openness and closure of the boundary of the locality in their own terms. In other cases this can lead to what McCannell (1992: 31) refers to as "the hostile Indian act", in which ex-primitives typically engage in hatred, sullen silence and freezing out. For their part, the cannibal tourists can achieve a safe package version replete with vicarious thrills of the "heart of darkness", while fulfilling a theme in the popular imagination: a visit to the place of "the Other" – with the proviso that at the end of each day they can return to their home comforts and familiar Western surroundings of the cruise ship.

There are cases, however, where it is possible for tourists to take part in tribal life on a more complete basis, as is the case with some communities of Inuit in Alaska. Here the tourist lives with the tribe and takes part in a wide range of activities – there is no tour ship to retreat to and only individuals or small groups are admitted to the tribe on a strictly regulated basis under the supervision of government agencies. The Inuit use the money they get to buy essential supplies and equipment (bullets for hunting rifles, etc.) in order to maintain a partly modernized, yet independent version of their traditional way of life. They are in a situation in which they possess sufficient power resources to be able to manipulate the boundary of their community to their own advantage and maintain their sense of cultural identity. A further example would be of the Ainu. A "hunter and gatherer" people, they largely inhabit the northern Japanese island of Hokkaido, which only became officially integrated into Japan after the Meiji Restoration (1868). During the 1970s an Ainu cultural movement developed which not only established schools for the teaching of their language and traditions, but also in certain areas established traditional village structures to produce handicraft goods, so that tourists could come to witness their traditional lifestyle (Friedman, 1990: 320). Tourism, then, has been consciously manipulated for the purposes of the reconstitution of Ainu cultural identity.

For other cultural movements tourism may cease to be seen as a resource, but may be identified as a major element in the process which is destroying localism and ethnic identities. The Hawaiian cultural movement which has developed since the 1970s has reacted against the long-term process that has incorporated Hawaii into the US economy. This has seen the development of a multi-ethnic Hawaii in which Hawaiians became a minority in their own land, with their numbers reduced from 600,000 to 40,000 during the first century of contact, along with the stigmatization and disintegration of the Hawaiian language and customs. The tourist industry, the dominant force since the decline of the plantation economy, became identified with the taking of land and the commodification and trivialization of Hawaiian culture as exotica. Instead of the old system with its homogeneous model of Western modernist identity at the top and backward and quaint Hawaiians at the bottom, and with those at the bottom threatened with assimilation, it is argued that in its place a polycentric system has emerged (Friedman, 1992). The new model revolves around the Hawaiian cultural movement's opposition to tourist development and attempts to establish and defend their authentic sense of the past, and the newer more upmarket tourism which seeks both to modernize and develop and define those who stand in its way as lazy and backward, and to recreate a nostalgic vision of the former plantation Hawaii. A vision that has little acceptance from the Hawaiian movement, which wishes to develop a particular identity and way of life which resists the whole enterprise of being an object for someone else's gaze (for a further account of the complexity of localized identities in Hawaii see Kirkpatrick, 1989).

Concluding Remarks

Anthony King (1995) has remarked that all "globalizing theories are self-representations of the dominant particular", acutely pointing to the problem of the location of the theorist who necessarily writes from a particular place and within a particular tradition of discourse which endow him or her with differential power resources not only to be able to speak, but also to be listened to. Many of our Western taken-for-granted assumptions about the world have immense power because their very self-evident quality does not encourage the possibility of dialogue. Hence we have a number of theories about the ways in which the West was able to impose its particular vision of the "exotic Other" on distant parts of the world. Yet this should not allow us to remain bound to the view that our representations must remain trapped within the particularism of our fantasy-laden projections, for the question of evidence cannot be completely dispensed with.

It took an American anthropologist of Sri Lankan origins to raise doubts about one of the powerful Western myths about the Pacific: that Captain Cook was deified by the Hawaiians. Obeyeskere (1992) demonstrates through careful research that it wasn't the Hawaiians who deified Captain Cook, but the Europeans who projected the myth of native deification on to the Hawaiians to bolster their own civilizing myths. The discovery of this reversal was made possible in part through Obeyeskere's knowledge of Asian societies – he could find no local evidence to support assumptions of the deifications of Westerners by over-credulous natives – and in part by his attribution of commonsense practical rationality to the Hawaiians; the latter is in contrast to those who emphasize the enduring strength of their culture through the inflexibility of their cosmological categories. As members of "the rest" come increasingly to reside in the West and are able to make their voices heard, we can expect many more accounts which challenge the "self-representations of the dominant particular". At the same time, important as the drive for deconceptualization is, there remains the problem of reconceptualization, the possibility of the construction of higher-level, more abstract general models of the globe. Here we can make a number of points.

The first is to do with how we conceptualize the globe. To identify it as a single place is perhaps to give it a sense of false concreteness and unity (see

Tagg, 1991). For many of the people in the world the consciousness of the process of globalization, that they inhabit the same place, may be absent or limited, or occur only spasmodically. To some extent an appropriate model to represent this might be a heap, a congeries or aggregate (see Elias, 1987; S. F. Moore, 1989). Clearly, this is one way of understanding the notion of a global culture: the sense of heaps, congeries and aggregates of cultural particularities juxtaposed together on the same field, the same bounded space, in which the fact that they are different and do not fit together, or want to fit together, becomes noticeable and a source of practical problems. The study of culture, our interest in doing justice to the description of particularities and differences, necessarily directs us towards an ideographic mode in which we are acutely aware of the danger of hypostatizations and over-generalizations.

At the same time there are clearly systemic tendencies in social life which derive from the expansive and integrating power of economic processes and the hegemonizing efforts of particular nation-states or blocs. From this perspective there is a need for practical knowledge which is modelled in systematic form and which yields technically useful information and rational planning; for models in which differences have to become domesticated, turned into variables to further integration. In this sense certain aspects of the world are becoming more amenable to systems analysis as the world becomes more integrated through systemic practices and takes on systemic properties. Yet when we consider the relationship between the system and culture, a shift away from the powerful hegemonic control over the system could be accompanied by a concomitant shift in cultural categories. Friedman (1988), for example, has argued that while all cultures are plural and creole in terms of their origins, whether or not they identify themselves as such depends upon further processes. Hence our capacity to notice, look for or advocate pluralism and the defence of particularity may not depend upon the actual extent of these characteristics, but be a function of relative changes in our situation which now gives us "permission" to see them:

In fact it might well be argued that the pluralist conception of the world is a distinctly western mode of apprehending the current fragmentation of the system, a confusion of our own identity space. When hegemony is strong or increasing cultural space is similarly homo-genized, spaghetti becomes Italian, a plural set of dialects become a national language in which cultural differences are translated into a continuum of correct to incorrect, or standard to nonstandard. (Friedman, 1988: 458)

In some ways this conception is similar to that developed by Elias in which he argues that in situations in which established groups are firmly in control relationships with outsider groups are more hierarchical and the dominant group is able to colonize the weaker with its own pattern of conduct. The established are able to develop a collective "we-image" based upon a sense of superiority and "group charisma", an image which is inseparable from the imposition and internalization of a sense of "group disgrace", a stigmatized sense of unworthiness and inferiority by the outsider group. The outsiders are invariably characterized as "dirty, morally unreliable and lazy" (Mennell, 1989: 122). This colonization phase of the relationship between the established and the outsiders can give way with a shift in interdependencies and the relative power balance to a second phase, that of "functional democratization". In this second phase of differentiation and emancipation, people become enmeshed in longer and denser webs of interdependencies, which the established group finds difficulty in controlling. Outsider groups gain in social power and confidence and the contrasts and tensions in society increase. It can be added that in this second phase it is possible that many of the unified models which are seen as doing an injustice to particularity and complexity become subjected to critique and rejection. Interest develops in constructing models and theories which allow for notions of syncretism, complexity and seemingly random and arbitrary patterns (Serres, 1991). These concluding remarks are, of course, speculative, and there are many difficulties in trying to use established-outsider models in situations where there are increasing numbers of participants in the global "game" and the boundaries between collectivities can be breached or ignored, yet at the very least it perhaps does suggest that we should not be too hasty in dispensing with theories of social relations altogether.

Notes

1. For discussions of localism and locality see Cooke (1990), Bell and Newby (1971) and Cohen (1985).

2. It is interesting to note that the term "Wigan Pier" was coined by George Formby Sr, who ironically confounded the grime of a mining town with the delights of a seaside resort (Richards, 1984: 191).
3. Some of these criticisms apply to the recent work of Giddens (1990, 1991) on modernity. For a critique of his neglect of the cultural dimension and assumption that globalization is merely modernity writ large, see Robertson (1992b).
4. Canevacci (1992), for example, mentions how the Brazilian Indios at Iguacu Falls not only were fans of Italian football and identified with Rud Guillot of Milan, but also used video cameras both to communicate amongst themselves and to produce images for the outside world.
5. This is not just a question of the flow between the West as the centre and "the rest" as the periphery. As Abu-Lughod (1991) has indicated, we have to consider the proliferation of multiple cores, and especially how the cultures of the rising cores in Asia are diffusing within their own circuits. This also means raising the question of the relations between the hosts and migrants into these new cores – e.g. Japan.

References

Abu-Lughod, J. (1991) "Going beyond the global babble", in A. D. King (ed.), *Culture, Globalization and the World-system*. London: Macmillan.

Anderson, B. (1991) *Imagined Communities*, revised edn. London: Verso.

Appadurai, A. (1990) "Disjunction and difference in the global cultural economy", *Theory, Culture & Society*, 7 (2–3).

Arensberg, C. M. (1968) *The Irish Countrymen*. Garden City, NY: Natural History Press, orig. publ. 1937.

Arensberg, C. M. and Kimball, S. T. (1940) *Family and Community in Ireland*. London: Peter Smith.

Arnason, J. (1987a) "The modern constellation and the Japanese enigma", Part I, *Thesis Eleven*, 17.

Arnason, J. (1987b) "The modern constellation and the Japanese enigma", Part II, *Thesis Eleven*, 18.

Arnason, J. (1990) "Nationalism, globalization and modernity", in M. Featherstone (ed.), *Global Culture*. London: Sage.

Bauman, Z. (1991) *Modernity and Ambivalence*. Cambridge: Polity.

Bauman, Z. (1992) *Intimations of Postmodernity*. London: Routledge.

Bell, C. and Newby, H. (1971) *Community Studies*. London: Allen & Unwin.

Bergesen, A. (1990) "Turning world-system theory on its head", in M. Featherstone (ed.), *Global Culture*. London: Sage.

Berner, E. and Korff, R. (1992) "Strategies and counter-strategies: globalization and localization from the perspective of the sociology of group conflict", University of Bielefeld, mimeo.

Bhabha, H. K. (1991) " 'Race', time and the revision of modernity", *Oxford Literary Review*, 13.

Bourdieu, P. (1984) *Distinction: A Social Critique of the Judgement of Taste*, trans. R. Nice. London: Routledge.

Brennan, T. (1990) "The national longing for form", in H. Bhabha (ed.), *Nation and Narration*. London: Routledge.

Bruner, E. M. (1989) "Of cannibals, tourists and ethnographers", *Cultural Anthropology*, 4 (4).

Burke, P. (1978) *Popular Culture in Early Modern Europe*. London: Temple Smith.

Canevacci, M. (1992) "Image accumulation and cultural syncretism", *Theory, Culture & Society*, 9 (3).

Chaney, D. (1986) "The symbolic form of ritual in mass communication", in P. Golding (ed.), *Communicating Politics*. Leicester: Leicester University Press.

Clifford, J. (1989) "Notes on travel and theory", *Inscriptions*, 5: 177–88.

Cohen, A. (1985) *The Symbolic Construction of Community*. London: Tavistock.

Cooke, P. (1988) "Modernity, postmodernity and the city", *Theory, Culture & Society*, 5 (2–3).

Cooke, P. (1990) "Locality, structure and agency: a theoretical analysis", *Cultural Anthropology*, 5 (1).

Critcher, C. (1979) "Sociology, cultural studies and the postwar working class", in J. Clarke, C. Critcher and R. Johnson (eds), *Working Class Culture*. London: Hutchinson.

Dezalay, Y. (1990) "The big bang and the law", in M. Featherstone (ed.), *Global Culture*. London: Sage.

Donaldson, P. (1975) *Edward VIII*. Philadelphia.

Douglas, M. and Isherwood, B. (1980) *The World of Goods*. Harmondsworth: Penguin.

Durkheim, E. (1961) *The Elementary Forms of the Religious Life*. New York: Collier.

Dyan, D. and Katz, E. (1988) "Articulating consensus: the ritual and rhetoric of media events", in J. C. Alexander (ed.), *Durkheimian Sociology: Cultural Studies*. Cambridge: Cambridge University Press.

Elias, N. (1978) *The Civilizing Process, Volume 1: the History of Manners*. Oxford: Blackwell.

Elias, N. (1987) *Involvement and Detachment*. Oxford: Blackwell.

Elias, N. and Scotson, J. L. (1994) *The Established and the Outsiders*, revised edn. London: Sage.

Featherstone, M. (1991) *Consumer Culture and Postmodernism*. London: Sage.

Featherstone, M. (1995) *Undoing Culture*. London: Sage.

Featherstone, M. and Lash, S. (1995) "Globalization, modernity and the specialization of social theory", in M. Featherstone, S. Lash and R. Robertson (eds), *Global Modernities*. London: Sage.

Fiske, J., Hodge, B. and Turner, G. (eds) (1987) *Myths of Oz*. Sydney: Allen & Unwin.

Fjellman, S. J. (1992) *Vinyl Leaves: Walt Disney World and America*. Boulder, CO: Westview Press.

Frankenberg, R. (1966) *Communities in Britain*. Harmondsworth: Penguin.

Friedman, J. (1988) "Cultural logics of the global system", *Theory, Culture & Society*, 5 (2–3), special issue on postmodernism.

Friedman, J. (1992) "Narcissism, roots and postmodernity: the constitution of selfhood in the global crisis", in S. Lash and J. Friedman (eds), *Modernity and Identity*. Oxford: Blackwell.

Fussell, P. (1980) *Abroad. British Literary Travelling between the Wars*. Oxford: Oxford University Press.

Game, A. (1990) "Nation and identity: Bondi", *New Formations*, 11.

Gellner, E. (1983) *Nations and Nationalism*. Oxford: Blackwell.

Gessner, V. and Schade, A. (1990) "Conflicts of culture in cross-border legal relations", *Theory, Culture & Society*, 7 (2–3).

Giddens, A. (1990) *The Consequence of Modernity*. Cambridge: Polity.

Giddens, A. (1991) *Modernity and Self-Identity*. Cambridge: Polity.

Gupta, A. and Ferguson, J. (1992) "Beyond 'culture': space, identity, and the politics of difference", *Cultural Anthropology*, 7 (1): 6–23.

Haferkamp, H. (1987) "Beyond the iron cage of modernity", *Theory, Culture & Society*, 4 (1).

Halbwachs, M. (1992) *On Collective Memory*. Chicago: Chicago University Press.

Hall, S. (1991) "Old and new identities", in A. King (ed.), *Culture*. London: Sage.

Hall, S. (1992) "The rest and the West: discourse and power", in S. Hall and B. Gieben (eds), *Formation of Modernity*. Cambridge: Polity.

Hannerz, U. (1991) "Scenarios for peripheral cultures", in A. King (ed.), *Culture, Globalization and the World-System*. London: Macmillan.

Higson, A. (1989) "The concept of national cinema", *Screen*, 30 (4).

Hoggart, R. (1957) *The Uses of Literacy*. Harmondsworth: Penguin.

Iyer, P. (1989) *Video Nights in Kathmandu: Reports from the Not-So-Far East*. London: Black Swan.

Jackson, B. (1968) *Working Class Community*. London: Routledge.

King, A. D. (1990) *Global Cities*. London: Routledge.

King, A. D. (1995) "The times and spaces of modernity (or who needs postmodernism?)" in M. Featherstone, S. Lash and R. Robertson (eds), *Global Modernities*. London: Sage.

Kirkpatrick, John (1989) "Trials of identity in America", *Cultural Anthropology*, 4 (3): 301–11.

Knorr-Cetina, K. (1994) "Primitive classification and postmodernity: towards a sociological notion of fiction", *Theory, Culture & Society*, 11 (3).

Laing, S. (1986) *Representations of Working Class Life 1957–1964*. London: Macmillan.

Ley, D. (1989) "Modernism, post-modernism and the struggle for place", in J. A. Agnew and J. A. Duncan (eds), *The Power of Place*. London: Unwin Hyman.

Luke, T. (1995) "New world order or new world orders? Power, politics and ideology in the informationalizing glocal order", in M. Featherstone, S. Lash and R. Robertson (eds), *Global Modernities*. London: Sage.

Lutkehaus, N. C. (1989) " 'Excuse me, everything is not all right': an interview with film-maker Dennis O'Rourke", *Cultural Anthropology*, 4 (4).

Lynd, D. and Lynd, H. (1929) *Middletown*. New York: Harcourt Brace.

Lynd, D. and Lynd, H. (1937) *Middletown in Transition*. New York: Harcourt Brace.

McCannell, D. (1992) *Empty Meeting Grounds. The Tourist Papers*. London: Routledge.

Maffesoli, M. (1995) *The Time of the Tribes*. London: Sage.

Marcus, G. (1992) "Past, present and emergent identities: requirements for ethnography in late twentieth century modernity", in S. Lash and J. Friedman (eds), *Modernity and Identity*. Oxford: Blackwell.

Martin, B. (1981) *A Sociology of Contemporary Cultural Change*. Oxford: Blackwell.

Maruyama, M. (1969) *Thought and Behaviour in Japanese Politics*. London: Oxford University Press.

Maybury-Lewis, D. (1992a) "On the importance of being tribal", *Utney Reader*, 52 (July–August).

Maybury-Lewis, D. (1992b) *Millennium: Tribal Wisdom and the Modern World*. New York: Viking Penguin.

Mennell, S. (1989) *Norbert Elias*. Oxford: Blackwell.

Meyrowitz, J. (1985) *No Sense of Place*. Oxford: Oxford University Press.

Middleton, D. and Edwards, D. (eds) (1990) *Collective Remembering*. London: Sage.

Minh-ha, Trinh T. (1989) *Woman, Native, Other. Writing Postcoloniality and Feminism*. Bloomington: Indiana University Press.

Mitsuhiro, Y. (1989) "Postmodernism and mass images in Japan", *Public Culture*, 1 (2).

Moore, S. F. (1989) "The production of cultural pluralism as a process", *Public Culture*, 1 (2).

Morley, D. (1991) "Where the global meets the local: notes from the sitting room", *Screen*, 32 (1).

Morris, M. (1990) "Banality in cultural studies", in P. Mellencamp (ed.), *Logics of Television*. Bloomington: Indiana University Press.

Obeyeskere, G. (1992) *The Apotheosis of Captain Cook*. Princeton: Princeton University Press.

Pearson, G. (1985) "Lawlessness, Modernity and Social Change", *Theory, Culture & Society*, 2 (3).

Richards, J. (1984) *The Age of the Dream Palace: Cinema and Society in Britain 1930–1939*. London: Routledge.

Robertson, R. (1992a) *Globalization*. London: Sage.

Robertson, R. (1992b) "Globality and modernity", *Theory, Culture & Society*, 9 (2).

Robertson, R. (1995) "Glocalization: time-space and homogeneity-heterogeneity", in M. Featherstone,

S. Lash and R. Robertson (eds), *Global Modernities*. London: Sage.

Sakai, N. (1989) "Modernity and its critique: the problem of universalism and particularism", in M. Miyoshi and H. D. Harootunian (eds), *Postmodernism and Japan*. Durham, NC: Duke University Press.

Sassen, S. (1991) *Global Cities: New York, London, Tokyo*. Princeton: Princeton University Press.

Serres, M. (1991) *Rome: The Book of Foundations*. Stanford, CA: Stanford University Press.

Smith, A. D. (1990) "Towards a global culture?" *Theory, Culture & Society*, 5 (2–3).

Stein, M. (1960) *Eclipse of Community*. New York: Harper.

Tagg, J. (1991) "Globalization, totalization and the discursive field", in A. King (ed.), *Culture, Globalization and the World-System*. London: Macmillan.

Theroux, P. (1992) *The Happy Isles of Oceania: Paddling the Pacific*. New York: Putnam.

Tomlinson, J. (1991) *Cultural Imperialism*. London: Pinter.

Tönnies, F. (1955) *Community and Association*. London: Routledge.

Turner, B. S. (1987) "A note on nostalgia", *Theory, Culture & Society*, 4 (1).

Turner, V. (1969) *The Ritual Process: Structure and AntiStructure*. Harmondsworth: Allen Lane.

Urry, J. (1990) *The Tourist Gaze*. London: Sage.

Urry, J. (1992) "The tourist gaze and the 'environment' ", *Theory, Culture & Society*, 9 (3).

Viddich, A. and Bensman, J. (1958) *Small Town in Mass Society*. Princeton, NJ: Princeton University Press.

Warner, W. L. and Lunt, P. S. (1941) *The Social Life of a Modern Community*. New Haven: Yale University Press.

Watier, P. (1991) "The war writings of Georg Simmel", *Theory, Culture & Society*, 8 (3), special issue on Georg Simmel.

White, R. (1981) *Inventing Australia*. Sydney: Allen & Unwin.

Williams, R. (1983) *Towards 2000*. London: Chatto & Windus.

Williamson, B. (1982) *Class, Culture and Community*. London: Routledge.

Zukin, S. (1988) "The postmodern debate over urban form", *Theory, Culture & Society*, 5 (2–3).

Zukin, S. (1991) *Landscapes of Power, From Detroit to Disney World*. Berkeley: California University Press.

32

Universalism, Particularism and the Question of Identity

Ernesto Laclau

There is today a lot of talk about social, ethnic, national and political identities. The "death of the subject", which was proudly proclaimed *urbi et orbi* not so long ago, has been succeeded by a new and widespread interest in the multiple identities that are emerging and proliferating in our contemporary world. These two movements are not, however, in such a complete and dramatic contrast as we would be tempted to believe at first sight. Perhaps the death of *the* Subject (with a capital "S") has been the main precondition of this renewed interest in the question of subjectivity. It is perhaps the very impossibility of any longer referring the concrete and finite expressions of a multifarious subjectivity to a transcendental centre that makes it possible to concentrate our attention on the multiplicity itself. The founding gestures of the 1960s are still with us, making possible the political and theoretical explorations in which we are today engaged.

If there was, however, this temporal gap between what had become theoretically thinkable and what was actually achieved, it is because a second and more subtle temptation haunted the intellectual imaginary of the Left for a while: that of replacing the transcendental subject with its symmetrical other, that of reinscribing the multifarious forms of undomesticated subjectivities in an objective totality. From this derived a concept which had a great deal of currency in our immediate prehistory: that of "subject positions". But this was not, of course, a real transcending of the problematic of transcendental subjectivity (something which haunts us as an absence is, indeed, very much present). "History is a process without a subject." Perhaps. But how do we know it? Is not the very possibility of such an assertion already requir-

ing what one was trying to avoid? If history as a totality is a possible object of experience and discourse, who could be the subject of such an experience but the subject of an absolute knowledge? Now, if we try to avoid this pitfall, and negate the terrain that would make that assertion a meaningful one, what becomes problematic is the very notion of "subject position".

What could such a position be but a special location within a totality, and what could this totality be but the object of experience of an absolute subject? At the very moment in which the terrain of absolute subjectivity collapses, it also collapses *the very possibility* of an absolute object. There is no real alternative between Spinoza and Hegel. But this locates us in a very different terrain: one in which the very possibility of the subject/object distinction is the simple result of the impossibility of constituting either of its two terms. I am a subject precisely *because* I cannot be an absolute consciousness, because something constitutively alien confronts me; and there can be no pure object as a result of this opaqueness/alienation which shows the traces of the subject in the object. Thus, once objectivism disappeared as an "epistemological obstacle", it became possible to develop the full implications of the "death of the subject". At that point, the latter showed the secret poison that inhabited it, the possibility of its second death: "the death of the death of the subject"; the re-emergence of the subject as a result of its own death; the proliferation of concrete finitudes whose limitations are the source of their strength; the realization that there can be "subjects" because the gap that "the Subject" was supposed to bridge is actually unbridgeable.

This is not just abstract speculation; it is instead an intellectual way opened by the very terrain in which history has thrown us: the multiplication of new – and not so new – identities as a result of the collapse of the places from which the universal subjects spoke – the explosion of ethnic and national identities in Eastern Europe and in the territories of the former USSR, struggles of immigrant groups in Western Europe, new forms of multicultural protest and self-assertion in the USA, to which we have to add the gamut of forms of contestation associated with the new social movements. Now, the question arises: is this proliferation thinkable *just as* proliferation – that is, simply in terms of its multiplicity? To put the problem in its simplest terms: is particularism thinkable *just as* particularism, only out of the differential dimension that it asserts? Are the relations between universalism and particularism simple relations of mutual exclusion? Or, if we address the matter from the opposite angle: does the alternative between an essential objectivism and a transcendental subjectivism exhaust the range of language games that it is possible to play with the "universal"?

These are the main questions that I am going to address. I will not pretend that the *place* of questioning does not affect the nature of the questions, and that the latter do not predetermine the kind of answer to be expected. Not all roads lead to Rome. But by confessing the tendentious nature of my intervention, I am giving the reader the only freedom that it is in my power to grant: that of stepping outside of my discourse and rejecting its validity in terms which are entirely incommensurable with it. So, in offering you some surfaces of inscription for the formulation of *questions* rather than answers, I am engaging in a power struggle for which there is a name: hegemony.

Let us start by considering the historical forms in which the relationship between universality and particularity has been thought. A first approach asserts: (a) that there is an uncontaminated dividing line between the universal and the particular; and (b) that the pole of the universal is entirely graspable by reason. In that case, there is no possible mediation between universality and particularity: the particular can only *corrupt* the universal. We are in the terrain of classical ancient philosophy. Either the particular realizes in itself the universal – that is it eliminates itself as particular and transforms itself in a transparent medium through which universality operates – or it negates the uni-

versal by asserting its particularism (but as the latter is purely irrational, it has no entity of its own and can only exist as corruption of being). The obvious question concerns the frontier dividing universality and particularity: is it universal or particular? If the latter, universality can only be a particularity which defines itself in terms of a limitless exclusion; if the former, the particular itself becomes part of the universal and the dividing line is again blurred. But the very possibility of formulating this last question would require that the *form* of universality as such is subjected to a clear differentiation from the actual *contents* to which it is associated. The thought of this difference, however, is not available to ancient philosophy.

The second possibility in thinking of the relation between universality and particularity is related to Christianity. A point of view of the totality exists but it is God's, not ours, so that it is not accessible to human reason. *Credo quia absurdum.* Thus, the universal is mere event in an eschatological succession, only accessible to us through revelation. This involves an entirely different conception of the relationship between particularity and universality. The dividing line cannot be, as in ancient thought, that between rationality and irrationality, between a deep and a superficial layer *within the thing*, but that between two series of events: those of a finite and contingent succession on the one hand, and those of the eschatological series on the other. Because the designs of God are inscrutable, the deep layer cannot be a timeless world of rational forms, but a temporal succession of essential events which are opaque to human reason; and because each of these universal moments has to realize itself in a finite reality which has no common measure with them, the relation between the two orders also has to be an opaque and incomprehensible one. This type of relation was called incarnation, its distinctive feature being that between the universal and the body incarnating it there is no rational connection whatsoever. God is the only and absolute mediator. A subtle logic destined to have a profound influence on our intellectual tradition was started in this way: that of the *privileged agent of history*, the agent whose particular body was the expression of a universality transcending it. The modern idea of a "universal class" and the various forms of Eurocentrism are nothing but the distant historical effects of the logic of incarnation.

Not entirely so, however, because modernity at its highest point was, to a large extent, the attempt to interrupt the logic of incarnation. God, as the absolute source of everything existing, was replaced in its function of universal guarantor by reason, but a *rational* ground and source has a logic of its own, which is very different from that of a divine intervention – the main difference being that the effects of a rational grounding have to be fully transparent to human reason. Now, this requirement is entirely incompatible with the logic of incarnation; if everything has to be transparent to reason, the connection between the universal and the body incarnating it also has to be so; in that case, the incommensurability between the universal to be incarnated and the incarnating body has to be eliminated. We have to postulate a body which is, in and of itself, the universal.

The full realization of these implications took several centuries. Descartes postulated a dualism in which the ideal of a full rationality still refused to become a principle of reorganization of the social and political world; but the main currents of the Enlightenment were going to establish a sharp frontier between the past, which was the realm of mistakes and follies of men, and a rational future, which had to be the result of an act of absolute institution. A last stage in the advance of this rationalistic hegemony took place when the gap between the rational and the irrational was closed through the representation of the act of its cancellation as a necessary moment in the self-development of reason: this was the task of Hegel and Marx, who asserted the total transparency, in absolute knowledge, of the real to reason. The body of the proletariat is no longer a particular body in which a universality external to it has to be incarnated: it is instead a body in which the distinction between particularity and universality is cancelled and, as a result, the need for any incarnation is definitely eradicated.

This was the point, however, at which social reality refused to abandon its resistance to universalistic rationalism. For an unsolved problem still remained. The universal had found its own body, but this was still the body of a certain particularity – European culture of the nineteenth century. So European culture was a particular one, and at the same time the expression – no longer the incarnation – of universal human essence (as the USSR was going to be considered later the "motherland" of socialism). The crucial issue here is that there was no intellectual means of distinguishing between European particularism and the universal functions that it was supposed to incarnate, given that European universalism had constructed its identity precisely through the cancellation of the logic of incarnation and, as a result, through the universalization of its own particularism. So, European imperialist expansion had to be presented in terms of a universal civilizing function, modernization and so forth. The resistances of other cultures were, as a result, presented not as struggles between particular identities and cultures, but as part of an all-embracing and epochal struggle between universality and particularisms – the notion of peoples without history expressing precisely their incapacity to represent the universal.

This argument could be conceived in very explicit racist terms, as in the various forms of social Darwinism, but it could also be given some more "progressive" versions – as in some sectors of the Second International – by asserting that the civilizing mission of Europe would finish with the establishment of a universally freed society of planetary dimensions. Thus, the logic of incarnation was reintroduced – Europe having to represent, for a certain period, universal human interests. In the case of Marxism, a similar reintroduction of the logic of incarnation takes place. Between the universal character of the tasks of the working class and the particularity of its concrete demands an increasing gap opened, which had to be filled by the Party as representative of the historical interests of the proletariat. The gap between class itself and class for itself opened the way to a succession of substitutions: the Party replaced the class, the autocrat the Party, and so on. Now, this well-known migration of the universal through the successive bodies incarnating it differed in one crucial point from Christian incarnation. In the latter a supernatural power was responsible both for the advent of the universal event and for the body which had to incarnate the latter. Human beings were on an equal footing *vis-à-vis* a power that transcended all of them. In the case of a secular eschatology, however, as the source of the universal is not external but internal to the world, the universal can only manifest itself through the establishment of an *essential* inequality between the objective positions of the social agents. Some of them are going to be privileged agents of historical change, not as a result of a contingent relation of forces but because they are incarnations of the universal. The same type of logic operating in Eurocentrism will establish the ontological privilege of the proletariat.

As this ontological privilege is the result of a process which was conceived as entirely rational, it was doubled into an epistemological privilege: the point of view of the proletariat supersedes the opposition subject/object. In a classless society, social relations will finally be fully transparent. It is true that if the increasing simplification of the social structure under capitalism had taken place in the way predicted by Marx, the consequences of this approach would not necessarily have been authoritarian, because the position of the proletariat as bearer of the viewpoint of social totality and the position of the vast majority of the population would have overlapped. But if the process moved – as it did – in the opposite direction, the successive bodies incarnating the viewpoint of the universal class had to have an increasingly restricted social base. The vanguard party, as concrete particularity, had to claim to have knowledge of the "objective meaning" of any event, and the viewpoint of the other particular social forces had to be dismissed as false consciousness. From this point on, the authoritarian turn was unavoidable.

This whole story is apparently leading to an inevitable conclusion: the chasm between the universal and the particular is unbridgeable – which is the same as saying that the universal is no more than a particular that at some moment has become dominant, that there is no way of reaching a reconciled society. And, in actual fact, the spectacle of the social and political struggles of the 1990s seems to confront us, as we said before, with a proliferation of particularisms, while the point of view of universality is increasingly put aside as an old-fashioned totalitarian dream. However, I will argue that an appeal to pure particularism is no solution to the problems that we are facing in contemporary societies. In the first place, the assertion of pure particularism, independently of any content and of the appeal to a universality transcending it, is a self-defeating enterprise. For if it is the only accepted normative principle, it confronts us with an unsolvable paradox. I can defend the right of sexual, racial and national minorities in the name of particularism; but if particularism is the only valid principle, I have to also accept the rights to self-determination of all kinds of reactionary groups involved in antisocial practices. Even more: as the demands of various groups will necessarily clash with each other, we have to appeal – short of postulating some kind of pre-established harmony – to some more general principles in order to regulate such clashes. In actual fact, there is no particularism which does not make appeal to such principles in the construction of its own identity. These principles can be progressive in our appreciation, such as the right of peoples to self-determination – or reactionary, such as social Darwinism or the right to *Lebensraum* – but they are always there, and for essential reasons.

There is a second and perhaps more important reason why pure particularism is self-defeating. Let us accept, for the sake of the argument, that the above-mentioned pre-established harmony is possible. In that case, the various particularisms would not be in antagonistic relation with each other, but would coexist one with the other in a coherent whole. This hypothesis shows clearly why the argument for pure particularism is ultimately inconsistent. For if each identity is in a differential, non-antagonistic relation to all other identities, then the identity in question is purely differential and relational; so it presupposes not only the presence of all the other identities but also the total ground which constitutes the differences as differences. Even worse: we know very well that the relations between groups are constituted as relations of power – that is, that each group is not only different from the others but constitutes in many cases such difference on the basis of the exclusion and subordination of other groups. Now, if the particularity asserts itself as mere particularity, in a purely differential relation with other particularities, it is sanctioning the *status quo* in the relation of power between the groups. This is exactly the notion of "separate developments" as formulated in apartheid: only the differential aspect is stressed, while the relations of power on which the latter is based are systematically ignored.

This last example is important because, coming from a discursive universe – South African apartheid – which is quite opposite to that of the new particularisms that we are discussing, and revealing, however, the same ambiguities in the construction of any difference, it opens the way to an understanding of a dimension of the relationship particularism/universalism which has generally been disregarded. The basic point is this: I cannot assert a differential identity without distinguishing it from a context, and, in the process of making the distinction, I am asserting the context at the same time. And the opposite is also true: I cannot destroy a context without destroying at the same time the identity of the particular subject who carries out the destruction. It is a very well known historical fact that an oppositionist force whose identity is constructed within a certain system of power is ambiguous *vis-à-vis* that system, because the latter is what prevents the constitution of the identity and it is, at the same time, its condition of existence. And any victory against the system also destabilizes the identity of the victorious force.

Now, an important corollary of this argument is that if a fully achieved difference eliminates the antagonistic dimension as constitutive of any identity, the possibility of maintaining this dimension depends on the very failure in the full constitution of a differential identity. It is here that the "universal" enters into the scene. Let us suppose that we are dealing with the constitution of the identity of an ethnic minority for instance. As we said earlier, if this differential identity is fully achieved, it can only be so within a context – for instance, a nation-state – and the price to be paid for total victory *within the context* is total integration with it. If, on the contrary, total integration *does not* take place, it is because that identity is not fully achieved – there are, for instance, unsatisfied demands concerning access to education, to employment, to consumer goods and so on. These demands cannot be made in terms of difference, but of some universal principles that the ethnic minority shares with the rest of the community: the right of everybody to have access to good schools, or live a decent life, or participate in the public space of citizenship, and so on.

This means that the universal is part of my identity as far as I am penetrated by a constitutive lack, that is as far as my differential identity has failed in its process of constitution. The universal emerges out of the particular not as some principle underlying and explaining the particular, but as an incomplete horizon suturing a dislocated particular identity. This points to a way of conceiving the relations between the universal and the particular which is different from those that we have explored earlier. In the case of the logic of incarnation, the universal and the particular were fully constituted but totally separated identities, whose connection was the result of a divine intervention, impenetrable to human reason. In the case of secularized eschatologies, the particular had to be eliminated entirely: the universal class was conceived as the cancellation of all differences. In the case of extreme particularism there is no universal body – but, as the ensemble of non-antagonistic particularities purely and simply reconstructs the

notion of social totality, the classical notion of the universal is not put into question in the least. (A universal conceived as a homogeneous space differentiated by its internal articulations and a *system* of differences constituting a unified ensemble are exactly the same.) Now we are pointing to a fourth alternative: the universal is the symbol of a missing fullness and the particular exists only in the contradictory movement of asserting at the same time a differential identity and cancelling it through its subsumption in the non-differential medium.

I will devote the rest of this paper to discussing three important political conclusions that one can derive from this fourth alternative. The first is that the construction of differential identities on the basis of total closure to what is outside them is not a viable or progressive political alternative. It would be a reactionary policy in Western Europe today, for instance, for immigrants from Northern Africa or Jamaica to abstain from all participation in Western European institutions, with the justification that theirs is a different cultural identity and that European institutions are not their concern. In this way, all forms of subordination and exclusion would be consolidated with the excuse of maintaining pure identities. The logic of apartheid is not only a discourse of the dominant groups; as we said before, it can also permeate the identities of the oppressed. At its very limit, understood as *mere* difference, the discourse of the oppressor and the discourse of the oppressed cannot be distinguished. The reason for this we have given earlier: if the oppressed is defined by its difference from the oppressor, such a difference is an essential component of the identity of the oppressed. But in that case, the latter cannot assert its identity without asserting that of the oppressor as well:

> Il y a bien des dangers à invoquer des différences pures, libérées de l'identique, devenues indépendantes du négatif. Le plus grand danger est de tomber dans les représentations de la belle-âme: rien que des différences, conciliables et fédérables, loin des luttes sanglantes. La belle-âme dit: nous sommes différentes, main non pas opposés.[1]

The idea of "negative" implicit in the dialectical notion of contradiction is unable to take us beyond this conservative logic of pure difference. A negative which is part of the determination of a positive content is an integral part of the latter. This is what shows the two faces of Hegel's *Logic*: if, on the one hand, the inversion defining the speculative proposition means that the predicate becomes subject, and that a universality transcending all particular determinations "circulates" through the latter, on the other hand, that circulation has a direction dictated by the movement of the particular determinations themselves, and is strictly reduced to it. Dialectical negativity does not question in the least the logic of identity (= the logic of pure difference).

This shows the ambiguity which is inherent in all forms of radical opposition: the opposition, in order to be radical, has to put in a common ground both what it asserts and what it excludes, so that the exclusion becomes a particular form of assertion. But this means that a particularism really committed to change can only do so by rejecting both what denies its own identity and that identity itself. There is no clear-cut solution to the paradox of radically negating a system of power while remaining in secret dependency on it. It is well known how opposition to certain forms of power requires identification with the very places from which the opposition takes place; as the latter are, however, internal to the opposed system, there is a certain conservatism inherent in *all* opposition. The reason why this is unavoidable is that the ambiguity inherent in *all* antagonistic relation is something we can negotiate with but not actually supersede – we can play with both sides of the ambiguity and produce results by preventing any of them prevailing in an exclusive way, but the ambiguity as such cannot be properly *resolved*. To surpass an ambiguity involves going beyond both its poles, but this means that there can be no simple politics of preservation of an identity. If the racial or cultural minority, for instance, has to assert its identity in new social surroundings, it will have to take into account new situations which will inevitably transform that identity. This means, of course, moving away from the idea of negation as radical reversal.[2] The main consequence that follows is that, if the politics of difference means continuity of difference by being always an *other*, the rejection of the other cannot be radical elimination either, but constant renegotiation of the forms of his presence. Aletta J. Norval asked herself recently about identities in a post-apartheid society:

The question looming on the horizon is this: what are the implications of recognizing that

the identity of the other is constitutive of the self, in a situation where apartheid itself will have become something of the past? That is, how do we think of social and political identities as post-apartheid?

And after asserting that:

[I]f the other is merely rejected, externalized *in toto* in the movement in which apartheid receives its signified, we would have effected a reversal of the order, remaining in effect in the terrain in which apartheid has organized and ruled . . .

she points to a different possibility:

Through a remembrance of apartheid as other, post-apartheid could become the site from which the final closure and suturing of identities is to be prevented. Paradoxically, a post-apartheid society will then only be radically beyond apartheid in so far as apartheid itself is present in it as its other. Instead of being effaced once and for all, "apartheid" itself would have to play the role of the element keeping open the relation to the other, of serving as watchword against any discourse claiming to be able to create a final unity.[3]

This argument can be generalized. Everything hinges on which of the two equally possible movements leading to the suppression of oppression is initiated. None can avoid maintaining the reference to the "other", but they do so in two completely different ways. If we simply *invert* the relation of oppression, the other (the former oppressor) is maintained as what is now oppressed and repressed, but this inversion of the *contents* leaves the form of oppression unchanged. And as the identity of the newly emancipated groups has been constituted through the rejection of the old dominant ones, the latter continue shaping the identity of the former. The operation of inversion takes place entirely within the old *formal* system of power. But as we have seen, all political identity is internally split, because no particularity can be constituted except by maintaining an internal reference to universality as that which is missing. But in that case, the identity of the oppressor will equally be split: on the one hand, he will represent a particular system of oppression; on the other, he will symbolize the *form* of oppression as such. This is what makes the second move suggested in Norval's text possible: instead of inverting a particular relation of oppression/closure in what it has of concrete particularity, inverting it in what it has of universality: the *form* of oppression and closure as such. The reference to the other is also maintained here but, as the inversion takes place at the level of the universal reference and not of the concrete contents of an oppressive system, the identities of *both* oppressors and oppressed are radically changed. A similar argument was made by Walter Benjamin with reference to Sorel's distinction between political strike and proletarian strike: while the political strike aims at obtaining concrete reforms that change a system of power and thereby constitute a new power, the proletarian strike aims at the destruction of power as such, of the very form of power, and in this sense it does not have any particular objective.[4]

These remarks allow us to throw some light on the divergent courses of action that current struggles in defence of multiculturalism can follow. One possible way is to affirm, purely and simply, the right of the various cultural and ethnic groups to assert their differences and their separate development. This is the route to self-apartheid, and it is sometimes accompanied by the claim that Western cultural values and institutions are the preserve of white, male Europeans or Anglo-Americans and have nothing to do with the identity of other groups living in the same territory. What is advocated in this way is total segregationism, the mere opposition of one particularism to another. Now, it is true that the assertion of any particular identity involves, as one of its dimensions, the affirmation of the right to a separate existence. But it is here that the difficult questions start, because the separation – or better, the right to difference – has to be asserted within the global community – that is within a space in which that particular group has to coexist with other groups. Now, how could that coexistence be possible without some shared universal values, without a sense of belonging to a community larger than each of the particular groups in question? Here people sometimes say that any agreement should be reached through *negotiation*. Negotiation, however, is an ambiguous term that can mean very different things. One of these is a process of mutual pressures and concessions whose outcome depends only on the balance of power between antagonistic groups. It is obvious that no sense of community can be constructed through

that type of negotiation. The relation between groups can only be one of potential war. *Vis pacis para bellum.* This is not far away from the conception of the nature of the agreement between groups implicit in the Leninist conception of class alliances: the agreement concerns only circumstantial matters, but the identity of the forces entering it remains uncontaminated by the process of negotiation. Translated into the cultural field, this affirmation of an extreme separatism led to the sharp distinction between bourgeois science and proletarian science. Gramsci was well aware that, in spite of the extreme diversity of the social forces that had to enter into the construction of a hegemonic identity, no collective will and no sense of community could result from such a conception of negotiation and alliances.

The dilemma of the defenders of extreme particularism is that their political action is anchored in a perpetual incoherence. On the one hand, they defend the right to difference as a universal right, and this defence involves their engagement in struggles for changes in legislation, for the protection of minorities in courts, against the violation of civil rights, and so forth. That is they are engaged in a struggle for the internal reform of the present institutional setting. But on the other hand, as they simultaneously assert both that this setting is necessarily rooted in the cultural and political values of the traditional dominant sectors of the West *and that they have nothing to do with that tradition*, their demands cannot be articulated into any wider hegemonic operation to reform the system. This condemns them to an ambiguous peripheral relation with the existing institutions, which can have only paralyzing political effects.

This is not, however, the only possible course of action for those engaged in particularistic struggles – and this is our second conclusion. As we have seen before, a system of oppression (that is of closure) can be combated in two different ways – either by an operation of inversion which performs a new closure, or by negating in that system its universal dimension: the principle of closure as such. It is one thing to say that the universalistic values of the West are the preserve of its traditional dominant groups; it is very different to assert that the historical link between the two is a contingent and unacceptable fact which can be modified through political and social struggles. When Mary Wollstonecraft, in the wake of the French Revolution, defended the rights of women, she did not present the exclusion of women from the declaration of the rights of man and citizen as a proof that the latter are intrinsically male rights, but tried, on the contrary, to deepen the democratic revolution by showing the incoherence of establishing universal rights which were restricted to particular sectors of the population. The democratic process in present-day societies can be considerably deepened and expanded if it is made accountable to the demands of large sections of the population – minorities, ethnic groups and so on – who traditionally have been excluded from it. Liberal democratic theory and institutions have in this sense to be deconstructed. As they were originally thought for societies which were far more homogeneous than the present ones, they were based on all kinds of unexpressed assumptions which no longer obtain in the present situation. Present-day social and political struggles can bring to the fore this game of decisions taken in an undecidable terrain, and help us to move in the direction of new democratic practices and a new democratic theory which is fully adapted to the present circumstances. That political participation can lead to political and social integration is certainly true, but for the reasons we gave before, political and cultural segregation can lead to exactly the same result. Anyway, the decline of the integrationist abilities of the Western states make political conformism a rather unlikely outcome. I would argue that the unresolved tension between universalism and particularism opens the way to a movement away from Western Eurocentrism, through the operation that we could call a systematic decentring of the West. As we have seen, Eurocentrism was the result of a discourse which did not differentiate between the universal values that the West was advocating and the concrete social agents that were incarnating them. Now, however, we can proceed to a separation of these two aspects. If social struggles of new social actors show that the concrete practices of our society restrict the universalism of our political ideals to limited sectors of the population, it becomes possible to retain the universal dimension while widening the spheres of its application – which, in turn, will define the concrete contents of such universality. Through this process, universalism as a horizon is expanded at the same time as its necessary attachment to any particular content is broken. The opposite policy – that of rejecting universalism *in toto* as the particular content of the ethnia of the West – can only lead to a political blind alley.

This leaves us, however, with an apparent paradox – and its analysis will be my last conclusion. The universal, as we have seen, does not have a concrete content of its own (which would close it on itself), but is an always receding horizon resulting from the expansion of an indefinite chain of equivalent demands. The conclusion seems to be that universality is incommensurable with any particularity but cannot, however, exist apart from the particular. In terms of our previous analysis: if only particular actors, or constellations of particular actors can actualize the universal at any moment, in that case, the possibility of making visible the nonclosure inherent to a post-dominated society – that is a society that attempts to transcend the very form of domination – depends on making the asymmetry between the universal and the particular permanent. The universal is incommensurable with the particular, but cannot, however, exist without the latter. How is this relation possible? My answer is that this paradox cannot be solved, but that its non-solution is the very precondition of democracy. The solution of the paradox would imply that a particular body had been found, which would be the *true* body of the universal. But in that case, the universal would have found its necessary location, and democracy would be impossible. If democracy is possible, it is because the universal has no necessary body and no necessary content; different groups, instead, compete between themselves to temporarily give to their particularisms a function of universal representation. Society generates a whole vocabulary of empty signifiers whose temporary signifieds are the result of a political competition. It is this final failure of society to constitute itself as society – which is the same thing as the failure of constituting difference as difference – which makes the distance between the universal and the particular unbridgeable and, as a result, burdens concrete social agents with the impossible task of making democratic interaction achievable.

Notes

1. Gilles Deleuze, *Différence et Répétition*, Paris, Presses Universitaires de France 1989, p. 2.
2. It is at this point that, in my recent work, I have tried to complement the idea of radical antagonism – which still involves the possibility of a radical representability – with the notion of dislocation which is previous to any kind of antagonistic representation. Some of the dimensions of this duality have been explored by

Bobby Sayyid and Lilian Zac in a short, written presentation to a Ph.D. seminar on Ideology and Discourse Analysis, University of Essex, December 1990.

3. Aletta J. Norval, "Letter to Ernesto", in Ernesto Laclau, *New Reflections on the Revolution of our Time*, London, Verso 1990, p. 157.

4. Cf. Walter Benjamin, "Zur Kritik der Gewalt", in R. Tiedemann and H. Schweppenhauser (eds.), *Gesemmelte Schriften*, 179, 1977. See a commentary on Benjamin's text in Werner Hamacher, "Afformative, Strike", *Cardozo Law Review*, vol. 13, no. 4, December 1991.

33

A Manifesto for Cyborgs: Science, Technology, and Socialist Feminism in the 1980s

Donna Haraway

An Ironic Dream of a Common Language for Women in the Integrated Circuit

This essay is an effort to build an ironic political myth faithful to feminism, socialism, and material- ism. Perhaps more faithful as blasphemy is faith- ful, than as reverent worship and identification. Blasphemy has always seemed to require taking things very seriously. I know no better stance to adopt from within the secular-religious, evangel- ical traditions of United States politics, including the politics of socialist-feminism. Blasphemy pro- tects one from the moral majority within, while still insisting on the need for community. Blasphemy is not apostasy. Irony is about contradictions that do not resolve into larger wholes, even dialectically, about the tension of holding incompatible things together because both or all are necessary and true. Irony is about humor and serious play. It is also a rhetorical strategy and a political method, one I would like to see more honored within socialist feminism. At the center of my ironic faith, my blasphemy, is the image of the cyborg.

A cyborg is a cybernetic organism, a hybrid of machine and organism, a creature of social reality as well as a creature of fiction. Social reality is lived social relations, our most important political construction, a world-changing fiction. The inter- national women's movements have constructed

"women's experience," as well as uncovered or dis- covered this crucial collective object. This experi- ence is a fiction and fact of the most crucial, political kind. Liberation rests on the construction of the consciousness, the imaginative apprehension, of oppression, and so of possibility. The cyborg is a matter of fiction and lived experience that changes what counts as women's experience in the late twentieth century. This is a struggle over life and death, but the boundary between science fiction and social reality is an optical illusion.

Contemporary science fiction is full of cyborgs – creatures simultaneously animal and machine, who populate worlds ambiguously natural and crafted. Modern medicine is also full of cyborgs, of coup- lings between organism and machine, each con- ceived as coded devices, in an intimacy and with a power that was not generated in the history of sexuality. Cyborg "sex" restores some of the lovely replicative baroque of ferns and invertebrates (such nice organic prophylactics against heterosexism). Cyborg replication is uncoupled from organic repro- duction. Modern production seems like a dream of cyborg colonization of work, a dream that makes the nightmare of Taylorism seem idyllic. And modern war is a cyborg orgy, coded by c^3I, command- control-communication-intelligence, an $84 billion item in 1984's US defense budget. I am making an argument for the cyborg as a fiction mapping our social and bodily reality and as an imaginative resource suggesting some very fruitful couplings. Foucault's biopolitics is a flaccid premonition of cyborg politics, a very open field.

By the late twentieth century, our time, a mythic time, we are all chimeras, theorized and fabricated hybrids of machine and organism; in short, we are cyborgs. The cyborg is our ontology; it gives us our politics. The cyborg is a condensed image of both imagination and material reality, the two joined centers structuring any possibility of historical transformation. In the traditions of "Western" science and politics – the tradition of racist, male-dominant capitalism; the tradition of progress; the tradition of the appropriation of nature as resource for the productions of culture; the tradition of reproduction of the self from the reflections of the other – the relation between organism and machine has been a border war. The stakes in the border war have been the territories of production, reproduction, and imagination. This essay is an argument for *pleasure* in the confusion of boundaries and for *responsibility* in their construction. It is also an effort to contribute to socialist-feminist culture and theory in a post-modernist, non-naturalist mode and in the utopian tradition of imagining a world without gender, which is perhaps a world without genesis, but maybe also a world without end. The cyborg incarnation is outside salvation history.

The cyborg is a creature in a post-gender world; it has no truck with bisexuality, pre-Oedipal symbiosis, unalienated labor, or other seductions to organic wholeness through a final appropriation of all the powers of the parts into a higher unity. In a sense, the cyborg has no origin story in the Western sense; a "final" irony since the cyborg is also the awful apocalyptic *telos* of the "West's" escalating dominations of abstract individuation, an ultimate self untied at last from all dependency, a man in space. An origin story in the "Western," humanist sense depends on the myth of original unity, fullness, bliss and terror, represented by the phallic mother from whom all humans must separate, the task of individual development and of history, the twin potent myths inscribed most powerfully for us in psychoanalysis and Marxism. Hilary Klein has argued that both Marxism and psychoanalysis, in their concepts of labor and of individuation and gender formation, depend on the plot of original unity out of which difference must be produced and enlisted in a drama of escalating domination of woman/nature. The cyborg skips the step of original unity, of identification with nature in the Western sense. This is its illegitimate promise that might lead to subversion of its teleology as star wars.

The cyborg is resolutely committed to partiality, irony, intimacy, and perversity. It is oppositional, utopian, and completely without innocence. No longer structured by the polarity of public and private, the cyborg defines a technological polis based partly on a revolution of social relations in the *oikos*, the household. Nature and culture are reworked; the one can no longer be the resource for appropriation or incorporation by the other. The relationships for forming wholes from parts, including those of polarity and hierarchical domination, are at issue in the cyborg world. Unlike the hopes of Frankenstein's monster, the cyborg does not expect its father to save it through a restoration of the garden; i.e., through the fabrication of a heterosexual mate, through its completion in a finished whole, a city and cosmos. The cyborg does not dream of community on the model of the organic family, this time without the Oedipal project. The cyborg would not recognize the Garden of Eden; it is not made of mud and cannot dream of returning to dust. Perhaps that is why I want to see if cyborgs can subvert the apocalypse of returning to nuclear dust in the manic compulsion to name the Enemy. Cyborgs are not reverent; they do not re-member the cosmos. They are wary of holism, but needy for connection – they seem to have a natural feel for united front politics, but without the vanguard party. The main trouble with cyborgs, of course, is that they are the illegitimate offspring of militarism and patriarchal capitalism, not to mention state socialism. But illegitimate offspring are often exceedingly unfaithful to their origins. Their fathers, after all, are inessential.

I will return to the science fiction of cyborgs at the end of this essay, but now I want to signal three crucial boundary breakdowns that make the following political fictional (political scientific) analysis possible. By the late twentieth century in United States scientific culture, the boundary between human and animal is thoroughly breached. The last beachheads of uniqueness have been polluted if not turned into amusement parks – language, tool use, social behavior, mental events, nothing really convincingly settles the separation of human and animal. And many people no longer feel the need of such a separation; indeed, many branches of feminist culture affirm the pleasure of connection of human and other living creatures. Movements for animal rights are not irrational denials of human uniqueness; they are clear-sighted recognition of connection across the discredited breach of nature and culture. Biology and evolutionary theory over the last two centuries have simultaneously produced modern organisms as objects of knowledge and reduced the line between humans and animals to a faint trace re-etched in ideological struggle or professional disputes between life and social sciences. Within this framework, teaching modern Christian creationism should be fought as a form of child abuse.

Biological-determinist ideology is only one position opened up in scientific culture for arguing the meanings of human animality. There is much room for radical political people to contest for the meanings of the breached boundary.[1] The cyborg appears in myth precisely where the boundary between human and animal is transgressed. Far from signaling a walling off of people from other living beings, cyborgs signal disturbingly and pleasurably tight coupling. Bestiality has a new status in this cycle of marriage exchange.

The second leaky distinction is between animal-human (organism) and machine. Pre-cybernetic machines could be haunted; there was always the specter of the ghost in the machine. This dualism structured the dialogue between materialism and idealism that was settled by a dialectical progeny, called spirit or history, according to taste. But basically machines were not self-moving, self-designing, autonomous. They could not achieve man's dream, only mock it. They were not man, an author to himself, but only a caricature of that masculinist reproductive dream. To think they were otherwise was paranoid. Now we are not so sure. Late-twentieth-century machines have made thoroughly ambiguous the difference between natural and artificial, mind and body, self-developing and externally-designed, and many other distinctions that used to apply to organisms and machines. Our machines are disturbingly lively, and we ourselves frighteningly inert.

Technological determinism is only one ideological space opened up by the reconceptions of machine and organism as coded texts through which we engage in the play of writing and reading the world.[2] "Textualization" of everything in post-structuralist, post-modernist theory has been damned by Marxists and socialist feminists for its utopian disregard for lived relations of domination that ground the "play" of arbitrary reading.[3] It is certainly true that post-modernist strategies, like my

cyborg myth, subvert myriad organic wholes (e.g., the poem, the primitive culture, the biological organism). In short, the certainty of what counts as nature – a source of insight and a promise of innocence – is undermined, probably fatally. The transcendent authorization of interpretation is lost, and with it the ontology grounding "Western" epistemology. But the alternative is not cynicism or faithlessness, i.e., some version of abstract existence, like the accounts of technological determinism destroying "man" by the "machine" or "meaningful political action" by the "text." Who cyborgs will be is a radical question; the answers are a matter of survival. Both chimpanzees and artifacts have politics, so why shouldn't we?[4]

The third distinction is a subset of the second: the boundary between physical and non-physical is very imprecise for us. Pop physics books on the consequences of quantum theory and the indeterminacy principle are a kind of popular scientific equivalent to the Harlequin romances as a marker of radical change in American white heterosexuality: they get it wrong, but they are on the right subject. Modern machines are quintessentially microelectronic devices: they are everywhere and they are invisible. Modern machinery is an irreverant upstart god, mocking the Father's ubiquity and spirituality. The silicon chip is a surface for writing; it is etched in molecular scales disturbed only by atomic noise, the ultimate interference for nuclear scores. Writing, power, and technology are old partners in Western stories of the origin of civilization, but miniaturization has changed our experience of mechanism. Miniaturization has turned out to be about power; small is not so much beautiful as pre-eminently dangerous, as in cruise missiles. Contrast the TV sets of the 1950s or the news cameras of the 1970s with the TV wrist bands or hand-sized video cameras now advertised. Our best machines are made of sunshine; they are all light and clean because they are nothing but signals, electromagnetic waves, a section of a spectrum. And these machines are eminently portable, mobile – a matter of immense human pain in Detroit and Singapore. People are nowhere near so fluid, being both material and opaque. Cyborgs are ether, quintessence.

The ubiquity and invisibility of cyborgs is precisely why these sunshine-belt machines are so deadly. They are as hard to see politically as materially. They are about consciousness – or its simulation.[5] They are floating signifiers moving in pickup trucks across Europe, blocked more effectively by the witch-weavings of the displaced and so unnatural Greenham women, who read the cyborg webs of power very well, than by the militant labor of older masculinist politics, whose natural constituency needs defense jobs. Ultimately the "hardest" science is about the realm of greatest boundary confusion, the realm of pure number, pure spirit, C^3I, cryptography, and the preservation of potent secrets. The new machines are so clean and light. Their engineers are sun-worshipers mediating a new scientific revolution associated with the night dream of post-industrial society. The diseases evoked by these clean machines are "no more" than the miniscule coding changes of an antigen in the immune system, "no more" than the experience of stress. The nimble little fingers of "Oriental" women, the old fascination of little Anglo-Saxon Victorian girls with doll houses, women's enforced attention to the small take on quite new dimensions in this world. There might be a cyborg Alice taking account of these new dimensions. Ironically, it might be the un-natural cyborg women making chips in Asia and spiral dancing in Santa Rita whose constructed unities will guide effective oppositional strategies.

So my cyborg myth is about transgressed boundaries, potent fusions, and dangerous possibilities which progressive people might explore as one part of needed political work. One of my premises is that most American socialists and feminists see deepened dualisms of mind and body, animal and machine, idealism and materialism in the social practices, symbolic formulations, and physical artifacts associated with "high technology" and scientific culture. From *One-Dimensional Man* to *The Death of Nature*,[6] the analytic resources developed by progressives have insisted on the necessary domination of technics and recalled us to an imagined organic body to integrate our resistance. Another of my premises is that the need for unity of people trying to resist worldwide intensification of domination has never been more acute. But a slightly perverse shift of perspective might better enable us to contest for meanings, as well as for other forms of power and pleasure in technologically-mediated societies.

From one perspective, a cyborg world is about the final imposition of a grid of control on the planet, about the final abstraction embodied in a Star War apocalypse waged in the name of defense, about the final appropriation of women's bodies in a masculinist orgy of war.[7] From another perspective, a cyborg world might be about lived social and bodily realities in which people are not afraid of their joint kinship with animals and machines, not afraid of permanently partial identities and contradictory standpoints. The political struggle is to see from both perspectives at once because each reveals both dominations and possibilities unimaginable from the other vantage point. Single vision produces worse illusions than double vision or many-headed monsters. Cyborg unities are monstrous and illegitimate; in our present political circumstances, we could hardly hope for more potent myths for resistance and recoupling. I like to imagine LAG, the Livermore Action Group, as a kind of cyborg society, dedicated to realistically converting the laboratories that most fiercely embody and spew out the tools of technological apocalypse, and committed to building a political form that actually manages to hold together witches, engineers, elders, perverts, Christians, mothers, and Leninists long enough to disarm the state. Fission Impossible is the name of the affinity group in my town. (Affinity: related not by blood but by choice, the appeal of one chemical nuclear group for another, avidity.)

Fractured Identities

It has become difficult to name one's feminism by a single adjective – or even to insist in every circumstance upon the noun. Consciousness of exclusion through naming is acute. Identities seem contradictory, partial, and strategic. With the hard-won recognition of their social and historical constitution, gender, race, and class cannot provide the basis for belief in "essential" unity. There is nothing about being "female" that naturally binds women. There is not even such a state as "being" female, itself a highly complex category constructed in contested sexual scientific discourses and other social practices. Gender, race, or class consciousness is an achievement forced on us by the terrible historical experience of the contradictory social realities of patriarchy, colonialism, and capitalism. And who counts as "us" in my own rhetoric? Which identities are available to ground such a potent political myth called "us," and what could motivate enlistment in this collectivity? Painful fragmentation among feminists (not to mention among women) along every possible fault line has made the concept of *woman* elusive, an excuse for the matrix of women's dominations of each other. For me – and for many who share a similar historical location in white, professional middle class, female, radical, North American, mid-adult bodies – the sources of a crisis in political identity are legion. The recent history for much of the US left and US feminism has been a response to this kind of crisis by endless splitting and searches for a new essential unity. But there has also been a growing recognition of another response through coalition – affinity, not identity.[8]

Chela Sandoval, from a consideration of specific historical moments in the formation of the new political voice called women of color, has theorized a hopeful model of political identity called "oppositional consciousness," born of the skills for reading webs of power by those refused stable membership in the social categories of race, sex, or class.[9] "Women of color," a name contested at its origins by those whom it would incorporate, as well as a historical consciousness marking systematic breakdown of all the signs of Man in "Western" traditions, constructs a kind of post-modernist identity out of otherness and difference. This post-modernist identity is fully political, whatever might be said about other possible post-modernisms.

Sandoval emphasizes the lack of any essential criterion for identifying who is a woman of color. She notes that the definition of the group has been by conscious appropriation of negation. For example, a Chicana or US black woman has not been able to speak as a woman or as a black person or as a Chicano. Thus, she was at the bottom of a cascade of negative identities, left out of even the privileged oppressed authorial categories called "women and blacks," who claimed to make the important revolutions. The category "woman" negated all non-white women; "black" negated all non-black people, as well as all black women. But there was also no "she," no singularity, but a sea of differences among US women who have affirmed their historical identity as US women of color. This identity marks out a self-consciously constructed space that cannot affirm the capacity to act on the basis of natural identification, but only on the basis of conscious coalition, of affinity, of political kinship.[10] Unlike the "woman" of some streams of the white women's movement in the United States, there is no naturalization of the matrix, or at least this is what Sandoval argues is uniquely available through the power of oppositional consciousness.

Sandoval's argument has to be seen as one potent formulation for feminists out of the worldwide development of anti-colonialist discourse, i.e., discourse dissolving the "West" and its highest product – the one who is not animal, barbarian, or woman; i.e., man, the author of a cosmos called history. As orientalism is deconstructed politically and semiotically, the identities of the occident destabilize, including those of feminists.[11] Sandoval argues that "women of color" have a chance to build an effective unity that does not replicate the imperializing, totalizing revolutionary subjects of previous Marxisms and feminisms which had not faced the consequences of the disorderly polyphony emerging from decolonization.

Katie King has emphasized the limits of identification and the political/poetic mechanics of identification built into reading "the poem," that generative core of cultural feminism. King criticizes the persistent tendency among contemporary feminists from different "moments" or "conversations" in feminist practice to taxonomize the women's movement to make one's own political tendencies appear to be the *telos* of the whole. These taxonomies tend to remake feminist history to appear to be an ideological struggle among coherent types persisting over time, especially those typical units called radical, liberal, and socialist feminism. Literally, all other feminisms are either incorporated or marginalized, usually by building an explicit ontology and epistemology.[12] Taxonomies of feminism produce epistemologies to police deviation from official women's experience. And of course, "women's culture," like women of color, is consciously created by mechanisms inducing affinity. The rituals of poetry, music, and certain forms of academic practice have been pre-eminent. The politics of race and culture in the US women's movements are intimately interwoven. The common achievement of King and Sandoval is learning how to craft a poetic/political unity without relying on a logic of appropriation, incorporation, and taxonomic identification.

The theoretical and practical struggle against unity-through-domination or unity-through-incorporation ironically not only undermines the justifications for patriarchy, colonialism, humanism, positivism, essentialism, scientism, and other unlamented -isms, but *all* claims for an organic or natural standpoint. I think that radical and socialist/Marxist feminisms have also undermined their/our own epistemological strategies and that this is a crucially valuable step in imagining possible unities. It remains to be seen whether all "epistemologies" as Western political people have known them fail us in the task to build effective affinities.

It is important to note that the effort to construct revolutionary standpoints, epistemologies as achievements of people committed to changing the world, has been part of the process showing the limits of identification. The acid tools of post-modernist theory and the constructive tools of ontological discourse about revolutionary subjects might be seen as ironic allies in dissolving Western selves in the interests of survival. We are excruciatingly conscious of what it means to have a historically constituted body. But with the loss of innocence in our origin, there is no expulsion from the Garden either. Our politics lose the indulgence of guilt with the naïveté of innocence. But what would another political myth for socialist feminism look like? What kind of politics could embrace partial, contradictory, permanently unclosed constructions of personal and collective selves and still be faithful, effective – and, ironically, socialist feminist?

I do not know of any other time in history when there was greater need for political unity to confront effectively the dominations of "race," "gender," "sexuality," and "class." I also do not know of any other time when the kind of unity we might help build could have been possible. None of "us" have any longer the symbolic or material capability of dictating the shape of reality to any of "them." Or at least "we" cannot claim innocence from practicing such dominations. White women, including socialist feminists, discovered (i.e., were forced kicking and screaming to notice) the non-innocence of the category "woman." That consciousness changes the geography of all previous categories; it denatures them as heat denatures a fragile protein. Cyborg feminists have to argue that "we" do not want any more natural matrix of unity and that no construction is whole. Innocence, and the corollary insistence on victimhood as the only ground for insight, has done enough damage. But the constructed revolutionary subject must give late-twentieth-century people pause as well. In the fraying of identities and in the reflexive strategies for constructing them, the possibility opens up for weaving something other than a shroud for the day after the apocalypse that so prophetically ends salvation history.

Both Marxist/socialist feminisms and radical feminisms have simultaneously naturalized and denatured the category "woman" and consciousness of the social lives of "women." Perhaps a schematic caricature can highlight both kinds of moves. Marxian socialism is rooted in an analysis of wage labor which reveals class structure. The consequence of the wage relationship is systematic alienation, as the worker is dissociated from his (*sic*) product. Abstraction and illusion rule in knowledge, domination rules in practice. Labor is the pre-eminently privileged category enabling the Marxist to overcome illusion and find that point of view which is necessary for changing the world. Labor is the humanizing activity that makes man; labor is an ontological category permitting the knowledge of a subject, and so the knowledge of subjugation and alienation.

In faithful filiation, socialist feminism advanced by allying itself with the basic analytic strategies of Marxism. The main achievement of both Marxist feminists and socialist feminists was to expand the category of labor to accommodate what (some) women did, even when the wage relation was subordinated to a more comprehensive view of labor under capitalist patriarchy. In particular, women's labor in the household and women's activity as mothers generally, i.e., reproduction in the socialist feminist sense, entered theory on the authority of analogy to the Marxian concept of labor. The unity of women here rests on an epistemology based on the ontological structure of "labor." Marxist/socialist feminism does not "naturalize" unity; it is a possible achievement based on a possible standpoint rooted in social relations. The essentializing move is in the ontological structure of labor or of its analogue, women's activity.[13] The inheritance of Marxian humanism, with its pre-eminently Western self, is the difficulty for me. The contribution from these formulations has been the emphasis on the daily responsibility of real women to build unities, rather than to naturalize them.

Catharine MacKinnon's version of radical feminism is itself a caricature of the appropriating, incorporating, totalizing tendencies of Western theories of identity grounding action.[14] It is factually and politically wrong to assimilate all of the diverse "moments" or "conversations" in recent women's politics named radical feminism to MacKinnon's version. But the teleological logic of her theory shows how an epistemology and ontology – including their negations – erase or police difference. Only one of the effects of MacKinnon's theory is the rewriting of the history of the polymorphous field called radical feminism. The major effect is the production of a theory of experience, of women's identity, that is a kind of apocalypse for all revolutionary standpoints. That is, the totalization built into this tale of radical feminism achieves its end – the unity of women – by enforcing the experience of and testimony to radical non-being. As for the Marxist/socialist feminist, consciousness is an achievement, not a natural fact. And MacKinnon's theory eliminates some of the difficulties built into humanist revolutionary subjects, but at the cost of radical reductionism.

MacKinnon argues that radical feminism necessarily adopted a different analytical strategy from Marxism, looking first not at the structure of class, but at the structure of sex/gender and its generative relationship, men's constitution and appropriation of women sexually. Ironically, MacKinnon's "ontology" constructs a non-subject, a non-being. Another's desire, not the self's labor, is the origin of "woman." She therefore develops a theory of consciousness that enforces what can count as "women's" experience – anything that names sexual violation, indeed, sex itself as far as "women" can be concerned. Feminist practice is the construction of this form of consciousness; i.e., the self-knowledge of a self-who-is-not.

Perversely, sexual appropriation in this radical feminism still has the epistemological status of labor, i.e., the point from which analysis able to contribute to changing the world must flow. But sexual objectification, not alienation, is the consequence of the structure of sex/gender. In the realm of knowledge, the result of sexual objectification is illusion and abstraction. However, a woman is not simply alienated from her product, but in a deep sense does not exist as a subject, or even potential subject, since she owes her existence as a woman to sexual appropriation. To be constituted by another's desire is not the same thing as to be alienated in the violent separation of the laborer from his product.

MacKinnon's radical theory of experience is totalizing in the extreme; it does not so much marginalize as obliterate the authority of any other women's political speech and action. It is a totalization producing what Western patriarchy itself never succeeded in doing – feminists' consciousness of the non-existence of women, except as products of men's desire. I think MacKinnon correctly argues that no Marxian version of identity can firmly ground women's unity. But in solving the problem of the contradictions of any Western revolutionary subject for feminist purposes, she develops an even more authoritarian doctrine of experience. If my complaint about socialist/Marxian standpoints is their unintended erasure of polyvocal, unassimilable, radical difference made visible in anti-colonial discourse and practice, MacKinnon's intentional erasure of all difference through the device of the "essential" non-existence of women is not reassuring.

In my taxonomy, which like any other taxonomy is a reinscription of history, radical feminism can accommodate all the activities of women named by socialist feminists as forms of labor only if the activity can somehow be sexualized. Reproduction

had different tones of meanings for the two tendencies, one rooted in labor, one in sex, both calling the consequences of domination and ignorance of social and personal reality "false consciousness."

Beyond either the difficulties or the contributions in the argument of any one author, neither Marxist nor radical feminist points of view have tended to embrace the status of a partial explanation; both were regularly constituted as totalities. Western explanation has demanded as much; how else could the "Western" author incorporate its others? Each tried to annex other forms of domination by expanding its basic categories through analogy, simple listing, or addition. Embarrassed silence about race among white radical and socialist feminists was one major, devastating political consequence. History and polyvocality disappear into political taxonomies that try to establish genealogies. There was no structural room for race (or for much else) in theory claiming to reveal the construction of the category woman and social group women as a unified or totalizable whole. The structure of my caricature looks like this:

Socialist Feminism –
    structure of class//wage labor//alienation
    labor, by analogy reproduction, by extension
      sex, by addition race
Radical Feminism —
    structure of gender//sexual appropriation//
      objectification
    sex, by analogy labor, by extension reproduction, by addition race

In another context, the French theorist Julia Kristeva claimed women appeared as a historical group after World War II, along with groups like youth. Her dates are doubtful; but we are now accustomed to remembering that as objects of knowledge and as historical actors, "race" did not always exist, "class" has a historical genesis, and "homosexuals" are quite junior. It is no accident that the symbolic system of the family of man – and so the essence of woman – breaks up at the same moment that networks of connection among people on the planet are unprecedentedly multiple, pregnant, and complex. "Advanced capitalism" is inadequate to convey the structure of this historical moment. In the "Western" sense, the end of man is at stake. It is no accident that woman disintegrates into women in our time. Perhaps socialist feminists were not substantially guilty of producing essentialist theory that suppressed women's particularity and contradictory interests. I think we have been, at least through unreflective participation in the logics, languages, and practices of white humanism and through searching for a single ground of domination to secure our revolutionary voice. Now we have less excuse. But in the consciousness of our failures, we risk lapsing into boundless difference and giving up on the confusing task of making partial, real connection. Some differences are playful; some are poles of world historical systems of domination. "Epistemology" is about knowing the difference.

The Informatics of Domination

In this attempt at an epistemological and political position, I would like to sketch a picture of possible unity, a picture indebted to socialist and feminist principles of design. The frame for my sketch is set by the extent and importance of rearrangements in worldwide social relations tied to science and technology. I argue for a politics rooted in claims about fundamental changes in the nature of class, race, and gender in an emerging system of world order analogous in its novelty and scope to that created by industrial capitalism; we are living through a movement from an organic, industrial society to a polymorphous, information system – from all work to all play, a deadly game. Simultaneously material and ideological, the dichotomies may be expressed in the following chart of transitions from the comfortable old hierarchical dominations to the scary new networks I have called the informatics of domination:

Representation	Simulation
Bourgeois novel, realism	Science fiction, post-modernism
Organism	Biotic component
Depth, integrity	Surface, boundary
Heat	Noise
Biology as clinical practice	Biology as inscription
Physiology	Communications engineering
Small group	Subsystem
Perfection	Optimization
Eugenics	Population control
Decadence, *Magic Mountain*	Obsolescence, *Future Shock*
Hygiene	Stress Management
Microbiology, tuberculosis	Immunology, AIDS
Organic division of labor	Ergonomics/cybernetics of labor
Functional specialization	Modular construction
Reproduction	Replication
Organic sex role specialization	Optimal genetic strategies
Biological determinism	Evolutionary inertia, constraints
Community ecology	Ecosystem
Racial chain of being	Neo-imperialism, United Nations humanism
Scientific management in home/factory	Global factory/Electronic cottage
Family/Market/Factory	Women in the Integrated Circuit
Family wage	Comparable worth
Public/Private	Cyborg citizenship
Nature/Culture	Fields of difference
Cooperation	Communications enhancement
Freud	Lacan
Sex	Genetic engineering
Labor	Robotics
Mind	Artificial Intelligence
World War II	Star Wars
White Capitalist Patriarchy	Informatics of Domination

A Manifesto for Cyborgs

This list suggests several interesting things.[15] First, the objects on the right-hand side cannot be coded as "natural," a realization that subverts naturalistic coding for the left-hand side as well. We cannot go back ideologically or materially. It's not just that "god" is dead; so is the "goddess." In relation to objects like biotic components, one must think not in terms of essential properties, but in terms of strategies of design, boundary constraints, rates of flows, systems logics, costs of lowering constraints. Sexual reproduction is one kind of reproductive strategy among many, with costs and benefits as a function of the system environment. Ideologies of sexual reproduction can no longer reasonably call on the notions of sex and sex role as organic aspects in natural objects like organisms and families. Such reasoning will be unmasked as irrational, and ironically corporate executives reading *Playboy* and antiporn radical feminists will make strange bedfellows in jointly unmasking the irrationalism.

Likewise for race, ideologies about human diversity have to be formulated in terms of frequencies of parameters, like blood groups or intelligence scores. It is "irrational" to invoke concepts like primitive and civilized. For liberals and radicals, the search for integrated social systems gives way to a new practice called "experimental ethnography" in which an organic object dissipates in attention to the play of writing. At the level of ideology, we see translations of racism and colonialism into languages of development and underdevelopment, rates and constraints of modernization. Any objects or persons can be reasonably thought of in terms of disassembly and reassembly; no "natural" architectures constrain system design. The financial districts in all the world's cities, as well as the export-processing and free-trade zones, proclaim this elementary fact of "late capitalism." The entire universe of objects that can be known scientifically must be formulated as problems in communications engineering (for the managers) or theories of the text (for those who would resist). Both are cyborg semiologies.

One should expect control strategies to concentrate on boundary conditions and interfaces, on rates of flow across boundaries – and not on the integrity of natural objects. "Integrity" or "sincerity" of the Western self gives way to decision procedures and expert systems. For example, control strategies applied to women's capacities to give birth to new human beings will be developed in the languages of population control and maximization of goal achievement for individual decision-makers.

Control strategies will be formulated in terms of rates, costs of constraints, degrees of freedom. Human beings, like any other component or subsystem, must be localized in a system architecture whose basic modes of operation are probabilistic, statistical. No objects, spaces, or bodies are sacred in themselves; any component can be interfaced with any other if the proper standard, the proper code, can be constructed for processing signals in a common language. Exchange in this world transcends the universal translation effected by capitalist markets that Marx analyzed so well. The privileged pathology affecting all kinds of components in this universe is stress – communications breakdown.[16] The cyborg is not subject to Foucault's biopolitics; the cyborg simulates politics, a much more potent field of operations.

This kind of analysis of scientific and cultural objects of knowledge which have appeared historically since World War II prepares us to notice some important inadequacies in feminist analysis which has proceeded as if the organic, hierarchical dualisms ordering discourse in "the West" since Aristotle still ruled. They have been cannibalized, or as Zoe Sofia (Sofoulis) might put it, they have been "techno-digested." The dichotomies between mind and body, animal and human, organism and machine, public and private, nature and culture, men and women, primitive and civilized are all in question ideologically. The actual situation of women is their integration/exploitation into a world system of production/reproduction and communication called the informatics of domination. The home, workplace, market, public arena, the body itself – all can be dispersed and interfaced in nearly infinite, polymorphous ways, with large consequences for women and others – consequences that themselves are very different for different people and which make potent oppositional international movements difficult to imagine and essential for survival. One important route for reconstructing socialist-feminist politics is through theory and practice addressed to the social relations of science and technology, including crucially the systems of myth and meanings structuring our imaginations. The cyborg is a kind of disassembled and reassembled, post-modern collective and personal self. This is the self feminists must code.

Communications technologies and biotechnologies are the crucial tools recrafting our bodies. These tools embody and enforce new social relations for women worldwide. Technologies and scientific discourses can be partially understood as formalizations, i.e., as frozen moments, of the fluid social interactions constituting them, but they should also be viewed as instruments for enforcing meanings. The boundary is permeable between tool and myth, instrument and concept, historical systems of social relations and historical anatomies of possible bodies, including objects of knowledge. Indeed, myth and tool mutually constitute each other.

Furthermore, communications sciences and modern biologies are constructed by a common move – *the translation of the world into a problem of coding*, a search for a common language in which all resistance to instrumental control disappears and all heterogeneity can be submitted to disassembly, reassembly, investment, and exchange.

In communications sciences, the translation of the world into a problem in coding can be illustrated by looking at cybernetic (feedback controlled) systems theories applied to telephone technology, computer design, weapons deployment, or data base construction and maintenance. In each case, solution to the key questions rests on a theory of language and control; the key operation is determining the rates, directions, and probabilities of flow of a quantity called information. The world is subdivided by boundaries differentially permeable to information. Information is just that kind of quantifiable element (unit, basis of unity) which allows universal translation, and so unhindered instrumental power (called effective communication). The biggest threat to such power is interruption of communication. Any system breakdown is a function of stress. The fundamentals of this technology can be condensed into the metaphor c^3I, command-control-communication-intelligence, the military's symbol for its operations theory.

In modern biologies, the translation of the world into a problem in coding can be illustrated by molecular genetics, ecology, sociobiological evolutionary theory, and immunobiology. The organism has been translated into problems of genetic coding and read-out. Biotechnology, a writing technology, informs research broadly.[17] In a sense, organisms have ceased to exist as objects of knowledge, giving way to biotic components, i.e., special kinds of information processing devices. The analogous moves in ecology could be examined by probing the history and utility of the concept of the ecosystem. Immunobiology and associated medical practices are rich exemplars of the privilege of coding and recognition systems as objects of knowledge, as constructions of bodily reality for us. Biology is here a kind of cryptography. Research is necessarily a kind of intelligence activity. Ironies abound. A stressed system goes awry; its communication processes break down; it fails to recognize the difference between self and other. Human babies with baboon hearts evoke national ethical perplexity – for animal-rights activists at least as much as for guardians of human purity. Gay men, Haitian immigrants, and intravenous drug users are the "privileged" victims of an awful immune-system disease that marks (inscribes on the body) confusion of boundaries and moral pollution.

But these excursions into communications sciences and biology have been at a rarefied level; there is a mundane, largely economic reality to support my claim that these sciences and technologies indicate fundamental transformations in the structure of the world for us. Communications technologies depend on electronics. Modern states, multinational corporations, military power, welfare-state apparatuses, satellite systems, political processes, fabrication of our imaginations, labor-control systems, medical constructions of our bodies, commercial pornography, the international division of labor, and religious evangelism depend intimately upon electronics. Microelectronics is the technical basis of simulacra, i.e., of copies without originals.

Microelectronics mediates the translations of *labor* into robotics and word processing; *sex* into genetic engineering and reproductive technologies; and *mind* into artificial intelligence and decision procedures. The new biotechnologies concern more than human reproduction. Biology as a powerful engineering science for redesigning materials and processes has revolutionary implications for industry, perhaps most obvious today in areas of fermentation, agriculture, and energy. Communications sciences and biology are constructions of natural-technical objects of knowledge in which the difference between machine and organism is thoroughly blurred; mind, body, and tool are on very intimate terms. The "multinational" material organization of the production and reproduction of daily life and the symbolic organization of the production and reproduction of culture and imagination seem equally implicated. The boundary-maintaining images of base and superstructure, public and private, or material and ideal never seemed more feeble.

I have used Rachel Grossman's image of women in the integrated circuit to name the situation of women in a world so intimately restructured through the social relations of science and technology.[18] I use the odd circumlocution, "the social relations of science and technology," to indicate that we are not dealing with a technological determinism, but with a historical system depending upon structured relations among people. But the phrase should also indicate that science and technology provide fresh sources of power, that we need fresh sources of analysis and political action.[19] Some of the rearrangements of race, sex, and class rooted in high-tech-facilitated social relations can make socialist feminism more relevant to effective progressive politics.

The Homework Economy

The "new industrial revolution" is producing a new worldwide working class. The extreme mobility of capital and the emerging international division of labor are intertwined with the emergence of new collectivities, and the weakening of familiar groupings. These developments are neither gender- nor race-neutral. White men in advanced industrial societies have become newly vulnerable to permanent job loss, and women are not disappearing from the job rolls at the same rates as men. It is not simply that women in third-world countries are the preferred labor force for the science-based multinationals in the export-processing sectors, particularly in electronics. The picture is more systematic and involves reproduction, sexuality, culture, consumption, and production. In the prototypical Silicon Valley, many women's lives have been structured around employment in electronics-dependent jobs, and their intimate realities include serial heterosexual monogamy, negotiating childcare, distance from extended kin or most other forms of traditional community, a high likelihood of loneliness and extreme economic vulnerability as they age. The ethnic and racial diversity of women in Silicon Valley structures a microcosm of conflicting differences in culture, family, religion, education, language.

Richard Gordon has called this new situation the homework economy.[20] Although he includes the phenomenon of literal homework emerging in connection with electronics assembly, Gordon intends "homework economy" to name a restructuring of work that broadly has the characteristics formerly ascribed to female jobs, jobs literally done only by women. Work is being redefined as both literally female and feminized, whether performed by men or women. To be feminized means to be made extremely vulnerable; able to be disassembled, reassembled, exploited as a reserve labor force; seen less as workers than as servers; subjected to time arrangements on and off the paid job that make a mockery of a limited work day; leading an existence that always borders on being obscene, out of place, and reducible to sex. Deskilling is an old strategy newly applicable to formerly privileged workers. However, the homework economy does not refer only to large-scale deskilling, nor does it deny that new areas of high skill are emerging, even for women and men previously excluded from skilled employment. Rather, the concept indicates that factory, home, and market are integrated on a new scale and that the places of women are crucial – and need to be analyzed for differences among women and for meanings for relations between men and women in various situations.

The homework economy as a world capitalist organizational structure is made possible by (not caused by) the new technologies. The success of the attack on relatively privileged, mostly white, men's unionized jobs is tied to the power of the new communications technologies to integrate and control labor despite extensive dispersion and decentralization. The consequences of the new technologies are felt by women both in the loss of the family (male) wage (if they ever had access to this white privilege) and in the character of their own jobs, which are becoming capital-intensive, e.g., office work and nursing.

The new economic and technological arrangements are also related to the collapsing welfare state and the ensuing intensification of demands on women to sustain daily life for themselves as well as for men, children, and old people. The feminization of poverty – generated by dismantling the welfare state, by the homework economy where stable jobs become the exception, and sustained by the expectation that women's wage will not be matched by a male income for the support of children – has become an urgent focus. The causes of various women-headed households are a function of race, class, or sexuality; but their increasing generality is a ground for coalitions of women on many issues. That women regularly sustain daily life partly as a function of their enforced status as mothers is hardly new; the kind of integration with the overall capitalist and progressively war-based economy is new. The particular pressure, for example, on US black women, who have achieved an escape from (barely) paid domestic service and who now hold clerical and similar jobs in large numbers, has large implications for continued enforced black poverty *with* employment. Teenage women in industrializing areas of the third world increasingly find themselves the sole or major source of a cash wage for their families, while access to land is ever more problematic. These developments must have major consequences in the psychodynamics and politics of gender and race.

Within the framework of three major stages of capitalism (commercial/early industrial, monopoly, multinational) – tied to nationalism, imperialism, and multinationalism, and related to Jameson's three dominant aesthetic periods of realism, modernism, and post-modernism – I would argue that specific forms of families dialectically relate to forms of capital and to its political and cultural concomitants. Although lived problematically and unequally, ideal forms of these families might be schematized as (1) the patriarchal nuclear family, structured by the dichotomy between public and private and accompanied by the white bourgeois ideology of separate spheres and nineteenth-century Anglo-American bourgeois feminism; (2) the modern family mediated (or enforced) by the welfare state and institutions like the family wage, with a flowering of a-feminist heterosexual ideologies, including their radical versions represented in Greenwich Village around World War I; and (3) the "family" of the homework economy with its oxymoronic structure of women-headed households and its explosion of feminisms and the paradoxical intensification and erosion of gender itself.

This is the context in which the projections for worldwide structural unemployment stemming from the new technologies are part of the picture of the homework economy. As robotics and related technologies put men out of work in "developed" countries and exacerbate failure to generate male jobs in third-world "development," and as the automated office becomes the rule even in labor-surplus countries, the feminization of work intensifies. Black women in the United States have long known what it looks like to face the structural underemployment ("feminization") of black men, as well as their own highly vulnerable position in the wage economy. It is no longer a secret that sexuality, reproduction, family, and community life are interwoven with this economic structure in myriad ways which have also differentiated the situations of white and black women. Many more women and men will contend

with similar situations, which will make cross-gender and race alliances on issues of basic life support (with or without jobs) necessary, not just nice.

The new technologies also have a profound effect on hunger and on food production for subsistence worldwide. Rae Lessor Blumberg estimates that women produce about fifty per cent of the world's subsistence food.[21] Women are excluded generally from benefiting from the increased high-tech commodification of food and energy crops, their days are made more arduous because their responsibilities to provide food do not diminish, and their reproductive situations are made more complex. Green Revolution technologies interact with other high-tech industrial production to alter gender divisions of labor and differential gender migration patterns.

The new technologies seem deeply involved in the forms of "privatization" that Ros Petchesky has analyzed, in which militarization, right-wing family ideologies and policies, and intensified definitions of corporate property as private synergistically interact.[22] The new communications technologies are fundamental to the eradication of "public life" for everyone. This facilitates the mushrooming of a permanent high-tech military establishment at the cultural and economic expense of most people, but especially of women. Technologies like video games and highly miniaturized television seem crucial to production of modern forms of "private life." The culture of video games is heavily oriented to individual competition and extraterrestrial warfare. High-tech, gendered imaginations are produced here, imaginations that can contemplate destruction of the planet and a sci-fi escape from its consequences. More than our imaginations is militarized; and the other realities of electronic and nuclear warfare are inescapable.

The new technologies affect the social relations of both sexuality and of reproduction, and not always in the same ways. The close ties of sexuality and instrumentality, of views of the body as a kind of private satisfaction- and utility-maximizing machine, are described nicely in sociobiological origin stories that stress a genetic calculus and explain the inevitable dialectic of domination of male and female gender roles.[23] These sociobiological stories depend on a high-tech view of the body as a biotic component or cybernetic communications system. Among the many transformations of reproductive situations is the medical one, where women's bodies have boundaries newly permeable to both "visualization" and "intervention." Of course, who controls the interpretation of bodily boundaries in medical hermeneutics is a major feminist issue. The speculum served as an icon of women's claiming their bodies in the 1970s; that hand-craft tool is inadequate to express our needed body politics in the negotiation of reality in the practices of cyborg reproduction. Self-help is not enough. The technologies of visualization recall the important cultural practice of hunting with the camera and the deeply predatory nature of a photographic consciousness.[24] Sex, sexuality, and reproduction are central actors in high-tech myth systems structuring our imaginations of personal and social possibility.

Another critical aspect of the social relations of the new technologies is the reformulation of expectations, culture, work, and reproduction for the large scientific and technical work force. A major social and political danger is the formation of a strongly bimodal social structure, with the masses of women and men of all ethnic groups, but especially people of color, confined to a homework economy, illiteracy of several varieties, and general redundancy and impotence, controlled by high-tech repressive apparatuses ranging from entertainment to surveillance and disappearance. An adequate socialist-feminist politics should address women in the privileged occupational categories, and particularly in the production of science and technology that constructs scientific-technical discourses, processes, and objects.[25]

This issue is only one aspect of inquiry into the possibility of a feminist science, but it is important. What kind of constitutive role in the production of knowledge, imagination, and practice can new groups doing science have? How can these groups be allied with progressive social and political movements? What kind of political accountability can be constructed to tie women together across the scientific-technical hierarchies separating us? Might there be ways of developing feminist science/technology politics in alliance with anti-military science facility conversion action groups? Many scientific and technical workers in Silicon Valley, the high-tech cowboys included, do not want to work on military science.[26] Can these personal preferences and cultural tendencies be welded into progressive politics among this professional middle class in which women, including women of color, are coming to be fairly numerous?

Women in the Integrated Circuit

Let me summarize the picture of women's historical locations in advanced industrial societies, as these positions have been restructured partly through the social relations of science and technology. If it was ever possible ideologically to characterize women's lives by the distinction of public and private domains – suggested by images of the division of working-class life into factory and home, of bourgeois life into market and home, and of gender existence into personal and political realms – it is now a totally misleading ideology, even to show how both terms of these dichotomies construct each other in practice and in theory. I prefer a network ideological image, suggesting the profusion of spaces and identities and the permeability of boundaries in the personal body and in the body politic. "Networking" is both a feminist practice and a multinational corporate strategy – weaving is for oppositional cyborgs.

The only way to characterize the informatics of domination is as a massive intensification of insecurity and cultural impoverishment, with common failure of subsistence networks for the most vulnerable. Since much of this picture interweaves with the social relations of science and technology, the urgency of a socialist-feminist politics addressed to science and technology is plain. There is much now being done, and the grounds for political work are rich. For example, the efforts to develop forms of collective struggle for women in paid work, like SEIU's District 925, should be a high priority for all of us. These efforts are profoundly tied to technical restructuring of labor processes and reformations of working classes. These efforts also are providing understanding of a more comprehensive kind of labor organization, involving community, sexuality, and family issues never privileged in the largely white male industrial unions.

The structural rearrangements related to the social relations of science and technology evoke strong ambivalence. But it is not necessary to be ultimately depressed by the implications of late-twentieth-century women's relation to all aspects of work, culture, production of knowledge, sexuality, and reproduction. For excellent reasons, most Marxisms see domination best and have trouble understanding what can only look like false consciousness and people's complicity in their own domination in late capitalism. It is crucial to remember that what is lost, perhaps especially from women's points of view, is often virulent forms of oppression, nostalgically naturalized in the face of current violation. Ambivalence toward the disrupted unities mediated by high-tech culture requires not sorting consciousness into categories of "clear-sighted critique grounding a solid political epistemology" versus "manipulated false consciousness," but subtle understanding of emerging pleasures, experiences, and powers with serious potential for changing the rules of the game.

There are grounds for hope in the emerging bases for new kinds of unity across race, gender, and class, as these elementary units of socialist-feminist analysis themselves suffer protean transformations. Intensifications of hardship experienced worldwide in connection with the social relations of science and technology are severe. But what people are experiencing is not transparently clear, and we lack sufficiently subtle connections for collectively building effective theories of experience. Present efforts – Marxist, psychoanalytic, feminist, anthropological – to clarify even "our" experience are rudimentary.

I am conscious of the odd perspective provided by my historical position – a Ph.D. in biology for an Irish Catholic girl was made possible by Sputnik's impact on US national science-education policy. I have a body and mind as much constructed by the post-World War II arms race and cold war as by the women's movements. There are more grounds for hope by focusing on the contradictory effects of politics designed to produce loyal American technocrats, which as well produced large numbers of dissidents, rather than by focusing on the present defeats.

The permanent partiality of feminist points of view has consequences for our expectations of forms of political organization and participation. We do not need a totality in order to work well. The feminist dream of a common language, like all dreams for a perfectly true language, of perfectly faithful naming of experience, is a totalizing and imperialist one. In that sense, dialectics too is a dream language, longing to resolve contradiction. Perhaps, ironically, we can learn from our fusions with animals and machines how not to be Man, the embodiment of Western logos. From the point of view of pleasure in these potent and taboo fusions, made inevitable by the social relations of science and technology, there might indeed be a feminist science.

Cyborgs: A Myth of Political Identity

I want to conclude with a myth about identity and boundaries which might inform late-twentieth-century political imaginations. I am indebted in this story to writers like Joanna Russ, Samuel Delaney, John Varley, James Tiptree, Jr., Octavia Butler, Monique Wittig, and Vonda McIntyre.[27] These are our storytellers exploring what it means to be embodied in high-tech worlds. They are theorists for cyborgs. Exploring conceptions of bodily boundaries and social order, the anthropologist Mary Douglas should be credited with helping us to consciousness about how fundamental body imagery is to world view, and so to political language.[28] French feminists like Luce Irigaray and Monique Wittig, for all their differences, know how to write the body, how to weave eroticism, cosmology, and politics from imagery of embodiment, and especially for Wittig, from imagery of fragmentation and reconstitution of bodies.[29]

American radical feminists like Susan Griffin, Audre Lorde, and Adrienne Rich have profoundly affected our political imaginations – and perhaps restricted too much what we allow as a friendly body and political language.[30] They insist on the organic, opposing it to the technological. But their symbolic systems and the related positions of ecofeminism and feminist paganism, replete with organicisms, can only be understood in Sandoval's terms as oppositional ideologies fitting the late twentieth century. They would simply bewilder anyone not preoccupied with the machines and consciousness of late capitalism. In that sense they are part of the cyborg world. But there are also great riches for feminists in explicitly embracing the possibilities inherent in the breakdown of clean distinctions between organism and machine and similar distinctions structuring the Western self. It is the simultaneity of breakdowns that cracks the matrices of domination and opens geometric possibilities. What might be learned from personal and political "technological" pollution? I will look briefly at two overlapping groups of texts for their insight into the construction of a potentially helpful cyborg myth: constructions of women of color and monstrous selves in feminist science fiction.

Earlier I suggested that "women of color" might be understood as a cyborg identity, a potent subjectivity synthesized from fusions of outsider identities. There are material and cultural grids mapping this potential. Audre Lorde captures the tone in the title of her *Sister Outsider*. In my political myth, Sister Outsider is the offshore woman, whom US workers, female and feminized, are supposed to regard as the enemy preventing their solidarity, threatening their security. Onshore, inside the boundary of the United States, Sister Outsider is a potential amidst the races and ethnic identities of women manipulated for division, competition, and exploitation in the same industries. "Women of color" are the preferred labor force for the science-based industries, the real women for whom the worldwide sexual market, labor market, and politics of reproduction kaleidoscope into daily life. Young Korean women hired in the sex industry and in electronics assembly are recruited from high schools, educated for the integrated circuit. Literacy, especially in English, distinguishes the "cheap" female labor so attractive to the multinationals.

Contrary to orientalist stereotypes of the "oral primitive," literacy is a special mark of women of color, acquired by US black women as well as men through a history of risking death to learn and to teach reading and writing. Writing has a special significance for all colonized groups. Writing has been crucial to the Western myth of the distinction of oral and written cultures, primitive and civilized mentalities, and more recently to the erosion of that distinction in "post-modernist" theories attacking the phallogocentrism of the West, with its worship of the monotheistic, phallic, authoritative, and singular word, the unique and perfect name.[31] Contests for the meanings of writing are a major form of contemporary political struggle. Releasing the play of writing is deadly serious. The poetry and stories of US women of color are repeatedly about writing, about access to the power to signify; but this time that power must be neither phallic nor innocent. Cyborg writing must not be about the Fall, the imagination of a once-upon-a-time wholeness before language, before writing, before Man. Cyborg writing is about the power to survive, not on the basis of original innocence, but on the basis of seizing the tools to mark the world that marked them as other.

The tools are often stories, retold stories, versions that reverse and displace the hierarchical dualisms of naturalized identities. In retelling origin stories, cyborg authors subvert the central myths of origin of Western culture. We have all been colonized by those origin myths, with their longing for fulfillment in apocalypse. The phallogocentric origin stories most crucial for feminist cyborgs are built into the literal technologies – technologies that write the world, biotechnology and microelectronics – that have recently textualized our bodies as code problems on the grid of C^3I. Feminist cyborg stories have the task of recoding communication and intelligence to subvert command and control.

Figuratively and literally, language politics pervade the struggles of women of color; and stories about language have a special power in the rich contemporary writing by US women of color. For example, retellings of the story of the indigenous woman Malinche, mother of the mestizo "bastard" race of the new world, master of languages, and mistress of Cortés, carry special meaning for Chicana constructions of identity. Cherrie Moraga in *Loving in the War Years* explores the themes of identity when one never possessed the original language, never told the original story, never resided in the harmony of legitimate heterosexuality in the garden of culture, and so cannot base identity on a myth or a fall from innocence and right to natural names, mother's or father's.[32] Moraga's writing, her superb literacy, is presented in her poetry as the same kind of violation as Malinche's mastery of the conquerer's language – a violation, an illegitimate production, that allows survival. Moraga's language is not "whole"; it is self-consciously spliced, a chimera of English and Spanish, both conqueror's languages. But it is this chimeric monster, without claim to an original language before violation, that crafts the erotic, competent, potent identities of women of color. Sister Outsider hints at the possibility of world survival not because of her innocence, but because of her ability to live on the boundaries, to write without the founding myth of original wholeness, with its inescapable apocalypse of final return to a deathly oneness that Man has imagined to be the innocent and all-powerful Mother, freed at the End from another spiral of appropriation by her son. Writing marks Moraga's body, affirms it as the body of a woman of color, against the possibility of passing into the unmarked category of the Anglo father or into the orientalist myth of "original illiteracy" of a mother that never was. Malinche was mother here, not Eve before eating the forbidden fruit. Writing affirms Sister Outsider, not the Woman-before-the-Fall-into-Writing needed by the phallogocentric Family of Man.

Writing is pre-eminently the technology of cyborgs, etched surfaces of the late twentieth century. Cyborg politics is the struggle for language and the struggle against perfect communication, against the one code that translates all meaning perfectly, the central dogma of phallogocentrism. That is why cyborg politics insist on noise and advocate pollution, rejoicing in the illegitimate fusions of animal and machine. These are the couplings which make Man and Woman so problematic, subverting the structure of desire, the force imagined to generate language and gender, and so subverting the structure and modes of reproduction of "Western" identity, of nature and culture, of mirror and eye, slave and master, body and mind. "We" did not originally choose to be cyborgs, but choice grounds a liberal politics and epistemology that imagines the reproduction of individuals before the wider replications of "texts."

From the perspective of cyborgs, freed of the need to ground politics in "our" privileged position of the oppression that incorporates all other dominations, the innocence of the merely violated, the ground of those closer to nature, we can see powerful possibilities. Feminisms and Marxisms have run aground on Western epistemological imperatives to construct a revolutionary subject from the perspective of a hierarchy of oppressions and/or a latent position of moral superiority, innocence, and greater closeness to nature. With no available original dream of a common language or original symbiosis promising protection from hostile "masculine" separation, but written into the play of a text that has no finally privileged reading or salvation history, to recognize "oneself" as fully implicated in the world, frees us of the need to root politics in identification, vanguard parties, purity, and mothering. Stripped of identity, the bastard race teaches about the power of the margins and the importance of a mother like Malinche. Women of color have transformed her from the evil mother of masculinist fear into the originally literate mother who teaches survival.

This is not just literary deconstruction, but liminal transformation. Every story that begins with original innocence and privileges the return to wholeness imagines the drama of life to be individuation, separation, the birth of the self, the tragedy of autonomy, the fall into writing, alienation; i.e., war, tempered by imaginary respite in the bosom of the Other. These plots are ruled by a reproductive politics – rebirth without flaw, perfection, abstraction. In this plot women are imagined either better or worse off, but all agree they have less selfhood, weaker individuation, more fusion to the oral, to Mother, less at stake in masculine autonomy. But there is another route to having less at stake in masculine autonomy, a route that does not pass through Woman, Primitive, Zero, the Mirror Stage

and its imaginary. It passes through women and other present-tense, illegitimate cyborgs, not of Woman born, who refuse the ideological resources of victimization so as to have a real life. These cyborgs are the people who refuse to disappear on cue, no matter how many times a "Western" commentator remarks on the sad passing of another primitive, another organic group done in by "Western" technology, by writing.[33] These real-life cyborgs, e.g., the Southeast Asian village women workers in Japanese and US electronics firms described by Aiwa Ong, are actively rewriting the texts of their bodies and societies. Survival is the stakes in this play of readings.

To recapitulate, certain dualisms have been persistent in Western traditions; they have all been systemic to the logics and practices of domination of women, people of color, nature, workers, animals – in short, domination of all constituted as *others*, whose task is to mirror the self. Chief among these troubling dualisms are self/other, mind/body, culture/nature, male/female, civilized/primitive, reality/appearance, whole/part, agent/resource, maker/made, active/passive, right/wrong, truth/illusion, total/partial, God/man. The self is the One who is not dominated, who knows that by the service of the other; the other is the one who holds the future, who knows that by the experience of domination which gives the lie to the autonomy of the self. To be One is to be autonomous, to be powerful, to be God; but to be One is to be an illusion, and so to be involved in a dialectic of apocalypse with the other. Yet to be other is to be multiple, without clear boundary, frayed, insubstantial. One is too few, but two are too many.

High-tech culture challenges these dualisms in intriguing ways. It is not clear who makes and who is made in the relation between human and machine. It is not clear what is mind and what body in machines that resolve into coding practices. Insofar as we know ourselves in both formal discourse (e.g., biology) and in daily practice (e.g., the homework economy in the integrated circuit), we find ourselves to be cyborgs, hybrids, mosaics, chimeras. Biological organisms have become biotic systems, communications devices like others. There is no fundamental, ontological separation in our formal knowledge of machine and organism, of technical and organic.

One consequence is that our sense of connection to our tools is heightened. The trance state experienced by many computer users has become a staple of science-fiction film and cultural jokes. Perhaps paraplegics and other severely handicapped people can (and sometimes do) have the most intense experiences of complex hybridization with other communication devices. Anne McCaffrey's *The Ship Who Sang* explored the consciousness of a cyborg, hybrid of girl's brain and complex machinery, formed after the birth of a severely handicapped child. Gender, sexuality, embodiment, skill: all were reconstituted in the story. Why should our bodies end at the skin, or include at best other beings encapsulated by skin? From the seventeenth century till now, machines could be animated – given ghostly souls to make them speak or move or to account for their orderly development and mental capacities. Or organisms could be mechanized – reduced to body understood as resource of mind. These machine/organism relationships are obsolete, unnecessary. For us, in imagination and in other practice, machines can be prosthetic devices, intimate components, friendly selves. We don't need organic holism to give impermeable wholeness, the total woman and her feminist variants (mutants?). Let me conclude this point by a very partial reading of the logic of the cyborg monsters of my second group of texts, feminist science fiction.

The cyborgs populating feminist science fiction make very problematic the statuses of man or woman, human, artifact, member of a race, individual identity, or body. Katie King clarifies how pleasure in reading these fictions is not largely based on identification. Students facing Joanna Russ for the first time, students who have learned to take modernist writers like James Joyce or Virginia Woolf without flinching, do not know what to make of *The Adventures of Alyx* or *The Female Man*, where characters refuse the reader's search for innocent wholeness while granting the wish for heroic quests, exuberant eroticism, and serious politics. *The Female Man* is the story of four versions of one genotype, all of whom meet, but even taken together do not make a whole, resolve the dilemmas of violent moral action, nor remove the growing scandal of gender. The feminist science fiction of Samuel Delany, especially *Tales of Neveryon*, mocks stories of origin by redoing the neolithic revolution, replaying the founding moves of Western civilization to subvert their plausibility. James Tiptree, Jr., an author whose fiction was regarded as particularly manly until her "true" gender was revealed, tells tales of

reproduction based on non-mammalian technologies like alternation of generations or male brood pouches and male nurturing. John Varley constructs a supreme cyborg in his arch-feminist exploration of Gaea, a mad goddess-planet-trickster-old woman-technological device on whose surface an extraordinary array of post-cyborg symbioses are spawned. Octavia Butler writes of an African sorceress pitting her powers of transformation against the genetic manipulations of her rival (*Wild Seed*), of time warps that bring a modern US black woman into slavery where her actions in relation to her white master-ancestor determine the possibility of her own birth (*Kindred*), and of the illegitimate insights into identity and community of an adopted cross-species child who came to know the enemy as self (*Survivor*).

Because it is particularly rich in boundary transgressions, Vonda McIntyre's *Superluminal* can close this truncated catalogue of promising monsters who help redefine the pleasures and politics of embodiment and feminist writing. In a fiction where no character is "simply" human, human status is highly problematic. Orca, a genetically altered diver, can speak with killer whales and survive deep ocean conditions, but she longs to explore space as a pilot, necessitating bionic implants jeopardizing her kinship with the divers and cetaceans. Transformations are effected by virus vectors carrying a new developmental code, by transplant surgery, by implants of microelectronic devices, by analogue doubles, and other means. Laenea becomes a pilot by accepting a heart implant and a host of other alterations allowing survival in transit at speeds exceeding that of light. Radu Dracul survives a virus-caused plague on his outerworld planet to find himself with a time sense that changes the boundaries of spatial perception for the whole species. All the characters explore the limits of language, the dream of communicating experience, and the necessity of limitation, partiality, and intimacy even in this world of protean transformation and connection.

Monsters have always defined the limits of community in Western imaginations. The Centaurs and Amazons of ancient Greece established the limits of the centered polis of the Greek male human by their disruption of marriage and boundary pollutions of the warrior with animality and woman. Unseparated twins and hermaphrodites were the confused human material in early modern France who grounded discourse on the natural and supernatural, medical and legal, portents and diseases – all crucial to establishing modern identity.[34] The evolutionary and behavioral sciences of monkeys and apes have marked the multiple boundaries of late-twentieth-century industrial identities. Cyborg monsters in feminist science fiction define quite different political possibilities and limits from those proposed by the mundane fiction of Man and Woman.

There are several consequences to taking seriously the imagery of cyborgs as other than our enemies. Our bodies, ourselves; bodies are maps of power and identity. Cyborgs are no exceptions. A cyborg body is not innocent; it was not born in a garden; it does not seek unitary identity and so generate antagonistic dualisms without end (or until the world ends); it takes irony for granted. One is too few, and two is only one possibility. Intense pleasure in skill, machine skill, ceases to be a sin, but an aspect of embodiment. The machine is not an *it* to be animated, worshiped and dominated. The machine is us, our processes, an aspect of our embodiment. We can be responsible for machines; *they* do not dominate or threaten us. We are responsible for boundaries; we are they. Up till now (once upon a time), female embodiment seemed to be given, organic, necessary; and female embodiment seemed to mean skill in mothering and its metaphoric extensions. Only by being out of place could we take intense pleasure in machines, and then with excuses that this was organic activity after all, appropriate to females. Cyborgs might consider more seriously the partial, fluid, sometimes aspect of sex and sexual embodiment. Gender might not be global identity after all.

The ideologically charged question of what counts as daily activity, as experience, can be approached by exploiting the cyborg image. Feminists have recently claimed that women are given to dailiness, that women more than men somehow sustain daily life, and so have a privileged epistemological position potentially. There is a compelling aspect to this claim, one that makes visible unvalued female activity and names it as the ground of life. But *the* ground of life? What about all the ignorance of women, all the exclusions and failures of knowledge and skill? What about men's access to daily competence, to knowing how to build things, to take them apart, to play? What about other embodiments? Cyborg gender is a local possibility taking a global vengeance. Race, gender, and capital require a cyborg theory of wholes and parts. There is no drive in cyborgs to produce total theory, but there is an intimate experience of boundaries, their construction and deconstruction. There is a myth system waiting to become a political language to ground one way of looking at science and technology and challenging the informatics of domination.

One last image: organisms and organismic, holistic politics depend on metaphors of rebirth and invariably call on the resources of reproductive sex. I would suggest that cyborgs have more to do with regeneration and are suspicious of the reproductive matrix and of most birthing. For salamanders, regeneration after injury, such as the loss of a limb, involves regrowth of structure and restoration of function with the constant possibility of twinning or other odd topographical productions at the site of former injury. The regrown limb can be monstrous, duplicated, potent. We have all been injured, profoundly. We require regeneration, not rebirth, and the possibilities for our reconstitution include the utopian dream of the hope for a monstrous world without gender.

Cyborg imagery can help express two crucial arguments in this essay: (1) the production of universal, totalizing theory is a major mistake that misses most of reality, probably always, but certainly now; (2) taking responsibility for the social relations of science and technology means refusing an anti-science metaphysics, a demonology of technology, and so means embracing the skillful task of reconstructing the boundaries of daily life, in partial connection with others, in communication with all of our parts. It is not just that science and technology are possible means of great human satisfaction, as well as a matrix of complex dominations. Cyborg imagery can suggest a way out of the maze of dualisms in which we have explained our bodies and our tools to ourselves. This is a dream not of a common language, but of a powerful infidel heteroglossia. It is an imagination of a feminist speaking in tongues to strike fear into the circuits of the super-savers of the new right. It means both building and destroying machines, identities, categories, relationships, spaces, stories. Though both are bound in the spiral dance, I would rather be a cyborg than a goddess.

Notes

Research was funded by an Academic Senate Faculty Research Grant from the University of California, Santa Cruz. An earlier version of the paper on genetic engineering appeared as "Lieber Kyborg als Gottin: Für eine sozialistisch-feministische Unterwanderung der

Gentechnologie," in Bernd-Peter Lange and Anna Marie Stuby, eds., *1984* (Berlin: Argument-Sonderband 105, 1984), pp. 66–84. The cyborg manifesto grew from "New Machines, New Bodies, New Communities: Political Dilemmas of a Cyborg Feminist," *The Scholar and the Feminist x: The Question of Technology*, Conference, April 1983.

The people associated with the History of Consciousness Board of UCSC have had an enormous influence on this paper, so that it feels collectively authored more than most, although those I cite may not recognize their ideas. In particular, members of graduate and undergraduate feminist theory, science and politics, and theory and methods courses have contributed to the cyborg manifesto. Particular debts here are due Hilary Klein ("Marxism, Psychoanalysis, and Mother Nature"); Paul Edwards ("Border Wars: The Science and Politics of Artificial Intelligence"); Lisa Lowe ("Julia Kristeva's *Des Chinoises*: Representing Cultural and Sexual Others"); Jim Clifford, "On Ethnographic Allegory: Essays," forthcoming.

Parts of the paper were my contribution to a collectively developed session, Poetic Tools and Political Bodies: Feminist Approaches to High Technology Culture, 1984 California American Studies Association, with History of Consciousness graduate students Zoe Sofoulis, "Jupiter Space"; Katie King, "The Pleasures of Repetition and the Limits of Identification in Feminist Science Fiction: Reimaginations of the Body after the Cyborg"; and Chela Sandoval, "The Construction of Subjectivity and Oppositional Consciousness in Feminist Film and Video." Sandoval's theory of oppositional consciousness was published as "Women Respond to Racism: A Report on the National Women's Studies Association Conference," Center for Third World Organizing, Oakland, California, n.d. For Sofoulis's semiotic-psychoanalytic readings of nuclear culture, see Z. Sofia, "Exterminating Fetuses: Abortion, Disarmament and the Sexo-Semiotics of Extraterrestrialism," Nuclear Criticism issue, *Diacritics*, vol. 14, no. 2 (1984), pp. 47–59. King's manuscripts ("Questioning Tradition: Canon Formation and the Veiling of Power"; "Gender and Genre: Reading the Science Fiction of Joanna Russ"; "Varley's *Titan* and *Wizard*: Feminist Parodies of Nature, Culture, and Hardware") deeply inform the cyborg manifesto.

Barbara Epstein, Jeff Escoffier, Rusten Hogness, and Jaye Miller gave extensive discussion and editorial help. Members of the Silicon Valley Research Project of USCS and participants in SVRP conferences and workshops have been very important, especially Rick Gordon, Linda Kimball, Nancy Snyder, Langdon Winner, Judith Stacey, Linda Lim, Patricia Fernandez-Kelly, and Judith Gregory. Finally, I want to thank Nancy Hartsock for years of friendship and discussion on feminist theory and feminist science fiction.

1. Useful references to left and/or feminist radical science movements and theory and to biological/

biotechnological issues include: Ruth Bleier, *Science and Gender: A Critique of Biology and Its Themes on Women* (New York: Pergamon, 1984); Elizabeth Fee, "Critiques of Modern Science: The Relationship of Feminist and Other Radical Epistemologies," and Evelyn Hammonds, "Women of Color, Feminism and Science," papers for Symposium on Feminist Perspectives on Science, University of Wisconsin, 11–12 April, 1985 (proceedings to be published by Pergamon); Stephen J. Gould, *Mismeasure of Man* (New York: Norton, 1981); Ruth Hubbard, Mary Sue Henifin, Barbara Fried, eds., *Biological Woman, the Convenient Myth* (Cambridge, Mass.: Schenkman, 1982); Evelyn Fox Keller, *Reflections on Gender and Science* (New Haven: Yale University Press, 1985); R. C. Lewontin, Steve Rose, and Leon Kamin, *Not in Our Genes* (New York: Pantheon, 1984); *Radical Science Journal*, 26 Freegrove Road, London N7 9RQ; *Science for the People*, 897 Main St., Cambridge, MA 02139.

2. Starting points for left and/or feminist approaches to technology and politics include: Ruth Schwartz Cowan, *More Work for Mother: The Ironies of Household Technology from the Open Hearth to the Microwave* (New York: Basic Books, 1983); Joan Rothschild, *Machina ex Dea: Feminist Perspectives on Technology* (New York: Pergamon, 1983); Sharon Traweek, "Uptime, Downtime, Spacetime, and Power: An Ethnography of U.S. and Japanese Particle Physics," Ph.D. thesis, UC Santa Cruz, History of Consciousness, 1982; R. M. Young and Les Levidov, eds., *Science, Technology, and the Labour Process*, vols. 1–3 (London: CSE Books); Joseph Weizenbaum, *Computer Power and Human Reason* (San Francisco: Freeman, 1976); Langdon Winner, *Autonomous Technology: Technics Out of Control as a Theme in Political Thought* (Cambridge, Mass.: MIT Press, 1977); Langdon Winner, "Paths in Technopolis," esp. "Mythinformation in the High Tech Era" (in ms., forthcoming); Jan Zimmerman, ed., *The Technological Woman: Interfacing with Tomorrow* (New York: Praeger, 1983); *Global Electronics Newsletter*, 867 West Dana St., #204, Mountain View, CA 94041; *Processed World*, 55 Sutter St., San Francisco, CA 94104; ISIS, Women's International Information and Communication Service, P.O. Box 50 (Cornavin), 1211 Geneva 2, Switzerland, and Via Santa Maria dell'Anima 30, 00186 Rome, Italy. Fundamental approaches to modern social studies of science that do not continue the liberal mystification that it all started with Thomas Kuhn include: Karin Knorr-Cetina, *The Manufacture of Knowledge* (Oxford: Pergamon, 1981); K. D. Knorr-Cetina and Michael Mulkay, eds., *Science Observed: Perspectives on the Social Study of Science* (Beverly Hills, Calif.: Sage, 1983); Bruno Latour and Steve Woolgar, *Laboratory Life: The Social Construction of Scientific Facts*

(Beverly Hills, Calif.: Sage, 1979); Robert M. Young, "Interpreting the Production of Science," *New Scientist*, vol. 29 (March 1979), pp. 1026–8. More is claimed than is known about room for contesting productions of science in the mythic/material space of "the laboratory"; the 1984 Directory of the Network for the Ethnographic Study of Science, Technology, and Organizations lists a wide range of people and projects crucial to better radical analysis; available from NESSTO, P.O. Box 11442, Stanford, CA 94305.

3. Frederic Jameson, "Post Modernism, or the Cultural Logic of Late Capitalism," *New Left Review*, July/August 1984, pp. 53–94. See Marjorie Perloff, "'Dirty' Language and Scramble Systems," *Sulfur* 11 (1984), pp. 178–83; Kathleen Fraser, *Something (Even Human Voices) in the Foreground, a Lake* (Berkeley, Calif.: Kelsey St. Press, 1984).

A provocative, comprehensive argument about the politics and theories of "post-modernism" is made by Frederick Jameson, who argues that post-modernism is not an option, a style among others, but a cultural dominant requiring radical reinvention of left politics from within; there is no longer any place from without that gives meaning to the comforting fiction of critical distance. Jameson also makes clear why one cannot be for or against post-modernism, an essentially moralist move. My position is that feminists (and others) need continuous cultural reinvention, post-modernist critique, and historical materialism; only a cyborg would have a chance. The old dominations of white capitalist patriarchy seem nostalgically innocent now: they normalized heterogeneity, e.g., into man and woman, white and black. "Advanced capitalism" and post-modernism release heterogeneity without a norm, and we are flattened, without subjectivity, which requires depth, even unfriendly and drowning depths. It is time to write *The Death of the Clinic*. The clinic's methods required bodies and works; we have texts and surfaces. Our dominations don't work by medicalization and normalization anymore; they work by networking, communications redesign, stress management. Normalization gives way to automation, utter redundancy. Michel Foucault's *Birth of the Clinic, History of Sexuality*, and *Discipline and Punish* name a form of power at its moment of implosion. The discourse of biopolitics gives way to technobabble, the language of the spliced substantive; no noun is left whole by the multinationals. These are their names, listed from one issue of *Science*: Tech-Knowledge, Genentech, Allergen, Hybritech, Compupro, Genen-cor, Syntex, Allelix, Agrigenetics Corp., Syntro, Codon, Repligen, Micro-Angelo from Scion Corp., Percom Data, Inter Systems, Cyborg Corp., Statcom Corp., Intertec. If we are imprisoned by language, then escape from that prison house

requires language poets, a kind of cultural restriction enzyme to cut the code; cyborg heteroglossia is one form of radical culture politics.

4. Frans de Waal, *Chimpanzee Politics: Power and Sex among the Apes* (New York: Harper & Row, 1982); Langdon Winner, "Do artifacts have politics?" *Daedalus*, Winter 1980.

5. Jean Baudrillard, *Simulations*, trans. P. Foss, P. Patton, P. Beitchman (New York: Semiotext(e), 1983). Jameson ("Post modernism," p. 66) points out that Plato's definition of the simulacrum is the copy for which there is no original, i.e., the world of advanced capitalism; of pure exchange.

6. Herbert Marcuse, *One-Dimensional Man* (Boston: Beacon, 1964); Carolyn Merchant, *Death of Nature* (San Francisco: Harper & Row, 1980).

7. Zoe Sofia, "Exterminating Fetuses," *Diacritics*, vol. 14, no. 2 (Summer 1984), pp. 47–59, and "Jupiter Space" (Pomona, Calif: American Studies Association, 1984).

8. Powerful developments of coalition politics emerge from "third world" speakers, speaking from nowhere, the displaced center of the universe, earth: "We live on the third planet from the sun" – *Sun Poem* by Jamaican writer Edward Kamau Braithwaite, review by Nathaniel Mackey, *Sulfur*, 11 (1984), pp. 200–5. *Home Girls*, ed. Barbara Smith (New York: Kitchen Table, Women of Color Press, 1983), ironically subverts naturalized identities precisely while constructing a place from which to speak called home. See esp. Bernice Reagan, "Coalition Politics, Turning the Century," pp. 356–68.

9. Chela Sandoval, "Dis-Illusionment and the Poetry of the Future: The Making of Oppositional Consciousness," Ph.D. qualifying essay, UCSC, 1984.

10. Bell Hooks, *Ain't I a Woman?* (Boston: South End Press, 1981); Gloria Hull, Patricia Bell Scott, and Barbara Smith, eds., *All the Women Are White, All the Men Are Black, But Some of Us Are Brave: Black Women's Studies* (Old Westbury, Conn.: Feminist Press, 1982). Toni Cade Bambara, in *The Salt Eaters* (New York: Vintage/Random House, 1981), writes an extraordinary post-modernist novel, in which the women of color theater group, The Seven Sisters, explores a form of unity. Thanks to Elliott Evans's readings of Bambara, Ph.D. qualifying essay, UCSC, 1984.

11. On orientalism in feminist works and elsewhere, see Lisa Lowe, "Orientation: Representations of Cultural and Sexual 'Others,'" Ph.D. thesis, UCSC; Edward Said, *Orientalism* (New York: Pantheon, 1978).

12. Katie King has developed a theoretically sensitive treatment of the workings of feminist taxonomies as genealogies of power in feminist ideology and polemic: "Prospectus," *Gender and Genre: Academic Practice and the Making of Criticism* (Santa Cruz, Calif.: University of California Press, 1984). King

examines an intelligent, problematic example of taxonomizing feminisms to make a little machine producing the desired final position: Alison Jaggar, *Feminist Politics and Human Nature* (Totowa, N.J.: Rowman & Allanheld, 1983). My caricature here of socialist and radical feminism is also an example.

13. The feminist standpoint argument is being developed by: Jane Flax, "Political Philosophy and the Patriarchal Unconsciousness," in Sandra Harding and Merill Hintikka, eds., *Discovering Reality* (Dordrecht: Reidel, 1983); Sandra Harding, "The Contradictions and Ambivalence of a Feminist Science," ms.; Harding and Hintikka, *Discovering Reality*; Nancy Hartsock, *Money, Sex, and Power* (New York: Longman, 1983) and "The Feminist Standpoint: Developing the Ground for a Specifically Feminist Historical Materialism," in Harding and Hintikka, *Discovering Reality*; Mary O'Brien, *The Politics of Reproduction* (New York: Routledge & Kegan Paul, 1981); Hilary Rose, "Hand, Brain, and Heart: A Feminist Epistemology for the Natural Sciences," *Signs*, vol. 9, no. 1 (1983), pp. 73–90; Dorothy Smith, "Women's Perspective as a Radical Critique of Sociology," *Sociological Inquiry* 44 (1974), and "A Sociology of Women," in J. Sherman and E. T. Beck, ed., *The Prism of Sex* (Madison: University of Wisconsin Press, 1979).

   The central role of object-relations versions of psychoanalysis and related strong universalizing moves in discussing reproduction, caring work, and mothering in many approaches to epistemology underline their authors' resistance to what I am calling post-modernism. For me, both the universalizing moves and the versions of psychoanalysis make analysis of "women's place in the integrated circuit" difficult and lead to systematic difficulties in accounting for or even seeing major aspects of the construction of gender and gendered social life.

14. Catharine MacKinnon, "Feminism, Marxism, Method, and the State: An Agenda for Theory," *Signs*, vol. 7, no. 3 (Spring 1982), pp. 515–44. A critique indebted to MacKinnon, but without the reductionism and with an elegant feminist account of Foucault's paradoxical conservatism on sexual violence (rape), is Teresa de Lauretis, "Violence Engendered," forthcoming in *Semiotica*, special issue on "The Rhetoric of Violence," ed. Nancy Armstrong, 1985. A theoretically elegant feminist social-historical examination of family violence, that insists on women's, men's, children's complex agency without losing sight of the material structures of male domination, race, and class, is Linda Gordon, *Cruelty, Love, and Dependence: Family Violence and Social Control, Boston 1880–1960*, forthcoming with Pantheon.

15. My previous efforts to understand biology as a cybernetic command-control discourse and organisms

as "natural-technical objects of knowledge" are: "The High Cost of Information in Post-World War II Evolutionary Biology," *Philosophical Forum*, vol. 13, nos. 2–3 (1979), pp. 206–37; "Signs of Dominance: From a Physiology to a Cybernetics of Primate Society," *Studies in History of Biology* 6 (1983), pp. 129–219; "Class, Race, Sex, Scientific Objects of Knowledge: A Socialist-Feminist Perspective on the Social Construction of Productive Knowledge and Some Political Consequences," in Violet Haas and Carolyn Perucci, eds., *Women in Scientific and Engineering Professions* (Ann Arbor: University of Michigan Press, 1984), pp. 212–29.

16. E. Rusten Hogness, "Why Stress? A Look at the Making of Stress, 1936–56," available from the author, 4437 Mill Creek Rd., Healdsburg, CA 95448.

17. A left entry to the biotechnology debate: *GeneWatch*, a Bulletin of the Committee for Responsible Genetics, 5 Doane St., 4th floor, Boston, MA 02109; Susan Wright, forthcoming book and "Recombinant DNA: The Status of Hazards and Controls," *Environment*, July/August 1982; Edward Yoxen, *The Gene Business* (New York: Harper & Row, 1983).

18. Starting references for "women in the integrated circuit": Pamela D'Onofrio-Flores and Sheila M. Pfafflin, eds., *Scientific-Technological Change and the Role of Women in Development* (Boulder, Colo.: Westview Press, 1982); Maria Patricia Fernandez-Kelly, *For We Are Sold, I and My People* (Albany, N.Y.: SUNY Press, 1983); Annette Fuentes and Barbara Ehrenreich, *Women in the Global Factory* (Boston: South End Press, 1983), with an especially useful list of resources and organizations; Rachael Grossman, "Women's Place in the Integrated Circuit," *Radical America*, vol. 14, no. 1 (1980), pp. 29–50; June Nash and M. P. Fernandez-Kelly, eds., *Women and Men and the International Division of Labor* (Albany, N.Y.: SUNY Press, 1983); Aiwa Ong, "Japanese Factories, Malay Workers: Industrialization and the Cultural Construction of Gender in West Malaysia," in Shelley Errington and Jane Atkinson, eds., *The Construction of Gender*, forthcoming; Science Policy Research Unit, *Microelectronics and Women's Employment in Britain* (University of Sussex, 1982).

19. The best example is Bruno Latour, *Les Microbes: Guerre et Paix, suivi de Irreductions* (Paris: Metailie, 1984).

20. For the homework economy and some supporting arguments: Richard Gordon, "The Computerization of Daily Life, the Sexual Division of Labor, and the Homework Economy," in R. Gordon, ed., *Microelectronics in Transition* (Norwood, N.J.: Ablex, 1985); Patricia Hill Collins, "Third World Women in America," and Sara G. Burr, "Women and Work," in Barbara K. Haber, ed., *The Women's Annual, 1981* (Boston: G. K. Hall, 1982); Judith Gregory and Karen Nussbaum, "Race against Time: Automation

of the Office," *Office: Technology and People* 1 (1982),
pp. 197–236; Frances Fox Piven and Richard
Cloward, *The New Class War: Reagan's Attack on
the Welfare State and Its Consequences* (New York:
Pantheon, 1982); Microelectronics Group, *Microelectronics: Capitalist Technology and the Working
Class* (London: CSE, 1980); Karin Stallard, Barbara
Ehrenreich, and Holly Sklar, *Poverty in the American Dream* (Boston: South End Press, 1983), including a useful organization and resource list.

21. Rae Lessor Blumberg, "A General Theory of Sex
Stratification and Its Application to the Position of
Women in Today's World Economy," paper deliv-
ered to Sociology Board, UCSC, February 1983. Also
Blumberg, *Stratification: Socioeconomic and Sexual
Inequality* (Boston: Brown, 1981). See also Sally
Hacker, "Doing It the Hard Way: Ethnographic
Studies in the Agribusiness and Engineering Class-
room," California American Studies Association,
Pomona, 1984, forthcoming in *Humanity and Soci-
ety*; S. Hacker and Lisa Bovit, "Agriculture to
Agribusiness: Technical Imperatives and Changing
Roles," *Proceedings* of the Society for the History of
Technology, Milwaukee, 1981; Lawrence Busch and
William Lacy, *Science, Agriculture, and the Politics of
Research* (Boulder, Colo.: Westview Press, 1983);
Denis Wilfred, "Capital and Agriculture, a Review
of Marxian Problematics," *Studies in Political
Economy*, no. 7 (1982), pp. 127–54; Carolyn Sachs,
*The Invisible Farmers: Women in Agricultural Pro-
duction* (Totowa, N.J.: Rowman & Allanheld, 1983).
Thanks to Elizabeth Bird, "Green Revolution
Imperialism," I & II, ms. UCSC, 1984.

The conjunction of the Green Revolution's social
relations with biotechnologies like plant genetic engineering makes the pressures on land in the third
world increasingly intense. AID's estimates (*New
York Times*, 14 October 1984) used at the 1984 World
Food Day are that in Africa, women produce about
90 per cent of rural food supplies, about 60–80 per
cent in Asia, and provide 40 per cent of agricultural
labor in the Near East and Latin America. Blumberg
charges that world organizations' agricultural politics, as well as those of multinationals and national
governments in the third world, generally ignore
fundamental issues in the sexual division of labor.
The present tragedy of famine in Africa might
owe as much to male supremacy as to capitalism,
colonialism, and rain patterns. More accurately,
capitalism and racism are usually structurally male
dominant.

22. Cynthia Enloe, "Women Textile Workers in the
Militarization of Southeast Asia," in Nash and
Fernandez-Kelly, *Women and Men*; Rosalind
Petchesky, "Abortion, Anti-Feminism, and the Rise
of the New Right," *Feminist Studies*, vol. 7, no. 2
(1981).

23. For a feminist version of this logic, see Sarah Blaffer
Hrdy, *The Woman That Never Evolved* (Cambridge,
Mass.: Harvard University Press, 1981). For an
analysis of scientific women's story-telling practices,
especially in relation to sociobiology, in evolutionary debates around child abuse and infanticide, see
Donna Haraway, "The Contest for Primate Nature:
Daughters of Man the Hunter in the Field, 1960–
80," in Mark Kann, ed., *The Future of American
Democracy* (Philadelphia: Temple University Press,
1993), pp. 175–208.

24. For the moment of transition of hunting with
guns to hunting with cameras in the construction of
popular meanings of nature for an American urban
immigrant public, see Donna Haraway, "Teddy
Bear Patriarchy," *Social Text*, forthcoming, 1985;
Roderick Nash, "The Exporting and Importing of
Nature: Nature-Appreciation as a Commodity, 1850–
1980," *Perspectives in American History*, vol. 3 (1979),
pp. 517–60; Susan Sontag, *On Photography* (New
York: Dell, 1977); and Douglas Preston, "Shooting
in Paradise," *Natural History*, vol. 93, no. 12
(December 1984), pp. 14–19.

25. For crucial guidance for thinking about the polit-
ical/cultural implications of the history of women
doing science in the United States, see: Violet Haas
and Carolyn Perucci, eds., *Women in Scientific and
Engineering Professions* (Ann Arbor: University of
Michigan Press, 1984); Sally Hacker, "The Culture
of Engineering: Women, Workplace, and Machine,"
Women's Studies International Quarterly, vol. 4, no. 3
(1981), pp. 341–53; Evelyn Fox Keller, *A Feeling
for the Organism* (San Francisco: Freeman, 1983);
National Science Foundation, *Women and Minorities
in Science and Engineering* (Washington, D.C.: NSF,
1982); Margaret Rossiter, *Women Scientists in America*
(Baltimore: Johns Hopkins University Press, 1982).

26. John Markoff and Lenny Siegel, "Military Micros,"
UCSC Silicon Valley Research Project conference,
1983, forthcoming in *Microelectronics and Industrial Transformation*. High Technology Professionals
for Peace and Computer Professionals for Social
Responsibility are promising organizations.

27. Katie King, "The Pleasure of Repetition and the
Limits of Identification in Feminist Science Fic-
tion: Reimaginations of the Body after the Cyborg,"
California American Studies Association, Pomona,
1984. An abbreviated list of feminist science fiction
underlying themes of this essay: Octavia Butler, *Wild
Seed, Mind of My Mind, Kindred, Survivor*; Suzy
McKee Charnas, *Motherliness*; Samuel Delany, *Tales
of Neveryon*; Anne McCaffery, *The Ship Who Sang,
Dinosaur Planet*; Vonda McIntyre, *Superluminal,
Dreamsnake*; Joanna Russ, *Adventures of Alix, The
Female Man*; James Tiptree, Jr., *Star Songs of an
Old Primate, Up the Walls of the World*; John Varley,
Titan, Wizard, Demon.

28. Mary Douglas, *Purity and Danger* (London: Routledge & Kegan Paul, 1966), *Natural Symbols* (London: Cresset Press, 1970).

29. French feminisms contribute to cyborg heteroglossia. Carolyn Burke, "Irigaray through the Looking Glass," *Feminist Studies*, vol. 7, no. 2 (Summer 1981), pp. 288–306; Luce Irigaray, *Ce sexe qui n'en est pas un* (Paris: Minuit, 1977); L. Irigaray, *Et l'une ne bouge pas sans l'autre* (Paris: Minuit, 1979); Elaine Marks and Isabelle de Courtivron, ed., *New French Feminisms* (Amherst: University of Massachusetts Press, 1980); *Signs*, vol. 7, no. 1 (Autumn, 1981), special issue on French feminism; Monique Wittig, *The Lesbian Body*, trans. David LeVay (New York: Avon, 1975; *Le corps lesbien*, 1973).

30. But all these poets are very complex, not least in treatment of themes of lying and erotic, decentered collective and personal identities. Susan Griffin, *Women and Nature: The Roaring Inside Her* (New York: Harper & Row, 1978); Audre Lorde, *Sister Outsider* (New York: Crossing Press, 1984); Adrienne Rich, *The Dream of a Common Language* (New York: Norton, 1978).

31. Jacques Derrida, *Of Grammatology*, trans. and introd. G. C. Spivak (Baltimore: Johns Hopkins University Press, 1976), esp. part II, "Nature, Culture, Writing"; Claude Lévi-Strauss, *Tristes Tropiques*, trans. John Russell (New York, 1961), esp. "The Writing Lesson."

32. Cherrie Moraga, *Loving in the War Years* (Boston: South End Press, 1983). The sharp relation of women of color to writing as theme and politics can be approached through: "The Black Woman and the Diaspora: Hidden Connections and Extended Acknowledgments," An International Literary Conference, Michigan State University, October 1985; Mari Evans, ed., *Black Women Writers: A Critical Evaluation* (Garden City, N.Y.: Doubleday/Anchor, 1984); Dexter Fisher, ed., *The Third Woman: Minority Women Writers of the United States* (Boston: Houghton Mifflin, 1980); several issues of *Frontiers*, esp. vol. 5 (1980), "Chicanas en el Ambiente Nacional" and vol. 7 (1983), "Feminisms in the Non-Western World"; Maxine Hong Kingston, *China Men* (New York: Knopf, 1977); Gerda Lerner, ed., *Black Women in White America: A Documentary History* (New York: Vintage, 1973); Cherrie Moraga and Gloria Anzaldua, eds., *This Bridge Called My Back: Writings by Radical Women of Color* (Watertown, Mass.: Persephone, 1981); Robin Morgan, ed., *Sisterhood Is Global* (Garden City, N.Y.: Anchor/Doubleday, 1984). The writing of white women has had similar meanings: Sandra Gilbert and Susan Gubar, *The Madwoman in the Attic* (New Haven: Yale University Press, 1979); Joanna Russ, *How to Suppress Women's Writing* (Austin: University of Texas Press, 1983).

33. James Clifford argues persuasively for recognition of continuous cultural reinvention, the stubborn non-disappearance of those "marked" by Western imperializing practices; see "On Ethnographic Allegory: Essays," forthcoming 1985, and "On Ethnographic Authority," *Representations*, vol. 1, no. 2 (1983), pp. 118–46.

34. Page DuBois, *Centaurs and Amazons* (Ann Arbor: University of Michigan Press, 1982); Lorraine Daston and Katharine Park, "Hermaphrodites in Renaissance France," ms., n.d.; Katharine Park and Lorraine Daston, "Unnatural Conceptions: The Study of Monsters in 16th and 17th Century France and England," *Past and Present*, no. 92 (August 1981), pp. 20–54.

34

The Epistemic Status of Cultural Identity

Satya P. Mohanty

Several closely related practical and theoretical questions concerning identity emerge from current debates about cultural diversity. If multiculturalism is to be a goal of educational and political institutions, we need a workable notion of how a social group is unified by a common culture, as well as the ability to identify genuine cultural differences (and similarities) across groups. Whether cultures are inherited or consciously and deliberately created, basic problems of definition – who belongs where or with whom, who belongs and who doesn't – are unavoidable the moment we translate our dreams of diversity into social visions and agendas. Debates about minority literatures, for instance, often get bogged down in tedious disputes over genuineness or authenticity, but it is difficult to eliminate these disputes entirely. That is because they point to what is in many cases a practical problem: who can be trusted to represent the real interests of the group without fear of betrayal or misrepresentation? Every "obvious" answer (such as "It'll have to be one of us, of course!") begs the question, indicating why our views about cultural identity always involve theoretical presuppositions. The most basic questions about identity call for a more general reexamination of the relation between personal experience and public meanings – subjective choices and evaluations, on the one hand, and objective social location, on the other.

So it is not surprising that recent theoretical writings on cultural identity have focused on the status of our personal experiences, examining the claims to representativeness we might make on their behalf. The two dominant alternative views on cultural identity – the view associated with identity politics and characterized as essentialism and the

position of postmodernism – are in fact seen as providing conflicting definitions of identity because they understand the relation between the experiences of social actors and the theoretical construct we call "their identity" very differently. Simply put, the essentialist view would be that the identity common to members of a social group is stable and more or less unchanging, since it is based on the experiences they share. Opponents of essentialism often find this view seriously misleading, since it ignores historical changes and glosses over internal differences within a group by privileging only the experiences that are common to everyone. Postmodernists in particular insist that identities are fabricated and constructed rather than self-evidently deduced from experience, since – they claim – experience cannot be a source of objective knowledge.[1]

My central task here is to show, first, that the relation between experience and identity is a genuine philosophical or theoretical issue, and, second, that there is a better way to think about identity than might be suggested by the alternatives provided by the essentialists and the postmodernists. I develop this view by examining what I shall call the epistemic status of cultural identity. [. . .]

One of the main components of the postmodernist case against identity politics is the charge that "experience" is not a self-evident or even reliable source of knowledge and cannot be seen as grounding a social identity. Postmodernists typically warn against the desire to consider experience a foundation of other social meanings; they point out that personal experiences are basically rather unstable or slippery, and since they can only be interpreted in terms of linguistic or other signs, they must be heir to all the exegetical and interpretive problems that accompany social signification. This specifically poststructuralist view contains an epistemological thesis. Jonathan Culler's formulation of the thesis in his 1982 discussion of experience and "reading" is one that is most frequently cited: " 'Experience' always has [a] divided, duplicitous character: it has always already occurred and yet is still to be produced – an indispensable point of reference, yet never simply there" (*On Deconstruction* 63). This claim, with its Derridean allusions (Derrida usually couches it as a critique of specifically idealist or phenomenological notions of experience), leads to the following conclusion about the relation between experience and identity: "For a woman to read as a woman is not to repeat an identity or an experience that is given but to play a role she constructs with reference to her identity as a woman, which is also a construct, so that the series can continue: a woman reading as a woman reading as a woman. The noncoincidence reveals an interval, a division within woman or within any reading subject and the 'experience' of that subject" (64; emphasis added).[2]

I think, however, that this argument about the relation between experience and cultural identity can be best appreciated as part of the more general suspicion of foundationalism in contemporary thought, for there is nothing peculiar to experience as such which warrants its rejection on epistemological grounds. The critique of epistemological foundationalism contains the suggestion that we naturalize epistemology, that is, examine the production, justification, and regulation of belief as social processes. Many antifoundationalists contend that the growth of empirical knowledge about the practices and protocols of justification in the various sciences ought to shape our understanding of epistemological questions. In this sense, neither a "method" of justification nor some privileged class of foundational beliefs can be seen as existing outside the social contexts of inquiry.[3]

I suggest that we consider the postmodernist critique of identity politics in analogous terms, as a critique of experiential foundationalism. If we were not to specify the critique in this way, the general postmodernist skepticism toward experience could lead to the strange conclusion that the experiences of social actors are irrelevant to explain, say, their moral or political growth. Alternatively, we could be led to conclude that moral or political change (growth or decline) is never real because it is tied

to experience and can thus never be justified. The antifoundationalist thesis I have tried to retrieve from postmodernism brings into focus the accurate and damaging critique that postmodernists can make of identity politics, but by itself it does not entail either of the two extreme conclusions to which their skepticism can lead us. The naturalist-realist account of experience I defend here is neither foundationalist nor skeptical; it maintains that experience, properly interpreted, can yield reliable and genuine knowledge, just as it can point up instances and sources of real mystification. Central to this account is the claim that the experience of social subjects has a cognitive component. Experiences can be "true" or "false," can be evaluated as justified or illegitimate in relation to the subject and his world, for "experience" refers very simply to the variety of ways humans process information. (This conception carries none of the normative baggage that comes with Hegelian *Erfahrung*, which is always tied to a particular model of ethical development. Neither does it presuppose, as Dilthey's conception of *Erlebnis* does, a necessary opposition between "lived experience" and scientific thinking.) It is on the basis of this revised understanding of experience that we can construct a realist theory of social or cultural identity, in which experiences would not serve as foundations because of their self-evident authenticity but would provide some of the raw material with which we construct identities. As we shall see, to say that experiences and identities are constructed is not to prejudge the question of their epistemic status.[4] Radical skepticism about the cognitive implications of cultural identity is not the only alternative to an ahistorical essentialism.

A Realist Approach to Culture and Politics

The first claim I wish to advance is that "personal experience" is socially and "theoretically" constructed, and it is precisely in this mediated way that it yields knowledge. Let me develop this idea by drawing in part on work done by feminist theorists in the last decade and a half, beginning with an insightful essay by the philosopher Naomi Scheman.[5]

Writing from an explicitly anti-individualist perspective on such things as emotions and feelings, Scheman explains how the notion of our emotions as our own "inner" possessions is fundamentally misleading. She focuses on the anger that women who have been members of feminist consciousness-raising groups often come to feel. This anger, Scheman says, should not be seen as a fully formed emotion that was waiting to be released or expressed in the context of the group. Rather, the emotion becomes what it is through the mediation of the social and emotional environment that the consciousness-raising group provides. Part of what constitutes this environment is an alternative narrative or account of the individual's relationship with the world, and these alternative accounts are unavoidably theoretical. They involve notions of what a woman is supposed to be angry about, what she should not tolerate, what is worth valuing, notions that are not merely moral but also social-theoretical in nature. They imply social visions and critiques of what exists; at the very least they suggest that it is perfectly okay to feel dissatisfied about certain relationships and social arrangements. Scheman's point is that in many important instances such alternative accounts and notions help organize inchoate or confused feelings to produce an emotion that is experienced more directly and fully. It follows, then, that this new emotion, say, anger, and the ways it is experienced are not purely personal or individual. A necessary part of its form and shape is determined by the nonindividual social meanings that the theories and accounts supply. It would be false to say that this emotion is the individual's own "inner" possession and that she alone has "privileged access" to its meaning or significance ("Anger" 179). Rather, our emotions provide evidence of the extent to which even our deepest personal experiences are socially constructed, mediated by visions and values that are "political" in nature, that refer outward to the world beyond the individual.

> The structure that consciousness-raising groups provide for the interpretation of feelings and behavior is overtly political; it should be immediately obvious that one is presented with a particular way of making sense of one's experience, a way intimately linked with certain controversial political views. Consciousness-raising groups are not, however, unique in this respect. What they are is unusually honest: the political framework is explicit (though often vague) and openly argued for. The alternative is not "a clear space in which to get your head together"

> but a hidden political framework that pretends not to be one. (186)

There are different ways of making sense of an experience, and the way we make sense of it can in fact create a new experience.

Consider Scheman's example, Alice, who joins a consciousness-raising group and in the safe and supportive environment provided by other women like her learns to recognize that her depression and guilt, though sincerely felt, may not be legitimate. In fact, they hide from her her real needs and feelings, as well as the real nature of her situation. "The guilt and depression," the group might argue and Alice might come to acknowledge, "are a response to and a cover for those other feelings, notably feelings of anger. Alice is urged to recognize her anger as legitimate and justifiable in this situation" (177). Here is where the "political" nature of the views Alice is now asked to ponder comes in: she is not seen as merely bringing to the surface something she, as a lone individual, knew and felt all along. Rather, her emotion (the anger) is constituted in part by the "views" about the world, about herself in it, and the details of what is acceptable and unacceptable in this new theoretical picture. She comes to experience anger by reinterpreting her old feelings of depression, guilt, and so on, but she does so unavoidably with the aid of theory, an alternative, socially produced construction of herself and the world. Now, "we may describe [Alice] as having discovered that she had been angry, though she hadn't previously recognized it. She would, in fact, have denied it if she were asked: 'Why *should* I be angry?'" "It is significant," Scheman goes on, "that a denial that one is angry often takes the form of a denial that one would be justified in being angry. Thus one's discovery of anger can often occur not from focusing on one's feelings but from a political redescription of one's situation" (177). The reason we say that Alice "discovers" she has been angry is that the anger underlay her vague or confused feelings of depression or guilt; now it organizes these feelings, giving them coherence and clarity. And our judgment that the anger is deeper than the depression or guilt is derived from (and corroborated by) our understanding of Alice's changing personal and social situation, an understanding that is based in part on a "theory."[6]

Here we discern what might be the strongest argument against the essentialist picture of cultural identity. The constructed nature of experience shows why there is no guarantee that my experiences will lead me to some common core of values or beliefs that link me with every other member of my cultural group. Our experiences do not have self-evident meanings, for they are in part theoretical affairs, and our access to our remotest personal feelings is dependent on social narratives, paradigms, and even ideologies. In fact, drawing on a Nietzschean theme, the postmodernist might declare that we need to go further, that the kind of theory dependence I have just identified leads to a radical perspectivism or relativism. When we choose among these alternative ways of organizing and interpreting experience, we make a purely arbitrary choice, determined by our social locations or our prerational ideological commitments. "Experience" remains unstable and unreliable. Why, then, speak of the cognitive component of personal experience, as though we might be able to glean objective knowledge from it?[7]

Oddly enough, this postmodernist response turns out to reveal a disguised form of foundationalism, for it remains within a specifically positivist conception of objectivity and knowledge. It assumes that the only kind of objective knowledge we can have is independent of (socially produced and revisable) theoretical presuppositions and concludes that the theory dependence of experience is evidence that it is always epistemically suspect. But what if we reject as overly abstract and limiting this conception of objectivity as presupposition-free knowledge? What if we give up both radical perspectivism and the dream of a "view from nowhere" in order to grant that all the knowledge we can ever have is necessarily dependent on theories and perspectives? We might then be able to see that there are different kinds and degrees of theory dependence and understand how theory-laden and socially constructed experiences can lead to a knowledge that is accurate and reliable.

Consider Scheman's example again. Alice's emotion, "anger," is the result of a political redescription of herself and her world, but if that new description happens to explain adequately and cogently – as social, psychological, and moral theory – the constituent features of Alice's situation, then Alice's experience of the emotion anger leads us to conclude that she has just come to know something, something not merely about her repressed feelings but also about her self, her personhood, and the range of its moral and political claims and needs. She comes to this knowledge by discovering or understanding features of the social and cultural

arrangements of her world that define her sense of self, the choices she is taught to have, the range of personal capacities she is expected to exploit and exercise. And she does so in the process of learning to trust her judgments about herself, recognizing how others like her have done so as well. If this is the case, Alice's anger is not merely a personal or private thing inside, as it were, her own "innermost" self; rather, her anger is the theoretical prism through which she views her world and herself in it correctly. Hers is then an objective assessment of her situation, and in this strong sense, her anger is rational and justified.[8]

The example also suggests why emotions do not have to be seen as fully explicit beliefs or clear processes of reasoning for us to appreciate their cognitive role. We misunderstand the way Alice's anger gives coherence and shape to her previously confused feelings if we do not also appreciate the extent to which her experience of anger is a process whereby she weighs one vaguely felt hunch against another, reinterprets and reevaluates the information she considered relevant to her feelings and her situation, and thus redefines the contours of "her world." This sifting and reinterpretation of information sometimes happens quite suddenly; at other times, it becomes clearer and more lucid slowly and only in retrospect. The emotion is this not-entirely-explicit way Alice learns to reanalyze or even discern crucial features of her situation.

Emotions fall somewhere between conscious reasoning and reflexlike instinctual responses to stimuli. They are, as Ronald de Sousa has proposed, ways of paying attention to the world. They fill the "gaps" between our instinctually driven desires, on the one hand, and our fully developed reasoning faculties, on the other, especially when we need to decide what to do or believe. Emotions are "determinate patterns of salience"; like Kuhn's scientific paradigms, says de Sousa, they provide our half-articulated "questions" about the world. Emotions are "what we see the world 'in terms of,'" and therefore, like the scientific paradigm, they "cannot be articulated propositions" ("The Rationality" 136–8). It is significant that the focus her anger provides allows Alice to discover some of the constitutive features of her world. Emotions enable and encourage specific interpretations or evaluations of the world, and our judgment that Alice's anger is rational, justified, or "appropriate" (de Sousa's term) is a judgment about the accuracy of the interpretation and the objectivity of the evaluation. In Aristotelian terms, an essential component of Alice's moral development would be the increased capacity of her analytical and affective faculties to work together for cognitive purposes. Emotional growth would be central to moral growth, and both presuppose the postpositivist notion of theory-mediated objectivity I am defending.[9]

There is no commitment here to the silly idea that all emotions are equally justified or rational. Questions about the legitimacy of emotions are answered by looking at the features of the subject in her world, and it is possible to glean an accurate picture of these features not only through the right theory (or narrative or description) but also through the relevant information that we can examine and share. "The difference between someone who is irrationally angry and someone who is not," Scheman explains, "may not be a difference in what they *feel* so much as a difference in what sorts of feelings, under what sorts of circumstances they are ready to take as anger. When we judge that people are right to deny the name of anger to their irrational reactions, we are often judging that their situation, unlike Alice's, does not really call for anger" (178–9). If Alice's father or husband were to become angry at Alice for supposedly betraying their trust by going to the consciousness-raising group meetings and by becoming dissatisfied with her personal relationships, we would evaluate these emotions as we do Alice's. The anger may be sincerely felt, but whether or not we consider it justified or legitimate would depend on what we think of the underlying political and moral views of these men about the role of women in society, as well as the information (about themselves, about their society, and so on) they draw on – or ignore – to support these views. This kind of assessment is naturally both complex and difficult. But the difficulty is not due to anything peculiar to emotions. All experience – and emotions offer the paradigm case here – is socially constructed, but the constructedness does not make it arbitrary or unstable in advance. Experiences are crucial indexes of our relationships with our world (including our relationships with ourselves), and to stress their cognitive nature is to argue that they can be susceptible to varying degrees of socially constructed truth or error and can serve as sources of objective knowledge or socially produced mystification.

This kind of argument about the cognitive component of experience helps strengthen the claim made by feminist standpoint theorists that in a gender-stratified society women's experiences are often significant repositories of oppositional knowledge, but this does not mean that experience serves to ground feminist knowledge. "It is rather," Sandra Harding maintains, "the subsequently articulated observations of and theory about the rest of nature and social relations" which help us make sense of "women's lives" in our sexist social structure (*Whose Science?* 124). "Women's lives" constitute an "objective location" (123) from which feminist research should examine the world, because without it we would not be able to explain a significant feature of our society. "Women's lives" is a theoretical notion or construct, but it involves the kind of social theory without which we could not make sense of – explain – a central feature of our world. The theoretical notion "women's lives" refers not just to the experiences of women but also to a particular social arrangement of gender relations and hierarchies which can be analyzed and evaluated. The standpoint of women in this society is not self-evidently deduced from the "lived experience" of individual women or groups of women. Rather, the standpoint is based in "women's lives" to the extent that it articulates their material and epistemological interests. Such interests are discovered by an explanatory empirical account of the nature of gender stratification, how it is reproduced and regulated, and the particular social groups and values it legitimates. Our definition of social location is thus closely tied to our understanding of social interests.[10]

An important metatheoretical consequence follows from this. Objectivity is inextricably tied to social and historical conditions, and objective knowledge is the product not of disinterested theoretical inquiry so much as of particular kinds of social practice. In the case of social phenomena such as sexism and racism, whose distorted representation benefits the powerful and established groups and institutions, an attempt at an objective explanation is necessarily continuous with oppositional political struggles. Objective knowledge of such social phenomena is in fact often dependent on the theoretical knowledge that activism creates, for without these alternative constructions and accounts, Harding notes, our capacity to interpret and understand the dominant ideologies and institutions is limited to those created or sanctioned by these very ideologies and institutions (127). Moreover, as Richard Boyd shows in an important essay, even moral knowledge (for example, knowledge of "fundamental human goods") is to a great extent "experimental knowledge," dependent on social and political experiments. "We would not have been able to explore the dimensions of our needs for artistic expression and appreciation," Boyd points out, "had not social and technological developments made possible cultures in which, for some classes at least, there was the leisure to produce and consume art. We would not have understood the role of political democracy in [shaping our conception of the human] good had the conditions not arisen in which the first limited democracies developed. Only after the moral insights gained from the first democratic experiments were in hand, were we equipped to see the depth of the moral peculiarity of slavery. Only since the establishment of the first socialist societies are we even beginning to obtain the data necessary to assess the role of egalitarian social practices in fostering the good" ("How to Be a Moral Realist" 205).

The claim that political activity is in various ways continuous with attempts to seek scientific, objective explanations of social reality underscores that objective knowledge should not be sought by metatheoretically sundering the realm of "hard facts" from the realm of values. In the postpositivist picture of knowledge I am outlining here, some evaluations – from vaguely felt ethical judgments to more developed normative theories of right and wrong – can in crucial instances enable and facilitate greater accuracy in representing social reality, providing better ways of organizing the relevant or salient facts, urging us to look in newer and more productive ways. We have seen in the case of Alice how this epistemic reorientation takes place on a very personal level, where an individual's recognition and conscious acceptance of her feelings makes possible the process of search and discovery through which she comes to discern crucial features of her situation. For such emotional growth is a form of epistemic training as well. When we speak of collective political struggles and oppositional social movements, we can see how the political is continuous with the epistemological. In fact one may interpret Marx's famous eleventh thesis on Feuerbach as making just such an epistemological argument. It does not urge us to give up the job of interpreting the world (in the interest of changing it) but instead points out how the possibility of interpreting our world accurately depends fundamentally on our coming to know what it would take to change it, on our identifying the central relations of power and privilege that sustain it and make the world what it is. And we learn to identify these

relations through our various attempts to change the world, not merely to contemplate it as it is.[11]

We can thus see how the unavoidability of theory, one of the key ideas of postpositivist intellectual culture, leads to an important nonrelativist insight about the political moorings of knowledge; there are better or worse social and political theories, and we can seek less distorted and more objective knowledge of social phenomena by creating the conditions for the production of better knowledge. Given the pervasiveness of both sexism and individualism in Alice's culture, it is more likely that she will come to discover the reality about herself and her situation in a feminist consciousness-raising group than by herself at home. Research institutions that employ scientists from a wide variety of social backgrounds (and do not confine decision making about research topics or the allocation of funds to a handful of individuals from the socially advantaged groups) will be less likely than other institutions to betray unconscious racial or gender bias in their research agendas. Objectivity is something we struggle for, in a number of direct and not so obvious ways, and this puts into perspective the epistemic privilege "experience" might give us. Feminist standpoint theorists like Harding both develop and clarify Marx's argument about the political bases of knowledge production. A standpoint, says Harding, "is not something that anyone can have simply by claiming it" (127). Since "experience" is only the raw material for the kind of political and social knowledge that constitutes a feminist standpoint, it cannot guarantee or ground it. A standpoint is thus "an achievement" (127), both theoretical and political. The objectivity we achieve is thus profoundly theory dependent and thus postpositivist. It is based on our developing understanding of the various causes of distortion and mystification. I believe a naturalistic conception of human inquiry best suits the various examples I have been discussing. An essential part of this conception of inquiry would be an understanding of fallibility which is developed and specified through our explanations of how different kinds and degrees of error arise. Precision and depth in understanding the sources and causes of error or mystification help us define the nature of objectivity, and central to this definition would be the possibility of its revision and improvement on the basis of new information. This conception of fallibility is thus based on a dialectical opposition between objectivity and error. Since error in this view is opposed not to certainty but rather to objectivity as a theory-dependent, socially realizable goal, the possibility of error does not sanction skepticism about the possibility of knowledge. Such skepticism (postmodernist or otherwise) is usually the flip side of the quest for certainty.[12]

My proposal is that we reorient our theorizing of cultural identity in the following way: instead of conceiving identities as self-evidently based on the authentic experiences of members of a cultural or social group (the conception that underlies identity politics) or as all equally unreal to the extent that they lay any claim to the real experiences of real people because experience is a radically mystifying term (this is the postmodernist alternative), we need to explore the possibility of a theoretical understanding of social and cultural identity in terms of objective social location. To do so, we need a cognitivist conception of experience, as I have been suggesting, a conception that will allow for both legitimate and illegitimate experience, enabling us to see experience as source of both real knowledge and social mystification. Both the knowledge and the mystification are, however, open to analysis on the basis of empirical information about our social situation and a theoretical account of our current social and political arrangements. Whether we inherit an identity – masculinity, being black – or we actively choose one on the basis of our political predilections – radical lesbianism, black nationalism, socialism – our identities are ways of making sense of our experiences. Identities are theoretical constructions that enable us to read the world in specific ways. It is in this sense that they are valuable, and their epistemic status should be taken very seriously. In them, and through them, we learn to define and reshape our values and our commitments, we give texture and form to our collective futures. Both the essentialism of identity politics and the skepticism of the postmodernist position seriously underread the real epistemic and political complexities of our social and cultural identities.

[. . .]

Cultural Difference and Social Power

Let me summarize part of my central argument in outlining some of the advantages of the realist view of experience and identity. First, this account of cultural identity explains an important way in which identities can be both constructed (socially,

linguistically, theoretically, and so on) and "real" at the same time. Their "reality" consists in their referring outward, to causally significant features of the social world. Alice's gendered identity is theoretically constructed, to be sure, insofar as she elaborates and consolidates it in the context of the consciousness-raising group and the alternative descriptions of the world she encounters and debates there. But if this description happens to be accurate as an explanation of the key causal factors that make this world what it is, that is, make this world this world, then Alice's new feminist cultural and political identity is "real" in the following sense: it refers accurately to her social location and interests. Alice discovers that what defines her life in her society is the fact that she belongs to a group defined by gender. Gender is a social fact that is causally relevant for the experiences she has and the choices and possibilities that are available to her. Her world is what it is because in it social power is sustained through the hierarchical organization of gendered groups, including the cultural meanings they share. The collective identity Alice consciously forges through reexamination of the accepted cultural meanings and values, the given definition of her personal and political interests, is then as much her discovery as it is a construction. For good social and political theories do not only organize pregiven facts about the world; they also make it possible for us to detect new ones. They do so by guiding us to new patterns of salience and relevance, teaching us what to take seriously and what to reinterpret. To say that theories and identities "refer" is thus to understand the complex way they provide us knowledge about the world. Beyond the elementary descriptive relationship that individual signs might have with unique and static objects, "reference," postpositivist realists say, should be understood dialectically and socially as providing us degrees of "epistemic access" to reality. On this view, there can be both partial and successful reference. In some cases, theories (like signs) can fail to refer accurately, but reference should not be conceived as an all–or–nothing affair. Thus, when I say that cultural identities refer, I am suggesting that they can be evaluated using the same complex epistemic criteria we use to evaluate "theories."[13]

So the second advantage a realist theory of identity offers is this: it helps explain how we can distinguish legitimate identities from spurious ones. In fact it gives us the way to appreciate different degrees of legitimacy and spuriousness. It does so by urging us to take the epistemic status of personal experience very seriously, seriously enough in fact to consider why Alice's anger and her father's are not equally justified. [. . .] Alice's evolving personal experience plays an epistemic role since it reveals to her some of the determining features of her social location and her world, and where, objectively speaking, her personal interests might lie. To say that Alice [. . .] learns from her experience is to emphasize that under certain conditions personal experience yields reliable knowledge about oneself and one's situation.[14] And since different experiences and identities refer to different aspects of one world, one complex causal structure that we call "social reality," the realist theory of identity implies that we can evaluate them comparatively by considering how adequately they explain this structure. This comparison is often a complex and difficult negotiation (since it can involve competing interpretations and only partially overlapping bodies of information), but it is facilitated by making buried explanations explicit, by examining the social and political views that are involved in what seem like purely personal choices and predilections. Experiences and identities – and theories about them – are bits of social and political theory themselves and are to be evaluated as such.

The cultural radicalism of the postmodernist position I identified earlier is based on the argument that all identities are constructed and are thus contingent and changeable. But it cannot adequately explain what difference different kinds of construction make. Since it refuses to take the epistemic dimension of experience seriously, it cannot explain how (as, say, in the case of Alice [. . .]) changes in our cultural identity reflect moral and political growth, an increase both in our personal capacities and in knowledge. Once we consider the theoretical option to postmodernism provided by the realist account of identity I have proposed here, it might also be clearer why we should not frame our questions about cultural identity in terms of a rigid opposition between essentialism, claiming unchanging "reality," and (social) constructionism, emphasizing social and historical ideology. Both this unhelpful opposition and efforts to transcend it through such weak theoretical compromises as are suggested by such terms as "strategic essentialism"[15] are based on an evasion of the difficult but unavoidable epistemological questions that the postmodernist confronts. If the identities of social

actors cannot be deduced from experiences whose meanings are self-evident, is there anything objective we can say about these identities? How do we determine that one social identity is more legitimate than another? How do we justify one "strategy" over another? Is such justification purely a matter of pragmatic calculation, or does it obey some epistemic constraints as well? Does what we know about the world (independently of specific questions about identity) have any bearing on our understanding of this justification? I have suggested some answers to these questions by emphasizing the continuity of accounts of cultural identity with accounts of the social justification of knowledge, especially the knowledge involved in our ethical and political claims and commitments.

The third, more specific, advantage of the realist approach to experience and identity is that it explains how the oppressed may have epistemic privilege, but it does so without espousing a self-defeating or dubious kind of relativism with separatist implications. To have a cognitivist view of experience is to claim that its truth content can be evaluated, and thus potentially shared with others. As we saw in my discussion of a theory of emotions, the individualist "privileged access" theory is wrong because it denies that personal experience is fundamentally theory mediated. A realist theory of the kind I have outlined would both acknowledge the constitutive role played by theory and respect the ways specific theories – and social situations, conditions of research, and so on – provide better or worse ways of detecting new and relevant information about our world. I have said (drawing on Harding, Boyd, and Marx) that certain social arrangements and conditions – social struggles of dominated groups, for instance – can help produce more objective knowledge about a world that is constitutively defined by relations of domination. That would help explain why granting the possibility of epistemic privilege to the oppressed might be more than a sentimental gesture; in many cases in fact it is the only way to push us toward greater social objectivity. For granting that the oppressed have this privilege opens up the possibility that our own epistemic perspective is partial, shaped by our social location, and that it needs to be understood and revised hermeneutically. [. . .]

This is a general lesson whose implications every historian confronts, as theorists have lately been pointing out. Reviewing the recent cultural debate among German historians about the centrality of the Holocaust in the writing of objective national history, Dominick LaCapra shows why the historian of the period must overcome the kind of false objectivity that is derived from a denial of one's "subject position." What is needed, instead, is an understanding of the variety of affective responses to the past, responses shaped by one's location. For the historian's interpretation to be more objective than might otherwise be possible, she must attend to the ethical implications of her discursive stances.

> The Holocaust presents the historian with transference in the most traumatic form conceivable – but in a form that will vary with the difference in subject position of the analyst. Whether the historian or analyst is a survivor, a relative of survivors, a former Nazi, a former collaborator, a relative of former Nazis or collaborators, a younger Jew or German distanced from more immediate contact with survival, participation, or collaboration, or a relative "outsider" to these problems will make a difference even in the meaning of statements that may be formally identical. Certain statements or even entire orientations may seem appropriate for someone in a given subject position but not in others. (It would, for example, be ridiculous if I tried to assume the voice of Elie Wiesel or Saul Friedlander. There is a sense in which I have no right to these voices. There is also a sense in which, experiencing a lack of a viable voice, I am constrained to resort to quotation and commentary more often than I otherwise might be.) Thus although any historian must be "invested" in a distinctive way in the events of the Holocaust, not all investments (or cathexes) are the same and not all statements, rhetorics, or orientations are equally available to different historians. ("Representing the Holocaust" 110)

LaCapra goes on to characterize "statements, rhetorics, or orientations" as specific choices about "how language is used" (110), but in the context of my present discussion it is possible to see that they point to epistemic choices and stances as well. They "orient" inquiry by suggesting where we might be reflexive or critical, where attention to seemingly irrelevant subjective information can lead to greater objectivity. When we acknowledge that the experiences of victims might be repositories of valuable knowledge, and thus allow that they have epistemic privilege, we are not thereby reduced to sentimen-

tal silence. Entailed in our acknowledgment is the need to pay attention to the way our social locations facilitate or inhibit knowledge by predisposing us to register and interpret information in certain ways. Our relation to social power produces forms of blindness just as it enables degrees of lucidity. The notion of epistemic privilege is thus inseparable from the cognitivist account of experience and cultural identity I have sketched, and it explains how objectivity in historical and moral inquiry can be found not by denying our perspectives or locations but rather by interrogating their epistemic consequences.

My arguments should indicate that these consequences are not so severe that we need to retreat into skepticism. Even when we are discussing such slippery things as personal experiences and cultural meanings, it is not clear that postmodernist skepticism is warranted. Either to base definitions of identity on an idealized conception of experience (as essentialists do) or to deny experience any cognitive value whatsoever (as postmodernists might) is to cut with too blunt a theoretical knife. The realist-cognitivist account of identity I have proposed here [. . .] might suggest to some a viable alternative to these dominant theoretical positions.

Concluding Remarks

One implication of the realist account of identity I have provided may surprise some readers. This theory reconciles the claims of certain forms of identity politics with moral universalism. Indeed, it enables us to respect social difference while deepening the radical potential of universalist moral and political claims. The notion of epistemic privilege I outlined, a notion central to the realist understanding of identity, shows us why this should be the case. If our views about our identities are partly explanations of the world in which we live and these explanations are based on the knowledge we gather from our social activities, then the claim that oppressed social groups have a special kind of knowledge about the world as it affects them is hardly a mysterious one requiring idealist assumptions about cultural essences or inaccessible particularities. Rather it is an empirical claim, tied to a wider (empirical and theoretical) account of the society in which these groups live. And therefore any claim about the epistemic privilege of a particular social group will be only as convincing as the social theory and description that accompany it. On the view I am defending, claims about the epistemic privilege of a particular group are necessarily embedded in wider explanatory theories of history and of the society in which the group lives. Both the claim of epistemic privilege and the identity politics based on it need to be evaluated as any social and historical explanation should be; they are prone, like all explanatory accounts of the world, to error – both empirical and theoretical.

But when such a claim about a particular social group is true, its implications are general, not merely limited to the subjective experiences of the group in question. The knowledge we gain is "objective." This conclusion shows why we need to be wary of those overly abstract universalist visions of morality or social justice which focus on only the most general features that the various social groups (or individuals) have in common and exclude consideration of relevant particularities, relevant contextual information. [. . .]

[. . .] Subjective, particular perspectives often contain deep sources of information and knowledge, or even alternative theoretical pictures and accounts of the world we all share. An adequate appreciation of such "particular" perspectives and viewpoints makes possible a richer general picture, a deeper and more nuanced universalist view of human needs and vulnerabilities, as well as – by implication – human flourishing. In such cases, the (cultural or historical) particular and the (moral) universal complement and substantiate each other.

This explains why, with all their flaws and obvious limitations, identity-based political struggles can be built on genuine political insights. Once we acknowledge, as the realist theory requires, that such struggles cannot be based on a priori claims to political or moral knowledge, we can understand how they can legitimately draw on personal experiences and histories to deepen our knowledge of society. A feminist political consciousness often develops, for instance, through a recognition of the overwhelming significance of the personal, of the way gender relations and inequalities are played out in our most intimate relationships (including our relationships with ourselves). As we saw in Alice's case, an adequate appreciation of the political effects of gender often depends on a personal reorientation or growth, involving both the affective and the deliberative faculties. And the relation between the personal and the political is complex and indeed dialectical. The recovery of an indi-

vidual's sense of personal worth and the development of her capacity for the right kind of anger or indignation partly depend on finding the right social and political theory. In Alice's case, such a theory or such deeply theoretical hypotheses are what the consciousness-raising group provides. The group also provides Alice with the appropriate epistemic and emotional context in which to examine such hypotheses, and thus Alice's political growth, the growth in her knowledge about herself, her capacities, and her world, is predicated on her acknowledgment of her inherited social identity and its effects.

What cultural and social conditions make identitarian politics a necessary (though certainly not sufficient) form of social struggle, even of social inquiry? Alice's situation is by no means uncommon. What makes Alice's "identity" so central to the process of her moral and political growth is a very crucial feature of the world in which we all live: hierarchical and unequal gender relations are produced and reproduced by a process through which Alice is taught in effect to devalue her personal experiences as a source of knowledge about her world, and even about herself as a person – that is, as someone with genuine needs and capacities, rights and entitlements. Alice learns to value these experiences again and to glean from them – as well as from the fact that she had been taught to ignore them – crucial information about both herself and her world. "Learning" to value and imagine in such new ways is relevant not only for the disadvantaged but also for the historically privileged, for both privilege and privation can produce (different kinds of) moral and political blindness. Cultural decolonization often involves an interrogation of the epistemic and affective consequences of our social location, of historically learned habits of thinking and feeling. [. . .]

For [. . .] so many [. . .] in modern society, an identity-based politics becomes a necessary first step in coming to know what an oppressive social and cultural system obscures. Such "obscuring" is often a highly mediated and almost invisible process, implicit in traditional forms of schooling as well as in less formal practices of education and socialization. The institutions of social reproduction and cultural transmission – schools, libraries, newspapers, and museums, for instance – are oriented to the dominant cultural and social perspectives. Much of their bias is often invisible because of the relatively benign form the transmission of cultural

5

information takes: it seems utterly natural, part of the scheme of things. In such instances, cultural assimilation amounts to a repression of alternative sources of experience and value. That repression would explain why the feelings of minority groups about their "racial" or cultural identities are so tenacious, for instance, or why claims about the significance of gender or sexual identity are more than the simple "politics of recognition."[16] Quite often, such claims and feelings embody alternative and antihegemonic accounts of what is significant and in fact necessary for a more accurate understanding of the world we all share.

Thus, in analyzing identity-based politics, claims about the general social significance of a particular identity should be evaluated together with its accompanying assumptions or arguments about how the current social or cultural system makes some experiences intelligible and others obscure or irrelevant, how it treats some as legitimate sources of knowledge about the world while relegating others to the level of the narrowly personal. Both the claims and the underlying assumptions refer to the social world; they amount to explanatory theses with both empirical and theoretical content. They need to be engaged as such, and evaluated as we evaluate other such descriptions and theories about society. This realist attitude toward identity politics does not guarantee that a particular version of identity politics is justified; that justification will depend on the details of what is being claimed. We need to ask if these details mesh with the world as we know it, and to see how the accompanying theories compare with our best moral and political accounts. Thus, for instance, parallel claims and assumptions can be made by both the kind of feminist identity politics that Alice practices and a retrograde form of religious fundamentalism, and we have no way of choosing between them in advance. It would be hasty to dismiss both Alice's feminist identity and the fundamentalist religious identity *in the same way*, simply because both appeal to personal experience and make some claim to epistemic privilege. As I have been emphasizing, realism about identity requires that we see identities as complex theories about (and explanations of) the social world, and the only way to evaluate such theories is to look at how well they work as explanations. "Good" social and cultural identities are quite simply (based on) good explanations of the social world. Such explanations are not purely empirical, and what makes them "good" is in part

the cogency of the background theories they draw on, which often necessarily have deep moral and evaluative content. But such necessary interdependence of the empirical and the theoretical, the factual and the evaluative, is, the postpositivist realist will point out, not evidence of the unique epistemic status of cultural identities; this interdependence is a feature of all inquiry, scientific and moral, and adjudicating between different identity claims is not fundamentally all that different from adjudicating between two fairly complex accounts of the natural or social world. There simply is no easy way out, for a lot depends on the details. What we lose by looking for an easy way out – for example, by denying all identities validity because they are always tied to personal experience and subjective judgments – is the capacity to make useful and important distinctions between different kinds of identity, different kinds of value and judgment.

Notes

This chapter has been excerpted from Satya P. Mohanty's *Literary Theory and the Claims of History*. An earlier version, without the concluding remarks, appeared in *Cultural Critique* 24 (Spring 1993): 41–80.

[This essay has been edited for reasons of space to exclude the analysis of Toni Morrison's *Beloved*: Editors' note.]

1. Diana Fuss, in *Essentially Speaking*, provides an intelligent discussion of various kinds of essentialism and identity politics. Since my focus here is primarily on postmodernism, I have found it expedient to initially accept the simple definition of identity politics in terms of an ahistorical essentialism. Later, however, I attempt to answer some of the fundamental questions raised by proponents of identity politics (e.g., the status of experience, the epistemological privilege that the oppressed might have, etc.) in terms that are not available through the postmodernist-essentialist debate as it is currently understood, even in resourceful reinterpretations such as the one Fuss provides.

2. For a selective survey of the various critiques of experience in modern European philosophy, see Jardine 145–55. Jardine is however not too helpful when it comes to basic distinctions such as that between Hegel's *Erfahrung* and the ordinary idea of everyday experience Culler and other poststructuralist critics wish to question. For a useful account of some of the responses to Culler's position, see Fuss 23–37. For a postmodernist position on identity that draws on a variety of sources and identifies

itself as "postcolonial," see Bhabha 183–209; the relevant epistemological claims (as I understand them) are presented on pp. 191–4.

The current skepticism about the claims of experience can be traced back to Nietzsche, especially his critique of idealist notions of consciousness and subjectivity as self-sufficient and self-authorizing (see, e.g., *The Will to Power* 263–7, secs. 477–80). Nietzsche's central argument is an antipositivist one about the theory dependence of experience and facts. Whether recognition of theory dependence should lead to a denial of objectivity is one of the main questions I am addressing here. Postmodernists say that it does; Nietzsche was at least ambiguous on the subject. For Nietzsche's conception of objectivity (through the mediation of theories or perspectives), see *On the Genealogy of Morals* 555, Third Essay, sec. 12, a conception that is compatible with the antirelativist theory I am outlining here.

3. For a brief statement of the naturalistic view of philosophy as "continuous with science" rather than an "a priori propadeutic or groundwork for science," see Quine, *Ontological Relativity* 126–8.

4. I think it is a belief in the cognitive component of experience (and the knowledge it can give us about our social location) that is behind Houston Baker's impatience with Anthony Appiah's "debunking" account of the reality of race (both in Gates, *"Race," Writing, and Difference*). Appiah's critique of racial essentialism is not based on postmodernist premises, but his response to Baker on the question of experience is evasive (see "The Conservation of 'Race'" 39–44) and might point to a vagueness in his conception of identity.

One way of evaluating my theory of experience and identity is to see how it responds to the challenge the historian Joan Scott has formulated quite well: "Experience is not a word we can do without, although it is tempting, given its usage to essentialize identity and reify the subject, to abandon it altogether. . . . But [experience] serves as a way of talking about what happened, of establishing difference and similarity, of claiming knowledge. . . . Given the ubiquity of the term, it seems to me more useful to work with it, to analyze its operations and redefine its meaning. . . . The study of experience . . . must call into question its originary status in historical explanation" (37). Scott points out that postmodernist attacks on experience are a critique of a certain kind of epistemological view. I am not sure, however, that I agree with her assumption that a "genuinely non-foundational[ist] history" is possible only "when historians take as their project not the reproduction and transmission of knowledge said to be arrived at through experience, but the analysis of the production of that knowledge itself" (37). I would suggest that once we acknowledge the cognitive status of experience, as well as the way it is necessarily theory dependent, we can conceive of legitimate ways of reproducing and transmitting "knowledge said to be arrived at through experience." As will be clear from what I argue below, this is in fact the best way to understand the "epistemic privilege" of, say, the oppressed, as well as how it demands hermeneutical respect from the historian.

5. See Scheman, "Anger and the Politics of Naming."

6. This theory-mediated process of coming to acknowledge one's genuine feelings is central to any form of political consciousness raising. The antiracist work done by the "freedom schools" in the South also drew on normative theories of personhood and racial justice in order to enable victims of racism to accurately interpret their experiences and their needs. Such "interpretations" are, as I hope to suggest, never purely intellectual.

7. I am thinking here of the kind of extreme thesis about "drives" and "needs" that Nietzsche sometimes combined with his valid antipositivist insights: "Against positivism, which halts at phenomena – 'There are only *facts*' – I would say: No, facts [*sic*] is precisely what there is not, only interpretations. We cannot establish any fact 'in itself': perhaps it is folly to want to do such a thing. . . . It is our needs that interpret the world; our drives and their For and Against. Every drive is a kind of lust to rule; each one has its perspective that it would like to compel all the other drives to accept as a norm" (*Will* 267, sec. 481).

8. In emphasizing the fact that Alice comes to know something about her world through her emotion, I wish to show how Scheman's account of emotion is a realist one. Scheman does not identify her position as realist, perhaps because she thinks (wrongly, to my mind) that realism about emotions can only lead to a sort of physicalism: e.g., "types of psychological states (like being angry or in pain) actually are types of physical states (like certain patterns of neurons firing)" ("Individualism" 225). My interpretation of emotions in this essay should suggest a better conception of the realist view. For a cognitivist-realist understanding of emotions that is compatible with mine, see the many valuable suggestions in Lorde, esp. 54–8.

9. "A person of practical insight," writes Martha Nussbaum, imaginatively and resourcefully elaborating Aristotle's view of moral development, "will cultivate emotional openness and responsiveness in approaching a new situation. Frequently, it will be her passional response, rather than detached thinking, that will guide her to the appropriate recognitions. 'Here is a case where a friend needs my help': this will often be 'seen' first by the feelings that are constituent parts of friendship, rather than

by pure intellect. Intellect will often want to consult these feelings to get information about the true nature of the situation. Without them its approach to a new situation would be blind and obtuse.... Without feeling, a part of the correct perception is missing" (78–9).

10. This explanatory notion of "objective interests" implies comparison with other competing explanations of the same phenomena. When Marxists talk about the objective interests of the working class, they are trying to explain the location of the class in terms, on the one hand, of the relations of production and, on the other, of their theories about human freedom and social justice. Ernesto Laclau and Chantal Mouffe's criticism of the notion of objective interests thus seems to be either hasty or disingenuous. "In our view," they write, "... it is necessary to ... discard the idea of a perfectly unified and homogeneous agent, such as the working class of classical discourse.... [F]undamental interests in socialism cannot be *logically* deduced from determinate positions in the economic process" (84). The theoretical assumption here is that "fundamental interests in socialism" can either be "logically deduced" on the basis of "determinate positions in the economic process" or else not discovered at all. The view that "interests" might be inferred (or deduced, in their stronger language) solely on the basis of "determinate positions" without the mediation of any theory is clearly based on a positivist understanding of explanation. Having rejected this view, Laclau and Mouffe leap to the postmodernist conclusion that a social group's interests cannot be identified through an objective explanation: There is "no constitutive principle for social agents [interests or anything else] which can be fixed in an ultimate class core." This leads to the more general assertion that "unfixity [is] the condition of every social identity" (85). The glib antiobjectivism of many postmodernist positions is based on such positivist presuppositions about the nature of inquiry. For a useful point of contrast, see the accounts of Marx's conception of scientific and moral objectivity in Railton 763–73; and Gilbert 154–83.

11. See Railton, esp. 770–1.

12. One way to evaluate different versions of postmodernism is to examine the conception of objectivity they define themselves against; another is to look carefully at how precisely they develop their notion of fallibility. Donna Haraway has suggested in a well-known essay that we need to go beyond "realism" (by which I think she means positivism) to conceive the world (i.e., the object of knowledge) as a "coding trickster with whom we must learn to converse" (esp. 198–9, 201). "The Coyote or Trickster," she argues, "embodied in American Southwest Indian accounts, suggests our situation when we give up mastery but keep searching for fidelity,

knowing all the while we will be hoodwinked" (199). The image suggests the epistemological injunction to acknowledge "the agency of the world" by "mak[ing] room for some unsettling possibilities, including a sense of the world's independent sense of humour" (199). This view is for the most part compatible with the postpositivist epistemology I am developing here, but Haraway's conception of fallibility is not precise enough to be very helpful. It is important to know more than the fact that "we will be hoodwinked," which is here formulated as a generalized possibility. We do not begin to understand the hoodwinking until we appreciate why and where we were wrong in our expectations (or theories). In many situations – many more than Haraway's image suggests – it is barely useful to know that we were wrong unless we are also led to a more precise understanding of the sources of our error. I agree with Haraway that we should give up (foundationalist) "mastery," and opt for (postpositivist) "fidelity"; but our conception of that fidelity will be richer to the extent that we can specify and deepen our understanding of the conditions that lead to our "hoodwinking." Objectivity and error are the products of social practice, and we should attempt to understand as much as we legitimately can about them (in naturalistic terms) before we generalize about our condition of original epistemic sinfulness.

13. This way of understanding reference builds on the "causal" account discussed in chapter 2 of my *Literary Theory and the Claims of History*. Also see Boyd, "Metaphor and Theory Change" 356–408, for a useful development of the causal theory.

14. For two realist accounts that define political identity by reference to social location, common interests, and shared contexts of struggle, see Sivanandan (on "black" people in Britain) and Chandra Talpade Mohanty (on "Third World women"). I discussed Sivanandan's essay briefly in my *Literary Theory and the Claims of History* 17.

15. See Spivak 202–11; and for a position that is both more complex and more lucidly discussed, Fuss, esp. 118–19. I think Fuss's overall project would be better served by a fully developed realist theory of experience than by the Althusserian one she invokes in her concluding discussion.

16. Charles Taylor sees contemporary demands for multiculturalism as primarily the demand for "recognition"; see "The Politics of Recognition" 25–73. It should be evident by now why I would think that this is an underestimation of the multiculturalist claim.

References

Appiah, Anthony. "The Conservation of 'Race.'" *Black American Literature Forum* 23.1 (Spring 1989): 37–69.

———. "The Uncompleted Argument: Du Bois and the Illusion of Race." *Critical Inquiry* 12.1 (1985): 21–37.

Baker, Houston A., Jr. "Caliban's Triple Play." *"Race," Writing, and Difference*. Ed. Henry Louis Gates. Vol. 12, no. 1. Chicago: University of Chicago Press. 381–95.

Bhabha, Homi K. "Interrogating Identity: The Postcolonial Prerogative." *Anatomy of Racism*. Ed. David Theo Goldberg. Minneapolis: University of Minnesota Press, 1990. 183–209.

Boyd, Richard N. "How to Be a Moral Realist." *Essays on Moral Realism*. Ed. Geoffrey Sayre-McCord. Ithaca: Cornell University Press, 1988. 181–228.

———. "Metaphor and Theory Change: What Is 'Metaphor' a Metaphor For?" *Metaphor and Thought*. Ed. Andrew Ortony. New York: Cambridge University Press, 1979. 356–408.

Culler, Jonathan. *On Deconstruction: Theory and Criticism after Structuralism*. Ithaca: Cornell University Press, 1982.

de Sousa, Ronald. "The Rationality of Emotions." *Explaining Emotions*. Ed. Amelie O. Rorty. Berkeley: University of California Press, 1980. 127–51.

Fuss, Diana. *Essentially Speaking: Feminism, Nature & Difference*. New York: Routledge, 1989.

Gates, Henry Louis, ed. *"Race," Writing, and Difference*. Vol. 12, no. 1. Chicago: University of Chicago Press, 1985.

Gilbert, Alan. "Marx's Moral Realism: Eudaimonism and Moral Progress." *After Marx*. Ed. Terence Ball and James Farr. New York: Cambridge University Press, 1984. 154–83.

Haraway, Donna J. "Situated Knowledges: The Science Question in Feminism and the Privilege of Partial Perspective." *Simians, Cyborgs, and Women*. New York: Routledge, 1991. 183–201, 248–50.

Harding, Sandra. *Whose Science? Whose Knowledge? Thinking from Women's Lives*. Ithaca: Cornell University Press, 1991.

Jardine, Alice A. *Gynesis*. Ithaca: Cornell University Press, 1985.

LaCapra, Dominick. "Representing the Holocaust: Reflections on Historians' Debate." *Probing the Limits of Representation: Nazism and the "Final Solution."* Ed. Saul Friedlander. Cambridge, MA: Harvard University Press, 1992. 108–27, 356–60.

Laclau, Ernesto, and Chantal Mouffe. *Hegemony & Socialist Strategy: Towards a Radical Democratic Politics*. Trans. Winston Moore and Paul Cammack. London: Verso, 1985.

Lorde, Audre. *Sister Outsider*. Freedom, CA: Crossing Press, 1984.

Mohanty, Chandra Talpade. "Cartographies of Struggle: Third World Women and the Politics of Feminism." *Third World Women and the Politics of Feminism*. Ed. Chandra Talpade Mohanty, Ann Russo, and Lourdes Torres. Bloomington: Indiana University Press, 1991. 1–47.

Mohanty, Satya. *Literary Theory and the Claims of History: Postmodernism, Objectivity, Multicultural Politics*. Ithaca: Cornell University Press, 1997.

———. "Us and Them: On the Philosophical Basis of Political Criticism." *Yale Journal of Criticism* 2.2 (1989): 1–31.

Mohanty, Satya P., and Jonathan Monroe. "John Ashbery and the Articulation of the Social." *Diacritics* 17.2 (Summer 1987): 37–63.

Nietzsche, Friedrich. *On the Genealogy of Morals. Basic Writings of Nietzsche*. Trans. and ed. Walter Kaufmann. New York: Modern Library, 1969. 449–599.

———. *The Will to Power*. Trans. Walter Kaufmann and R. J. Hollingdale. Ed. Walter Kaufmann. New York: Vintage, 1968.

Nussbaum, Martha. *Love's Knowledge*. New York: Oxford University Press, 1990.

Putnam, Hilary. "Explanation and Reference." *Mind, Language and Reality*. New York: Cambridge University Press, 1975. 196–214.

———. "The Meaning of 'Meaning.'" *Mind, Language and Reality*. 215–71.

Quine, W. V. O. "Epistemology Naturalized." *Naturalizing Epistemology*. Ed. Hilary Kornblith. Cambridge, MA: MIT Press, 1985. 15–29.

———. *Ontological Relativity and Other Essays*. New York: Columbia University Press, 1969. 126–8.

Railton, Peter. "Marx and the Objectivity of Science." *The Philosophy of Science*. Ed. Richard Boyd, Philip Gasper, and J. D. Trout. Cambridge, MA: MIT Press, 1991. 763–73.

Scheman, Naomi. "Anger and the Politics of Naming." *Women and Language in Literature and Society*. Ed. Sally McConnell-Ginet, Ruth Borker, and Nelly Furman. New York: Praeger, 1980. 174–87.

———. "Individualism and the Objects of Psychology." *Discovering Reality*. Ed. Sandra Harding and Merril B. Hintikka. Dordrecht: D. Riedel, 1983. 225–44.

Scott, Joan. "'Experience.'" *Feminists Theorize the Political*. Ed. Judith Butler and Joan Scott. New York: Routledge, 1992. 22–40.

Sivanandan, A. "RAT and the Degradation of Black Struggle." *Communities of Resistance: Writings on Black Struggles for Socialism*. London: Verso, 1990. 77–122.

Taylor, Charles. "The Politics of Recognition." *Multiculturalism and the Politics of Recognition: An Essay by Charles Taylor*. Ed. Amy Gutmann. Princeton: Princeton University Press, 1992. 25–73.

Afterword
Identities: Postcolonial and Global

Eduardo Mendieta

We endure, we endure creatively due to our imperative ability to say "No" to reality, to build fictions of alterity, of dreamt or willed or awaited "otherness" for our consciousness to inhabit. It is in this precise sense that the utopian and the messianic are figures of syntax.

George Steiner[1]

Ich bin du, wenn ich ich bin

Paul Celan[2]

People increasingly believe in what they see and they buy what they believe in. . . . People use, drive, wear, eat and buy what they see in the movies.

Wim Wenders[3]

[I]ntersubjectivity *stricto sensu* involves the subject's radical decenteredness: only when my self-consciousness is externalized in an object do I begin to look for it in another subject.

Slavo Zizek[4]

The Bookend and Bookmark

At the end of a massive and ecumenical anthology like the one the reader is holding, these closing remarks can only hope to be a bookend. They hope to merely trace lines of approach and departure. In this way, they offer a sort of map, which, like all maps, is circumscribed and conditional. These remarks, then, aim at offering an impressionistic sketch that draws lines of resemblance but also possible horizons for future study.

Even a cursory glance at the table of contents of this volume will make the following evident: we are always many, synchronically and diachronically. Our identities are never discovered. They are always constituted, constructed, invented, imagined, imposed, projected, suffered, and celebrated. Identities are never univocal, stable, or innocent. They are always an accomplishment and a ceaseless project. For this reason, in the process of constituting them

and negotiating them, we discover that we *were* like we never imagined ourselves to have been. And, simultaneously, we discover that we have *become* or are now something that has little resemblance to what we thought we were. In this play between what we were, but did not know we were, and what we have become, and perhaps are reluctant to face, enters another factor: namely, how we get a glimpse or take a glance at that identity that was and that we have become. Identities have a lot to do with images, imaginaries, and the imagination. A version of an identity is crystallized or captured as a portrait by a certain image. Let us think of a Norman Rockwell – a whole train of ideology runs through his pictures of middle-class, white America, with its racial economy, its good old American values, and its almost mythical solidness. Of course, before there was a Rockwell, we had the great painters of bourgeois portraits. Museums, where these portraits are enshrined as high art, are national albums – they archive the ways in which nations and cultures have represented themselves. For this reason, they are central to the processes of national identity construction, and, consequently, they are always objects of political contestation. Yet neither portraits nor museums are self-evident, and for this reason a plurality of forms, techniques, and genres of making sense of them have emerged. Images are not legible by themselves. And in this way, even our images of us, of our national and cultural pasts, have been catalogued, exegeted, commented, analyzed, criticized, and studied perennially. In this way, we may say, we have made a full circle: our identities are always plural, because the ways we have represented and captured those identities have been plural. In tandem, the techniques for making sense of these forms of representation have also been plural. This much also has been announced: the way in which identities were or might have been constituted; how they are presently being constituted; the shift in the means and objects for their representation have become plural; and the equally urgent questions about the transformation in the conceptual tools for reflecting on those images and representations of identities.

The Way We Were (Not)

This volume might be taken to be constructing a narrative that goes something like this. Subjects or selves were constituted by a matrix of vectors: nation, class, gender, race, sexuality, and ethnicity. These were the most salient vectors, although the editors could also have included subsections on age and religion. The relationship of these vectors was not always one of parallelism, or even tangentiality and perpendicularity. At times, these vectors have entered into multiple alliances, or convergences. Class and race have conspired to project a certain national identity. Gender has also always had a synergetic effect. In conjunction with race and class, the nation has been imagined as emasculated or violated, virile or effeminate. The nation is clearly marked by a sexual imaginary and image. Think of Uncle Sam, or the Statue of Liberty. Which image is mobilized has to do with the nature of the threat and the aim of the mobilization. Are we about to enter a war against an external foe, or are we about to wage a metaphorical war on "poverty," "illiteracy," or "malnutrition"? Depending on the nature of the threat, we mobilize different images

about ourselves. In this way, the person, as a social agent, finds herself at the vortex of these converging vectors. We are many, and we are always being torn asunder by the many forces that impinge upon us and that make claims on us. We negotiate these forces, and thus we gain a foothold on an imaginary place: the sovereignty of our selves.

The entwinement between forces that converge in synergy to create the space for the emergence of identities is further complicated by an equivocal synchronicity. Put differently, we have no timetable for the ordering of sequences. More explicitly, we cannot say that class is prior to nation; or rather, affirmatively, that class is co-constitutive of and co-originary with nationhood and nationality. Alternatively, we can ask, is race prior to class, or is class constituted through a play on nation and race, in such a way that one must exclude the other, or the latter is a contaminant of the former? Similarly, religion seems to predate the order of nation and class, yet there is a way in which Irish Catholicism, American Judaism, Southern Baptism, or Midwestern evangelical Protestantism are very unique formations that emerged from the interaction between class, race, and nationality. It should not go without mention that race and gender have a double valence, or polarity, that complicates further the nature of the interactions. It is not just a question of blackness and masculinity, but also of whiteness and femininity, and their respective interactions. The obstinacy and opaqueness of these forces *vis-à-vis* how we constitute our identities is once again best illustrated in terms of an image, or lack thereof: when we think of "America," when we seek to imagine America, why are our images of that America not just gendered but also raced, and raced in such a way that we would never, or rather, very infrequently, imagine and image (as a verb) that America as a black woman?

Our identities, then, we may aver, are a matter of positionality, or locality. An identity is not a *prius*, object, or substratum, or essential substance. It is a social locus, and a social locus is an imagined and imaginary topos. This place or locality is a function of a social topography, or how forces determine a field of forces. We move, or are in the process of moving, through those fields of forces. Social topographies themselves have changed in accordance with the stability and potentiality of some of the forces that constituted the web of forces determining the space of social interaction. At the very least, however, for several hundred years, identities have been determined and constituted by the framework of the national economy, fairly stable class identities, gender and race relations that have entered into interaction with each other within the political economy of the nation-states. These nation-states in turn formed part of geopolitical units. Nation-states themselves developed through and in the midst of imperial and colonial projects, projects that have been sanctioned and required by civilizational missions. These civilizational missions were themselves the remnants of millennial cultural and political matrixes of social interaction. For at one time, identities were thought of in terms of Christendom versus Islam, or versus the infidels, or barbarians. Nation-states became the carriers of civilizational missions: England, France, Italy, or Germany would take up the burden of the white man, but also of all of Western culture. These burdens – this mission – would be carried out not only through internal wars of pacification and unification, but also through imperial wars for the sake of the expansion of civilization. In the language of world-system analysis, we may say that at different times the managing center of the system has shifted from nation to nation, depending on which nation is in control not only of the principal tool of management of the world economy, but also of the military might, and the power to condition the imaginary of that world system. Paraphrasing Marx, the ruling imaginary of the world system is the imaginary of the ruling nation within the world system. And thus, we have had anglophilia, francophilia, germanophilia, and more recently americanophilia.

At any given time, then, we are not just negotiating our localities or positions *vis-à-vis* race, class, gender, and nationality, but also positionalities within a geopolitical system. We are not solely working-class, white, secular/Protestant/civil religion, males, living our masculinity vicariously through a mass culture and mass consumerist mediated imaginary; we are also Westerners, in Europe or North America, who benefit from participating in the consumption of a culture that is taken as the norm for all other cultures across the world. There are invisible privileges that are attached to both race and gender, but also to "culture" in the broadest sense of what world historians such as Arnold Toynbee, William McNeill, and Eric Voegelin have called "civilizational units." We reflect as little on what it feels, or means, to be a white male as we reflect on what it means to be a white Westerner.

Yet, whether we belong to "Western," Muslim, African, Latin American, and so on, cultures conditions our position within a field of forces, and field of production of possibilities or lack thereof. Our identities are global products. Some not so mundane examples: British identity and tea time, French café au lait, lattes and cappuccinos, North American green and fruit salads. These are not merely anecdotal bookmarks. Behind a whole national *modus vivendi* and comportment, there stand intricate webs of commercial, political, and colonial dependencies and hegemonies. For this reason the world system, since its formalization and consolidation in the sixteenth century, has been ever since then a modern colonial world system, as Walter Mignolo has argued.[5] In this way, what has been called the "wages of whiteness"[6] and masculinity must be thought simultaneously in terms of a "coloniality of power," that is, the way in which cultural, political, economic, and social relations are shot through with the traces of colonial relations. Positionality is conditioned by a topology of simultaneous webs of power, which harbor and preserve the traces of their historical origins. This is what Anibal Quijano has felicitously called "coloniality of power."[7] Power is an effect of modern, colonial, geopolitical positions within a world system, and, in turn, someone's position within this world system enables or disables certain forms of force and coercion, resistance or subjugation. Our identities are many; they are always negotiated, and they always carry the mark of the coloniality of power.

How We Are Becoming Different Again

The consolidation of the modern colonial world system was accompanied by the rise of violent, intransigent, and differential forms of nationalisms that mobilized all substrata of sociality for the sake of "imagined communities."[8] Regimes of masculinity and femininity were constituted for the sake of the domestication and management of social imaginaries that made of social subjects docile weapons and tools of wars and genocidal industries. Within these regimes of masculinity, or compulsive heterosexuality, and domestic femininity, or solicitous docility, as some sort of lymphatic fluid, there flows the bad blood of racism. Racism is a capillary to the sociality of both masculinity and femininity. Yet racism is never solely a national affair, although we can talk about particular forms of racisms (German, French, British, North American, etc.). It is constitutive of cultural and civilizational orientations. Using a Foucauldian lexicon, we may say that racism was deployed in order to create a condition in which an internal threat had to be monitored, studied, regimented, and submitted to the vigilance and violence of sanctioned authorities.[9] Modern nation-states, as units within a world system, emerged from the domestication and regimentation of a social body. In this way, nationalism was and is a biopolitics – that is, a politics of the gendered, raced, and classed bodies. The goal of this biopolitics was to make available to the nation the body of its subjects. Nationalisms, then, have been a form of "animal husbandry,"[10] in which the full apparatus of the state creates the conditions for the survival of its subjects, and to the same extent abrogates for itself the full authority of letting or making live, and thus, of letting or making die (killing by means of a sanctioned death penalty) in accordance with a calculus of national (or international) justice and lawfulness. Nationalisms are forms of power over life, as Etienne Balibar puts it, glossing Foucault.[11] For this reason, racisms are the acme of this sovereign power over the life of social subjects. Racism is the normalization, and institutionalization, of the sanction to kill an imagined, whether it is internal or external, threat.[12]

It makes sense at this point to ask: to what extent has this regimentation of the social body undergone a structural transformation as a result of two processes: globalization and postcolonialism? By globalization, we should not understand here merely the planetarization of a certain form of economic imperialism, i.e. the expansion of multinationals, the interdependence of finance markets, the subjugation of national economies to the policies of the World Bank, the International Monetary Fund, etc. Globalization has to do also with processes of political, cultural, and social integration that in many ways antecede economic globalization.[13] Here one can briefly make reference to movements such as the green, peace, and women's movements, which have been proto-globalization movements. A global polity has nominally emerged via the rhetoric and protection of universal human rights. A global, or postnational, form of legality has begun to emerge through the precedents of the Nuremberg trials, the prosecutions of crimes against humanity, and the legal precedents that allow for extradition of war criminals such as Augusto Pinochet, Slobodan Milosevic, Pol Pot, and even possibly Henry Kissinger.[14]

In parallel, at the level of what Arjun Appadurai has called cultural flows,[15] we have not just the globalization of an "American" imaginary, but instead a more complicated interaction between the local and the global. Thus we have the emergence of cultural formations and trends that are not easily reducible to national forms of cultural sovereignty and affirmation. Such musical, fashion, and even literary productions are, rather, a product of the interaction between local contexts and global trends. At one point, in anthropology and religious studies, these processes of cultural appropriation were called acculturation and enculturation. Today we talk about *glocalization*.[16] But the import of these references has to do with what Jürgen Habermas has called a "post-national" constellation in which the forces and challenges that communities face are directly linked to dynamics and processes that overflow the boundaries and constitutions of nation-states.[17]

On the other hand, we have the challenge of postcolonial conditions, which have to do with the same processes that are generally described under the rubric of globalization theory, but which are described from the perspective of the "coloniality of power." A provisional formulation would be that while globalization theories erase the conditions of the emergence of global relations, postcolonial theory wants to make such conditions the very object of reflection. And while globalization theories would like to disaggregate and make opaque the relations between political-economic and cultural power, not just within but also without the nation, postcolonial forms of theorizing seek to foreground the interdependence between cultural formations and economic and political powers. Another difference between these different ways of looking at the same phenomena is that globalization theories seem to operate with the assumption of the *fait accompli* character of globalization processes, and in this way, they seem, or would like to, dispense with history. Postcolonial forms of critique and theorizing aim at thematizing in tandem the power of history and the history of power.[18]

With those reflections in place, we can ask once again: what are the new contexts for the construction and constitutions of identities or identity formations? We must at the very least speak of both global and postcolonial identities. Such identities have to do with generalized expectations about the inviolability of personal integrity. At the very least, and very nominally, persons across the world can appeal to a transnational political realm that offers them the guarantee and warrant for recourse against totalitarian states. And, in this way, identity has shifted one of its referents, jumping over the nation–state and its conditional constitutions. Human rights project a political identity that obeys a different logic than that of the nation–state, with its atavistic and virulent nationalisms. Economically, for a section of the globe of course, a certain standard of living has become a norm, even an entitlement. In a non-equivocating way, it has become clear that mass communication and culture has conspired to planetarize a regime of mass consumption. An attendant consequence of this planetarized mass consumption is the homogenization of expectations of commodity entitlements. In this way, needs are dictated by the market, or rather needs are transformed in compulsions to consume what the market offers. It goes without saying that this holy trinity of mass culture, communication, and consumption have forged a *lingua franca*, or, more precisely, a transnational pidgin that is made up of the acronyms and brand names of global commodities.

Even when forms and processes of resistance to these new transnational or postcolonial formations emerge, their languages are already conditioned by the global forms of communication. Religious fundamentalism is an obvious example, but other forms of localized resistance could be used to illustrate this dialectic of using the tools and objects of a global culture to contest and challenge it. In the case of religious fundamentalism, whether it is Islamic or Christian, there is a deployment of the whole spectrum of channels as well as images of the global order to transmit and foment an anti-globalization or anti-modern message. The use of extremely sophisticated channels of communication, as well as the tools of international finance markets, and up-to-date technology, is accompanied by the mobilization of archaic icons and rituals. For this reason, one may speculate that these forms of anti-modernism and anti-globalization movements are less mobilizations external to the global processes themselves, and more internal forms of resistance whose grammars of critique and rejection are determined by the global and postcolonial condition.

The emergence of this planetarized mass culture, furthermore, has been accompanied by a generalization of mass mobilization, nomadism, and transnational flows of populations. These terms might rightly be dismissed as being too Aesopian. Indeed, the almost global condition of mass immigration and intra- and trans-continental flows of populations have had to do less with benign conditions of free access and relocation, and more with the devastations of civil and international wars. Immigrations, exiles, and refugees: this is the other side of planetarized uprootedness. We would be concealing the dark underside of our global age were we to think of it merely in terms of the cosmopolitan world traveler who displaces herself across continents and crosses passport checkpoints effortlessly.[19] As Saskia Sassen has so eloquently argued, the twentieth century has normalized, in the most detrimental and inhuman way, the condition of the exile and the refuge.[20] Yet without endorsing a theodicy in which all is for the good of humanity *in the long run*, or as the cunning of reason would reconcile *post festum*, it must be granted that from these massive, devastating, and uprooting exiles and mobilizations new cultures have and are emerging (not just in Europe and Africa, but also in the American continent, where over the last hundred years we have witnessed massive population moves northward).

Perhaps a last – but only in the order of narrative and not in terms of the whole spectrum of elements and forces that constitute our global and postnational condition – point of reference for the emergent topography of postnational and postcolonial identities is the unprecedented mega-urbanization of the planet. Close to half of humanity lives in mega-urbes, and these are mostly located in the geographical south. Cities have become the point of destination of most of the displaced and exiled masses of the world. Cities, at the same time, have become nodes in a network of transnational flows (economic, political, cultural, and of working humanity). In this way, cities have become what Sassen has called the locus for the territorialization of global process. At the same time, cities have become the locus for the contestation of the national; that is, they have become places where the national is undone and reconstituted. This takes the form not only of the emergence of cosmopolitan civic cultures, but also the development of urban, legal, and political formations that short-circuit the national and nationalistic order.[21] Cities are the frontiers in which national identities are formed and recontextualized. The most notorious example of this logic of formation and recontextualization is the way in which Latinos in the US have become a major force in the urban renaissance of major US cities such as Los Angeles, New York, San Francisco, Chicago, and Miami, as Mike Davis has recently shown.[22] The point: at the same time that we are witnessing the emergence of postnational and postcolonial identities, we are also witnessing the emergence of identities that are more likely to be city-focused or oriented. Thus, it is inevitable that New Yorkers, Berliners, Barcelonans, Parisians, Londoners, Tokyoans, and so on, share more in common among themselves than with their respective compatriots or native nationals.

If we accept the definition of identity as locality and positionality determined by a social topography, then we must realize that the cartography of contemporary identities has been and is being redrawn. The lines of demarcation are shifting, as boundaries move with mass migrations, as cities become global nodes in a transnational nexus of forces, and televisions, portable CD players, magazines, movies, and even novels project a postcolonial and postnational imaginary.

How We Look at Ourselves Looking at Ourselves

Identities are not only unstable because they are fragile negotiations, but also because they are always succumbing to the shock of visual misrecognition. More often than not, identities fail to recognize themselves in the images that are projected of them and for them. In an alternative formulation, one may say that identities are not only ephemeral and always in the process of being redrawn because they are ideological sedimentations, but also because the images that are mobilized and painted of them and for them are always fragmenting and tearing under the pressure of visual scrutiny. The auguring of identity theorizations and the politics of identity are not entirely dissociated from the hegemony of the visual, or the rise of an occularocentric culture. Yet it is precisely that visual or ocular regime that renders them suspect. For the image is the focus of concentration of the imagination and the imaginary. An image is a crystallization of an act of imagination that is informed by a certain imaginary. Yet such images, as coagulated ideology, inevitably ossify. For this reason, it is not necessary to wax metaphysical, Lacanian, or metaphorical in order to offer enough warrant for what is taken as the *conditio sine qua non* of the advertising industry: namely,

that an image is worth a thousand words, and that ideologies speak their imaginations and imaginaries through the language of images. Who is able to control the images a society projects for itself is able to manipulate the social imagination and imaginary, and in this way to coin the currency of what is representable, criticizable, and fathomable. By imagination, we understand what a social group or group of social agents can foreseeably anticipate – it is the faculty by means of which agents give form and meaning to their web of relations. The imaginary is a horizon of meaningfulness, of possibilities and lacks, of what is at all thinkable and what remains illegible and unfathomable. Image, imagination, and imaginary stand in a continuum of concreteness and metaphoricality, of representation and representability, of lexicality and symbolicality. They also stand conditioned by the technical infrastructures that enable the commerce in images. This is another way of saying that in the age of the electronic and mechanical reproduction of images, in the age of the digitization of all forms of information, we have the boundless dissemination and depthless manipulability of all images and information that may be represented in the form of images. The objection will be quickly raised: the new mediatization of culture affects not just what is represented and visualized, but also what might be heard and worn. There is a feedback effect. The pervasiveness of all electronic means of communication have made certain images ubiquitous; these images in turn sanction, insinuate, and command certain fashions and cultural images that come to be taken as the common currency of cultures across the globe.

A logical consequence of the emergence of digitally reproducible and the manipulability of images and the imagination is the elimination of the distinction between high and low culture, as well as the evisceration of a differential culture that discriminated between the young and old. We live in a postcultural culture, and post-ageist society. It is postcultural inasmuch as culture made reference to something that only a very educated and select public could understand, appreciate, and enjoy. The rise of a mass culture has meant that what was before low culture has become mainstream culture, while what was high culture has become part of mass culture. Seen in this way, it is perhaps pointless to try to say whether the cultural elitist or the cultural populist has won. For elements of both have been appropriate in a culture that many call no-brow culture, a culture without invidious and exclusionary distinctions.

One may rightly point out that age has become less important to a very small population of the world: namely, those populations within the developed and industrialized nations of the geographical north of the planet. Yet the issue of age is not only related to longer life expectancies that have been achieved because of incredible advances in medicine, better nutrition, and socialized healthcare (in particular in Europe, where most of these trends are true), but also because of other factors, most notorious among them being perhaps the perpetual transformation of the labor market, in these advanced and highly informaticized economies, on the one hand, and the not always generalized practices of socialized higher education and the re-education of the labor force, on the other hand.[23] In conjunction with this general flux of the labor market, which has literally transformed the conditions for the construction of male identities that were so fundamentally fixed and determined by stable jobs and professions – to the extent that entire family generations engage in the same trade and profession, and the already vanishing phenomenon of a breadwinner who might have spent the better part of his adult life doing the same type of job – we have to add the emergence of a cultural marketplace that appeals to all ages simultaneously. This latter trend might be transitory and perhaps only a function of a generational overlap having to do with global recessions and the coming-of-age of baby-boomers. Yet there is the peculiar contemporary situation in which middle-age persons are enjoying the same kinds of music and participating in the same kinds of cultural icon that teenagers are consuming and referring to in their own identity constructions.

There is a general cultural jam, so to speak, in which generations meet in the beltway of cultural dialogue and there is a pandemonium in which it is difficult to differentiate between what responds to and speaks for which generation. Cultures, then, have become market options, rather than inevitable ascriptions, or fated lifelines. Ulrich Beck, as well as Anthony Giddens, has called this the rise of the post-traditional society.[24] Traditions were the way of anchoring cultural practices as well as life options and personal choices. Personal character was linked to a tradition. In the market cacophony of the cultural jam in which we may opt for this or that culture, tradition itself has become less a stable compass, and more a contingent and perhaps irrelevant option. This is, of course, viewed from the worst angle. At best, traditions themselves have become more self-reflexive than we have ever allowed them to be. The conditions of the acceptability of a tradition have now become open to debate and deliberation. In other words, traditions themselves have become objects of critical reflection and criticizable claims. In this way, to live in a post-traditional society means that we live in societies in which we critically appropriate the ways in which we decide to position ourselves to our past and our future. And in this way, once again we have come full circle: what is taken to be tradition is itself a choice made available to us by the very conditions of postnational and postcolonial society. For this reason, fundamentalisms, of any sort whatsoever, are not options against modernity, but options that modernity itself has made available to modern/postcolonial/global subjects. When we seek to find out who we are, the question is no longer what identity we seek to discover, but rather into what mirrors we look, and how we may be able to look in different mirrors at the same time.

Heterotopias or Second Order Observations

The fact that these remarks are a bookend at the end of a wide-ranging and interdisciplinary anthology gathering classic and reverberating analyses on identity is perhaps too thin a veneer to conceal the promiscuous and polygenic character of what has thus far been presented. The question of identity – at least this much should have been taken away from a volume like this – is not a mere passing cultural fad. Nor are the diverse studies and theories about it an apologia poorly disguised as political correctness. It is an enduring question, a perennial human question. Next, this much should also have been taken away: a variety of disciplines have emerged that have tried to deal explicitly with the issues relating to the question of identity, and not just for aleatory reasons. Identity has defied and will continue to defy easy encapsulation by one or even a group of disciplines. For identity has to do with the most fundamental, but also wide-spanning, aspects of human existence. There is in fact a way in which narratives could be told of different, if not all disciplines, in terms of their specific and original confrontation with the question of identity. Whether it is sociology, political theory, economics, philosophy, or history, in one way or another, they have been constitutively determined by the way they have broached the question of identity.[25]

The constitutive relationship between the human and social sciences, on the one hand, and the question of identity, on the other, can best be illustrated by looking briefly at the way this relationship has played itself out with respect to philosophy. At first blush, one can easily note that identity has been an enduring philosopheme that runs through the entire Western philosophical tradition, at least since its putative birth in Ionia. We find reflections about the issue in Heraclitus, Plato, Aristotle, Augustine, Plotinus, Boethius, Ockham, Aquinas, Suarez, Descartes, Montaigne, Spinoza, Kant, Vico, Hegel – to name just a few of the salient names of philosophers in the canon. As a philosopheme, it has been approached from a variety of philosophical sub-fields: metaphysics, theology, ontology, epistemology; but also approaches: anthropological, linguistic, mathematical, logical, etc. Indeed, the very structure and coherence of philosophical traditions has been determined by how they have dealt with the question of identity. Thus, we have had monists and pluralists, nominalists and realists, pantheists and monotheists, and so on. Indeed, where one stands with respect to the tradition depends on how one sees the "one" as being related to the "many," or on how one sees the identity, or non-identity, between the creator and the created, or "ideas" in the mind and the "signs" that point to what ideas stand for in the "real world," which are all questions having to do with the identity of the world, signs, ideas, and persons.

From the perspective of the philosopher as a historical and hermeneutically embedded agent, the question of identity has been equally determining. Yet Western philosophers have rejected with equal vehemence the dependence of their thinking on their own personhood. Whether this rejection is a fundamental tenet of Western philosophy is not as revealing as is what Western philosophers have been doing while rejecting their own embeddedness within a tradition. Performatively, in the praxis of their calling and discipline, they proved precisely what they so anxiously seek to refute. In their *modus operandi*, philosophers philosophize in terms of how the tradition is either betrayed or preserved, of how there is a conceptual core and coherence which is to be nurtured and protected through an abidance to and reverence for certain texts and philosophemes.

But such preservation and transmittal of the tradition(s) are always functions of specific historical contexts. A philosopher is enabled by a tradition, but also by a national and geopolitical context. A philosopher is always a disciple, or master, within a unique national, continental, and world-system context. The identity of the philosopher matters to what he or she is able to think about, and think through. A language, first and foremost, then a school of thinking, with its masters and epigones, then a whole infrastructure of readers, publishers, journals, schools, universities, and so on, and, last but not least, the essential belief that a dialogue across ages is being carried on. It is this inescapable rootedness of philosophers in their own cultural identities which may allow us to talk of a "philosophical identity," that has been foregrounded by the thawing of tensions along the border of the misnamed analytical–Continental divide. For once British and North American philosophers were forced to recognize that what they called philosophy *as such* was a peculiar by-product of Cold War politics, and ideological realignment in the age of a *pax Americana*, then the particular British and North American character of their thinking became explicit. In other words, the divide was not just a matter of styles of doing philosophy, but of how certain countries and schools stood in relationship to the tradition. The struggle over what counted as "real" philosophy was a struggle over who inherited the tradition most faithfully. In parallel, so-called Continentalists are recognizing their own embeddedness. Thus, we have seen a proliferation of histories of philosophies by country. Behind the moniker "Continental" is concealed the fact that we have extremely fractured and pugnacious philosophical divides (the most notorious one being that between the Germans and the French, with the Italians and Spanish determining their identity *vis-à-vis* these two alternatives). The history of philosophy is the history of the identities of philosophers, and how those identities were impacted by national, continental, and geopolitical contexts. In this way, the question of identity has been determining for philosophy.

Finally, we need to discuss how the question of identity has been a serious concern to philosophy not just as a philosopheme, or object of concern, but also in terms of philosophy's own identity, as a practice, a doing, a coherent and unique way of thinking. Indeed, philosophy has, since its emergence from its roots in myth, religion, poetry, and theology, asked about its identity. It has always defined itself in terms of what makes it different from other forms of human questioning and investigation. What counts as philosophy? And, conversely, what may be an appropriate concern of true philosophy and how might it be articulated in a way that is properly philosophical? These are questions that have decided the very identity of philosophy. Is philosophy a form of literature, and if not, what is the difference between works such as Augustine's *Confessions*, Descartes' *Meditations*, Sartre's *Nausea*, and Heidegger's *Being and Time*, works which are as generative as they are profoundly dissimilar? Lacking either a Dewey or a Library of Congress cataloguing system, could we separate in a library those texts that are merely philosophical and those that are merely literary? The same kinds of question may be asked with respect to theology, the social and the natural sciences. Here, we may conclude with the note that identity has been not just an abstract, albeit constant, object of reflection of the human and social sciences, to use that redundant neoplasm, but also, and just as determining, identity has been a practical, material, and especially existential, concern of thinkers who have tried to understand the relationship between social agents, their worlds, and the world of their ideas, and how their interactions crystallize in identity formations.

Notes

1. George Steiner, *After Babel: Aspects of Language and Translation* (Oxford and New York: Oxford University Press, 1992), xiv.

2. Paul Celan, quoted in Emmanuel Levinas, *De Otro Modo que Ser, O mas Alla de la Esencia* (Salamanca: Ediciones Sígueme, 1987), 163.

3. Wim Wenders, quoted in David Cystal, *English as a Global Language* (Cambridge: Cambridge University Press, 1997), 91.

4. Slavoj Zizek, *Tarrying with the Negative: Kant, Hegel, and the Critique of Ideology* (Durham, NC: Duke University Press, 1994), 68.

5. Walter Mignolo, *Local Histories/Global Designs: Coloniality, Subaltern Knowledges, and Border Thinking* (Princeton: Princeton University Press, 2000).

6. David R. Roediger, *The Wages of Whiteness: Race and the Making of the American White Working Class* (London: Verso, 1991).

7. Anibal Quijano, "Coloniality of Power, Eurocentrism, and Latin America," *Nepantla: Views from the South*, 1.3 (2000): 533–80.

8. Benedict Anderson, *Imagined Communities: Reflections on the Origin and Spread of Nationalism* (London and New York: Verso, 1991).

9. See Eduardo Mendieta, "The Modernity of Race and the Race of Modernity: On Foucault's Genealogy of Racism," forthcoming; Michel Foucault, "Il faut défendre la société," *Cours au Collège de France (1975–1976)* (Février: Seuil/Gallimard, 1997); and Ann Laura Stoler, *Race and the Education of Desire: Foucault's History of Sexuality and the Colonial Order of Things* (Durham, NC: Duke University Press, 1995).

10. Peter Sloterdijk, *Regel für den Menschenpark: Ein Antwortschreiben zu Heideggers Brief über den Humanismus* (Frankfurt am Main: Suhrkamp Verlag, 1999).

11. Etienne Balibar and Immanuel Wallerstein, *Race, Nation, Class: Ambiguous Identities* (London and New York: Verso, 1991), as well as Balibar's *Masses, Classes, Ideas: Studies on Politics and Philosophy Before and After Marx* (New York: Routledge, 1993).

12. Foucault, "Il faut défendre la société," p. 227.

13. Eduardo Mendieta, "Invisible Cities: A Phenomenology of Globalization from Below," *City*, 5.1 (2001): 7–26; David Held, Anthony McGrew, David Goldblatt, and Jonathan Perraton, *Global Transformations: Politics, Economics, and Culture* (Stanford: Stanford University Press, 1999).

14. Christopher Hitchens, *The Trial of Henry Kissinger* (New York and London: Verso, 2001).

15. Arjun Appadurai, *Modernity at Large: Cultural Dimensions of Globalization* (Minneapolis: University of Minnesota Press, 1996).

16. Roland Robertson, "Globalisation or Glocalisation?" *The Journal of International Communication*, 1.1 (1994): 33–52.

17. Jürgen Habermas, *The Postnational Constellation: Political Essays* (Cambridge, MA: The MIT Press, 2001).

18. Dipesh Chakrabarty, *Provincializing Europe: Postcolonial Thought and Historical Difference* (Princeton: Princeton University Press, 2000), and his essay "Minority Histories, Subaltern Pasts" in *Postcolonial Studies*, 1.1 (1998): 15–29. See also Gayatri Chakravorty Spivak, *A Critique of Postcolonial Reason: Toward a History of the Vanishing Present* (Cambridge, MA: Harvard University Press, 1999).

19. Zygmut Bauman, *Globalization: The Human Consequences* (New York: Columbia University Press, 1998).

20. Saskia Sassen, *Guests and Aliens* (New York: New Press, 1999).

21. Manuel Castells, *The Information Age: Economy, Society and Culture*, Vol. 1: *The Rise of the Network Society*; Vol. 2: *The Power of Identity*; Vol 3: *End of Millennium* (Malden, MA and Oxford: Blackwell Publishers, 1996–8); Saskia Sassen, *Cities in a World Economy*, 2nd edn (Thousand Oaks: Pine Forge Press, 2000).

22. Mike Davis, *Magical Urbanism: Latinos Reinvent the US Big City*, 2nd revised edn (London: Verso, 2001); Victor M. Valle, Rodolfo D. Torres, eds., *Latino Metropolis* (Minneapolis: University of Minnesota Press, 2000).

23. Jeremy Rifkin, *The End of Work: The Decline of the Global Labor Force and the Dawn of the Post-Market Era* (New York: Putnam's, 1995); Ulrich Beck, *The Brave New World of Work* (Malden, MA: Polity, 2000).

24. Ulrich Beck, Anthony Giddens, and Scott Lash, *Reflexive Modernization: Politics, Tradition, and Aesthetics in the Modern Social Order* (Stanford: Stanford University Press, 1994); Paul Heelas, Scott Lash, and Paul Morris, eds., *Detraditionalization: Critical Reflections on Authority and Identity* (Cambridge, MA: Blackwell Publishers, 1996).

25. Craig J. Calhoun, *Critical Social Theory: Culture, History, and the Challenge of Difference* (Cambridge, MA: Blackwell, 1995).

Subject Index

Name Index

Ackerley, J. R., 228
Acosta-Belén, Edna, 290
Agostinho, P., 287
Albinus, Clodius, 217
Albrow, M., 300–3
Ali, Shahrazad, 179
Allen, Carolyn, 247
Amin, Samir, 321
Amodio, Emanuel, 285
Anderson, Benedict, 97, 282, 284, 346
Anzaldúa, Gloria, 250
Appadurai, Arjun, 322, 352, 410
Aquinas, Thomas, 149, 150, 153, 218, 414
Archer, M., 302
Ardao, Arturo, 286
Arensberg, C. M., 343
Aristophanes, 152, 216, 217, 230–1
Aristotle, 150, 153, 218, 221, 245, 377, 395, 414
Arnason, J., 347–8
Aron, M., 297
Artaud, Antonin, 66
Artemidorus, 221, 235–6
Augustine, 153, 246, 414, 415
Aurelianus, Caelius, 232–3

Balibar, Etienne, 304, 410
Barnes, Djuna, 246, 247, 250
Barre, Poulain de la, 153
Basch, Linda, 289
Bauer, Bruno, 17–28
Baum, R. C., 297
Bauman, Z., 353
Beaumont, Gustave de, 19, 24
Beauvoir, Simone de, 1, 3, 158, 159, 164–5
Beck, Ulrich, 413
Benjamin, Harry, 259–60

Benjamin, Walter, 324, 366
Bensman, J., 343
Bentham, Jeremy, 79
Bergesen, A., 349
Bergson, Henri, 65
Berner, E., 352
Bhabha, Homi, 313, 322, 323, 353
Birke, Lynda, 259
Blades, Rubén, 281–2, 289, 291–2
Blanchard, Ray, 259, 263
Blumberg, Rae Lessor, 380
Bockting, Walter, 260
Boethius, 414
Bohan, Janis, 265
Bolin, Anne, 260–1, 265
Bolívar, Simón, 289
Booth, Charles, 344
Boswell, John, 229, 230–1
Botasso, Juan, 285
Bourdieu, P., 344
Bowen, Gary, 264
Bowers v. *Hardwick*, 245
Boyd, Richard, 396–7, 399
Bradley, Susan, 259
Brennan, T., 346
Breytenbach, Breyten, 271–2
Brossard, Nicole, 250
Brown v. *Board of Education*, 192
Bruner, E., 354
Brysk, Alison, 285
Burke, P., 346
Butler, Judith, 3, 262, 265
Butler, Octavia, 382, 385

Caicedo, José María Torres, 286
Canevacci, M., 352